Ninth International Conference on Computational Semantics 2011

(IWCS 2011)

Oxford, UK
12-14 January 2011

Editors:

Johan Bos
Stephen Pulman

ISBN: 978-1-61839-239-8

Printed from e-media with permission by:

Curran Associates, Inc.
57 Morehouse Lane
Red Hook, NY 12571

CURRAN ASSOCIATES INC. proceedings.com

Some format issues inherent in the e-media version may also appear in this print version.

Printed by Curran Associates, Inc. (2011)

Association for Computational Linguistics
209 N. Eighth Street
Stroudsburg, Pennsylvania 18360

Phone: 1-570-476-8006
Fax: 1-570-476-0860

acl@aclweb.org

Additional copies of this publication are available from:

Curran Associates, Inc.
57 Morehouse Lane
Red Hook, NY 12571 USA
Phone: 845-758-0400
Fax: 845-758-2634
Email: curran@proceedings.com
Web: www.proceedings.com

Contents

Invited Talks

Regular Papers

Short Papers

Preface

Hibernation is certainly not one of the activities of computational semanticists. In the midst of winter they defy sub-zero temperatures, vicious snowstorms, and ice-covered roads to attend the mother of all computational semantics conferences: IWCS. This has been an almost biennial tradition since December 1994, when the first IWCS was initiated by Harry Bunt and held in Tilburg, Netherlands. The workshop turned out to be a successful event, and seven more IWCS meetings were organised — all by Harry Bunt, and all in Tilburg — between 1997 and 2009.

The ninth episode of IWCS, however, is different from various points of view. For the first time in its history, it is not taking place in Tilburg, and not organised by Harry Bunt. IWCS released itself, crossed the channel and landed in Oxford. Yet many of its key characteristics remain as they were. For instance the IWCS logo, inspired by the park "Oude Warande" near the traditional IWCS site at Tilburg University, continues to decorate the cover of the proceedings.

The call for papers for IWCS-2011 triggered a record number of 110 submissions, of which 75 were submitted as regular papers, and 35 as short papers. The programme committee, based on a total of 328 reviews, selected 50 of these — 30 long and 20 short (three regular papers were accepted as short papers). This gives an overall acceptance rate of 50/110 = 45% (30/72 = 42% for regular papers, and 20/38 = 53% for short papers). Two papers (one regular, one short) were withdrawn by their authors after the notification of acceptance.

It remains to say that we hope to offer you an exciting selection of state-of-the-art work in computational semantics at IWCS-2011. We wish you a pleasant stay in Oxford!

Johan Bos, University of Groningen

Stephen Pulman, Oxford University

http://www.sigsem.org
IWCS is endorsed by SIGSEM, the ACL special interest group on computational semantics.

Programme Chairs
Johan Bos, Stephen Pulman

Programme Committee
Rodrigo Agerri, Marco Baroni, Anja Belz, Patrick Blackburn, António Branco, Harry Bunt, Aljoscha Burchardt, Nicoletta Calzolari, Rui Chaves, Philipp Cimiano, Peter Clark, Ariel Cohen, Robin Cooper, Ann Copestake, Rodolfo Delmonte, Markus Egg, Katrin Erk, Raquel Fernández, Anette Frank, Claire Gardent, Jonathan Ginzburg, Jerry Hobbs, Laura Kallmeyer, Lauri Karttunen, Ralf Klabunde, Alexander Koller, Emiel Krahmer, Shalom Lappin, Alex Lascarides, Kiyong Lee, Leonardo Lesmo, Bernd Ludwig, Bill MacCartney, Katja Markert, Paul Mc Kevitt, Sergei Nirenburg, Malvina Nissim, Sebastian Padó, Vincenzo Pallotta, Martha Palmer, Manfred Pinkal, Paul Piwek, Massimo Poesio, Sylvain Pogodalla, Richard Power, James Pustejovsky, Allan Ramsay, German Rigau, Mike Rosner, Rolf Schwitter, Jennifer Spenader, Manfred Stede, Mary Swift, Stefan Thater, Peter Turney, Benjamin Van Durme, Carl Vogel, Kees van Deemter, Jan van Eijck, Josef van Genabith

External Reviewers
Raffaella Bernardi, Cristina Bosco, Susan W. Brown, Christophe Cerisara, Francisco Costa, Georgiana Dinu, Dmitriy Dligach, Sascha Fendrich, Andrew Gargett, Konstantina Garoufi, Rosa Del Gaudio, Patricia Gonçalves, Matthias Hartung, Abdelati Hawwari, Jena Hwang, Alessandro Mazzei John McCrae, Courtney Napoles, Ulrike Padó, Daniele Radicioni, Livio Robaldo, João Silva, Dennis Spohr, Christina Unger, Ashwini Vaidya, Jonathan Weese

Local Organization
Stephen Pulman, Elizabeth Walsh

Invited Speakers

Harry Bunt

Eduard Hovy

The Semantics of Dialogue Acts

Harry Bunt
TiCC, Tilburg Center for Cognition and Communication
Tilburg University, The Netherlands
harry.bunt@uvt.nl

Abstract

This paper presents an update semantic for dialogue acts, defined in terms of combinations of very simple 'elementary update functions'. This approach allows fine-grained distinctions to be made between related types of dialogue acts, and relations like entailment and exclusion between dialogue acts to be established. The approach is applied to dialogue act representations as defined in the Dialogue Act Markup Language (DiAML), part of the recently proposed ISO standard 24617-2 for dialogue act annotation.

1 Introduction

The notion of a dialogue act plays a key role in studies of dialogue, in particular in the interpretation of the behaviour of dialogue participants and in the design of spoken dialogue systems. But in spite of their popularity, their status is nearly always reduced to that of informal, intuitive concepts which lack proper definitions (see Poesio and Traum, 1998 for one of the few attempts at formalization). A wide range of alternative dialogue act taxonomies and inventories have been proposed, causing considerable terminological and conceptual confusion, and problems for reusing annotated corpora. This has motivated the International Organisation for Standards ISO to develop a standard for interoperable dialogue act annotation, ISO 24617-2 (see ISO 2010). This proposed standard is partly based on the comprehensive DIT^{++} taxonomy, which has added to the earlier DIT taxonomy (Bunt, 1994) a number of concepts from other proposals and studies. Semantically, the DIT^{++} taxonomy is based on the dynamic approach to utterance meaning taken in Dynamic Interpretation Theory (DIT), which views dialogue acts as corresponding to update operations on the information states of participants in the dialogue; an approach commonly known as the 'information-state update approach' to meaning in dialogue – see e.g. Bunt (2000); Traum & Larsson (2003). A dialogue act, on this approach, has two main components: a semantic content, which describes the objects, properties, relations, or actions that the dialogue act is about, and a communicative function, which specifies how an addressee should update his information state with the semantic content.

Utterances in dialogue are often multifunctional, i.e., they have more than one communicative function. Dialogue analysis and annotation frameworks are therefore often 'multidimensional' in the sense of allowing the assignment of multiple functions to functional segments. The DAMSL annotation scheme for example (DAMSL = Dialogue Act Markup using Several Layers) distinguishes nine 'dimensions' as mutually exclusive groups of function tags.

Bunt (2006) introduces a notion of dimension based on the observation that participation in a dialogue involves, beyond activities strictly related to performing the underlying task, sharing information about the processing of utterances, managing the use of time, taking turns, and various other types of communicative activity, and defines dimensions as corresponding to such aspects of communication. Each dimension in this sense constitutes a category of communicative activity, and the dialogue acts involved in these activities are concerned with different types of information: feedback acts with the success of processing previous utterances; turn management acts with the allocation of the speaker role, task-related acts with the dialogue task; and so on. Dimensions thus classify semantic content.

Petukhova & Bunt (2009a; 2009b) formulate criteria for distinguishing dimensions, and apply these in the analysis of the dimensions that occur in 18 existing annotation schemes, showing that the 10 dimensions of DIT^{++} form a well-founded set of dimensions. These are the following:

(1)
1. Task/Activity: dialogue acts for performing the task or activity underlying the dialogue
2. Auto-Feedback: providing information about the speaker's processing of previous utterances.
3. Allo-Feedback: the speaker expresses opinions or elicits information about the addressee's processing of previous utterances;
4. Contact Management: dialogue acts for establishing and maintaining contact;
5. Turn Management: concerned with grabbing, keeping, giving, or accepting the speaker role;
6. Time Management: the speaker indicates to need some extra time to formulate his contribution;
7. Discourse Structuring: dialogue acts for explicitly structuring the conversation;
8. Own Communication Management: dialogue acts for editing the speaker's current utterance;
9. Partner Communication Management: dialogue acts to assists or correct the current speaker;
10. Social Obligations Management: dialogue acts that take care of social conventions such as greetings, apologies, and expressions of gratitude.

Some communicative functions are specific for a particular dimension; for instance *Turn Accept* and *Turn Release* are specific for turn management; *Stalling* and *Pausing* for time management. Other functions can be applied in any dimension; for instance a *Check Question* can be used with task-related semantic content, but also for checking correct understanding (feedback). Similarly for commissive and directive functions. These functions are therefore called *general-purpose* functions, as opposed to *dimension-specific* functions. The DIT^{++} taxonomy therefore consists of two parts: a taxonomy of *general-purpose functions* and one of *dimension-specific functions* - see Appendix A and `http://dit.uvt.nl`.

2 DiAML: Dialogue Act Markup Language

The Dialogue Act Markup Language (DiAML) which is part of the ISO standard under development for dialogue act annotation (see Bunt et al., 2010, and `http://semantic-annotation.uvt.nl`) has been designed in accordance with the ISO Linguistic Annotation Framework (Ide & Romary, 2004), which makes a distinction between *annotation* and *representation*; 'annotation' refers to the linguistic information that is added to segments of language data, independent of format; 'representation' refers to the format in which an annotation is rendered, independent of content. This distinction is implemented in the DiAML definition by a syntax that specifies, besides a class of XML-based *representation structures*, also a class of more abstract *annotation structures*. These two components are called the *concrete* and *abstract syntax*, respectively.

The abstract syntax defines a class of set-theoretical structures, called 'annotation structures'. It consists of: (a) a specification of the elements from which annotation structures are built up, called a 'conceptual inventory', and (b) a specification of the possible ways of combining these elements. The conceptual inventory consists of finite sets of elements called 'functional segments', 'dimensions', 'communicative functions', 'qualifiers', and 'rhetorical relations'.

An annotation structure consists of a set of *entity structures* and a set of *link structures*. Entity structures contain semantic information about a functional segment; link structures describe semantic relations between segments. The most important kind of entity structure is a so-called *'dialogue act structure'*, which is a quadruple $\langle S, A, d, f \rangle$ where S and A are the sender and addressee of a dialogue act; d is a dimension; and f is a communicative function or a pair $\langle f, q \rangle$, where q is a list of qualifiers.

The concrete syntax defines a rendering of annotation structures in XML. It is defined in accordance with the methodology for defining semantic annotation languages described in Bunt (2010), which introduces the notion of an *ideal representation format*, defined as one where every representation represents a uniquely determined annotation structureThe semantics of the language is then defined for the structures defined by the *abstract* syntax. This has the effect that any two 'ideal' representation formats are semantically equivalent; every representation in one such format can be converted by a meaning-preserving mapping into any other such format.[1] The concrete syntax of DiAML is illustrated in (3) and (2). P2's utterance is segmented into two overlapping functional segments: one (fs2.1) in the Auto-Feedback dimension and one (fs2.2) in the Task dimension, with value 'answer' qualified as 'uncertain'. (#-prefixed elements are assumed to be identified in the metadata of the source material or in another layer of annotation.)

(2)

1.	P1:	*What time does the next train to Utrecht leave?*
TA:	fs1:	*What time does the next train to Utrecht leave?*
2.	P2:	*The next train to Utrecht leaves I think at 8:32.*
AuFB	fs2.1:	*The next train to Utrecht*
TA	fs2.2:	*The next train to Utrecht leaves I think at 8:32.*

(3)

```
<diaml xmlns:"http://www.iso.org/diaml/">
<dialogueAct xml:id="da1" target="#fs1"
  sender="#p1" addressee="#p2"
communicativeFunction="setQuestion" dimension="task"
  conditionality="conditional"/>
<dialogueAct xml:id="da2" target="#fs2"
  sender="#p2" addressee="#p1"
  communicativeFunction="autoPositive" dimension="autoFeedback"/>
<feedbackDependence dact="#da2.1" fbSegment="#fs1"/>
<dialogueAct xml:id="da3" target="#fs2.2"
  sender="#p2" addressee="#p1"
  communicativeFunction="answer" certainty="uncertain"
  dimension="task" />
<functionalDependence dact="#da3" functAntecedent="#da1"/>
</diaml>
```

3 Context Model Structure and Content

As the proposed semantics of dialogue acts is in terms of information-state updates, the question arises as to what exactly is an information state in this context; what information does it contain, and how is it structured. An information state will be assumed to have a number of components, an assumption which is shared between all proposals for information states (e.g. Poesio & Traum, 1998; Bunt, 2000; Ahn, 2001; Cooper, 2004); moreover, certain types of information can be argued to be required in information states. The details of an information-state update semantics also depend on whether only the information state of an *addressee* is considered to be updated by dialogue acts, or also that of the sender, and on whether these updates involve *mutual* beliefs, as e.g. argued in Bunt (2000). We consider here only the updates of a single addressee's information state, disregarding mutual beliefs; this is anyway the basis for more complex approaches involving multiple information states and mutual beliefs. In DIT, it is customary to speak of 'contexts' or context models', rather than 'information states', and we will use this terminology in the rest of this paper.

A fundamental requirement for an adequate context model is that, for a given range of dialogue act types, the model contains the kinds of information that are updated by a dialogue act. Bunt (forthc.) argues that an agent's context model does not necessarily have a separate component for each DIT dimension, but that it is convenient to distinguish the following five components:

(4)
1. Linguistic Context, which contains a record of the dialogue history, information about discourse plans (if any), and wishes concerning the occupation of the speaker role;
2. Semantic Context, which contains the agent's information and goals relating to the dialogue task, as well as his assumptions about the dialogue partner's task-related goals and beliefs;
3. Cognitive Context, which contains information about the agent's cognitive processes concerned with the processing and production of dialogue utterances, including time estimates for these processes;

[1]See Bunt (2010) for formal definitions and proofs relating to alternative representation formats sharing the same abstract syntax, and Ide & Bunt (2010) for applying this to the GrAF framework for linguistic annotation.

4. Physical/Perceptual Context, which contains information about physical and perceptual properties of the interactive situation;
5. Social Context, which contains information relevant for interpreting and generating 'social' acts like greetings, apologies, expressions of gratitude.

Versions of such a 5-component context model have been implemented in the PARADIME dialogue manager (Keizer and Bunt, 2006; 2007) and for experimentation by Petukhova et al. (2010).

An update semantics has to take into account that update operations should not undermine the consistency of the context model. A dialogue participant may change his mind during the dialogue, as an effect of receiving some unexpected information, which can have the effect that the participant brings in new information which contradicts something that was already grounded, and hence cannot simply be added without making the context model inconsistent. Rather then building consistency checks into the semantics of each dialogue act, we exploit the DIT distinction of five levels of utterance processing: (1) attention, (2) perception, (3) understanding, (4) evaluation, and (5) execution. The level of *understanding* determines the meaning of a dialogue segment in terms of dialogue acts. The *evaluation* level checks whether the corresponding updates would keep the current context model consistent. If so, it performs the updates. One way to implement this approach is to add to a context model a part called the *pending context*, which serves as a buffer for items to be inserted in the main context once their consistency with the current content of the main context has been established.[2] Updating the pending context is a matter of simply *adding* items to it. For convenience we will assume the pending context A' of an agent A's context model to be structured in the same way as the main context. We will use the notation (5a) to specify the update consisting of adding the information z to component A'_i i of A's pending context. If f is the update (5a) and g the update $A'_j =\!\!+u$, then (5b) designates the combination of the two updates.[3]

(5) a. $A'_i =\!\!+z$
b. $f \sqcup g$

An analysis of the definitions of the DIT^{++} communicative functions shows that a formal description of the update effects of dialogue acts with a general-purpose function requires the basic concepts listed in Table 1. For convenience, we also introduce the following abbreviations: **Bel**(S,p) abbreviates **Bel**S,p, firm); **Wk-Bel**(S,p) abbreviates **Bel**S,p, weak); **Assumes(S,p)** abbreviates **Bel(S,p)** $\vee$ **Wk-Bel(S,p)**. In all action-related attitude operators we suppress the argument $\top$ representing the 'empty' condition, hence **WilDo**(S,α) abbreviates **WilDo**$(S,\alpha,\top)$, and so on.

description	notation	meaning
believes that	**Bel**(S,p,σ)	*S believes that p*; σ indicates whether this is a firm belief or an uncertain belief (σ can have the values 'firm' and 'weak')
knows value of	**Know-val**(S,z)	*S possesses the information z*
has goal	**Wantl**(S,p)	*S has the goal that p*
is able to do	**CanDo**(S,α)	*S is able to perform the action* α
is willing to do	**WilDo**(S,α,C_α)	*S is willing to perform the action* α *if the condition* C_α *is* fulfilled; C_α may be the universally true statement $\top$
is committed to do	**CommitDo**(S,α,C_α)	*S is committed to perform the action* α *if the condition* C_α *is* fulfilled; the condition C_α may be 'empty' ($\top$)
is committed to refrain from doing	**RefrainDo**(S,α,C_α)	*S is committed to refrain from performing the action* α *if the condition* C_α *is fulfilled* C_α may be 'empty' ($\top$)
is considering to be done	**ConsidDo** (X,α,Y,C_α)	*X is considering the action* α*, to be performed by Y, if the condition* C_α *is fulfilled* C_α may be 'empty' ($\top$)
is in the interest of	**Interest**(Y,α)	action α is of interest to agent Y.

Table 1: Basic semantic concepts for general-purpose communicative function interpretation

[2]This approach has been implemented in the multimodal DenK dialogue system; see Kievit et al. (2001).

[3]The combined update $(f \sqcup g)$ is undefined if the order of performing the two updates would make a difference.

Dimension	*Primitives*
Auto- and Allo-feedback	**Attended, Perceived, Understood, Accepted, Executed, Attention-Problem, Perception-Problem, Interpretation-Problem, Evaluation-Problem, Execution-Problem**
Turn Management	**Current-Speaker, Next-Speaker**
Time Mangement	**Time-Need, small, substantial**
Contact Management	**Present**
Discourse Structuring	**Ready, Available, Start-Dialogue, Close-Dialogue**
Own and Partner Communication Man.	**Delete, Replace, Append**
Social Obligations Man.	**Available, Thankful, Regretful, Knows-id, Final**

Table 2: Dimension-specific semantic primitives

Dimension-specific communicative functions are always concerned with a specific category of semantic content, which requires certain specific semantic primitives for its representation. Table 2 lists the basic concepts for describing their update semantics.

For expressing the semantics of a feedback act which is underspecified for the level of processing, we introduce in (6) the predicates **Succes-Processing**, defined as successful at least at the level of understanding, and **Unsuccessful-Processing**, defined as unsuccessful at the level of understanding or lower.

(6) a. **Succes-Processing** = **Understood** $\vee$ **Accepted** $\vee$ **Executed**
    b. **Unsuccessful-Processing** = **Interpretation-Problem** $\vee$ **Perception-Problem** $\vee$ **Attention-Problem**

4 Dialogue Act Semantics

In this section we outline a semantics of dialogue acts in the form of an update semantics for the 'dialogue act structures' defined by the DiAML abstract syntax. A dialogue act structure does not correspond to a full-blown dialogue act representation, since it does not include the full semantic content, but only the dimension which classifies the semantic content. The semantics of a dialogue act structure should therefore be something which can be combined with a semantic content in order to form the interpretation of a full-blown dialogue act. This is precisely the case, for the recursive interpretation of a dialogue act structure $\langle S, A, d, f\rangle$ is defined through the recursive valuation function V as specified in (7). Of the four arguments of V in the left-hand side of (7), *S, A,* and d are elements of the categories of the DiAML conceptual inventory, so there is no recursion in their interpretation; for such elements, the valuation function is defined by a value assignment function F, playing the same role as that of a 'model assignment' function in model-theoretic semantics; F for example assigns to a sender and an addressee certain individuals, identified in the metadata of an annotated dialogue (cf. $\#p1$ and $\#p2$ in (3)). To the dimension argument d, F assigns that component of an information state that should be updated.

(7) V(<S, A, d, f>) = $(V(\text{f}))(F(S), F(A), F(d))$

4.1 The Update Semantics of Communicative Functions

A communicative function will be interpreted as a function which, applied to a given speaker, addressee, and dimension, results in a function which can be applied to a semantic content in order to obtain a context-update specification. Since related communicative functions often share parts of their defining preconditions, we will construct such interpretations as *combinations of elementary update functions*, each of which takes care of the update corresponding to a single dialogue act precondition; see Table 3 and Table 4 for illustration: Table 3 lists the definitions of the update semantics of the communicative functions of the information-providing class, while Table 4 lists the elementary elementary update functions used in these definitions.

4.1.1 General-Purpose Communicative Functions

The class of general-purpose communicative functions in the DIT^{++} taxonomy falls apart into the *information-transfer functions* and *action-discussion functions*, further subdivided into information-providing and information-seeking functions, and commissives and directives, respectively.

a. Information-Providing and Information-Seeking Functions The class of information-providing functions has a hierarchical structure, with the communicative function Inform as the mother of all information-providing functions; all other functions are specializations of this function. These functions all have in common that (1) the speaker wants the addressee to possess certain information which (2) the speaker assumes to be correct.

Using the epistemic operators introduced in Section 5, these preconditions are formalized as follows:

(8) 1. $\textbf{Want}(S, U, \textbf{Bel}(A, p, \sigma))$
2. $\textbf{Bel}(A, p, \sigma)$

The semantics of the Inform function, specified in Table 3, binds the variable σ, representing the belief strength for both the elementary update functions involved. (See further below, section 4.2.)

The update semantics in terms of combinations of elementary update functions often brings out immediately that some communicative functions are specializations of others (as visualized in Appendix A), for instance, the update semantics of the Answer function shares with the Inform function the updates defined by the elementary update functions U_1 and U_2, and adds to that the effects of U_7 and U_9; the semantic of the Confirm function adds to that the update defined by U_8. Hence Confirm is a specialization of Answer, which is a specialization of Inform, or in other words Confirm entails Answer entails Inform.

F(Inform)	=	$\lambda s.\lambda X.\lambda Y.\lambda D_i.\lambda p.U_1(X,Y,D_i,p,s) \sqcup U_2(X,Y,D_i,p,s)$
F(Agreement)	=	$\lambda s.\lambda X.\lambda Y.\lambda D_i.\lambda p.U_1(X,Y,D_i,p,s) \sqcup U_2(X,Y,D_i,p,s) \sqcup U_5(X,Y,D_i,p)$
F(Disagreement)	=	$\lambda s.\lambda X.\lambda Y.\lambda D_i.\lambda p.U_1(X,Y,D_i,\neg p,s) \sqcup U_2(X,Y,D_i,\neg p,s) \sqcup U_5(X,Y,D_i,p)$
F(Correction)	=	$\lambda s.\lambda X.\lambda Y.\lambda D_i.\lambda p.U_1(X,Y,D_i,p_1,s) \sqcup U_2(X,Y,D_i,\neg p_1,s) \sqcup U_6(X,Y,D_i,p_2)$
F(Answer)	=	$\lambda s.\lambda X.\lambda Y.\lambda D_i.\lambda p.U_1(X,Y,D_i,p,s) \sqcup U_2(X,Y,D_i,p,s) \sqcup U_9(X,Y,D_i,p)$ $\sqcup U_7(X,Y,D_i,p)$
F(Confirm)	=	$\lambda s.\lambda X.\lambda Y.\lambda D_i.\lambda p.U_1(X,Y,D_i,p,s) \sqcup U_2(X,Y,D_i,p,s) \sqcup U_8(X,Y,D_i,p)$ $\sqcup U_9(X,Y,D_i,p,s) \sqcup U_7(X,Y,D_i,p)$
F(Disconfirm)	=	$\lambda s.\lambda X.\lambda Y.\lambda D_i.\lambda p.U_1(X,Y,D_i,\neg p,s) \sqcup U_2(X,Y,D_i,\neg p,s) \sqcup U_8(X,Y,D_i,\neg p,s)$ $\sqcup U_9(X,Y,D_i,p) \sqcup U_7(X,Y,D_i,p)$
F(Question)	=	$\lambda X.\lambda Y.\lambda D_i.\lambda z.U_{10}(X,Y,D_i,z) \sqcup U_{11}(X,Y,D_i,z)$
F(Prop.Question)	=	$\lambda X.\lambda Y.\lambda D_i.\lambda p.U_{10}(X,Y,D_i,p) \sqcup U_{11}(X,Y,D_i,p) \sqcup U_{12}(X,Y,D_i,p)$
F(CheckQuestion)	=	$\lambda X.\lambda Y.\lambda D_i.\lambda z.U_{10}(X,Y,D_i,p) \sqcup U_{11}(X,Y,D_i,p) \sqcup U_4(X,Y,D_i,p)$
F(SetQuestion)	=	$\lambda X.\lambda Y.\lambda D_i.\lambda z.U_{10}(X,Y,D_i,P) \sqcup U_{11}(X,Y,D_i,P) \sqcup U_{13}(X,Y,D_i,P)$
F(ChoiceQuestion)	=	$\lambda X.\lambda Y.\lambda D_i.\lambda p.U_{15a}(X,Y,D_i,p) \sqcup U_{15}(X,Y,D_i,p) \sqcup U_{16}(X,Y,D_i,p)$

Table 3: Update semantics for information-providing and information-seeking communicative functions

As an illustration of the update semantics of information-providing functions, consider the case of the answer in (9.2).

(9) 1. D: twenty-five euros, how much is that in pounds?
2. C: twenty-five euros is something like 20 pounds

Applying the semantics of the Answer function (see Table 3) to the participants C and D and the semantic content of (9.2), we obtain:

(10) F(Answer)(C, D, Task, EU25=BP20) = U_1(C,D,SemC, EU25=BP20) $\sqcup$
$\sqcup$ U_2(C,D,Task, EU25=BP20) $\sqcup$ U_9(C, D, Task, EU25=BP20) $\sqcup$ U_7(C, D, Task, EU25=BP20) =
D'_{SemC} $=\!\!+$ **Bel**(D, **Want**(C, **Bel**(D, EU25=BP20))); D'_{SemC} $=\!\!+$ **Bel**(D, **Bel**(C, EU25=BP20));
D'_{SemC} $=\!\!+$ **Bel**(D, **Bel**(C, **Want**(D, **Know-val**(D, EU25=BP20)))); D'_{SemC} $=\!\!+$ **Bel**(D, **Bel**(C, **Assume**(D, **Know-val**(C, EU25=BP20))))

Hence the following beliefs are added to D's pending Semantic Context: (1) C wants D to know that EU25=BP20; (2) C believes that EU25=BP20; (3) C believes that D wants to know whether EU25=BP20; and (4) C believes that D assumes C to know whether EU25=BP20.

$U_1(X,Y,D_i,p,s)$	$Y_i' =\!\!+ \textbf{Bel}(Y, \textbf{Want}(X, \textbf{Bel}(Y,p,s)))$
$U_2(X,Y,D_i,p,s)$	$Y_i' =\!\!+ \textbf{Bel}(Y, \textbf{Bel}(X,p,s))$
$U_3(X,Y,D_i,p)$	$Y_i' =\!\!+ \textbf{Bel}(Y, \textbf{Assume}(X,p))$
$U_4(X,Y,D_i,p)$	$Y_i' =\!\!+ \textbf{Bel}(Y, \textbf{Wk-Bel}(X,p))$
$U_5(X,Y,D_i,p)$	$Y_i' =\!\!+ \textbf{Bel}(Y, \textbf{Bel}(X, \textbf{Assume}(Y,p)))$
$U_6(X,Y,D_i,p)$	$Y_i' =\!\!+ \textbf{Bel}(Y, \textbf{Assume}(X, \textbf{Assume}(Y,p)))$
$U_7(X,Y,D_i,p)$	$Y_i' =\!\!+ \textbf{Bel}(Y, \textbf{Bel}(X, \textbf{Assume}(Y, \textbf{Know-val}(X,P))))$
$U_8(X,Y,D_i,p)$	$Y_i' =\!\!+ \textbf{Bel}(Y, \textbf{Assume}(X, \textbf{Wk-Bel}(Y,p)))$
$U_9(X,Y,D_i,p)$	$Y_i' =\!\!+ \textbf{Bel}(Y, \textbf{Bel}(X, \textbf{Want}(Y, \textbf{Know-val}(Y,p))))$
$U_{10}(X,Y,D_i,p)$	$Y_i' =\!\!+ \textbf{Bel}(Y, \textbf{Want}(X, \textbf{Know-val}(X,)))$
$U_{11}(X,Y,D_i,p)$	$Y_i' =\!\!+ \textbf{Bel}(Y, \textbf{Assume}(X, \textbf{Know-val}(Y,p)))$
$U_{12}(X,Y,D_i,p)$	$Y_i' =\!\!+ \textbf{Bel}(Y, \textbf{Bel}(X, p \vee \neg p))$
$U_{15}(X,Y,D_i,p)$	$Y_i' =\!\!+ \textbf{Bel}(Y, \textbf{Assume}(X, p_1 \; xor \; p_2))$
$U_{15a}(X,Y,D_i,p)$	$Y_i' =\!\!+ \textbf{Bel}(Y, \textbf{Want}(X, \textbf{Bel}(X,p_1) \vee \textbf{Bel}(X,p_2))))$
$U_{16}(X,Y,D_i,p)$	$Y_i' =\!\!+ \textbf{Bel}(Y, \textbf{Assume}(X, \textbf{Bel}(Y,p_1) \vee \textbf{Bel}(Y,p_2))))$

Table 4: Elementary update functions used in the semantics of information-transfer functions

b. Commissive and Directive Functions For the classes of commissive and directive communicative functions, we provide for reasons of space the semantics of only a small selection of functions; see Bunt (2011a) for more.

F(Offer)	$= \lambda C_\alpha.\lambda X.\lambda Y.\lambda D_i.\lambda \alpha.U_{25a}(X,Y,D_i,\alpha) \sqcup U_{20}(X,Y,D_i,\alpha,C_\alpha)$
F(AddressRequest)	$= \lambda C_\alpha.\lambda X.\lambda Y.\lambda D_i.\lambda \alpha.U_{17a}(X,Y,D_i,\alpha,C_\alpha) \sqcup U_{18}(X,Y,D_i,\alpha) \sqcup U_{26b}(X,Y,D_i,\alpha)$
F(AcceptRequest)	$= \lambda C_\alpha.\lambda X.\lambda Y.\lambda D_i.\lambda \alpha.U_{17}(X,Y,D_i,\alpha,C_\alpha) \sqcup U_{18}(X,Y,D_i,\alpha) \sqcup U_{26b}(X,Y,D_i,\alpha)$
F(DeclineRequest)	$= \lambda C_\alpha.\lambda X.\lambda Y.\lambda D_i.\lambda \alpha.U_{27}(X,Y,D_i,\alpha,C_\alpha) \sqcup U_{18}(X,Y,D_i,\alpha) \sqcup U_{26b}(X,Y,D_i,\alpha)$
F(Request)	$= \lambda C_\alpha.\lambda X.\lambda Y.\lambda D_i.\lambda \alpha.U_{23}(X,Y,D_i,\alpha,C_\alpha) \sqcup U_{26}(X,Y,D_i,\alpha)$
F(Instruct)	$= \lambda C_\alpha.\lambda X.\lambda Y.\lambda D_i.\lambda \alpha.U_{24}(X,Y,D_i,\alpha,C_\alpha) \sqcup U_{26}(X,Y,D_i,\alpha) \sqcup U_{25}(X,Y,D_i,\alpha)$
F(AddressOffer)	$= \lambda C_\alpha.\lambda X.\lambda Y.\lambda D_i.\lambda \alpha.U_{17b}(X,Y,D_i,\alpha,C_\alpha) \sqcup U_{25}(X,Y,D_i,\alpha) \sqcup U_{25b}(X,Y,D_i,\alpha)$
F(AcceptOffer)	$= \lambda C_\alpha.\lambda X.\lambda Y.\lambda D_i.\lambda \alpha.U_{24}(X,Y,D_i,\alpha) \sqcup U_{25}(X,Y,D_i,\alpha) \sqcup U_{25b}(X,Y,D_i,\alpha)$

Table 5: Update semantics for a selection of commissive and directive functions

As an example of the interpretation of a directive dialogue act, consider the request in (11.2):

(11) 1. A: (...)
2. B: Could you please repeat that?

Applied to the participants A and B and the semantic content Repeat(u1), which situates the Request act in the Auto-Feedback dimension, the definition of the Request semantics in Table 5 leads to:

(12) F(Request)(A, B, Auto-Feedback, $\langle$Repeat(u1), unconditional$\rangle$) = $\lambda C_\alpha.\lambda X.\lambda Y.\lambda D_i.\lambda \alpha.)$
$U_{23}(X,Y,D_i,\alpha,C_\alpha \sqcup U_{26}(X,Y,D_i,\alpha)$(A, B, Auto-Feedback, Repeat(u1), $\top$) =
= U_{23}(A,B, CC, Repeat(u1), $\top$) $\sqcup$ U_{26}(A,B, C, Repeat(u1)) =
$B'_{CC} =\!\!+ \textbf{Bel}(B, \textbf{Want}(A, [\textbf{WilDo}(A, Repeat(u1) \rightarrow \textbf{CommitDo}(B, Repeat(u1))]));$
$B'_{CC} =\!\!+ \textbf{Bel}(B, \textbf{Bel}(A, \textbf{CanDo}(B, Repeat(u1))))$

where 'CC' stands for Cognitive Context.

4.1.2 Dimension-Specific Communicative Functions

4.1.2.1 Feedback Functions The communicative functions for providing and eliciting feedback in DIT^{++} fall apart in those concerned with the speaker's own processing of previous utterances (Auto-Feedback)

$U_{17}(X, Y, D_i, \alpha, C_\alpha)$	$Y_i' =\!\!+ \textbf{Bel}(Y, \textbf{CommitDo}(X, \alpha, C_\alpha))$
$U_{17a}(X, Y, D_i, \alpha, C_\alpha)$	$Y_i' =\!\!+ \textbf{Bel}(Y, \textbf{ConsidDo}(X, \alpha, X, C_\alpha))$
$U_{17b}(X, Y, D_i, \alpha, C_\alpha)$	$Y_i' =\!\!+ \textbf{Bel}(Y, \textbf{ConsidDo}(X, \alpha, Y, C_\alpha))$
$U_{18}(X, Y, D_i, \alpha)$	$Y_i' =\!\!+ \textbf{Bel}(Y, \textbf{Bel}(X, \textbf{Want}(Y, \textbf{CommitDo}(X, \alpha, C_\alpha)))$
$U_{20}(X, Y, D_i, \alpha, C_\alpha)$	$Y_i' =\!\!+ \textbf{Bel}(Y, \textbf{WilDo}(X, \alpha, C_\alpha))$
$U_{21}(X, Y, D_i, \alpha)$	$Y_i' =\!\!+ \textbf{Bel}(Y, \textbf{Bel}(X, \textbf{Interest}(\alpha, Y)))$
$U_{23}(X, Y, D_i, \alpha)$	$Y_i' =\!\!+ \textbf{Bel}(Y, \textbf{Want}(X, [\textbf{WilDo}(Y, \alpha, C_\alpha) \rightarrow \textbf{CommitDo}(Y, \alpha, C_\alpha)]))$
$U_{24}(X, Y, D_i, \alpha)$	$Y_i' =\!\!+ \textbf{Bel}(Y, \textbf{Want}(X, \textbf{CommitDo}(Y, \alpha)))$
$U_{25}(X, Y, D_i, \alpha, C_\alpha)$	$Y_i' =\!\!+ \textbf{Bel}(Y, \textbf{Bel}(X, \textbf{WilDo}(Y, \alpha, C_\alpha)))$
$U_{25a}(X, Y, D_i, \alpha, C_\alpha)$	$Y_i' =\!\!+ \textbf{Bel}(Y, \textbf{Want}(X, \textbf{Bel}(Y, \textbf{WilDo}(X, \alpha, C_\alpha))))$
$U_{25b}(X, Y, D_i, \alpha, C_\alpha)$	$Y_i' =\!\!+ \textbf{Bel}(Y, \textbf{Bel}(X, \textbf{Want}(Y, \textbf{Bel}(X, \textbf{WilDo}(Y, \alpha, C_\alpha)))))$
$U_{26}(X, Y, D_i, \alpha)$	$Y_i' =\!\!+ \textbf{Bel}(Y, \textbf{Assume}(X, \textbf{CanDo}(Y, \alpha)))$
$U_{26b}(X, Y, D_i, \alpha)$	$Y_i' =\!\!+ \textbf{Bel}(Y, \textbf{Bel}(X, \textbf{Assume}(Y, \textbf{CanDo}(X, \alpha)))$
$U_{27}(X, Y, D_i, \alpha, C_\alpha)$	$Y_i' =\!\!+ \textbf{Bel}(Y, \textbf{CommitRefrain}(X, \alpha, C_\alpha))$

Table 6: Elementary update functions used in the semantics of action-discussion functions.

and those concerned with the addressee's processing, as perceived by the speaker (Allo-Feedback). The elementary update functions for both dimensions are nearly identical, only differing in whose processing is concerned. Tables 7 and 8 show the update semantics of a small, representative subset of the (25) DIT^{++} communicative functions for providing and eliciting feedback.

$U_{31}(X, Y, D_i, z)$	$Y'_{CC} =\!\!+$ **Bel**$(Y,$ **Want**(X, **Bel**(Y, **Succes-Processing**$(X, z)))$
$U_{35}(X, Y, D_i, z)$	$Y'_{CC} =\!\!+$ **Bel**$(Y,$ **Want**(X, **Bel**(Y, **Accepted**$(X, z)))$
$U_{79}(X, Y, D_i, z)$	$Y'_{CC} =\!\!+$ **Bel**$(Y,$ **Want**(X, **Bel**(Y, **Perception-Problem**$(Y, z)))$
$U_{76}(X, Y, D_i, z)$	$Y'_{CC} =\!\!+$ **Bel**$(Y,$ **Want**(X, **Bel**(Y, **Execution-Problem**$(Y, z)))$
$U_{61}(X, Y, D_i, z)$	$Y'_{CC} =\!\!+$ **Bel**$(Y,$ **Bel**(X, **Success-Processing**$(X, z)))$
$U_{64}(X, Y, D_i, z)$	$Y'_{CC} =\!\!+$ **Bel**$(Y,$ **Bel**(X, **Accepted**$(X, z)))$
$U_{67}(X, Y, D_i, z)$	$Y'_{CC} =\!\!+$ **Bel**$(Y,$ **Bel**(X, **Perception-Problem**$(X, z)))$
$U_{85}(X, Y, D_i, z)$	$Y'_{CC} =\!\!+$ **Bel**$(Y,$ **Bel**(X, **Execution-Problem**$(Y, z)))$

Table 7: Elementary update schemes for the semantics of auto- and allo-feedback functions (selection).

F(AutoPositive)	=	$\lambda X.\lambda Y.\lambda D_i.\lambda p.U_{31}(X, Y, D_i, p) \sqcup U_{61}(X, Y, D_i)$
F(AlloPerceptionNegative)	=	$\lambda X.\lambda Y.\lambda D_i.\lambda p.U_{33}(X, Y, D_i, p) \sqcup U_{62}(X, Y, D_i)$
F(AutoEvaluationPositive)	=	$\lambda X.\lambda Y.\lambda D_i.\lambda p.U_{35}(X, Y, D_i, p) \sqcup U_{64}(X, Y, D_i)$
F(AlloExecutionNegative)	=	$\lambda X.\lambda Y.\lambda D_i.\lambda p.U_{76}(X, Y, D_i, p) \sqcup U_{85}(X, Y, D_i)$

Table 8: Semantics of feedback functions (selection)

4.1.2.2 Turn Management Functions

The communicative functions for turn management serve to decide who has or will have the speaker role. Hence the various functions for taking, accepting, grabbing, keeping, releasing, or assigning the turn are all defined in terms in who currently occupies the speaker and who wants or should have it next.

For example, assigning the turn to somebody (Turn Assign) means that the participant A, who currently occupies the speaker role, wants the indicated other participant, B, to occupy the speaker role next. This is expressed in the form of a combination of elementary update functions as shown in (13):

(13) $F(\text{TurnAssign})(A, B) = [\lambda X.\lambda Y.U_{101}(X, Y, TurnM) \sqcup U_{102}(X, Y, TurnM](A, B) =$
$= U_{101}(A, B, TurnM) \sqcup U_{102}(X, Y, TurnM) =$
$= B'_{LiC} =\!\!+ \textbf{Bel}(A, \textbf{Current-Speaker}(A)); B'_{LiC} =\!\!+ \textbf{Want}(A, \textbf{Next-Speaker}(B))$

In other words, the Linguistic Context component of B's pending context is updated to contain the beliefs that A is the current speaker and wants B to be the next speaker.

$U_{101}(X, Y, TurnM)$	Y'_{LiC} =+ **Bel**(X, **Current-Speaker**(X))
$U_{102}(X, Y, TurnM)$	Y'_{LiC} =+ **Want**(X, **Next-Speaker**(Y))
$U_{103}(X, Y, TurnM)$	Y'_{LiC} =+ **Bel**(X, **Current-Speaker**(Y))
$U_{104}(X, Y, TurnM)$	Y'_{LiC} =+ **Wants**(X, **Current-Speaker**(X))
$U_{105}(X, Y, TurnM)$	Y'_{LiC} =+ **Wants**(X, **Next-Speaker**(X))
$U_{105}(X, Y, TurnM)$	Y'_{LiC} =+ **Want**(X, ¬ **Next-Speaker**(X))
$U_{107}(X, Y, TurnM)$	Y'_{LiC} =+ **Bel**(X, ¬ **Next-Speaker**(X) ∧ ¬ **Next-Speaker**(Y))
$U_{108}(X, Y, TurnM)$	Y'_{LiC} =+ **Bel**(X, **Want**(Y, **Next-Speaker**(X)))

Table 9: Elementary update schemes for the semantics of turn management functions.

F(TurnAccept)	=	$\lambda X.\lambda Y.\lambda D_i.U_{103}(X, Y, D_i) \sqcup U_{105}(X, Y, D_i) \sqcup U_{107}(X, Y, D_i)$
F(TurnAssign)	=	$\lambda X.\lambda Y.\lambda D_i.U_{101}(X, Y, D_i) \sqcup U_{102}(X, Y, D_i)$
F(TurnGrab)	=	$\lambda X.\lambda Y.\lambda D_i.U_{103}(X, Y, D_i) \sqcup U_{104}(X, Y, D_i)$
F(TurnKeep)	=	$\lambda X.\lambda Y.\lambda D_i.U_{101}(X, Y, D_i) \sqcup U_{105}(X, Y, D_i)$
F(TurnRelease)	=	$\lambda X.\lambda Y.\lambda D_i.U_{101}(X, Y, D_i) \sqcup U_{106}(X, Y, D_i)$
F(TurnTake)	=	$\lambda X.\lambda Y.\lambda D_i.U_{105}(X, Y, D_i) \sqcup U_{107}(X, Y, D_i)$

Table 10: Update semantics of turn management functions

4.1.2.3 Time Management Functions Time management acts are used by a speaker to indicate that he needs some time to compose his utterance, as signalled for instance by protracting (decreasing his speech tempo) or filled pauses; or that he needs so much time that he suspends the dialogue as in *Just a moment.* The semantics of such acts requires a context model to contain beliefs about the amount of time needed by cetain cognitive processes; the DIT context model therefore assumes the representation of estimates of amount of time to be represented in the Cognitive Context component, which also contains other information about the speaker's cognitive processing.

Consider for example consider the update semantics of a Stalling act:

(14)
$$\begin{aligned} V(<Sys, Usr, \text{TimeM}, \text{Stalling}>) &= F(\text{Stalling})(Sys, Usr, \text{CogC}) \\ &= U_{111}(Sys, Usr, CogC, \textbf{Time-Need}(Sys, \textbf{small})) \\ &= Usr'_{CC} =+ \textbf{TimeNeed}(Sys, \textbf{small}) \end{aligned}$$

This update operation adds to the pending cognitive context of *Usr* the information that *Sys* needs a small amount of time.

$U_{111}(X, Y, CC)$	Y'_{CC} =+	**TimeNeed**(X, **small**)
$U_{112}(X, Y, CC)$	Y'_{CC} =+	**TimeNeed**(X, **substantial**)
$U_{111}(X, Y, CC)$	Y'_{CC} =+	**TimeNeed**(X, **small**)
$U_{112}(X, Y, CC)$	Y'_{CC} =+	**TimeNeed**(X, **substantial**)

Table 11: Elementary update schemes for the semantics of time management functions.

4.1.2.4 Other Communicative Functions

The semantics of the dimension-specific communicative functions for Contact Management, Discourse Structuring, Own Communication Management, Partner Communication Management, and Social Obligations Management is quite similar to that of the dimension-specific communicative functions that considered above. the main difference being the use of other, dimension-specific predicates.

4.2 The Interpretation of Communicative Function Qualifiers

Communicative function qualifiers come in two varieties, 'q-specifiers' and 'q-additives'. Q-specifiers make preconditions of the communicative function that they qualify more specific, for instance specifying for an answer that there is some uncertainty about the correctness of its content. Q-additives enrich a communicative function, for instance adding that an offer is accepted *happily*. Currently DIT distinguishes two classes of q-specifiers, the 'certainty' and 'conditionality' qualifiers, and one type of q-additive, for 'sentiment' representation.Qualifiers can apply only to general-purpose communicative functions; certainty qualifiers to information-providing functions, and conditionality qualifiers to action-discussion functions. Sentiment qualifiers can be attached in principle to every communicative function.

For the semantics of qualified communicative functions we thus have three possible cases to consider, where f_i is an unqualified communicative function: (a) $\langle f_i, qs_j \rangle$ where qs_j is a q-specifier; (b) $\langle f_i, qa_k \rangle$ where qa_k is a q-additive; and (c) $\langle f_i, qs_j, as_k \rangle$ where qs_j is a q-specifier and qa_k is a q-additive. The following clauses in the definition of the recursive valuation function V for DiAML specify the semantic interpretation in each of these cases:

(15) a. $V(\langle f_i, qs_j \rangle) = (F(f_i))(F(qs_j))$

b. $V(\langle f_i, qa_k \rangle) = \lambda S.\lambda z.[(F(f_i))(S, z) \sqcup (F(qa_k))(S, z)]$

c. $V(\langle f_i, qs_j, qa_k \rangle) = \lambda S.\lambda z.[((F(f_i))(F(qs_j)))(S, z) \sqcup (F(qa_k))(S, z)]$

The semantics of each of the individual qualifiers is defined as follows:

(16)

F(certain)	=	'firm'
F(uncertain)	=	'weak'
F(conditional)	=	'cond'
F(unconditional)	=	$\top$ (the 'empty' condition)
F(sentiment$_k$)	=	$\lambda X.\lambda u.$ SENTIMENT-PREDICATE$_k(X, u)$

We consider two examples. The first illustrates the semantics of an answer, qualified as uncertain, as in (17) ('p5' abbreviates the proposition that the train to Tilburg leaves from platform 5):

(17) 1. A: Does the train to Tilburg leave from platform 5?
2. B: I think so, probably yes.

(18)
$$V(\langle B, A, \text{Task}, p5, \langle \text{Answer, uncertain}\rangle\rangle) = V(\langle \text{Answer, uncertain}\rangle)(A, B, \text{Task}, p5)$$
$$= B_i' =\!\!+ \textbf{Bel}(B, U_1(A, B, \text{Task}, p5, \text{weak}) \sqcup U_2(A, B, \text{Task}, p5, \text{weak}) \sqcup U_9(A, B, Task, p)$$
$$\sqcup U_7(A, B, Tak, p)$$
$$= A'_{SemC} =\!\!+ \textbf{Bel}(A, \textbf{Want}(B, \textbf{Bel}(A, p, \text{weak}))); A'_{SemC} =\!\!+ \textbf{Bel}(A, \textbf{Bel}(B, p, \text{weak}));$$
$$A'_{SemC} =\!\!+ \textbf{Bel}(A, \textbf{Bel}(B, \textbf{Want}(A, \textbf{Know-val}(A, p))));$$
$$A'_{SemC} =\!\!+ \textbf{Bel}(A, \textbf{Bel}(B, \textbf{Assume}(A, \textbf{Know-val}(B, p))))$$

This means that A's pending semantic context is extended with the following pieces of information:

(19) 1. **Bel**$(B, p5,\text{weak})$, or equivalently: **Wk-Bel**$(B, p5)$; i.e., B holds the uncertain belief that $p5$;
2. **Want**$(B,$ **Wk-Bel**$(A, p5))$, i.e. B has the goal that A also holds this uncertain belief;
3. **Bel**$(B,$ **Want**$(A,$ **Know-val**$(A, p)))$, i.e. B believes that A wants to know whether $p5$.
4. **Bel**$(B,$**Assume**$(A,$ **Know-val**$(B, p)))$: B believes that A assumes that B knows whether $p5$.

Second, example (20) illustrates the semantics of an unconditional Accept Offer with a happy sentiment (as in A: *How about a cup of coffee?* B: *Oh yes, that would be wonderful!*), using (15c).

(20)
$$V(\langle \text{AcceptOffer, unconditional, happy}\rangle) =$$
$$= \lambda S.\lambda z.[[F(\text{AcceptOffer})(F(\text{unconditional}))](S, z) \sqcup [F(\text{happy})](S, z)]$$
$$= \lambda S.\lambda z.[[[\lambda X.\lambda Y.\lambda D_i.\lambda \alpha.\lambda C_\alpha.\ U_{24}(X, Y, D_i, \alpha) \sqcup U_{25}(X, Y, D_i, \alpha, C_\alpha) \sqcup$$
$$U_{25b}(X, Y, D_i, \alpha, C_\alpha)](\top)](S, z) \sqcup \text{HAPPY}(S, z))]$$
$$= [[\lambda S.\lambda Y.\lambda D_i.\lambda z.\lambda C_z.\ U_{24}(S, Y, D_i, z) \sqcup U_{25}(S, Y, D_i, z, \top) \sqcup$$
$$U_{25b}(S, Y, D_i, z, \top)] \sqcup \text{HAPPY}(S, z))]$$

Applied to the participants A and B and the action 'coffee', we obtain:

(21)
$$= A'_{Task} =\!\!+ \textbf{Bel}(A, \textbf{Want}(B, \textbf{CommitDo}(A, \text{coffee})));$$
$$A'_{Task} =\!\!+ \textbf{Bel}(A, \textbf{Bel}(B, \textbf{WilDo}(A, \text{coffee})));$$
$$A'_{Task} =\!\!+ \textbf{Bel}(A, \textbf{Bel}(B, \textbf{Want}(A, \textbf{Bel}(B, \textbf{WilDo}(A, \text{coffee})))));$$
$$A'_{CC} =\!\!+ \text{HAPPY}(B, \text{coffee}))]$$

In other words, the Task component of A's pending context is extended with the beliefs that B wants A to commit himself to arrange coffee; that A is willing to do s o; and that A wants B to believe that. Moreover, the understanding that B is happy to get some coffee is represented in the cognitive component of A's pending context.

Concerning the certainty regarding the correctness of provided information, as represented through certainty qualifiers, the unmarked case in natural language is *certain*. A speaker who is quite certain about something may indicate this by expressions like *definitely, most certainly*, but this tends to occur only when doubt or disbelief has expressed about something that was claimed. When there is no expression of uncertainty, the speaker's utterance is therefore interpreted as expressing certainty. For conditionality, the unmarked case is *unconditional*; an unconditional commitment or willingness to perform a certain action can be expressed explicitly, but this tends to occur only if some doubt has been expressed about someone's commitment or willingness. When no conditions for performing an action are expressed, we therefore interpret the utterance as unconditional.

5 Conclusion and Future Work

This paper has outlined an update semantics of dialogue acts, associated with annotation structures defined by the abstract syntax of the DIAML language for semantic annotation, which forms part of ISO standard (24617-2) under development for dialogue act annotation.

Future work that's crying to be done includes further implementation, testing and evaluation beyond what has already been done (see Petukhova, Bunt and Malchanau, 2010; Keizer, Bunt and Petukhova, 2010), and supplementing the approach with an interpretation of the relations between dialogue acts and other units in dialogue (see Petukhova, Prévot and Bunt, 2011).

Acknowledgements

I thank the members of the Tilburg Dialogue Club, who over the years have contributed to shaping Dynamic Interpretation Theory, as well as PhD students and colleagues in related projects. This includes Volha Petukhova, Jeroen Geertzen, Simon Keizer, Roser Morante, Amanda Schiffrin, Ielka van der Sluis, Hans van Dam, Yann Girard, Rintse van der Werff, Elyon Dekoven, Paul Piwek, Robbert-Jan Beun, René Ahn, and Leen Kievit. Important contributions have also come from collaborative work in ISO project 24617-2 "Semantic Annotation Framework, Part 2: Dialogue Acts", in particular with David Traum.

References

Ahn, R. (2001). *Agents, Object and Events: A computational approach to knowledge, observation and communication.* PhD Thesis, Eindhoven University of Technology.

Bunt, H. (2000). Dialogue pragmatics and context specification. In H. Bunt and W. Black (Eds.), *Abduction, Belief and Context in Dialogue. Studies in Computational Pragmatics*, pp. 81–150. Amsterdam: John Benjamins.

Bunt, H. (2006). Dimensions in dialogue annotation. In *Proceedings of the 5th International Conference on Language Resources and Evaluation (LREC 2006), Genova, Italy*, Paris, pp. 919–924. ELRA.

Bunt, H. (2009). Multifunctionality and muldimensional dialogue semantics. In *Proceedings of Dia-Holmia, 13th Workshop on the Semantics and Pragmatics of Dialogue*, Stockholm, pp. 3–14.

Bunt, H. (2010). A methodology for designing semantic annotation languages. In *Proceedings of the 2nd International Conference on Global Interoperability for Language Resources*, Hong Kong, pp. 29–46.

Bunt, H. (2011a). Formal specification of an update semantics for dialogue acts. TiCC Technical Report TR 2011-001, Tilburg Center for Cognition and Communication.

Bunt, H. (2011b). Multifunctionality in dialogue and its interpretation. *Computer, Speech and Language* (25), 225 – 245.

Bunt, H. (forthc.). Interpretation and generation of dialogue with multidimensional context models. In A. Esposito (Ed.), *Toward Autonomous, adaptive, and context-aware multimedia interfaces*, pp. 81–131. Berlin: Springer.

Bunt, H., J. Alexandersson, J. Carletta, J.-W. Choe, A. Fang, K. Hasida, K. Lee, V. Petukhova, A. Popescu-Belis, L. Romary, C. Soria, and Traum (2010). Towards an ISO standard for dialogue act formal annotation. In *Proceedings 7th International Conference on Language Resources and Evaluation (LREC 2010)*, Malta. Paris: ELRA.

Cooper, R. (2000). Information states, attitudes and dependent record types. In L. Cavedon, P. Blackburn, N. Braisby, and A. Shimojima (Eds.), *Logic, Language and Computation, Vol 3*, pp. 85–106. Stanford: CSLI Publications.

Core, M. and J. Allen (1997). Coding dialogs with the DAMSL annotation schema. In *AAAI Fall Symposium on Communicative Action in Humans and Machines*, Boston, MA.

Ide, N. and H. Bunt (2010). Anatomy of semantic annotation schemes: Mappings to GrAF. In *Proceedings of the4th Linguistic Annotation Workshop (LAW-IV)*, Uppsala.

Ide, N. and L. Romary (2004). International standard for a linguistic annotation framework. *Natural Language engineering 10*, 211–225.

ISO (2010). *DIS 24617-2: Semantic annotation framework Part 2: Dialogue acts.* ISO, Geneva: Draft International Standard, July 2010.

Kievit, L., P.Piwek, R.-J. Beun, and H. Bunt (2001). Multimodal cooperative resolution of referential expressions in the DenK system. In H. Bunt and R.-J. Beun (Eds.), *Cooperative Multimodal Communication*, pp. 197–214. Berlin: Springer.

Morante, R. (2007). *Computing meaning in interaction.* Ph.D. Dissertation, Tilburg University.

Petukhova, V. and H. Bunt (2009a). Dimensions in communication. TiCC Technical Report TR 2009-003, Tilburg University.

Petukhova, V. and H. Bunt (2009b). The independence of dimensions in multidimensional dialogue act annotation. In *Proceedings NAACL HLT Conference, Boulder, Colorado.*

Petukhova, V., H. Bunt, and A. Malchanau (2010). Empirical and theoretical constraints on dialogue act combinations. In *Proceedings 14th Workshop on the Semantics and Pragmatics of Dialogue, Poznan.*

Poesio, M. and D. Traum (1998). Towards an axiomatisation of dialogue acts. In *Proceedings of the twente Workshop on the Semantics and Pragmatics of Dialogue*, Enschede, pp. 207 – 222.

Traum, D. and S. Larsson (2003). The information state approach to dialogue management. In *Current and New Directions in Discourse and Dialogue, Kluwer, Dordrecht, pp. 325 – 345.*

Appendix: The DIT++ taxonomy of communicative functions

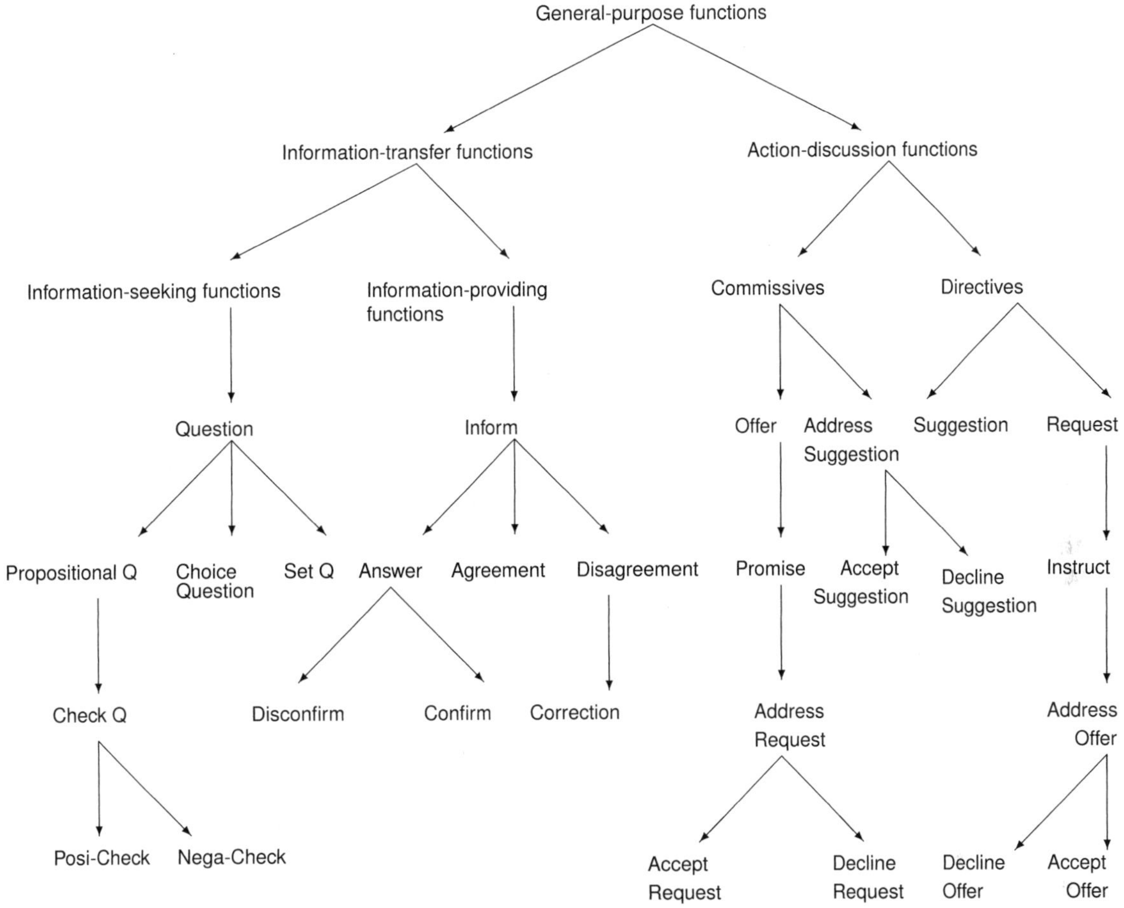

Figure 1: General-purpose functions

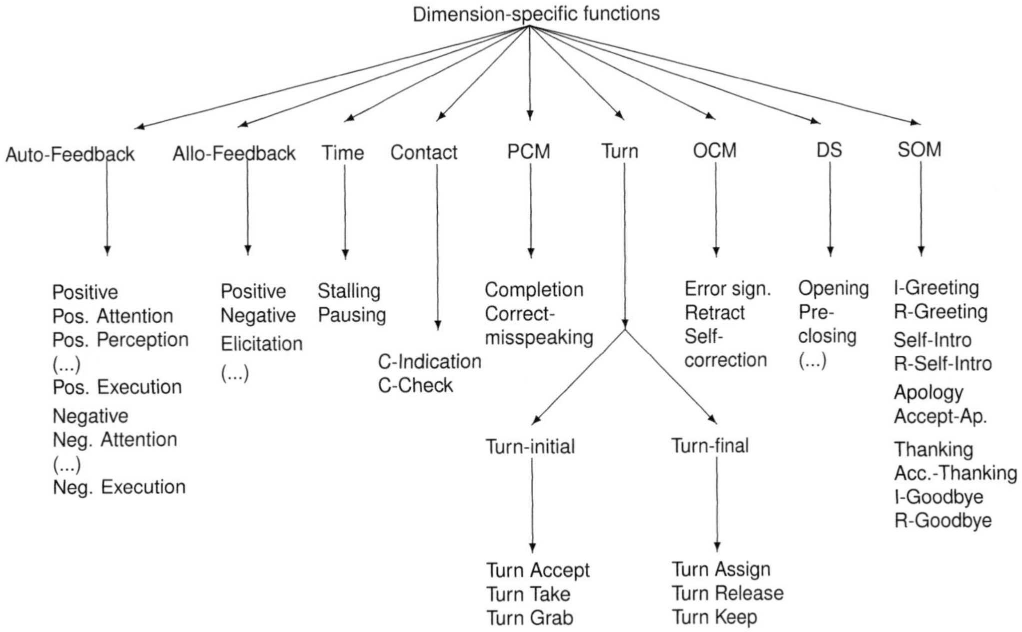

Figure 2: Dimension-specific communicative functions

A New Semantics:
Merging Propositional and Distributional Information

Eduard Hovy

Information Sciences Institute
University of Southern California
hovy@isi.edu

Despite hundreds of years of study on semantics, theories and representations of semantic *content*—the actual meaning of the symbols used in semantic propositions—remain impoverished. The traditional extensional and intensional models of semantics are difficult to actually flesh out in practice, and no large-scale models of this kind exist. Recently, researchers in Natural Language Processing (NLP) have increasingly treated *topic signature word distributions* (also called 'context vectors', 'topic models', 'language models', etc.) as a de facto placeholder for semantics at various levels of granularity. This talk argues for a new kind of semantics that combines traditional symbolic logic-based proposition-style semantics (of the kind used in older NLP) with (computation-based) statistical word distribution information (what is being called Distributional Semantics in modern NLP). The core resource is a single lexico-semantic 'lexicon' that can be used for a variety of tasks. I show how to define such a lexicon, how to build and format it, and how to use it for various tasks. Combining the two views of semantics opens many fascinating questions that beg study, including the operation of logical operators such as negation and modalities over word(sense) distributions, the nature of ontological facets required to define concepts, and the action of compositionality over statistical concepts.

Deterministic Statistical Mapping of Sentences to Underspecified Semantics

Hiyan Alshawi
Google, Inc.
(hiyan@google.com)

Pi-Chuan Chang
Google, Inc.
(pichuan@google.com)

Michael Ringgaard
Google, Inc.
(ringgaard@google.com)

Abstract

We present a method for training a statistical model for mapping natural language sentences to semantic expressions. The semantics are expressions of an underspecified logical form that has properties making it particularly suitable for statistical mapping from text. An encoding of the semantic expressions into dependency trees with automatically generated labels allows application of existing methods for statistical dependency parsing to the mapping task (without the need for separate traditional dependency labels or parts of speech). The encoding also results in a natural per-word semantic-mapping accuracy measure. We report on the results of training and testing statistical models for mapping sentences of the Penn Treebank into the semantic expressions, for which per-word semantic mapping accuracy ranges between 79% and 86% depending on the experimental conditions. The particular choice of algorithms used also means that our trained mapping is deterministic (in the sense of deterministic parsing), paving the way for large-scale text-to-semantic mapping.

1 Introduction

Producing semantic representations of text is motivated not only by theoretical considerations but also by the hypothesis that semantics can be used to improve automatic systems for tasks that are intrinsically semantic in nature such as question answering, textual entailment, machine translation, and more generally any natural language task that might benefit from inference in order to more closely approximate human performance. Since formal logics have formal denotational semantics, and are good candidates for supporting inference, they have often been taken to be the targets for mapping text to semantic representations, with frameworks emphasizing (more) tractable inference choosing first order predicate logic (Stickel, 1985) while those emphasizing representational power favoring one of the many available higher order logics (van Benthem, 1995).

It was later recognized that in order to support some tasks, fully specifying certain aspects of a logic representation, such as quantifier scope, or reference resolution, is often not necessary. For example, for semantic translation, most ambiguities of quantifier scope can be carried over from the source language to the target language without being resolved. This led to the development of underspecified semantic representations (e.g. QLF, Alshawi and Crouch (1992) and MRS, Copestake et al (2005)) which are easier to produce from text without contextual inference but which can be further specified as necessary for the task being performed.

While traditionally mapping text to formal representations was predominantly rule-based, for both the syntactic and semantic components (Montague (1973), Pereira and Shieber (1987), Alshawi (1992)), good progress in statistical syntactic parsing (e.g. Collins (1999), Charniak (2000)) led to systems that applied rules for semantic interpretation to the output of a statistical syntactic parser (e.g. Bos et al. (2004)). More recently researchers have looked at statistical methods to provide robust and trainable methods for mapping text to formal representations of meaning (Zettlemoyer and Collins, 2005).

In this paper we further develop the two strands of work mentioned above, i.e. mapping text to underspecified semantic representations and using statistical parsing methods to perform the analysis.

Here we take a more direct route, starting from scratch by designing an underspecified semantic representation (Natural Logical Form, or NLF) that is purpose-built for statistical text-to-semantics mapping. An underspecified logic whose constructs are motivated by natural language and that is amenable to trainable direct semantic mapping from text without an intervening layer of syntactic representation. In contrast, the approach taken by (Zettlemoyer and Collins, 2005), for example, maps into traditional logic via lambda expressions, and the approach taken by (Poon and Domingos, 2009) depends on an initial step of syntactic parsing.

In this paper, we describe a supervised training method for mapping text to NLF, that is, producing a statistical model for this mapping starting from training pairs consisting of sentences and their corresponding NLF expressions. This method makes use of an encoding of NLF expressions into dependency trees in which the set of labels is automatically generated from the encoding process (rather than being pre-supplied by a linguistically motivated dependency grammar). This encoding allows us to perform the text-to-NLF mapping using any existing statistical methods for labeled dependency parsing (e.g. Eisner (1996), Yamada and Matsumoto (2003), McDonald, Crammer, Pereira (2005)). A side benefit of the encoding is that it leads to a natural per-word measure for semantic mapping accuracy which we use for evaluation purposes. By combing our method with deterministic statistical dependency models together with deterministic (hard) clusters instead of parts of speech, we obtain a deterministic statistical text-to-semantics mapper, opening the way to feasible mapping of text-to-semantics at a large scale, for example the entire web.

This paper concentrates on the text-to-semantics mapping which depends, in part, on some properties of NLF. We will not attempt to defend the semantic representation choices for specific constructions illustrated here. NLF is akin to a variable-free variant of QLF or an MRS in which some handle constraints are determined during parsing. For the purposes of this paper it is sufficient to note that NLF has roughly the same granularity of semantic representation as these earlier underspecified representations.

We outline the steps of our text-to-semantics mapping method in Section 2, introduce NLF in Section 3, explain the encoding of NLF expressions as formal dependency trees in Section 4, and report on experiments for training and testing statistical models for mapping text to NLF expressions in Section 5.

2 Direct Semantic Mapping

Our method for mapping text to natural semantics expressions proceeds as follows:

1. Create a corpus of pairs consisting of text sentences and their corresponding NLF semantic expressions.

2. For each of the sentence-semantics pairs in the corpus, align the words of the sentence to the tokens of the NLF expressions.

3. "Encode" each alignment pair as an ordered dependency tree in which the labels are generated by the encoding process.

4. Train a statistical dependency parsing model with the set of dependency trees.

5. For a new input sentence S, apply the statistical parsing model to S, producing a labeled dependency tree D_S.

6. "Decode" D_S into a semantic expression for S.

For step 1, the experiments in this paper (Section 5) obtain the corpus by converting an existing constituency treebank into semantic expressions. However, direct annotation of a corpus with semantic expressions *is* a viable alternative, and indeed we are separately exploring that possibility for a different, open domain, text corpus.

For steps 4 and 5, any method for training and applying a dependency model from a corpus of labeled dependency trees may be used. As described in Section 5, for the experiments reported here we use an algorithm similar to that of Nivre (2003).

For steps 2, 3 and 6, the encoding of NLF semantic expressions as dependency trees with automatically constructed labels is described in Section 4.

3 Semantic Expressions

NLF expressions are by design amenable to facilitating training of text-to-semantics mappings. For this purpose, NLF has a number of desirable properties:

1. Apart from a few built-in logical connectives, all the symbols appearing in NLF expressions are natural language words.
2. For an NLF semantic expression corresponding to a sentence, the word tokens of the sentence appear exactly once in the NLF expression.
3. The NLF notation is variable-free.

Technically, NLF expressions are expression of an underspecified logic, i.e. a semantic representation that leaves open the interpretation of certain constructs (for example the scope of quantifiers and some operators and the referents of terms such as anaphora, and certain implicit relations such as those for compound nominals). NLF is similar in some ways to Quasi Logical Form, or QLF (Alshawi, 1992), but the properties listed above keep NLF closer to natural language than QLF, hence *natural* logical form. [1] There is no explicit formal connection between NLF and Natural Logic (van Benthem, 1986), though it may turn out that NLF is a convenient starting point for some Natural Logic inferences.

In contrast to statements of a fully specified logic in which denotations are typically taken to be *functions* from possible worlds to truth values (Montague, 1973), denotations of a statement in an underspecified logic are typically taken to be *relations* between possible worlds and truth values (Alshawi and Crouch (1992), Alshawi (1996)). Formal denotations for NLF expressions are beyond the scope of this paper and will be described elsewhere.

3.1 Connectives and Examples

A NLF expression for the sentence

> *In 2002, Chirpy Systems stealthily acquired two profitable companies producing pet accessories.*

is shown in Figure 1.

The NLF constructs and connectives are explained in Table 1. For variable-free abstraction, an NLF expression `[p, ^, a]` corresponds to $\lambda x.p(x,a)$. Note that some common logical operators are not built-in since they will appear directly as words such as *not*.[2] We currently use the unknown/unspecified operator, `%`, mainly for linguistic constructions that are beyond the coverage of a particular semantic mapping model. A simple example that includes `%` in our converted WSJ corpus is *Other analysts are nearly as pessimistic* for which the NLF expression is

```
[are, analysts.other, pessimistic%nearly%as]
```

In Section 5 we give some statistics on the number of semantic expressions containing `%` in the data used for our experiments and explain how it affects our accruracy results.

[1]The term QLF is now sometimes used informally (e.g. Liakata and Pulman (2002), Poon and Domingos (2009)) for any logic-like semantic representation without explicit quantifier scope.

[2]NLF does include Horn clauses, which implictly encode negation, but since Horn clauses are not part of the experiments reported in this paper, we will not discuss them further here.

```
[acquired
     /stealthily
     :[in, ^, 2002],
 Chirpy+Systems,
 companies.two
     :profitable
     :[producing,
        ^,
       pet+accessories]]
```

Figure 1: Example of an NLF semantic expression.

Operator	Example	Denotation	Language Constructs
`[...]`	`[sold, Chirpy, Growler]`	predication tuple	clauses, prepositions, ...
`:`	`company:profitable`	intersection	adjectives, relative clauses, ...
`.`	`companies.two`	(unscoped) quantification	determiners, measure terms
`^`	`[in, ^, 2005]`	variable-free abstract	prepositions, relatives, ...
`_`	`[eating, _, apples]`	unspecified argument	missing verb arguments, ...
`{...}`	`and{Chirpy, Growler}`	collection	noun phrase coordination, ...
`/`	`acquired/stealthily`	type-preserving operator	adverbs, modals, ...
`+`	`Chirpy+Systems`	implicit relation	compound nominals, ...
`@`	`meeting@yesterday`	temporal restriction	bare temporal modifiers, ...
`&`	`[...] & [...]`	conjunction	sentences, ...
`|...|`	`|Dublin, Paris, Bonn|`	sequence	paragraphs, fragments, lists, ...
`%`	`met%as`	uncovered op	constructs not covered

Table 1: NLF constructs and connectives.

4 Encoding Semantics as Dependencies

We encode NLF semantic expressions as labeled dependency trees in which the label set is generated automatically by the encoding process. This is in contrast to conventional dependency trees for which the label sets are presupplied (e.g. by a linguistic theory of dependency grammar). The purpose of the encoding is to enable training of a statistical dependency parser and converting the output of that parser for a new sentence into a semantic expression. The encoding involves three aspects: Alignment, headedness, and label construction.

4.1 Alignment

Since, by design, each word token corresponds to a symbol token (the same word type) in the NLF expression, the only substantive issue in determining the alignment is the occurrence of multiple tokens of the same word type in the sentence. Depending on the source of the sentence-NLF pairs used for training, a particular word in the sentence may or may not already be associated with its corresponding word position in the sentence. For example, in some of the experiments reported in this paper, this correspondence is provided by the semantic expressions obtained by converting a constituency treebank (the well-known Penn WSJ treebank). For situations in which the pairs are provided without this information, as is the case for direct annotation of sentences with NLF expressions, we currently use a heuristic greedy algorithm for deciding the alignment. This algorithm tries to ensure that dependents are near their heads, with a preference for projective dependency trees. To guage the importance of including correct alignments in the input pairs (as opposed to training with inferred alignments), we will present accuracy results for semantic mapping for both correct and automatically infererred alignments.

4.2 Headedness

The encoding requires a definition of headedness for words in an NLF expression, i.e., a head-function h from dependent words to head words. We define h in terms of a head-function g from an NLF (sub)expression e to a word w appearing in that (sub)expression, so that, recursively:

$$g(w) = w$$
$$g([e_1, ..., e_n]) = g(e_1)$$
$$g(e_1 : e_2) = g(e_1)$$
$$g(e_1.e_2) = g(e_1)$$
$$g(e_1/e_2) = g(e_1)$$
$$g(e_1@e_2) = g(e_1)$$
$$g(e_1\&e2) = g(e_1)$$
$$g(|e_1, ..., e_n|) = g(e1)$$
$$g(e_1\{e_2, ..., e_n\}) = g(e_1)$$
$$g(e_1 + ... + e_n) = g(e_n)$$
$$g(e_1\%e_2) = g(e_1)$$

Then a head word $h(w)$ for a dependent w is defined in terms of the smallest (sub)expression e containing w for which

$$h(w) = g(e) \neq w$$

For example, for the NLF expression in Figure 1, this yields the heads shown in Table 3. (The labels shown in that table will be explained in the following section.)

This definition of headedness is not the only possible one, and other variations could be argued for. The specific definition for NLF heads turns out to be fairly close to the notion of head in traditional dependency grammars. This is perhaps not surprising since traditional dependency grammars are often partly motivated by semantic considerations, if only informally.

4.3 Label Construction

As mentioned, the labels used during the encoding of a semantic expression into a dependency tree are derived so as to enable reconstruction of the expression from a labeled dependency tree. In a general sense, the labels may be regarded as a kind of formal semantic label, though more specifically, a label is interpretable as a sequence of instructions for constructing the part of a semantic expression that links a dependent to its head, given that part of the semantic expression, including that derived from the head, has already been constructed. The string for a label thus consists of a sequence of atomic instructions, where the decoder keeps track of a current expression and the parent of that expression in the expression tree being constructed. When a new expression is created it becomes the current expression whose parent is the old current expression. The atomic instructions (each expressed by a single character) are shown in Table 2.

A sequence of instructions in a label can typically (but not always) be paraphrased informally as "starting from head word w_h, move to a suitable node (at or above w_h) in the expression tree, add specified NLF constructs (connectives, tuples, abstracted arguments) and then add w_d as a tuple or connective argument."

Continuing with our running example, the labels for each of the words are shown in Table 3.

Algorithmically, we find it convenient to transform semantic expressions into dependency trees and vice versa via a derivation tree for the semantic expression in which the atomic instruction symbols listed above are associated with individual nodes in the derivation tree.

The output of the statistical parser may contain inconsistent trees with formal labels, in particular trees in which two different arguments are predicated to fill the same position in a semantic expression tuple. For such cases, the decoder that produces the semantic expression applies the simple heuristic

Instruction	Decoding action
[, {, |	Set the current expression to a newly created tuple, collection, or sequence.
:, /, ., +, &, @, %	Attach the current subexpression to its parent with the specified connective.
⋆	Set the current expression to a newly created symbol from the dependent word.
0, 1, ...	Add the current expression at the specified parent tuple position.
^, _	Set the current subexpression to a newly created abstracted-over or unspecfied argument.
-	Set the current subexpression to be the parent of the current expression.

Table 2: Atomic instructions in formal label sequences.

Dependent	Head	Label
In	acquired	[:^1-⋆0
2002	in	-⋆2
Chirpy	Systems	⋆+
Systems	acquired	-⋆1
stealthily	acquired	⋆/
acquired		[⋆0
two	companies	⋆.
profitable	companies	⋆:
companies	acquired	-⋆2
producing	companies	[:^1-⋆0
pet	accessories	⋆+
accessories	producing	-⋆2

Table 3: Formal labels for an example sentence.

Dataset	Null Labels?	Auto Align?	WSJ sections	Sentences
Train+Null-AAlign	yes	no	2-21	39213
Train-Null-AAlign	no	no	2-21	24110
Train+Null+AAlign	yes	yes	2-21	35778
Train-Null+AAlign	no	yes	2-21	22611
Test+Null-AAlign	yes	no	23	2416
Test-Null-AAlign	no	no	23	1479

Table 4: Datasets used in experiments.

of using the next available tuple position when such a conflicting configuration is predicated. In our experiments, we are measuring per-word semantic head-and-label accuracy, so this heuristic does not play a part in that evaluation measure.

5 Experiments

5.1 Data Preparation

In the experiments reported here, we derive our sentence-semantics pairs for training and testing from the Penn WSJ Treebank. This choice reflects the lack, to our knowledge, of a set of such pairs for a reasonably sized publicly available corpus, at least for NLF expressions. Our first step in preparing the data was to convert the WSJ phrase structure trees into semantic expressions. This conversion is done by programming the Stanford treebank toolkit to produce NLF trees bottom-up from the phrase structure trees. This conversion process is not particularly noteworthy in itself (being a traditional rule-based syntax-to-semantics translation process) except perhaps to the extent that the closeness of NLF to natural language perhaps makes the conversion somewhat easier than, say, conversion to a fully resolved logical form.

Since our main goal is to investigate trainable mappings from text strings to semantic expressions, we only use the WSJ phrase structure trees in data preparation: the phrase structure trees are not used as inputs when training a semantic mapping model, or when applying such a model. For the same reason, in these experiments, we do not use the part-of-speech information associated with the phrase structure trees in training or applying a semantic mapping model. Instead of parts-of-speech we use word cluster features from a hierarchical clustering produced with the unsupervised Brown clustering method (Brown et al, 1992); specifically we use the publicly available clusters reported in Koo et al. (2008).

Constructions in the WSJ that are beyond the explicit coverage of the conversion rules used for data preparation result in expressions that include the unknown/unspecified (or 'Null') operator `%`. We report on different experimental settings in which we vary how we treat training or testing expressions with `%`. This gives rise to the data sets in Table 4 which have +Null (i.e., including `%`), and -Null (i.e., not including `%`) in the data set names.

Another attribute we vary in the experiments is whether to align the words in the semantic expressions to the words in the sentence automatically, or whether to use the correct alignment (in this case preserved from the conversion process, but could equally be provided as part of a manual semantic annotation scheme, for example). In our current experiments, we discard non-projective dependency trees from training sets. Automatic alignment results in additional non-projective trees, giving rise to different effective training sets when auto-alignment is used: these sets are marked with +AAlign, otherwise -AAlign. The training set numbers shown in Table 4 are the resulting sets after removal of non-projective trees.

Training	Test	Accuracy(%)
+Null-AAlign	+Null-AAlign	81.2
-Null-AAlign	+Null-AAlign	78.9
-Null-AAlign	-Null-AAlign	86.1
+Null-AAlign	-Null-AAlign	86.5

Table 5: Per-word semantic accuracy when training with the correct alignment.

Training	Test	Accuracy(%)
+Null+AAlign	+Null-AAlign	80.4
-Null+AAlign	+Null-AAlign	78.0
-Null+AAlign	-Null-AAlign	85.5
+Null+AAlign	-Null-AAlign	85.8

Table 6: Per-word semantic accuracy when training with an auto-alignment.

5.2 Parser

As mentioned earlier, our method can make use of any trainable statistical dependency parsing algorithm. The parser is trained on a set of dependency trees with formal labels as explained in Sections 2 and 4. The specific parsing algorithm we use in these experiments is a deterministic shift reduce algorithm (Nivre, 2003), and the specific implementation of the algorithm uses a linear SVM classifier for predicting parsing actions (Chang et al., 2010). As noted above, hierarchical cluster features are used instead of parts-of-speech; some of the features use coarse (6-bit) or finer (12-bit) clusters from the hierarchy. More specifically, the full set of features is:

- The words for the current and next input tokens, for the top of the stack, and for the head of the top of the stack.
- The formal labels for the top-of-stack token and its leftmost and rightmost children, and for the leftmost child of the current token.
- The cluster for the current and next three input tokens and for the top of the stack and the token below the top of the stack.
- Pairs of features combining 6-bit clusters for these tokens together with 12-bit clusters for the top of stack and next input token.

5.3 Results

Tables 5 and 6 show the *per-word semantic accuracy* for different training and test sets. This measure is simply the percentage of words in the test set for which both the predicted formal label and the head word are correct. In syntactic dependency evaluation terminology, this corresponds to the labeled attachment score.

All tests are with respect to the correct alignment; we vary whether the correct alignment (Table 5) or auto-alignment (Table 6) is used for training to give an idea of how much our heuristic alignment is hurting the semantic mapping model. As shown by comparing the two tables, the loss in accuracy due to using the automatic alignment is only about 1%, so while the automatic alignment algorithm can probably be improved, the resulting increase in accuracy would be relatively small.

As shown in the Tables 5 and 6, two versions of the test set are used: one that includes the 'Null' operator `%`, and a smaller test set with which we are testing only the subset of sentences for which the semantic expressions do not include this label. The highest accuracies (mid 80's) shown are for the

# Labels	# Train Sents	Accuracy(%)
151 (all)	22611	85.5
100	22499	85.5
50	21945	85.5
25	17669	83.8
12	7008	73.4

Table 7: Per-word semantic accuracy after pruning label sets in Train-Null+AAlign (and testing with Test-Null-AAlign).

(easier) test set which excludes examples in which the test semantic expressions contain Null operators. The strictest settings, in which semantic expressions with Null are not included in training but included in the test set effectively treat prediction of Null operators as errors. The lower accuracy (high 70's) for such stricter settings thus incorporates a penalty for our incomplete coverage of semantics for the WSJ sentences. The less strict Test+Null settings in which `%` is treated as a valid output may be relevant to applications that can tolerate some unknown operators between subexpressions in the output semantics.

Next we look at the effect of limiting the size of the automatically generated formal label set prior to training. For this we take the configuration using the TrainWSJ-Null+AAlign training set and the TestWSJ-Null-AAlign test set (the third row in Table refPerWordSemanticAccuracyAAlign for which auto-alignment is used and only labels without the NULL operator `%` are included). For this training set there are 151 formal labels. We then limit the training set to instances that only include the most frequent k labels, for $k = 100, 50, 25, 12$, while keeping the test set the same. As can be seen in Table 7, the accuracy is unaffected when the training set is limited to the 100 most frequent or 50 most frequent labels. There is a slight loss when training is limited to 25 labels and a large loss if it is limited to 12 labels. This appears to show that, for this corpus, the core label set needed to construct the majority of semantic expressions has a size somewhere between 25 and 50. It is perhaps interesting that this is roughly the size of hand-produced traditional dependency label sets. On the other hand, it needs to be emphasized that since Table 7 ignores beyond-coverage constructions that presently include Null labels, it is likely that a larger label set would be needed for more complete semantic coverage.

6 Conclusion and Further Work

We've shown that by designing an underspecified logical form that is motivated by, and closely related to, natural language constructions, it is possible to train a direct statistical mapping from pairs of sentences and their corresponding semantic expressions, with per-word accuracies ranging from 79% to 86% depending on the strictness of the experimental setup. The input to training does not require any traditional syntactic categories or parts of speech. We also showed, more specifically, that we can train a model that can be applied deterministically at runtime (using a deterministic shift reduce algorithm combined with deterministic clusters), making large-scale text-to-semantics mapping feasible.

In traditional formal semantic mapping methods (Montague (1973), Bos et al. (2004)), and even some recent statistical mapping methods (Zettlemoyer and Collins, 2005), the semantic representation is overloaded to performs two functions: (i) representing the final meaning, and (ii) composing meanings from the meanings of subconstituents (e.g. through application of higher order lambda functions). In our view, this leads to what are perhaps overly complex semantic representations of some basic linguistic constructions. In contrast, in the method we presented, these two concerns (meaning representation and semantic construction) are separated, enabling us to keep the semantics of constituents simple, while turning the construction of semantic expressions into a separate structured learning problem (with its own internal prediction and decoding mechanisms).

Although, in the experiments we reported here we *do* prepare the training data from a traditional treebank, we are encouraged by the results and believe that annotation of a corpus with only semantic expressions is sufficient for building an efficient and reasonably accurate text-to-semantics mapper. Indeed, we have started building such a corpus for a question answering application, and hope to report results for that corpus in the future. Other further work includes a formal denotational semantics of the underspecified logical form and elaboration of practical inference operations with the semantic expressions. This work may also be seen as a step towards viewing semantic interpretation of language as the interaction between a pattern recognition process (described here) and an inference process.

References

Hiyan Alshawi and Richard Crouch. 1992. Monotonic Semantic Interpretation. *Proceedings of the 30th Annual Meeting of the Association for Computational Linguistics.* Newark, Delaware, 32–39.

Hiyan Alshawi, ed. 1992. *The Core Language Engine.* MIT Press, Cambridge, Massachusetts.

Hiyan Alshawi. 1996. Underspecified First Order Logics. In *Semantic Ambiguity and Underspecification*, edited by Kees van Deemter and Stanley Peters, CSLI Publications, Stanford, California.

Johan van Benthem. 1986. *Essays in Logical Semantics.* Reidel, Dordrecht.

Johan van Benthem. 1995. *Language in Action: Categories, Lambdas, and Dynamic Logic.* MIT Press, Cambridge, Massachusetts.

Bos, Johan, Stephen Clark, Mark Steedman, James R. Curran, and Julia Hockenmaier. 2004. Wide-coverage semantic representations from a CCG parser. *Proceedings of the 20th International Conference on Computational Linguistics.* Geneva, Switzerland, 1240–1246.

P. Brown, V. Pietra, P. Souza, J. Lai, and R. Mercer. 1992. Class-based n-gram models of natural language. *Computational Linguistics*, 18(4):467–479.

Eugene Charniak. 2000. A maximum entropy inspired parser. *Proceedings of the 1st Conference of the North American Chapter of the Association for Computational Linguistics*, Seattle, Washington.

Michael Collins. 1999. *Head Driven Statistical Models for Natural Language Parsing.* Ph.D. thesis, University of Pennsylvania.

A. Copestake, D. Flickinger, I. Sag, C. Pollard. 2005. Minimal Recursion Semantics, An Introduction. *Research on Language and Computation*, 3(23):281-332.

D. Davidson. 1967. The Logical Form of Action Sentences. In *The Logic of Decision and Action*, edited by N. Rescher, University of Pittsburgh Press, Pittsburgh, Pennsylvania.

Jason Eisner. 1996. Three New Probabilistic Models for Dependency Parsing: An Exploration. *Proceedings of the 16th International Conference on Computational Linguistics (COLING-96*, 340–345.

T. Koo, X. Carreras, and M. Collins. 2008. Simple Semisupervised Dependency Parsing. *Proceedings of the Annual Meeting of the Association for Computational Linguistics.*

Maria Liakata and Stephen Pulman. 2002. From trees to predicate-argument structures. *Proceedings of the 19th International Conference on Computational Linguistics.* Taipei, Taiwan, 563–569.

Chang, Y.-W., C.-J. Hsieh, K.-W. Chang, M. Ringgaard, and C.-J. Lin. 2010. Training and Testing Low-degree Polynomial Data Mappings via Linear SVM. *Journal of Machine Learning Research*, 11, 1471–1490.

Ryan McDonald, Koby Crammer and Fernando Pereira 2005. Online Large-Margin Training of Dependency Parsers. *Proceedomgs of the 43rd Annual Meeting of the Association for Computational Linguistics.*.

R. Montague. 1973. The Proper Treatment of Quantification in Ordinary English. In *Formal Philosophy*, edited by R. Thomason, Yale University Press, New Haven.

Fernando Pereira and Stuart Shieber. 1987. *Prolog and Natural Language Analysis.* Center for the Study of Language and Information, Stanford, California.

Joakim Nivre 2003 An Efficient Algorithm for Projective Dependency Parsing. *Proceedings of the 8th International Workshop on Parsing Technologies*, 149–160.

H. Poon and P. Domingos 2009. Unsupervised semantic parsing. *Proceedings of the 2009 Conference on Empirical Methods in Natural Language Processing*, Singapore, 2009.

Mark Stickel. 1985. Automated deduction by theory resolution. *Journal of Automated Reasoning*, 1, 4.

Hiroyasu Yamada and Yuji Matsumoto 2003. Statistical dependency analysis with support vector machines. *Proceedings of the 8th International Workshop on Parsing Technologies*, 195–206.

Zettlemoyer, Luke S. and Michael Collins. 2005. Learning to map sentences to logical form: Structured classification with probabilistic categorial grammars. *Proceedings of the 21st Conference on Uncertainty in Artificial Intelligence.* Edinburgh, Scotland, 658–666.

Word Sense Disambiguation with Multilingual Features

Carmen Banea and Rada Mihalcea
Department of Computer Science and Engineering
University of North Texas
carmenbanea@my.unt.edu, rada@cs.unt.edu

Abstract

This paper explores the role played by a multilingual feature representation for the task of word sense disambiguation. We translate the context of an ambiguous word in multiple languages, and show through experiments on standard datasets that by using a multilingual vector space we can obtain error rate reductions of up to 25%, as compared to a monolingual classifier.

1 Introduction

Ambiguity is inherent to human language. In particular, word sense ambiguity is prevalent in all natural languages, with a large number of the words in any given language carrying more than one meaning. For instance, the English noun *plant* can mean *green plant* or *factory*; similarly the French word *feuille* can mean *leaf* or *paper*. The correct sense of an ambiguous word can be selected based on the context where it occurs, and correspondingly the problem of *word sense disambiguation* is defined as the task of automatically assigning the most appropriate meaning to a polysemous word within a given context.

Among the various knowledge-based (Lesk, 1986; Mihalcea et al., 2004) and data-driven (Yarowsky, 1995; Ng and Lee, 1996) word sense disambiguation methods that have been proposed to date, supervised systems have been constantly observed as leading to the highest performance. In these systems, the sense disambiguation problem is formulated as a supervised learning task, where each sense-tagged occurrence of a particular word is transformed into a feature vector which is then used in an automatic learning process. One of the main drawbacks associated with these methods is the fact that their performance is closely connected to the amount of labeled data available at hand.

In this paper, we investigate a new supervised word sense disambiguation method that is able to take additional advantage of the sense-labeled examples by exploiting the information that can be obtained from a multilingual representation. We show that by representing the features in a multilingual space, we are able to improve the performance of a word sense disambiguation system by a significant margin, as compared to a traditional system that uses only monolingual features.

2 Related Work

Despite the large number of word sense disambiguation methods that have been proposed so far, targeting the resolution of word ambiguity in different languages, there are only a few methods that try to explore more than one language at a time. The work that is perhaps most closely related to ours is the bilingual bootstrapping method introduced in (Li and Li, 2002), where word translations are automatically disambiguated using information iteratively drawn from two languages. Unlike that approach, which iterates between two languages to select the correct translation for a given target word, in our method we *simultaneously* use the features extracted from several languages. In fact, our method can handle more than two languages at a time, and we show that the accuracy of the disambiguation algorithm increases with the number of languages used.

There have also been a number of attempts to exploit parallel corpora for word sense disambiguation (Resnik and Yarowsky, 1999; Diab and Resnik, 2002; Ng et al., 2003), but in that line of work the parallel texts were mainly used as a way to induce word senses or to create sense-tagged corpora, rather than as a source of additional multilingual views for the disambiguation features. Another related technique is concerned with the selection of correct word senses in context using large corpora in a second language (Dagan and Itai, 1994), but as before, the additional language is used to help distinguishing between the word senses in the original language, and not as a source of additional information for the disambiguation context.

Also related is the recent SEMEVAL task that has been proposed for cross-lingual lexical substitution, where the word sense disambiguation task was more flexibly formulated as the identification of cross-lingual lexical substitutes in context (Mihalcea et al., 2010). A number of different approaches have been proposed by the teams participating in the task, and although several of them involved the translation of contexts or substitutes from one language to another, none of them attempted to make simultaneous use of the information available in the two languages.

Finally, although the multilingual subjectivity classifier proposed in Banea et al. (2010) is not directly applicable to the disambiguation task we address in this paper, their findings are similar to ours. In that paper, the authors showed how a natural language task can benefit from the use of features drawn from multiple languages, thus supporting the hypothesis that multilingual features can be effectively used to improve the accuracy of a monolingual classifier.

3 Motivation

Our work seeks to explore the expansion of a monolingual feature set with features drawn from multiple languages in order to generate a more robust and more effective vector-space representation that can be used for the task of word sense disambiguation. While traditional monolingual representations allow a supervised learning systems to achieve a certain accuracy, we try to surpass this limitation by infusing additional information in the model, mainly in the form of features extracted from the machine translated view of the monolingual data. A statistical machine translation (MT) engine does not only provide a dictionary-based translation of the words surrounding a given ambiguous word, but it also encodes the translation knowledge derived from very large parallel corpora, thus accounting for the contextual dependencies between the words.

In order to better explain why a multilingual vector space provides for a better representation for the word sense disambiguation task, consider the following examples centered around the ambiguous verb **build**.[1] For illustration purposes, we only show examples for four out of the ten possible meanings in WordNet (Fellbaum, 1998), and we only show the translations in one language (French). All the translations are performed using the Google Translate engine.

En 1: Telegraph Co. said it will spend $20 million to **build** a factory in Guadalajara, Mexico, to make telephone answering machines. (*sense id 1*)
Fr 1: Telegraph Co. a annoncé qu'il dépensera 20 millions de dollars pour **construire** une usine á Guadalajara, au Mexique, pour faire répondeurs téléphoniques.

En 2: A member in the House leadership and skilled legislator, Mr. Fazio nonetheless found himself burdened not only by California's needs but by Hurricane Hugo amendments he accepted in a vain effort to **build** support in the panel. (*sense id 3*)
Fr 2: Un membre de la direction de la Chambre et le législateur compétent, M. Fazio a néanmoins conclu lui-même souffre, non seulement par les besoins de la Californie, mais par l'ouragan Hugo amendements qu'il a accepté dans un vain effort pour **renforcer** le soutien dans le panneau.

En 3: Burmah Oil PLC, a British independent oil and specialty-chemicals marketing concern, said SHV Holdings N.V. has **built** up a 7.5% stake in the company. (*sense id 3*)

[1]The sentences provided and their annotations are extracted from the SEMEVAL corpus.

Fr 3: Burmah Oil PLC, une huile indépendant britannique et le souci de commercialisation des produits chimiques de spécialité, a déclaré SHV Holdings NV a **acquis** une participation de 7,5% dans la société.

En 4: Plaintiffs' lawyers say that buildings become "sick" when inadequate fresh air and poor ventilation systems lead pollutants to **build** up inside. (*sense id 2*)
Fr 4: Avocats des plaignants disent que les bâtiments tombent malades quand l'insuffisance d'air frais et des systèmes de ventilation insuffisante de plomb polluants de s'**accumuler** à l'intérieur.

As illustrated by these examples, the multilingual representation helps in two important ways. First, it attempts to disambiguate the target ambiguous word by assigning it a different translation depending on the context where it occurs. For instance, the first example includes a usage for the verb **build** in its most frequent sense, namely that of **construct** (WordNet: *make by combining materials and parts*), and this sense is correctly translated into French as **construire**. In the second sentence, **build** is used as part of the verbal expression **build support** where it means *to form or accumulate steadily* (WordNet), and it is accurately translated in both French sentences as **renforcer**. For sentences three and four, **build** is followed by the adverb **up**, yet in the first case, its sense id in WordNet is 3, *build or establish something abstract*, while in the second one is 2, *form or accumulate steadily*. Being able to infer from the co-occurrence of additional words appearing the context, the MT engine differentiates the two usages in French, translating the first occurrence as **acquis** and the second one as **accumuler**.

Second, the multilingual representation also significantly enriches the feature space, by adding features drawn from multiple languages. For instance, the feature vector for the first example will not only include English features such as *factory* and *make*, but it will also include additional French features such as *usine* and *faire*. Similarly, the second example will have a feature vector including words such as *buildings* and *systems*, and also *bâtiments* and *systèmes*. While this multilingual representation can sometime result in redundancy when there is a one-to-one translation between languages, in most cases however the translations will enrich the feature space, by either indicating that two features in English share the same meaning (e.g., the words *manufactory* and *factory* will both be translated as *usine* in French), or by disambiguating ambiguous English features using different translations (e.g., the context word *plant* will be translated in French as *usine* or *plante*, depending on its meaning).

Appending therefore multilingual features to the monolingual vector generates a more orthogonal vector space. If, previously, the different senses of **build** were completely dependent on their surrounding context in the source language, now they are additionally dependent on the disambiguated translation of **build** given its context, as well as the context itself and the translation of the context.

4 Multilingual Vector Space Representations for WSD

4.1 Datasets

We test our model on two publicly available word sense disambiguation datasets. Each dataset includes a number of ambiguous words. For each word, a number of sample contexts were extracted and then manually labeled with their correct sense. Therefore, both datasets follow a Zipfian distribution of senses in context, given their natural usage. Note also that senses do not cross part-of-speech boundaries.

The TWA[2] (two-way ambiguities) dataset contains sense tagged examples for six words that have two-way ambiguities (bass, crane, motion, palm, plant, tank). These are words that have been previously used in word sense disambiguation experiments reported in (Yarowsky, 1995; Mihalcea, 2003). Each word has approximately 100 to 200 examples extracted from the British National Corpus. Since the words included in this dataset have only two homonym senses, the classification task is easier.

[2] http://www.cse.unt.edu/~rada/downloads.html\#twa

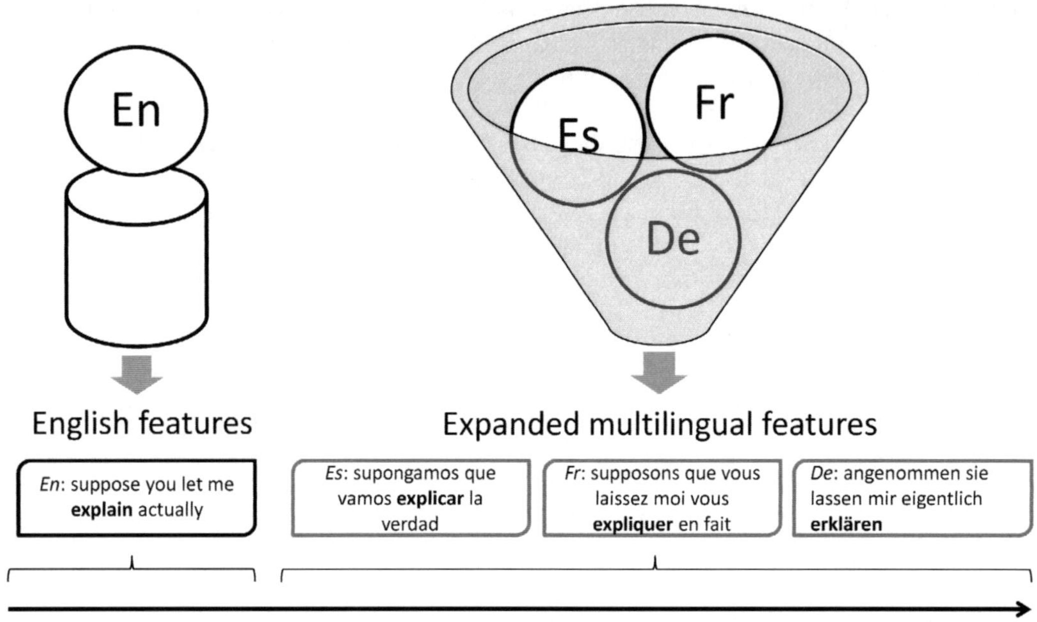

Figure 1: Construction of a multilingual vector (combinations of target languages $C(3, k)$, where $k = 0..3$

The second dataset is the SEMEVAL corpus 2007 (Pradhan et al., 2007),[3] consisting of a sample of 35 nouns and 65 verbs with usage examples extracted from the Penn Treebank as well as the Brown corpus, and annotated with OntoNotes sense tags (Hovy et al., 2006). These senses are more coarse grained when compared to the traditional sense repository encoded in the WordNet lexical database. While OntoNotes attains over 90% inter-annotator agreement, rendering it particularly useful for supervised learning approaches, WordNet is too fine grained even for human judges to agree (Hovy et al., 2006). The number of examples available per word and per sense varies greatly; some words have as few as 50 examples, while some others can have as many as 2,000 examples. Some of these contexts are considerably longer than those appearing in TWA, containing around 200 words. For the experiments reported in this paper, given the limitations imposed by the number of contexts that can be translated by the online translation engine,[4] we randomly selected a subset of 31 nouns and verbs from this dataset.

4.2 Model

In order to generate a multilingual representation for the TWA and SEMEVAL datasets, we rely on the method proposed in Banea et al. (2010) and use Google Translate to transfer the data from English into several other languages and produce multilingual representations. We experiment with three languages, namely French (Fr), German (De) and Spanish (Es). Our choice is motivated by the fact that when Google made public their statistical machine translation system in 2007, these were the only languages covered by their service, and we therefore assume that the underlying statistical translation models are also the most robust. Upon translation, the data is aligned at instance level, so that the original English context is augmented with three mirroring contexts in French, German, and Spanish, respectively.

We extract the word unigrams from each of these contexts, and then generate vectors that consist of the original English unigrams followed by the multilingual portion resulted from all possible combinations of the three languages taken 0 through 3 at a time, or more formally $C(3, k)$, where $k = 0..3$ (see Figure 1). For instance, a vector resulting from $C(3, 0)$ is the traditional monolingual vector, whereas a vector built from the combination $C(3, 3)$ contains features extracted from all languages.

[3] `http://nlp.cs.swarthmore.edu/semeval/tasks/task17/description.shtml`

[4] We use Google Translate (`http://translate.google.com/`), which has a limitation of 1,000 translations per day.

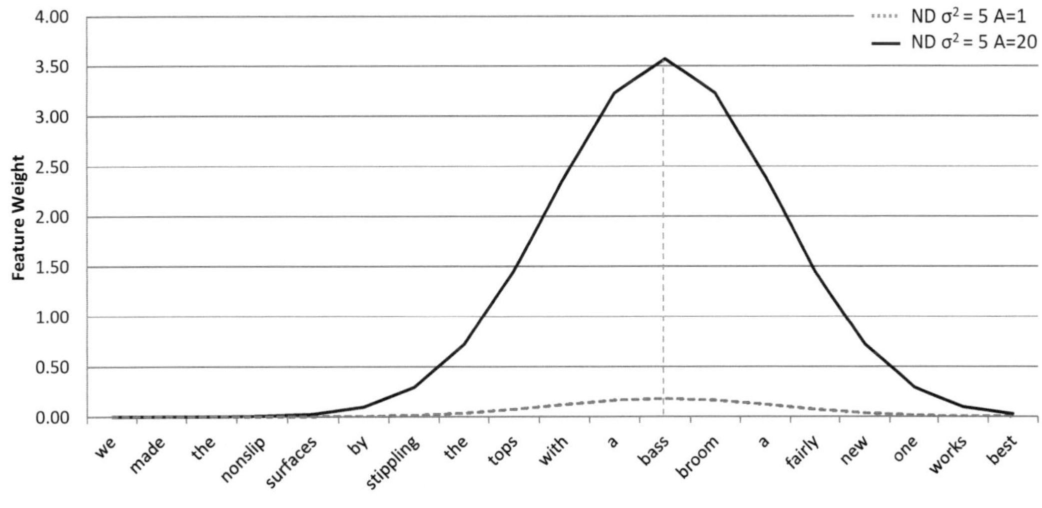

Figure 2: Example of sentence whose words are weighted based on a normal distribution with variance of 5, and an amplification factor of 20

4.2.1 Feature Weighting

For weighting, we use a parametrized weighting based on a normal distribution scheme, to better leverage the multilingual features. Let us consider the following sentence:

> We made the non-slip surfaces by stippling the tops with a <head> bass </head> broom a fairly new one works best.

Every instance in our datasets contains an XML-marking before and after the word to be disambiguated (also known as a headword), in order to identify it from the context. For instance, in the example above, the headword is **bass**. The position of this headword in the context can be considered the mean of a normal distribution. When considering a $\sigma^2 = 5$, five words to the left and right of the mean are activated with a value above 10^{-2} (see the dotted line in Figure 2). However, all the features are actually activated by some amount, allowing this weighting model to capture a continuous weight distribution across the entire context. In order to attain a higher level of discrepancy between the weight of consecutive words, we amplify the normal distribution curve by an empirically determined factor of 20, effectively mapping the values to an interval ranging from 0 to 4. We apply this amplified activation to every occurrence of a headword in a context. If two activation curves overlap, meaning that a given word has two possible weights, the final weight is set to the highest (generated by the closest headword in context). Similar weighting is also performed on the translated contexts, allowing for the highest weight to be attained by the headword translated into the target language, and a decrementally lower weight for its surrounding context.

This method therefore allows the vector-space model to capture information pertaining to both the headword and its translations in the other languages, as well as a language dependent gradient of the neighboring context usage. While a traditional bigram or trigram model only captures an exact expression, a normal distribution based model is able to account for wild cards, and transforms the traditionally sparse feature space into one that is richer and more compact at the same time.

4.3 Adjustments

We encountered several technical difficulties in translating the XML-formatted datasets, which we will expand on in this section.

4.3.1 XML-formatting and alignment

First of all, as every instance in our datasets contains an XML-marked headword (as shown in Section 4.2.1), the tags interfere with the MT system, and we had to remove them from the context before proceeding with the translation. The difficulty came from the fact that the translated context provides no way of identifying the translation of the original headword. In order to acquire candidate translations of the English headword we query the Google Multilingual Dictionary[5] (setting the dictionary direction from English to the target language) and consider only the candidates listed under the correct part-of-speech. We then scan the translated context for any of the occurrences mined from the dictionary, and locate the candidates.

In some of the cases we also identify candidate headwords in the translated context that do not mirror the occurrence of a headword in the English context (i.e., the number of candidates is higher than the number of headwords in English). We solve this problem by relying on the assumption that there is an ideal position for a headword candidate, and this ideal position should reflect the relative position of the original headword with regard to its context. This alignment procedure is supported by the fact that the languages we use follow a somewhat similar sentence structure; given parallel paragraphs of text, these cross-lingual "context anchors" will lie in close vicinity. We therefore create two lists: the first list is the reference English list, and contains the indexes of the English headwords (normalized to 100); the second list contains the normalized indexes of the candidate headwords in the target language context. For each candidate headword in the target language, we calculate the shortest distance to a headword appearing in the reference English list. Once the overall shortest distance is found, both the candidate headword's index in the target language and its corresponding English headword's index are removed from their respective list. The process continues until the reference English list is empty.

4.3.2 Inflections

There are also cases when we are not able to identify a headword due to the fact that we are trying to find the lemma (extracted from the multilingual dictionary) in a fully inflected context, where most probably the candidate translation is inflected as well. As French, German and Spanish are all highly inflected languages, we are faced with two options: to either lemmatize the contexts in each of the languages, which requires a lemmatizer tuned for each language individually, or to stem them. We chose the latter option, and used the Lingua::Stem::Snowball,[6] which is a publicly available implementation of the Porter stemmer in multiple languages.

To summarize, all the translations are stemmed to obtain maximum coverage, and alignment is performed when the number of candidate entries found in a translated context does not match the frequency of candidate headwords in the reference English context. Also, all the contexts are processed to remove any special symbols and numbers.

5 Results and Discussion

5.1 Experimental Setup

In order to determine the effect of the multilingual expanded feature space on word sense disambiguation, we conduct several experiments using the TWA and SEMEVAL datasets. The results are shown in Tables 1 and 2.

Our proposed model relies on a multilingual vector space, where each individual feature is weighted using a scheme based on a modified normal distribution (Section 4.2.1). As eight possible combinations are available when selecting one main language (English) and combinations of three additional languages

[5] `http://www.google.com/dictionary`

[6] `http://search.cpan.org/dist/Lingua-Stem-Snowball/lib/Lingua/Stem/Snowball.pm`

taken 0 through 3 at a time (Spanish, French and German), we train eight Naïve Bayes learners[7] on the resulted datasets: one monolingual (En), three bilingual (En-De, En-Fr, En-Es), three tri-lingual (En-De-Es, En-De-Fr, En-Fr-Es), and one quadri-lingual (En-Fr-De-Es). Each dataset is evaluated using ten fold cross-validation; the resulting micro-accuracy measures are averaged across each of the language groupings and they appear in Tables 1 and 2 in ND-L1 (column 4), ND-L2 (column 5), ND-L3 (column 6), and ND-L4 (column 7), respectively. Our hypothesis is that as more languages are added to the mix (and therefore the number of features increases), the learner will be able to distinguish better between the various senses.

5.2 Baselines

Our baseline consists of the predictions made by a majority class learner, which labels all examples with the predominant sense encountered in the training data.[8] Note that the most frequent sense baseline is often times difficult to surpass because many of the words exhibit a disproportionate usage of their main sense (i.e., higher than 90%), such as the noun *bass* or the verb *approve*. Despite the fact that the majority vote learner provides us with a supervised baseline, it does not take into consideration actual features pertaining to the instances. We therefore introduce a second, more informed baseline that relies on binary-weighted features extracted from the English view of the datasets and we train a multinomial Naïve Bayes learner on this data. For every word included in our datasets, the binary-weighted Naïve Bayes learner achieves the same or higher accuracy as the most frequent sense baseline.

5.3 Experiments

Comparing the accuracies obtained when training on the monolingual data, the binary weighted baseline surpasses the normal distribution-based weighting model in only three out of six cases on the TWA dataset (difference ranging from .5% to 4.81%), and in 6 out of 31 cases on the SEMEVAL dataset (difference ranging from .53% to 7.57%, where for 5 of the words, the difference is lower than 3%). The normal distribution-based model is thus able to activate regions around a particular headword, and not an entire context, ensuring more accurate sense boundaries, and allowing this behavior to be expressed in multilingual vector spaces as well (as seen in columns 7-9 in Tables 1 and 2).

When comparing the normal distribution-based model using one language versus more languages, 5 out of 6 words in TWA score highest when the expanded feature space includes all languages, and one scores highest for combinations of 3 languages (only .17% higher than the accuracy obtained for all languages). We notice the same behavior in the SEMEVAL dataset, where 18 of the words exhibit their highest accuracy when all four languages are taken into consideration, and 3 achieve the highest score for three-language groupings (at most .37% higher than the accuracy obtained for the four language grouping). While the model displays a steady improvement as more languages are added to the mix, four of the SEMEVAL words are unable to benefit from this expansion, namely the verbs buy (-0.61%), care (-1.45%), feel (-0.29%) and propose (-2.94%). Even so, we are able to achieve error rate reductions ranging from 6.52% to 63.41% for TWA, and from 3.33% to 34.62% for SEMEVAL.

To summarize the performance of the model based on the expanded feature set and the proposed baselines, we aggregate all the accuracies from Tables 1 and 2, and present the results obtained in Table 3. The monolingual modified normal-distribution model is able to exceed the most common sense baseline and the binary-weighted Naïve Bayes learner for both datasets, proving its superiority as compared to a purely binary-weighted model. Furthermore, we notice a consistent increase in accuracy as more languages are added to the vector space, displaying an average increment of 1.7% at every step for TWA, and 0.67% for SEMEVAL. The highest accuracy is achieved when all languages are taken into consideration: 86.02% for TWA and 83.36% for SEMEVAL, corresponding to an error reduction of 25.96% and 10.58%, respectively.

[7]We use the multinomial Naïve Bayes implementation provided by the Weka machine learning software (Hall et al., 2009).

[8]Our baseline it is not the same as the traditional most common sense baseline that uses WordNet's first sense heuristic, because our data sets are not annotated with WordNet senses.

1 Word	2 # Inst	3 # Senses	4 MCS	5 BIN-L1	6 ND-L1	7 ND-L2	8 ND-L3	9 ND-L4	10 Error Red.
bass.n	107	2	90.65	90.65	90.65	91.28	91.90	**92.52**	20.00
crane.n	95	2	75.79	75.79	76.84	76.14	76.49	**78.95**	9.09
motion.n	201	2	70.65	81.09	79.60	86.73	89.88	**92.54**	63.41
palm.n	201	2	71.14	73.13	87.06	88.89	**89.72**	89.55	19.23
plant.n	187	2	54.55	79.14	74.33	77.90	81.82	**83.96**	37.50
tank.n	201	2	62.69	77.61	77.11	76.29	76.45	**78.61**	6.52

Table 1: Accuracies obtained on the TWA dataset; Columns: **1** - words contained in the corpus, **2** - number of examples for a given word, **3** - number of senses covered by the examples, **4** - micro-accuracy obtained when using the most common sense (MCS), **5** - micro-accuracy obtained using the multinomial Naïve Bayes classifier on binary weighted monolingual features in English, **6** - **9** - average micro-accuracy computed over all possible combinations of English and 3 languages taken 0 through 3 at a time, resulted from features weighted following a modified normal distribution with $\sigma^2 = 5$ and an amplification factor of 20 using a multinomial Naïve Bayes learner, where **6** - one language, **7** - 2 languages, **8** - 3 languages, **9** - 4 languages, **10** - error reduction calculated between ND-L1 (6) and ND-L4 (9)

6 Conclusion

This paper explored the cumulative ability of features originating from multiple languages to improve on the monolingual word sense disambiguation task. We showed that a multilingual model is suited to better leverage two aspects of the semantics of text by using a machine translation engine. First, the various senses of a target word may be translated into other languages by using different words, which constitute unique, yet highly salient features that effectively expand the target word's space. Second, the translated context words themselves embed co-occurrence information that a translation engine gathers from very large parallel corpora. This information is infused in the model and allows for thematic spaces to emerge, where features from multiple languages can be grouped together based on their semantics, leading to a more effective context representation for word sense disambiguation. The average micro-accuracy results showed a steadily increasing progression as more languages are added to the vector space. Using two standard word sense disambiguation datasets, we showed that a classifier based on a multilingual representation can lead to an error reduction ranging from 10.58% (SEMEVAL) to 25.96% (TWA) as compared to the monolingual classifier.

Acknowledgments

This material is based in part upon work supported by the National Science Foundation CAREER award #0747340 and IIS award #1018613. Any opinions, findings, and conclusions or recommendations expressed in this material are those of the authors and do not necessarily reflect the views of the National Science Foundation.

References

Banea, C., R. Mihalcea, and J. Wiebe (2010, August). Multilingual subjectivity: Are more languages better? In *Proceedings of the 23rd International Conference on Computational Linguistics (Coling 2010)*, Beijing, China, pp. 28–36.

Dagan, I. and A. Itai (1994). Word sense disambiguation using a second language monolingual corpus. *Computational Linguistics 20*(4), 563–596.

Diab, M. and P. Resnik (2002, July). An unsupervised method for word sense tagging using parallel corpora. In *Proceedings of the 40st Annual Meeting of the Association for Computational Linguistics (ACL 2002)*, Philadelphia, PA.

1 Word	2 # Inst	3 # Senses	4 MCS	5 BIN-L1	6 ND-L1	7 ND-L2	8 ND-L3	9 ND-L4	10 Error Red.
approve.v	53	2	94.34	94.34	94.34	94.34	95.60	**96.23**	33.33
ask.v	348	6	64.94	68.39	72.41	73.66	74.71	**75.00**	9.37
bill.n	404	3	65.10	88.12	90.59	91.75	92.41	**92.82**	23.68
buy.v	164	5	**78.66**	**78.66**	78.05	77.64	77.44	77.44	-2.78
capital.n	278	4	92.81	92.81	92.81	92.81	93.17	**93.53**	10.00
care.v	69	3	78.26	78.26	**86.96**	86.47	85.99	85.51	-11.11
effect.n	178	3	82.02	82.02	84.83	85.96	**86.33**	85.96	7.41
exchange.n	363	5	71.90	73.83	78.51	82.37	84.85	**85.95**	34.62
explain.v	85	2	88.24	88.24	88.24	88.24	88.24	88.24	0.00
feel.v	347	3	**82.13**	**82.13**	**82.13**	82.04	81.94	81.84	-1.61
grant.v	19	2	63.16	73.68	73.68	71.93	71.93	**78.95**	20.00
hold.v	129	8	34.88	**45.74**	43.41	43.41	43.41	43.41	0.00
hour.n	187	4	**84.49**	**84.49**	83.96	83.78	83.78	**84.49**	3.33
job.n	188	3	74.47	74.47	80.32	80.67	82.62	**84.04**	18.92
part.n	481	4	81.91	81.91	82.12	83.30	84.13	**85.45**	18.60
people.n	754	4	91.11	91.11	91.11	91.29	92.22	**93.37**	25.37
point.n	469	9	71.64	73.99	77.61	82.09	83.51	**84.22**	29.52
position.n	268	7	27.61	60.82	61.19	66.17	**68.91**	68.66	19.23
power.n	251	3	47.81	**84.46**	76.89	81.94	82.87	83.27	27.59
president.n	879	3	86.23	89.87	87.14	88.28	89.34	**90.79**	28.32
promise.v	50	2	**88.00**	**88.00**	86.00	86.67	87.33	**88.00**	14.29
propose.v	34	2	85.29	85.29	**88.24**	87.25	86.27	85.29	-25.00
rate.n	1009	2	84.64	86.92	87.02	88.07	88.64	**89.30**	17.56
remember.v	121	2	99.17	99.17	99.17	99.17	99.17	99.17	0.00
rush.v	28	2	92.86	92.86	92.86	92.86	92.86	92.86	0.00
say.v	2161	5	97.78	97.78	97.78	97.78	97.78	97.78	0.00
see.v	158	6	44.94	47.47	49.37	51.05	51.69	**52.53**	6.25
state.n	617	3	83.14	83.95	85.25	85.25	85.47	**85.74**	3.30
system.n	450	5	55.56	72.44	74.00	73.85	75.26	**75.78**	6.84
value.n	335	3	89.25	89.25	89.25	89.35	89.45	**89.85**	5.56
work.v	230	7	64.78	65.65	66.96	68.26	**68.99**	68.70	5.26

Table 2: Accuracies obtained on the SEMEVAL dataset; Columns: **1** - words contained in the corpus, **2** - number of examples for a given word, **3** - number of senses covered by the examples, **4** - micro-accuracy obtained when using the most common sense (MCS), **5** - micro-accuracy obtained using the multinomial Naïve Bayes classifier on binary weighted monolingual features in English, **6** - **9** - average micro-accuracy computed over all possible combinations of English and 3 languages taken 0 through 3 at a time, resulted from features weighted following a modified normal distribution with $\sigma^2 = 5$ and an amplification factor of 20 using a multinomial Naïve Bayes learner, where **6** - one language, **7** - 2 languages, **8** - 3 languages, **9** - 4 languages, **10** - error reduction calculated between ND-L1 (6) and ND-L4 (9)

1 Dataset	2 MCS	3 BIN-L1	4 ND-L1	5 ND-L2	6 ND-L3	7 ND-L4	8 Error Red.
TWA	70.91	79.57	80.93	82.87	84.38	86.02	25.96
SEMEVAL	75.71	80.52	81.36	82.18	82.78	83.36	10.58

Table 3: Aggregate accuracies obtained on the TWA and SEMEVAL datasets; Columns: **1** - dataset, **2** - average micro-accuracy obtained when using the most common sense (MCS), **3** - average micro-accuracy obtained using the multinomial Naïve Bayes classifier on binary weighted monolingual features in English, **4** - **7** - average micro-accuracy computed over all possible combinations of English and 3 languages taken 0 through 3 at a time, resulted from features weighted following a modified normal distribution with $\sigma^2 = 5$ and an amplification factor of 20 using a multinomial Naïve Bayes learner, where **4** - one language, **5** - 2 languages, **6** - 3 languages, **7** - 4 languages, **8** - error reduction calculated between ND-L1 (4) and ND-L4 (7)

Fellbaum, C. (1998). *WordNet, An Electronic Lexical Database*. The MIT Press.

Hall, M., E. Frank, G. Holmes, B. Pfahringer, P. Reutemann, and I. H. Witten (2009). The weka data mining software: An update. *SIGKDD Explorations 11*(1).

Hovy, E., M. Marcus, M. Palmer, L. Ramshaw, and R. Weischedel (2006). Ontonotes: the 90In *Proceedings of the Human Language Technology Conference of the NAACL, Companion Volume: Short Papers on XX*, NAACL '06, Morristown, NJ, USA, pp. 57–60. Association for Computational Linguistics.

Lesk, M. (1986, June). Automatic sense disambiguation using machine readable dictionaries: How to tell a pine cone from an ice cream cone. In *Proceedings of the SIGDOC Conference 1986*, Toronto.

Li, C. and H. Li (2002). Word translation disambiguation using bilingual bootstrapping. In *Proceedings of 40th Annual Meeting of the Association for Computational Linguistics*, Philadelphia, Pennsylvania.

Mihalcea, R. (2003, September). The role of non-ambiguous words in natural language disambiguation. In *Proceedings of the conference on Recent Advances in Natural Language Processing RANLP-2003*, Borovetz, Bulgaria.

Mihalcea, R., R. Sinha, and D. McCarthy (2010). Semeval-2010 task 2: Cross-lingual lexical substitution. In *Proceedings of the ACL Workshop on Semantic Evaluations*, Uppsala, Sweden.

Mihalcea, R., P. Tarau, and E. Figa (2004). PageRank on semantic networks, with application to word sense disambiguation. In *Proceedings of the 20st International Conference on Computational Linguistics (COLING 2004)*, Geneva, Switzerland.

Ng, H. and H. Lee (1996). Integrating multiple knowledge sources to disambiguate word sense: An examplar-based approach. In *Proceedings of the 34th Annual Meeting of the Association for Computational Linguistics (ACL 1996)*, Santa Cruz.

Ng, H., B. Wang, and Y. Chan (2003, July). Exploiting parallel texts for word sense disambiguation: An empirical study. In *Proceedings of the 41st Annual Meeting of the Association for Computational Linguistics (ACL 2003)*, Sapporo, Japan.

Pradhan, S., E. Loper, D. Dligach, and M. Palmer (2007, June). Semeval-2007 task-17: English lexical sample, srl and all words. In *Proceedings of the Fourth International Workshop on Semantic Evaluations (SemEval-2007)*, Prague, Czech Republic.

Resnik, P. and D. Yarowsky (1999). Distinguishing systems and distinguishing senses: new evaluation methods for word sense disambiguation. *Natural Language Engineering* 5(2), 113–134.

Yarowsky, D. (1995, June). Unsupervised word sense disambiguation rivaling supervised methods. In *Proceedings of the 33rd Annual Meeting of the Association for Computational Linguistics (ACL 1995)*, Cambridge, MA.

Using Inverse λ and Generalization to Translate English to Formal Languages

Chitta Baral
Arizona State University
chitta@asu.edu

Juraj Dzifcak
Arizona State University
juraj.dzifcak@asu.edu

Marcos Alvarez Gonzalez
Arizona State University
malvar@asu.edu

Jiayu Zhou
Arizona State University
Jiayu.Zhou@asu.edu

Abstract

We present a system to translate natural language sentences to formulas in a formal or a knowledge representation language. Our system uses two inverse λ-calculus operators and using them can take as input the semantic representation of some words, phrases and sentences and from that derive the semantic representation of other words and phrases. Our inverse λ operator works on many formal languages including first order logic, database query languages and answer set programming. Our system uses a syntactic combinatorial categorial parser to parse natural language sentences and also to construct the semantic meaning of the sentences as directed by their parsing. The same parser is used for both. In addition to the inverse λ-calculus operators, our system uses a notion of generalization to learn semantic representation of words from the semantic representation of other words that are of the same category. Together with this, we use an existing statistical learning approach to assign weights to deal with multiple meanings of words. Our system produces improved results on standard corpora on natural language interfaces for robot command and control and database queries.

1 Introduction

Our long term goal is to develop general methodologies to translate natural language text into a formal knowledge representation (KR) language. In the absence of a single KR language that is appropriate for expressing all the nuances of a natural language, currently, depending on the need different KR languages are used. For example, while first-order logic is appropriate for mathematical knowledge, one of its subset Description logic is considered appropriate for expressing ontologies, temporal logics are considered appropriate for expressing goals of agents and robots, and various non-monotonic logics have been proposed to express common-sense knowledge. Thus, one of of our goals in this paper is to develop general methodologies that can be used in translating natural language to a desired KR language.

There have been several learning based approaches, mainly from two groups at MIT and Austin. These include the following works: Zettlemoyer and Collins (2005), Kate and Mooney (2006), Wong and Mooney (2006), Wong and Mooney (2007), Lu et al. (2008), Zettlemoyer and Collins (2007) and Ge and Mooney (2009). Given a training corpus of natural language sentences coupled with their desired representations, these approaches learn a model capable of translating sentences to a desired meaning representation. For example, in the work by Zettlemoyer and Collins (2005), a set of hand crafted rules is used to learn syntactic categories and semantic representations of words based on combinatorial categorial grammar (CCG), as described by Steedman (2000), and λ-calculus formulas, as discussed by Gamut (1991). The later work of Zettlemoyer and Collins (2007), also uses *hand crafted rules*. The Austin group has several papers over the years. Many of their works including the one by Ge and Mooney (2009) use a word alignment method to learn semantic lexicon and learn rules for composing meaning representation.

Similar to the work by Ge and Mooney (2009), we use an existing syntactic parser to parse natural language. However we use a CCG parser, as described by Clark and Curran (2007), to parse sentences, use lambda calculus for meaning representation, use the CCG parsing to compose meaning and have an initial dictionary. Note that unlike the work by Ge and Mooney (2009), we do not need to learn rules for composing meaning representation. We use a novel method to learn semantic lexicon which is based on two inverse lambda operators that allow us to compute F given G and H such that $F@G = H$ or $G@F = H$. Compared to the work by Zettlemoyer and Collins (2005), we use the same learning approach but use a completely different approach in lexical generation. Our inverse λ operator has been tested to work for many languages including first order logic, database query language, CLANG by Chen et al. (2003), answer set programming (ASP) as described by Baral (2003), and temporal logic. Thus our approach is not dependent on the language used to represent the semantics, nor limited by a fixed set of rules. Rather, the new λ-calculus formulas and their semantic models, corresponding to the semantic or meaning representations, are directly obtained from known semantic representations which were provided with the data or learned before. The richness of λ calculus allows us to rely only on the syntactic parse itself without the need to have separate rules for composing the semantics. The provided method yields improved experimental results on existing corpora on robot command and control and database queries.

2 Motivation and Background

We now illustrate how one can use CCG parsing and λ-calculus applications to obtain database query representation of sentences. We then motivate and explain the role of our "inverse λ" operator. A syntactic and semantic parse tree for the sentence "Give me the largest state." is given in Table 1.

Give me	the	largest	state.
S/NP	NP/N	N/N	N
S/NP	NP/N	N	
S/NP	NP		
S			

Give me	the	largest	state.
$\lambda x.answer(A, x@A)$	$\lambda x.x$	$\lambda x.\lambda y.largest(y, x@y)$	$\lambda z.state(z)$
$\lambda x.answer(A, x@A)$	$\lambda x.x$	$\lambda y.largest(y, state(y))$	
$\lambda x.answer(A, x@A)$	$\lambda y.largest(y, state(y))$		
$answer(A, largest(A, state(A)))$			

Table 1: CCG and λ-calculus derivation for "Give me the largest state."

The upper portion of the figure lists the nodes corresponding to the CCG categories which are used to syntactically parse the sentence. These are assigned to each word and then combined using combinatorial rules, as described by Steedman (2000), to obtain the categories corresponding to parts of the sentence and finally the complete sentence itself. For example, the category for "largest", N/N is combined with the category of "state.", N, to obtain the category of "largest state.", which is N. In a similar manner, each word is assigned a semantic meaning in the form of a λ-calculus formula, as indicated by the lower portion of the figure. The language used to represent the semantics of words and the sentence is the database query language used in the robocup domain. The formulas corresponding to words are combined by applying one to another, as dictated by the syntactic parse tree to obtain the semantic representation of the whole sentence. For example, the semantics of "the largest state.", $\lambda y.largest(y, state(y))$ is applied to the semantics of "Give me", $\lambda x.answer(A, x@A)$, to obtain the semantics of "Give me the largest state.", $answer(A, largest(A, state(A)))$.

The given example illustrates how to obtain the semantics of the sentence given the semantics of words. However, what happens if the semantics of the word "largest" is not given? It might be either missing completely, or the current semantics of "largest" in the dictionary might simply not be applicable for the sentence "Give me the largest state.".

Let us assume that the semantic representation of "largest" is not known, while the semantic representation of the rest of the sentence is known. We can then obtain the semantic representation of "largest" as follows. Given the formula $answer(A, largest(A, state(A)))$ for the whole sentence "Give me the largest state." and the formula $\lambda x.answer(A, x@A)$ for "Give me", we can perform some kind of an *inverse application* [1] to obtain the semantics representation of "the largest state", $\lambda y.largest(y, state(y))$. Similarly, we can then use the known semantics of "the", to obtain the semantic representation of "largest state." as $\lambda y.largest(y, state(y))$. Finally, using the known semantics of state, $\lambda z.state(z)$ we can obtain the the semantics of "largest" as $\lambda x.\lambda y.largest(y, x@y)$.

It is important to note that using @ we are able to construct relatively complex semantic representations that are properly mapped to the required syntax.

Given a set of training sentences with their desired semantic representations, a syntactic parser, such as the one by Clark and Curran (2007), and an initial dictionary, we can apply the above idea on each of the sentences to learn the missing semantic representations of words. We can then apply a learning model, such as the one used by Zettlemoyer and Collins (2005), on these new semantic representations and assign weights to different semantic representations. These can then be used to parse and represent the semantics of new sentences. This briefly sums up our approach to learn and compute new semantic representations. It is easy to see that this approach can be applied with respect to any language that can be handled by "inverse λ" operators and is not limited in the set of new representations it provides.

We will consider two domains to evaluate our approach. The fist one is the GEOQUERY domain used by Zelle and Mooney (1996), which uses a Prolog based language to query a database with geographical information about the U.S. It should be noted that this language uses higher-order predicates. An example query is provided in Table 1. The second domain is the ROBOCUP domain of Chen et al. (2003). This is a multi-agent domain where agents compete against each other in a simulated soccer game. The language CLANG of Chen et al. (2003) is a formal language used to provide instructions to the agents. An example query with the corresponding natural language sentence is given below.

- If the ball is in our midfield, position player 3 at (-5, -23).
- *((bpos (midfield our)) (do (player our 3) (pos (pt -5 -23))))*

3 Learning Approach

We adopt the learning model given by Zettlemoyer and Collins (2005, 2007, 2009) and use it to assign weights to the semantic representations of words. Since a word can have multiple possible syntactic and semantic representations assigned to it, such as $John$ may be represented as $John$ as well as $\lambda x.x@John$, we use the probabilistic model to assign weights to these representations.

The main differences between our algorithm and the one given by Zettlemoyer and Collins (2005) are the way in which new semantic representations are obtained. While Zettlemoyer and Collins (2005) uses a predefined table to obtain these, we obtain the new semantic representations by using inverse λ operators and generalization.

3.1 Learning model and parsing

We assume that complete syntactic parses are available[2]. The parsing uses a probabilistic combinatorial categorial grammar framework similar to the one given by Zettlemoyer and Collins (2005). We assume a probabilistic categorial grammar (PCCG) based on a log linear model. Let S denote a sentence, L denote the semantic representation of the sentence, and T denote it's parse tree. We assume a mapping $\bar{f}$ of a triple (L, T, S) to feature vectors R^d and a vector of parameters $\bar{\Theta} \in R^d$ representing the weights. Then the probability of a particular syntactic and semantic parse is given as:

[1] Thus instead of applying G to F to obtain H, $G@F = H$, we try to find an F such that $G@F = H$ given G and H.

[2] A sentence can have several different parses.

$$P(L,T|S;\bar{\Theta}) = \frac{e^{\bar{f}(L,T,S).\bar{\Theta}}}{\sum_{(L,T)} e^{\bar{f}(L,T,S).\bar{\Theta}}}$$

We use only lexical features. Each feature f_j counts the number of times that the lexical entry is used in T.

Parsing a sentence under PCCG includes finding L such that $P(L|S;\bar{\Theta})$ is maximized.

$$argmax_L P(L|S;\bar{\Theta}) =$$
$$argmax_L \sum_T P(L,T|S;\bar{\Theta})$$

We use dynamic programming techniques to calculate the most probable parse for a sentence.

3.2 The inverse λ operators

For lack of space, we present only one of the two Inverse λ operators, $Inverse_L$ and $Inverse_R$ of Gonzalez (2010). The objective of these two algorithms is that given typed λ-calculus formulas H and G, we want to compute the formula F such that $F@G = H$ and $G@F = H$. First, we introduce the different symbols used in the algorithm and their meaning :

- Let G, H represent typed λ-calculus formulas, J^1,J^2,...,J^n represent typed terms, v_1 to v_n, v and w represent variables and σ_1,...,σ_n represent typed atomic terms.
- Let $f()$ represent a typed atomic formula. Atomic formulas may have a different arity than the one specified and still satisfy the conditions of the algorithm if they contain the necessary typed atomic terms.
- Typed terms that are sub terms of a typed term J are denoted as J_i.
- If the formulas we are processing within the algorithm do not satisfy any of the if conditions then the algorithm returns $null$.

Definition 1 (operator :) *Consider two lists of typed λ-elements A and B, $(a_i, ..., a_n)$ and $(b_j, ..., b_n)$ respectively and a formula H. The result of the operation $H(A : B)$ is obtained by replacing a_i by b_i, for each appearance of A in H.*

Next, we present the definition of an inverse operators[3] $Inverse_R(H, G)$:

Definition 2 ($Inverse_R(H, G)$) *The function $Inverse_R(H, G)$, is defined as:*
Given G and H:

1. *If G is $\lambda v.v@J$, set $F = Inverse_L(H, J)$*
2. *If J is a sub term of H and G is $\lambda v.H(J : v)$ then F = J.*
3. *If G is not $\lambda v.v@J$, J is a sub term of H and G is $\lambda w.H(J(J_1, ..., J_m) : w@J_p, ..., @J_q)$ with 1 $\leq$ p,q,s $\leq$ m. then $F = \lambda v_1, ..., v_s.J(J_1, ..., J_m : v_p, ..., v_q)$.*

The function $Inverse_L(H, G)$ is defined similarly.

Illustration: Inverse$_R$ - Case 3:
Suppose H = $in(river, Texas)$ and G = $\lambda v.v@Texas@river$
G is not of the form $\lambda v.v@J$ since J = $Texas@river$ is not a formula. Thus the first condition is not satisfied. Similarly, there is no J that satisfies the second condition. Thus let us try to find a suitable J that satisfies third condition. If we take J_1 = $river$ and J_2 = $Texas$, then the third condition is satisfied by G = $\lambda x.H((J(J_1, J_2) : x@J_2@J_1)$, which in this case corresponds to G = $\lambda x.H(in(river, Texas) : x@Texas@river)$. Thus, F = $\lambda v_1, v_2.J(J_1, J_2 : v_2, v_1)$ and so F = $\lambda v_1, v_2.in(v_2, v_1)$.
It is easy to see that G @ F = H.

[3]This is the operator that was used in this implementation. In a companion work we develop an enhancement of this operator which is proven sound and complete.

3.3 Generalization

Using $INVERSE\_L$ and $INVERSE\_R$, we are able to obtain new semantic representations of particular words in the sentence. However, without any form of generalization, we are not able to extend these to words beyond the ones actually contained in the training data. Since our goal is to go beyond that, we strive to generalize the new semantic representations beyond those words.

To extend our coverage, a function that will take any new learned semantic expressions and the current lexicon and will try to use them to obtain new semantic expressions for words of the same category has to be designed. It will use the following idea. Consider the non-transitive verb "fly" of category $S\backslash NP$. Lets assume we obtain a new semantic expression for "fly" as $\lambda x.fly(x)$ using $INVERSE\_L$ and $INVERSE\_R$. The $GENERALIZE$ function looks up all the words of the same syntactic category, $S\backslash NP$. It then identifies the part of the semantic expression in which "fly" is involved. In our particular case, it's the subexpression fly. It then proceeds to search the dictionary for all the words of category $S\backslash NP$. For each such word w, it will add a new semantic expression $\lambda x.w(x)$ to the dictionary. For example for the verb "swim", it would add $\lambda x.swim(x)$.

However, the above idea also comes with a drawback. It can produce a vast amount of new semantics representations that are not necessary for most of the sentences, and thus have a negative impact on performance. Thus instead of applying the above idea on the whole dictionary, we perform generalization "on demand". That is, if a sentence contains words with unknown semantics, we look for words of the same category and use the same idea to find their semantics. Let us assume $IDENTIFY(word, semantics)$ identifies the parts of $semantics$ in which $word$ is involved and $REPLACE(s, a, b)$ replaces a with b in s. We assume that each lexical entry is a triple (w, cat, sem) where w is the actual word, cat is the syntactic category and sem is the semantic expression corresponding to w and cat.

$GENERALIZE_D(L, \alpha)$

- For each $l_j \in L$
  - If $l_j(cat) = \alpha(cat)$
    - $I = IDENTIFY(l_j(w), l_j(sem))$
    - $S = REPLACE(l_j(sem), I, \alpha(w))$
    - $L = L \cup (\alpha(w), \alpha(cat), S)$

As an example, consider the sentence "Give me the largest state." from Table 1. Let us assume that the semantics of the word "largest" as well as "the" is not known, however the semantics of "longest" is given by the dictionary as $\lambda x.\lambda y.longest(y, x@y)$. Normally, the system would be unable to parse this sentence and would continue on. However, upon calling $GENERALIZE_D(L,\text{"}largest\text{"})$, the word longest is found in the dictionary with the same syntactic category. Thus this function takes the semantic representation of "longest" $\lambda x.\lambda y.longest(y, x@y)$, modifies it accordingly for largest, giving $\lambda x.\lambda y.largest(y, x@y)$ and stores it in the lexicon. After that, the $INVERSE_L$ and $INVERSE_R$ can be applied to obtain the semantics of "the".

3.4 Trivial inverse solutions

Even with on demand generalization, we might still be missing large amounts of semantics information to be able to use $INVERSE_L$ and $INVERSE_R$. To make up for this, we allow trivial solutions under certain conditions. A trivial solution is a solution, where one of the formulas is assigned a $\lambda x.x$ representation. For example, given H, we are looking for F such that $H = G@F$. If we set G to be $\lambda x.x$, then trivially $F = H$. Thus we can try to carefully set some unknown semantics of words as $\lambda x.x$ which will allow us to compute the semantics of the remaining words using $INVERSE_L$ and $INVERSE_R$. The question then becomes, when do we allow these? In our approach, we allow these for words that do not seem to have any contribution to the final semantic meaning of the text. In some cases, articles such as "the", while having a specific place in the English language, might not contribute anything to the actual meaning representation of the sentence. In general, any word not present in the final semantics is a potential candidate to be assigned the trivial semantic representation $\lambda x.x$. These are added with very low weights compared to the semantics found using $INVERSE_L$ and $INVERSE_R$, so that if at one point a non-trivial semantic representation is found, the system will attempt to use it over the trivial one.

As an example, consider again the sentence "Give me the largest state." from Table 1 with the semantics $answer(A, largest(A, state(A)))$. Let us assume the semantic representations of "the" and "largest" are not known. Under normal circumstances the algorithm would be unable to find the semantics of "largest" using $INVERSE_L$ and $INVERSE_R$ as it is missing the semantics of "the". However, as "the" is not present in the desired semantics, the system will attempt to assign $\lambda x.x$ as its semantic representation. After doing that, $INVERSE_L$ and $INVERSE_R$ can be used to compute the semantic representation of "largest" as $\lambda x.\lambda y.largest(y, x@y)$.

3.5 The overall learning algorithm.

The complete learning algorithm used within our approach is shown below. The input to the algorithm is an initial lexicon L_0 and a set of pairs $(S_i, L_i), i = 1, ..., n$, where S_i is a sentence and L_i its corresponding logical form. The output of the algorithm is a PCCG defined by the lexicon L_T and a parameter vector Θ_T.

The parameter vector Θ_i is updated at each iteration of the algorithm. It stores a real number for each item in the dictionary. The initial values were set to 0.1. The algorithm is divided into two major steps, lexical generation and parameters update. The goal of the algorithm is to extract as much information as possible given the provided training data.

In the first step, the algorithm iterates over all the sentences n times and for each sentence constructs a syntactic and (potentially incomplete) semantic parse tree. Using the semantic parse tree, it then attempts to obtain new λ-calculus formulas by traversing the tree and performing regular applications and inverse computations where possible. Any new semantics are then generalized and stored in the lexicon.

The main reason to iterate over all the sentences n times is to extract all the possible information given the current parameter vector. There may be cases where the information learned from the last sentence can be used to learn additional information from the third sentence, which can then be used to learn new semantics from the second sentence etc. By looping over all sentences n times, we ensure we capture and learn as much information as possible.

Note that the semantic parse trees of the sentences may change once the parameters of words change. Thus even though we are looping over all the sentences T times, the semantic parse tree of a sentence might change as a result of a change in the parameter vector. This change can be very minor, such as change in the semantics of a single word, or in a rare case a major one where most of the semantic expressions present in the tree change. Thus we might learn different semantics of words given different parameter vectors.

In the second step, the parameter vector Θ_i is updated using stochastic gradient descent. Steps one and two are performed T times. In our experiments, the value of T ranged from 50 to 100.

Overall, steps one and two form an exhaustive search which optimizes the log-likelihood of the training model.

- **Input:**

  A set of training sentences with their corresponding desired representations $S = \{(S_i, L_i) : i = 1...n\}$ where S_i are sentences and L_i are desired expressions. Weights are given an initial value of 0.1.

  An initial lexicon L_0. An initial feature vector Θ_0.

- **Output:**

  An updated lexicon L_{T+1}. An updated feature vector Θ_{T+1}.

- **Algorithm:**
  - For t = 1 . . . T
  - Step 1: (Lexical generation)
  - For i = 1...n.
    * For j = 1...n.
    * Parse sentence S_j to obtain T_j
    * Traverse T_j
      - apply $INVERSE\_L$, $INVERSE\_R$ and $GENERALIZE_D$ to find new λ-calculus expressions of words and phrases α.
    * Set $L_{t+1} = L_t \cup \alpha$
  - Step 2: (Parameter Estimation)
  - Set $\Theta_{t+1} = UPDATE(\Theta_t, L_{t+1})$[4]
- return $GENERALIZE(L_T, L_T), \Theta(T)$

4 Experimental Evaluation

4.1 The data

To evaluate our algorithm, we used the standard corpus in GEOQUERY and CLANG. The GEOQUERY corpus contained 880 English sentences with respective database queries. The CLANG corpus contained 300 entries specifying rules, conditions and definitions in CLANG. The GEOQUERY corpus contained relatively short sentences with the sentences ranging from four to seventeen words of quite similar syntactic structure. The sentences in CLANG are much longer, with more complex structure with length ranging from five to thirty eight words.

For our experiments, we used the $C\&C$ parser of Clark and Curran (2007) to provide syntactic parses for sentences. For CLANG corpus, the position vectors and compound nouns with numbers were pre-processed and consequently treated as single noun.

Our experiments were done using a 10 fold cross validation and were conducted as follows. A set of training and testing examples was generated from the respective corpus. These were parsed by the $C\&C$ parser to obtain the syntactic tree structure. These together with the training sets containing the training sentences with their corresponding semantic representations (SRs) and an initial dictionary was used to train a new dictionary with corresponding parameters. This dictionary was generalized with respect of all the words in the test sentences. Note that it is possible that many of the words were still missing their SRs. This dictionary was then used to parse the test sentences and highest scoring parse was used to determine precision and recall. Since many words might have been missing their SRs, the system might not have returned a proper complete semantic parse.

To measure precision and recall, we adopted the measures given by Ge and Mooney (2009). *Precision* denotes the percentage of of returned SRs that were correct, while *Recall* denotes the percentage of test examples with pre-specified SRs returned. *F-measure* is the standard harmonic mean of precision and recall. For database querying, an SR was considered correct if it retrieved the same answer as the standard query. For CLANG, an SR was correct if it was an exact match of the desired SR, except for argument ordering of conjunctions and other commutative predicates. Additionally, a set of additional experiments was run with "(definec" and "(definer" treated as being equal.

We evaluated two different version of our system. The first one, $INVERSE$, uses $INVERSE_L$ and $INVERSE_R$ and regular generalization which is applied after each step. The second version, $INVERSE+$, uses trivial inverse solutions as well as on demand generalization. Both systems were

[4]For details on Θ computation, please see the work by Zettlemoyer and Collins (2005)

evaluated on the same data sets using 10 fold cross validation and the $C\&C$ parser using an equal number of train and test sentences, randomly chosen from their respective corpus. The initial dictionary contained a few nouns, with the addition of one randomly selected word from the set $\{what, where, which\}$ in case of GEOQUERY. For CLANG, the initial dictionary also contained a few nouns, together with the addition of one randomly selected word from the set $\{if, when, during\}$. The learning parameters were set to the values used by Zettlemoyer and Collins (2005).

4.2 Results

We compared our systems with the performance results of several alternative systems for which the performance data is available in the literature. In particular, we used the performance data given by Ge and Mooney (2009). The systems that we compared with are: The SYN0, SYN20 and GOLDSYN systems by Ge and Mooney (2009), the system SCISSOR by Ge and Mooney (2005), an SVM based system KRIPS by Kate and Mooney (2006), a synchronous grammar based system WASP by Wong and Mooney (2007), the CCG based system by Zettlemoyer and Collins (2007) and the work by Lu et al. (2008). Please note that many of these approaches require different parsers, human supervision or other additional tools, while our approach requires a syntactic parse of the sentences and an initial dictionary.

Our and their reported results for the respective corpora are given in the Tables 2 and 3.

	Precision	Recall	F-measure
INVERSE+	93.41	89.04	91.17
INVERSE	91.12	85.78	88.37
GOLDSYN	91.94	88.18	90.02
WASP	91.95	86.59	89.19
Z&C	91.63	86.07	88.76
SCISSOR	95.50	77.20	85.38
KRISP	93.34	71.70	81.10
Lu at al.	89.30	81.50	85.20

Table 2: Performance on GEOQUERY.

	Precision	Recall	F-measure
INVERSE+(i)	87.67	79.08	83.15
INVERSE+	85.74	76.63	80.92
GOLDSYN	84.73	74.00	79.00
SYN20	85.37	70.00	76.92
SYN0	87.01	67.00	75.71
WASP	88.85	61.93	72.99
KRISP	85.20	61.85	71.67
SCISSOR	89.50	73.70	80.80
Lu at al.	82.50	67.70	74.40

Table 3: Performance on CLANG.

The $INVERSE + (i)$ denotes training where "(definec" and "(definer" at the start of SRs were treated as being equal. The main reason for this was that there seems to be no way to distinguish in between them. Even as a human, we found it hard to be able to distinguish between them.

4.3 Analysis

Our testing showed that our method is capable of outperforming all of the existing parsers in F-measure. However, there are parsers which can produce greater precision, such as WASP and SCISSOR on CLANG corpus, however they do at the cost in recall. As discussed by Ge and Mooney (2009), the GEOQUERY results for SCISSOR, KRISP and Lu's work use a different, less accurate representation language FUNSQL which may skew the results. Also, SCISSOR outperforms our system on GEOQUERY corpus in terms of precision, but at the cost of additional human supervision.

Our system is particularly accurate for shorter sentences, or a corpus where many sentences have similar general structure, such as GEOQUERY. However, it is also capable of handling longer sentences, in particular if they in fact consists of several shorter sentences, such as for example "If the ball is in our midfield, position player 3 at (-5,-23).", which can be looked at as "IF A, B" where "A" and "B" are smaller complete sentences themselves. The system is capable of learning the semantics of several basic categories such as verbs, after which most of the training sentences are easily parsed and missing semantics is learned quickly. The inability to parse other sentences mostly comes from two sources. First one is if the test sentence contains a syntactic category not seen in the training data. Our generalization model is not capable of generalizing these and thus fails to produce a semantic parse. The second problem comes from ambiguity of SRs. During training, many words will be assigned several SRs based on the training data. The parses are then ranked and in several cases, the correct SR might not be on the top. Re-ranking might help alleviate the second issue.

Unlike the other systems, we do not make use of a grammar for the semantics of the sentence. The reason it is not required is that the actual semantics is analyzed in computing the inverse lambdas, and the richness of λ-calculus allows us to compute relatively complex formulas to represent the semantic of words.

We also run examples with increased size of training data. These produced larger dictionaries and in general did not significantly affect the results. The main reason is that as discussed before, once the most common categories of words have their semantics assigned, most of the sentences can be properly parsed. Increasing the amount of training data increases the coverage in terms of the rare syntactic categories, but these are also rarely present in the testing data. The used training sample was in all cases sufficient to learn almost all of the categories. This might not be the case in general, for example if we had a corpus with all of the sentences of a particular length and structure, our method might not be capable of learning any new semantics. In such cases, additional words would have to be added to the initial dictionary, or additional sentences of varying lengths would have to be added.

The $C\&C$ parser of Clark and Curran (2007) was primarily trained on news paper text and thus did have some problems with these different domains and in some cases resulted in complex semantic representations of words. This could be improved by using a different parser, or by simply adjusting some of the parse trees. In addition, our system can be gradually improved by increasing the size of initial dictionary.

5 Conclusions and Discussion

We presented a new approach to map natural language sentences to their semantic representations. We used an existing syntactic parser, a novel inverse λ operator and several generalization techniques to learn the semantic representations of words. Our method is largely independent of the target representation language and directly computes the semantic representations based on the syntactic structure of the syntactic parse tree and known semantic representations. We used statistical learning methods to assign weights to different semantic representation of words and sentences.

Our results indicate that our approach outperforms many of the existing systems on the standard corpora of database querying and robot command and control.

We envision several directions of future work. One direction is to experiment our system with corpora where the natural language semantics is given through other Knowledge Representation languages such as answer set programming (ASP)[5] and temporal logic. We are currently building such corpora. Another direction is to improve the statistical learning part of the system. An initial experimentation with a different learning algorithm shows significant decrease in training time with slight reduction in performance. Finally, since our system uses an initial dictionary, which we tried to minimize by only having a few nouns and one of the query words, exploring how to reduce it further and possibly completely eliminating it is a future direction of research.

References

Baral, C. (2003). *Knowledge Representation, Reasoning, and Declarative Problem Solving*. Cambridge University Press.

Chen, M., E. Foroughi, F. Heintz, S. Kapetanakis, K. Kostadis, J. Kummeneje, I. Noda, O. Obst, P. Riley, T. Steffens, and Y. W. X. Yin (2003). Users manual: Robocup soccer server manula for soccer server version 7.07 and later. In *Avaliable at http://sourceforge.net/projects/sserver/.*

[5] A preliminary evaluation with respect to a corpus with newspaper text translated into ASP resulted in a precision of 77%, recall of 82% with F-measure at 80 using a much smaller training set.

Clark, S. and J. R. Curran (2007). Wide-coverage efficient statistical parsing with ccg and log-linear models. *Computational Linguistics 33*.

Gamut, L. (1991). *Logic, Language, and Meaning*. The University of Chicago Press.

Ge, R. and R. J. Mooney (2005). A statistical semantic parser that integrates syntax and semantics. In *In Proceedings of the Ninth Conference on Computational Natural Language Learning.*, pp. 9–16.

Ge, R. and R. J. Mooney (2009). Learning a compositional semantic parser using an existing syntactic parser. In *In Proceedings of the Joint Conference of the 47th Annual Meeting of the Association for Computational Linguistics and the 4th International Joint Conference on Natural Language Processing of the Asian Federation of Natural Language Processing (ACL-IJCNLP 2009).*, pp. 611–619.

Gonzalez, M. A. (2010). An inverse lambda calculus algorithm for natural language processing. Master's thesis, Arizona State University.

Kate, R. J. and R. J. Mooney (2006). Using string-kernels for learning semantic parsers. In *In Proceedings of the 21st Intl. Conference on Computational Linguistics.*, pp. 439–446.

Lu, W., H. T. Ng, W. S. Lee, and L. S. Zettlemoyer (2008). A generative model for parsing natural language to meaning representations. In *In Proceedings of the Conference on Empirical Methods in Natural Language Pricessing (EMNLP-08).*

Steedman, M. (2000). *The syntactic process*. MIT Press.

Wong, Y. W. and R. J. Mooney (2006). Learning for semantic parsing with statistical machine translation. In *In Proceedings of the Human Language Technology Conference of the North American Chapter of the Association for Computational Linguistics (HLT/NAACL-2006).*, pp. 439–446.

Wong, Y. W. and R. J. Mooney (2007). Learning synchronous grammars for semantic parsing with lambda calculus. In *In Proceedings of the 45th Annual Meeting of the Association for Computational Linguistics (ACL-07).*, pp. 960–967.

Zelle, J. M. and R. J. Mooney (1996). Learning to parse database queries using inductive logic programming. In *14th National Conference on Artificial Intelligence*.

Zettlemoyer, L. and M. Collins (2005). Learning to map sentences to logical form: Structured classification with probabilistic categorial grammars. In *21th Annual Conference on Uncertainty in Artificial Intelligence*, pp. 658–666.

Zettlemoyer, L. and M. Collins (2007). Online learning of relaxed ccg grammars for parsing to logical form. In *Proceedings of the 2007 Joint Conference on Empirical Methods in Natural Language Processing and Computational Natural Language Learning*, pp. 678–687.

Zettlemoyer, L. and M. Collins (2009). Learning context-dependent mappings from sentences to logical form. In *ACL*.

A Model for Composing Semantic Relations

Eduardo Blanco and Dan Moldovan
Human Language Technology Research Institute
The University of Texas at Dallas
{eduardo,moldovan}@hlt.utdallas.edu

Abstract

This paper presents a model to compose semantic relations. The model is independent of any particular set of relations and uses an extended definition for semantic relations. This extended definition includes restrictions on the domain and range of relations and utilizes semantic primitives to characterize them. Primitives capture elementary properties between the arguments of a relation. An algebra for composing semantic primitives is used to automatically identify the resulting relation of composing a pair of compatible relations. Inference axioms are obtained. Axioms take as input a pair of semantic relations and output a new, previously ignored relation. The usefulness of this proposed model is shown using PropBank relations. Eight inference axioms are obtained and their accuracy and productivity are evaluated. The model offers an unsupervised way of accurately extracting additional semantics from text.

1 Introduction

Semantic representation of text is an important step toward text understanding, performing inferences and reasoning. Potentially, it could dramatically improve the performance of several Natural Language Processing applications.

Semantic relations have been studied in linguistics for decades. They are unidirectional underlying connections between concepts. For example, the sentence *The construction slowed down the traffic* encodes a CAUSE and detecting it would help answer the question *Why is traffic slower?*

In Computational Linguistics, there have been several proposals to detect semantic relations. Current approaches focus on a particular set of relations and given a text they output relations. There have been competitions aiming at detecting semantic roles (i.e., relations between a verb and its arguments) (Carreras and Màrquez, 2005), and between nominals (Girju et al., 2007; Hendrickx et al., 2009).

In this paper, we propose a model to compose semantic relations to extract previously ignored relations. The model allows us to automatically obtain inference axioms given a set of relations and is not coupled to any particular set. Axioms take as their input semantic relations and yield a new semantic relation as their conclusion.

Consider the sentence *John went to the shop to buy flowers*. Figure 1 shows semantic role annotation with solid arrows. By composing this basic annotation with inference axioms, one can obtain the relations shown with discontinuous arrows: *John* had the intention to *buy*, the *buying* event took place *at the shop* and *John* and the *flowers* were at some point *in the shop*.

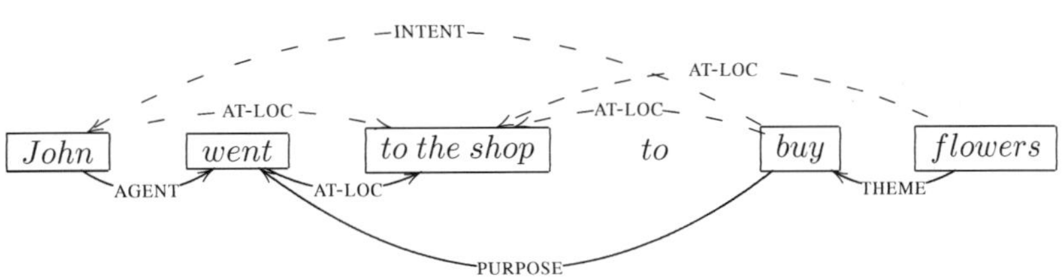

Figure 1: Semantic representation of the sentence *John went to the shop to buy flowers*.

2 Semantic Relations

Semantic relations are the underlying relations between concepts expressed by words or phrases. In other words, semantic relations are implicit associations between concepts in text.

In general, a semantic relation is defined by stating the kind of connection linking two concepts. For example, Hendrickx et al. (2009) loosely define ENTITY-ORIGIN as *an entity is coming or is derived from an origin (e.g., position or material)* and give one example: *Earth is located in the Milky Way*. We find this kind of definition weak and prone to confusion.

Following Helbig (2005), we propose an extended definition for semantic relations, including semantic restrictions for its domain and range. For example, DOMAIN(AGENT) must be an animate concrete object and RANGE(AGENT) must be a situation.

Moreover, we propose to characterize relations by semantic primitives. Primitives indicate if a certain property holds between the arguments of a relation. For example, the primitive *temporal* indicates if the first argument must happen before the second in order for the relation to hold. This primitive holds for CAUSE (a cause must *precede* its effect) and it does not apply to PART-WHOLE since the later relation does not consider time.

Besides having a better understanding of each relation, this extended definition allows us to create a model that automatically obtains inference axioms for composing semantic relations. The model detects possible combinations of relations and identifies the conclusion of composing them.

Formally, we represent a relation R as R(x, y), where R is the relation type and x and y are the first and second argument respectively. R(x, y) should be read *x is* R *of* Y. DOMAIN(R) and RANGE(R) are the sorts of concepts that can be part of the first and second argument respectively. Any ontology can be used to define domains and ranges, e.g., Helbig (2005) defined one to define a set of 89 relations. Primitives are represented by an array P_{R} of length n, where n is the number of primitives and P^i_{R} indicates the value R takes for the ith primitive.

The inverse of R is denoted R^{-1} and can be obtained by simply switching the arguments of R. Given R(x, y), $\text{R}^{-1}(y, x)$ always holds. We can easily define R^{-1} given the definition for R: DOMAIN(R^{-1}) = RANGE(R), RANGE(R^{-1}) = DOMAIN(R), and $P_{\text{R}^{-1}}$ is defined according to the fourth column of Table 1 for each primitive, i.e., $\forall i \in [1, n] : P^i_{R^{-1}} = Inverse(P^i_R)$.

2.1 Semantic Primitives

Relation primitives capture deep characteristics of relations. Huhns and Stephens (1989) define them as:

> They [primitives] are independently determinable for each relation and relatively self-explanatory. They specify a relationship between an element of the domain and an element of the range of the semantic relation being described.

Relation primitives are fundamental properties that cannot be explained using other primitives; they are elemental. They specify basic attributes of a relation by stating if a particular property must hold by definition between the domain and range.

Each relation takes a value for each primitive from the set $V = \{+, -, 0\}$, where '+' indicates that the property holds, '−' that it does not hold and '0' that it does not apply. For example, the primitive *volitional* indicates if a relation requires volition between domain and range. AGENT takes as value + for this primitive and PART-WHOLE takes 0.

Primitives complement the definition of a relation by stating if a particular property holds between its arguments. They help to understand the inter-relation differences and clustering relations. Primitives can be used as conditions to be fulfilled in order to determine if a potential relation holds. They are general enough to be determined for a relation, not a particular instantiation. In other words, they state properties that hold for all instances of a relation by definition.

Our set of primitives (Table 1) is inspired on previous work in Knowledge Bases (Huhns and Stephens, 1989). We only select from them useful primitives for our purpose and add more primitives. The additional primitives are justified by the fact that we aim at combining relations capturing semantics

No.	Primitive	Description	Inverse	Ref.
1	Composable	Relation can be meaningfully composed with other relations due to their fundamental characteristics	same	[3]
2	Functional	Domain is in a specific spatial or temporal position with respect to the range in order for the connection to exist	same	[1]
3	Separable	Domain can be temporally or spatially separated from the range, and can thus exist independently of the range	same	[1]
4	Temporal	Domain temporally precedes the range	opposite	[2]
5	Connected	Domain is physically or temporally connected to the range; connection might be indirect.	same	[3]
6	Intrinsic	Relation is an attribute of the essence/stufflike nature of the domain or range	same	[3]
7	Volitional	Relation requires volition between the arguments	same	-
8	Fully Implicational	The existence of the domain implies the existence of the range	opposite	-
9	Weakly Implicational	The existence of the domain generally implies the existence of the range	opposite	-

Table 1: Primitives for characterizing semantic relations, values for the inverse relation and references. In the fifth column, [1] stands for Winston et al. (1987), [2] for Cohen and Losielle (1988) and [3] for Huhns and Stephens (1989). '-' indicates new primitive.

1: **Composable**

	R2		
R1	-	0	+
-	×	0	×
0	0	0	0
+	×	0	+

2: **Functional**

	R2		
R1	-	0	+
-	-	0	+
0	0	0	0
+	+	0	+

3: **Separable**

	R2		
R1	-	0	+
-	-	-	-
0	-	0	+
+	-	+	+

4: **Temporal**

	R2		
R1	-	0	+
-	-	-	×
0	-	0	+
+	×	+	+

5: **Connected**

	R2		
R1	-	0	+
-	-	-	+
0	-	0	+
+	+	+	+

6: **Intrinsic**

	R2		
R1	-	0	+
-	-	0	-
0	0	0	0
+	-	0	+

7: **Volitional**

	R2		
R1	-	0	+
-	-	0	+
0	0	0	0
+	+	0	+

8: **F Impl.**

	R2		
R1	-	0	+
-	-	0	-
0	0	0	0
+	-	0	+

9: **W Impl.**

	R2		
R1	-	0	+
-	-	0	-
0	0	0	0
+	-	0	+

Table 2: Algebra for composing semantic primitives. Each cell of the ith table indicates $P^i_{R_1} \circ P^i_{R_2}$.

from natural language. Whatever the set of chosen relations, it will describe the characteristics of events (who/when/where/how something happened), which elements were involved, connections between events (e.g. CAUSE, CORRELATION). Time (whether an argument is guaranteed to happen before than the other), space and volition (whether or not there must be volition between the arguments) also play an important role.

The fourth column in Table 1 indicates the value of the primitive for the inverse relation. *Same* means the inverse relation takes the same value, *opposite* means it takes the opposite. The opposite of $-$ is $+$, the opposite of $-$ is $+$, and the opposite of 0 is 0.

For example, $P_{\text{AGENT}} = \{+, +, +, 0, -, -, +, 0, 0\}$, indicating that $P^5_{\text{AGENT}} = -$ and $P^7_{\text{AGENT}} = +$, i.e., AGENT(x, y) does not require x and y to be *connected* and it requires *volition* between the arguments. Note that $P_{\text{AGENT}}{}^{-1} = P_{\text{AGENT}}$.

2.2 An Algebra for Composing Semantic Relations

The key to automatically obtaining inference axioms is the ability to know beforehand the result of composing semantic primitives using an algebra. This way, one can identify prohibited combinations of relations and determine conclusions for the composition of valid combinations.

Given $P^i_{R_1}$ and $P^i_{R_2}$, i.e., the values of R_1 and R_2 for a primitive p_i, we define an algebra that indicates the result of composing them (i.e., $P^i_{R_1} \circ P^i_{R_2}$). Composing two primitives can yield three values: $+$, $-$ or 0, indicating if the primitive holds, does not hold or does not apply to the composition of R_1 and R_2. Additionally, the composition can be prohibited, indicated with $\times$. After composing all the primitives for R_1 and R_2, we obtain the primitives values for the composition of R_1 and R_2 (i.e., $P_{R_1} \circ P_{R_2}$).

We define the values for the composition using a table for each primitive. Table 2 depicts the whole algebra. The ith table indicates the rules for composing the ith primitive. For example, regarding the *intrinsic* primitive, we have the following rules:

- If both relations are *intrinsic*, the composition is *intrinsic*;
- else if *intrinsic* does not apply to either relation, the primitive does not apply to the composition;
- else, the composition is not *intrinsic*.

Other rules stated by the algebra are: (1) two relations shall not compose if they have different opposite values for the primitive *temporal*; (2) the composition of R_1 and R_2 is not *separable* if either relation is not *separable*; and (3) if either R_1 or R_2 are *connected*, then the composition is *connected*.

3 Necessary Conditions for Composing Semantic Relations

In principle, one could define axioms for every single possible combination of relations. However, there are two necessary conditions in order to compose R_1 and R_2:

1. They have to be compatible. A pair of relations is compatible if it is possible, from a theoretical point of view, to compose them. Formally, R_1 and R_2 are compatible iff $\text{RANGE}(R_1) \cap \text{DOMAIN}(R_2) \neq \emptyset$.
2. A third relation R_3 must fit as conclusion, that is, $\exists R_3$ such that $\text{DOMAIN}(R_3) \cap \text{DOMAIN}(R_1) \neq \emptyset$ and $\text{RANGE}(R_3) \cap \text{RANGE}(R_2) \neq \emptyset$.
   Furthermore, P_{R_3} must be compatible with the result of composing P_{R_1} and P_{R_2}.

It is important to note that domain and range compatibility is not enough to compose two relations. For example, given KINSHIP(*Mary*, *John*) and AT-LOCATION(*John*, *Dallas*), no relation can be inferred between *Mary* and *Dallas*.

4 Inference Axioms

An axiom is defined as a set of relations called premises and a conclusion. The composition operator $\circ$ is the basic way of combining two relations to form an axiom. We denote an inference axiom as $R_1(x, y) \circ R_2(y, z) \rightarrow R_3(x, z)$, where R_1 and R_2 are the premises and R_3 the conclusion. In order to instantiate an axiom the premises must have an argument in common, *y*.

In general, for n relations there are $\binom{n}{2} = \frac{n(n-1)}{2}$ different pairs. For each pair, taking into account the two relations and their inverses, there are $4 \times 4 = 16$ different possible combinations.

We note that $R_1 \circ R_2 = ({R_2}^{-1} \circ {R_1}^{-1})^{-1}$, reducing the total number of different combinations to 10. Out of these 10, (1) 4 combine R_1, R_2 and their inverses (Table 3); (2) 3 combine R_1 and its inverse; and (3) 3 combine R_2 and its inverse. The most interesting combinations to use as premises for an axiom fall into category (1), since the other two can be resolved by the transitivity property of a relation and its inverse. Therefore, for n relations there are $2n^2+n$ potential axioms: $\binom{n}{2} \times 4 + 3n = 2 \times n(n-1) + 3n = 2n^2 - 2n + 3n = 2n^2 + n$.

4.1 An Algorithm for Obtaining Inference Axioms

Given a set of relations R defined using the extended definition, one can automatically obtain inference axioms using the following steps for each pair of relations $R_1 \in R$ and $R_2 \in R$, where $R_1 \neq R_2$:

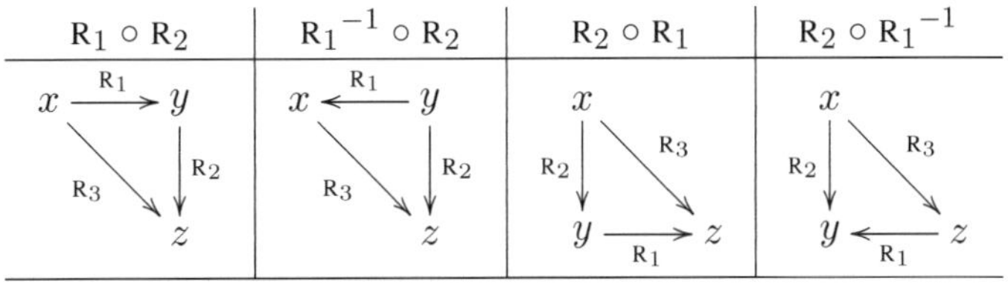

Table 3: The four unique axioms taking as premises R_1 and R_2. R_3 indicates the conclusion.

Role	Composable	Functional	Separable	Temporal	Connected	Intrinsic	Volitional	Fully Impl.	Weakly Impl.	Role	Composable	Functional	Separable	Temporal	Connected	Intrinsic	Volitional	Fully Impl.	Weakly Impl.
ARG0	+	+	+	0	-	-	+	0	0	ARG0^{-1}	+	+	+	0	-	-	+	0	0
ARG1	+	-	+	0	-	-	-	0	0	ARG1^{-1}	+	-	+	0	-	-	-	0	0
MLOC	+	+	0	0	+	-	0	0	0	MLOC^{-1}	+	+	0	0	+	-	0	0	0
MCAU	+	+	+	+	-	+	0	+	+	MCAU^{-1}	+	+	+	-	-	+	0	-	-
MTMP	+	+	0	0	+	-	0	0	0	MTMP^{-1}	+	+	0	0	+	-	0	0	0
MPNC	+	-	+	-	-	-	-	0	-	MPNC^{-1}	+	-	+	+	-	-	-	0	+
MMNR	+	-	+	0	-	-	+	0	0	MMNR^{-1}	+	-	+	0	-	-	+	0	0

Table 4: Semantic Roles in PropBank, their inverses and their primitives.

Repeat Steps 1, 2 and 3 for $(R_i, R_j) \in [(R_1, R_2), ({R_1}^{-1}, R_2), (R_2, R_1), (R_2, {R_1}^{-1})]$:

1. **Domain and range compatibility**
   If $\text{RANGE}(R_i) \cap \text{DOMAIN}(R_j) = \emptyset$, **break**
2. **Primitives composition**
   Using the algebra for composing semantic primitives, calculate $P_{R_i} \circ P_{R_j}$
3. **Conclusion match** Repeat for $R_3 \in R$
   If $\text{DOMAIN}(R_3) \cap \text{DOMAIN}(R_i) \neq \emptyset$ **and** $\text{RANGE}(R_3) \cap \text{RANGE}(R_j) \neq \emptyset$
   and $consistent(P_{R_3}, P_{R_i} \circ P_{R_j})$, **then**
   $inference\_axioms$ += $R_i(x, y) \circ R_j(y, z) \rightarrow R_3(x, z)$

The method $consistent(P_1, P_2)$ is a simple procedure that compares the values assigned to each primitive one by one. Two values for the same primitive are compatible unless they have different opposites or either value is '×' (i.e., prohibited).

5 Case Study: PropBank

PropBank (Palmer et al., 2005) adds a layer of predicate-argument information, or semantic role labels, on top of the syntactic trees provided by the Penn TreeBank. Along with FrameNet, it is the resource most widely used for semantic role annotation.

PropBank uses a series of numeric core roles (ARG0 - ARG5) and a set of more general roles, ARGMs (e.g. MTMP, MLOC, MMNR). The interpretation of the numeric roles is determined by a verb-specific framesets, although ARG0 and ARG1 usually correspond to the prototypical AGENT and THEME. On the other hand, the meaning of AGRMs generalize across verbs.

An example of PropBank annotation is the following: $[\text{Winston}]_{\text{ARG0}}$ $[\text{procrastinated}]_{rel}$ $[\text{a lot}]_{\text{MADV}}$ $[\text{due to his nervous demeanor}]_{\text{MCAU}}$. Palmer et al. (2005) discuss the creation of PropBank. For more information about the semantics of each role, we refer the reader to the annotation guidelines[1].

Since ARG2, AGR3, ARG4 and ARG5 do not have a common meaning across verbs, they become not *composable*. For example, ARG2 is used for INSTRUMENT in the frameset *kick.01* and for BENEFACTIVE in the frameset *call.02*.

[1]http://verbs.colorado.edu/~m palmer/projects/ace/PBguidelines.pdf

	R_2						
R_1	a: ARG0^{-1}	b: ARG1^{-1}	c: MLOC^{-1}	d: MCAU^{-1}	e: MTMP^{-1}	f: MPNC^{-1}	g: MMNR^{-1}
a: ARG0	=	-	-	a	-	a	-
b: ARG1	-	=	-	-	-	b	-
c: MLOC	-	-	=	c	-	c	-
d: MCAU	a	-	c	=	e	-	-
e: MTMP	-	-	-	e	=	e	-
f: MPNC	a	b	c	-	e	=	g
g: MMNR	-	-	-	-	-	g	=

Table 5: Results after applying the steps depicted in Section 4.1 using PropBank semantic roles. A letter indicates an inference axiom $R_1 \circ R_2 \rightarrow R_3$ by indicating the conclusion R_3. '-' indicates that the combination is not prohibited but a relation compatible with $P_{R_1} \circ P_{R_2}$ could not be found; '=' indicates that the cell corresponds to a relation and its inverse.

The remaining labels (ARG0, ARG1 and all ARGMs) do generalize in meaning across verbs. Roles MEXT, MDIS, MADV, MNEG, MMOD, MDIR, are not *composable* because they encode a very narrow semantic connection. Manual examination of several examples leads to this conclusion.

Table 4 depicts the primitives for the roles which are *composable* and their inverses. Note that for any two relations their primitives are different.

PropBank does not provide domains and ranges for its roles, although we can specify our own. We do so by using the ontology defined by Helbig (2005). All relations in PropBank are denoted as $R(x, y)$, where x is an argument of y, and y is a verb. The range of all relations is a situation. The domain of AGR0 and ARG1 are objects, the domain of MLOC and MTMP local and temporal descriptors respectively, the domain of MMNR qualities or states, and the domain of MPNC and MCAU are situations.

5.1 Inference Axioms from PropBank

Out of the four possible axioms between any pair of relations (Table 3), the only way to compose two relations from PropBank is by using as common argument y a verb. This restriction is due to the fact that PropBank exclusively annotates relations between a verb and its arguments. Thus, the only possible axiom for any pair of roles R_1 and R_2 is $R_1(x, y) \circ R_2^{-1}(y, z) \rightarrow R_3(x, z)$, where y is a verb.

Table 5 shows the eight inference axioms obtained after following the steps depicted in Section 4.1. Note that the matrix is symmetric as stated by the property $R_1 \circ R_2 = (R_2^{-1} \circ R_1^{-1})^{-1}$.

Some of the axioms obtained are:

- MCAU $\circ$ MLOC^{-1} $\rightarrow$ MLOC^{-1}, *the location of a cause is the same than the location of its effect.*
- MPNC $\circ$ ARG0^{-1} $\rightarrow$ ARG0^{-1}, *the agent of an action is inherited by its purpose.*
- MPNC $\circ$ MMNR^{-1} $\rightarrow$ MMNR^{-1}, *the manner of an action is inherited by its purpose.*

5.2 Evaluation

First, we evaluated all the instantiations of axiom MPNC $\circ$ MMNR^{-1} $\rightarrow$ MMNR^{-1}. This axiom can be instantiated 237 times using PropBank annotation, yielding 189 new MANNER not present in PropBank. The overall accuracy is 0.797, superior to state-of-the art semantic role labelers.

Second, we have evaluated the accuracy of the eight inference axioms (Table 5). Since PropBank is a large corpus, the amount of instantiations found for all axioms is too large to be checked by hand. We have manually evaluated the first 1,000 sentences that are an instantiation of any axiom. Since a sentence may instantiate several axioms, we have actually evaluated 1,412 instantiations. The first 1,000 sentences which are an instantiation of any axiom are found within the first 31,450 sentences in PropBank. Table 6 shows the number of roles PropBank annotates for these sentences.

Role	No. Instances
CAUSE	421
PURPOSE	768
AGENT	22,525
THEME	29,738
AT-LOCATION	2,024
AT-TIME	5,743
MANNER	2,212

Table 6: Number of relations in PropBank for the first 31,450 sentences.

		no heuristic			with heuristic		
No.	Axiom	No. Inst.	Acc.	Produc.	No. Inst.	Acc.	Produc.
1	CAU ∘ AGT^{-1} → AGT^{-1}	201	0.40	0.89%	75	0.67	0.33%
2	CAU ∘ AT-L → AT-L	17	0.82	0.84%	15	0.93	0.74%
3	CAU ∘ AT-T → AT-T	72	0.85	1.25%	69	0.87	1.20%
1-3	CAU ∘ R_2 → R_3	290	0.53	0.96%	159	0.78	0.53%
4	PRP ∘ AGT^{-1} → AGT^{-1}	375	0.89	1.66%	347	0.94	1.54%
5	PRP ∘ THM^{-1} → THM^{-1}	489	0.12	1.64%	87	0.65	0.29%
6	PRP ∘ AT-L → AT-L	49	0.90	2.42%	48	0.92	2.37%
7	PRP ∘ AT-T → AT-T	138	0.84	2.40%	129	0.88	2.25%
8	PRP ∘ MNR^{-1} → MNR^{-1}	71	0.82	3.21%	70	0.83	3.16%
4-8	PRP ∘ R_2 → R_3	1,122	0.54	1.80%	681	0.88	1.09%
1-8	**All**	1,412	0.54	2.26%	**840**	**0.86**	**1.35%**

Table 7: Axioms used during evaluation, number of instances, accuracy and productivity. Results are reported both using and not using the heuristic. Productivity refers to the number of relations added by the axiom in relative terms.

Table 7 depicts the total number of instantiations for each axiom and its accuracy (columns 3 and 4). Accuracies range from 0.12 to 0.90, showing that the plausibility of an axiom depends on the axiom. The average accuracy for axioms involving MCAU is 0.53 and for axioms involving MPNC is 0.54.

Axiom MCAU ∘ ARG0^{-1} → ARG0^{-1} adds 201 relations, which corresponds to 0.89% in relative terms. Its accuracy is low, 0.40. Other axioms are less productive overall, but have a greater relative impact and accuracy. For example, axiom MPNC ∘ MMNR^{-1} → MMNR^{-1}, only yields 71 new MMNR, and yet it is adding 3.21% in relative terms with an accuracy of 0.82.

It is worth noting that overall, applying the eight axioms used during evaluation adds 1,412 relations on top of the ones already present (2.26% in relative terms) with an accuracy of 0.54.

5.3 Error Analysis

Because of the low accuracy of axioms 1 and 5, an error analysis was performed. We found that unlike other axioms, these axioms often yield a relation type that is already present in the semantic representation. Specifically, axioms 1 and 5 often yield R(*x*, *z*) when R(*x'*, *z*) is already known.

An example can be found in Figure 4, where axiom 5 yields ARG1(*orders, to buy*) when the relation ARG1(*the basket, to buy*) is already present. We use the following heuristic in order to improve the accuracy of axioms 1 and 5: *do not instantiate an axiom* $R_1(x, y) \circ R_2(y, z) \rightarrow R_3(x, z)$ *if a relation of the form* $R_3(x', z)$ *is already known.*

This simple heuristic allows us to augment the accuracy of the inferences at the cost of lowering their productivity. The last three columns in Table 7 show results when using the heuristic. The eight axioms add 840 relations (1.35% in relative terms) with an accuracy of 0.86.

5.4 Examples

In this section we present several examples of instantiations. We provide the full text of each example, but only the relevant semantic annotation for instantiating axioms. For all examples, solid arrows indicate semantic role annotation from PropBank, and discontinuous arrows inferred relations.

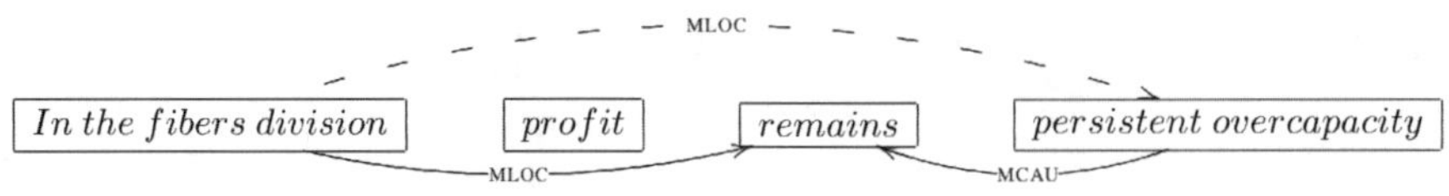

Figure 2: *In the fibers division, profit remains weak, largely because of persistent overcapacity.* (wsj_0552, 28).

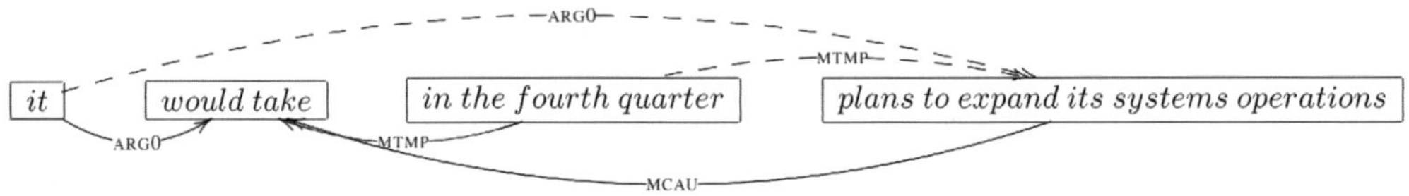

Figure 3: *First Tennessee National Corp. said it would take a $4 million charge in the fourth quarter, as a result of plans to expand its systems operation.* (wsj_0621, 0).

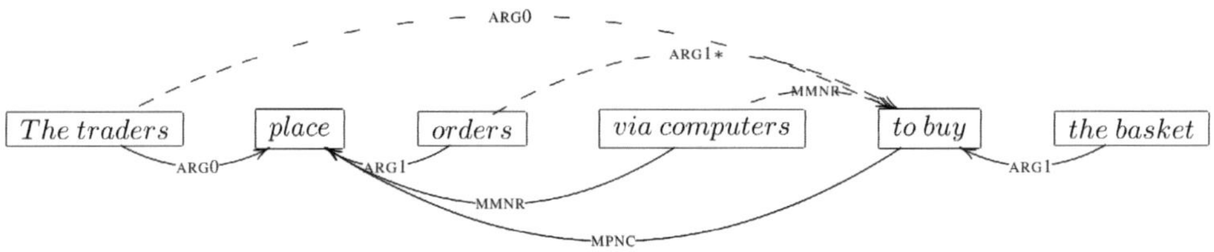

Figure 4: *When it occurs, the traders place orders via computers to buy the basket of stocks ... in whichever market is cheaper and sell them in the more expensive market; ...* (wsj_0118, 48).

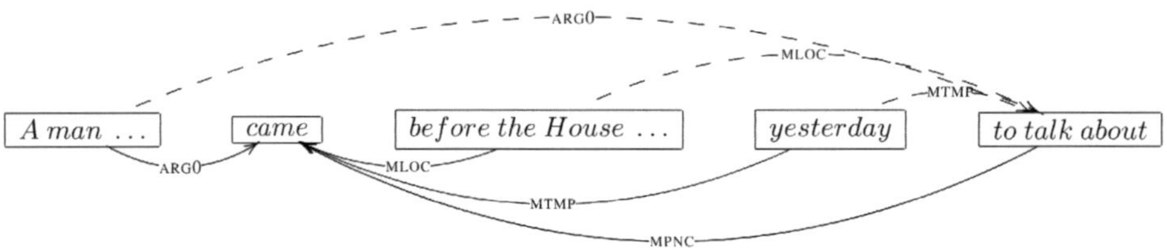

Figure 5: *A man from the Bush administration came before the House Agriculture Committee yesterday to talk about ...* (wsj_0134, 0).

Figures 2 and 3 instantiate axioms 1, 2 and 3. For these examples, all inferences are correct.

Figures 4 and 5 instantiate the rest of axioms. Not using the heuristic leads to a wrong inference in the example shown in Figure 4, indicated with *. Using the heuristic, all inferences are correct.

6 Comparison with Previous Work

There have been abundant proposals to detect semantic relations without taking into account composition of relations. All these approaches, regardless of their particular details, take as their input text and output the relations found in it. In contrast, the framework proposed in this article obtains axioms that take as their input relations found in text and output more relations previously ignored.

Generally, efforts to extract semantic relations have concentrated on particular sets of relations or a single relation, e.g. CAUSE (Bethard and Martin, 2008; Chang and Choi, 2006) and PART-WHOLE (Girju et al., 2006). Automatic detection of semantic roles has received a lot of attention lately (Màrquez et al., 2008; Carreras and Màrquez, 2005). The SemEval-2007 Task 04 (Girju et al., 2007) and SemEval-2010 Task 08 (Hendrickx et al., 2009) aimed at relations between nominals. There has been work on detecting relations within noun phrases (Moldovan et al., 2004; Nulty, 2007), clauses (Szpakowicz et al., 1995) and syntax-based comma resolution (Srikumar et al., 2008).

Previous research has exploited the idea of using semantic primitives to define and classify semantic relations under different names. Among others, the literature uses *relation elements*, *deep structure*, *aspects* and *primitives*. To the best of our knowledge, the first effort on describing semantic relations using primitives was made by Chaffin and Herrmann (1987). They introduce Relation Element Theory, and differentiate relations by *relation elements*. The authors describe a set of 31 relations clustered in five groups (CONTRAST, SIMILARS, CLASS INCLUSION, CASE-RELATIONS, PART-WHOLE), and distinguish each relation by its *relations elements* and not just a definition and examples. Their 30 *relation elements* are clustered into five groups (elements of intensional force, dimension elements, elements of agreement, propositional elements, elements of part-whole inclusion). They only use the *elements* to define relations, not to compose relations.

Winston et al. (1987) work with six subtypes of PART-WHOLE and uses 3 relation elements (*functional, homeomerous* and *separable*) to distinguish the subtypes. Cohen and Losielle (1988) introduce the notion of *deep structure* and characterize it using two aspects: *hierarchical* and *temporal*. Huhns and Stephens (1989) extend previous works by considering an extended set of 10 primitives.

In Computational Linguistics there have been previous proposals to combine semantic relations. Harabagiu and Moldovan (1998) manually extract plausible inference axioms using WordNet relations. Helbig (2005) transforms chains of relations into theoretical axioms. On the other hand, the model presented in this paper extracts inference axioms automatically.

Composing relations has been proposed before in the more general field of Artificial Intelligence, in particular in the context of Knowledge Bases. Cohen and Losielle (1988) point out that two relations shall combine if and only if they do not have contradictory values for the aspect *hierarchical* or *temporal*. They work with a set of nine specific relations (CAUSES, COMPONENT-OF, FOCUS-OF, MECHANISM-OF, PRODUCT-OF, PURPOSE-OF, SETTING-OF, SUBJECT-OF and SUBFIELD-OF) and their inverses. Huhns and Stephens (1989) are the first to propose an algebra for composing semantic primitives. Unlike ours, their set of relations is not linguistically motivated; ten of them map to some sort of PART-WHOLE (e.g. PIECE-OF, SUBREGION-OF).

7 Conclusions

In this paper, we have presented a model to compose semantic relations. The model is independent of any particular set of relations and is able to obtain inference axioms. These axioms take as their input two semantic relations and yield a previously ignored relation as conclusion.

The model is based on an extended definition of semantic relations, including restrictions on domains and ranges and values for a set of semantic primitives. We have defined an algebra for composing semantic primitives. This algebra is the key to automatically identify the resulting relation of composing a pair of compatible relations and to form an axiom.

The proposed algorithm to compose semantic relations identifies eight inference axioms using PropBank relations. When instantiated in a subset of PropBank, these axioms add 2.26% of annotation in relative terms with an accuracy of 0.54. We believe these results are worthwhile for a completely unsupervised approach to obtain semantic relations. Adding a simple heuristic improves the accuracy to 0.86, lowering the productivity in relative terms to 1.35%.

The model has limitations and is not always correct. First, relations are defined manually and mistakes could be made when assigning values to their primitives. Second, the algebra for composing primitives is also manually defined.

We find the first problem easy to overcome. Whatever the set of relations one might use, we believe thinking in terms of primitives helps to understand the nature of the relations and their differences. An issue might be that the proposed set of primitives is not enough for a particular set, but more primitives could be added to solve this eventuality.

A further issue with the algebra is the fact that primitives are composed orthogonally. This is a simplification, but we have shown that this simplified algebra works.

Even though different sets of semantic relations may call for different ontologies to define domains and ranges, and possibly an extended set of primitives, we believe the model presented in this paper is applicable to any set. As far as we are concerned, this is a novel way to compose semantic relations in the field of Computational Linguistics.

References

Bethard, S. and J. H. Martin (2008). Learning Semantic Links from a Corpus of Parallel Temporal and Causal Relations. In *Proceedings of ACL-08: HLT, Short Papers*, Columbus, OH.

Carreras, X. and L. Màrquez (2005). Introduction to the CoNLL-2005 shared task: semantic role labeling. In *Proc. of the 9th Conf. on Computational Natural Language Learning*, Morristown, NJ.

Chaffin, R. and D. J. Herrmann (1987). Relation Element Theory: A New Account of the Representation and Processing of Semantic Relations. In D. S. Gorfein and R. R. Hoffman (Eds.), *Memory and Learning. The Ebbinghaus Centennial Conference*.

Chang, D. S. and K. S. Choi (2006). Incremental cue phrase learning and bootstrapping method for causality extraction using cue phrase and word pair probabilities. *Information Processing & Management 42*(3), 662–678.

Cohen, P. R. and C. L. Losielle (1988). Beyond ISA: Structures for Plausible Inference in Semantic Networks. In *Proceedings of the Seventh National conference on Artificial Intelligence*, St. Paul, MN.

Girju, R., A. Badulescu, and D. Moldovan (2006). Automatic Discovery of Part-Whole Relations. *Computational Linguistics 32*(1), 83–135.

Girju, R., P. Nakov, V. Nastase, S. Szpakowicz, P. Turney, and D. Yuret (2007). SemEval-2007 Task 04: Classification of Semantic Relations between Nominals. In *Proceedings of the Fourth International Workshop on Semantic Evaluations*, Prague, Czech Republic.

Harabagiu, S. and D. Moldovan (1998). Knowledge Processing on an Extended WordNet. In C. Fellbaum (Ed.), *WordNet: An Electronic Lexical Database and Some of its Applications*, Chapter 17, pp. 684–714. The MIT Press.

Helbig, H. (2005). *Knowledge Representation and the Semantics of Natural Language* (1st ed.). Springer.

Hendrickx, I., S. N. Kim, Z. Kozareva, P. Nakov, Diarmuid, S. Padó, M. Pennacchiotti, L. Romano, and S. Szpakowicz (2009). SemEval-2010 Task 8: Multi-Way Classification of Semantic Relations Between Pairs of Nominals. In *Proceedings of the Workshop on Semantic Evaluations*, Boulder, CO.

Huhns, M. N. and L. M. Stephens (1989). Plausible Inferencing Using Extended Composition. In *IJCAI'89: Proceedings of the 11th international joint conference on AI*, San Francisco, CA.

Màrquez, L., X. Carreras, K. C. Litkowski, and S. Stevenson (2008, June). Semantic Role Labeling: An Introduction to the Special Issue. *Computational Linguistics 34*(2), 145–159.

Moldovan, D., A. Badulescu, M. Tatu, D. Antohe, and R. Girju (2004). Models for the Semantic Classification of Noun Phrases. In *HLT-NAACL 2004: Workshop on Computational Lexical Semantics*.

Nulty, P. (2007). Semantic Classification of Noun Phrases Using Web Counts and Learning Algorithms. In *Proceedings of the ACL 2007 Student Research Workshop*, Prague, Czech Republic.

Palmer, M., D. Gildea, and P. Kingsbury (2005). The Proposition Bank: An Annotated Corpus of Semantic Roles. *Computational Linguistics 31*(1), 71–106.

Srikumar, V., R. Reichart, M. Sammons, A. Rappoport, and D. Roth (2008). Extraction of Entailed Semantic Relations Through Syntax-Based Comma Resolution. In *Proceedings of ACL-08: HLT*, Columbus, OH.

Szpakowicz, B., K. Barker, and S. Szpakowicz (1995). Interactive semantic analysis of Clause-Level Relationships. In *Proc. of the 2nd Conference of the Pacific Association for Computational Linguistics*.

Winston, M. E., R. Chaffin, and D. Herrmann (1987). A Taxonomy of Part-Whole Relations. *Cognitive Science 11*(4), 417–444.

Implementing Weighted Abduction in Markov Logic

James Blythe
USC ISI
blythe@isi.edu

Jerry R. Hobbs
USC ISI
hobbs@isi.edu

Pedro Domingos
University of Washington
pedrod@cs.washington.edu

Rohit J. Kate
University of Wisconsin-Milwaukee
katerj@uwm.edu

Raymond J. Mooney
University of Texas at Austin
mooney@cs.utexas.edu

Abstract

Abduction is a method for finding the best explanation for observations. Arguably the most advanced approach to abduction, especially for natural language processing, is weighted abduction, which uses logical formulas with costs to guide inference. But it has no clear probabilistic semantics. In this paper we propose an approach that implements weighted abduction in Markov logic, which uses weighted first-order formulas to represent probabilistic knowledge, pointing toward a sound probabilistic semantics for weighted abduction. Application to a series of challenge problems shows the power and coverage of our approach.

1 Introduction

Abduction is inference to the best explanation.[1] Typically, one uses it to find the best hypothesis explaining a set of observations, e.g., in diagnosis and plan recognition. In natural language processing the content of an utterance can be viewed as a set of observations, and the best explanation then constitutes the interpretation of the utterance. Hobbs et al. [7] described a variety of abduction called "weighted abduction" for interpreting natural language discourse. The key idea was that the best interpretation of a text is the best explanation or proof of the logical form of the text, allowing for assumptions. What counted as "best" was defined in terms of a cost function which favored proofs with the fewest number of assumptions and the most salient and plausible axioms, and in which the pervasive redundancy implicit in natural language discourse was exploited. It was argued in that paper that such interpretation problems as coreference and syntactic ambiguity resolution, determining the specific meanings of vague predicates and lexical ambiguity resolution, metonymy resolution, metaphor interpretation, and the recognition of discourse structure could be seen to "fall out" of the best abductive proof.

Specifically, weighted abduction has the following features:

1. In a goal expression consisting of an existentially quantified conjunction of positive literals, each literal is given a cost that represents the utility of proving that literal as opposed to assuming it. That is, a low cost on a literal will make it more likely for it to be assumed, whereas a high cost will result in a greater effort to find a proof.

[1]We are indebted to Jesse Davis, Parag Singla and Marc Sumner for discussions about this work. This research was supported in part by the Defense Advanced Research Projects Agency (DARPA) Machine Reading Program under Air Force Research Laboratory (AFRL) prime contract no. FA8750-09-C-0172, in part by the Office of Naval Research under contract no. N00014-09-1-1029, and in part by the Army Research Office under grant W911NF-08-1-0242. Any opinions, findings, and conclusions or recommendations expressed in this material are those of the authors and do not necessarily reflect the view of the DARPA, AFRL, ONR, ARO, or the US government.

2. Costs are passed back across the implication in Horn clauses according to weights on the conjuncts in the antecedents. Specifically, if a consequent costs $\$c$ and the weight on a conjunct in the antecedent is v, then the cost on that conjunct will be $\$vc$. Note that if the weights add up to less than one, backchaining on the rule will be favored, as the cost of the antecedent will be less than the cost of the consequent. If the weights add up to more than one, backchaining will be disfavored unless a proof can be found for one or more of the conjuncts in the antecedent, thereby providing partial evidence for the consequent.

3. Two literals can be factored or unified, where the result is given the minimum cost of the two, providing no contradiction would result. This is a frequent mechanism for coreference resolution. In practice, only a shallow or heuristic check for contradiction is done.

4. The lowest-cost proof is the best interpretation, or the best abductive proof of the goal expression.

However, there are two significant problems with weighted abduction as it was originally presented. First, it required a large knowledge base of commonsense knowledge. This was not available when weighted abduction was first described, but since that time there have been substantial efforts to build up knowledge bases for various purposes, and at least two of these have been used with promising results in an abductive setting—Extended WordNet [6] for question-answering and FrameNet [11] for textual inference.

The second problem with weighted abduction was that the weights and costs did not have a probabilistic semantics. This, for example, hampers automatic learning of weights from data or existing resources. That is the issue we address in the present paper.

In the last decade and a half, a number of formalisms for adding uncertain reasoning to predicate logic have been developed that are well-founded in probability theory. Among the most widely investigated is Markov logic [14, 4]. In this paper we show how weighted abduction can be implemented in Markov logic. This demonstrates that Markov logic networks can be used as a powerful mechanism for interpreting natural language discourse, and at the same time provides weighted abduction with something like a probabilistic semantics.

In Section 2 we briefly describe Markov logic and Markov logic networks. Section 3 then describes how weighted abduction can be implemented in Markov logic. In Section 4 we describe experiments in which fourteen published examples of the use of weighted abduction in natural language understanding are implemented in Markov logic networks, with good results. Section 5 on current and future directions briefly describes an ongoing experiment in which we are attempting to scale up to apply this procedure to the textual inference problem with a knowledge base derived from FrameNet with tens of thousands of axioms.

2 Markov Logic Networks and Related Work

Markov logic [14, 4] is a recently developed theoretically sound framework for combining first-order logic and probabilistic graphical models. A traditional first-order knowledge base can be seen as a set of hard constraints on the set of possible worlds: if a world violates even one formula, its probability is zero. In order to soften these constraints, Markov logic attaches a weight to each first-order logic formula in the knowledge base. Such a set of weighted first-order logic formulae is called a *Markov logic network* (MLN). A formula's weight reflects how strong a constraint it imposes on the set of possible worlds: the higher the weight, the lower the probability of a world that violates it; however, that probability need not be zero. An MLN with all infinite weights reduces to a traditional first-order knowledge base with only hard constraints.

Formally, an MLN L is a set of formula–weight pairs (F_i, w_i). Given a set of constants, it defines a joint probability distribution over a set of boolean variables $X = (X_1, X_2...)$ corresponding to the possible groundings (using the given constants) of the literals present in the first-order formulae:

$$P(X = x) = \frac{1}{Z} exp(\sum_i w_i n_i(x))$$

where $n_i(x)$ is the number of true groundings of F_i in x and Z is a normalization term obtained by summing $P(X = x)$ over all values of X.

Semantically, an MLN can be viewed as a set of templates for constructing Markov networks [12], the undirected counterparts of Bayesian networks. An MLN and a set of constants produce a Markov network in which each ground literal is a node and every pair of ground literals that appear together in some grounding of some formula are connected by an edge. Different sets of constants produce different Markov networks; however, there are certain regularities in their structure and parameters. For example, all groundings of the same formula have the same weight.

Probabilistic inference for an MLN (such as finding the most probable truth assignment for a given set of ground literals, or finding the probability that a particular formula holds) can be performed by first producing the ground Markov network and then using well known inference techniques for Markov networks, like Gibbs sampling. Given a knowledge base as a set of first-order logic formulae, and a database of training examples each consisting of a set of true ground literals, it is also possible to learn appropriate weights for the MLN formulae which maximize the probability of the training data. An open-source software package for MLNs, called Alchemy [2], is also available with many built-in algorithms for performing inference and learning.

Much of the early work on abduction was done in a purely logical framework (e.g., [13, 3, 9, 10]. Typically the choice between alternative explanations is made on the basis of parsimony; the shortest proofs with the fewest assumptions are favored. However, a significant limitation of these purely logical approaches is that they are unable to reason under uncertainty or estimate the likelihood of alternative explanations. A probabilistic form of abduction is needed in order to account for uncertainty in the background knowledge and to handle noisy and incomplete observations.

In Bayesian networks [12] background knowledge with its uncertainties is encoded in a directed graph. Then, given a set of observations, probabilistic inference over the graph structure is done to compute the posterior probability of alternative explanations. However, Bayesian networks are based on propositional logic and cannot handle structured representations, hence preventing their use in situations, characteristic of natural language processing, that involve an unbounded number of entities with a variety of relations between them.

In recent years there have been a number of proposals attempting to combine the probabilistic nature of Bayesian networks with structured first-order representations. It is impossible here to review this literature here. A a good review of much of it can be found in [5], and in [14] there are detailed comparisonss of various models to MLNs.

Charniak and Shimony [2] define a variant of weighted abduction, called "cost-based abduction" in which weights are attached to terms rather than to rules or to antecedents in rules. Thus, the term P_i has the same cost whatever rule it is used in. The cost of an assignment to the variables in the domain is the sum of the costs of the variables that are true in the assignment. Charniak and Shimony provide a probabilistic semantics for their approach by showing how to construct a Bayesian network from a domain such that a most probable explanation solution to the Bayes net corresponds to a lowest-cost solution to the abduction problem. However, in natural language applications the utility of proving a proposition can vary by context; weighted abduction accomodates this, whereas cost-based abduction does not.

[2] http://alchemy.cs.washington.edu

3 Weighted Abduction and MLNs

Kate and Mooney [8] show how logical abduction can be implemented in Markov logic networks. They use forward inference in MLNs to perform abduction by adding clauses with reverse implications. Universally quantified variables from the left hand side of rules are converted to existentially quantified variables in the reversed clause. For example, suppose we have the following rule saying that mosquito bites transmit malaria:

$$mosquito(x) \land infected(x, Malaria) \land bite(x, y) \supset infected(y, Malaria)$$

This would be translated into the soft rule

$$[w]\ infected(y, Malaria) \supset \exists x[mosquito(x) \land infected(x, Malaria) \land bite(x, y)]$$

Where there is more than one possible explanation, they include a closure axiom saying that one of the explanations must hold. Since blood transfusions also cause malaria, they have the hard rule

$$\begin{aligned} &infected(y, Malaria) \supset \\ &\quad \exists x[mosquito(x) \land infected(x, Malaria) \land bite(x, y)] \\ &\quad \lor \exists x[infected(x, Malaria) \land transfuse(Blood, x, y)]. \end{aligned}$$

Kate and Mooney also add a soft mutual exclusivity clause that states that no more than one of the possible explanations is true.

In translating between weighted abduction and Markov logic, we need similarly to specify the axioms in Markov logic that correspond to a Horn clause axiom in weighted abduction. In addition, we need to describe the relation between the numbers in weighted abduction and the weights on the Markov logic axioms. Hobbs et al. [7] give only broad, informal guidelines about how the numbers correspond to probabilities. In this development, we elaborate on how the numbers can be defined more precisely within these guidelines in a way that links with the weights in Markov logic, thereby pointing to a probabilistic semantics for the weighted abduction numbers.

There are two sorts of numbers in weighted abduction—the weights on conjuncts in the antecedents of Horn clause axioms, and the costs on conjuncts in goal expressions, which are existentially quantified conjunctions of positive literals. We deal first with the weights, then with the costs.

The space of events over which probabilities are taken is the set of proof graphs constituting the best interpretations of a set of texts in a corpus. Thus, by the probability of $p(x)$ given $q(x)$, we mean the probability that $p(x)$ will occur in a proof graph in which $q(x)$ occurs.

The translation from weighted abduction axioms to Markov logic axioms can be broken into two steps. First we consider the "or" node case, determining the relative costs of axioms that have the same consequent. Then we look at the "and" node case, determining how the weights should be distributed across the conjuncts in the antecedent of a Horn clause, given the total weight for the antecedent.

Weights on Antecedents in Axioms. First consider a set of Horn clause axioms all with the same consequent, where we collapse the antecedent into a single literal, and for simplicity allow x to stand for all the universally quantified variables in the antecedent, and assume the consequent to have only those variables. That is, we convert all axioms of the form

$$p_1(x) \land \ldots \supset q(x)$$

into axioms of the form

$$A_i(x) \supset q(x), \text{ where } p_1(x) \land \ldots \equiv A_i(x)$$

To convert this into Markov logic, we first introduce the hard constraint

$$A_i(x) \supset q(x).$$

In addition, given a goal of proving $q(x)$, in weighted abduction we will want to backchain on at least (and usually at most) one of these axioms or we will want simply to assume $q(x)$. Thus, we can introduce another hard constraint with the disjunction of these antecedents as well as a literal $AssumeQ(x)$ that means $q(x)$ is assumed rather than proved.

$q(x) \supset A_1(x) \vee A_2(x) \vee \ldots \vee A_n(x) \vee AssumeQ(x)$.

Then we need to introduce soft constraints to indicate that each of these disjuncts is a possible explanation, or proof, of $q(x)$, with an associated probability, or weight.

$[w_i]\ q(x) \supset A_i(x), \ldots$
$[w_0]\ q(x) \supset AssumeQ(x)$

The probability that $AssumeQ(x)$ is true is the conditional probability P_0 that none of the antecedents is true given that $q(x)$ is true.

$$P_0 = P(\neg[A_1(x) \vee A_2(x) \vee \ldots \vee A_n(x)] \mid q(x))$$

In weighted abduction, when the antecedent weight is greater than one, we prefer assuming the consequent to assuming the antecedent. When the antecedent weight is less than one we prefer to assume the antecedent. If the probability that an antecedent $A_i(x)$ is the explanation of $q(x)$ is greater than P_0, it should be given a weighted abduction weight v_i less than 1, making it more likely to be chosen.[3] Correspondingly, if it is less than P_0, it should be given a weight v_i greater than 1, making it less likely to be chosen. In general, the weighted abduction weights should be in reverse order of the conditional probabilities P_i that $A_i(x)$ is the explanation of $q(x)$.

$$P_i = P(A_i(x) \mid q(x))$$

If we assign the weights v_i in weighted abduction to be

$$v_i = \frac{logP_i}{logP_0}$$

then this is consistent with informal guidelines in [7] on the meaning of these weights. We use the logs of the probabilities rather than the probabilities themselves to moderate the effect of one axiom being very much more probable than any of the others.

Kate and Mooney [8], in their translation of logical abduction into Markov logic, also include soft constraints stipulating that the different possible explanations $A_i(x)$ are normally mutually exclusive. We do not do that here, but we get a kind of soft mutual exclusivity constraint by virtue of the axioms below that levy a cost for any literal that is taken to be true. In general, more parimonious explanations will be favored.

Nevertheless, in most cases a single explanation will suffice. When this is true, the probability of $A_i(x)$ holding when $q(x)$ holds is $\frac{e^{w_i}}{Z}$. Then a reasonable approximation for the relation between the weighted abduction weights v_i and the Markov logic weights w_i is

$$w_i = -v_i logP_0$$

Weights on Conjuncts in Antecedents. Next consider how cost is spread across the conjuncts in the antecedent of a Horn clause in weighted abduction. Here we use u's to represent the weighted abduction weights on the conjuncts.

$$p_1(x)^{u_1} \wedge p_2(x)^{u_2} \wedge \ldots \equiv A(x)$$

The u's should somehow represent the semantic contribution of each conjunct to the conclusion. That is, given that the conjunct is true, what is the probability that it is part of an explanation of the consequent? Conjuncts with a higher such probability should be given higher weights u; they play a more significant role in explaining $A(x)$.

Let P_i be the conditional probability of the consequent given the ith conjunct in the antecedent.

$$P_i = P(A(x)|p_i(x))$$

and let Z be a normalization factor.

$$Z = \sum_{i=1}^{n} P_i$$

[3] We use v_i for these weighted abduction weights and w_i for Markov logic weights.

Let v be the weight of the entire antecedent as determined above.

Then it is consistent with the guidelines in [7] to define the weights on the conjuncts as follows:

$$u_i = \frac{vP_i}{Z}$$

The weights u_i will sum to v and each will correspond to the semantic contribution of its conjunct to the consequent.

In Markov logic, weights apply only to axioms as a whole, not parts of axioms. Thus, the single axiom above must be decomposed into one axiom for each conjunct and the dependencies must be written as

$$[w_i]\ p_i(x) \supset A(x), \ldots$$

The relation between the weighted abduction weights u_i and the Markov logic weights w_i can be approximated by

$$u_i = \frac{ve^{-w_i}}{Z}$$

Costs on Goals. The other numbers in weighted abduction are the costs associated with the conjuncts in the goal expression. In weighted abduction these costs function as utilities. Some parts of the goal expression are more important to interpret correctly than others; we should try harder to prove these parts, rather than simply assuming them. In language it is important to recognize the referential anchor of an utterance in shared knowledge. Thus, those parts of a sentence most likely to provide this anchor have the highest utility. If we simply assume them, we lose their connection with what is already known. Those parts of a sentence most likely to be new information will have a lower cost, because we usually would not be able to prove them in any case.

Consider the two sentences

The smart man is tall.
The tall man is smart.

The logical form for each of them will be

$$(\exists\, x)[smart(x) \wedge tall(x) \wedge man(x)]$$

In weighted abduction, an interpretation of the sentence is a proof of the logical form, allowing assumptions. In the first sentence we want to prove $smart(x)$ to anchor the sentence referentially. Then $tall(x)$ is new information; it will have to be assumed. We will want to have a high cost on $smart(x)$ to force the proof procedure to find this referential anchor. The cost on $tall(x)$ will be low, to allow it to be assumed without expending too much effort in trying to locate that fact in shared knowledge.

In the second sentence, the case is the reverse.

Let's focus on the first sentence and assume we know that educated people are smart and big people are tall, and furthermore that John is educated and Bill is big.

$$educated(x)^{1.2} \supset smart(x)$$
$$big(x)^{1.2} \supset tall(x)$$
$$educated(J), big(B)$$

In weighted abduction, the best interpretation will be that the smart man is John, because he is educated, and we pay the cost for assuming he is tall. The interpretation we want to avoid is one that says x is Bill; he is tall because he is big, and we pay the cost of assuming he is smart. Weighted abduction with its differential costs on conjuncts in the goal expression favors the first and disfavors the second.

In weighted abduction, only assumptions cost; literals that are proved cost nothing. When the above axioms are translated into Markov logic, it would be natural to capture the differential costs by attaching a negative weight to $smart(x)$ to model the cost associated with assuming it. However, this weight would apply to any assignment in which $smart(J)$ is true, regardless of whether it was assumed, derived from an assumed fact, or derived from a known fact. A potential solution might be to attach the negative weight to $AssumeSmart(x)$. But the first axiom above allows us to bypass the negative weight on $smart(x)$. We can hypothesize that x is Bill, pay a low cost on $AssumeEducated(B)$, derive $smart(B)$, and get the wrong assignment. Thus it is not enough to attach a negative weight to high-cost conjuncts in the goal expression. This negative weight would have to be passed back through the whole knowledge base, making the complexity of setting the weights at problem time in the MLN knowledge base equal to the complexity of running the inference problem.

An alternative solution, which avoids this problem when the forward inferences are exact, is to use a set of predicates that express knowing a fact without any assumptions. In the current example, we would add $Ksmart(x)$ for knowing that an entity is smart. The facts asserted in the data base are now $Keducated(J)$ and $Kbig(B)$. For each hard axiom involving non-K predicates, we have a corresponding axiom that expresses the relation between the K-predicates, and we have a soft axiom allowing us to cross the border between the K predicates and their non-K counterparts.

$Keducated(x) \supset Ksmart(x).,\ldots$
$[w]\ Ksmart(x) \supset smart(x),\ldots$

Here the positive weight w attached is chosen to counteract the negative weight we would attach to $smart(x)$ to reflect the high cost of assuming it.

This removes the weight associated with assuming $smart(x)$ regardless of the inference path that leads to knowing $smart(x)$ ($KSmart(x)$)). Further, this translation takes linear time in the size of the goal expression to compute, since we do not need to know the equivalent weighted abduction cost assigned to the possible antecedents of $smart(x)$.

If the initial facts do not include $KEducated(B)$ and instead $educated(B)$ must be assumed, then the negative weight associated with $smart(B)$ is still present. In this solution, there is no danger that the inference process can by-pass the cost of assuming $smart(B)$, since it is attached to the required predicate and can only be removed by inferring $KSmart(B)$.

Finally, there is a tendency in Markov logic networks for assignments of high probability for propositions for which there is no evidence one way or the other. To suppress this, we associate a small negative weight with every predicate. In practice, it has turned out that a weight of -1 effectively suppresses this behavior.

4 Experimental Results

We have tested our approach on a set of fourteen challenge problems from [7] and subsequent papers, designed to exercise the principal features of weighted abduction and show its utility for solving natural language interpretation problems. The knowledge bases used for each of these problems are sparse, consisting of only the axioms required for solving the problems plus a few distractors.

An example of a relatively simple problem is #5 in the table below, resolving "he" in the text

I saw my doctor last week. He told me to get more exercise.

where we are given a knowledge base that says a doctor is a person and a male person is a "he". Solving the problem requires assuming the doctor is male.

$(\forall x)[doctor(x)^{1.2} \supset person(x)]$
$(\forall x)[male(x)^{.6} \wedge person(x)^{.6} \supset he(x)]$

The logical form fragment to prove is $(\exists x)he(x)$, where we know $doctor(D)$.

A problem of intermediate difficulty (#7) is resolving the three lexical ambiguities in the sentence

The plane taxied to the terminal.

where we are given a knowledge base saying that airplanes and wood smoothers are planes, planes moving on the ground and people taking taxis are both described as "taxiing", and computer terminals and airport terminals are both terminals.

An example of a difficult problem is #12, finding the coherence relation, thereby resolving the pronoun "they", between the sentences

The police prohibited the women from demonstrating. They feared violence.

The axioms specify relations between fearing, not wanting, and prohibiting, as well as the defeasible transitivity of causality and the fact that a causal relation between sentences makes the discourse coherent.

The weights in the axioms were mostly distributed evenly across the conjuncts in the antecedents and summed to 1.2.

For each of these problems, we compare the performance of the method described here with a manually constructed gold standard and also with a method based on Kate and Mooney's (KM) approach. In this method, weights were assigned to the reversed clauses based on the negative log of the sum of weights in the original clause. This approach does not capture different weights for different antecedents of the same rule, and so has less fidelity to weighted abduction than our approach. In each case, we used Alchemy's probabilistic inference to determine the most probable explanation (MPE) [12].

In some of the problems the system should make more than one assumption, so there are 22 assumptions in total over all 14 problems in the gold standard. Using our method, 18 of the assumptions were found, while 15 were found using the KM method. Table 1 shows the number of correct assumptions found and the running time for the two approaches for each problem. Our method in particular provides good coverage, with a recall of over 80% of the assumptions made in the gold standard. It has a shorter running time overall, approximately 5.3 seconds versus 8.7 seconds for the reversal method. This is largely due to one problem in the test set, problem #9, where the running time for the KM method is relatively high because the technique finds a less sparse network, leading to larger cliques. There were two problems in the test set that neither approach could solve. One of these contains predicates that have a large number of arguments, leading to large clique sizes.

5 Current and Future Directions

In other work [11] we are experimenting with using weighted abduction with a knowledge base with tens of thousands of axioms derived from FrameNet for solving problems in recognizing textual entailment (RTE2) from the Pascal dataset [1]. For a direct comparison between standard weighted abduction and the Markov logic approach described here, we are also experimenting with using the latter on the same task with the same knowledge base.

For each text-hypothesis pair, the sentences are parsed and a logical form is produced. The output for the first sentence forms the specific knowledge the system has while the output for the second sentence is used as the target to be explained. If the cost of the best explanation is below a threshold we take the target sentence to be true given the initial information.

It is a major challenge to scale our approach to handle all the problems from the RTE2 development and test sets. We are not yet able to address the most complex of these using inference in Markov logic networks. However, we have devised a number of pre-processing steps to reduce the complexity of the resultant network, which significantly increase the number of problems that are tractable.

The FrameNet knowledge base contains a large number of axioms with general coverage. For any individual entailment problem, most of them are irrelevant and can be removed after a simple graphical analysis. We are able to remove more irrelevant axioms and predicates with an iterative approach that in

	Our Method		KM Method		Gold
Problem	score	seconds	score	seconds	standard
1	3	300	3	16	3
2	1	250	1	265	1
3	1	234	1	266	1
4	2	234	2	203	2
5	1	218	1	218	1
6	1	218	0	265	1
7	3	300	3	218	3
8	1	200	1	250	1
9	2	421	0	5000	2
10	1	2500	1	1500	3
11	0		0		1
12	0		0		1
13	1	250	1	250	1
14	1	219	1	219	1
Total	18	5344	15	8670	22

Table 1: Performance on each problem in our test set, comparing two encodings of weighted abduction into Markov logic networks and a gold standard.

each iteration both drops axioms that are shown to be irrelevant and simplifies remaining axioms in such a way as not to change the probability of entailment.

We also simplify predications by removing unnecessary arguments. The most natural way to convert FrameNet frames to axioms is to treat a frame as a predicate whose arguments are the frame elements for all of its roles. After converting to Markov logic, this results in rules having large numbers of existentially quantified variables in the consequent. This can lead to a combinatorial explosion in the number of possible ground rules. Many of the variables in the frame predicate are for general use and can be pruned in the particular entailment. Our approach essentially creates abstractions of the original predicates that preserve all the information that is relevant to the current problem but greatly reduces the number of ground instances to consider.

Before implementing these pre-processing steps, only two or three problems could be run to completion on a Macbook Pro with 8 gigabytes of RAM. After making them, 28 of the initial 100 problems could be run to completion.

Work on this effort continues.

6 Summary

Weighted abduction is a logical reasoning framework that has been successfully applied to solve a number of interesting and important problems in computational natural-language semantics ranging from word sense disambiguation to coreference resolution. However, its method for representing and combining assumption costs to determine the most preferred explanation is ad hoc and without a firm theoretical foundation. Markov Logic is a recently developed formalism for combining first-order logic with probabilistic graphical models that has a well-defined formal semantics in terms of specifying a probability distribution over possible worlds. This paper has presented a method for mapping weighted abduction to Markov logic, thereby providing a sound probabilistic semantics for the approach and also allowing it to exploit the growing toolbox of inference and learning algorithms available for Markov logic. Complementarily, it has also demonstrated how Markov logic can thereby be applied to help solve important problems in computational semantics.

References

[1] Roy Bar-Haim, Ido Dagan, Bill Dolan, Lisa Ferro, Danilo Giampiccolo, Bernardo Magnini, and Idan Szpektor. The second pascal recognising textual entailment challenge. In *Proceedings of the Second PASCAL Challenges Workshop on Recognising Textual Entailment*, Venice, Italy, 2006.

[2] Eugene Charniak and Solomon E. Shimony. Cost-based abduction and map explanation. *Artificial Artificial Intelligence Journal*, 66(2):345–374, 1994.

[3] P. T. Cox and T. Pietrzykowski. Causes for events: Their computation and applications. In J. Siekmann, editor, *8th International Conference on Automated Deduction (CADE-8)*, Berlin, 1986. Springer-Verlag.

[4] P. Domingos and D. Lowd. *Markov Logic: An Interface Layer for Artificial Intelligence*. Morgan & Claypool, San Rafael, CA, 2009.

[5] L. Getoor and B. Taskar, editors. *Introduction to Statistical Relational Learning*. MIT Press, Cambridge, MA, 2007.

[6] S. Harabagiu and D.I. Moldovan. Lcc's question answering system. In *11th Text Retrieval Conference, TREC-11*, Gaithersburg, MD., 2002.

[7] Jerry R. Hobbs, Mark E. Stickel, Douglas E. Appelt, and Paul A. Martin. Interpretation as abduction. *Artificial Intelligence*, 63(1-2):69–142, 1993.

[8] Rohit Kate and Ray Mooney. Probabilistic abduction using markov logic networks. In *IJCAI 09 Workshop on Plan, Activity and Intent Recognition*, 2009.

[9] Hector J. Levesque. A knowledge-level account of abduction. In *Eleventh International Joint Conference on Artificial Intelligence*, volume 2, pages 1061–1067, Detroit, Michigan, 1989.

[10] Hwee Tou Ng and Raymond J. Mooney. The role of coherence in constructing and evaluating abductive explanations. In P. O'Rorke, editor, *Working Notes, AAAI Spring Symposium on Automated Abduction*, Stanford, California, March 1990.

[11] E. Ovchinnikova, N. Montazeri, T. Alexandrov, J. Hobbs, M. McCord, and R. Mulkar-Mehta. Abductive reasoning with a large knowledge base for discourse processing. In *Proceedings of the 9th International Conference on Computational Semantics*, Oxford, United Kingdom, 2011.

[12] J. Pearl. *Probabilistic Reasoning in Intelligent Systems: Networks of Plausible Inference*. Morgan Kaufmann, San Francisco, CA, 1988.

[13] Harry E. Pople. On the mechanization of abductive logic. In *Third International Joint Conference on Artificial Intelligence*, pages 147–152, Stanford, California, August 1973.

[14] M. Richardson and P. Domingos. Markov logic networks. *Machine Learning*, 62:107–136, 2006.

Modular Graph Rewriting to Compute Semantics

Guillaume Bonfante
Nancy-Université - LORIA
bonfante@loria.fr

Bruno Guillaume
INRIA - LORIA
guillaum@loria.fr

Mathieu Morey
Nancy-Université - LORIA
moreymat@loria.fr

Guy Perrier
Nancy-Université - LORIA
perrier@loria.fr

Abstract

Taking an asynchronous perspective on the syntax-semantics interface, we propose to use modular graph rewriting systems as the model of computation. We formally define them and demonstrate their use with a set of modules which produce underspecified semantic representations from a syntactic dependency graph. We experimentally validate this approach on a set of sentences. The results open the way for the production of underspecified semantic dependency structures from corpora annotated with syntactic dependencies and, more generally, for a broader use of modular rewriting systems for computational linguistics.

Introduction

The aim of our work is to produce a semantic representation of sentences on a large scale using a formal and exact approach based on linguistic knowledge. In this perspective, the design of the syntax-semantics interface is crucial.

Based on the compositionality principle, most models of the syntax-semantics interface use a synchronous approach: the semantic representation of a sentence is built step by step in parallel with its syntactic structure. According to the choice of the syntactic formalism, this approach is implemented in different ways: in a Context-Free Grammars (CFG) style framework, every syntactic rule of a grammar is associated with a semantic composition rule, as in the classical textbook by Heim and Kratzer (1998); following the principles introduced by Montague, Categorial Grammars use an homomorphism from the syntax to the semantics (Carpenter (1992)). HPSG integrates the semantic and syntactic representations in feature structures which combine by unification (Copestake et al. (2005)). LFG follows a similar principle (Dalrymple (2001)). In a synchronous approach, the syntax-semantics interface closely depends on the grammatical formalism. Building such an interface can be very costly, especially if we aim at a large coverage for the grammar.

In our work, we have chosen an asynchronous approach in the sense that we start from a given syntactic analysis of a sentence to produce a semantic representation. With respect to the synchronous approach, a drawback is that the reaction of the semantics on the syntax is delayed. On the other hand, the computation of the semantics is made relatively independent from the syntactic formalism. The only constraint is the shape of the output of the syntactic analysis.

In the formalisms mentioned above, the syntactic structure most often takes the form of a phrase structure, but the choice of constituency for the syntax makes the relationship with the semantics more complicated. We have chosen *dependency graphs*, because syntactic dependencies are closely related to predicate-argument relations. Moreover, they can be enriched with relations derived from the syntax, which are usually ignored, such as the arguments of infinitives or the anaphora determined by the syntax. One may observe that our syntactic representation of sentences involves plain graphs and not trees. Indeed, these relations can give rise to multiple governors and dependency cycles. On the semantic side, we have also chosen graphs, which are widely used in different formalisms and theories, such as DMRS (Copestake (2009)) or MTT (Mel'čuk (1988)) .

The principles being fixed, our problem was then to choose a model of computation well suited to transforming syntactic graphs into semantic graphs. The λ-calculus, which is widely used in formal semantics, is not a good candidate because it is appropriate for computing on trees but not on graphs. Our choice naturally went to *graph rewriting*. Graph rewriting is barely used in computational linguistics; it could be due to the difficulty to manage large sets of rules. Among the pioneers in the use of graph rewriting, we mention Hyvönen (1984); Bohnet and Wanner (2001); Crouch (2005); Jijkoun and de Rijke (2007); Bédaride and Gardent (2009); Chaumartin and Kahane (2010).

A graph rewriting system is defined as a set of *graph rewrite rules* and a computation is a sequence of rewrite rule applications to a given graph. The application of a rule is triggered via a mechanism of pattern matching, hence a sub-graph is isolated from its context and the result is a local modification of the input. This allows a linguistic phenomenon to be easily isolated for applying a transformation.

Since each step of computation is fired by some local conditions in the whole graph, it is well known that one has no grip on the sequence of rewriting steps. The more rules, the more interaction between rules, and the consistency of the whole rule system becomes difficult to maintain. This bothers our ambition of a large coverage for the grammar. To solve this problem, we propose to organize rules in *modules*. A module is a set of rules that is linguistically consistent and represents a particular step of the transformation. For instance, in our proposal, there is a module transforming the syntactic arguments of verbs, predicative nouns and adjectives into their semantic arguments. Another module resolves the anaphoric links which are internal to the sentence and determined by the syntax.

From a computational point of view, the grouping of a small number of rules inside a module allows some optimizations in their application, thus leading to efficiency. For instance, the confluence of rewriting is a critical feature — one computes only one normal form, not all of them — for the performance of the program. Since the underlying relation from syntax to semantics is not functional but relational, the system cannot be globally confluent. Then, it is particularly interesting to isolate subsets of confluent rules. Second point, with a small number of rules, one gets much more control on their output. In particular, it is possible to automatically infer some invariant properties of graphs along the computation within a particular module. Thus, it simplifies the writing of the rules for the next modules. It is also possible to plan a strategy in the global evaluation process.

It is well known that syntactic parsers produce outputs in various formats. As a by-product of our approach, we show that the choice of the input format (that is the syntax) seems to be of low importance overall. Indeed, as far as two formats contain the same linguistic information with different representations, a system of rewrite rules can be designed to transform any graph from one format to another as a preliminary step. The same remark holds for the output formats.

To illustrate our proposal, we have chosen the *Paris7 TreeBank* (hereafter *P7TB*) dependency format defined by Candito et al. (2010) as the syntactic input format and the *Dependency MRS* format (hereafter *DMRS*) defined by Copestake (2009) as the semantic output format. We chose those two formats because the information they represent, if it is not complete, is relatively consensual and because both draw on large scale experiments: statistical dependency parsing for French[1] on the one hand and the DELPH-IN project[2] on the other hand.

Actually, in our experiments, since we do not have an appropriate corpus annotated according to the *P7TB* standard, we used our syntactic parser LEOPAR[3] whose outputs differ from this standard and we designed a rewriting system to go from one format to the other.

The paper is organized as follows. In section 1, we define our graph rewriting calculus, the β-calculus. In Section 2, we describe the particular rewriting system that is used to transform graphs from the syntactic *P7TB* format into the *DMRS* semantic format. In Section 3, we present experimental results on a test suite of sentences.

---

[1] http://alpage.inria.fr/statgram/frdep/fr_stat_dep_parsing.html

[2] http://www.delph-in.net/

[3] http://leopar.loria.fr

1 The β-calculus, a graph rewriting calculus

Term rewriting and tree rewriting can be defined in a straightforward and canonical way. Graph rewriting is much more problematic and there is unfortunately no canonical definition of a graph rewriting system. Graph rewriting can be defined through a categorical approach like SPO or DPO (Rozenberg (1997)). But, in practice, it is much easier to use a more operational view of rewriting where modification of the graph (the "right-hand side" of a rule) is defined by means of a set of commands; the control of the way rules are applied (the "left hand-side") still uses pattern matching as this is done in traditional graph rewriting.

In this context, a *rule* is a pair of a *pattern* and a sequence of *commands*. We give below the formal materials about graphs, patterns, matchings and commands. We illustrate the section with examples of rules and of rewriting.

1.1 Graph definition

In the following, we suppose given a finite set $\mathcal{L}$ of edge labels corresponding to the kind of dependencies used to describe sentences. They may correspond to syntax or to semantics. For instance, we use $\mathcal{L} = \{\text{SUJ}, \text{OBJ}, \text{ARG1}, \text{ANT}, \ldots\}$.

To decorate vertices, we use the standard notion of feature structures. Let $\mathcal{N}$ be a finite set of *feature names* and $\mathcal{A}$ be a finite set of *atomic feature values*. In our example, $\mathcal{N} = \{\text{cat}, \text{mood}, \ldots\}$ and $\mathcal{A} = \{\text{passive}, \text{v}, \text{n}, \ldots\}$. A *feature* is a pair made of a feature name and a set of atomic values. The feature $(cat, \{v, aux\})$ means that the feature name cat is associated to either the value v or aux. In the sequel, we use the notation $cat = v|aux$ for this feature. Two features $f = v$ and $f' = v'$ are compatible whenever $f = f'$ and $v \cap v' \neq \emptyset$.

A *feature structure* is a finite set of features such that each feature name occurs at most once. $\mathcal{F}$ denotes the set of feature structures. Two feature structures are compatible if their respective features with the same name are pairwise compatible.

A graph $\mathcal{G}$ is then defined by a 6-tuple $(\mathcal{V}, \textbf{fs}, \mathcal{E}, \textbf{lab}, \sigma, \tau)$ with:

- a finite set $\mathcal{V}$ of vertices;
- a labelling function $\textbf{fs}$ from $\mathcal{V}$ to $\mathcal{F}$;
- a finite set $\mathcal{E}$ of edges;
- a labelling function $\textbf{lab}$ from $\mathcal{E}$ to $\mathcal{L}$;
- two functions σ and τ from $\mathcal{E}$ to $\mathcal{V}$ which give the source and the target of each edge.

Moreover, we require that two edges between the same couple of nodes cannot have the same label.

1.2 Patterns and matchings

Formally, a *pattern* is a graph and a *matching* ϕ of a pattern $\mathcal{P} = (\mathcal{V}', \textbf{fs}', \mathcal{E}', \textbf{lab}', \sigma', \tau')$ into a graph $\mathcal{G} = (\mathcal{V}, \textbf{fs}, \mathcal{E}, \textbf{lab}, \sigma, \tau)$ is an *injective* graph morphism from $\mathcal{P}$ to $\mathcal{G}$. More precisely, ϕ is a couple of injective functions: $\phi_\mathcal{V}$ from $\mathcal{V}'$ to $\mathcal{V}$ and $\phi_\mathcal{E}$ from $\mathcal{E}'$ to $\mathcal{E}$ which:

- respects vertex labelling: $\textbf{fs}(\phi_\mathcal{V}(v))$ and $\textbf{fs}'(v)$ are compatible;
- respects edge labelling: $\textbf{lab}(\phi_\mathcal{E}(e)) = \textbf{lab}'(e)$;
- respects edge sources: $\sigma(\phi_\mathcal{E}(e)) = \phi_\mathcal{V}(\sigma'(e))$;
- respects edge targets: $\tau(\phi_\mathcal{E}(e)) = \phi_\mathcal{V}(\tau'(e))$.

1.3 Commands

Commands are low-level operations on graphs that are used to describe the rewriting of the graph within a rule application. In the description below, we suppose to be given a pattern matching $\phi : \mathcal{P} \to \mathcal{G}$. We describe here the set of commands which we used in our experiment so far. Naturally, this set could be extended.

- **del_edge**(α, β, ℓ) removes the edge labelled ℓ between α and β. More formally, we suppose that $\alpha \in \mathcal{V}_\mathcal{P}$, $\beta \in \mathcal{V}_\mathcal{P}$ and $\mathcal{P}$ contains an edge e from α to β with label $\ell \in \mathcal{L}$. Then, **del_edge**$(\alpha, \beta, \ell)(\mathcal{G})$ is the graph $\mathcal{G}$ without the edge $\phi(e)$. In the following, we give only the intuitive definition of the command: thanks to injectivity of the matching ϕ, we implicitly forget the distinction between x and $\phi(x)$.

- **add_edge**(α, β, ℓ) adds an edge labelled ℓ between α and β. Such an edge is supposed not to exist in $\mathcal{G}$.

- **shift_edge**(α, β) modifies all edges that are incident to α: each edge starting from α is moved to start from β; similarly each edge ending on α is moved to end on β;

- **del_node**(α) removes the α node in $\mathcal{G}$. If $\mathcal{G}$ contains edges starting from α or ending on α, they are silently removed.

- **add_node**(β) adds a new node with identifier β (a fresh name).

- **add_feat**$(\alpha, f = v)$ adds the feature $f = v$ to the node α. If α already contains a feature name f, it is replaced by the new one.

- **copy_feat**(α, β, f) copies the value of the feature named f from the node α to the node β. If α does not contain a feature named f, nothing is done. If β already contains a feature named f, it is replaced by the new value.

Note that commands define a partial function on graphs: the action **add_edge**(α, β, ℓ) is undefined on a graph which already contains an edge labelled ℓ from α to β.

The action of a sequence of commands is the composition of actions of each command. Sequences of commands are supposed to be consistent with the pattern:

- **del_edge** always refers to an edge described in the pattern and not previously modified by a **del_edge** or a **shift_edge** command;

- each command refers only to identifiers defined either in the pattern or in a previous **add_node**;

- no command refers to a node previously deleted by a **del_node** command.

Finally, we define a *rewrite rule* to be a pair of a pattern and a consistent sequence of commands.

A first example of a rule is given below with the pattern on the left and the sequence of commands on the right. This rule called INIT_PASSIVE is used to remove the node corresponding to the auxiliary of the passive construction and to modify the features accordingly.

INIT_PASSIVE

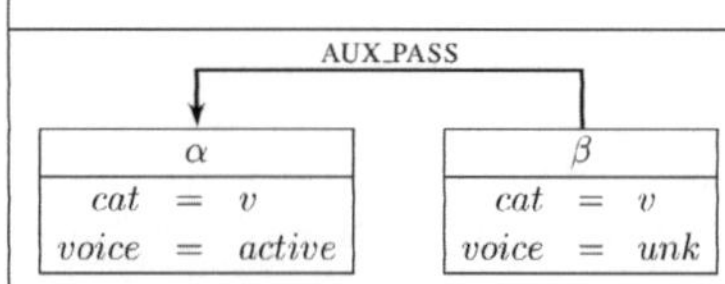

$c_1 =$ **copy_feat**$(\alpha, \beta, mood)$ $c_4 =$ **del_edge**$(\beta, \alpha, \text{AUX\_PASS})$
$c_2 =$ **copy_feat**$(\alpha, \beta, tense)$ $c_5 =$ **shift_edge**(α, β)
$c_3 =$ **add_feat**$(\beta, voice = passive)$ $c_6 =$ **del_node**(α)

Our second example (PASSIVE_ATS) illustrates the **add_node** command. It is used in a passive construction where the semantic subject of the verb is not realized syntactically.

PASSIVE_ATS

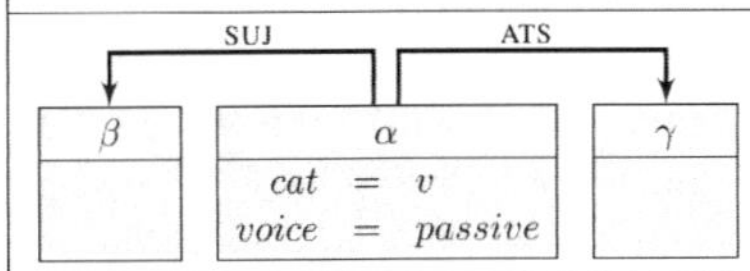

$c_1 = \textbf{del\_edge}(\alpha, \beta, \text{SUJ})$
$c_2 = \textbf{add\_edge}(\alpha, \beta, \text{OBJ})$
$c_3 = \textbf{del\_edge}(\alpha, \gamma, \text{ATS})$
$c_4 = \textbf{add\_edge}(\alpha, \gamma, \text{ATO})$
$c_5 = \textbf{add\_feat}(\alpha, voice = active)$
$c_6 = \textbf{add\_node}(\delta)$
$c_7 = \textbf{add\_edge}(\alpha, \text{SUJ}, \delta)$

1.4 Rewriting

We consider a graph $\mathcal{G}$ and a rewrite rule $r = (\mathcal{P}, [c_1, \ldots, c_k])$. We say that $\mathcal{G}'$ is obtained from $\mathcal{G}$ by a rewrite step with the r rule (written $\mathcal{G} \longrightarrow_r \mathcal{G}'$) if there is a matching morphism $\phi : \mathcal{P} \to \mathcal{G}$ and $\mathcal{G}'$ is obtained from $\mathcal{G}$ by applying the composition of commands $c_k \circ \ldots \circ c_1$.

Let us now illustrate two rewrite steps with the rules above. Consider the first graph below which is a syntactic dependency structure for the French sentence *"Marie est considérée comme brillante"* [*Mary is considered as bright*]. The second graph is obtained by application of the INIT_PASSIVE rewrite rule and the last one with the PASSIVE_ATS rewrite rule.

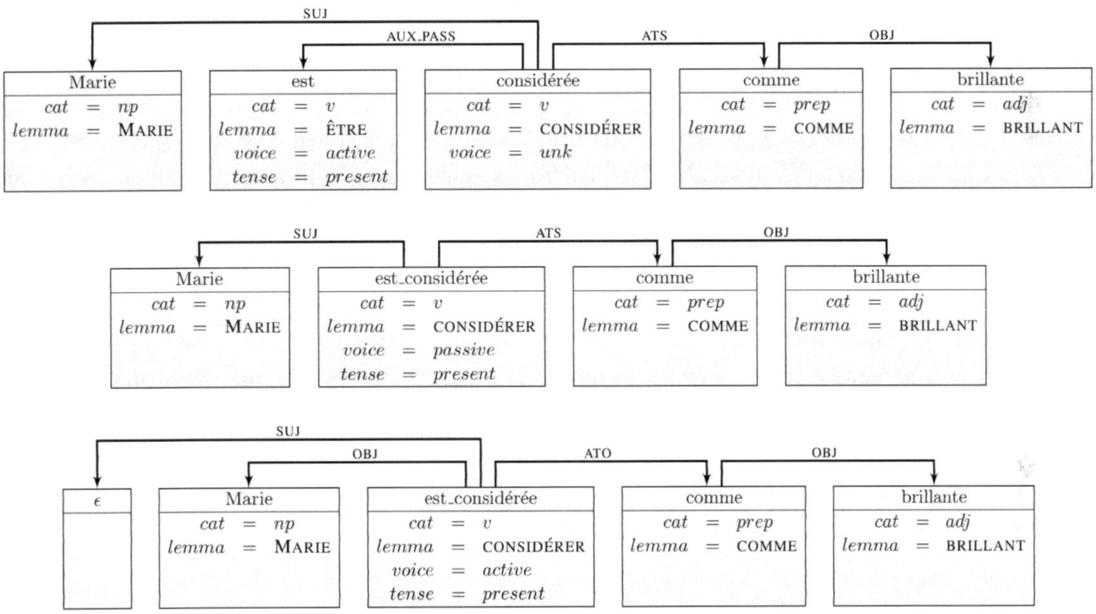

1.5 Modules and normal forms

A *module* contains a set of rewrite rules but, in order to have a finer control on the output of these modules, it is useful to declare some forbidden patterns. Hence a module is defined by a set $\mathcal{R}$ of rules and a set $\mathcal{P}$ of forbidden patterns.

For a given module $\mathcal{M} = (\mathcal{R}, \mathcal{P})$, we say that $\mathcal{G}'$ is an $\mathcal{M}$-*normal form* of the graph $\mathcal{G}$ if there is a sequence of rewriting steps with rules of $\mathcal{R}$ from $\mathcal{G}$ to $\mathcal{G}'$: $\mathcal{G} \longrightarrow_{r_1} \mathcal{G}_1 \longrightarrow_{r_2} \mathcal{G}_2 \ldots \longrightarrow_{r_k} \mathcal{G}'$, if no rule of $\mathcal{R}$ can be applied to $\mathcal{G}'$ and no pattern of $\mathcal{P}$ matches in $\mathcal{G}'$.

In our experiment, forbidden patterns are often used to control the subset of edges allowed in normal forms. For instance, the *NORMAL* module contains the forbidden pattern: $\square \xrightarrow{\text{AUX\_PASS}} \square$. Hence, we can then safely suppose that no graph contains any AUX_PASS edge afterward.

2 From syntactic dependency graphs to semantic graphs

Linguistic theories diverge on many issues including the exact definition of the linguistic levels and the relationships between them. Our aim here is not to commit to any linguistic theory but rather to demonstrate that graph rewriting is an adequate and realistic computational framework for the syntax-semantics interface. Consequently, our approach is bound to neither the (syntactic and semantic) formats we have chosen nor the transformation modules we have designed; both are mainly meant to exemplify our proposal.

2.1 Representational formats

Our syntactic and semantic formats both rely on the notion of linguistic dependency. The syntactic format is an enrichment of the one which was designed to annotate the French Treebank (Abeillé and Barrier (2004)) with surface syntactic dependencies (Candito et al. (2010)). The enrichment is twofold:

- if they are present in the sentence, the deep arguments of infinitives and participles (from participial subordinate clauses) are marked with the usual labels of syntactic functions,
- the anaphora relations that are predictable from the syntax (i.e. the antecedents of relative, reflexive and repeated pronouns) are marked with a special label ANT.

This additional information can already be provided by many syntactic parsers and is particularly interesting to compute semantics.

The semantic format is Dependency Minimal Recursion Semantics (*DMRS*) which was introduced by Copestake (2009) as a compact and easily readable equivalent to Robust Minimal Recursion Semantics (RMRS), which was defined by Copestake (2007). This underspecified semantic formalism was designed for large scale experiments without committing to fine-grained semantic choices. *DMRS* graphs contain the predicate-argument relations, the restriction of generalized quantifiers and the mode of combination between predicates. Predicate-argument relations are labelled ARGi, where i is an integer following a fixed order of obliqueness SUJ, OBJ, ATS, ATO, A-OBJ, DE-OBJ.... Naturally, the lexicon must be consistent with this ordering. The restrictions of generalized quantifiers are labelled RSTR ; their bodies are not overtly expressed but can be retrieved from the graph. There are three ways of combining predicates:

- EQ when two predicates are elements of a same conjunction;
- H when a predicate is in the scope of another predicate; it is not necessarily one of its arguments because quantifiers may occur between them;
- NEQ for all other cases.

2.2 Modular rewriting system

Graph rewriting allows to proceed step by step to the transformation of a syntactic graph into a semantic one, by associating a rewrite rule to each linguistic rule. While the effect of every rule is local, grouping rules in modules allows a better control on the global effect of all rules.

We do not have the space here to propose a system of rules that covers the whole French grammar. We however propose six modules which cover a significative part of this grammar (cleft clauses, coordination, enumeration, comparatives and ellipses are left aside but they can be handled by other rewrite modules):

- *NORMAL* handles the regular syntactic transformations involving predicates: it computes tense and transforms all redistributions of arguments (passive and middle voices, impersonal constructions and the combination of them) to the active canonical form. This reduces the number of rules required to produce the predicate-argument relations in the *ARG* module below.
- *PREP* removes affixes, prepositions and complementizers.
- *ARG* transforms the verbal, nominal and adjectival predicative phrases into predicate-argument relations.

- *DET* translates the determiner dependencies (denoted DET) to generalized quantifiers.
- *MOD* interprets the various modifier dependencies (denoted MOD), according to their specificity: adjectives, adverbs, adjunct prepositional phrases, participial clauses, relative clauses, adjunct clauses.
- *ANA* interprets all anaphoric relations that are determined by the syntax (denoted ANT).

Modules provide an easy way to control the order in which rules are fired. In order to properly set up the rules in modules, we first have to fix the global ordering of the modules. Some ordering constraints are evident: for instance, *NORMAL* must precede *PREP*, which must precede *ARG*. The rules we present in the following are based on the order *NORMAL, PREP, ARG, DET, MOD, ANA*.

2.2.1 Normalization of syntactic dependencies

The *NORMAL* module has two effects: it merges tense and voice auxiliaries with their past participle and brings all the argument redistributions back to the canonical active form. This module accounts for the passive and middle voices and the impersonal construction for verbs that are not essentially impersonal. The combination of the two voices with the impersonal construction is naturally expressed by the composition of the corresponding rewrite rules. The two rules given in section 1.4 are part of this module. The first rule (INIT_PASSIVE) merges the past participle of the verb with its passive auxiliary. The auxiliary brings its mood and tense to the verb, which is marked as being passive. The second rule (PASSIVE_ATS) transforms a passive verb with a subject and an attribute of the subject into its active equivalent with a semantically undetermined subject, an object (which corresponds to the subject of the passive form) and an attribute of the object (which corresponds to the attribute of the subject of the passive form).

2.2.2 Erasure of affixes, prepositions and complementizers

The *PREP* module removes affixes, prepositions and complementizers. For example, the rule given here merges prepositions with the attribute of the object that they introduce. The value of the preposition is kept to compute the semantics.

PREP_ATO

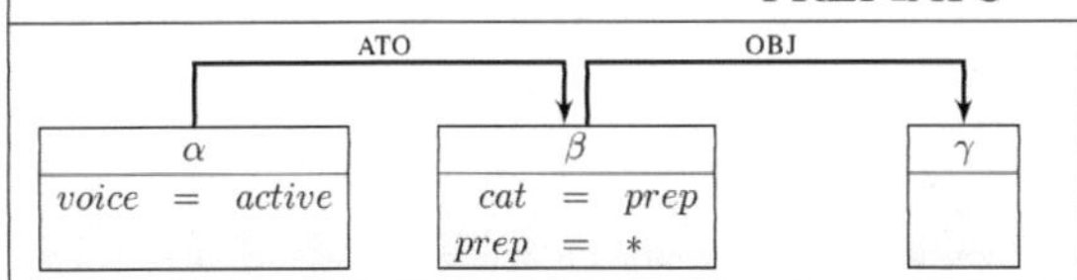

$c_1 = \mathbf{copy\_feat}(\beta, \gamma, prep)$
$c_2 = \mathbf{del\_edge}(\beta, \gamma, \text{OBJ})$
$c_3 = \mathbf{shift\_edge}(\beta, \gamma)$
$c_4 = \mathbf{del\_node}(\beta)$

2.2.3 From lexical predicative phrases to semantic predicates

The *ARG* module transforms the syntactic arguments of a predicative word (a verb, a common noun or an adjective) into its semantic arguments. Following *DMRS*, the predicate-argument relations are not labelled with thematic roles but only numbered. The numbering reflects the syntactic obliqueness.

ARG_OBJ

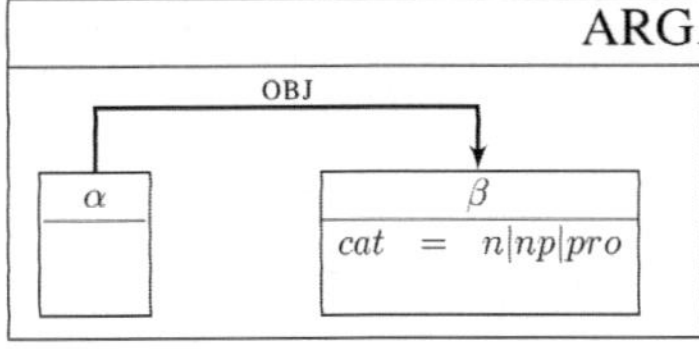

$c_1 = \mathbf{del\_edge}(\alpha, \beta, \text{OBJ})$
$c_2 = \mathbf{add\_edge}(\alpha, \beta, \text{ARG2})$
$c_3 = \mathbf{add\_edge}(\alpha, \beta, \text{NEQ})$

2.2.4 From determiners to generalized quantifiers

DET reverts the determiner dependencies (labelled DET) from common nouns to determiners into dependencies of type RSTR from the corresponding generalized quantifier to the nominal predicate which is the core of their restriction.

DET	
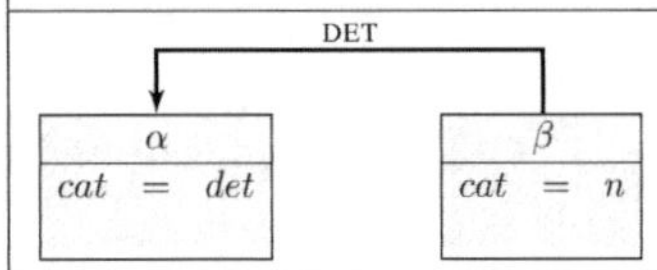	$c_1 = \textbf{del\_edge}(\beta, \alpha, \text{DET})$ $c_2 = \textbf{add\_edge}(\alpha, \beta, \text{RSTR})$ $c_3 = \textbf{add\_edge}(\alpha, \beta, \text{H})$

2.2.5 Interpretation of different kinds of modification

MOD deals with the modifier dependencies (labelled MOD, MOD_REL and MOD_LOC), providing rules for the different kinds of modifiers. Adjectives and adverbs are translated as predicates whose first argument is the modified entity. The modifier and modified entities are in a conjunction (EQ), except for scopal adverbs which take scope (H) over the modified predicate. Because only lexical information enables to differentiate scopal from non-scopal adverbs, we consider all adverbs to be systematically ambiguous at the moment. Adjunct prepositional phrases (resp. clauses) have a similar rule except that their corresponding predicate is the translation of the preposition (resp. complementizer), which has two arguments: the modified entity and the noun (resp. verb) which heads the phrase (resp. clause). Participial and relative clauses exhibit a relation labelled EQ or NEQ between the head of the clause and the antecedent, depending on the restrictive or appositive type of the clause.

2.2.6 Resolution of syntactic anaphora

ANA deals with dependencies of type ANT and merges their source and their target. We apply them to reflexive, relative and repeated pronouns.

3 Experiments

For the experimentation, we are interested in a test suite which is at the same time small enough to be manually validated and large enough to cover a rich variety of linguistic phenomena. As said earlier, we use the P7 surface dependency format as input, so the first attempt at building a test suite is to consider examples in the guide which describes the format. By nature, an annotation guide tries to cover a large range of phenomena with a small set of examples.

The latest version[4] of this guide (Candito et al. (2010)) contains 186 linguistic examples. In our current implementation of the semantic constructions, we leave out clefts, coordinations and comparatives. We also leave out a small set of exotic sentences for which we are not able to give a sensible syntactic structure. Finally, our experiment runs on 116 French sentences. Syntactic structures following P7 specifications are obtained with some graph rewriting on the output of our parser. Each syntactic structure was manually checked and corrected when needed. Then, graph rewriting with the modules described in the previous section is performed.

For all of these sentences, we produce at least one normal form. Even if *DMRS* is underspecified, our system can output several semantic representations for one syntactic structure (for instance, for appositive and restrictive relative clauses). We sometimes overgenerate because we do not use lexical information like the difference between scopal and non-scopal adverbs.

The result for three sentences is given below and the full set is available on a web page [5].

[4] version 1.1, january 2010

[5] http://leopar.loria.fr/doku.php?id=iwcs2011

[012] *"Le français se parle de moins en moins dans les conférences."* [*The French language is less and less spoken in conferences.*]

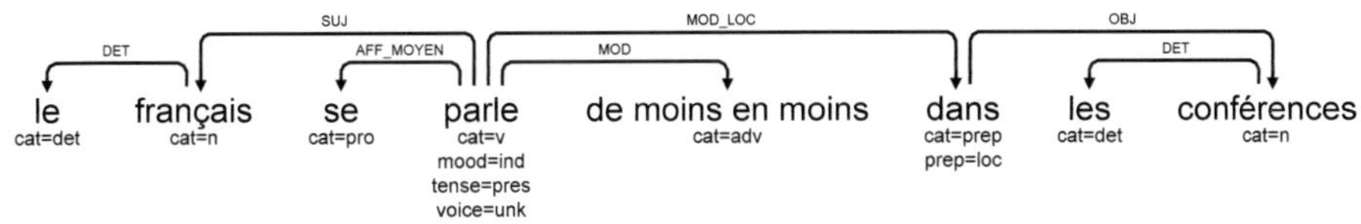

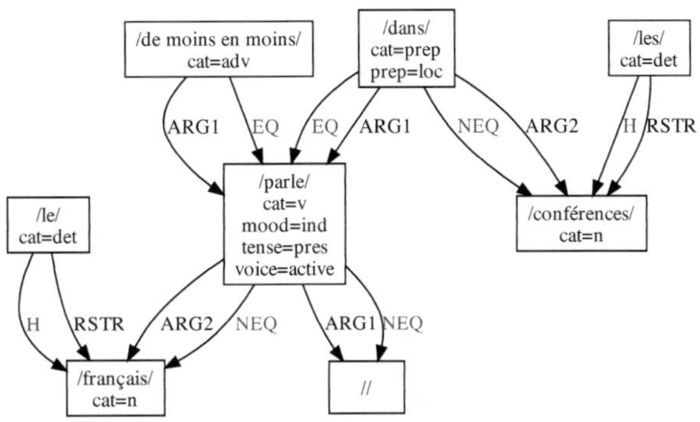

[057] *"J'encourage Marie à venir."* [*I invite Mary to come.*]

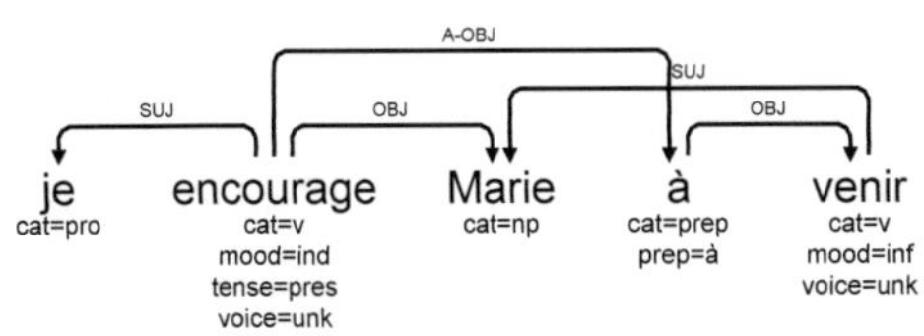

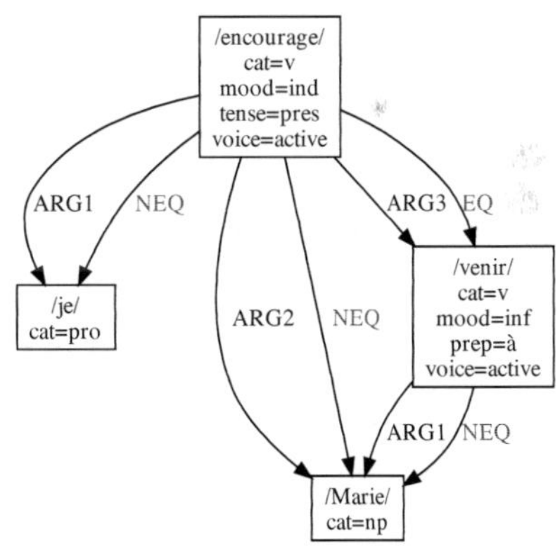

[106] *"La série dont Pierre connaît la fin"* [*The story Peter knows the end of*]

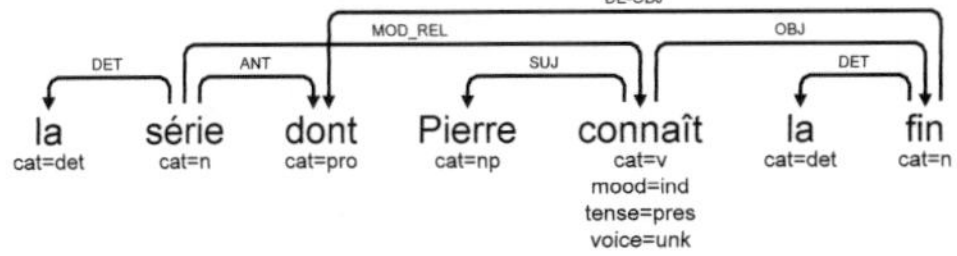

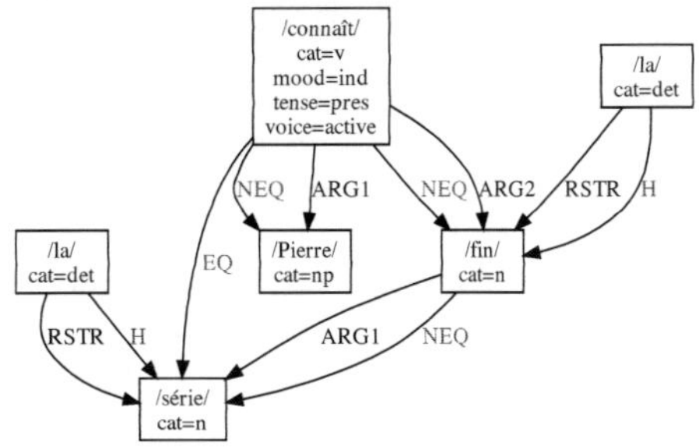

Conclusion

In this paper, we have shown the relevance of modular graph rewriting to compute semantic representations from graph-shaped syntactic structures. The positive results of our experiments on a test suite of varied sentences make us confident that the method can apply to large corpora.

The particular modular graph rewriting system presented in the paper was merely here to illustrate the method, which can be used for other input and output formats. There is another aspect to the flexibility of the method: we may start from the same system of rules and enrich it with new rules to get a finer semantic analysis — if *DMRS* is considered as providing a minimal analysis — or integrate lexical information. The method allows the semantic ambiguity to remain unsolved within underspecified representations or to be solved with a rule system aiming at computing models of underspecified representations. Moreover, we believe that its flexibility makes graph rewriting a convenient framework to deal with idiomatic expressions.

References

Abeillé, A. and N. Barrier (2004). Enriching a french treebank. In *Proceedings of LREC.*

Bédaride, P. and C. Gardent (2009). Semantic Normalisation : a Framework and an Experiment. In *Proceedings of IWCS*, Tilburg Netherlands.

Bohnet, B. and L. Wanner (2001). On using a parallel graph rewriting formalism in generation. In *Proceedings of EWNLG '01*, pp. 1–11. Association for Computational Linguistics.

Candito, M., B. Crabbé, and P. Denis (2010). Statistical french dependency parsing: Treebank conversion and first results. *Proceedings of LREC2010.*

Candito, M., B. Crabbé, and M. Falco (2010). *Dépendances syntaxiques de surface pour le français.*

Carpenter, B. (1992). *The logic of typed feature structures.* Cambridge: Cambridge University Press.

Chaumartin, F.-R. and S. Kahane (2010). Une approche paresseuse de l'analyse sémantique ou comment construire une interface syntaxe-sémantique à partir d'exemples. In *TALN 2010, Montreal, Canada.*

Copestake, A. (2007). Semantic composition with (robust) minimal recursion semantics. In *Proceedings of the Workshop on Deep Linguistic Processing*, pp. 73–80. Association for Computational Linguistics.

Copestake, A. (2009). *Invited Talk:* Slacker semantics: Why superficiality, dependency and avoidance of commitment can be the right way to go. In *Proceedings of EACL 2009*, Athens, Greece, pp. 1–9.

Copestake, A., D. Flickinger, C. Pollard, and I. Sag (2005). Minimal Recursion Semantics - an Introduction. *Research on Language and Computation 3*, 281–332.

Crouch, D. (2005). Packed Rewriting for Mapping Semantics to KR. In *Proceedings of IWCS.*

Dalrymple, M. (2001). *Lexical Functional Grammar.* New York: Academic Press.

Heim, I. and A. Kratzer (1998). *Semantics in generative grammar.* Wiley-Blackwell.

Hyvönen, E. (1984). Semantic Parsing as Graph Language Transformation - a Multidimensional Approach to Parsing Highly Inflectional Languages. In *COLING*, pp. 517–520.

Jijkoun, V. and M. de Rijke (2007). Learning to transform linguistic graphs. In *Second Workshop on TextGraphs: Graph-Based Algorithms for Natural Language Processing, Rochester, NY, USA.*

Mel'čuk, I. (1988). *Dependency Syntax: Theory and Practice.* Albany: State Univ. of New York Press.

Rozenberg, G. (Ed.) (1997). *Handbook of Graph Grammars and Computing by Graph Transformations, Volume 1: Foundations.* World Scientific.

Interpreting tractable versus intractable reciprocal sentences

Oliver Bott[a], Fabian Schlotterbeck[a] & Jakub Szymanik[b]
SFB 833, University of Tübingen[a], University of Stockholm[b]
oliver.bott@uni-tuebingen.de
fabian.schlotterbeck@uni-tuebingen.de
jakub.szymanik@gmail.com

Abstract

In three experiments, we investigated the computational complexity of German reciprocal sentences with different quantificational antecedents. Building upon the *tractable cognition thesis* (van Rooij, 2008) and its application to the verification of quantifiers (Szymanik, 2010) we predicted complexity differences among these sentences. Reciprocals with *all*-antecedents are expected to preferably receive a strong interpretation (Dalrymple et al., 1998), but reciprocals with proportional or numerical quantifier antecedents should be interpreted weakly. Experiment 1, where participants completed pictures according to their preferred interpretation, provides evidence for these predictions. Experiment 2 was a picture verification task. The results show that the strong interpretation was in fact possible for tractable *all but one*-reciprocals, but not for *exactly n*. The last experiment manipulated monotonicity of the quantifier antecedents.

Formal semantics hasn't paid much attention to issues of computational complexity when the meaning of an expression is derived. However, when it comes to semantic processing in humans (and computers) with limited processing resources, computational tractability becomes one of the most important constraints a cognitively realistic semantics must face. Two consequences come to mind immediately. If there is a choice between algorithms, we should choose tractable ones over intractable ones. And secondly, meanings which cannot be effectively computed shouldn't be posited for natural language expressions. In this paper we present three psycholinguistic experiments investigating the latter aspect.

Following traditions in computer science, a number of cognitive scientists have defined computational tractability as polynomial-time-computability (for an overview see van Rooij, 2008) leading to the *P-Cognition Hypothesis* (PCH): cognitive capacities are limited to those functions that can be computed in polynomial time. These functions are input-output functions in the sense of Marr (1982)'s first level. One objection against the PCH is that computational complexity is defined in terms of limit behavior as the input increases. In practice, however, the input may be rather small. van Rooij (2008) points out that the input size can be parametrized turning a problem that is intractable for a large input size into a tractable one for small inputs. We manipulated the input size in an experiment to test this more refined version of the PCH.

An interesting test case for the PCH are quantified sentences containing reciprocal expressions of the form *Q of the As R each other*. Consider (1-a) – (1-c).

(1) a. Most of the dots are connected to each other.

b. Four of the dots are connected to each other.

c. All dots are connected to each other.

It has been commonly observed that such sentences are highly ambiguous (see eg. Dalrymple et al., 1998). For instance, under its logically strongest interpretation (1-a) is true iff given n dots there is a subset of more than $\frac{n}{2}$ dots which are pairwise connected. But there are weaker readings of reciprocity, too, i.e. connectedness by a path (a continuous path runs through Q of the dots) or – even weaker – Q of the dots are interconnected, but no path has to connect them all. Following Dalrymple et al. (1998) we call these reciprocal meanings *strong*, *intermediate*, and *weak*, respectively. As for verification, Szymanik (2010) has shown that the various meanings assigned to reciprocals with quantified antecedents differ drastically in their computational complexity. In particular, the strong meanings of reciprocal sentences with proportional and counting[1] quantifiers in their antecedents are intractable, i.e. the verification problem for those readings is NP-complete. This is due to the combinatorial explosion in identifying the relevant completely-connected subsets for these two types of quantifiers (cf. CLIQUE problem, see Garey and Johnson (1979, problem GT19)) which does not emerge with *all*. However, intermediate and weak interpretations are PTIME computable. For example, going through all the elements in the model, thereby listing all the paths, and then evaluating the paths against the quantifier in the antecedent solves the problem in ploynomial time. The PCH thus allows us to derive the following predictions. A strong interpretation should be impossible for sentences (1-a) and (1-b), but possible for the tractable sentence (1-c). Therefore, Szymanik (2010) suggests that if the processor initially tries to establish a strong interpretation, there should be a change in the meanings of sentences (1-a) and (1-b) to one of the weaker interpretations.

In an attempt to explain variations in the literal meaning of the reciprocal expressions Dalrymple et al. (1998) proposed the *Strong Meaning Hypothesis* (SMH). According to the SMH, the reading associated with the reciprocal is the strongest available reading which is consistent with the properties of the reciprocal relation and the relevant information supplied by the context. Consider (2-a) to (2-c).

(2) a. All members of parliament refer to each other indirectly.

b. All Boston pitchers sat alongside each other.

c. All pirates were staring at each other in surprise.

The interpretation of reciprocity differs among those sentences. Sentence (2-a) implies that each parliament member refers to each of the other parliament members indirectly. In other words, the strong interpretation seems to be the most natural reading. This is different in (2-b) and (2-c) which receive intermediate and weak interpretations, respectively. Here the predicates *sit alongside* and *stare at* arguably constrain the meaning. Observations like these lend intuitive support to the SMH. Kerem et al. (2010) modified the SMH and provided experimental evidence that comprehenders are biased towards

[1]It is natural to assume that people have one quantifier concept *Exactly* k, for every natural number k, rather than the infinite set of concepts *Exactly* 1, *Exactly* 2, and so on. Mathematically, we can account for this idea by introducing the counting quantifier $\mathsf{C}^{=\mathsf{A}}$ saying that the number of elements satisfying some property is equal to the cardinality of the set A. The idea here is that determiners like *Exactly* k express a relation between the number of elements satisfying a certain property and the cardinality of some prototypical set A (see Szymanik (2010) for more discussion).

the most typical interpretation of the reciprocal relation. Thus, the reciprocal relation seems to constrain the meaning. Neither the original SMH nor Kerem et al. (2010)'s account leads us to expect that the three quantifiers in (1-a) – (1-c) should differ with respect to how they constrain reciprocal meanings. With 'neutral' predicates like *to be connected by lines* the SMH predicts an overall preference for the strong interpretation in all three sentences. A property that should matter, though, is the monotonicity of the quantificational antecedent. Since monotone decreasing quantifiers have the exact opposite entailment pattern as increasing ones, the SMH leads us to expect that preferences should be reversed in monotone decreasing quantificational antecedents.

We tested the PCH and the SMH in three experiments. In the first we surveyed the default interpretation of reciprocal sentences with quantificational antecedents like (1-a) – (1-c) by having participants complete dot pictures. The second experiment tested the availability of strong and intermediate interpretations in a picture verification task using clearly disambiguated pictures where, in addition, the input size was manipulated. The last experiment compared upward increasing and decreasing quantifiers.

Experiment 1: what is the preferred interpretation?

According to the SMH, sentences like (3-a) are preferably interpreted with their strong meaning in (3-b).

(3) a. All/Most/Four of the dots are connected to each other.
  b. $\exists X \subseteq DOTS[Q(DOTS, X) \wedge \forall x, y \in X(x \neq y \rightarrow connect(x, y))]$,
  where Q is ALL, $MOST$ or $FOUR$.

The PCH, on the other hand, predicts differences between the three quantifiers. While the strong meaning of *reciprocal all* can be checked in polynomial time, verifying the strong interpretation of *reciprocal most* and *reciprocal four* is NP-hard[2]. By contrast, the weaker readings are computable in polynomial time for all three types of quantifiers. It is thus expected that the choice of Q should affect the preference for strong vs. intermediate/weak interpretations. Bringing the SMH and the PCH together we get the following predictions: *reciprocal all* should receive a strong reading, but *reciprocal most/four* should receive an intermediate or weak one.

Method

These predictions were tested in a paper-and-pencil questionnaire. 23 German native speakers (mean age 24.3 years; 10 female) received a series of sentences, each paired with a picture of unconnected dots. Their task was to connect the dots in such a way that the resulting picture matched their interpretation of the sentence. We tested German sentences in the following three conditions (*all* vs. *most* vs. *four*).

(4) Alle / Die meisten / Vier Punkte sind miteinander verbunden.
  All / The most / Four dots are with-one-other connected.
  All / Most / Four dots are connected with each other.

All-sentences were always paired with a picture consisting of four dots, whereas *most* and *four* had pictures with seven dots. Each participant completed five pictures for each quantifier. For this purpose, we

[2] See footnote 1.

drew 15 pictures with randomly distributed dots. In addition, we included 48 filler sentences. Half of them clearly required a complete (sub)graph, just like the experimental sentences in their strong interpretation. The other half were only consistent with a path. We constructed four pseudorandomized orders, making sure that two adjacent items were separated by at least two fillers and each condition was as often preceded by a complete graph filler as it was by a path filler. The latter was done to prevent participants from being biased towards either strong or intermediate interpretations in any of the conditions.

The completed pictures were labeled with respect to the chosen interpretation taking both truth conditions and scalar implicatures into account[3]. A picture was judged to show a strong meaning if the truth conditions in (3-b) were met and no implicatures of Q were violated. It was classified as intermediate if a (sub)graph of appropriate size was connected by a continuous path, but there was no complete graph connecting these nodes. Finally, a picture was labeled *weak* if Q nodes all had some connections, but there was no path connecting them all. Since we didn't find any weak readings, we will just consider the strong and intermediate readings in the analysis. Cases that did not correspond to any of these readings were coded as mistakes. Here is an example:

(5) Most of the dots are connected to each other.

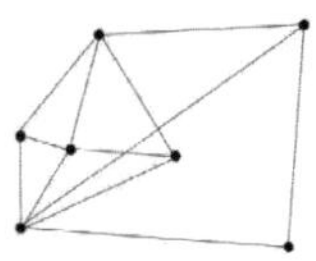

Since the strong meaning of (5) requires at least four dots to form a complete subgraph, (5) is clearly false in this reading. The intermediate or weak reading is ruled out pragmatically, since all dots are connected by a continuous path. We checked whether participants obeyed pragmatic principles by analyzing sentences in the condition with *four*. In this condition participants (except for six cases) never connected more than four dots suggesting that they paid attention to implicatures.

Results

The proportions of strong meanings in the three conditions were analyzed using logit mixed effects model analyses (see eg. Jäger (2009)) with *quantifier* as a fixed effect and participants and items as random effects. We computed three pairwise comparisons: *all* vs. *most*, *all* vs. *four* and *most* vs. *four*. In all of these analyses, we only included the correct pictures.

Participants chose strong meanings in the *all*-condition 47.0% of the time, 22.9% in the *most*-condition and 17.4% in the *four*-condition. The logit mixed effects model analyses revealed a significant difference between *all* and *most* ($estimate = -1.82$; $z = -3.99$; $p < .01$) and between *all* and *four* ($estimate = -3.16$; $z = -5.51$; $p < .01$), but only a marginally significant difference between *four* and *most* ($estimate = .80$; $z = 1.65$; $p = .10$).

The error rates differed between conditions. Participants did not make a single mistake in the *all*-condition. In the *four*-condition 94.8% of the answers were correct. In the *most*-condition the proportion of correct pictures dropped down to 83.5%. Two pairwise comparisons using Fisher's exact test revealed

[3]Implicatures were only an issue in the four- and the most-conditions, but not in the all-condition.

a significant difference between *all* and *four* ($p < .05$) and a significant difference between *four* and *most* ($p < .01$).

Discussion

The results provide evidence against the SMH. Participants overwhelmingly drew pictures which do not satisfy a strong reading. In the *all* condition our data provide evidence for a real ambiguity between the strong and the intermediate interpretation. This is unexpected under the SMH; if the predicate *to be connected* is neutral, a strong interpretation should be favored. For the quantifiers *most* and *four*, the results provide even stronger evidence against the SMH. In these two conditions intermediate readings were clearly preferred over strong ones which were hardly, if at all, available.

The PCH, on the other hand, receives initial support by our findings, in particular by the observed difference in the proportion of strong interpretations between *reciprocal all*, *reciprocal most* and *reciprocal four*. The error rates provide further support for the PCH. *Most* and *four* led to more errors than *all* did. This can be accounted for if we assume that participants sometimes tried to compute a strong interpretation but due to the complexity of the task failed to do so. To clarify whether this explanation is on the right track we clearly need real-time data on the interpretation process. This has to be left to future research. Another open question is whether the strong readings of *reciprocal most* and *reciprocal four* are just dispreferred or completely unavailable. This cannot be decided on the basis of the current experiment. What is needed instead is a task which allows us to determine whether a particular reading is possible or not.

Experiment 2: which readings are available?

The second experiment employed a picture verification task using clearly disambiguating pictures for strong vs. intermediate readings. Unfortunately, the quantifiers we used in the last experiment are all upward monotone in their right argument and therefore their strong interpretation implies the intermediate reading. Hence, even if the diagrams supporting the strong reading were judged to be true, we still wouldn't know which interpretation subjects had in mind. Luckily, in sentences that contain non-monotone quantifiers neither reading entails the other. We therefore chose the quantifiers *all but one*, *most* and *exactly n* in (6). *All but one* and *exactly four* are clearly non-monotone. For *most*, if we take the implicature *most, but not all* into account, it is possible to construct strong pictures in a way that the other readings are ruled out pragmatically. Crucially, the strong reading of *all but one* is still PTIME computable, although it is more complex than *all*. For instance, for verifying a model of size n, only the n subsets of size $n - 1$ have to be considered. By contrast, verifying the strong meaning of (6-b,c) is intractable.

(6) a. Alle Punkte bis auf einen sind miteinander verbunden.
All dots except for one are with-one-another connected.

b. Die meisten Punkte sind miteinander verbunden.
The most dots are with-one-another connected.

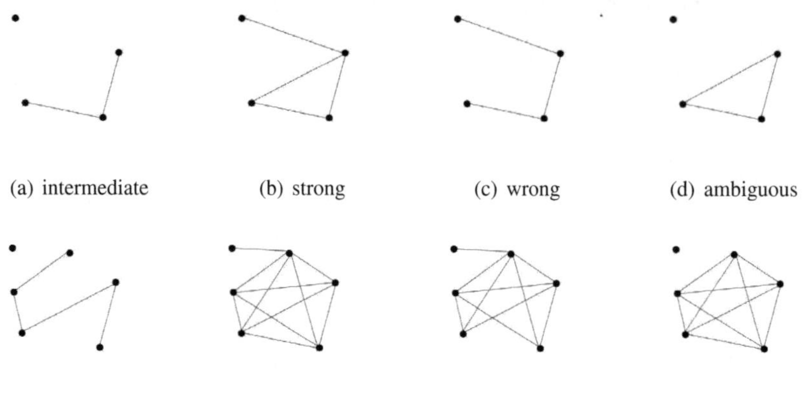

(a) intermediate (b) strong (c) wrong (d) ambiguous

(e) intermediate (f) strong (g) wrong (h) ambiguous

Figure 1: Diagrams used in Exp. 2

c. Genau drei Punkte sind miteinander verbunden.
Exactly three dots are with-one-another connected.

We paired these sentences with diagrams disambiguating towards the intermediate or strong reading. Sample diagrams are depicted in Figure 1(a) and 1(b). For strong pictures, the PCH predicts lower acceptance rates for (6-b,c) than for (6-a). In order to find out whether the strong readings of (6-b,c) are dispreferred or completely unavailable we also paired them with false control diagrams (see Figure1(c)). The wrong pictures differed from the strong ones in that a single line was removed from the completely connected subset. If the strong reading is available for these two sentences at all, we expect more positive judgments following a strong diagram than following a false control. Furthermore, we included ambiguous diagrams as an upper bound for the intermediate pictures (cf. Figure 1(d)). If the strong meaning should conflict with an intermediate picture, we would expect more positive responses following an ambiguous diagram than following an intermediate diagram.

Secondly, as mentioned in the introduction we wanted to investigate whether availability of the strong reading in sentences with counting or proportional quantifiers depends on the size of the model. The strong meaning of (6-b,c) may be easy to verify in small universes, but not in larger ones. To test this possibility we manipulated the number of dots. Small models always contained four dots and large models six dots. We chose small models only consisting of four dots because this is the smallest number for which the strong meaning can be distinguished from the intermediate interpretation, so we could be sure that the task would be doable at all[4]. For the more complex six-dot pictures we presented sentences with *exactly five* instead of *exactly three*. Example diagrams are given in Figure 1[5]. In total, this yielded 24 conditions according to a 3 (*quantifier*) $\times$ 4 (*picture type*) $\times$ 2 (*size*) factorial design.

[4]We had the intuitive impression that pictures with ten dots were already far too complex to be evaluated by naive informants.

[5]The wrong pictures with six dots were slightly different for *most*. In these diagrams, all dots were connected by lines, but there was no subset containing four or more elements forming a complete graph.

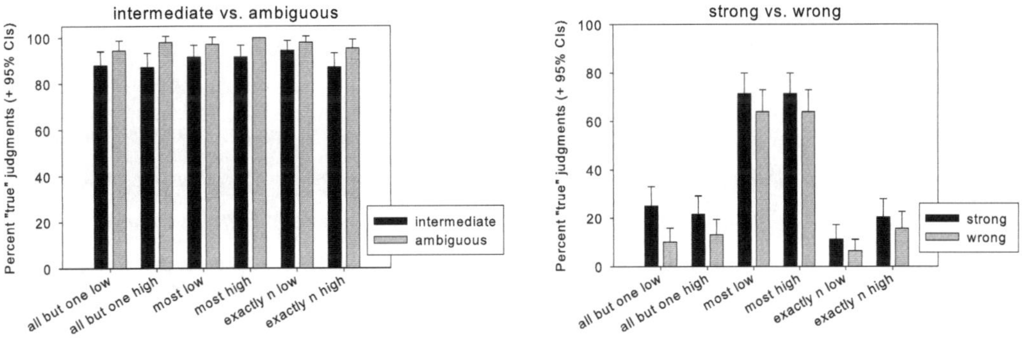

Figure 2: Mean judgments in Exp. 2 (*low* = pictures with 4 dots; *high* = pictures with 6 dots)

Method

Each participant provided three judgments per condition yielding a total of 72 experimental trials. We added 54 filler trials (20 false/34 true) and the 12 monotonicity trials from Experiment 3.

36 German native speakers (mean age 26.9 years; 23 female) read reciprocal quantified sentences on a computer screen in a self-paced fashion. When they finished reading the sentence, it disappeared from the screen and a dot picture was presented for which a truth value judgment had to be provided within a time limit of 10s[6]. Participants received feedback about how fast they had responded. This was done to trigger the first interpretation they had in mind. We collected judgments and judgment times, but because of space limitations will only report the former. The experiment started with a practice session of 10 trials, followed by the experiment with 138 trials in an individually randomized order. An experimental session lasted approximately 15 minutes.

Results

Two kinds of analyses were conducted on the proportion of 'true' judgments. The upper bound analyses concerned the default status of the intermediate interpretation by comparing intermediate picture conditions with ambiguous conditions. Lower bound analyses aimed at clarifying the status of the strong interpretation by comparing strong picture conditions with wrong conditions. The mean judgments of both analyses are presented in Figure 2.

Upper bound analysis: A logit mixed effects model analysis including *quantifier*, *reading* (*ambiguous* vs. *intermediate*), *complexity* and their interactions as fixed effects and participants and items as random effects only revealed a significant main effect of *reading* ($estimate = -2.37$; $z = -2.88$; $p < .01$). This main effect was due to an across-the-board preference (7.3% on average) of ambiguous pictures to pictures disambiguating towards an intermediate interpretation.

Lower bound analyses: We computed a logit mixed effects model analysis including *quantifier*, *truth* (*strong* vs. *wrong*), *complexity* and their interactions as fixed effects and participants and items as random effects. The only reliable effect was the fixed effect of *quantifier* ($estimate = 3.31$; $z = 8.10$; $p < .01$). The effect of *truth* was marginal ($estimate = 0.72$; $z = 1.77$; $p = .07$). As it turned

[6]Participants were very fast. On average they spent 2.5s reading the sentence and 1.8s to provide a judgment.

out, a simpler model taking into account only these two main effects and the random effects accounted for the data with a comparable fit. This was revealed by a comparison of the log-likelihood of the saturated and the simpler model ($\chi^2_{(8)} = 12.36$; $p = .14$). Thus, *complexity* had no significant influence on the judgments. The simple model revealed a significant main effect of *truth* ($estimate = 0.67$; $z = 4.08$; $p < .01$) which was due to 7.9% more 'true' judgments on average in the strong conditions than in the wrong conditions. The main effect of *quantifier* was also significant (*most* vs. *all/exactly*: $estimate = 3.21$; $z = 15.10$; $p < .01$). This was due to more than 60% acceptance for all *most* conditions but much lower acceptance for the other two quantifiers.

We analyzed the data by computing separate logit mixed effect models with fixed effects of *truth*, *complexity* and their interaction for all three quantifiers and simplified the models when a fixed effect failed to contribute to model fit. The best model for *all but one* contained only the fixed effect of *truth* which was reliable ($estimate = 1.04$; $z = 3.47$; $p < .01$), but neither *complexity* nor the interaction enhanced model fit ($\chi^2_{(2)} = 1.04$; $p = .60$). Thus, independently of *complexity* strong pictures were more often accepted than wrong pictures. The same held for *most* (fixed effect of *truth*: $estimate = 0.98$; $z = 2.71$; $p < .01$). *Exactly n* was different in that the fixed effect of *truth* and the interaction didn't matter ($\chi^2_{(2)} = 2.68$; $p = .26$), but *complexity* was significant ($estimate = -0.97$; $z = -2.96$; $p < .01$). This effect was due to more errors in complex pictures than in simpler ones.

Discussion

Overall, the intermediate reading was overwhelmingly preferred to the strong one. However, both the upper bound and the lower bound analyses provide evidence that the strong reading is available to some degree. Both analyses revealed a significant effect of picture type. Intermediate diagrams were less often accepted than the ambiguous diagrams. Moreover, strong diagrams were more often accepted than false ones. Focussing on *all but one* and *exactly n* with respect to the difference between the strong and wrong conditions the pattern looks as predicted by the PCH. The strong reading was possible for tractable *all but one* reciprocals but less so for intractable *exactly n* reciprocals. With *most*, the picture looks different. Even though verification of its strong meaning should be intractable, there was a reliable difference between the strong and wrong conditions. Thus, participants seemed to sometimes choose strong readings. An intractable problem can of course be innocuous under certain circumstances, for instance, when the input size is sufficiently small. The lack of effects of the number of dots manipulation points in this direction. Perhaps even the 'complex' conditions with six dots presented a relatively easy task. This brings us to a parametrized version of the PCH. A hard verification problem may be easy if we include parameters like the size and arrangement of the model. Although far from conclusive, we take our results as pointing in this direction.

Surprisingly, *most* was accepted quite often in the strong and the allegedly wrong conditions. The high acceptance rates in the latter indicate that participants were canceling the implicature of *most* and interpreting it as the upward monotone *more than half*. This also explains the high acceptance of the strong *most* conditions which were, without implicature, consistent with an intermediate interpretation.

Experiment 3: monotone increasing vs. decreasing antecedents

So far, we have been investigating reciprocal sentences with the upward monotone quantifiers *all*, *most*, *four* (Exp. 1) and the non-monotone quantifiers *all but one* and *exactly n* (Exp. 2). As it looks, only *all* licenses a strong interpretation easily. This finding may follow from the monotonicity plus implicatures. According to Dalrymple et al. (1998)'s SMH strong readings are preferred in sentences with upward monotone quantificational antecedents. For downward monotone quantifiers, on the other hand, intermediate readings should be preferred to strong readings. The reverse preferences are triggered by opposite entailment patterns. In the present experiment we compared upward monotone *more than n* with downward monotone antecedents *fewer than n+2*.

We paired diagrams like Figure 1(f) vs. Figure 1(e) with the two sentences in (7) according to a 2 (*monotonicity*) $\times$ 2 (*truth*) factorial design. The diagrams of the first type were identical to the strong pictures of the last experiment. With monotone increasing quantifiers they were ambiguous between strong and intermediate interpretations while in the monotone decreasing cases they disambiguated towards a strong interpretation. The second type of pictures disambiguated towards weak readings in monotone increasing quantifiers, but were ambiguous for monotone decreasing quantificational antecedents. On the basis of the first two experiments we expected high acceptance of both picture types with monotone increasing quantifiers, but much lower acceptance rates for (7-b) with strong than with ambiguous pictures. We constructed six items and collected three judgments from each participant in each condition. The experiment was run together with Experiment 2 using the same method.

(7) a. Mehr als vier Punkte sind miteinander verbunden.
More than four dots are with-one-another connected.

b. Weniger als sechs Punkte sind miteinander verbunden.
Fewer than six dots are with-one-another connected.

Results and Discussion

As expected, *upward monotone* antecedents were accepted in both picture types (ambiguous 98.1%; intermediate 92.5%). A logit mixed effect model analysis revealed no significant difference between the picture types ($estimate$ = 1.53; z = 1.60; p = .11). This was completely different in sentences with monotone decreasing antecedents where strong pictures were only accepted in 13.0% of all trials while ambiguous pictures were accepted 92.6% of the time. This asymmetric distribution provides clear evidence that the predicate *be connected to each other* induced a bias towards the intermediate reading. Thus, although intended to be neutral we apparently chose a predicate that is far from optimal.

Conclusions

We have presented evidence that the kind of quantificational antecedent influences the amount of ambiguity displayed by reciprocal sentences. For example, in Exp. 1 only *all* reciprocals were fully ambiguous. Furthermore, comparing tractable reciprocals with antecedents *all* and *all but one* to intractable reciprocals with *n* and *exactly n* we found support for the predictions of the PCH. In reciprocals with *all* and *all but one* strong readings were possible whereas *exactly n* blocked a strong interpretation. As for *most* the results are somewhat mixed. In Exp. 1 the strong reading was hardly available, but Exp. 2 showed that although dispreferred it is nevertheless possible.

At first sight, our findings provide evidence against the SMH. Strong interpretations were not the default in Exp. 1 and for the monotone increasing quantifiers in Exp. 3 weak interpretations were just as acceptable as the ambiguous pictures. However, contrary to our initial assumptions *be connected* doesn't seem to be neutral but seems to bias towards an intermediate interpretation. This may have to do with the transitivity of the relation. If two dots are only indirectly connected, it seems impossible to say that they are *not connected*, yet possible to say they are *not directly connected.* A next step, therefore, will be to apply the design of Exp. 2 to other predicates like *to know someone*, a relation that is clearly not transitive.

Another route to pursue is increasing the size of the models. A particularly strong test for the PCH would be to increase the model size up to a point where the acceptance rate for the strong reading of proportional quantifiers drops to the level of wrong pictures and see whether tractable antecedents still exhibit their strong interpretation. Exp. 2 was a first step in that direction but the size of the models was obviously still too small.

To conclude, we hope to have shown that relatively innocent looking reciprocal sentences with quantificational antecedents are an interesting test case for considerations of tractability in verification. More generally, within this domain research can be applied to a number of different constructions (for instance, branching quantifiers), so claims about computational complexity can be validated extending the test case investigated in the present study.

References

Dalrymple, M., M. Kanazawa, Y. Kim, S. McHombo, and S. Peters (1998). Reciprocal expressions and the concept of reciprocity. *Linguistics and Philosophy 21*(2), 159–210.

Garey, M. and D. Johnson (1979). *Computers and Intractability.* San Francisco: W.H. Freeman and Co.

Jäger, F. (2009). Categorical data analysis: away from anovas (transformation or not) and towards logit mixed models. *Journal of Memory and Language 59*(4), 434–446.

Kerem, N., N. Friedmann, and Y. Winter (2010). Typicality effects and the logic of reciprocity. In *Proceedings of SALT XIX.*

Marr, D. (1982). *Vision: A Computational Investigation into the Human Representation and Processing of Visual Information.* New York: Freeman.

Szymanik, J. (2010). Computational complexity of polyadic lifts of generalized quantifiers in natural language. *Linguistics and Philosophy.* DOI: 10.1007/s10988-010-9076-z.

van Rooij, I. (2008). The tractable cognition hypothesis. *Cognitive Science 32*, 939–984.

VerbNet Class Assignment as a WSD Task

Susan Windisch Brown
University of Colorado
susanwbrown@colorado.edu

Dmitriy Dligach
University of Colorado
dmitriy.dligach@colorado.edu

Martha Palmer
University of Colorado
martha.palmer@colorado.edu

Abstract

The VerbNet lexical resource classifies English verbs based on semantic and syntactic regularities and has been used for numerous NLP tasks, most notably, semantic role labeling. Since, in addition to thematic roles, it also provides semantic predicates, it can serve as a foundation for further inferencing. Many verbs belong to multiple VerbNet classes, with each class membership corresponding roughly to a different sense of the verb. A VerbNet token classifier is essential for current applications using the resource and could provide the basis for a deep semantic parsing system, one that made full use of VerbNet's extensive syntactic and semantic information. We describe our VerbNet classifier, which uses rich syntactic and semantic features to label verb instances with their appropriate VerbNet class. It achieves an accuracy of 88.67% with multiclass verbs, which is a 49% error reduction over the most frequent class baseline.

1 Introduction

Rich verb representations are central to deep semantic parsing, requiring the identification of not only a verb's meaning but also how it connects the participants in the sentence. Disambiguating verbs using a lexicon that has already been enriched with syntactic and semantic information, rather than a more traditional lexicon, can bring end systems a step closer to accurate knowledge representation and reasoning. One such lexical resource, VerbNet, groups verbs into classes based on commonalities in their semantic and syntactic behavior. It is widely used for a number of semantic processing tasks, including semantic role labeling (Swier and Stevenson, 2004), the creation of conceptual graphs (Hensman and Dunion, 2004), and the creation of semantic parse trees (Shi and Mihalcea, 2005). In addition, the detailed semantic predicates associated with each VerbNet class have the potential to contribute to text-specific semantic representations and, thereby, to inferencing tasks. However, application of VerbNet's semantic and syntactic information to specific text requires first identifying the appropriate VerbNet class of each verb token, a task very similar to word sense disambiguation.

Studies that have made use of VerbNet have dealt with the issue of multiclass verbs in different ways. When deciding on the class for a particular token of a verb in text, Zapirain et al. (2008) simply assigned the most frequent class for the verb rather than attempt to disambiguate. Their data consisted of any sentences in the Semlink corpus (Loper et al., 2007) in which the thematic roles mapped completely between PropBank and VerbNet, which resulted in a corpus that contained about 56% of the original. For the data in their study, the most frequent class label was accurate 97% of the time. Multiclass verbs throughout the entire Semlink corpus, however, have a most frequent class baseline of 73.8%.

Other systems seem to have set aside the problem of multiclass verbs. For example, Bobrow et al. (2007) describe using VerbNet's semantic predicates in PARC's question-answering system to derive pre- and post-conditions of events, such as the change of location of entities. For a verb like *leave,* the system attempts to use the semantic predicates provided by the VerbNet Leave-51.2 class:

MOTION(DURING(E), THEME)LOCATION(START(E), THEME, SOURCE)
NOT(LOCATION(END(E), THEME, SOURCE))DIRECTION(DURING(E), FROM, THEME, SOURCE)

to show that an entity was located in one place before the event and was in another location after the event. However, *leave* has multiple usages, not all of them involving physical change of location.

Table 1 shows its VerbNet classes and their semantic predicates. The PARC system would need to identify only those instances in their data where *leave* has the change of location meaning.

VerbNet class	Example	VerbNet semantics
Escape-51.1	The students left.	MOTION(DURING(E), THEME) DIRECTION(DURING(E), PREP_DIR, THEME)
Leave-51.2	Elvis has left the building.	MOTION(DURING(E), THEME) LOCATION(START(E), THEME, SOURCE) NOT(LOCATION(END(E), THEME, SOURCE)) DIRECTION(DURING(E), FROM, THEME, SOURCE)
Resign-10.11	He left Microsoft in 2008.	CAUSE(AGENT, E) LOCATION(START(E), SOURCE) NOT(LOCATION(END(E), SOURCE))
Fulfilling-13.1.4	He left the tenant with his business card.	HAS_POSSESSION(START(E), AGENT, THEME) HAS_POSSESSION(END(E), RECIPIENT, THEME) TRANSFER(DURING(E), THEME) CAUSE(AGENT, E)
Future_having-13.3	He left Sam his stamp collection.	HAS_POSSESSION(START(E), AGENT, THEME) FUTURE_POSSESSION(END(E), RECIPIENT, THEME) CAUSE(AGENT, E)
Keep-15.2	She left the papers in her desk	PREP(DURING(E), THEME, LOCATION) CAUSE(AGENT, E)

Table 1: VerbNet classes and semantic predicates for the verb *leave*

Zaenen et al. (2008, p. 387) explain that the problem of automatically selecting only those instances that fit the desired class remains to be solved, especially in terms of dividing metaphorical from literal tokens of a verb: “We ignore the problem of metaphorical extensions for the relevant verbs. Resources other than VerbNet will need to be exploited to insure that these non-physical interpretations are excluded.”Although they do not state which ones are the relevant verbs, for many verbs this problem could be alleviated by disambiguating the class assignment for a specific verb instance. To continue our example, *leave* has six VerbNet classes: *Escape, Fulfilling, Future_having, Keep, Leave* and *Resign*. Only the *Leave* class and the *Resign* class have the start location and end location information they are looking for, and, for the *Resign* class, the change of location is metaphorical. Therefore, the *Leave* class is the only class for this verb that suits their purposes. Classifying instances with the appropriate VerbNet class would enable them to apply the Location predicate to only those instances that are relevant. For the Semlink corpus, applying a most frequent class heuristic for *leave* would result in only 59% accuracy. This is only one example of how an accurate, automatic VerbNet classifier would be useful.

2 Related Work

We know of only two previous efforts to create a VerbNet class disambiguator for verb tokens, those of Girju et al. (2005) and Abend et al. (2008). Girju et al. used a supervised machine learning methodology, with features from the words within three positions of the verb. These features included lemma, part of speech tag, phrase type from a syntactic chunker and named entity information. First, however, they faced the problem of creating a training set tagged with VerbNet class labels. They automatically constructed one by mapping from PropBank roleset labels to VerbNet classes, choosing to label only those verb instances in which the PropBank roleset mapped to only one VerbNet class. This methodology resulted in a set of target verbs in which 96% belonged to only one VerbNet class. The high most-frequent-class baseline of 96.5% reflects the predominance of monosemous verbs and explains the low level of improvement over it: only 2%. Because our classifier uses only multiclass verbs and a gold standard corpus with VerbNet class labels, it is not comparable to the Girju classifier.

The disambiguator developed by Abend et al. (2008) supports a much closer comparison. They also approach the task as a supervised machine learning problem, training and testing on the Semlink corpus. Polysemous verbs account for 58% of their data, and they report results for all verbs and for just polysemous verbs. The Semlink corpus has annotated the verbs in the Wall Street Journal corpus with VerbNet classes. They selected instances that had been labeled with a VerbNet class, disregarding those verb instances that had been labeled as having no appropriate VerbNet class. Their system achieved 96.4% accuracy, which was a 2.9% increase over the 93.7% baseline. The high baseline can also be attributed to the large number of monosemous verbs in their data. Considering only the polysemous verbs and the model using an automatic parser, the scenario most closely resembling our experimental setup, the most frequent class baseline was 88.6% and the system accuracy was 91.9%, which represents an error reduction of 28.95%.

The results of the Abend et al. study suggest that automatic disambiguation of VerbNet classes is a reasonable line of research, and a possible method for verb sense disambiguation. The classifier relies on lexical and syntactic features, such as part of speech and heads of phrases. The classifier we describe is similar in several ways, although it adds several unique syntactic and semantic features and trains and tests only on multiclass verbs. The following sections will include comparisons of features and results where appropriate.

3 Method

To achieve verb token classification with VerbNet classes, we use a supervised machine learning approach. Using a corpus annotated with VerbNet class labels, we create a feature vector for each verb instance. A learning algorithm is then applied to generate a classifier. The following sections describe the data, the features and the experimental setup.

3.1 The Data

The training and test data are drawn from the Semlink corpus (Loper et al., 2007), which consists of the Penn Treebank portions of the Wall Street Journal corpus. A combination of automatic and manual techniques was used to label each verb instance with the appropriate VerbNet class. The resulting corpus is the largest repository of VerbNet token classification available. The corpus contains 113K verb instances, 97K of which are verbs represented in at least one VerbNet class (i.e., 86%). Semlink includes 495 verbs that have instances labeled with more than one class (including verbs labeled with a single VerbNet class and None). We have trained and tested with all of these verbs that have 10 or more instances, resulting in a set of 344 verbs. The average number of classes for these verbs is 2.7, and the average number of instances was 133. All instances in the corpus for each verb were used, which created a dataset of 45,584 instances.

3.2 Features

We use a wide variety of features, including lexical, syntactic and semantic features, all derived automatically. Previous work has focused on lexical and syntactic features possibly because of the strong association of a VerbNet class to its syntactic alternations. However, a verb's membership in different classes also depends on its meaning, making the inclusion of semantic features a possible benefit. As mentioned earlier, multiple class memberships usually correlate with different senses of the verb, making VerbNet class disambiguation much like verb sense disambiguation. For this reason, we thought it was appropriate to treat the task as a verb sense disambiguation task. Some of the features are fairly standard ones used for general word sense disambiguation, but we have added some rich syntactic and semantic features that have proven useful for sense disambiguation of verbs. All features, which were previously also shown to be useful for WSD (Dligach and Palmer, 2008) are summarized in Table 2 and explained more fully in the sections that follow.

Lexical	All open class words from target sentence and the surrounding sentences
	The two words preceding the target and their POS tags
	The two words following the target and their POS tags
Syntactic	The path through the parse tree from the target verb to its arguments
	Whether the target has a subj or obj and their head words and POS.
	Whether the target has a subordinate clause
	Whether the target has a PP adjunct
	The subcategorization frame
	The verb's voice (active or passive)
Semantic	Named-entity tags of the target's arguments
	WN hypernyms of the target's arguments
	WN synonyms of the target's arguments
	Dynamic Dependency Neighbors (DDNs)

Table 2: Classifier features

3.2.1 Lexical features

The lexical features include all open class words drawn from the target sentence and the sentence directly before and the sentence directly after it. In addition, we use a feature that pairs each of the two words before and the two words after the target verb with their respective part of speech tag.

3.2.2 Syntactic features

The syntactic features are drawn from syntactic parses automatically created with the Bikel Parser (Bikel, 2004). These features focus on the type of patterns that often distinguish one verb sense from another and that help delineate VerbNet classes. These include whether the target verb is in an active or passive form, whether it has a subject, an object, a subordinate clause, or a prepositional phrase adjunct. For each of these dependent items, the head word and its part of speech are included as features.

We also implement several unusual syntactic features that seem particularly well suited for VerbNet class disambiguation. The first is the path through the parse tree from the target verb to the verb's arguments, and the second is the sentence's subcategorization frame, as used in semantic role labeling. Because syntactic alternations, or patterns of subcategorization frames, play a large role in the organization of VerbNet classes, we expect these final two features to be particularly useful.

3.2.3 Semantic features

Our use of semantic features is motivated by the work of Patrick Hanks (1996), who proposed that sense distinctions in verbs often rely on the membership of the verb's arguments in narrowly defined verb-specific semantic classes that he called lexical sets. A lexical set could consist, for example, of such nouns as *fist, finger, hand,* etc. (but not all body-parts); its members, when used as objects of *shake*, form instances of the communicative act sense of *shake*. This view corroborates our motivation that states the necessity of capturing the semantics of the verb's arguments and semantic similarities among them.

To illustrate with an example from our data, the verb *fix* falls into two VerbNet classes: (1) Preparing-26.3, (e.g., *He fixed lunch for the team; My mom fixed me a peanut butter and bacon sandwich*) and (2) Price-54.4, with the sense of "establish" (e.g., *They fixed the interest rate at 3%; The lawyers fixed the terms of the agreement at their last meeting*). These two senses can be distinguished largely on the basis of the objects *lunch, sandwich, rate* and *terms,* the first two indicating the Preparing-26.3 class and the latter two indicating the Price-54.4 class. Not surprisingly, semantic features drawn from a target verb's arguments have been shown to improve verb sense disambiguation above and beyond lexical and syntactic features (Dligach and Palmer, 2008).

Another study that reinforces a similar idea was reported by Federici et. al. (1999). They describe their SENSE system that relies on inter-contextual analogies between tagged and untagged instances of a word to infer that word's sense. For example, if a verb's sense is preserved when used with two different objects, it is often possible to conclude by analogy that the sense of another verb is also preserved when it is used with the same two objects.

In word sense disambiguation, the existing approaches to extracting semantic features are often based on obtaining lexical knowledge about the target verb's arguments from electronic dictionaries such as WordNet (Fellbaum, 1998). WordNet synonyms and hypernyms are often used as semantic features (Dang, 2002; Dligach, 2008). Named entity tags, another source of lexical knowledge, can be obtained from the output of a named-entity tagger such as IdentiFinder (Bikel, 1999).

Four types of semantic features are used, all derived from the arguments of the target verb: (1) named entity tags for all of the arguments of the target verb, extracted using IdentiFinder; (2) synonyms of the arguments as listed in their synonym sets in WordNet; (3) hypernyms of the arguments, also taken from WordNet; and (4) dynamic dependency neighbors (Dligach and Palmer, 2008), which connect objects of the verb based on the type of verbs they frequently occur with in object position. In this paper we utilized object-based DDNs to capture the semantics of the target verb's object. Elsewhere (citation below) we also experimented with subject-based DDNs in the context of verb sense disambiguation. We discovered that subject-based DDNs do not improve the performance over and above object-based DDNs. For these experiments the DDNs were calculated from the verbs' and objects' occurrence in the English Gigaword corpus, parsed with the dependency MaltParser (Nivre, 2007).

This last feature finds similarities between objects that can be missed by the other three, as can be seen in Table 3. The similarity in the first two objects, *price* and *terms*, is captured by the WordNet synset. The third object, *rate*, can be grouped with these via its WordNet hypernym. The fourth object, however, has none of these features in common with the others. Even moving up the WN hypernym hierarchy, *number* does not connect to the others until the very general category of Abstract Entity. However, objects with very different hypernyms or named entity tags may still be common objects of the same verbs. Objects grouped in this way can often help identify the particular sense of a verb (Dligach and Palmer, 2008). Comparing lists of the top 50 verbs that each object occurs with shows a great deal of overlap and notably draws the noun *number* into a group with the other three.

Object	NE tag	WN synset	WN hypernyms	Sample DDNs
price	n/a	price, terms, damage	cost	raise, bring, increase, put, reduce, cut, have, offer, set
terms	n/a	price, terms, damage	cost	reduce, cut, have, offer, set
rate	n/a	charge per unit	cost	raise, bring, increase, put, reduce, cut, have, offer, set
number	n/a	figure	amount	raise, bring, increase, put, reduce, cut, have, offer, set

Table 3: Semantic features for one sense of the verb *fix*

3.3 Experimental Setup

Like all supervised word sense disambiguation, each verb required the training and testing of its own classifier. We classified using support vector machines (Chang and Lin, 2001). Accuracy and error rates were computed with 5-fold cross validation. Baselines were established for each target verb type by calculating the accuracy that would be achieved if all instances of a verb were labeled with its most frequent VerbNet class. The average baseline for our verb set was 77.78%.

4 Results

The average accuracy of the system with the target verbs was 88.67%, which represents an error reduction of 49% over the baseline of 77.78%. The closest comparison to the Abend et al. classifier is to their results based on only polysemous verbs and using features drawn from an automatic parser. In this scenario, their classifier had an accuracy of 91.9%, with an error reduction of 28.95% over their baseline of 88.6%.

In order to assess the contribution of the features we use to the performance of the classifier, we developed several different models composed of various combinations of our features. In addition we created a dedicated test set using 30% of the Semlink corpus so that each model would be evaluated on identical training and test sets, assuring consistent comparisons. Using this test set, the overall performance of our classifier (the model with all features) was 84.64%. This result is somewhat lower than the classifier accuracy using 5-fold cross-validation described above, possibly because of the smaller amount of training data used for this method. Compared to the most frequent class baseline, this figure still represents an error reduction of 31%.

Lexical features are generally the most standard in supervised WSD systems and seem to contribute the most to the accuracy. Therefore, we used a model containing only the lexical features as our most stripped-down model. This model had an accuracy of 83.07%. The second model added syntactic features to that, and achieved an accuracy of 84.44%. Adding semantic features brought the accuracy to 84.65%. We were particularly interested in assessing the contribution of the DDN feature, given that it can be generated automatically and requires no manually built lexical resource. For that reason, we also created a model with all the features but the DDN and a model with all the features but the non-DDN semantic features, which resulted in accuracies of 84.12% and 84.89% respectively, validating the efficacy of the DDN feature. See Table 4 for a summary of these results, along with error reduction figures.

Model	Baseline (%)	Accuracy (%)	Error Reduction (%)
Lexical features only	77.78	83.07	23.81
Lexical + syntactic	77.78	84.44	29.97
Lexical + semantic	77.78	83.75	26.87
All but DDN	77.78	84.12	28.53
Lexical + syntactic + DDN	**77.78**	**84.89**	**32.00**
All features	77.78	84.65	30.92

Table 4: Accuracy and error reduction of models using various features

5 Discussion

The accuracy of our VerbNet classifier approaches 90%, the level that several researchers have indicated is needed for useful WSD (Sanderson, 2000; Ide and Wilks, 2006). Using VerbNet classes as sense distinctions makes available sets of semantic predicates that can be used for deeper analysis. WSD is not an end in itself; it is only useful in so far as it improves more complex applications. By substituting VerbNet classification for verb sense disambiguation, we would gain both a coarse-grained sense of the verb and direct mappings to VerbNet's class-specific syntactic and semantic information. With the goal of improving future VerbNet classifiers, we discuss several pertinent issues in the following sections.

5.1 Contributions of the Features

The difference between the model with only lexical features and that with both lexical and syntactic features was statistically significant (p=.0005)[1], suggesting that our syntactic features were a notable improvement to the model. Given the strong basis of VerbNet classes on syntactic alternations, we expected that syntactic features focused on argument structure would improve the system, and this comparison supports that hypothesis.

The semantic features showed a more complex pattern. A model with lexical and semantic features achieved an accuracy of 83.75%. Compared to the accuracy of the lexical-only model, this was a significant improvement (p=.0182), although less strongly so than the syntactic features. Interestingly, when the lexical+syntactic model (no semantic features) was compared to one with lexical, syntactic and semantic features, the difference in accuracy was not significant (p=.6982), suggesting that the small improvement we saw with the semantic features was only replicating some of the information the system was gaining from the syntactic features.

When the semantic features were tested separately, however, we found that the DDN feature substantially improved the system, while the other semantic features did not help the system. A model with all the features but the DDN feature showed no significant improvement over the lexical+syntactic model. This suggests that the named entity, WordNet synset, and WordNet hypernym features added nothing to the model. In a head-to-head comparison between the model with all features but the DDN and one with lexical, syntactic, and only DDNs, we found that the DDN feature significantly improved the system ($p<.05$). With an error reduction of 32%, the lexical + syntactic + DDN model performed the best of all those we tested.

These results suggest that the system could be streamlined by removing the named entity tag, WordNet synset, and WordNet hypernym features and leaving the DDNs as the only semantic features. This would reduce the system's dependence on other resources with no loss of accuracy. In addition, the DDN feature is created dynamically, and can be done with any corpus, increasing the portability of this system to new domains.

5.2 Semlink Annotation

A couple of matters came to light during a close examination of some of the Semlink annotation in our dataset. First, for some of the verbs, the mapping from PropBank to VerbNet that was the basis of the semiautomatic labeling inappropriately mapped some VerbNet classes. For example, the verb *fix* belongs to the Preparing class, which primarily describes events of food preparation. The thematic roles and semantic predicates for this class indicate the creation of some entity, such as *He fixed me a sandwich.* This class was used in the Semlink data to label such instances, but also to label instances of *fix* as a repair event, such as *We had to fix his car,* a usage that is currently not covered by any VerbNet class. Accuracy for this verb was still high at 89%, possibly because the feature patterns were still consistent when these instances were labeled with the Preparing class.

The consequences of inappropriate labeling in this case are mixed. If thematic roles were assigned based on this label, they would likely still be correct. Both senses of *fix* call for an Agent and a Patient. The subject in "We had to fix his car" would be correctly labeled as an Agent and the object would be correctly labeled as a Patient. For semantic role labeling, this sort of error should have little negative effect. Any inferences based on the semantic predicates, however, would be misleading. In a Repair event, such as *We had to fix his car* no new entity is created, but the Preparing class label would incorrectly imply that the car is a newly created entity. It is not clear whether such

[1] All tests of statistical significance in this section were performed using the Wilcoxon signed rank test.

inappropriate mapping is an isolated problem or not. In section 7 we discuss some methods for assessing the existing annotation and for efficiently augmenting it.

5.3 Metaphorical Interpretations

A more common issue concerns the extension of VerbNet classes to metaphorical or figurative usages of a verb. Although some classes include metaphorical usages of the member verbs, such as the *Amalgamate-22.2* class, others restrict the uses to literal events. For example, the *Bump-18.4* class describes events of contact between a Theme and a Location, such as *The grocery cart hit the wall.* The class restricts both the Theme and Location to [+concrete] arguments. A natural extension of this sense of *hit* would apply to abstract arguments and metaphorical events of contact, such as *The Bank of England was hit hard by the financial slump.* This usage of *hit* would not strictly fit the *Bump-18.4* class because the financial slump (the Theme) is not a concrete entity and the Bank of England would not qualify as a concrete location, at least as it is used in this sentence. There is currently no VerbNet class, however, that would accommodate this usage of *hit.*

For several verbs in our set, including *hit* and *pay,* class labels were applied to metaphorical sense extensions. It is unclear whether this affected the accuracy of the classifier; for these two examples, the accuracy for *hit* was 75%, whereas for *pay*, it was 97%. More importantly, in terms of applying the labeled data to further semantic processing, metaphorical extensions should have little detrimental effect. Any thematic roles assigned based on the class label would be correct, although the semantic restrictions on the roles (e.g., +concrete) would not. The semantic predicates would also be correct, as long as they were interpreted metaphorically as well.

6 Conclusion

The VerbNet class disambiguator we present in this paper achieves 89% accuracy with polysemous verbs, which is a 49% error reduction over the most frequent class baseline. Given that most applications that currently use verb mappings to VerbNet classes rely on a most-frequent-class heuristic (or hand-selected data), this classifier should improve the functioning of these applications.

In addition, we have demonstrated that VerbNet class disambiguation often corresponds to coarse-grained verb sense disambiguation. However, unlike sense disambiguation with more traditional lexicons, VerbNet class disambiguation would not only help disambiguate the senses of verbs in context, it would automatically connect that context to detailed information about likely thematic roles, semantic representations, and related verbs. In combination with a syntactic parse of the sentence, knowing the appropriate VerbNet class could help select a semantic representation of the events in the sentence. By choosing VerbNet as a sense inventory, the next steps in complex knowledge representation and reasoning tasks could be facilitated.

7 Future Work

Some additional steps can be taken to improve the usefulness of VerbNet class labeling. The coverage of verbs and verb senses could be improved, both in the Semlink corpus and in VerbNet itself: 25% of the verb tokens in the Semlink corpus have no VerbNet class label. However, Semlink is based on version 2.1 of VerbNet. The current version, 3.1, incorporates over 700 new verb senses, many of which introduce very common verbs, such as *seem, involve,* and *own.* Updating the corpus with annotations for these new verbs and verb senses would improve coverage. A more long-term goal is to annotate data from other types of corpora than the WSJ, which would likely improve any VerbNet classifier's portability to new domains.

We plan to increase VerbNet annotation in the Semlink corpus using methods that take advantage of existing mappings between PropBank and VerbNet and efficient manual annotation (Dligach, 2010).

SemLink expansion can be accomplished in two ways. First, more data can be labeled using some form of active learning (Settles, 2009) (e.g., batch mode uncertainty sampling). Once more annotated data has been acquired, it may be a good idea to double annotate all or parts of the data, leading to a more error-free labeled corpus. Various error detection techniques can be used to reduce the amount of the second round of annotation (Dligach, 2010). These methods can also be used to judge the reliability of the semiautomatic annotation that has already been done, which should indicate how widespread mislabeling is (such as with the verb *fix,* see section 5.2).

The question of metaphorical extensions in the VerbNet annotation is currently being addressed by the VerbNet team. Plans are underway to enhance VerbNet classes with metaphorical information, where appropriate. These enhancements will indicate any changes in thematic role restrictions with a metaphoric usage, and any changes necessary for a semantic predicate to be interpreted correctly.

Given the success of the DDN feature, we would like to see if expanding its contribution would further enhance our classifier. Currently, the DDN feature is only calculated for objects of the verb, but the feature could be encoded for the subject of the verb as well.

We see this classifier as an important step toward using VerbNet for deep semantic analysis. We have shown that verbs in multiple VerbNet classes can be disambiguated with close to 90% accuracy. Another related task, semantic role labeling, has made great strides lately (Palmer, Gildea and Xue, 2010). Using the output from both these tasks should enable us to identify the specific VerbNet frame and semantic predicate for the sentence. For example, VerbNet class disambiguation and semantic role labeling would identify the sentence "He left Sam his stamp collection" as

Agent V(class:Future-having-13.3)Recipient Theme

Only one frame in the Future-having-13.3 class has that pattern: the NP V NP-dative NP frame. Its semantic predicates are

HAS_POSSESSION(START(E), AGENT, THEME)
FUTURE_POSSESSION(END(E), RECIPIENT, THEME)
CAUSE(AGENT, E)

Given the argument labels from the semantic role labeling, it is straightforward to map from the original sentence to the semantic representation:

HAS_POSSESSION(START(E), HE, THE STAMP COLLECTION)
FUTURE_POSSESSION(END(E), SAM, THE STAMP COLLECTION)
CAUSE(HE, E)

Recent work in coreference resolution (Haghighi and Klein, 2009) and implicit argument resolution (Gerber and Chai, 2010) suggest how this representation could be enriched by identifying the referent of *he* from the surrounding text. All of these pieces of the semantic puzzle have the potential to fit together into a richer and deeper semantic representation of text. To further this goal, we intend to develop our classifier for all of the verbs in VerbNet and release the system to the public, along with an expanded version of the Semlink corpus.

References

Abend, Omri, Roy Reichart, and Ari Rappoport. 2008. A supervised algorithm for verb disambiguation into VerbNet classes. *Proceedings of the 22nd International Conference on Computational Linguistics* (Coling 2008), pp. 9–16. Manchester, August.

Bikel, Daniel M., Richard Schwartz, and Ralph M. Weischedel. 1999. An algorithm that learns what's in a name. *Machine Learning,* 34(1-3): 211-231. Special Issue on Natural Language Learning.

Bobrow, Danny, B. Cheslow, Cleo Condoravdi, Lauri Karttunen, Tracy H. King, Rowan Nairn, Valeria de Paiva, Charlotte Price, and Annie Zaenen. 2007. PARC's Bridge and Question Answering System. In *Proceedings of the Grammar Engineering Across Frameworks (GEAF07) Workshop,* pp. 46-66, CSLI Publications.

Chang, Chih-Chung, and Chih-Jen Lin. 2001. LIBSVM : A library for support vector machines, 2001. Software available at http://www.csie.ntu.edu.tw/~cjlin/libsvm.

Chen, Jinying, and Martha Palmer. 2005. Towards robust high performance word sense disambiguation of English verbs using rich linguistic features. In *Proceedings of the 2nd International Joint Conference on Natural Language Processing.* October 11-13, 2005, Jeju Island, Korea.

Dang, Hoa T., and Martha Palmer. 2002. Combining contextual features for word sense disambiguation. In *Proceedings of the SIGLEX/SENSEVAL Workshop on WSD: Recent Successes and Future Directions, in Conjunction with ACL-02,* Philadelphia.

Dligach, Dmitriy. 2010. High performance word sense disambiguation with less manual effort. Ph.D. diss. University of Colorado.

Dligach, Dmitriy, and Martha Palmer. 2008. Novel semantic features for word sense disambiguation. In *Proceedings of ACL-08: HLT, Short Papers,* pp. 29–32, Columbus, Ohio.

Federici, Stefano, Simonetta Montemagni, and Vito Pirrelli. 1999. SENSE: An analogy-based word sense disambiguation system. *Natural Language Engineering,* 5(2): 207-218.

Fellbaum, Christiane. 1998. *WordNet: An Electronic Lexical Database.*MIT Press, Cambridge, Mass.

Girju, Roxana, Dan Roth, and Mark Sammons. 2005. Token-level disambiguation of VerbNet classes. In *The Proceedings of the Interdisciplinary Workshop on the Identification and Representation of Verb Features and Verb Classes***,** K. Erk, A. Melinger, and S. Schulte im Walde (eds.), Saarland University, Saarbrucken, Germany.

Hanks, Patrick. 1996. Contextual dependencies and lexical sets. *The International Journal of Corpus Linguistics,* 1(1).

Hensman, Svetlana, and John Dunnion. 2004. Automatically building conceptual graphs using VerbNet and WordNet. In *Proceedings of the 3rd International Symposium on Information and Communication Technologies (ISICT)*, Las Vegas, NV.

Ide, Nancy, and Yorick Wilks. 2006. Making sense about sense. In Eneko Agirre and Philip Edmonds (eds.) *Word Sense Disambiguation: Algorithms and Applications.* Dordrecht, The Netherlands: Springer.

Kipper-Schuler, Karin. 2005. VerbNet: A broad-coverage, comprehensive verb lexicon. Ph.D. thesis, Computer and Information Science Dept., University of Pennsylvania, Philadelphia, June.

Levin, Beth. 1993. *English Verb Classes and Alternations.* Chicago: University of Chicago Press.

Loper, Edward, Szu ting Yi, and Martha Palmer. 2007. Combining lexical resources: Mapping between PropBank and VerbNet. In *The Proceedings of the 7th International Workshop on Computational Semantics*, Tilburg, the Netherlands.

Nivre, Joakim, Johann Hall, Jens Nilsson, et al. 2007. MaltParser: A language-independent system for data-driven dependency parsing. *Natural Language Engineering* 13(2): 95-135.

Palmer, Martha, Daniel Gildea, Nianwen Xue. 2010. *Semantic Role Labeling* (eBook), In Synthesis Lectures on Human Language Technologies, ed., Graeme Hirst. Morgan & Claypool.

Sanderson, Mark. 2000. Retrieving with good sense. *Information Retrieval.* 2(1): 49–69.

Shi, Lei, and Rada Mihalcea. 2005. Putting pieces together: Combining FrameNet, VerbNet and WordNet for robust semantic parsing. In *Proceedings of the Sixth International Conference on Intelligent Text Processing and Computational Linguistics*, Mexico City, Mexico.

Swier, R., and S. Stevenson. 2004. Unsupervised semantic role labeling. In *Proceedings of the 2004 Conf. on Empirical Methods in Natural Language Processing,* pp. 95–102, Barcelona, Spain.

Zaenen, A., D. G. Bobrow, C. Condoravdi. 2008. The encoding of lexical implications in VerbNet: Predicates of change of locations. In *LREC Proceedings* [http://www.lrec-conf.org/proceedings/lrec2008/pdf/101_paper.pdf]

Zapirain, Beñat, Eneko Agirre, and Lluís Màrquez. 2008. Robustness and generalization of role sets: PropBank vs. VerbNet. In *Proceedings of the 46th Annual Meeting of the Association of Computational Linguistics, ACL-08: HLT, Columbus, Ohio,* pp. 550-558.

Acquiring entailment pairs across languages and domains: A data analysis

Manaal Faruqui
Dept. of Computer Science and Engineering
Indian Institute of Technology
Kharagpur, India
manaal.iitkgp@gmail.com

Sebastian Padó
Seminar für Computerlinguistik
Universität Heidelberg
Heidelberg, Germany
pado@cl.uni-heidelberg.de

Abstract

Entailment pairs are sentence pairs of a premise and a hypothesis, where the premise textually entails the hypothesis. Such sentence pairs are important for the development of Textual Entailment systems. In this paper, we take a closer look at a prominent strategy for their automatic acquisition from newspaper corpora, pairing first sentences of articles with their titles. We propose a simple logistic regression model that incorporates and extends this heuristic and investigate its robustness across three languages and three domains. We manage to identify two predictors which predict entailment pairs with a fairly high accuracy across all languages. However, we find that robustness across domains within a language is more difficult to achieve.

1 Introduction

Semantic processing has become a major focus of attention in NLP. However, different applications such as Question Answering, Information Extraction and Machine Translation often adopt very different, task-specific semantic processing strategies. Textual entailment (TE) was introduced by Dagan et al. (2006) as a "meta-task" that can subsume a large part of the semantic processing requirements of such applications by providing a generic concept of inference that corresponds to "common sense" reasoning patterns. Textual Entailment is defined as a relation between two natural language utterances (a Premise P and a Hypothesis H) that holds if "a human reading P would infer that H is most likely true". See, e.g., the ACL "challenge paper" by Sammons et al. (2010) for further details.

The successive TE workshops that have taken place yearly since 2005 have produced annotation for English which amount to a total of several thousand entailing Premise-Hypothesis sentence pairs, which we will call *entailment pairs*:

(1) **P:** Swedish bond yields end 21 basis points higher.
H: Swedish bond yields rose further.

From the machine learning perspective assumed by many approaches to TE, this is a very small number of examples, given the complex nature of entailment. Given the problems of manual annotation, therefore, Burger and Ferro (2005) proposed to take advantage of the structural properties of a particular type of discourse – namely newspaper articles – to automatically harvest entailment pairs. They proposed to pair the title of each article with its first sentence, interpreting the first sentence as Premise and the title as Hypothesis. Their results were mixed, with an average of 50% actual entailment pairs among all pairs constructed in this manner. SVMs which identified "entailment-friendly" documents based on their bags of words lead to an accuracy of 77%. Building on the same general idea, Hickl et al. (2006) applied a simple unsupervised filter which removes all entailment pair candidates that "did not share an entity (or an NP)". They report an accuracy of 91.8% on a manually evaluated sample – considerably better Burger and Ferro. The article however does not mention the size of the original corpus, and whether "entity" is to be understood as named entity, so it is difficult to assess what its recall is, and whether it presupposes a high-quality NER system.

In this paper, we model the task using a logistic regression model that allows us to synchronously analyse the data and predict entailment pairs, and focus on the question of how well these results generalize across domains and languages, for many of which no entailment pairs are available at all. We make three main contributions: (a), we define an annotation scheme based on semantic and discourse phenomena that can break entailment and annotate two datasets with it; (b), we idenfiy two robust properties of sentence pairs that correlate strongly with entailment and which are robust enough to support high-precision entailment pair extraction; (c), we find that cross-domain differences are actually larger than cross-lingual differences, even for languages as different as German and Hindi.

Plan of the paper. Section 2 defines our annotation scheme. In Section 3, we sketch the logistic regression framework we use for analysis, and motivate our choice of predictors. Sections 4 and 5 present the two experiments on language and domain comparisons, respectively. We conclude in Section 6.

2 A fine-grained annotation scheme for entailment pairs

The motivation of our annotation scheme is to better understand why entailment breaks down between titles and first sentences of newswire articles. We subdivide the general *no* entailment category of earlier studies according to an inventory of reasons for non-entailment that we collected from an informal inspection of some dozen articles from an English-language newspaper. Additionally, we separate out sentences that are ill-formed in the sense of not forming one proposition.

2.1 Subtypes of non-entailment

No-par (Partial entailment). The Premise entails the Hypothesis almost, but not completely, in one of two ways: (a), The Hypothesis is a conjunction and the Premise entails just one conjunct; or (b), Premise and Hypothesis share the main event, but the Premise is missing an argument or adjunct that forms part of the Hypothesis. Presumably, in our setting, such information is provided by the other sentences in the article than the first one. In Ex. (1), if P and H were switched, this would be the case for the size of the rise.

No-pre (Presupposition): The Premise uses a construction which can only be understood with information from the Hypothesis, typically a definite description or an adjunct. This category arises because the title stands before the first sentence and is available as context. In the following example, the Premise NP "des Verbandes" can only be resolved through the mention of "VDA" (the German car manufacturer's association) in the Hypothesis.

(2) **P:** Herzog wird in dem vierköpfigen Führungsgremium des Verbands für die Teile-
Herzog will in the four-head management board of the association for the parts
und Zubehörindustrie zuständig sein.
and accessory business resposible be.

H: Martin Herzog wird VDA-Geschäftsführer.
Martin Herzog becomes VDA manager.

No-con (Contradiction): Direct contradiction of Premise and Hypothesis.

(3) **P:** Wie die innere Uhr [...] funktioniert, ist noch weitgehend unbekannt.
How the biological clock [...] works, is still mostly unknown.

H: Licht stellt die innere Uhr.
Light regulates the biological clock.

No-emb (Embedding): The Premise uses an embedding that breaks entailment (e.g., modal adverbials or non-factural embedding verb). In the following pair, the proposition in the Hypothesis is embedded under "expect".

(4) **P:** An Arkansas gambling amendment [...] is expected to be submitted to the state Supreme Court Monday for a rehearing, a court official said.
H: Arkansas gaming petition goes before court again Monday

No-oth (Other): All other negative examples where Premise and Hypothesis are well-formed, and which could not be assigned to a more specific category, are included under this tag. In this sense, "Other" is a catch-all category. Often, Premise and Hypothesis, taken in isolation, are simply unrelated:

(5) **P:** Victor the Parrot kept shrieking "Voda, Voda" – "Water, Water".
H: Thirsty jaguar procures water for Bulgarian zoo.

2.2 Ill-formed sentence pairs

Err (Error): These cases arise due to errors in sentence boundary detection: Premise or Hypothesis may be cut off in the middle of the sentence.

Ill (Ill-formed): Often, the titles are not single grammatical sentences and can therefore not be interpreted sensibly as the Hypothesis of an entailment pair. They can be incomplete proposition such as NPs or PPs ("Beautiful house situated in woods"), or, frequently, combinations of multiple sentences ("RESEARCH ALERT - Mexico upped, Chile cut.").

3 Modeling entailment with logistic regression

We will model the entailment annotation labels on candidate sentence pairs using a logistic regression model. From a machine learning point of view, logistic regression models can be seen as a rather simple statistical classifier which can be used to acquire new entailment pairs. From a linguistic point of view, they can be used to explain the phenomena in the data, see e.g., Bresnan et al. (2007).

Formally, logistic regression models assume that datapoints consist of a set of predictors x and a binary response variable y. They have the form

$$p(y = 1) = \frac{1}{1 + e^{-z}} \text{ with } z = \sum_i \beta_i x_i \tag{1}$$

where p is the probability of a datapoint x, β_i is the coefficient assigned to the linguistically motivated factor x_i. Model estimation sets the parameters β so that the likelihood of the observed data is maximized.

From the linguistics perspective, we are most interested in analysing the importance of the different predictors: for each predictor x_i, the comparison of the estimated value of its coefficient β_i can be compared to its estimated standard error, and it is possible to test the hypothesis that $\beta_i = 0$, i.e., the predictor does not significantly contribute to the model. Furthermore, the absolute value of β_i can be interpreted as the *log odds* – that is, as the change in the probability of the response variable being positive depending on x_i being positive.

$$e^{\beta_i} = \frac{P(y = 1|x = 1, \ldots)/P(y = 0|x = 1, \ldots)}{P(y = 1|x = 0, \ldots)/P(y = 0|x = 0, \ldots)} \tag{2}$$

The fact that z is just a linear combination of predictor weights encodes the assumption that the log odds combine linearly among factors.

From the natural language processing perspective, we would like to create predictions for new observations. Note, however, that simply assessing the significance of predictors on some dataset, as provided by the logistic regression model, corresponds to an evaluation of the model on the training set, which is prone to the problem of overfitting. We will therefore in our experiments always apply the models acquired from one dataset on another to see how well they generalize.

3.1 Choice of Predictors

Next, we need a set of plausible predictors that we can plug into the logistic regression framework. These predictors should ideally be language-independent. We analyse the categories of our annotation, as an inventory of phenomena that break entailment, to motivate a small set of robust predictors.

Following early work on textual entailment, we use word overlap as a strong indicator of entailment (Monz and de Rijke, 2001). Our **weighted overlap** predictor uses the well-known tf/idf weighting scheme to compute the overlap between P and H (Manning et al., 2008):

$$weightedOverlap(T, H, D) = \frac{\sum_{w \in T \cap H} \text{tf-idf}(w, D)}{\sum_{w \in H} \text{tf-idf}(w, D)} \tag{3}$$

where we treat each article as a separate document and the whole corpus as document collection D. We expect that No-oth pairs have generally the lowest weighted overlap, followed by No-par pairs, while Yes pairs have the highest weighted overlap. We also use a categorical version of this observation in the form of our **strict noun match** predictor. This predictor is similar in spirit to the proposal by Hickl et al. (2006) mentioned in Section 1. The boolean strict noun match predictor is true if all Hypothesis nouns are present in the Premise, and is therefore a predictor that is geared at precision rather than recall. A third predictor that was motivated by the No-par and No-oth categories was the number of words in the article: No-oth sentence pairs often come from long articles, where the first sentence provides merely an introduction. For this predictor, **log num words**, we count the total number of words in the article and logarithmize it.[1] The remaining subcategories of No were more difficult to model. No-pre pairs should be identifiable by testing whether the Premise contains a definite description that cannot be accommodated, a difficult problem that seems to require world knowledge. Similarly, the recognition of contradictions, as is required to find No-con pairs, is very difficult in itself (de Marneffe et al., 2008). Finally, No-emb requires the detection of a counterfactual context in the Premise. Since we do not currently see robust, language-independent ways of modelling these phenomena, we do not include specific predictors to address them.

The situation is similar with regard to the Err category. While it might be possible to detect incomplete sentences with the help of a parser, this again involves substantial knowledge about the language. The Ill category, however, appears easier to target: at least cases of Hypotheses consisting of multiple phrases case be detected easily by checking for sentence end markers in the middle of the Hypothesis (full stop, colon, dash). We call this predictor **punctuation**.

4 Experiment 1: Analysis by Language

4.1 Data sources and preparation

This experiment performs a cross-lingual comparison of three newswire corpora. We use English, German, and Hindi. All three belong to the Indo-European language family, but English and German are more closely related.

For English and German, we used the Reuters RCV2 Multilingual Corpus[2]. RCV2 contains over 487,000 news stories in 13 different languages. Almost all news stories cover the business and politics domains. The corpus marks the title of each article; we used the sentence splitter provided by Treetagger (Schmid, 1995) to extract the first sentences. Our Hindi corpus is extracted from the text collection of South Asian languages prepared by the EMILLE project (Xiao et al., 2004)[3]. We use the Hindi

[1]This makes the coefficiently easier to interpret. The predictive difference is minimal.
[2]`http://trec.nist.gov/data/reuters/reuters.html`
[3]`http://www.elda.org/catalogue/en/text/W0037.html`

No. of sentence pairs	English	German	Hindi
Original	473,874 (100%)	112,259 (100%)	20,209 (100%)
Filtered	264.711 (55.8%)	50.039 (44.5%)	10.475 (51.8%)

Table 1: Pair extraction statistics

Corpus	err	ill	no-con	no-emb	no-oth	no-par	no-pre	yes
English Reuters	3.5	2.9	0	0.2	3.7	7.4	0	82.3
German Reuters	2.1	11.0	0.4	0.2	4.3	2.1	0.2	79.7
Hindi Emille	1.1	2.5	0	0.3	14.7	5.7	0	75.7

Table 2: Exp.1: Distribution of annotation categories (in percent)

monolingual data, which was crawled from Webdunia,[4] an Indian daily online newspaper. The articles are predominantly political, with a focus on Indo-Pakistani and Indo-US affairs. We identify sentence boudaries with the Hindi sentence marker ('।'), which is used exclusively for this purpose.

We preprocessed the data by extracting the title and the first sentence, treating the first sentence as Premise and the title as Hypothesis. We applied a filter to remove pairs where the chance of entailment was impossible or very small. Specifically, our filter keeps only sentence pairs that (a) share at least one noun and where (b) both sentences include at least one verb and are not questions. Table 1 shows the corpus sizes before and after filtering. Note that the percentage of selected sentences across the languages are all in the 45%-55% range. This filter could presumably be improved by requiring a shared named entity, but since language-independent NER is still an open research issue, we did not follow up on this avenue. We randomly sampled 1,000 of the remaining sentence pairs per language for manual annotation.

4.2 Distribution of annotation categories

First, we compared the frequencies of the annotation categories defined in Section 3.1. The results are shown in Table 2. We find our simple preprocessing filter results in an accuracy of between 75 and 82%. This is still considerably below the results of Hickl et al., who report 92% accuracy on their English data.[5]

Even though the overall percentage of "yes" cases is quite similar among languages, the details of the distribution differ. One fairly surprising observation was the fairly large number of ill-formed sentence pairs. As described in Section 2, this category comprises cases where the Hypothesis (i.e., a title) is not a grammatical sentence. Further analysis of the category shows that the common patterns are participle constructions (Ex. (6)) and combinations of multiple statements (Ex. (7)). The participle construction is particularly prominent in German.

(6) Glencoe Electric, Minn., rated single-A by Moody's.

(7) Wieder Kämpfe in Südlibanon - Israeli getötet.
Again fights in Southern Lebanon - Israeli killed.

The "no"-categories make up a total of 11.3% (English), 6.6% (German), and 20.7% (Hindi). The "other" and "partial" categories clearly dominate. This is to be expected, in particular the high number of partial entailments. The "other" category mostly consists of cases where the title summarizes the whole article, but the first sentence provides only a gentle introduction to the topic:

(8) **P:** One automotive industry analyst has dubbed it the 'Lincoln Town Truck'.
H: Ford hopes Navigator will lure young buyers to Lincoln.

As regards the high ratio of "no-other" cases in the Hindi corpus, we found a high number of instances where the title states the gist of the article too differently from the first sentence to preserve entailment:

[4] http://www.webdunia.com

[5] We attribute the difference to the filtering scheme which is difficult to reconstruct from Hickl et al. (2006).

Predictor	German	sig	English	sig	Hindi	sig
weighted overlap	0.77	**	2.30	***	3.35	***
log num words	-0.05	–	0.03	–	-0.17	–
punctuation	-1.04	***	-0.43	**	-0.35	**
strict noun match	0.12	–	0.19	–	0.38	**

Table 3: Exp. 1: Predictors in the logreg model (*: p<0.05; **: p<0.01; ***: p<0.001)

(9) **P:** आज भी प्रिंसेस डायना की लोकप्रियता कम नहीं हुई है ।
Even today, Princess Diana's popularity has not decreased.
H: प्रिंसेस डायना के पत्र और कार्ड नीलाम होंगे ।
Bidding on Princess Diana's letter and cards would take place.

The remaining error categories (embedding, presupposition, contradiction) were, disappointingly, almost absent. Another sizable category is formed by errors, though. We find the highest percentage for English, where our sentence splitter misinterpreted full stops in abbreviations as sentence boundaries.

4.3 Modelling the data

We estimated logistic regression models on each dataset, using the predictors from Section 3.1. Considering the eventual goal of extracting entailment pairs, we use the decision yes vs. everything else as our response variable. The analysis was performed with `R`, using the `rms`[6] and `ROCR`[7] packages.

Analysis of predictors. The coefficients for the predictors and their significances are shown in Table 3. There is considerable parallelism between the languages. In all three languages, weighted overlap between H and P is a significant predictor: high overlap indicates entailment, and vice versa. Its effect size is large as well: Perfect overlap increases the probability of entailment for German by a factor of $e^{0.77} = 2.16$, for English by 10, and for Hindi even by 28. Similarly, the punctuation predictor comes out as a significant negative effect for all three languages, presumably by identifying ill-formed sentence pairs. In contrast, the length of the article (log num words) is not a significant predictor. This is a surprising result, given our hypothesis that long articles often involve an "introduction" which reduces the chance for entailment between the title and the first sentence. The explanation is that the two predictors, log num words and weighted overlap, are highly significantly correlated in all three corpora. Since weighted overlap is the predictive of the two, the model discards article length.

Finally, strict noun match, which requires that all nouns match between H and P, is assigned a positive coefficient for each language, but only reaches significance for Hindi. This is the only genuine cross-lingual difference: In our Hindi corpus, the titles are copied more verbatim from the text than for English and German (median weighted overlap: Hindi 0.76, English 0.72, German 0.69). Consequently, in English and German the filter discards too many entailment instances. For all three languages, though, the coefficient is small – for Hindi, where it is largest, it increases the odds by a factor of $e^{0.39} \approx 1.4$.

Evaluation. We trained models on the three corpora, using only the two predictors that contributed significantly in all languages (weighted overlap and punctuation), in order to avoid overfitting on the individual datasets.[8] We applied each model to each dataset. How such models should be evaluated depends on the intended purpose of the classification. We assume that it is fairly easy to obtain large corpora of newspaper text, which makes precision an issue rather than recall. The logistic regression classifier assigns a probability to each datapoint, so we can trade off recall and precision. We fix recall at a reasonable value (30%) and compare precision values.

[6]`http://biostat.mc.vanderbilt.edu/twiki/bin/view/Main/Design`
[7]`http://rocr.bioinf.mpi-sb.mpg.de/`
[8]Subsequent analysis of "full" models (with all features) showed that they did not generally improve over two-feature models.

Models / Data	German model	English model	Hindi model
German data	**91.6**	88.8	88.8
English data	93.2	94.3	**94.6**
Hindi data	98.7	98.7	**99.1**

Table 4: Exp. 1: Precision for the class "yes" (entailment) at 30% Recall

Our expectation is that each model will perform best on its own corpus (since this is basically the training data), and worse on the other languages. The size of the drop for the other languages reflects the differences between the corpora as well as the degree of overfitting models show to their training data.

The actual results are shown in Table 4.3. The precision is fairly high, generally over 90%, and well above the baseline percentage of entailment pairs. The German data is modelled best by the German model, with the two other models performing 3 percent worse. The situation is similar, although less pronounced, on Hindi data, where the Hindi-trained model is 0.4% better than the two other models. For English, the Hindi model even outperforms the English model by 0.3%[9], which in turn works about 1% better than the German model. In sum, the logistic regression models can be applied very well across languages, with little loss in precision. The German data with its high ratio of ill-formed headlines (cf. Table 2) is most difficult to model. Hindi is simplest, due to the tendency of title and first sentence to be almost identical (cf. the large weight for the overlap predictor).

5 Experiment 2: Analysis by Domain of German corpora

5.1 Data

This experiment compares three German corpora from different newspapers to study the impact of domain differences: Reuters, "Stuttgarter Zeitung", and "Die Zeit". These corpora differ in domain and in style. The Reuters corpus was already described in Section 4.1. "Stuttgarter Zeitung" (StuttZ) is a daily regional newspaper which covers international business and politics like Reuters, but does not draw its material completely from large news agencies and gives more importance to regional and local events. Its style is therefore less consistent. Our corpus covers some 80,000 sentences of text from StuttZ. The third corpus comprises over 4 million sentences of text from "Die Zeit", a major German national weekly. The text is predominantly from the 2000s, plus selected articles from the 1940s through 1990s. "Die Zeit" focuses on op-ed pieces and general discussions of political and social issues. It also covers arts and science, which the two other newspapers rarely do.

5.2 Distribution of annotation categories

We extracted and annotated entailment pair candidates in the same manner as before (cf. Section 4.1). The new breakdown of annotation categories in Table (10) shows, in comparison to the cross-lingual results in Table 2, a higher incidence of errors, which we attribute to formatting problems of these corpora. Compared to the German Reuters corpus we considered in Exp. 1, StuttZ and Die Zeit contain considerably fewer entailment pairs, most notably Die Zeit, where the percentage of entailment pairs is just 21.6% in our sample, compared to 82.3% for Reuters. Notably, there are almost no cases where the first sentence represents a partial entailment; in contrast, for more than one third of the examples (33.9%), there is no entailment relation between the title and the first sentence. This seems to be a domain-dependent, or even stylistic, effect: in "Die Zeit", titles are often designed solely as "bait" to interest readers in the article:

(10) **P:** Sat.1 sah [...] Doris dabei zu , wie sie [...] Auto fahren lernte.
Sat.1 watched [...] Doris , how she [...] to drive learned.

[9]The English model outperforms the Hindi model at higher recall levels, though.

Corpus	err	ill	no-con	no-emb	no-oth	no-par	no-pre	yes
Reuters	3.5	2.9	0	0.2	3.7	7.4	0	82.3
StuttZ	6.2	3.6	0.5	2.8	12.4	3.0	0.6	70.7
Die Zeit	2.3	39.0	0.5	1.8	33.9	0.9	0.0	21.6

Table 5: Exp. 2: Distribution of annotation categories on German corpora (in percent)

Predictor	Reuters	sig	StuttZ	sig	Die Zeit	sig
weighted overlap	0.77	**	1.82	***	2.60	***
log num words	-0.05	–	-0.24	–	-0.20	–
punctuation	-1.04	***	-0.01	–	-1.21	***
strict noun match	0.12	–	0.20	–	-0.01	–

Table 6: Exp. 2: Predictors in the logreg model (*: p<0.05; **: p<0.01; ***: p<0.001)

Models / Data	Reuters	StuttZ	Die Zeit
Reuters	**91.6**	85.4	**91.6**
StuttZ	**83.0**	**83.0**	82.6
Die Zeit	45.2	45.2	**46.7**

Table 7: Exp. 2: Precision for the class "yes" at 30% recall

H: Doris, es ist grün!
Doris, it is green!

Other titles are just noun or verb phrases, which accounts for the large number (39%) of ill-formed pairs.

5.3 Modelling the data

Predictors and evaluation. The predictors of the logistic regression models for the three German corpora are shown in Table 6. The picture is strikingly similar to the results of Exp. 1 (Table 3): weighted overlap and punctuation are highly significant predictors for all three corpora (except punctuation, which is insignificant for StuttZ); even the effect sizes are roughly similar. Again, neither sentence length nor strict noun match are significant. This indicates that the predictors we have identified work fairly robustly. Unfortunately, this does not imply that they always work well. Table 6 shows the precision of the predictors in Exp. 2, again at 30% Recall. Here, the difference to Exp. 1 (Table 4.3) is striking. First, overfitting of the predictors is worse across domains, with losses of 5% on Reuters and Die Zeit when they are classified with models trained on other corpora even though use just two generic features. Second, and more seriously, it is much more difficult to extract entailment pairs from the Stuttgarter Zeitung corpus and, especially, the Die Zeit corpus. For the latter, we can obtain a precision of at most 46.7%, compared to >90% in Exp. 1.

We interpret this result as evidence that domain adaptation may be an even greater challenge than multilinguality in the acquisition of entailment pairs. More specifically, our impression is that the heuristic of pairing title and first sentence works fairly well for a particular segment of newswire text, but not otherwise. This segment consists of factual, "no-nonsense" articles provided by large news agencies such as Reuters, which tend to be simple in their discourse structure and have an informative title. In domains where articles become longer, and the intent to entertain becomes more pertinent (as for Die Zeit), the heuristic fails very frequently. Note that the weighted overlap predictor cannot recover all negative cases. Example (10) is a case in point: one of the two informative words in H, "Doris" and "grün", is in fact in P.

Domain specificity. The fact that it is difficult to extract entailment pairs from some corpora is serious exactly because, according to our intuition, the "easier" news agency corpora (like Reuters) are domain-

Corpus	D(· | deWac)	words w with highest $P(w)/Q(w)$
Reuters	0.98	Händler (trader), Börse (exchange), Prozent (per cent), erklärte (stated)
StuttZ	0.93	DM (German Mark), Prozent (per cent), Millionen (millions), Geschäftsjahr (fiscal year), Milliarden (billions)
Die Zeit	0.64	heißt (means), weiß (knows), läßt (leaves/lets)

Table 8: Exp. 2: Domain specificity (KL distance from deWac); typical content words

specific. We quantify this intuition with an approach by Ciaramita and Baroni (2006), who propose to model the representativeness of web-crawled corpora as the KL divergence between their Laplace-smoothed unigram distribution P and that of a reference corpus, Q ($w \in W$ are vocabulary words):

$$D(P,Q) = \sum_{w \in W} P(w) \log \frac{P(w)}{Q(w)} \tag{4}$$

We use the deWac German web corpus (Baroni et al., 2009) as reference, making the idealizing assumption that it is representative for the German language. We interpret a large distance from deWac as domain specificity. The results in Table 8 bear out our hypothesis: Die Zeit is less domain specific than StuttZ, which in turn is less specific than Reuters. The table also lists the content words (nouns/verbs) that are most typical for each corpus, i.e., which have the highest value of $P(w)/Q(w)$. The lists bolster the interpretation that Reuters and StuttZ concentrate on the economical domain, while the typical terms of Die Zeit show an argumentative style, but no obvious domain bias. In sum, domain specificity is inversely correlated with the difficulty of extracting entailment pairs: from a representativity standpoint, we should draw entailment pairs from Die Zeit.

6 Conclusion

In this paper, we have discussed the robustness of extracting entailment pairs from the title and first sentence of newspaper articles. We have proposed a logistic regression model and have analysed its performance on two datasets that we have created: a cross-lingual one a cross-domain one. Our cross-lingual experiment shows a positive result: despite differences in the distribution of annotation categories across domains and languages, the predictors of all logistic regression models look remarkably similar. In particular, we have found two predictors which are correlated significantly with entailment across (almost) all languages and domains. These are (a), a tf/idf measure of word overlap between the title and the first sentence; and (b), the presence of punctuation indicating that the title is not a single grammatical sentence. These predictors extract entailment pairs from newswire text at a precision of $> 90\%$, at a recall of 30%, and represent a simple, cross-lingually robust method for entailment pair acquisition.

The cross-domain experiment, however, forces us to qualify this positive result. On two other German corpora from different newspapers, we see a substantial degradation of the model's performance. It may seem surprising that cross-domain robustness is a larger problem than cross-lingual robustness. Our interpretation is that the limiting factor is the degree to which the underlying assumption, namely that first sentence entails the title, is true. If the assumption is true only for a minority of sentences, our predictors cannot save the day. This assumption holds well in the Reuters corpora, but less so for the other newspapers. Unfortunately, we also found that the Reuters corpora are at the same time thematically constrained, and therefore only of limited use for extracting a representative corpus of entailment pairs. A second problem is that the addition of features we considered beyond the two mentioned above threatens to degrade the classifier due to overfitting, at least across domains.

Given these limitation of the present headline-based approach, other approaches that are more generally applicable may need to be explored. Entailment pairs have for example been extracted from Wikipedia (Bos et al., 2009). Another direction is to build on methods to extract paraphrases from comparable corpora (Barzilay and Lee, 2003), and extend them to capture asymmetrical pairs, where entailment holds in one, but not the other, direction.

Acknowledgments. The first author would like to acknowledge the support of a WISE scholarship granted by DAAD (German Academic Exchange Service).

References

Baroni, M., S. Bernardini, A. Ferraresi, and E. Zanchetta (2009). The wacky wide web: A collection of very large linguistically processed web-crawled corpora. *Journal of Language Resources and Evaluation 43*(3), 209–226.

Barzilay, R. and L. Lee (2003). Learning to paraphrase: An unsupervised approach using multiple-sequence alignment. In *Proceedings of HLT/NAACL*, Edmonton, AL, pp. 16–23.

Bos, J., M. Pennacchiotti, and F. M. Zanzotto (2009). Textual entailment at EVALITA 2009. In *Proceedings of IAAI*, Reggio Emilia.

Bresnan, J., A. Cueni, T. Nikitina, and H. Baayen (2007). Predicting the dative alternation. In G. Bouma, I. Kraemer, and J. Zwarts (Eds.), *Cognitive Foundations of Interpretation*, pp. 69–94. Royal Netherlands Academy of Science.

Burger, J. and L. Ferro (2005). Generating an entailment corpus from news headlines. In *Proceedings of the ACL Workshop on Empirical Modeling of Semantic Equivalence and Entailment*, pp. 49–54.

Ciaramita, M. and M. Baroni (2006). A figure of merit for the evaluation of web-corpus randomness. In *Proceedings of EACL*, Trento, Italy, pp. 217–224.

Dagan, I., O. Glickman, and B. Magnini (2006). The PASCAL recognising textual entailment challenge. In *Machine Learning Challenges*, Volume 3944 of *Lecture Notes in Computer Science*, pp. 177–190. Springer.

de Marneffe, M.-C., A. N. Rafferty, and C. D. Manning (2008). Finding contradictions in text. In *Proceedings of the ACL*, Columbus, Ohio, pp. 1039–1047.

Hickl, A., J. Williams, J. Bensley, K. Roberts, B. Rink, and Y. Shi (2006). Recognizing textual entailment with LCC's Groundhog system. In *Proceedings of the Second PASCAL Challenges Workshop*.

Manning, C. D., P. Raghavan, and H. Schütze (2008). *Introduction to Information Retrieval* (1st ed.). Cambridge University Press.

Monz, C. and M. de Rijke (2001). Light-weight entailment checking for computational semantics. In *Proceedings of ICoS*, Siena, Italy, pp. 59–72.

Sammons, M., V. Vydiswaran, and D. Roth (2010). "Ask Not What Textual Entailment Can Do for You...". In *Proceedings of ACL*, Uppsala, Sweden, pp. 1199–1208.

Schmid, H. (1995). Improvements in part-of-speech tagging with an application to german. In *Proceedings of the SIGDAT Workshop at ACL*, Cambridge, MA.

Xiao, Z., T. McEnery, P. Baker, and A. Hardie (2004). Developing Asian language corpora: Standards and practice. In *In Proceedings of the Fourth Workshop on Asian Language Resources*, Sanya, China, pp. 1–8.

Integrating Logical Representations with Probabilistic Information using Markov Logic

Dan Garrette
University of Texas at Austin
dhg@cs.utexas.edu

Katrin Erk
University of Texas at Austin
katrin.erk@mail.utexas.edu

Raymond Mooney
University of Texas at Austin
mooney@cs.utexas.edu

Abstract

First-order logic provides a powerful and flexible mechanism for representing natural language semantics. However, it is an open question of how best to integrate it with uncertain, probabilistic knowledge, for example regarding word meaning. This paper describes the first steps of an approach to recasting first-order semantics into the probabilistic models that are part of Statistical Relational AI. Specifically, we show how Discourse Representation Structures can be combined with distributional models for word meaning inside a Markov Logic Network and used to successfully perform inferences that take advantage of logical concepts such as factivity as well as probabilistic information on word meaning in context.

1 Introduction

Logic-based representations of natural language meaning have a long history. Representing the meaning of language in a first-order logical form is appealing because it provides a powerful and flexible way to express even complex propositions. However, systems built solely using first-order logical forms tend to be very brittle as they have no way of integrating uncertain knowledge. They, therefore, tend to have high precision at the cost of low recall (Bos and Markert, 2005).

Recent advances in computational linguistics have yielded robust methods that use weighted or probabilistic models. For example, distributional models of word meaning have been used successfully to judge paraphrase appropriateness. This has been done by representing the word meaning in context as a point in a high-dimensional semantics space (Erk and Padó, 2008; Thater et al., 2010; Erk and Padó, 2010). However, these models typically handle only individual phenomena instead of providing a meaning representation for complete sentences. It is a long-standing open question how best to integrate the weighted or probabilistic information coming from such modules with logic-based representations in a way that allows for reasoning over both. See, for example, Hobbs et al. (1993).

The goal of this work is to combine logic-based meaning representations with probabilities in a single unified framework. This will allow us to obtain the best of both situations: we will have the full expressivity of first-order logic and be able to reason with probabilities. We believe that this will allow for a more complete and robust approach to natural language understanding. In order to perform logical inference with probabilities, we draw from the large and active body of work related to Statistical Relational AI (Getoor and Taskar, 2007). Specifically, we make use of Markov Logic Networks (MLNs) (Richardson and Domingos, 2006) which employ weighted graphical models to represent first-order logical formulas. MLNs are appropriate for our approach because they provide an elegant method of assigning weights to first-order logical rules, combining a diverse set of inference rules, and performing inference in a probabilistic way.

While this is a large and complex task, this paper proposes a series of first steps toward our goal. In this paper, we focus on three natural language phenomena and their interaction: implicativity and factivity, word meaning, and coreference. Our framework parses natural language into a logical form, adds rule weights computed by external NLP modules, and performs inferences using an MLN. Our end-to-end approach integrates multiple existing tools. We use Boxer (Bos et al., 2004) to parse natural language into a logical form. We use Alchemy (Kok et al., 2005) for MLN inference. Finally, we use the exemplar-based distributional model of Erk and Padó (2010) to produce rule weights.

2 Background

Logic-based semantics. Boxer (Bos et al., 2004) is a software package for wide-coverage semantic analysis that provides semantic representations in the form of Discourse Representation Structures (Kamp and Reyle, 1993). It builds on the C&C CCG parser (Clark and Curran, 2004). Bos and Markert (2005) describe a system for Recognizing Textual Entailment (RTE) that uses Boxer to convert both the premise and hypothesis of an RTE pair into first-order logical semantic representations and then uses a theorem prover to check for logical entailment.

Distributional models for lexical meaning. Distributional models describe the meaning of a word through the context in which it appears (Landauer and Dumais, 1997; Lund and Burgess, 1996), where contexts can be documents, other words, or snippets of syntactic structure. Distributional models are able to predict semantic similarity between words based on distributional similarity and they can be learned in an unsupervised fashion. Recently distributional models have been used to predict the applicability of paraphrases in context (Mitchell and Lapata, 2008; Erk and Padó, 2008; Thater et al., 2010; Erk and Padó, 2010). For example, in "The wine left a stain", "result in" is a better paraphrase for "leave" than is "entrust", while the opposite is true in "He left the children with the nurse". Usually, the distributional representation for a word mixes all its usages (senses). For the paraphrase appropriateness task, these representations are then reweighted, extended, or filtered to focus on contextually appropriate usages.

Markov Logic. An MLN consists of a set of weighted first-order clauses. It provides a way of softening first-order logic by making situations in which not all clauses are satisfied less likely but not impossible (Richardson and Domingos, 2006). More formally, let X be the set of all propositions describing a world (i.e. the set of all ground atoms), $\mathcal{F}$ be the set of all clauses in the MLN, w_i be the weight associated with clause $f_i \in \mathcal{F}$, $\mathcal{G}_{f_i}$ be the set of all possible groundings of clause f_i, and $\mathcal{Z}$ be the normalization constant. Then the probability of a particular truth assignment $\mathbf{x}$ to the variables in X is defined as:

$$P(X = \mathbf{x}) = \frac{1}{\mathcal{Z}} \exp\left(\sum_{f_i \in \mathcal{F}} w_i \sum_{g \in \mathcal{G}_{f_i}} g(\mathbf{x})\right) = \frac{1}{\mathcal{Z}} \exp\left(\sum_{f_i \in \mathcal{F}} w_i n_i(\mathbf{x})\right) \quad (1)$$

where $g(\mathbf{x})$ is 1 if g is satisfied and 0 otherwise, and $n_i(\mathbf{x}) = \sum_{g \in \mathcal{G}_{f_i}} g(\mathbf{x})$ is the number of groundings of f_i that are satisfied given the current truth assignment to the variables in X. This means that the probability of a truth assignment rises exponentially with the number of groundings that are satisfied.

Markov Logic has been used previously in other NLP application (e.g. Poon and Domingos (2009)). However, this paper marks the first attempt at representing deep logical semantics in an MLN.

While it is possible learn rule weights in an MLN directly from training data, our approach at this time focuses on incorporating weights computed by external knowledge sources. Weights for word meaning rules are computed from the distributional model of lexical meaning and then injected into the MLN. Rules governing implicativity and coreference are given infinite weight (hard constraints).

3 Evaluation and phenomena

Textual entailment offers a good framework for testing whether a system performs correct analyses and thus draws the right inferences from a given text. For example, to test whether a system correctly handles implicative verbs, one can use the *premise* p along with the *hypothesis* h in (1) below. If the system analyses the two sentences correctly, it should infer that h holds. While the most prominent forum using textual entailment is the Recognizing Textual Entailment (RTE) challenge (Dagan et al., 2005), the RTE datasets do not test the phenomena in which we are interested. For example, in order to evaluate our system's ability to determine word meaning in context, the RTE pair would have to specifically test word sense confusion by having a word's context in the hypothesis be different from the context of the premise. However, this simply does not occur in the RTE corpora. In order to properly test our phenomena, we construct hand-tailored premises and hypotheses based on real-world texts.

In this paper, we focus on three natural language phenomena and their interaction: implicativity and factivity, word meaning, and coreference. The first phenomenon, implicativity and factivity, is concerned with analyzing the truth conditions of nested propositions. For example, in the premise of the entailment pair shown in example (1), "arrange that" falls under the scope of "forget to" and "fail" is under the scope of "arrange that". Correctly recognizing nested propositions is necessary for preventing false inferences such as the one in example (2).

(1) p: Ed did not forget to arrange that Dave fail[1]
h: Dave failed

(2) p: The mayor hoped to build a new stadium[2]
h*: The mayor built a new stadium

For the second phenomenon, word meaning, we address paraphrasing and hypernymy. For example, in (3) "covering" is a good paraphrase for "sweeping" while "brushing" is not.

(3) p: A stadium craze is **sweeping** the country
h_1: A stadium craze is **covering** the country
h_2*: A stadium craze is **brushing** the country

The third phenomenon is coreference, as illustrated in (4). For this example, to correctly judge the hypothesis as entailed, it is necessary to recognize that "he" corefers with "Christopher" and "the new ballpark" corefers with "a replacement for Candlestick Park".

(4) p: George Christopher has been a critic of the plan to build a replacement for Candlestick Park. As a result, he won't endorse the new ballpark.
h: Christopher won't endorse a replacement for Candlestick Park.

Some natural language phenomena are most naturally treated as categorial, while others are more naturally treated using weights or probabilities. In this paper, we treat implicativity and coreference as categorial phenomena, while using a probabilistic approach to word meaning.

4 Transforming natural language text to logical form

In transforming natural language text to logical form, we build on the software package Boxer (Bos et al., 2004). We chose to use Boxer for two main reasons. First, Boxer is a wide-coverage system that can deal with arbitrary text. Second, the DRSs that Boxer produces are close to the standard first-order logical forms that are required for use by the MLN software package Alchemy. Our system transforms Boxer output into a format that Alchemy can read and augments it with additional information.

To demonstrate our transformation procedure, consider again the premise of example (1). When given to Boxer, the sentence produces the output given in Figure 1a. We then transform this output to the format given in Figure 1b.

Flat structure. In Boxer output, nested propositional statements are represented as nested sub-DRS structures. For example, in the premise of (1), the verbs "forget to" and "arrange that" both introduce nested propositions, as is shown in Figure 1a where DRS *x3* (the "arranging that") is the *theme* of "forget to" and DRS *x5* (the "failing") is the *theme* of "arrange that".

In order to write logical rules about the truth conditions of nested propositions, the structure has to be flattened. However, it is clearly not sufficient to just conjoin all propositions at the top level. Such an approach, applied to example (2), would yield $(hope(x_1) \wedge theme(x_1, x_2) \wedge build(x_2) \wedge \ldots)$, leading to the wrong inference that the stadium was built. Instead, we add a new argument to each predicate that

[1]Examples (1) and (16) and Figure 2 are based on examples by MacCartney and Manning (2009)

[2]Examples (2), (3), (4), and (18) are modified versions of sentences from document wsj_0126 from the Penn Treebank

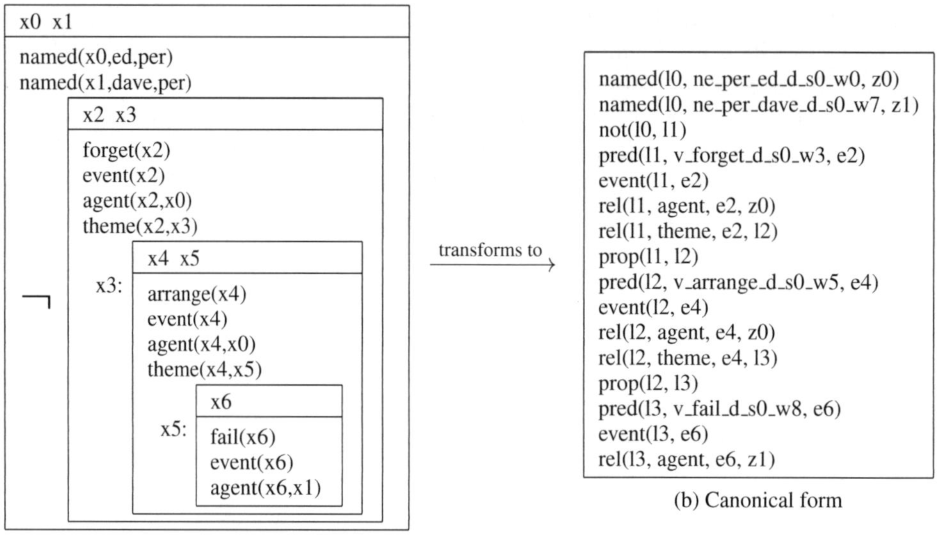

(b) Canonical form

(a) Output from Boxer

Figure 1: Converting the premise of (1) from Boxer output to MLN input

names the DRS in which the predicate originally occurred. Assigning the label *l1* to the DRS containing the predicate *forget*, we add *l1* as the first argument to the atom *pred(l1, v_forget_d_s0_w3, e2)*.[3] Having flattened the structure, we need to re-introduce the information about relations between DRSs. For this we use predicates *not*, *imp*, and *or* whose arguments are DRS labels. For example, $not(l0, l1)$ states that $l1$ is inside $l0$ and negated. Additionally, an atom $prop(l0, l1)$ indicates that DRS $l0$ has a subordinate DRS labeled $l1$.

One important consequence of our flat structure is that the truth conditions of our representation no longer coincide with the truth conditions of the underlying DRS being represented. For example, we do not directly express the fact that the "forgetting" is actually negated, since the negation is only expressed as a relation between DRS labels. To access the information encoded in relations between DRS labels, we add predicates that capture the truth conditions of the underlying DRS. We use the predicates $true(label)$ and $false(label)$ that state whether the DRS referenced by $label$ is *true* or *false*. We also add rules that govern how the predicates for logical operators interact with these truth values. For example, the rules in (5) state that if a DRS is *true*, then any negated subordinate must be *false* and vice versa.

$$\forall\, p\, n.[not(p, n) \rightarrow (true(p) \leftrightarrow false(n)) \wedge (false(p) \leftrightarrow true(n))] \quad (5)$$

Injecting additional information into the logical form. We want to augment Boxer output with additional information, for example gold coreference annotation for sentences that we subsequently analyze with Boxer. In order to do so, we need to be able to tie predicates in the Boxer output back to words in the original sentence. Fortunately, the optional "Prolog" output format from Boxer provides the sentence and word indices from the original sentence. When parsing the Boxer output, we extract these indices and concatenate them to the word lemma to specific the exact occurrence of the lemma that is under discussion. For example, the atom *pred(l1, v_forget_d_s0_w3, e2)* indicates that event *e2* refers to the lemma "forget" that appears in the 0th sentence of discourse *d* at word index 3.

Atomic formulas. We represent the words from the sentence as arguments instead of predicates in order to simplify the set of inference rules we need to specify. Because our flattened structure requires that the inference mechanism be reimplemented as a set of logical rules, it is desirable for us to be able to write general rules that govern the interaction of atoms. With the representation we have chosen, we can quantify over all predicates or all relations. For example, the rule in (6) states that a predicate is accessible if it is found in an out-scoping DRS.

[3]The extension to the word, such as *d_s0_w3* for "forget", is an index providing the location of the original word that triggered this atom; this is addressed in more detail shortly.

	signature	example
managed to	+/-	he managed to escape $\models$ he escaped he did not manage to escape $\models$ he did not escape
refused to	-/o	he refused to fight $\models$ he did not fight he did not refuse to fight $\not\models$ {he fought, he did not fight}

Figure 2: Implication Signatures

$$\forall\, l_1\, l_2.[outscopes(l_1, l_2) \rightarrow \forall\, p\, x.[pred(l_1, p, x) \rightarrow pred(l_2, p, x)]] \tag{6}$$

We use three different predicate symbols to distinguish three types of atomic concepts: predicates, named entities, and relations. Predicates and named entities represent words that appear in the text. For example, *named(l0, ne_per_ed_d_s0_w0, z0)* indicates that variable *z0* is a person named "Ed" while *pred(l1, v_forget_d_s0_w3, e2)* says that *e2* is a "forgetting to" event. Relations capture the relationships between words. For example, *rel(l1, agent, e2, z0)* indicates that *z0*, "Ed", is the "agent" of the "forgetting to" event *e2*.

5 Handling the phenomena

Implicatives and factives

Nairn et al. (2006) presented an approach to the treatment of inferences involving implicatives and factives. Their approach identifies an "implication signature" for every implicative or factive verb that determines the truth conditions for the verb's nested proposition, whether in a positive or negative environment. Implication signatures take the form "x/y" where x represents the implicativity in the the positive environment and y represents the implicativity in the negative environment. Both x and y have three possible values: "+" for positive entailment, meaning the nested proposition is entailed, "-" for negative entailment, meaning the negation of the proposition is entailed, and "o" for "null" entailment, meaning that neither the proposition nor its negation is entailed. Figure 2 gives concrete examples.

We use these implication signatures to automatically generate rules that license specific entailments in the MLN. Since "forget to" has implication signature "-/+", we generate the two rules in (7).

(7) (a) $\forall\, l_1\, l_2\, e.[(pred(l_1, \text{"}forget\text{"}, e) \wedge true(l_1) \wedge rel(l_1, \text{"}theme\text{"}, e, l_2) \wedge prop(l_1, l_2)) \rightarrow false(l_2)]]$[4]
(b) $\forall\, l_1\, l_2\, e.[(pred(l_1, \text{"}forget\text{"}, e) \wedge false(l_1) \wedge rel(l_1, \text{"}theme\text{"}, e, l_2) \wedge prop(l_1, l_2)) \rightarrow true(l_2)]$

To understand these rules, consider (7a). The rule says that if the atom for the verb "forget to" appears in a DRS that has been determined to be *true*, then the DRS representing any "theme" proposition of that verb should be considered *false*. Likewise, (7b) says that if the occurrence of "forget to" appears in a DRS determined to be *false*, then the theme DRS should be considered *true*.

Note that when the implication signature indicates a "null" entailment, no rule is generated for that case. This prevents the MLN from licensing entailments related directly to the nested proposition, but still allows for entailments that include the factive verb. So *he wanted to fly* entails neither *he flew* nor *he did not fly*, but it does still license *he wanted to fly*.

Ambiguity in word meaning

In order for our system to be able to make correct natural language inference, it must be able to handle paraphrasing and deal with hypernymy. For example, in order to license the entailment pair in (8), the system must recognize that "owns" is a valid paraphrase for "has", and that "car" is a hypernym of "convertible".

(8) *p:* Ed has a convertible
h: Ed owns a car

[4]Occurrence-indexing on the predicate "forget" has been left out for brevity.

In this section we discuss our probabilistic approach to paraphrasing. In the next section we discuss how this approach is extended to cover hypernymy. A central problem to solve in the context of paraphrases is that they are context-dependent. Consider again example (3) and its two hypotheses. The first hypothesis replaces the word "sweeping" with a paraphrase that is valid in the given context, while the second uses an incorrect paraphrase.

To incorporate paraphrasing information into our system, we first generate rules stating all paraphrase relationships that may *possibly* apply to a given predicate/hypothesis pair, using WordNet (Miller, 2009) as a resource. Then we associate those rules with weights to signal contextual adequacy. For any two occurrence-indexed words w_1, w_2 occurring anywhere in the premise or hypothesis, we check whether they co-occur in a WordNet synset. If w_1, w_2 have a common synset, we generate rules of the form $\forall\ l\ x.[pred(l, w_1, x) \leftrightarrow pred(l, w_2, x)]$ to connect them. For named entities, we perform a similar routine: for each pair of matching named entities found in the premise and hypothesis, we generate a rule $\forall\ l\ x.[named(l, w_1, x) \leftrightarrow named(l, w_2, x)]$.

We then use the distributional model of Erk and Padó (2010) to compute paraphrase appropriateness. In the case of (3) this means measuring the cosine similarity between the vectors for "sweep" and "cover" (and between "sweep" and "brush") in the sentential context of the premise. MLN formula weights are expected to be log-odds (i.e., $\log(P/(1-P))$ for some probability P), so we rank all possible paraphrases of a given word w by their cosine similarity to w and then give them probabilities that decrease by rank according to a Zipfian distribution. So, the kth closest paraphrase by cosine similarity will have probability P_k given by (9):

$$P_k \sim 1/k \tag{9}$$

The generated rules are given in (10) with the actual weights calculated for example (3). Note that the valid paraphrase "cover" is given a higher weight than the incorrect paraphrase "brush", which allows the MLN inference procedure to judge h_1 as a more likely entailment than h_2.[5] This same result would not be achieved if we did not take context into consideration because, without context, "brush" is a more likely paraphrase of "sweep" than "cover".

(10) (a) -2.602 $\forall\ l\ x.[pred(l, \text{“}v\_sweep\_p\_s0\_w4\text{”}, x) \leftrightarrow pred(l, \text{“}v\_cover\_h\_s0\_w4\text{”}, x)]$

(b) -3.842 $\forall\ l\ x.[pred(l, \text{“}v\_sweep\_p\_s0\_w4\text{”}, x) \leftrightarrow pred(l, \text{“}v\_brush\_h\_s0\_w4\text{”}, x)]$

Since Alchemy outputs a probability of entailment and not a binary judgment, it is necessary to specify a probability threshold indicating entailment. An appropriate threshold between "entailment" and "non-entailment" will be one that separates the probability of an inference with the valid rule from the probability of an inference with the invalid rule. While we plan to automatically induce a threshold in the future, our current implementation uses a value set manually.

Hypernymy

Like paraphrasehood, hypernymy is context-dependent: In "A bat flew out of the cave", "animal" is an appropriate hypernym for "bat", but "artifact" is not. So we again use distributional similarity to determine contextual appropriateness. However, we do not directly compute cosine similarities between a word and its potential hypernym. We can hardly assume "baseball bat" and "artifact" to occur in similar distributional contexts. So instead of checking for similarity of "bat" and "artifact" in a given context, we check "bat" and "club". That is, we pick a synonym or close hypernym of the word in question ("bat") that is also a WordNet hyponym of the hypernym to check ("artifact").

A second problem to take into account is the interaction of hypernymy and polarity. While (8) is a valid pair, (11) is not, because "have a convertible" is under negation. So, we create weighted rules of the form $hypernym(w, h)$, along with inference rules to guide their interaction with polarity. We create

[5] Because weights are calculated according to the equation $\log(P/(1-P))$, any paraphrase that has a probability of less than 0.5 will have a negative weight. Since most paraphrases will have probabilities less than 0.5, most will yield negative rule weights. However, the inferences are still handled properly in the MLN because the inference is dependent on the *relative* weights.

these rules for all pairs of words w, h in premise and hypothesis such that h is a hypernym of w, again using WordNet to determine potential hypernymy.

(11) *p:* Ed does not have a convertible
h: Ed does not own a car

Our inference rules governing the interaction of hypernymy and polarity are given in (12). The rule in (12a) states that in a positive environment, the hyponym entails the hypernym while the rule in (12b) states that in a negative environment, the opposite is true: the hypernym entails the hyponym.

(12) (a) $\forall\, l\; p_1\; p_2\; x.[(hypernym(p_1, p_2) \wedge true(l) \wedge pred(l, p_1, x)) \rightarrow pred(l, p_2, x)]]$
(b) $\forall\, l\; p_1\; p_2\; x.[(hypernym(p_1, p_2) \wedge false(l) \wedge pred(l, p_2, x)) \rightarrow pred(l, p_1, x)]]$

Making use of coreference information

As a test case for incorporating additional resources into Boxer's logical form, we used the coreference data in OntoNotes (Hovy et al., 2006). However, the same mechanism would allow us to transfer information into Boxer output from arbitrary additional NLP tools such as automatic coreference analysis tools or semantic role labelers. Our system uses coreference information into two distinct ways.

The first way we make use of coreference data is to copy atoms describing a particular variable to those variables that corefer. Consider again example (4) which has a two-sentence premise. This inference requires recognizing that the "he" in the second sentence of the premise refers to "George Christopher" from the first sentence. Boxer alone is unable to make this connection, but if we receive this information as input, either from gold-labeled data or a third-party coreference tool, we are able to incorporate it. Since Boxer is able to identify the index of the word that generated a particular predicate, we can tie each predicate to any related coreference chains. Then, for each atom on the chain, we can inject copies of all of the coreferring atoms, replacing the variables to match. For example, the word "he" generates an atom *pred(l0, male, z5)*[6] and "Christopher" generates atom *named(l0, christopher, x0)*. So, we can create a new atom by taking the atom for "christopher" and replacing the label and variable with that of the atom for "he", generating *named(l0, christopher, x5)*.

As a more complex example, the coreference information will inform us that "the new ballpark" corefers with "a replacement for Candlestick Park". However, our system is currently unable to handle this coreference correctly at this time because, unlike the previous example, the expression "a replacement for Candlestick Park" results in a complex three-atom conjunct with two separate variables: *pred(l2, replacement, x6)*, *rel(l2, for, x6, x7)*, and *named(l2, candlestick_park, x7)*. Now, unifying with the atom for "a ballpark", *pred(l0, ballpark, x3)*, is not as simple as replacing the variable because there are two variables to choose from. Note that it would *not* be correct to replace both variables since this would result in a unification of "ballpark" with "candlestick_park" which is wrong. Instead we must determine that *x6* should be the one to unify with *x3* while *x7* is replaced with a fresh variable. The way that we can accomplish this is to look at the dependency parse of the sentence that is produced by the C&C parser is a precursor to running Boxer. By looking up both "replacement" and "Candlestick Park" in the parse, we can determine that "replacement" is the head of the phrase, and thus is the atom whose variable should be unified. So, we would create new atoms, *pred(l0, replacement, x3)*, *rel(l0, for, x3, z0)*, and *named(l0, candlestick_park, z0)*, where *z0* is a fresh variable.

The second way that we make use of coreference information is to extend the sentential contexts used for calculating the appropriateness of paraphrases in the distributional model. In the simplest case, the sentential context of a word would simply be the other words in the sentence. However, consider the context of the word "lost" in the second sentence of (13).

(13) p_1: In [the final game of the season]$_1$, [the team]$_2$ held on to their lead until overtime
p_2: But despite that, [they]$_2$ eventually **lost** [it all]$_1$

[6] Atoms simplified for brevity

Here we would like to disambiguate "lost", but its immediate context, words like "despite" and "eventually", gives no indication as to its correct sense. Our procedure extends the context of the sentence by incorporating all of the words from all of the phrases that corefer with a word in the immediate context. Since coreference chains 1 and 2 have words in p_2, the context of "lost" ends up including "final", "game", "season", and "team" which give a strong indication of the sense of "lost". Note that using coreference data is stronger than simply expanding the window because coreferences can cover arbitrarily long distances.

6 Evaluation

As a preliminary evaluation of our system, we constructed a set of demonstrative examples to test our ability to handle the previously discussed phenomena and their interactions and ran each example with both a theorem prover and Alchemy. Note that when running an example in the theorem prover, weights are not possible, so any rule that would be weighted in an MLN is simply treated as a "hard clause" following Bos and Markert (2005).

Checking the logical form. We constructed a list of 72 simple examples that exhaustively cover cases of implicativity (positive, negative, null entailments in both positive and negative environments), hypernymy, quantification, and the interaction between implicativity and hypernymy. The purpose of these simple tests is to ensure that our flattened logical form and truth condition rules correctly maintain the semantics of the underlying DRSs. Examples are given in (14).

(14) (a) The mayor did not manage to build a stadium $\not\models$ The mayor built a stadium
(b) Fido is a dog and every dog walks $\models$ A dog walks

Examples in previous sections. Examples (1), (2), (3), (8), and (11) all come out as expected. Each of these examples demonstrates one of the phenomena in isolation. However, example (4) returns "not entailed", the incorrect answer. As discussed previously, this failure is a result of our system's inability to correctly incorporate the complex coreferring expression "a replacement for Candlestick Park". However, the system *is* able to correctly incorporate the coreference of "he" in the second sentence to "Christopher" in the first.

Implicativity and word sense. For example (15), "fail to" is a negatively entailing implicative in a positive environment. So, p correctly entails h_{good} in both the theorem prover and Alchemy. However, the theorem prover incorrectly licenses the entailment of h_{bad} while Alchemy does not. The probabilistic approach performs better in this situation because the categorial approach does not distinguish between a good paraphrase and a bad one. This example also demonstrates the advantage of using a context-sensitive distributional model to calculate the probabilities of paraphrases because "reward" is an *a priori* better paraphrase than "observe" according to WordNet since it appears in a higher ranked synset.

(15) p: The U.S. is watching closely as South Korea fails to honor U.S. patents[7]
h_{good}: South Korea does not **observe** U.S. patents
h_{bad}: South Korea does not **reward** U.S. patents

Implicativity and hypernymy. MacCartney and Manning (2009) extended the work by Nairn et al. (2006) in order to correctly treat inference involving monotonicity and exclusion. Our approaches to implicatives and factivity and hyper/hyponymy combine naturally to address these issues because of the structure of our logical representations and rules. For example, no additional work is required to license the entailments in (16).

(16) (a) John refused to dance $\models$ John didn't tango
(b) John did not forget to tango $\models$ John danced

[7]Example (15) is adapted from Penn Treebank document wsj_0020 while (17) is adapted from document wsj_2358

Example (17) demonstrates how our system combines categorial implicativity with a probabilistic approach to hypernymy. The verb "anticipate that" is positively entailing in the negative environment. The verb "moderate" can mean "chair" as in "chair a discussion" or "curb" as in "curb spending". Since "restrain" is a hypernym of "curb", it receives a weight based on the applicability of the word "curb" in the context. Similarly, "talk" receives a weight based on its hyponym "chair". Since our model predicts "curb" to be a more probable paraphrase of "moderate" in this context than "chair" (even though the priors according to WordNet are reversed), the system is able to infer h_{good} while rejecting h_{bad}.

(17) p: He did not anticipate that inflation would moderate this year
h_{good}: Inflation **restrained** this year
h_{bad}: Inflation **talked** this year

Word sense, coreference, and hypernymy. Example (18) demonstrates the interaction between paraphrase, hypernymy, and coreference incorporated into a single entailment. The relevant coreference chains are marked explicitly in the example. The correct inference relies on recognizing that "he" in the hypothesis refers to "Joe Robbie" and "it" to "coliseum", which is a hyponym of "stadium". Further, our model recognizes that "sizable" is a better paraphrase for "healthy" than "intelligent" even though WordNet has the reverse order.

(18) p: [Joe Robbie]$_{53}$ couldn't persuade the mayor , so [he]$_{53}$ built [[his]$_{53}$ own coliseum]$_{54}$. [He]$_{53}$ has used [it]$_{54}$ to turn a healthy profit.[8]
h_{good}: *Joe Robbie* used *a stadium* to turn a **sizable** profit
h_{bad-1}: *Joe Robbie* used *a stadium* to turn an **intelligent** profit
h_{bad-2}: *The mayor* used *a stadium* to turn a healthy profit

7 Future work

The next step is to execute a full-scale evaluation of our approach using more varied phenomena and naturally occurring sentences. However, the memory requirements of Alchemy are a limitation that prevents us from currently executing larger and more complex examples. The problem arises because Alchemy considers every possible grounding of every atom, even when a more focused subset of atoms and inference rules would suffice. There is on-going work to modify Alchemy so that only the required groundings are incorporated into the network, reducing the size of the model and thus making it possible to handle more complex inferences. We will be able to begin using this new version of Alchemy very soon and our task will provide an excellent test case for the modification.

Since Alchemy outputs a probability of entailment, it is necessary to fix a threshold that separates entailment from nonentailment. We plan to use machine learning techniques to compute an appropriate threshold automatically from a calibration dataset such as a corpus of valid and invalid paraphrases.

8 Conclusion

In this paper, we have introduced a system that implements a first step towards integrating logical semantic representations with probabilistic weights using methods from Statistical Relational AI, particularly Markov Logic. We have focused on three phenomena and their interaction: implicatives, coreference, and word meaning. Taking implicatives and coreference as categorial and word meaning as probabilistic, we have used a distributional model to generate paraphrase appropriateness ratings, which we then transformed into weights on first order formulas. The resulting MLN approach is able to correctly solve a number of difficult textual entailment problems that require handling complex combinations of these important semantic phenomena.

[8] Only relevent coreferences have been marked

References

Bos, J., S. Clark, M. Steedman, J. R. Curran, and J. Hockenmaier (2004). Wide-coverage semantic representations from a CCG parser. In *Proceedings of COLING 2004*, Geneva, Switzerland, pp. 1240–1246.

Bos, J. and K. Markert (2005). Recognising textual entailment with logical inference. In *Proceedings of EMNLP 2005*, pp. 628–635.

Clark, S. and J. R. Curran (2004). Parsing the WSJ using CCG and log-linear models. In *Proceedings of ACL 2004*, Barcelona, Spain, pp. 104–111.

Dagan, I., O. Glickman, and B. Magnini (2005). The pascal recognising textual entailment challenge. In *In Proceedings of the PASCAL Challenges Workshop on Recognising Textual Entailment.*

Erk, K. and S. Padó (2008). A structured vector space model for word meaning in context. In *Proceedings of EMNLP 2008*, Honolulu, HI, pp. 897–906.

Erk, K. and S. Padó (2010). Exemplar-based models for word meaning in context. In *Proceedings of ACL 2010*, Uppsala, Sweden, pp. 92–97.

Getoor, L. and B. Taskar (Eds.) (2007). *Introduction to Statistical Relational Learning*. Cambridge, MA: MIT Press.

Hobbs, J. R., M. Stickel, D. Appelt, and P. Martin (1993). Interpretation as abduction. *Artificial Intelligence 63*(1–2), 69–142.

Hovy, E., M. Marcus, M. Palmer, L. Ramshaw, and R. Weischedel (2006). Ontonotes: The 90% solution. In *Proceedings of HLT/NAACL 2006*, pp. 57–60.

Kamp, H. and U. Reyle (1993). *From Discourse to Logic; An Introduction to Modeltheoretic Semantics of Natural Language, Formal Logic and DRT*. Dordrecht: Kluwer.

Kok, S., P. Singla, M. Richardson, and P. Domingos (2005). The Alchemy system for statistical relational AI. Technical report, Department of Computer Science and Engineering, University of Washington. `http://www.cs.washington.edu/ai/alchemy`.

Landauer, T. and S. Dumais (1997). A solution to Platos problem: the latent semantic analysis theory of acquisition, induction, and representation of knowledge. *Psychological Review 104*(2), 211–240.

Lund, K. and C. Burgess (1996). Producing high-dimensional semantic spaces from lexical co-occurrence. *Behavior Research Methods, Instruments, and Computers 28*, 203—208.

MacCartney, B. and C. D. Manning (2009). An extended model of natural logic. In *Proceedings of the Eighth International Conference on Computational Semantics (IWCS-8)*, pp. 140–156.

Miller, G. A. (2009). Wordnet - about us. `http://wordnet.princeton.edu`.

Mitchell, J. and M. Lapata (2008). Vector-based models of semantic composition. In *Proceedings of ACL*, pp. 236–244.

Nairn, R., C. Condoravdi, and L. Karttunen (2006). Computing relative polarity for textual inference. In *Proceedings of Inference in Computational Semantics (ICoS-5)*, Buxton, UK.

Poon, H. and P. Domingos (2009). Unsupervised semantic parsing. In *Proceedings of EMNLP 2009*, pp. 1–10.

Richardson, M. and P. Domingos (2006). Markov logic networks. *Machine Learning 62*, 107–136.

Thater, S., H. Fürstenau, and M. Pinkal (2010). Contextualizing semantic representations using syntactically enriched vector models. In *Proceedings of ACL 2010*, Uppsala, Sweden, pp. 948–957.

An Abstract Schema for Representing Semantic Roles and Modelling the Syntax-Semantics Interface

Voula Gotsoulia
University of Essex
vghotsoulia@yahoo.co.uk

Abstract

This paper presents a novel approach to semantic role annotation implementing an entailment-based view of the concept of semantic role. I propose to represent arguments of predicates with grammatically relevant primitive properties entailed by the semantics of predicates. Such meaning components generalise over a range of semantic relations which humans tend to express systematically through language. In a preliminary study, I show that we can model linguistic knowledge at a general, principled syntax-semantics interface by incorporating a layer of skeletal, entailment-based representation of word meaning in large-scale corpus annotation.

1 Introduction

Large-scale lexical semantic resources that provide *relational* information about words have recently received much focus in the field of Natural Language Processing (NLP). In particular, data-driven models for lexical semantics require the creation of broad-coverage, hand-annotated corpora with *predicate-argument* information, i.e. rich information about words expressing a semantic relation having argument slots filled by the interpretations of their grammatical complements. Corpora combining semantic and syntactic annotations constitute the backbone for the development of probabilistic models that automatically identify the semantic relationships, or *semantic roles*, conveyed by sentential constituents (Gildea and Jurafsky, 2002). That is, given an input sentence and a target *predicator* the system labels constituents with general roles like Agent, Patient, Theme, etc., or more specific roles, as in (1).

(1) [$_{Cognizer}$ I] *admired* [$_{Evaluee}$ him] [$_{Degree}$ greatly] [$_{Reason}$ for his bravery and his cheerfulness].[1]

The task of *automatic semantic role labelling* (or *shallow semantic parsing*) is a first step towards text understanding and has found use in a variety of NLP applications including information extraction (Surdeanu et al., 2003), machine translation (Boas, 2002), question answering (Narayanan and Harabagiu, 2004), summarisation (Melli et al., 2005), recognition of textual entailment relations (Burchardt and Frank, 2006), etc.

Corpora with semantic role labels additionally lend themselves to extraction of linguistic knowledge at the *syntax-semantics interface*. The range of semantic and syntactic combinatorial properties (*valences*) of each word in each of its senses is documented in terms of annotated corpus attestations. For instance, the valence pattern for the use of *admire* in (1) is shown in (2).

(2) *Cognizer*: Noun Phrase (NP), Subject
Evaluee: Noun Phrase (NP), Object
Degree: Adverbial Dependent
Reason: Prepositional Dependent

[1] This annotated example is from the FrameNet lexicon (discussed in the next section). In all examples throughout the paper, predicators are marked in italics.

This data enables the quantitative study of various linguistic phenomena and the investigation of the relationship between the distinct linguistic layers comprised by predicate-argument analysis. Furthermore, the formulation of *generalisations* over predicate-specific annotations can capture how predicates relate in terms of both semantic and syntactic features. Such syntax-semantics mappings (so-called *linking generalisations*) encode regularities concerning the associations of semantic roles with grammatical functions and are essential for a *linguistic knowledge base* for NLP applications.

This paper addresses the problem of generalising over the valences of individual predicators and proposes an abstract semantic basis for the representation of participant roles. The definition of semantic notions at an appropriate level of abstraction is the prerequisite for the formulation of a general, principled syntax-semantics interface. This is in accordance with a somewhat intuitive conception of semantic roles as classificatory notions encoding semantic similarities across different types of events or situations in the world. In effect, all conceptions of semantic roles as opposed to predicate-specific roles, such as *admirer-admired*, posit some sort of semantic classification of arguments across predicators while indicating an acknowledgment that the syntax-semantics interface (referred to with the term *linking*) is not completely arbitrary. Put differently, semantic roles constitute a level of representation suitable for capturing semantic generalisations which humans tend to express *systematically* through language.

The structure of the paper is organised as follows. Section 2 looks at conceptions of semantic roles in state-of-the-art approaches to semantic annotation indicating problems or complications related to the question of whether or how these roles can support generalisations across predicates. Section 3 calls attention to the theoretical underpinnings of the notion of semantic role and introduces an annotation schema which departs from the traditional view of semantic roles as atomic, undecomposable categories. Following the insight of Dowty's (1991) theory of Proto-Roles, I will propose analytical representations of verbal arguments based on semantically well-founded, grammatically relevant meaning components entailed by the semantics of predicates (*Proto-Role entailments*). Finally, section 4 presents a study in which lexical entailments are marked in a corpus in accordance with the proposed schema. General syntax-semantics mappings are extracted from the annotated data and are formalised in abstract classes which readily encode generalisations concerning linking to syntactic form.

2 Corpora with Semantic Roles and Related Work

Semantically annotated corpora currently available for English implement two distinct approaches to the prickly notion of semantic role. The Proposition Bank (PropBank) (Kingsbury et al., 2002) is a one million word corpus in which predicate-argument relations are hand-annotated for every occurrence of every verb in the Wall Street Journal part of the Penn Treebank (Marcus et al., 1994). Verb senses are distinguished informally on the basis of semantic as well as syntactic criteria. The semantic arguments of a verb are numbered sequentially. PropBank uses a common set of role labels (Arg0 up to Arg5) for all predicators, but these labels are defined on a per-verb basis, i.e. they have verb-specific meanings. Example PropBank annotations:

(3) a. [$_{Arg0}$ John] *broke* [$_{Arg1}$ the window] [$_{Arg2}$ with a rock].
b. [$_{Arg0}$ John] *broke* [$_{Arg1}$ the window] [$_{Arg3}$ into a million pieces].
c. [$_{Arg1}$ The window] *broke* [$_{Arg3}$ into a million pieces].

(4) [$_{Arg0}$ Blue-chip consumer stocks] *provided* [$_{Arg1}$ a lift] [$_{Arg2}$ to the industrial average].

(5) In addition, [$_{Arg0}$ the bank] has an option to *buy* [$_{Arg1}$ a 30% stake in BIP] [$_{Arg2}$ from Societe Generale] [$_{ArgM-TMP}$ after Jan.1, 1990] [$_{Arg3}$ at 1,015 francs a share].[2]

As illustrated in (3), argument labels are consistent across alternate syntactic patterns of a given predicator in a given sense. However, PropBank refrains from formalising the semantics of the role labels and does not ensure their *coherence* across verbs. This is particularly clear with higher numbered labels,

[2] *ArgM-TMP* indicates a temporal adjunct modifier.

which correspond to distinct types of participants: Arg2 marks an Instrument for *break* (3), a Benefactive for *provide* (4), and a Source for *buy* (5). Lower-numbered labels denote various roles as well, but they are less arbitrary across verbs: Arg0 corresponds to traditional Agents, Experiencers, certain types of Theme, etc. which surface as subjects of transitive verbs and a class of intransitives called unergatives; Arg1, on the other hand, is assigned to objects of transitive verbs and subjects of unaccusatives and is the equivalent of traditional Patients, Themes, etc.

While the PropBank corpus enables empirical insight into a variety of linguistic phenomena (e.g. variations in the grammatical expression of arguments) providing useful frequency information for the uses of predicators, it does not lend itself to extraction of a principled linguistic knowledge base with semantic generalisations across predicates. Inasmuch as no consistent mapping is ensured between a label and a semantic role, the argument labels result seriously overloaded across verbs. This explains why role recognition models have particularly poor performance in assigning the labels Arg2-Arg5. In fact, an attempt is currently made to map PropBank argument labels to semantically coherent roles specified by VerbNet (Kipper et al., 2000) (i.e. a broad-coverage verb lexicon based on Levin's (1993) classification of English verbs according to *shared meaning and behaviour*). Even though VerbNet specifies a small list of abstract roles (23 in total) which are intended to support generalisations, these roles are not defined as global primitives, but are meaningful only within verb classes. Because mappings of labels to semantic roles with class-specific interpretations would lead to very sparse data, argument labels are subdivided into *groupings* of VerbNet roles. The latter are created manually on the basis of analysis of argument use.[3] The subdivided (more coherent) PropBank labels perform better for semantic role labelling (Loper et al., 2007).

A different paradigm for semantic role annotation is put forth by FrameNet. The Berkeley FrameNet project (Baker et al., 1998) is creating an online lexical database containing semantic descriptions of words based on Fillmore's (1985) theory of frame semantics. The basic unit of analysis is the semantic frame, i.e. a schematic representation of a stereotypical scene or situation. Each frame is associated with a set of predicates (including verbs, nouns, and adjectives) and a set of semantic roles (called *Frame Elements*, FEs) encoding the participants and props in the designated scene. FrameNet includes manually annotated example sentences from the British National Corpus incorporating additional layers of phrase structure and grammatical function annotation. It also includes two small corpora of full-text annotation intended to facilitate statistical analysis of frame-semantic structures. Currently it contains more than 960 frames covering more than 11,600 lexical items exemplified in more than 150,000 annotated sentences. The Judgment frame evoked by *admire* in (1) is shown in Table 3.

Frame: JUDGMENT	
Definition	A Cognizer makes a judgment about an Evaluee. The judgment may be *positive* (e.g. *respect*) or *negative* (e.g. *condemn*) and this information is recorded in the semantic types Positive and Negative on the Lexical Units of this frame. There may be a specific Reason for the Cognizer's judgment, or there may be a capacity or Role in which the Evaluee is judged.
FEs	**Cognizer**: [The boss] *appreciates* you for your diligence. **Evaluee**: The boss *appreciates* [you] for your diligence. **Expressor**: She viewed him with an *appreciative* [gaze]. **Reason**: I *admire* you [for your intellect].
Predicates	accolade.n, accuse.v, admiration.n, admire.v, admiring.a, applaud.v, appreciate.v, appreciation.n, appreciative.a, approbation.n, approving.a, blame.n, blame.v, boo.v, ...

Table 1: The Judgment frame

[3]This endeavour is part of the SemLink project which aims at developing computationally explicit connections between lexical semantic resources (PropBank, VerbNet, FrameNet, WordNet). The idea is to combine the advantages of these resources and overcome their limitations by bridging the complementary lexical information they offer. In a related vein, the LIRICS (i.e. Linguistic Infrastructure for Interoperable Resources and Systems) project has recently evaluated several approaches for semantic role annotation (PropBank, VerbNet, FrameNet, among others) aiming to propose ISO ratified standards for semantic representation that will enable the exchange and reuse of (multilingual) language resources (Petukhova and Bunt, 2008).

FrameNet avoids the difficulties of attempting to pin down a small set of general roles. Instead Frame Elements are defined *locally*, i.e. in terms of frames. Frames are situated in semantic space by means of directed (asymmetric) relations. Each frame-to-frame relation associates a less dependent or more general frame (*Super_frame*) with a more dependent or less general one (*Sub_frame*). The hierarchical organisation of frames along with FE identities or analogs across frames are intended to enable the formulation of generalisations concerning the combinatorial properties (valences) of predicates. In practice, however, the frame hierarchy turns out to be somewhat complicated. Inheritance (i.e. the strongest semantic relation and the most plausible to propagate valence information across frames) is conditioned on complex sets of semantic components underlying frame definitions, ranging from FE membership and relations to other frames to relationships among FEs and Semantic Types on frames and FEs.[4] This kind of frame dependence based on fine-grained semantic or ontological distinctions is doomed to miss argument structure commonalities in predicates evoking frames that are related at a more abstract, essentially structural semantic level. Section 4 includes a concrete example of the complications in generalising valence information across FrameNet frames.

Researchers working in the FrameNet paradigm have proposed different approaches for abstracting over the properties of individual predicators and increasing the size of training data for semantic role labelling systems. Gildea and Jurafsky (2002) attempt to generalise the behaviour of semantically related predicates experimenting with a small set of abstract semantic roles mapped to FrameNet roles. Frank (2004) discusses the potential of applying various generalisation 'filters' to corpus-induced syntax-semantics mappings for abstraction of a general linguistic knowledge base. The generalisations proposed by Frank are intended to apply within frames but not across frames. Baldewein et al. (2004) have trained semantic role classifiers re-using training instances of roles that are similar to the target role. As similarity measures, they use the FrameNet hierarchy, peripheral roles of FrameNet and clusters of roles constructed automatically. Matsubayashi et al. (2009) also explore various machine learning features for generalising semantic roles in FrameNet, namely role hierarchy, human-understandable descriptors of Frame Elements, Semantic Types of filler phrases, and mappings of FrameNet roles to roles of VerbNet. The experimental result of the role classification using these generalisation features shows significant improvements in the system. This is due to the fact that role generalisations can form a remedy for the severe problem of *sparse data* which is inherent in lexical semantic corpus annotation. Data sparseness, i.e. the insufficient coverage of the range of predicate senses and constructions within sensible sizes of manually annotated data, is a bottleneck both for acquisition of linguistic knowledge for the semantic lexicon and for automated techniques for semantic role assignment.

3 An Abstract Semantic Basis for the Representation of Participant Roles

From the presentation of different annotation projects it becomes evident that semantic role annotation is a complicated task whose product is deeply influenced by its initial design philosophy and underlying criteria.[5] Among these criteria the notion of semantic role itself is central. PropBank uses general role labels that lack semantic coherence. VerbNet and FrameNet, on the other hand, specify coherent roles at a more fine-grained level (i.e. roles with class-specific or frame-specific interpretations). In this section, I consider the linguistic contours of the concept of semantic role proposing an annotation schema based upon theoretically well-founded role concepts which meet the requirements of both *generality* and *coherence*. This schema is intended at enabling the formulation of a general syntax-semantics interface suitable for modelling the relations of predicates in terms of combinatorial features.

Espousing and extending Dowty's (1991) Proto-Role hypothesis, I propose to associate arguments of predicates with properties *entailed* by the semantics of predicates.[6] Mappings of entailments to syntactic

[4] *Semantic Types* encode information that is not representable in terms of frames and FE hierarchies, e.g. basic typing of fillers of FEs referring to some (external) ontological classification, descriptions of aspects of semantic variation between lexical units such as the Positive and Negative types in the Judgment frame above, etc.

[5] This point is discussed in detail by Ellsworth et al., 2004.

[6] The term *entailment* is used in the standard logical sense according to which one formula entails another if in every possible

constituents can be many-to-one. That is, an argument can be marked with one or more properties *necessarily* entailed by the meaning of the predicator.[7] Prepositional complements are also marked with verbal entailments to which prepositions may contribute more specific content. In this paper, I will make no attempt to formalise the content added by prepositions; prepositional semantics is represented solely in terms of the common entailment basis it shares with verbal meaning.

Each Proto-Role entailment indicates a grammatically pervasive concept, i.e. a property having direct effect on the grammatical behaviour of predicates. It is defined in terms of an abstract semantic *relation* underlying the lexical meaning of the predicate. Five such relations are identified in terms of which entailment-based representations are specified: Notion, Causation, Motion, Possession, Conditioning. Note that contrary to mere ontological labels, entailment-based representations encode structural characterisations of the semantics of arguments. Consider, for instance, the sentence in (1), repeated here as (6):

(6) [$_{Cognizer}$ I] *admired* [$_{Evaluee}$ him] [$_{Reason}$ for his bravery and his cheerfulness].

A structural representation of the meaning of this construction will explicitly encode the relationships between each of the arguments of *admire*, i.e. between the NP *I* and the NP *him*, between the NP *him* and the PP *for his bravery and his cheerfulness*, and between the NP *I* and the PP *for his bravery and his cheerfulness*. By contrast, the FrameNet roles shown above do not model the fact that the semantic content of an Evaluee *requires* a Cognizer, or that a Reason *requires* both a Cognizer and an Evaluee. The view that the semantic properties underlying lexical meaning are relational in nature (i.e. they are not to be conceived entirely independently of one another) has been advocated by several researchers, among others Wechsler (1995), Pinker (1989), Jackendoff (1990), and Davis (2001), on whose work I build.

In the rest of this section, I define a set of recurring entailments which underlie the semantics of a range of verbs displaying various syntactic patterns. Note that this set can be extended on the basis of additional primitive meaning components of the sort described above, covering the semantics of broad verb classes.

(7) [$_{Conceiver}$ The other two] *pondered* [$_{Conceived}$ over this morsel] as they tramped along behind him.[8]

(8) [$_{Conceiver,Intentional}$ They] *tested* [$_{Conceived}$ the software] [$_{Conceived\_bsoa}$ for similar errors].

(9) [$_{Conceiver,Intentional}$ The government] had *reneged* [$_{Conceived}$ on promises to give them land].

(10) [$_{Conceiver}$ He] likes *stereotyping* [$_{Conceived}$ people] [$_{Conceived\_bsoa}$ by appearance].

(11) [$_{Conceiver}$ The jury] has *found out* [$_{Conceived}$ the truth] [$_{Conceived\_bsoa}$ about the suspect].

(12) [$_{Conceiver}$ The court] *categorised* [$_{Conceived,Entity}$ the issue] [$_{Conceived,Property}$ as a collateral question].

---

situation (in every model) in which the first is true, the second is also true. For linguistic predicates, in particular, an entailment (or lexical entailment) is an analytic implication following from the meaning of the predicate in question.

[7]The presence of 'necessarily' in this sentence is somewhat redundant, in that its meaning is incorporated by the notion of entailment. I insist, however, on emphasising it to indicate that semantic properties that are accidentally associated with the meaning of a particular *use* of a verb will not be annotated. Dowty points out that entailments of the *predicate* must be distinguished from what follows from any one sentence as a whole (e.g. entailments that may arise from NP meanings) (Dowty, 1991:572, footnote 16). For example, in the sentence *Mary slapped John*, assuming that John is a human entity, it follows from the meaning of the sentence that John will perceive something as a result of the action of slapping. But this 'entailment' is not intrinsically tied to the meaning of *slap*, because the sentences *Mary slapped the table* or *Mary slapped the corpse* are also felicitous. That is, sentience of the direct object is not an essential component of the semantics of *slap*, in the way it is for a verb like *awaken*. The sentences *Mary awakened the table* and *Mary awakened the corpse* are clearly anomalous. True entailments of predicators (which are the ones that will be annotated) must be detectable in *every possible environment* in which the predicator is used.

[8]The examples used to illustrate the proposed schema are from the British National Corpus. Some of them are slightly modified for reasons of conciseness.

(13) [$_{Conceiver}$ Opposition members] *accuse* [$_{Conceived,Entity}$ the council] [$_{Conceived,Property}$ of acting purely ideologically].

The predicates in (7)-(13) are represented in terms of a Notion relation. That is, they involve a Conceiver who is entailed to have a notion or perception of a Conceived participant (while the reverse entailment does not necessarily go through).[9] In situation types in which a Conceiver is entailed to have a notion of more than one participant, Conceived arguments are distinguished on the basis of their *salience* in the overall semantics of the predicate. For instance, *test* (8) intuitively lexicalises a dyadic relation between a Conceiver (tester) and a Conceived (tested) entity. A sought entity denoted by a *for*-PP is represented as part of a secondary Notion relation situated at the background of the primary (testing) relation. Conceived entities that are peripheral to the essential relation lexicalised by the predicate are associated with a more specific property termed *Conceived_background_state_of_affairs* (*Conceived_bsoa*). These arguments receive less *focus* in the meaning of the predicate, in a sense that they are not absolutely necessary to understand the predicate's meaning. The representation of *test* (8), *stereotype* (10), and *find out* (11) in terms of two Notion relations, one of which is treated as more salient, reifies the concept of *relative significance* of Proto-Role properties in the verbal semantics. This concept is related to the weighting of entailments in the overall semantics of a verb, which plays a critical role in determining the syntactic patterns in which the verb appears (i.e. the grammatical realisations of its arguments).[10]

The verbs in (8) and (9) involve an additional entailment of Intentionality. This is used to mark entities characterised by conscious choice, decision, or control over the course of inherently intentional actions. Intentional participants necessarily have a notion/perception of some event participant(s). The annotations in (12) and (13) include the *Entity* and *Property* tags which are intended to distinguish Conceived arguments in terms of a predicative relation assigned in the Conceiver's mental model. The *Property* label corresponds to a representation of the form *P(x)* denoting a property *P* which is predicated of some object *x*.

The entailments of Notion are not applicable in the semantics of the predicates in (14)-(15) below. These verbs refer to situations with affected participants and are described in terms of an abstract relation of Causation. In the denoted events, a Causer is entailed to affect some entity (the Causee) either physically or mentally. Causally affected participants sometimes undergo radical changes in their (physical or mental) state, which are identified in terms of a readily observable transition from a source to a final (result) state, as shown in (15).

(14) [$_{Causer}$ Diet] *influences* [$_{Causee}$ disease].

(15) [$_{Causer}$ The sun] has *changed* [$_{Causee,Change\_of\_state}$ her hair color] [$_{Source\_state}$ from red] [$_{End\_state}$ to blue].

Verbs as in (16)-(17) are represented in terms of a Motion relation involving a Moving entity (i.e. an object entailed to change location) and Stationary reference frame. Locations at the start, end, or intermediate points of the stationary frame are tagged with the labels *Path_source*, *Path_goal*, and *Path*, respectively.

(16) [$_{Moving}$ The car] *passed* [$_{Stationary}$ the railway station].

(17) [$_{Moving}$ The river] *flowed* silently [$_{Path}$ through the forest].

Finally, verbs such as *own*, *possess*, *acquire*, *lack*, etc. are treated in terms of a Possession relation involving a Possessor and an entity entailed to be Possessed (18).

[9] The Notion relation, as defined by Wechsler (1995), essentially reconstructs the entailment of *sentience*, which was proposed by Dowty (1991).

[10] Arguments identified as *conceived_bsoas* have many of the syntactic properties of so-called semantic *adjuncts*. However, I refrain from invoking an argument versus adjunct division, in that it is known to involve serious theoretical pitfalls. Instead I classify conceived participants on the basis of the concept of importance of entailments, which lies exactly at the syntax-semantics interface. This concept is defined in terms of the *lexicalised* event rather than the real-world event that traditional analyses of adjuncthood appeal to.

(18) [$_{Possessor}$ This house] *lacks* [$_{Possessed}$ a guest room].

Verbs of caused Motion (19) or caused Possession (20) are represented in terms of both Causation and Motion/Possession, i.e. as meaning 'cause to move' (set to motion) or 'cause to possess'. This analysis posits a main (causal) event and a caused sub-event. The entailments associated with the latter are marked in square brackets.

(19) [$_{Causer}$ Lucie] *threw* [$_{Causee,[Moving]}$ him] [$_{[Path\_source]}$ from the parapet of a bridge] [$_{[Path\_goal]}$ into deep water].

(20) [$_{Causer}$ He] *handed* [$_{[Possessed]}$ the letter] [$_{[Possessor]}$ to Weir], who nodded.

Proto-Role entailments are defined in terms of inherently asymmetric semantic relations involving fixed role positions. Each of these relations (with the exception of Motion) can be thought of as instance of a more general relation entailing that properties of an entity β are dependent on an entity α. For example, a conceived entity in a Notion relation depends on the existence of a conceiver (it is taken to be within the scope of the conceiver's beliefs). An affected or possessed object in a causation or possession relation depends on the existence of some causer or possessor, respectively. I refer to this relation as Conditioning relation and associate it with appropriate Proto-Role properties capturing the semantics of a broad range of verbs for which none of the entailments specified so far seems to hold. These verbs conform to the basic transitivity pattern that motivated Dowty's Proto-Role hypothesis. Below are some characteristic examples:

(21) [$_{Condition}$ This game] *demands* [$_{Conditioned}$ great skill].

(22) [$_{Condition}$ Code 1425] *bans* [$_{Conditioned}$ large trucks in tunnels].

(23) [$_{Condition}$ The adjective 'beautiful'] *denotes* [$_{Conditioned}$ a quality which can be found in many different objects].

(24) [$_{Condition}$ Diversity] *characterises* [$_{Conditioned}$ the sociolinguistics domain].

A Conditioning relation encodes the asymmetries in such predicators in terms of the underlying entailment that the properties of a participant α impose a condition on properties of a participant β. In each of the sentences above we can conclude something about the object participant (e.g. that it is necessary, illegal, or linguistically expressed) on the basis of the subject referent (i.e. the characteristics of the game, the regulations specified by the code, the usage of the adjective 'beautiful'). By contrast, no property of the subject referent is necessarily conditioned on the object: the semantics of *ban*, for example, does not allow us to characterise code 1425 as fair/unfair, severe/lax, complete/incomplete, new/old, etc. on the basis of the object NP 'large trucks in tunnels'; similarly, we cannot infer the precise meaning of the word 'beautiful' or whether it is a verb or a noun or an adjective on the basis of the content of the NP 'a quality which can be found in many different objects'. A more precise definition of the Conditioning relation could state that the intrinsic (i.e. invariable) properties of a participant α determine or condition some non-intrinsic (i.e. variable or event-dependent) property of a participant β while the converse entailment does not go through. In (24), for example, the sociolinguistics domain is associated with a property of being diverse whereas the intrinsic properties of the domain have no significance for the definition of 'diversity' or what this notion may characterise.

4 Formulation of a General Syntax-Semantics Interface

A preliminary study has been carried out mapping state-of-the-art semantic role annotations to lexical entailment representations. In particular, a portion of the FrameNet corpora has been annotated with Proto-Role properties by a single annotator. The study focuses on a set of English verbs selected from 250 random FrameNet frames. For each verb in these frames, collections of example annotated sentences as well as sentences from the FrameNet full-text annotation corpora (where available) were extracted. More than 900 lexical units were considered in ~20K sentences. Proto-Role entailments were annotated on top of FrameNet's syntactic annotations in accordance with the schema sketched out above. The annotations were produced semi-automatically following a three-stage procedure: (i) mapping Frame Elements (FEs) to entailments at a frame level (ii) automatically adding this information to the data in a new annotation layer, (iii) manually correcting the novel annotations by examining the argument structures of individual predicators for finer semantic distinctions.

From the newly annotated data mappings of entailments to grammatical categories were acquired. The syntactic realisations of Proto-Role properties were found to readily generalise over combinatorial features of verbs pertaining to various FrameNet frames. Valence information can be formally rendered in entailment-based classes called *Lexicalisation Types* (*L-Types*) abstracting away from the semantics of predicators. L-Types are defined on the basis of grammatically relevant meaning components and encode linking generalisations cutting across FrameNet frames.

For instance, predicates such as *believe* and *desire* (evoking the frames Religious_Belief and Desiring, respectively) involve arguments that are equivalent in terms of entailments, as illustrated in (25)-(26) below. Hence they are categorised in the Notion L-Type shown in Table 2. Table 2 includes the correspondences between combinations of entailments and FrameNet Frame Elements.

Notion L-Type	Religious_belief	Desiring
Conceiver	Believer	Experiencer
Conceived, (Entity)	Element	Focal_participant
Conceived_bsoa, Property	Role	Role_of_focal_participant

Table 2: Mappings between Notion L-Type and FrameNet frames

(25) If [$_{Conceiver}$ he] *believes* [$_{Conceived,Entity}$ in Jesus] [$_{Conceived\_bsoa,Property}$ as his Saviour], he can be baptised.

(26) [$_{Conceiver}$ He] *wanted* [$_{Conceived,Entity}$ Smith] [$_{Conceived\_bsoa,Property}$ as the new producer].

In a similar fashion, *operate*, *research*, and *ratify* can be grouped together in a L-Type based on the underlying property of Intentionality. Examples (27)-(28) show that these verbs share common valence patterns despite the differences in the definition of the frames they evoke (Using, Research and Ratification): Role and Purpose are core Frame Elements in the Using frame, while Purpose is peripheral in Research and Ratification. Research and Ratification have no Role FE (but this kind of argument is clearly present in the constructions exemplified in (28b-c).

Intentionality L-Type	Using	Research	Ratification
Conceiver, Intentional	Agent	Researcher	Ratifier
Conceived, (Entity)	Instrument	Question	Proposal
Conceived_bsoa, Property	Role		
Conceived_bsoa, Intention	Purpose	Purpose	Purpose

Table 3: Mappings between Intentionality L-Type and FrameNet frames

(27) a. [$_{Conceiver,Intentional}$ We] *operate* [$_{Conceived}$ a menu] [$_{Conceived\_bsoa,Intention}$ to get the best out of rations].

b. [$_{Conceiver,Intentional}$ We] *research* [$_{Conceived}$ this fungus] [$_{Conceived\_bsoa,Intention}$ to fight aliments in tobacco and tomato fields].

c. [$_{Conceiver,Intentional}$ They] had to *ratify* [$_{Conceived}$ the amendments] [$_{Conceived\_bsoa,Intention}$ to be readmitted to the Union].

(28) a. There has been a long debate as to whether [$_{Conceived,Entity}$ the Severn Mill] *was operated* [$_{Conceived\_bsoa,Property}$ as a tide mill].

b. [$_{Conceived,Entity}$ Thin films] *are being researched* [$_{Conceived\_bsoa,Property}$ as a potential medium for integrated optical circuits].

c. [$_{Conceived,Entity}$ Such agreements] may *be ratified* [$_{Conceived\_bsoa,Property}$ as being in the public interest].

In the same Intentionality L-Type we also categorise verbs such as *carry out* and *visit* evoking the frames Intentionally_act and Visiting. It is important to note that despite the argument structure similarities of these predicators, it is not possible to establish an identity link between the Act FE of the Intentionally_act frame and the Entity FE of Visiting in terms of the frame hierarchy, because the FEs are associated with different Semantic Types in the corresponding frame definitions, i.e. Act is of type State_of_affairs whereas Entity is of type Physical_object. The examples (29)-(30) illustrate the common use of these verbs in the transitive construction. The (a) sentences show the FE annotation while the (b) sentences show the annotated entailments.

(29) a. [$_{Agent}$ They] had *carried out* [$_{Act}$ 113 uranium conversion experiments].

b. [$_{Conceiver,Intentional}$ They] had *carried out* [$_{Conceived}$ 113 uranium conversion experiments].

(30) a. [$_{Agent}$ You] have to *visit* [$_{Entity}$ your parents] every once in a while.

b. [$_{Conceiver,Intentional}$ You] have to *visit* [$_{Conceived}$ your parents] every once in a while.

Predicates grouped together in L-Types have some but not necessarily all their grammatical properties in common. This is in accordance with the fact that L-Types are essentially semantically-driven modelling recurring, abstract features in the semantics of predicators while disregarding ephemeral properties as well as lexical idiosyncrasies.[11] In addition to the set of entailments discussed in the previous section, L-Types may also incorporate more fine-grained properties that are clearly relevant to linking. For instance, verbs lexicalising a Desiring situation were found with prepositional complements introduced by *for*, *after*, *to*, *towards*, *of*, or *over* (e.g. *long for*, *hanker after*, *aspire to*, *pine over*, etc.), but not *on*, *upon*, *at*, or *about* (like other Notion verbs, such as *ponder*, *muse*, *think*, etc.). Inasmuch as a Desiring relation is identified as a recurring concept systematically associated with a particular grammatical relation (e.g. a *for*-PP), it can be represented in a separate L-Type inheriting from the Notion L-Type presented previously.[12] An initial classification like the one exemplified above captures general conditions which determine possible associations between the semantics of predicators and grammatical relations realising their arguments (e.g. the fact that a conceived entity can only surface in subject position in a passive sentence). It can be extended and refined on the basis of more specific semantic relations. Moreover, L-Types can be organised in hierarchical structures. They can form the upper portion of a principled hierarchy of classes encoding successively broader levels of generalisations concerning argument linking.

This study indicated that a small number of Lexicalisation Types abstracts over a wide range of FrameNet frames.[13] More precisely, in the annotated dataset 48 L-Types were identified based on various combinations of entailments: 9 Notion Types, 7 Intentionality Types, 10 Causation Types, 7 Communication (Caused_Notion) Types, 7 Motion (including Caused_Motion) Types, 7 Possession (including Caused_Possession) Types, and 1 Conditioning Type. These Types readily abstract over associations of semantic properties and grammatical functions attested in over 200 FrameNet frames.[14] In the FrameNet paradigm, L-Types can be modelled as non-lexicalised frames specifying syntactic mapping constraints.

[11] L-Types crucially differ from verb classes in VerbNet, which are based on a rigorous commitment to syntax. This commitment yields fine-grained distinctions that very often split semantically coherent classes. In fact, L-Types abstract over VerbNet classes encoding broader levels of linking generalisations.

[12] *For*-PPs are indeed associated with a desiderative sense with a wide range of verbs in various argument positions: 'He desperately hunted *for a new job*'. 'They searched the ground *for traces*'. 'John ran *for cover* when it started to rain'.

[13] Note that inasmuch as L-Types abstract over both VerbNet classes and FrameNet frames, they can also be useful for combining the two resources.

[14] About 30 frames contained predicates for which none of our entailments seemed to hold. Most of these verbs (e.g. *resemble*, *adjoin*, *concern*, *fit*, *suit*, etc.) involve what Dowty (1991) called *perspective-dependent* semantic roles traditionally described with labels such as Figure and Ground. The lexicalisation patterns of these verbs have been shown to depend on *pragmatic* or *discourse* factors rather than intrinsic semantic properties. Such predicates display great variability in their argument realisation options and are outside the scope of this study.

Mappings between FrameNet frames and L-Types can be stated by means of a separate relation in addition to the frame relations currently specified by FrameNet. A relation generalising the combinatorial properties of lexical items across frames would simplify the picture of the frame hierarchy, in that it would essentially decouple purely lexical semantic information (encoded by existing frame-to-frame relations) from information pertaining exactly to the interface of syntax and semantics. In future work, our intention is to test whether the proposed semantic role schema and the attested L-Types can be useful for dealing with the sparse data problem and increasing the performance of semantic role labelling systems.

References

[1] Baker, Collin F., Charles J. Fillmore, and John B. Lowe. 1998. The Berkeley FrameNet project. In Proceedings of the COLING-ACL. Montreal, Canada.

[2] Baldewein, Ulrike, Katrin Erk, Sebastian Padó, and Detlef Prescher. 2004. Semantic Role Labeling with Similarity-Based Generalisation Using EM-Based Clustering. In Proceedings of Senseval-3, pp. 64-68. Barcelona, Spain.

[3] Boas, Hans C. 2002. Bilingual FrameNet Dictionaries for Machine Translation. In Proceedings of the Third International Conference on Language Resources and Evaluation. Las Palmas, Spain. Vol. IV: pp. 1364-1371.

[4] Burchardt, Aljoscha and Anette Frank. 2006. Approximating Textual Entailment with LFG and FrameNet Frames. In Proceedings of the second PASCAL Recognizing Textual Entailment Workshop. Venice, Italy, pp. 92-97.

[5] Davis, Anthony. 2001. Linking by types in the hierarchical lexicon. CSLI Publications.

[6] Dowty, David. 1991. Thematic Proto-Roles and Argument Selection. Language 67.3, pp. 547-619.

[7] Ellsworth Michael, Katrin Erk, Paul Kingsbury, and Sebastian Padó. 2004. PropBank, SALSA, and FrameNet: How Design Determines Product. In Proceedings of the LREC 2004 Workshop on Building Lexical Resources from Semantically Annotated Corpora. Lisbon.

[8] Fillmore, Charles J. 1985. Frames and the semantics of understanding. Quaderni di Semantica 6.2, pp. 222-254.

[9] Frank, Anette. 2004. Generalizations over corpus-induced frame assignment rules. In Charles Fillmore, Manfred Pinkal, Collin Baker and Katrin Erk (eds.): Proceedings of the LREC 2004 Workshop on Building Lexical Resources from Semantically Annotated Corpora. Lisbon, Portugal, pp. 31-38.

[10] Gildea, Daniel and Daniel Jurafsky. 2002. Automatic labeling of semantic roles. Computational Linguistics 28 (3), pp. 245-288.

[11] Jackendoff, Ray. 1990. Semantic Structures. Cambridge, MA, MIT Press.

[12] Kingsbury, Paul and Martha Palmer. 2002. From Treebank to PropBank. In Proceedings of the LREC, Las Palmas, Canary Islands, Spain.

[13] Kipper, Karin, Hoa Trang Dang, and Martha Palmer. 2000. Class-based construction of a verb lexicon. In Proceedings of the Seventh National Conference on Artificial Intelligence (AAAI-2000), Austin,TX, July-August.

[14] Levin, Beth. 1993. English verb classes and alternations: A preliminary investigation. University of Chicago Press.

[15] Loper, Edward, Szu-ting Yi and Martha Palmer. 2007. Combining Lexical Resources: Mapping Between PropBank and VerbNet. Proceedings of the 7th International Workshop on Computational Semantics. Tilburg, the Netherlands.

[16] Marcus, Mitchell, Grace Kim, Mary Ann Marcinkiewicz, Robert MacIntyre, Ann Bies, Mark Ferguson, Karen Katz, and Britta Schasberger. 1994. The Penn Treebank: Annotating predicate argument structure. In Proceedings AR-PAHLT Workshop.

[17] Matsubayashi, Yuichiroh, Naoaki Okazaki, and Jun'ichi Tsujii. 2009. A Comparative Study on Generalization of Semantic Roles in FrameNet. In Proceedings of the 47th Annual Meeting of the ACL and the 4th IJCNLP of the AFNLP, pp.19-27. Suntec, Singapore.

[18] Melli, Gabor, Yang Wang, Yudong Liu, Mehdi M. Kashani, Zhongmin Shi, Baohua Gu, Anoop Sarkar, and Fred Popowich. 2005. Description of SQUASH, the SFU question answering summary handler for the DUC-2005 Summarization Task. In Proceedings of the HLT/EMNLP Document Understanding Workshop (DUC). Vancouver, Canada, available at http://duc.nist.gov/pubs/2005papers/simonfraseru.sarkar.pdf.

[19] Narayanan, Srini and Sanda Harabagiu. 2004. Question Answering Based on Semantic Structures. In Proceedings of the 20th International Conference on Computational Linguistics (COLING), pp. 693 - 701. Geneva, Switzerland.

[20] Petukhova, Volha and Harry Bunt. 2008. 'LIRICS semantic role annotation: design and evaluation of a set of data categories.' In Proceedings of the Sixth International Conference on Language Resources and Evaluation (LREC 2008), Marrakech, Morocco, May 28-30.

[21] Pinker, Steven. 1989. Learnability and Cognition. Cambridge, MA, MIT Press.

[22] Surdeanu, Mihai, Sanda Harabagiu, John Williams, and Paul Aarseth. 2003. Using Predicate Arguments Structures for Information Extraction. In Proceedings of the 41st Annual Meeting of the Association for Computational Linguistics, pp. 815. Sapporo, Japan.

[23] Wechsler, Stephen. 1995. The semantic basis of argument structure. Stanford, CA. CSLI Publications.

Concrete Sentence Spaces for Compositional Distributional Models of Meaning

Edward Grefenstette*, Mehrnoosh Sadrzadeh*, Stephen Clark†, Bob Coecke*, Stephen Pulman*
*Oxford University Computing Laboratory, †University of Cambridge Computer Laboratory
firstname.lastname@comlab.ox.ac.uk, stephen.clark@cl.cam.ac.uk

Abstract

Coecke, Sadrzadeh, and Clark [3] developed a compositional model of meaning for distributional semantics, in which each word in a sentence has a meaning vector and the distributional meaning of the sentence is a function of the tensor products of the word vectors. Abstractly speaking, this function is the morphism corresponding to the grammatical structure of the sentence in the category of finite dimensional vector spaces. In this paper, we provide a concrete method for implementing this linear meaning map, by constructing a corpus-based vector space for the type of sentence. Our construction method is based on structured vector spaces whereby meaning vectors of all sentences, regardless of their grammatical structure, live in the same vector space. Our proposed sentence space is the tensor product of two noun spaces, in which the basis vectors are pairs of words each augmented with a grammatical role. This enables us to compare meanings of sentences by simply taking the inner product of their vectors.

1 Background

Coecke, Sadrzadeh, and Clark [3] develop a mathematical framework for a compositional distributional model of meaning, based on the intuition that *syntactic analysis guides the semantic vector composition.* The setting consists of two parts: a formalism for a type-logical syntax and a formalism for vector space semantics. Each word is assigned a grammatical type and a meaning vector in the space corresponding to its type. The meaning of a sentence is obtained by applying the function corresponding to the grammatical structure of the sentence to the tensor product of the meanings of the words in the sentence. Based on the type-logic used, some words will have atomic types and some compound function types. The compound types live in a tensor space where the vectors are weighted sums (i.e. superpositions) of the pairs of bases from each space. Compound types are "applied" to their arguments by taking inner products, in a similar manner to how predicates are applied to their arguments in Montague semantics.

For the type-logic we use Lambek's Pregroup grammars [7]. The use of pregoups is not essential, but leads to a more elegant formalism, given its proximity to the categorical structure of vector spaces (see [3]). A Pregroup is a partially ordered monoid where each element has a right and left cancelling element, referred to as an *adjoint*. It can be seen as the algebraic counterpart of the cancellation calculus of Harris [6]. The operational difference between a Pregroup and Lambek's Syntactic Calculus is that, in the latter, the monoid multiplication of the algebra (used to model juxtaposition of the types of the words) has a right and a left adjoint, whereas in the pregroup it is the elements themselves which have adjoints. The adjoint types are used to denote functions, e.g. that of a transitive verb with a subject and object as input and a sentence as output. In the Pregroup setting, these function types are still denoted by adjoints, but this time the adjoints of the elements themselves.

As an example, consider the sentence "dogs chase cats". We assign the type n (for noun phrase) to "dog" and "cat", and $n^r s n^l$ to "chase", where n^r and n^l are the right and left adjoints of n and s is the type of a (declarative) sentence. The type $n^r s n^l$ expresses the fact that the verb is a predicate that takes two arguments of type n as input, on its right and left, and outputs the type s of a sentence. The parsing of the sentence is the following reduction:

$$n(n^r s n^l)n \leq 1s1 = s$$

This parse is based on the cancellation of n and n^r, and also n^l and n; i.e. $nn^r \leq 1$ and $n^l n \leq 1$ for 1 the unit of juxtaposition. The reduction expresses the fact that the juxtapositions of the types of the words reduce to the type of a sentence.

On the semantic side, we assign the vector space N to the type n, and the tensor space $N \otimes S \otimes N$ to the type $n^r s n^l$. Very briefly, and in order to introduce some notation, recall that the tensor space $A \otimes B$ has as a basis the cartesian product of a basis of A with a basis of B. Recall also that any vector can be expressed as a weighted sum of basis vectors; e.g. if $(\overrightarrow{v_1}, \ldots, \overrightarrow{v_n})$ is a basis of A then any vector $\overrightarrow{a} \in A$ can be written as $\overrightarrow{a} = \sum_i C_i \overrightarrow{v_i}$ where each $C_i \in \mathbb{R}$ is a weighting factor. Now for $(\overrightarrow{v_1}, \ldots, \overrightarrow{v_n})$ a basis of A and $(\overrightarrow{v'_1}, \ldots, \overrightarrow{v'_n})$ a basis of B, a vector $\overrightarrow{c}$ in the tensor space $A \otimes B$ can be expressed as follows:

$$\sum_{ij} C_{ij} \, (\overrightarrow{v_i} \otimes \overrightarrow{v'_j})$$

where the tensor of basis vectors $\overrightarrow{v_i} \otimes \overrightarrow{v'_j}$ stands for their pair $(\overrightarrow{v_i}, \overrightarrow{v'_j})$. In general $\overrightarrow{c}$ is not separable into the tensor of two vectors, except for the case when $\overrightarrow{c}$ is not *entangled*. For non-entangled vectors we can write $\overrightarrow{c} = \overrightarrow{a} \otimes \overrightarrow{b}$ for $\overrightarrow{a} = \sum_i C_i \overrightarrow{v_i}$ and $\overrightarrow{b} = \sum_j C'_j \overrightarrow{v'_j}$; hence the weighting factor of $\overrightarrow{c}$ can be obtained by simply multiplying the weights of its tensored counterparts, i.e. $C_{ij} = C_i \times C'_j$. In the entangled case these weights cannot be determined as such and range over all the possibilities. We take advantage of this fact to encode meanings of verbs, and in general all words that have compound types and are interpreted as predicates, relations, or functions. For a brief discussion see the last paragraph of this section. Finally, we use the Dirac notation to denote the dot or inner product of two vectors $\langle \overrightarrow{a} \mid \overrightarrow{b} \rangle \in \mathbb{R}$ defined by $\sum_i C_i \times C'_i$.

Returning to our example, for the meanings of nouns we have $\overrightarrow{\text{dogs}}, \overrightarrow{\text{cats}} \in N$, and for the meanings of verbs we have $\overrightarrow{\text{chase}} \in N \otimes S \otimes N$, i.e. the following superposition:

$$\sum_{ijk} C_{ijk} \, (\overrightarrow{n_i} \otimes \overrightarrow{s_j} \otimes \overrightarrow{n_k})$$

Here $\overrightarrow{n_i}$ and $\overrightarrow{n_k}$ are basis vectors of N and $\overrightarrow{s_j}$ is a basis vector of S. From the categorical translation method presented in [3] and the grammatical reduction $n(n^r s n^l)n \leq s$, we obtain the following linear map as the categorical morphism corresponding to the reduction:

$$\epsilon_N \otimes 1_s \otimes \epsilon_N : N \otimes (N \otimes S \otimes N) \otimes N \to S$$

Using this map, the meaning of the sentence is computed as follows:

$$\begin{aligned}
\overrightarrow{\text{dogs chase cats}} &= (\epsilon_N \otimes 1_s \otimes \epsilon_N) \left(\overrightarrow{\text{dogs}} \otimes \overrightarrow{\text{chase}} \otimes \overrightarrow{\text{cats}} \right) \\
&= (\epsilon_N \otimes 1_s \otimes \epsilon_N) \left(\overrightarrow{\text{dogs}} \otimes \left(\sum_{ijk} C_{ijk} (\overrightarrow{n_i} \otimes \overrightarrow{s_j} \otimes \overrightarrow{n_k}) \right) \otimes \overrightarrow{\text{cats}} \right) \\
&= \sum_{ijk} C_{ijk} \langle \overrightarrow{\text{dogs}} \mid \overrightarrow{n_i} \rangle \overrightarrow{s_j} \langle \overrightarrow{n_k} \mid \overrightarrow{\text{cats}} \rangle
\end{aligned}$$

The key features of this operation are, first, that the inner-products reduce dimensionality by ‘consuming’ tensored vectors and by virtue of the following component function:

$$\epsilon_N : N \otimes N \to \mathbb{R} :: \overrightarrow{a} \otimes \overrightarrow{b} \mapsto \langle \overrightarrow{a} \mid \overrightarrow{b} \rangle$$

Thus the tensored word vectors $\overrightarrow{\text{dogs}} \otimes \overrightarrow{\text{chase}} \otimes \overrightarrow{\text{cats}}$ are mapped into a sentence space S which is common to all sentences regardless of their grammatical structure or complexity. Second, note that the tensor product $\overrightarrow{\text{dogs}} \otimes \overrightarrow{\text{chase}} \otimes \overrightarrow{\text{cats}}$ does not need to be calculated, since all that is required for computation of the sentence vector are the noun vectors and the C_{ijk} weights for the verb. Note also that the inner product operations are simply picking out basis vectors in the noun space, an operation that can be performed in constant time. Hence this formalism avoids two problems faced by approaches in the vein of [9, 2], which use the tensor product as a composition operation: first, that the sentence meaning space is high dimensional and grammatically different sentences have representations with different dimensionalities, preventing them from being compared directly using inner products; and second, that the space complexity of the tensored representation grows exponentially with the length and grammatical complexity of the sentence. In constrast, the model we propose does not require the tensored vectors being combined to be represented explicitly.

Note that we have taken the vector of the transitive verb, e.g. $\overrightarrow{\text{chase}}$, to be an entangled vector in the tensor space $N \otimes S \otimes N$. But why can this not be a separable vector, in which case the meaning of the verb would be as follows:

$$\overrightarrow{\text{chase}} \quad = \quad \sum_i C_i \overrightarrow{n_i} \quad \otimes \quad \sum_j C'_j \overrightarrow{s_j} \quad \otimes \quad \sum_k C''_k \overrightarrow{n_k}$$

The meaning of the sentence would then become $\sigma_1 \sigma_2 \sum_j C'_j \overrightarrow{s_j}$ for $\sigma_1 = \sum_i C_i \langle \overrightarrow{\text{dogs}} \mid \overrightarrow{n_i} \rangle$ and $\sigma_2 = \sum_k C''_k \langle \overrightarrow{\text{cats}} \mid \overrightarrow{n_k} \rangle$. The problem is that this meaning only depends on the meaning of the verb and is independent of the meanings of the subject and object, whereas the meaning from the entangled case, i.e. $\sigma_1 \sigma_2 \sum_{ijk} C_{ijk} \overrightarrow{s_j}$, depends on the meanings of subject and object as well as the verb.

2 From Truth-Theoretic to Corpus-based Meaning

The model presented above is compositional and distributional, but still abstract. To make it concrete, N and S have to be constructed by providing a method for determining the C_{ijk} weightings. Coecke, Sadrzadeh, and Clark [3] show how a truth-theoretic meaning can be derived in the compositional framework. For example, assume that N is spanned by all animals and S is the two-dimensional space spanned by $\overrightarrow{\text{true}}$ and $\overrightarrow{\text{false}}$. We use the weighting factor to define a model-theoretic meaning for the verb as follows:

$$C_{ijk} \overrightarrow{s_j} = \begin{cases} \overrightarrow{\text{true}} & chase(\overrightarrow{n_i}, \overrightarrow{n_k}) = \text{true}\,, \\ \overrightarrow{\text{false}} & o.w. \end{cases}$$

The definition of our meaning map ensures that this value propagates to the meaning of the whole sentence. So $chase(\overrightarrow{dogs}, \overrightarrow{cats})$ becomes true whenever "dogs chase cats" is true and false otherwise. This is exactly how meaning is computed in the model-theoretic view on semantics. One way to generalise this truth-theoretic meaning is to assume that $chase(\overrightarrow{n_i}, \overrightarrow{n_k})$ has degrees of truth, for instance by defining $chase$ as a combination of run and $catch$, such as:

$$chase = \frac{2}{3} run + \frac{1}{3} catch$$

Again, the meaning map ensures that these degrees propagate to the meaning of the whole sentence. For a worked out example see [3]. But neither of these examples provide a *distributional* sentence meaning.

Here we take a first step towards a corpus-based distributional model, by attempting to recover a meaning for a sentence based on the meanings of the words derived from a corpus. But crucially this meaning goes beyond just composing the meanings of words using a vector operator, such as tensor product, summation or multiplication [8]. Our computation of sentence meaning treats some vectors as functions and others as function arguments, according to how the words in the sentence are typed, and uses the syntactic structure as a guide to determine how the functions are applied to their arguments. The intuition behind this approach is that *syntactic analysis guides semantic vector composition.*

The contribution of this paper is to introduce some concrete constructions for a compositional distributional model of meaning. These constructions demonstrate how the mathematical model of [3] can be implemented in a concrete setting which introduces a richer, not necessarily truth-theoretic, notion of natural language semantics which is closer to the ideas underlying standard distributional models of word meaning. We leave full evaluation to future work, in order to determine whether the following method in conjunction with word vectors built from large corpora leads to improved results on language processing tasks, such as computing sentence similarity and paraphrase evaluation.

Nouns and Transitive Verbs. We take N to be a *structured vector space*, as in [4, 5]. The bases of N are annotated by 'properties' obtained by combining dependency relations with nouns, verbs and adjectives. For example, basis vectors might be associated with properties such as "arg-fluffy", denoting the argument of the adjective fluffy, "subj-chase" denoting the subject of the verb chase, "obj-buy" denoting the object of the verb buy, and so on. We construct the vector for a noun by counting how many times in the corpus a word has been the argument of 'fluffy', the subject of 'chase', the object of 'buy', and so on.

The framework in [3] offers no guidance as to what the sentence space should consist of. Here we take the sentence space S to be $N \otimes N$, so its bases are of the form $\overrightarrow{s_j} = (\overrightarrow{n_i}, \overrightarrow{n_k})$. The intuition is that, for a transitive verb, the meaning of a sentence is determined by the meaning of the verb together with its subject and object.[1] The verb vectors $C_{ijk}(\overrightarrow{n_i}, \overrightarrow{n_k})$ are built by counting how many times a word that is n_i (e.g. has the property of being fluffy) has been subject of the verb and a word that is n_k (e.g. has the property that it's bought) has been its object, where the counts are moderated by the extent to which the subject and object exemplify each property (e.g. *how fluffy* the subject is). To give a rough paraphrase of the intuition behind this approach, the meaning of "dog chases cat" is given by: the extent to which a dog is fluffy and a cat is something that is bought (for the $N \otimes N$ property pair "arg-fluffy" and "obj-buy"), and the extent to which fluffy things *chase* things that are bought (accounting for the meaning of the verb for this particular property pair); plus the extent to which a dog is something that runs and a cat is something that is cute (for the $N \otimes N$ pair "subj-run" and "arg-cute"), and the extent to which things that run *chase* things that are cute (accounting for the meaning of the verb for this particular property pair); and so on for all noun property pairs.

Adjective Phrases. Adjectives are dealt with in a similar way. We give them the syntactic type nn^l and build their vectors in $N \otimes N$. The syntactic reduction $nn^l n \to n$ associated with applying an adjective to a noun gives us the map $1_N \otimes \epsilon_N$ by which we semantically compose an adjective with a noun, as follows:

$$\overrightarrow{\text{red fox}} = (1_N \otimes \epsilon_N)(\overrightarrow{\text{red}} \otimes \overrightarrow{\text{fox}}) = \sum_{ij} C_{ij} \overrightarrow{n_i} \langle \overrightarrow{n_j} \mid \overrightarrow{\text{fox}} \rangle$$

We can view the C_{ij} counts as determining what sorts of properties the arguments of a particular adjective typically have (e.g. arg-red, arg-colourful for the adjective "red").

Prepositional Phrases. We assign the type $n^r n$ to the whole prepositional phrase (when it modifies a noun), for example to "in the forest" in the sentence "dogs chase cats in the forest". The pregroup parsing is as follows:

$$n(n^r s n^l) n(n^r n) \le 1 s n^l 1 n \le s n^l n \le s1 = s$$

The vector space corresponding to the prepositional phrase will thus be the tensor space $N \otimes N$ and the categorification of the parse will be the composition of two morphisms: $(1_S \otimes \epsilon^l_N) \circ (\epsilon^r_N \otimes 1_S \otimes 1_N \otimes \epsilon^r_N \otimes 1_N)$.

[1] Intransitive and ditransitive verbs are interpreted in an analagous fashion; see §4.

The substitution specific to the prepositional phrase happens when computing the vector for "cats in the forest" as follows:

$$\begin{aligned}\overrightarrow{\text{cats in the forest}} &= (\epsilon_N^r \otimes 1_N)\left(\overrightarrow{\text{cats}} \otimes \overline{\text{in the forest}}\right)\\ &= (\epsilon_N^r \otimes 1_N)\left(\overrightarrow{\text{cats}} \otimes \sum_{lw} C_{lw}\overrightarrow{n_l} \otimes \overrightarrow{n_k}\right)\\ &= \sum_{lw} C_{lw}\langle \overrightarrow{\text{cats}} \mid \overrightarrow{n_l}\rangle \overrightarrow{n_w}\end{aligned}$$

Here we set the weights C_{lw} in a similar manner to the cases of adjective phrases and verbs with the counts determining what sorts of properties the noun modified by the prepositional phrase has, e.g. the number of times something that has attribute n_l has been in the forest.

Adverbs. We assign the type $s^r s$ to the adverb, for example to "quickly" in the sentence "Dogs chase cats quickly". The pregroup parsing is as follows:

$$n(n^r s n^l)n(s^r s) \leq 1s1s^r s = ss^r s \leq 1s = s$$

Its categorification will be a composition of two morphisms $(\epsilon_S^r \otimes 1_S) \circ (\epsilon_N^r \otimes 1_S \otimes \epsilon_N^l \otimes 1_S \otimes 1_S)$. The substitution specific to the adverb happens after computing the meaning of the sentence without it, i.e. that of "Dogs chase cats", and is as follows:

$$\begin{aligned}\overrightarrow{\text{Dogs chase cats quickly}} &= (\epsilon_S^r \otimes 1_S) \circ (\epsilon_N^r \otimes 1_S \otimes \epsilon_N^l \otimes 1_S \otimes 1_S)\left(\overrightarrow{\text{Dogs}} \otimes \overrightarrow{\text{chase}} \otimes \overrightarrow{\text{cats}} \otimes \overrightarrow{\text{quickly}}\right)\\ &= (\epsilon_S^r \otimes 1_S)\left(\sum_{ijk} C_{ijk}\langle \overrightarrow{\text{dogs}} \mid \overrightarrow{n_i}\rangle \overrightarrow{s_j}\langle \overrightarrow{n_k} \mid \overrightarrow{\text{cats}}\rangle \otimes \overrightarrow{\text{quickly}}\right)\\ &= (\epsilon_S^r \otimes 1_S)\left(\sum_{ijk} C_{ijk}\langle \overrightarrow{\text{dogs}} \mid \overrightarrow{n_i}\rangle \overrightarrow{s_j}\langle \overrightarrow{n_k} \mid \overrightarrow{\text{cats}}\rangle \otimes \sum_{lw} C_{lw}\overrightarrow{s_l} \otimes \overrightarrow{s_w}\right)\\ &= \sum_{lw} C_{lw}\left\langle \sum_{ijk} C_{ijk}\langle \overrightarrow{\text{dogs}} \mid \overrightarrow{n_i}\rangle \overrightarrow{s_j}\langle \overrightarrow{n_k} \mid \overrightarrow{\text{cats}}\rangle \mid \overrightarrow{s_l}\right\rangle \overrightarrow{s_k}\end{aligned}$$

The C_{lw} weights are defined in a similar manner to the above cases, i.e. according to the properties the adverb has, e.g. which verbs it has modified. Note that now the basis vectors $\overrightarrow{s_l}$ and $\overrightarrow{s_w}$ are themselves pairs of basis vectors from the noun space, $(\overrightarrow{n_i}, \overrightarrow{n_j})$. Hence, $C_{lw}(\overrightarrow{n_i}, \overrightarrow{n_j})$ can be set only for the case when $l = i$ and $w = j$; these counts determine what sorts of properties the verbs that happen quickly have (or more specifically what properties the subjects and objects of such verbs have). By taking the whole sentence into account in the interpretation of the adverb, we are in a better position to semantically distinguish between the meaning of adverbs such as "slowly" and "quickly", for instance in terms of the properties that the verb's subjects have. For example, it is possible that elephants are more likely to be the subject of a verb which is happening slowly, e.g. run slowly, and cheetahs are more likely to be the subject of a verb which is happening quickly.

3 Concrete Computations

In this section we first describe how to obtain the relevant counts from a parsed corpus, and then give some similarity calculations for some example sentence pairs.

Let C_l be the set of grammatical relations (GRs) for sentence s_l in the corpus. Define $verbs(C_l)$ to be the function which returns all instances of verbs in C_l, and $subj$ (and similarly obj) to be the function which returns the subject of an instance $V_{instance}$ of a verb V, for a particular set of GRs for a sentence:

$$subj(V_{instance}) = \begin{cases} noun & \text{if } V_{instance} \text{ is a verb with subject } noun \\ \varepsilon_n & o.w. \end{cases}$$

where ε_n is the empty string. We express C_{ijk} for a verb V as follows:

$$C_{ijk} = \begin{cases} \sum_l \sum_{v \in verbs(C_l)} \delta(v, V) \langle \overrightarrow{subj(v)} \mid \overrightarrow{n_i} \rangle \langle \overrightarrow{obj(v)} \mid \overrightarrow{n_k} \rangle & \text{if } \overrightarrow{s_j} = (\overrightarrow{n_i}, \overrightarrow{n_k}) \\ 0 & o.w. \end{cases}$$

where $\delta(v, V) = 1$ if $v = V$ and 0 otherwise. Thus we construct C_{ijk} for verb V only for cases where the subject property n_i and the object property n_k are paired in the basis $\overrightarrow{s_j}$. This is done by counting the number of times the subject of V has property n_i and the object of V has property n_k, then multiplying them, as prescribed by the inner products (which simply pick out the properties n_i and n_k from the noun vectors for the subjects and objects).

The procedure for calculating the verb vectors, based on the formulation above, is as follows:

1. For each GR in a sentence, if the relation is $subject$ and the head is a verb, then find the complementary GR with $object$ as a relation and the same head verb. If none, set the object to ε_n.

2. Retrieve the noun vectors $\overrightarrow{subject}, \overrightarrow{object}$ for the subject dependent and object dependent from previously constructed noun vectors.

3. For each $(n_i, n_k) \in basis(N) \times basis(N)$ compute the inner-product of $\overrightarrow{n_i}$ with $\overrightarrow{subject}$ and $\overrightarrow{n_k}$ with $\overrightarrow{object}$ (which involves simply picking out the relevant basis vectors from the noun vectors). Multiply the inner-products and add this to C_{ijk} for the verb, with j such that $\overrightarrow{s_j} = (\overrightarrow{n_i}, \overrightarrow{n_k})$.

The procedure for other grammatical types is similar, based on the definitions of C weights for the semantics of these types.

We now give a number of example calculations. We first manually define the distributions for nouns, which in practice would be obtained from a corpus:

	bankers	cats	dogs	stock	kittens
1. arg-fluffy	0	7	3	0	2
2. arg-ferocious	4	1	6	0	0
3. obj-buys	0	4	2	7	0
4. arg-shrewd	6	3	1	0	1
5. arg-valuable	0	1	2	8	0

We aim to make these counts match our intuitions, in that bankers are shrewd and a little ferocious but not furry, cats are furry but not typically valuable, and so on.

We also define the distributions for the transitive verbs 'chase', 'pursue' and 'sell', again manually specified according to our intuitions about how these verbs are used. Since in the formalism proposed above, $C_{ijk} = 0$ if $\overrightarrow{s_j} \neq (\overrightarrow{n_i}, \overrightarrow{n_k})$, we can simplify the weight matrices for transitive verbs to two dimensional C_{ik} matrices as shown below, where C_{ik} corresponds to the number of times the verb has a subject with attribute n_i and an object with attribute n_k. For example, the matrix below encodes the fact that something ferocious

$(i = 2)$ chases something fluffy $(k = 1)$ seven times in the hypothetical corpus from which we might have obtained these distributions.

$$C^{\text{chase}} = \begin{bmatrix} 1 & 0 & 0 & 0 & 0 \\ 7 & 1 & 2 & 3 & 1 \\ 0 & 0 & 0 & 0 & 0 \\ 2 & 0 & 1 & 0 & 1 \\ 1 & 0 & 0 & 0 & 0 \end{bmatrix} \quad C^{\text{pursue}} = \begin{bmatrix} 0 & 0 & 0 & 0 & 0 \\ 4 & 2 & 2 & 2 & 4 \\ 0 & 0 & 0 & 0 & 0 \\ 3 & 0 & 2 & 0 & 1 \\ 0 & 0 & 0 & 0 & 0 \end{bmatrix} \quad C^{\text{sell}} = \begin{bmatrix} 0 & 0 & 0 & 0 & 0 \\ 0 & 0 & 3 & 0 & 4 \\ 0 & 0 & 0 & 0 & 0 \\ 0 & 0 & 5 & 0 & 8 \\ 0 & 0 & 1 & 0 & 1 \end{bmatrix}$$

These matrices can be used to perform sentence comparisons:

$$\langle \overrightarrow{\text{dogs chase cats}} \mid \overrightarrow{\text{dogs pursue kittens}} \rangle =$$

$$= \left\langle \left(\sum_{ijk} C^{\text{chase}}_{ijk} \langle \overrightarrow{\text{dogs}} \mid \overrightarrow{n_i} \rangle \overrightarrow{s_j} \langle \overrightarrow{n_k} \mid \overrightarrow{\text{cats}} \rangle \right) \middle| \left(\sum_{ijk} C^{\text{pursue}}_{ijk} \langle \overrightarrow{\text{dogs}} \mid \overrightarrow{n_i} \rangle \overrightarrow{s_j} \langle \overrightarrow{n_k} \mid \overrightarrow{\text{kittens}} \rangle \right) \right\rangle$$

$$= \sum_{ijk} C^{\text{chase}}_{ijk} C^{\text{pursue}}_{ijk} \langle \overrightarrow{\text{dogs}} \mid \overrightarrow{n_i} \rangle \langle \overrightarrow{\text{dogs}} \mid \overrightarrow{n_i} \rangle \langle \overrightarrow{n_k} \mid \overrightarrow{\text{cats}} \rangle \langle \overrightarrow{n_k} \mid \overrightarrow{\text{kittens}} \rangle$$

The raw number obtained from the above calculation is 14844. Normalising it by the product of the length of both sentence vectors gives the cosine value of 0.979.

Consider now the sentence comparison $\langle \overrightarrow{\text{dogs chase cats}} \mid \overrightarrow{\text{cats chase dogs}} \rangle$. The sentences in this pair contain the same words but the different word orders give the sentences very different meanings. The raw number calculated from this inner product is 7341, and its normalised cosine measure is 0.656, which demonstrates the sharp drop in similarity obtained from changing sentence structure. We expect some similarity since there is some non-trivial overlap between the properties identifying cats and those identifying dogs (namely those salient to the act of chasing).

Our final example for transitive sentences is $\langle \overrightarrow{\text{dogs chase cats}} \mid \overrightarrow{\text{bankers sell stock}} \rangle$, as two sentences that diverge in meaning completely. The raw number for this inner product is 6024, and its cosine measure is 0.042, demonstrating the very low semantic similarity between these two sentences.

Next we consider some examples involving adjective-noun modification. The C_{ij} counts for an adjective A are obtained in a similar manner to transitive or intransitive verbs:

$$C_{ij} = \begin{cases} \sum_l \sum_{a \in adjs(\mathcal{C}_l)} \delta(a, A) \langle \overrightarrow{arg\text{-}of(a)} \mid \overrightarrow{n_i} \rangle & \text{if } \overrightarrow{n_i} = \overrightarrow{n_j} \\ 0 & o.w. \end{cases}$$

where $adjs(\mathcal{C}_l)$ returns all instances of adjectives in $\mathcal{C}_l$; $\delta(a, A) = 1$ if $a = A$ and 0 otherwise; and $arg\text{-}of(a) = noun$ if a is an adjective with argument $noun$, and ε_n otherwise.

As before, we stipulate the C_{ij} matrices by hand (and we eliminate all cases where $i \neq j$ since $C_{ij} = 0$ by definition in such cases):

$$C^{\text{fluffy}} = [9\ 3\ 4\ 2\ 2] \qquad C^{\text{shrewd}} = [0\ 3\ 1\ 9\ 1] \qquad C^{\text{valuable}} = [3\ 0\ 8\ 1\ 8]$$

We compute vectors for "fluffy dog" and "shrewd banker" as follows:

$$\overrightarrow{\text{fluffy dog}} = (3 \cdot 9)\, \overrightarrow{\text{arg-fluffy}} + (6 \cdot 3)\, \overrightarrow{\text{arg-ferocious}} + (2 \cdot 4)\, \overrightarrow{\text{obj-buys}} + (5 \cdot 2)\, \overrightarrow{\text{arg-shrewd}} + (2 \cdot 2)\, \overrightarrow{\text{arg-valuable}}$$

$$\overrightarrow{\text{shrewd banker}} = (0 \cdot 0)\, \overrightarrow{\text{arg-fluffy}} + (4 \cdot 3)\, \overrightarrow{\text{arg-ferocious}} + (0 \cdot 0)\, \overrightarrow{\text{obj-buys}} + (6 \cdot 9)\, \overrightarrow{\text{arg-shrewd}} + (0 \cdot 1)\, \overrightarrow{\text{arg-valuable}}$$

Vectors for $\overrightarrow{\text{fluffy cat}}$ and $\overrightarrow{\text{valuable stock}}$ are computed similarly. We obtain the following similarity measures:

$$cosine(\overrightarrow{\text{fluffy dog}}, \overrightarrow{\text{shrewd banker}}) = 0.389 \qquad cosine(\overrightarrow{\text{fluffy cat}}, \overrightarrow{\text{valuable stock}}) = 0.184$$

These calculations carry over to sentences which contain the adjective-noun pairings compositionally and we obtain an even lower similarity measure between sentences:

$$cosine(\overrightarrow{\text{fluffy dogs chase fluffy cats}}, \overrightarrow{\text{shrewd bankers sell valuable stock}}) = 0.016$$

To summarise, our example vectors provide us with the following similarity measures:

Sentence 1	**Sentence 2**	**Degree of similarity**
dogs chase cats	dogs pursue kittens	0.979
dogs chase cats	cats chase dogs	0.656
dogs chase cats	bankers sell stock	0.042
fluffy dogs chase fluffy cats	shrewd bankers sell valuable stock	0.016

4 Different Grammatical Structures

So far we have only presented the treatment of sentences with transitive verbs. For sentences with intransitive verbs, the sentence space suffices to be just N. To compare the meaning of a transitive sentence with an intransitive one, we embed the meaning of the latter from N into the former $N \otimes N$, by taking $\overrightarrow{\varepsilon_n}$ (the 'object' of an intransitive verb) to be $\sum_i \overrightarrow{n_i}$, i.e. the superposition of all basis vectors of N.

Following the method for the transitive verb, we calculate C_{ijk} for an instransitive verb V and basis pair $\overrightarrow{s_j} = (\overrightarrow{n_i}, \overrightarrow{n_k})$ as follows, where l ranges over the sentences in the corpus:

$$\sum_l \sum_{v \in verbs(\mathcal{C}_l)} \delta(v, V) \langle \overrightarrow{subj(v)} \mid \overrightarrow{n_i} \rangle \langle \overrightarrow{obj(v)} \mid \overrightarrow{n_k} \rangle = \sum_l \sum_{v \in verbs(\mathcal{C}_l)} \delta(v, V) \langle \overrightarrow{subj(v)} \mid \overrightarrow{n_i} \rangle \langle \overrightarrow{\varepsilon_n} \mid \overrightarrow{n_k} \rangle$$

and $\langle \overrightarrow{\varepsilon_n} \mid \overrightarrow{n_i} \rangle = 1$ for any basis vector n_i.

We can now compare the meanings of transitive and intransitive sentences by taking the inner product of their meanings (despite the different arities of the verbs) and then normalising it by vector length to obtain the cosine measure. For example:

$$\langle \overrightarrow{\text{dogs chase cats}} \mid \overrightarrow{\text{dogs chase}} \rangle = \left\langle \left(\sum_{ijk} C_{ijk} \langle \overrightarrow{\text{dogs}} \mid \overrightarrow{n_i} \rangle \overrightarrow{s_j} \langle \overrightarrow{n_k} \mid \overrightarrow{\text{cats}} \rangle \right) \middle| \left(\sum_{ijk} C'_{ijk} \langle \overrightarrow{\text{dogs}} \mid \overrightarrow{n_i} \rangle \overrightarrow{s_j} \right) \right\rangle$$

$$= \sum_{ijk} C_{ijk} C'_{ijk} \langle \overrightarrow{\text{dogs}} \mid \overrightarrow{n_i} \rangle \langle \overrightarrow{\text{dogs}} \mid \overrightarrow{n_i} \rangle \langle \overrightarrow{n_k} \mid \overrightarrow{\text{cats}} \rangle$$

The raw number for the inner product is 14092 and its normalised cosine measure is 0.961, indicating high similarity (but some difference) between a sentence with a transitive verb and one where the subject remains the same, but the verb is used intransitively.

Comparing sentences containing nouns modified by adjectives to sentences with unmodified nouns is straightforward:

$$\langle \overrightarrow{\text{fluffy dogs chase fluffy cats}} \mid \overrightarrow{\text{dogs chase cats}} \rangle =$$

$$\sum_{ij} C_i^{\text{fluffy}} C_j^{\text{fluffy}} C_{ij}^{\text{chase}} C_{ij}^{\text{chase}} \langle \overrightarrow{dogs} \mid \overrightarrow{n_i} \rangle^2 \langle \overrightarrow{n_j} \mid \overrightarrow{cats} \rangle^2 = 2437005$$

From the above we obtain the following similarity measure:

$$cosine(\overrightarrow{\text{fluffy dogs chase fluffy cats}}, \overrightarrow{\text{dogs chase cats}}) = 0.971$$

For sentences with ditransitive verbs, the sentence space changes to $N \otimes N \otimes N$, on the basis of the verb needing two objects; hence its grammatical type changes to $n^r s n^l n^l$. The transitive and intransitive verbs are embedded in this larger space in a similar manner to that described above; hence comparison of their meanings becomes possible.

5 Ambiguous Words

The two different meanings of a word can be distinguished by the different properties that they have. These properties are reflected in the corpus, by the different contexts in which the words appear. Consider the following example from [4]: the verb "catch" has two different meanings, "grab" and "contract". They are reflected in the two sentences "catch a ball" and "catch a disease". The compositional feature of our meaning computation enables us to realise the different properties of the context words via the grammatical roles they take in the corpus. For instance, the word 'ball' occurs as argument of 'round', and so has a high weight for the base 'arg-round', whereas the word 'disease' has a high weight for the base 'arg-contagious' and as 'mod-of-heart'. We extend our example corpus from previously to reflect these differences as follows:

	ball	disease
1. arg-fluffy	1	0
2. arg-ferocious	0	0
3. obj-buys	5	0
4. arg-shrewd	0	0
5. arg-valuable	1	0
6. arg-round	8	0
7. arg-contagious	0	7
8. mod-of-heart	0	6

In a similar way, we build a matrix for the verb 'catch' as follows:

$$C^{\text{catch}} = \begin{bmatrix} 3 & 2 & 3 & 3 & 3 & 8 & 6 & 2 \\ 3 & 2 & 3 & 0 & 1 & 4 & 7 & 4 \\ 2 & 4 & 7 & 1 & 1 & 6 & 2 & 2 \\ 3 & 1 & 2 & 0 & 0 & 3 & 6 & 2 \\ 1 & 1 & 1 & 0 & 0 & 2 & 0 & 1 \\ 0 & 0 & 0 & 0 & 0 & 0 & 0 & 0 \\ 0 & 0 & 0 & 0 & 0 & 0 & 0 & 0 \\ 0 & 0 & 0 & 0 & 0 & 0 & 0 & 0 \end{bmatrix}$$

The last three rows are zero because we have assumed that the words that can take these roles are mostly objects and hence cannot catch anything. Given these values, we compute the similarity measure between the two sentences "dogs catch a ball" and "dogs catch a disease" as follows:

$$\langle \overrightarrow{\text{dogs catch a ball}} \mid \overrightarrow{\text{dogs catch a disease}} \rangle \quad = \quad 0$$

In an idealised case like this where there is very little (or no) overlap between the properties of the objects associated with one sense of "catch" (e.g. a disease), and those properties of the objects associated with another sense (e.g. a ball), disambiguation is perfect in that there is no similarity between the resulting phrases.

In practice, in richer vector spaces, we would expect even diseases and balls to share some properties. However, as long as those shared properties are not those typically held by the object of catch, and as long as the usages of catch play to distinctive properties of diseases and balls, disambiguation will occur by the same mechanism as the idealised case above, and we can expect low similarity measures between such sentences.

6 Related Work

Mitchell and Lapata introduce and evaluate a multiplicative model for vector composition [8]. The particular concrete construction of this paper differs from that of [8] in that our framework subsumes truth-theoretic as well as corpus-based meaning, and our meaning construction relies on and is guided by the grammatical structure of the sentence. The approach of [4] is more in the spirit of ours, in that extra information about syntax is used to compose meaning. Similar to us, they use a structured vector space to integrate lexical information with selectional preferences. Finally, Baroni and Zamparelli model adjective-noun combinations by treating an adjective as a function from noun space to noun space, represented using a matrix, as we do in this paper [1].

References

[1] M. Baroni and R. Zamparelli. Nouns are vectors, adjectives are matrices: Representing adjective-noun constructions in semantic space. In *Conference on Empirical Methods in Natural Language Processing (EMNLP-10)*, Cambridge, MA, 2010.

[2] S. Clark and S. Pulman. Combining symbolic and distributional models of meaning. In *Proceedings of AAAI Spring Symposium on Quantum Interaction*. AAAI Press, 2007.

[3] B. Coecke, M. Sadrzadeh, and S. Clark. *Mathematical Foundations for a Compositional Distributional Model of Meaning*, volume 36. Linguistic Analysis (Lambek Festschrift), 2010. http://arxiv.org/abs/1003.4394.

[4] K. Erk and S. Padó. A structured vector space model for word meaning in context. In *Conference on Empirical Methods in Natural Language Processing (EMNLP-08)*, pages 897–906, Honolulu, Hawaii, 2008.

[5] G. Grefenstette. Use of syntactic context to produce term association lists for text retrieval. In Nicholas J. Belkin, Peter Ingwersen, and Annelise Mark Pejtersen, editors, *SIGIR*, pages 89–97. ACM, 1992.

[6] Z. Harris. *Mathematical Structures of Language*. Interscience Publishers John Wiley and Sons, 1968.

[7] J. Lambek. *From Word to Sentence*. Polimetrica, 2008.

[8] J. Mitchell and M. Lapata. Vector-based models of semantic composition. In *Proceedings of the 46th Annual Meeting of the Association for Computational Linguistics*, pages 236–244, Columbus, OH, 2008.

[9] P. Smolensky and G. Legendre. *The Harmonic Mind: From Neural Computation to Optimality-Theoretic Grammar Vol. I: Cognitive Architecture Vol. II: Linguistic and Philosophical Implications*. MIT Press, 2005.

Computing Semantic Compositionality in Distributional Semantics

Emiliano Guevara
Tekstlab, ILN, University of Oslo, `e.r.guevara@iln.uio.no`

Abstract

This article introduces and evaluates an approach to semantic compositionality in computational linguistics based on the combination of Distributional Semantics and supervised Machine Learning. In brief, distributional semantic spaces containing representations for complex constructions such as Adjective-Noun and Verb-Noun pairs, as well as for their constituent parts, are built. These representations are then used as feature vectors in a supervised learning model using multivariate multiple regression. In particular, the distributional semantic representations of the constituents are used to predict those of the complex structures. This approach outperforms the rivals in a series of experiments with Adjective-Noun pairs extracted from the BNC. In a second experimental setting based on Verb-Noun pairs, a comparatively much lower performance was obtained by all the models; however, the proposed approach gives the best results in combination with a Random Indexing semantic space.

1 Introduction

Probably the most important missing ingredient from the current NLP state-of-the-art is the ability to compute the meaning of complex structures, i.e. semantically compositional structures. In this paper, I propose a methodological approach and a series of experiments designed to teach computers the ability to compute the compositionality of (relatively simple) complex linguistic structures. This work uses a combination of Distributional Semantics and Machine Learning techniques. The starting data in the experiments reported below are multidimensional vectorial semantic representations extracted from electronic corpora. This work extends the basic methodology presented in Guevara (2010) with new data collection techniques, improved evaluation metrics and new case studies.

Compositionality is probably one of the defining properties of human language and, perhaps, a nearly uncontroversial notion among linguists. One of the best-known formulations of compositionality is:

(1) *The Principle of Compositionality:*
The meaning of a complex expression is a function of the meaning of its parts and of the syntactic rules by which they are combined. (Partee, ter Meulen and Wall, 1990: 318)

The Principle of Compositionality is a standard notion in many different fields of research, notably in logic, in philosophy of language, in linguistics and in computer science; this intrinsic multi-disciplinarity makes tracing back its recent history somewhat difficult.

The recent years have witnessed an ever-increasing interest in techniques that enable computers to automatically extract semantic information from linguistic corpora. In this paper I will refer to this new field in general as Distributional Semantics. Distributional Semantics, in short, extracts spatial representations of meaning from electronic corpora by using distributional (i.e. statistical) patterns of word usage. The main hypothesis in Distributional Semantics is the so-called *distributional hypothesis of meaning*, expressing the fact that "words that occur in the same contexts tend to have similar meanings" (Pantel, 2005). The distributional hypothesis of meaning is ascribed to Zellig Harris, who proposed a general distributional methodology for linguistics.

Since representations in Distributional Semantics are spatial in nature (e.g. vectors representing points in a multidimensional space), differences in meaning are captured through differences in location:

in the multidimensional space, two semantically (i.e. *distributionally*) similar words are *closer* than two words that are dissimilar. See Sahlgren (2006) and Turney and Pantel (2010) for detailed overviews of the methodology and applications of Distributional Semantics.

2 Compositionality in distributional semantics: state-of-the-art

I stressed above that computers are still not able to deal with the compositionality of meaning. However basically true, this statement should be qualified somewhat. Previous work in the field has produced a small number of operations to approximate the composition of vectorial representations of word meaning. In particular, given two independent vectors $v1$ and $v2$, the semantically compositional result $v3$ is modelled by one of the following four basic operations: vector addition, vector pointwise-multiplication, tensor product or linear regression.

In the literature on Information Retrieval, *vector addition* is the standard approach to model the composed meaning of a group of words (or a document) as the sum of their vectors (see, among many others, Widdows, 2004: ch. 5). More schematically:

(2) *Vector addition:* $v1_i + v2_i = v3_i$
Given two independent vectors $v1$ and $v2$, the compositional meaning of $v3$ consists of the sum of the corresponding components of the original vectors.

Mitchell and Lapata (2008) introduce a whole family of models of compositionality based on vector addition and pointwise-multiplication (and a weighted combination of both), evaluated on a sentence similarity task inspired by Kintsch (2001). While the additive model captures the compositionality of meaning by considering all available components, multiplicative models only operate on a subset of them, i.e. non-zero components. They claim that when we pointwise-multiply the vectors representing two words, we obtain an output that captures their composition; actually, this operation is keeping in the output only the components which had corresponding non-zero values: whether this operation has any relation with semantics is still unclear. However, in their experiments, Mitchell and Lapata prove that the pointwise-multiplicative model and the weighted combination of the additive and the multiplicative models perform equally well. Of these, only the simple multiplicative model will be tested in the experiments I present in the following section.

(3) *Vector pointwise multiplication:* $v1_i \times v2_i = v3_i$
Each corresponding pair of components of $v1$ and $v2$ is multiplied to obtain the corresponding component of $v3$.

Widdows (2008) proposes to apply a number of more complex vector operations imported from quantum mechanics to model composition in semantic spaces, in particular *tensor product* and the related operation of *convolution product*. Widdows (2008) obtains results indicating that both the tensor product and the convolution product perform better than the simple additive model in two small experiments (relation extraction and phrasal composition). Giesbrecht (2009) presents a more complex task, singling out non-compositional multiword expressions. Her results clearly show that tensor product outperforms vector addition, multiplication and convolution.

(4) *Tensor product:* $v1 \otimes v2 = v3$
where $v3$ is a matrix whose *ij*-th entry is equal to $v1_i \times v2_j$

However, since the tensor product (also called outer product) of two vectors produces a result with higher dimensionality (a matrix), it cannot be directly compared against the other methods, which instead generate compositional representations in the same original space. In the experiments reported in the following section, we will use the circular convolution composition method (Plate, 1991): in brief, circular convolution is a mathematical operation that effectively compresses the tensor product of two vectors onto the original space, thus allowing us to compare its outcome with that of the other methods here reviewed.

(5) *Circular convolution:* $v1 \otimes v2 = v3$
where $v3 = \sum_{j=0}^{n-1} v1_j v2_{i-j}$

It is interesting to note that a great deal of attention has recently been devoted to the tensor product as the basic operation for modelling compositionality, even at the sentential level (e.g. Grefenstette *et al.* 2010), through a combination of mathematical operations and symbolic models of logic (inspired by Clark and Pulman, 2007). Although extremely motivating and thought provoking, these proposals have not been tested on empirical grounds yet.

A common thread ties all the approaches briefly outlined above: all information that is present in the systems is conveyed by the vectors $v1$ and $v2$, e.g. the independent word representations, while completely disregarding $v3$ (the composed vector). Furthermore, all of these approaches are based on the application of a single geometric operation on the independent vectors $v1$ and $v2$. It seems highly unlikely that just one geometric operation could reliably represent *all* the semantic transformations introduced by *all* syntactic relations in *every* language.

Guevara (2010) and Baroni and Zamparelli (2010) introduce a different approach to model semantic compositionality in distributional spaces by extracting context vectors from the corpus also for the composed vector $v3$. For example, Guevara collects vector representations for *nice* and *house*, but also for the observed pair *nice_house*. With these data, a model of Adjective-Noun (AN) compositionality is built by using a supervised machine learning approach: multivariate multiple linear regression analysis by partial least squares. This method is able to learn the transformation function that best approximates $v3$ on the basis of both $v1$ and $v2$. Baroni and Zamparelli (2010) use a slightly different methodology: assuming that each adjective is a linear transformation function (i.e. the function to be learnt by the algorithm), they model AN compositionality by approximating $v3$ only on the basis of $v2$ (the noun) but running a different regression analysis for each adjective in their data.

The approach proposed by Guevara (2010) is really only an extension of the full additive model of Mitchell and Lapata (2008), the only difference being that adopting a supervised learning methodology ensures that the weight parameters in the function are estimated optimally by linear regression. In the following section, I present a new series of experiments that refine, extend and improve this approach to model the compositionality of adjacent AN and VN pairs by linear regression.

(6) *Compositionality by regression:* $Av1 + Bv2 = v3$
where A and B are weight matrices estimated by the supervised learning algorithm using multivariate multiple linear regression.

3 Compositionality by regression

Let us reconsider the highly underspecified definition of the Principle of Compositionality. Let us start by setting the *syntactic relation* that we want to focus on for the purposes of this study: following Guevara (2010) and Baroni and Zamparelli (2010), I model the semantic composition of adjacent Adjective-Noun pairs expressing attributive modification of a nominal head. In a second analogous experiment, I also model the *syntactic relation* between adjacent Verb-Noun expressing object selection by the verbal head.

The *complex expression* and its *parts* are, respectively, adjacent Adjective-Noun and Verb-Noun[1] pairs and their corresponding constituents (respectively, adjectives and nouns, verbs and nouns) extracted from the British National Corpus. Furthermore, the *meaning* of both complex expressions and their constituents is assumed to be the multidimensional context vectors obtained by building semantic spaces.

What remains to be done, therefore, is to model the *function* combining meanings of the constituent parts to yield the meaning of the resulting complex expression. This is precisely the main assumption made in this article. Since we are dealing with multidimensional vector representations of meaning, we suggest that compositionality can be interpreted as a *linear transformation function* mapping two

[1] Actually, the extracted Verb-Noun pairs are not always strictly adjacent, an optional determiner was allowed to occur between verb and noun. Thus, phrases such as "raise money" and "visit a client" were both included.

independent vectors in a multidimensional space into a composed vector in the same space. Moreover, considering that each component in the independent vectors $v1$ and $v2$ is a candidate predictor, and that each component in the composed vector $v3$ is a dependent variable, it is proposed to formulate compositionality of meaning in Distributional Semantics as a problem of multivariate multiple regression. Such a formulation allows us to model compositionality by applying well-known standard machine learning techniques such as the Multilayer Perceptron or Support Vector Machines.

However, since word sequences in corpora tend to have low frequency distributions (usually lower than the frequency of their constituents) and very sparse vectorial representations, it is very difficult to build datasets where the number of observations (the size of the dataset) is greater than the number of variables considered (the dimensions of the vector in the dataset). This issue is known as the *curse of dimensionality*, and specific mathematical techniques have been developed to deal with it. In our experiments, we use one such regression technique, Partial Least Squares.

3.1 Partial least squares regression

Partial Least Squares Regression (PLS) is a multivariate regression technique that has been designed specifically to treat cases where the curse of dimensionality is a serious issue. PLS has been successfully applied in a wide range of different scientific fields such as spectroscopy, chemistry, brain imaging and marketing (Mevik and Wehrens, 2007).

PLS predicts the output matrix Y from information found in both the input matrix X and in Y. It does so by looking for a set of *latent variables* in the data that perform a simultaneous decomposition of both matrices while trying to explain as much as possible of the covariance between X and Y. Next, PLS carries out regression using the decomposition of X to predict Y. Thus, PLS performs the prediction by extracting the latent variables with the best predictive power. PLS is a robust regression technique that is particularly efficient in situations with a high number of predictors and few observations (Abdi, 2007, Hastie *et al.*, 2009). Standard linear regression will fail in such cases.

3.2 Experimental setup

3.2.1 Corpus and construction of the dataset

Using a lemmatised and POS tagged version of the BNC, a list of adjacent AN pair candidates was extracted with simple regex-based queries targeting sequences composed of [Det/Art–A–N] (i.e. pairs expressing attributive modification of a nominal head like *'that little house'*). In order to ensure the computational attainability of the successive steps, the candidate list was filtered by frequency (> 400) obtaining 1,367 different AN pairs.

A new version of the BNC was then prepared to represent the selected AN lemma pairs as a single token; for example, while in the original BNC the phrase [*nice houses*] consists in two separate POS-tagged lemmas, *nice_AJ* and *house_NN*, in the processed corpus it appears as a single entry *nice_AJ_house_NN*). The corpus was also processed by stop-word removal (very high frequency items, mainly functional morphemes). The re-tokenization process of the BNC enables us to extract independent context vectors for each AN pair in our list ($v3$) and their corresponding constituents (A and N, respectively $v1$ and $v2$), while ensuring that the extracted vectors do not contain overlapping information.

The same preprocessing steps were carried out to extract VN pair candidates. Sequences composed of [V-(Det/Art)–N] with an optional determiner were targeted and filtered by frequency (> 400), resulting in a first list of 545 VN pairs. This list contained a large amount of noise due to lemmatisation and POS-tagging problems (e.g. *housing association*), and it also contained many very frequent lexicalized items (e.g. *thank goodness*). The list was manually cleaned, resulting in 193 different VN pairs.

3.2.2 Building semantic spaces and composition models

For each syntactic relation (AN and VN), two different semantic spaces were built with the S-Space package (Jurgen and Stevens, 2010): a *Hyperspace Analogue to Language* space (HAL, Burgess and

Lund, 1997) and a *Random Indexing* space (RI, Sahlgren, 2006). The spaces were built using the same vocabulary, the 23,222 elements in the corpus with a frequency $\geq$ 100 (comprising both individual lemmas and all the selected AN pairs) and the same contextual window of 5 words to the left and to the right of the target (either a word or a AN/VN pair).

HAL is a co-occurrence based semantic space that corresponds very closely to the well-known *term-by-term* matrix collection method. However, given the size of our vocabulary, the resulting matrix is extremely large (23,222 $\times$ 23,222). HAL reduces the dimensionality of the space by computing the variances of the row and column vectors for each word, and discarding the elements with lowest variance. The dimensionality of this space was reduced to the 500 most informative dimensions, thus ending with a size of 23,222 $\times$ 500. The vectors in this space were normalised before the successive steps.

RI avoids the problem of dimensionality of semantic spaces by applying a different strategy to collect the context vectors. Each word in the corpus is assigned an initial unique and randomly generated *index vector* of a fixed size. As the algorithm scans the corpus one token at a time, the vector of the target word is incrementally updated by combining it with the index vector of the context. In order to keep the comparability of the built spaces, the RI space was built with 500-dimensional index vectors, thus obtaining a space of 23,222 $\times$ 500 dimensions. The vectors in this space were also normalised.

With the AN/VN pair vectors and their corresponding constituents (respectively $v3$, $v1$ and $v2$), four different models of compositionality were built from each semantic space (HAL and RI) in each of the considered syntactic relations:

- an additive model (ADD) $v1_i + v2_i = v3_i$
- a simple multiplicative model (MUL) $v1_i \times v2_i = v3_i$
- a circular convolution model (CON) $v1 \otimes v2 = v3$
- a partial least squares regression model (PLS) $Av1 + Bv2 = v3$

In addition, two baseline models were introduced in the evaluation process. The baseline models were built by simply extracting the context vectors for the constituents in each pair from each space (A and N, V and N, respectively $v1$ and $v2$).

Of all the considered models, only PLS requires a stage of parameter estimation, i.e. training. In order to accomplish this, the data were randomly divided into a training set (1,000 AN pairs – 73%) and a test set (the remaining 367 AN pairs – 27%). In the much smaller VN dataset, the training set was built with 133 pairs (69%) and the test set with 60 pairs (31%). These parameters for the regression models were estimated by performing a 10-fold cross-validation in the training phase. All the models were built and evaluated using the R statistical computing environment and simple Python scripts. In particular, the regression analysis was carried out with the **pls** package (Mevik and Wehrens, 2007). After various preliminary trials, the PLS model's predictions were computed by using the first 50 latent variables.

3.3 Evaluation

The evaluation of models of compositionality is still a very uncertain and problematic issue. Previous work has relied mainly on "external" tasks such as rating sentence similarity or detection idioms. These evaluation strategies are "external" in the sense that each compared model produces a set of predictions which are then used in order to reproduce human annotation of datasets that do not have a representation in the semantic space under consideration. For example, Mitchell and Lapata (2008) use their models to approximate the human ratings in their sentence similarity dataset. Giesbrecht (2009) also uses human annotated data (manually classified collocations, compositional and non-compositional) in her evaluation task. However, any evaluation task requiring hand-annotated datasets will have a considerable cost in resource building. At present time, there are no suitable datasets in the public domain.

I propose instead to take a radically different point of view, developing "internal" evaluation tasks that try to measure how well the proposed models approximate the distributional patterns of corpus-extracted composed vectors. That is to say, I want to compare the predicted output of every model (i.e. a predicted context vector for $v3$) with the real observation of $v3$ that was collected from the corpus. The following subsections present a few experimental evaluation methods based on neighbour analysis and on the Euclidean measure of distance.

The evaluation strategies here presented rests on the sensible assumption that if a model of AN compositionality is reliable, its predicted output for any AN pair, e.g. *weird_banana*, should be in principle usable as a substitute for the corresponding corpus-attested AN vector. Moreover, if such a model performs acceptably, it could even be used predict the compositionality of unattested candidates like *shadowy_banana*: this kind of operations is the key to attaining human-like semantic performance.

3.3.1 Correlation analysis between modelled predictions and observations

Let us start the comparative evaluation of the modelled predictions by considering the results of a series of Mantel correlation tests. First, distance matrices were computed for the observations in the test sets and then the same was done for each of the prediction models. Then, each of the models' distance matrices was compared against the distance matrix of the observations trying to determine their degree of correlation. The null hypothesis in each Mantel test is that the distance matrices being compared are unrelated. The aim of this task is similar to the evaluation method used by Mitchell and Lapata (2008): we try to find out which model has the strongest correlation with the original data, with the difference that in our case no "external" human ratings are used.

	HAL		RI	
Model	*Correlation*	*Simul. p-value*	*Correlation*	*Simul. p-value*
PLS	**0.5438081**	0.001	**0.4341146**	0.001
ADD	0.5344057	0.001	0.3223733	0.001
MUL	0.3297359	0.001	0.1811038	0.002
CON	-0.05557023	0.956	-0.02584655	0.727

Table 1: Adjective-Noun pairs. Mantel tests of correlation (max. correlation = 1)

Considering the results for the AN dataset in Table 1, with the PLS and ADD models we can reject the null hypothesis that the two matrices (distance matrix between the observed AN pairs and distance matrix between each model's predictions) are unrelated with p-value = 0.001 in both the semantic spaces (HAL and RI). MUL also allows the null hypothesis to be rejected, but with a lower correlation (and with a greater p-value = 0.002 in RI). Having obtained the highest observed correlation in both settings, the PLS model is highly positively associated with the observed data. Also ADD and MUL have produced predictions that are positively correlated with the observed AN vectors. CON is not correlated with the original data. In other words, PLS and ADD seem to be much better that the remaining models in reproducing unseen AN pairs; overall, however, PLS produces the closest approximation of the corpus-based test set. Finally, although both semantic spaces (HAL and RI) produce the same ordering among the models, it seems that the predictions using the HAL space are relatively closer to the observed data.

	HAL		RI	
Model	*Correlation*	*Simul. p-value*	*Correlation*	*Simul. p-value*
PLS	0.2186435	0.003	0.1113741	0.116
ADD	**0.4094653**	0.001	**0.1290508**	0.124
MUL	0.1375934	0.042	-0.08865458	0.8
CON	0.05153776	0.174	-0.08186146	0.807

Table 2: Verb-Noun pairs. Mantel tests of correlation (max. correlation = 1)

Turning to the VN dataset, the obtained results are much less promising (see Table 2). As a general observation, the correlations between each of the models and the observations are very low, except for ADD in the HAL semantic space. In addition, ADD obtains the best correlation also in the RI space. PLS comes in second place. Given that PLS is based on the estimation of parameters from training data, its low performance can be attributed to the size of dataset (only 133 VN examples used for training). On the contrary, ADD, MUL and CON do not have this excuse and their extremely low performance must be due to other factors. Finally, it is very clear that HAL produces better correlations for all the models.

3.3.2 Observation-based neighbour analysis

For this and for the remaining evaluation protocols, a preliminary step was taken. Since our intention is to base the evaluation on the analysis of nearest neighbours, we extracted an identical subset of the built semantic spaces (HAL and RI, which originally had a vocabulary of 23,222 items) in order to compute a distance matrix of a manageable size.

In the Adjective-Noun dataset, the extracted subset comprises vectors for all the observed AN vectors in both the training and test sets (1,367 items), all the corresponding predictions, the NOUN- and ADJ-baseline models, the 2,500 most frequent nouns (not included in the baseline) and the 2,500 most frequent adjectives (not included in the baseline). The distance matrix for the selected sub-space was then created by using the Euclidean measure of distance, resulting in a 8,666 $\times$ 8,666 matrix.

The Verb-Noun dataset was treated in the same way, extracting vectors for all the VN observations, the corresponding predictions from each model, the VERB- and NOUN-baseline models and the 1,000 most frequent nouns and verbs in the space (not overlapping with the baselines); this resulted in a 2,420 $\times$ 2,420 distance matrix.

Following Guevara's (2010) neighbour analysis, for each observed AN pair in the test datasets, the list of n-top neighbours were extracted from the distance matrix (n=10 and n=20). Then, the resulting neighbour lists were analysed to see if any of the modelled predictions was to be found in the n-top list. The ADJ- and NOUN-baselines were introduced in the evaluation to further compare the appropriateness of each model. Below we only report the results obtained with n=20, but very similar results were obtained in the 10-top neighbour setting.

As can be observed from Table 3, in the HAL space, PLS obtains the highest score, followed by the NOUN-baseline at a short distance and then by the ADJ-baseline at a greater distance. The performance of the remaining models is negligible. A different situation can be seen for the RI space, where the winner is the NOUN-baseline followed by PLS and ADJ.

	HAL	RI
Model	*Predictions found*	*Predictions found*
ADD	0	0
CON	0	0
MUL	3	0
PLS	**152**	112
ADJ	32	53
NOUN	123	**144**

Table 3: AN pairs. Observation-based neighbour analysis (max. score = 367)

It is interesting to see that PLS is actually competing against the NOUN-baseline alone, being the rival models almost insensible to the evaluation task. This same pattern will be seen in the other evaluation tasks. Furthermore, the score differences obtained by PLS and the NOUN-baseline are significant (HAL p-value = 0.03275, RI p-value = 0.01635, 2-sample test for equality of proportions).

The VN dataset gave much poorer results, once more. In fact, it is almost pointless to comment anything except that only MUL was able to rank its predictions in top-20 neighbours six times (only in the HAL space) and that PLS managed to do the same 9 times (only in the RI space). The maximum score in this setting was 60.

3.3.3 Prediction-based neighbour analysis

Building on the previous neighbour analysis, a new task was set up by changing the starting point for neighbour extraction. In this case, for each modelled AN pair in the test dataset in each composition model, the list of n-top neighbours were extracted from the distance matrix (n=10 and n=20). Then, the resulting neighbour lists were analysed to see if the originally observed corresponding AN pair was to be found in the n-top list. The same procedure was used with the VN dataset.

Below we only report the results obtained with n=20, but very similar results were obtained in the 10-top neighbour setting. This task at first did not seem to be particularly difficult, but the obtained results were very poor.

	HAL	RI
Model	*Predictions found*	*Predictions found*
ADD	2	0
CON	0	0
MUL	0	0
PLS	**32**	**25**
ADJ	6	2
NOUN	26	16

Table 4: AN pairs. Prediction-based neighbour analysis (max. score = 367)

The winner in this experiment was PLS, once again followed by the NOUN-baseline. However, the score differences obtained by PLS and the NOUN-baseline are not significant (HAL p-value = 0.4939, RI p-value = 0.1985, 2-sample test for equality of proportions). The main observation to be made is that the obtained scores are surprisingly low if compared with the previous evaluation task. The reason for this difference is to be found in the homogeneity and specialization that characterizes each of the models' neighbour sets: each model produces predictions that are relatively very close to each other. This has the consequence that the nearest neighbour lists for each model's predictions are, by and large, populated by items generated in the same model, as shown in Table 5. In conclusion, although PLS obtained the highest score in this task, we cannot be sure that it performed better than the NOUN-baseline. In any case, the remaining composition models did not reach the performance of PLS.

Model	*Same-model items*
ADD	3626 (98,8 %)
CON	3670 (100 %)
MUL	3670 (100 %)
PLS	2767 (75,4 %)
NOUN	1524 (41,5 %)
ADJ	1382 (36,1 %)

Table 5: AN pairs. Same-model neighbours in each models' top-10 list of neighbours extracted from HAL semantic space (total items in each list = 3670)

The VN dataset once again did not produce interesting results. As a brief note, ADD won in the HAL space (but managing to score only two observations in its predictions' top-20 neighbours) while PLS won in the RI space as before, scoring 5 observations in its predictions' top-20 neighbours (max. score 60).

3.3.4 Gold-standard comparison of shared neighbours

Our previous evaluation methods targeted the distance between predictions and observations, i.e. the ability of each model to reproduce unseen AN/VN pairs. Changing perspective, it would be desirable to test if the models' predictions show a similar distributional behaviour with respect to the corresponding observed vector and to other words in the semantic space.

To test this idea, the n-top neighbour-lists (n=10 and n=20) for the observed AN/VN pairs were extracted and taken to be the gold-standard. Then, each prediction's n-top list of neighbours was analysed looking for shared neighbours with respect to the corresponding gold-standard list. Each time a shared neighbour was found, 1 point was awarded to the model.

Table 6 summarises the results obtained with n=20 (similar figures obtained with n=10) in the AN dataset. Although by a small margin, the winner in this task is PLS. Even if the obtained scores are still rather low (in the best cases, about 17% of all the available points were obtained), this experiment represents a significant improvement over Guevara's (2010) reported results, which reached only about 10% of the maximum score. Here again the same ordering of models can be observed: after PLS we find the NOUN- and ADJ-baselines, leaving the performance of the remaining models at a extremely modest level. Additionally, the score differences obtained by PLS and the NOUN-baseline are highly significant (HAL p-value = 2.363e-08, RI p-value = 0.0003983, 2-sample test for equality of proportions).

	HAL	RI
Model	*Shared neighbours*	*Shared neighbours*
ADD	28	0
CON	0	0
MUL	5	0
PLS	**1299**	**1267**
ADJ	259	534
NOU	1050	1108
Total shared:	2641	2909

Table 6: AN pairs. Gold-standard comparison of shared neighbours (max. score = 7340)

Table 7 summarises the results obtained in the VN dataset, which show a considerable improvement over the preceding evaluation methods. Here we have to clear winners, ADD in the HAL space and PLS in the RI space. Interestingly, although the numbers are still on the low side, ADD obtained 8.6% of the total points, with shared neighbours for 35 out of 60 VN pairs; PLS obtained 21% of the total, with shared neighbours for 40 out of 60 VN pairs. In particular this last score is (21%) is the highest one ever obtained with gold-standard comparison of shared neighbours (also considering Guevara's 2010 results).

	HAL	RI
Model	*Shared neighbours*	*Shared neighbours*
ADD	**103**	0
CON	0	0
MUL	31	0
PLS	0	**253**
VERB	0	0
NOUN	0	0
Total shared:	134	253

Table 7: VN pairs. Gold-standard comparison of shared neighbours (max. score = 1200)

4 Conclusions

This paper proposes an improved framework to model the compositionality of meaning in Distributional Semantics. The method, Partial Least Squares Regression, is well known in other data-intensive fields of research, but to our knowledge had never been put to work in computational semantics.

PLS outperformed all the competing models in the reported experiments with AN pairs. In particular, the PLS model generates compositional predictions that are closer to the observed composed vectors than those of its rivals. This is an extremely promising result, indicating that it is possible to generalize linear transformation functions beyond single lexical items in Distributional Semantics' spaces.

It is remarkable that PLS did not actually have to compete against any of the previously proposed approaches to compositionality, but only against the NOUN- and ADJ-baselines, and in particular against the former. This fact is expected from a theoretical point of view: since the Noun is the head of the AN pair, it is likely that the complex expression and its head share much of their distributional properties. PLS nearly always outperformed the NOUN-baseline, but only by small margins, which indicates that there is a still plenty of space for improvement. Our experiments also show that AN compositionality by regression performs nearly equally well in semantic spaces of very different nature (HAL and RI).

The second dataset used in this paper contained VN pairs. Generally, this dataset did not produce good results with any of the considered approaches to model compositionality. This rather negative result may be due to its relatively smaller size, but this excuse may only be applied to PLS, the only model that relies on parameter estimation. Surprisingly, though, the gold-standard comparison of shared neighbours gave much better results, with ADD performing well in the HAL space and PLS performing very well in the RI space. Even if the VN dataset did not produce excellent results, it highlights some interesting issues. First, not all syntactic relations may be equally "easy" to model. Second, different evaluation methods may favor competing approaches. Finally, some approaches may be particularly successful with a specific distributional space architecture (like PLS and RI, and ADD and HAL).

This work has intentionally left the data as raw as possible, in order to keep the noise present in the models at a realistic level. The combination of Machine Learning and Distributional Semantics here advocated suggests a very promising perspective: transformation functions corresponding to different syntactic relations could be learned from suitably processed corpora and then combined to model larger, more complex structures, probably also recursive phenomena. It remains to prove if this approach is able to model the symbolic, logic-inspired kind of compositionality that is common in Formal Semantics; being inherently based on functional items, it is at present time very difficult and computationally intensive to attain, but hopefully this will change in the near future.

References

Abdi, H. (2007). Partial least squares regression. In N. Salkind (Ed.) *Encyclopaedia of Measurement and Statistics*. Thousand Oaks (CA), Sage.

Baroni, M. and A. Lenci. (2009). One semantic memory, many semantic tasks. In *Proc. of the EACL Workshop on Geometrical Models of Natural Language Semantics*, 3–11. Athens, ACL.

Baroni, M. and R. Zamparelli. (2010, to appear). Nouns are vectors, adjectives are matrices: Representing adjective-noun constructions in semantic space. In *Proceedings of EMNLP 2010*.

Burgess, C. and K. Lund. (1997). Modeling parsing constraints with high-dimensional context space. *"Language and Cognitive Processes"*, 12, 177-210.

Clark, S. and S. Pulman. (2007). Combining symbolic and distributional models of meaning. In *Proceedings of the AAAI Spring Symposium on Quantum Interaction,* 52–55. Stanford (CA).

Giesbrecht, E. (2009). In Search of Semantic Compositionality in Vector Spaces. In *Proceedings of ICCS 2009*, Moscow, Russia, 173–184. Berlin, Springer.

Grefenstette, E. Bob Coecke, S Pulman, S. Clark and M. Sadrzadeh. (2010). Concrete Compositional Sentence Spaces. Talk presented at ESSLLI 2010, August 16-20, 2010, University of Copenhagen.

Guevara, E. (2010). A Regression Model of Adjective-Noun Compositionality in Distributional Semantics. In *Proc. of the 2010 Workshop on Geometrical Models of Natural Language Semantics*, 33-37. Uppsala, ACL.

Jurgens, D. and K. Stevens. (2010). The S-Space Package: An Open Source Package for Word Space Models. In *Proceedings of the ACL 2010 System Demonstrations,* 30-35. Uppsala, ACL.

Kintsch, W. 2001. Predication. *"Cognitive Science"*, 25 (2), 173–202.

Mevik, B.-H. and R. Wehrens. (2007). The pls package: principal component and partial least squares regression in R. *"Journal of Statistical Software"*, 18 (2), 1–24.

Mitchell, J. and M. Lapata. (2008). Vector- based Models of Semantic Composition. In *Proceedings of the 46th Annual Meeting of the ACL*, 236–244. Columbus, OH, ACL.

Pantel, P. (2005). Inducing ontological co-occurrence vectors. In *Proceedings of the 43rd Conference of the ACL*, 125–132. Morristown, ACL.

Partee, B.H., A. ter Meulen and R.E. Wall. (1990). *Mathematical methods in linguistics*. Dordrecht, Kluwer.

Plate, T.A. (1991). Holographic reduced representations: Convolution algebra for compositional distributed representations. In *Proceedings of the 12th International Joint Conference on Artificial Intelligence*, 30–35. Sydney.

Sahlgren, M. (2006). *The Word Space Model*. Ph.D. dissertation. Stockholm University.

Turney, P. and P. Pantel. (2010). From frequency to meaning: Vector space models of semantics. *"Journal of Artificial Intelligence Research"*, 37, 141–188.

Widdows, D. (2004). *Geometry and Meaning*. Stanford, CSLI publications.

Widdows, D. (2008). Semantic Vector Products: Some Initial Investigations. Paper presented at the *Second AAAI Symposium on Quantum Interaction*. Oxford, 26th–28th March 2008.

Using Query Patterns to Learn the Duration of Events

Andrey Gusev Nathanael Chambers Pranav Khaitan Divye Khilnani
Steven Bethard Dan Jurafsky
Department of Computer Science, Stanford University
{agusev,nc,pranavkh,divyeraj,bethard,jurafsky}@cs.stanford.edu

Abstract

We present the first approach to learning the durations of events without annotated training data, employing web query patterns to infer duration distributions. For example, we learn that "war" lasts *years* or *decades*, while "look" lasts *seconds* or *minutes*. Learning aspectual information is an important goal for computational semantics and duration information may help enable rich document understanding. We first describe and improve a supervised baseline that relies on event duration annotations. We then show how web queries for linguistic patterns can help learn the duration of events without labeled data, producing fine-grained duration judgments that surpass the supervised system. We evaluate on the TimeBank duration corpus, and also investigate how an event's participants (arguments) effect its duration using a corpus collected through Amazon's Mechanical Turk. We make available a new database of events and their duration distributions for use in research involving the temporal and aspectual properties of events.

1 Introduction

Bridging the gap between lexical knowledge and world knowledge is crucial for achieving natural language understanding. For example, knowing whether a nominal is a person or organization and whether a person is male or female substantially improves coreference resolution, even when such knowledge is gathered through noisy unsupervised approaches (Bergsma, 2005; Haghighi and Klein, 2009). However, existing algorithms and resources for such semantic knowledge have focused primarily on static properties of nominals (e.g. gender or entity type), not dynamic properties of verbs and events.

This paper shows how to learn one such property: the typical duration of events. Since an event's duration is highly dependent on context, our algorithm models this aspectual property as a distribution over durations rather than a single mean duration. For example, a "war" typically lasts *years*, sometimes *months*, but almost never *seconds*, while "look" typically lasts *seconds* or *minutes*, but rarely *years* or *decades*. Our approach uses web queries to model an event's typical distribution in the real world.

Learning such rich aspectual properties of events is an important area for computational semantics, and should enrich applications like event coreference (e.g., Chen and Ji, 2009) in much the same way that gender has benefited nominal coreference systems. Event durations are also key to building event timelines and other deeper temporal understandings of a text (Verhagen et al., 2007; Pustejovsky and Verhagen, 2009).

The contributions of this work are:

- Demonstrating how to acquire event duration distributions by querying the web with patterns.
- Showing that a system that predicts event durations based only on our web count distributions can outperform a supervised system that requires manually annotated training data.
- Making available an event duration lexicon with duration distributions for common English events.

We first review previous work and describe our re-implementation and augmentation of the latest supervised system for predicting event durations. Next, we present our approach to learning event distributions based on web counts. We then evaluate both of these models on an existing annotated corpus of event durations and make comparisons to durations we collected using Amazon's Mechanical Turk. Finally, we present a generated database of event durations.

2 Previous Work

Early work on extracting event properties focused on linguistic aspect, for example, automatically distinguishing *culminated* events that have an end point from *non-culminated* events that do not (Siegel and McKeown, 2000). The more fine-grained task of predicting the duration of events was first proposed by Pan et al. (2006), who annotated each event in a small section of the TimeBank (Pustejovsky et al., 2003) with duration lower and upper bounds. They then trained support vector machines on their annotated corpus for two prediction tasks: *less-than-a-day* vs. *more-than-a-day*, and bins like *seconds*, *minutes*, *hours*, etc. Their models used features like bags of words, heads of syntactic subjects and objects, and WordNet hypernyms of the events. This work provides a valuable resource in its annotated corpus and is also a good baseline. We replicate their work and also add new features as described below.

Our approach to the duration problem is inspired by the standard use of web patterns for the acquisition of relational lexical knowledge. Hearst (1998) first observed that a phrase like "...algae, such as Gelidium..." indicates that "Gelidium" is a type of "algae", and so hypernym-hyponym relations can be identified by querying a text collection with patterns like "such <noun> as <noun>" and "<noun> , including <noun>". A wide variety of pattern-based work followed, including the application of the idea in VerbOcean to acquire aspects and temporal structure such as happens-before, using patterns like "to <verb> and then <verb>" (Chklovski and Pantel, 2004).

More recent work has learned nominal gender and animacy by matching patterns like "<noun> * himself" and "<noun> and her" to a corpus of Web n-grams (Bergsma, 2005; Ji and Lin, 2009). Phrases like "John Joseph", which were observed often with masculine pronouns and never with feminine or neuter pronouns, can thus have their gender identified as masculine. Ji and Lin found that such web-counts can predict person names as well as a fully supervised named entity recognition system.

Our goal, then, is to integrate these two strands in the literature, applying pattern/web approaches to the task of estimating event durations. One difference from previous work is the distributional nature of the extracted knowledge. In the time domain, unlike in most previous relation-extraction domains, there is rarely a single correct answer: "war" may last *months*, *years* or *decades*, though *years* is the most likely. Our goal is thus to produce a distribution over durations rather than a single mean duration.

3 Duration Prediction Tasks

In both our supervised and unsupervised models, we consider two types of event duration predictions: a *coarse-grained* task in which we only want to know whether the event lasts more or less than a day, and a *fine-grained* task in which we want to know whether the event lasts *seconds*, *minutes*, *hours*, *days*, *weeks*, *months* or *years*. These two duration prediction tasks were originally suggested by Pan et al. (2006), based on their annotation of a subset of newspaper articles in the Timebank corpus (Pustejovsky et al., 2003). Events were annotated with a minimum and maximum duration like the following:

- **5 minutes – 1 hour**: A Brooklyn woman who was *watching* her clothes dry in a laundromat.
- **1 week – 3 months**: Eileen Collins will be named commander of the Space Shuttle *mission*.
- **3 days – 2 months**: President Clinton says he is *committed* to a possible strike against Iraq...

Pan et al. suggested the *coarse-grained* binary classification task because they found that the mean event durations from their annotations were distributed bimodally across the corpus, roughly split into short events (less than a day) and long events (more than a day). The *fine-grained* classification task provides additional information beyond this simple two way distinction.

For both tasks, we must convert the minimum/maximum duration annotations into single labels. We follow Pan et al. (2006) and take the arithmetic mean of the minimum and maximum durations in seconds. For example, in the first event above, *5 minutes* would be converted into 300 seconds, *1 hour* would be converted into 3600 seconds, the resulting mean would be 1950 seconds, and therefore this event would be labeled *less-than-a-day* for the *coarse-grained* task, and *minutes* for the *fine-grained* task. These labels can then be used directly to train and evaluate our models.

4 Supervised Approach

Before describing our query-based approach, we describe our baseline, a replication and extension of the supervised system from Pan et al. (2006). We first briefly describe their features, which are shared across the coarse and fine-grained tasks, and then suggest new features.

4.1 Pan et. al. Features

The Pan et al. (2006) system included the following features which we also replicate:

Event Properties: The event token, lemma and part of speech (POS) tag.

Bag of Words: The n tokens to the left and right of the event word. However, because Pan et al. found that $n = 0$ performed best, we omit this feature.

Subject and Object: The head word of the syntactic subject and object of the event, along with their lemmas and POS tags. Subjects and objects provide important context. For example, "saw Europe" lasts for *weeks* or *months* while "saw the goal" lasts only *seconds*.

Hypernyms: WordNet hypernyms for the event, its subject and its object. Starting from the first synset of each lemma, three hypernyms were extracted from the WordNet hierarchy. Hypernyms can help cluster similar events together. For example, the event *plan* had three hypernym ancestors as features: *idea*, *content* and *cognition*.

4.2 New Features

We present results for our implementation of the Pan et al. (2006) system in Section 8. However, we also implemented additional features.

Event Attributes: Timebank annotates individual events with four attributes: the event word's tense (past, present, future, none), aspect (e.g., progressive), modality (e.g., *could, would, can,* etc.), and event class (occurrence, aspectual, state, etc.). We use each of these as a feature in our classifier. The aspect and tense of the event, in particular, are well known indicators of the temporal shape of events (Vendler, 1976).

Named Entity Classes: Pan et al. found the subject and object of the events to be useful features, helping to identify the particular sense of the event. We used a named entity recognizer to add more information about the subjects and objects, labeling them as *persons, organizations, locations*, or *other*.

Typed Dependencies: We coded aspects of the subcategorization frame of a predicate, such as transitivity, or the presence of prepositional objects or adverbial modifiers, by adding a binary feature for each typed dependency[1] seen with a verb or noun. We experimented with including the head of the argument itself, but results were best when only the dependency type was included.

Reporting Verbs: Many of the events in Timebank are reporting verbs (*say, report, reply,* etc.). We used a list of reporting verbs to identify these events with a binary feature.

4.3 Classifier

Both the Pan et al. feature set and our extended feature set were used to train supervised classifiers for the two event duration prediction tasks. We experimented with naive bayes, logistic regression, maximum entropy and support vector machine classifiers, but as discussed in Section 8, the maximum entropy model performed best in cross-validations on the training data.

5 Unsupervised Approach

While supervised learning is effective for many NLP tasks, it is sensitive to the amount of available training data. Unfortunately, the training data for event durations is very small, consisting of only 58 news articles (Pan et al., 2006), and labeling further data is quite expensive. This motivates our desire to find an

[1] We parsed the documents into typed dependencies with the Stanford Parser (Klein and Manning, 2003).

approach that does not rely on labeled data, but instead utilizes the large amounts of text available on the Web to search for duration-specific patterns. This section describes our web-based approach to learning event durations.

5.1 Web Query Patterns

Temporal properties of events are often described explicitly in language-specific constructions which can help us infer an event's duration. Consider the following two sentences from our corpus:

- Many *spend hours* surfing the Internet.
- The answer is coming up *in a few minutes.*

These sentences explicitly describe the duration of the events. In the first, the dominating clause *spend hours* tells us how long surfing the Internet lasts (*hours*, not *seconds*), and in the second, the preposition attachment serves a similar role. These examples are very rare in the corpus, but as can be seen, are extremely informative when present. We developed several such informative patterns, and searched the Web to find instances of them being used with our target events.

For each pattern described below, we use Yahoo! to search for the patterns occurring with our events. We collect the total hit counts and use them as indicators of duration. The Yahoo! search API returns two numbers for a query: *totalhits* and *deephits*. The former excludes duplicate pages and limits the number of documents per domain while the latter includes all duplicates. We take the sum of these two numbers as our count (this worked better than either of the two individually on the training data and provides a balance between the benefits of each estimate) and normalize the results as described in Section 5.2. Queries are submitted as complete phrases with quotation marks, so the results only include exact phrase matches. This greatly reduces the number of hits, but results in more precise distributions.

5.1.1 Coarse-Grained Patterns

The coarse grained task is a binary decision: *less than a day* or *more than a day*. We can model this task directly by looking for constructions that can only be used with events that take less than a day. The adverb *yesterday* fills this role nicely; an event modified by *yesterday* strongly implies that it took place within a single day's time. For example, *'shares closed at $18 yesterday'* implies that the *closing* happened in less than a day. We thus consider the following two query patterns:

- <event$_{past}$> yesterday
- <event$_{pastp}$> yesterday

where <event$_{past}$> is the past tense (preterite) form of the event (e.g., *ran*), and <event$_{pastp}$> is the past progressive form of the event (e.g., *was running*).

5.1.2 Fine-Grained Patterns

For the fine-grained task, we need patterns that can identify when an event falls into any of the various buckets: *seconds, minutes, hours*, etc. Thus, our fine-grained patterns are parameterized both by the event and by the bucket of interest. We use the following patterns inspired in part by Dowty (1979):

1. <event$_{past}$> for * <bucket>
2. <event$_{pastp}$> for * <bucket>
3. spent * <bucket> <event$_{ger}$>

where <event$_{past}$> and <event$_{pastp}$> are defined as above, <event$_{ger}$> is the gerund form of the event (e.g., *running*), and the wildcard '*' can match any single token[2].

The following three patterns ultimately did not improve the system's performance on the training data:

4. <event$_{past}$> in * <bucket>
5. takes * <bucket> to <event>
6. <event$_{past}$> last <bucket>

Pattern 4 returned a lot of hits, but had low precision as it picked up many non-durative expressions. Pattern 5 was very precise but typically returned few hits, and pattern 6 worked for, e.g., *last week*, but did not work for shorter durations. All reported systems use patterns 1-3 and do not include 4-6.

[2]We experimented with varying numbers of wildcards but found little difference in performance on the training data.

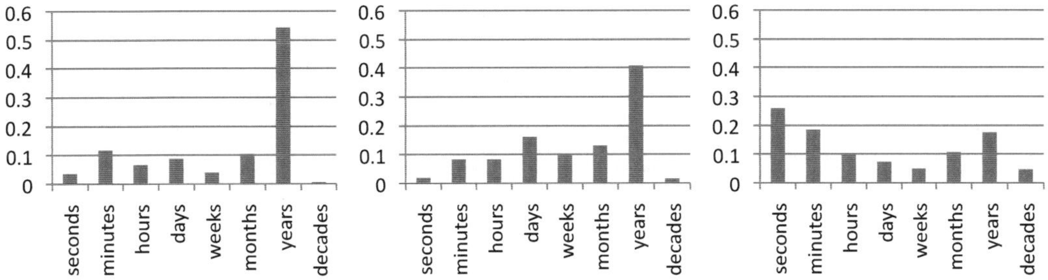

(a) "was saying for <bucket>" (b) "for <bucket>" (c) (a) counts divided by (b) counts

Figure 1: Normalizing the distribution for the pattern "was saying for <bucket>".

We also tried adding subjects and/or objects to the patterns when they were present for an event. However, we found that the benefit of the extra context was outweighed by the significantly fewer hits that resulted. We implemented several backoff approaches that removed the subject and object from the query, however, the counts from these backoff approaches were less reliable than just using the base event.

5.2 Predicting Durations from Patterns

To predict the duration of an event from the above patterns, we first insert the event into each pattern template and query the web to see how often the filled template occurs. These counts form a distribution over each of the bins of interest, e.g., in the fine-grained task we have counts for *seconds*, *minutes*, *hours*, etc. We discard pattern distributions with very low total counts, and normalize the remaining pattern distributions based on the frequency with which the pattern occurs in general. Finally, we uniformly merge the distributions from all patterns, and use the resulting distribution to select a duration label for the event. The following sections detail this process.

5.2.1 Coarse-Grained Prediction

For the coarse-grained task of less than a day vs. more than a day, we collect counts using the two *yesterday* patterns described above. We then normalize these counts by the count of the event's occurrence in general. For example, given the event *run*, we query for "ran yesterday" and divide by the count of "ran". This gives us the probability of seeing *yesterday* given that we saw *ran*. We average the probabilities from the two *yesterday* patterns, and classify an event as lasting less than a day if its average probability exceeds a threshold t. We optimized t to our training set ($t = .002$). This basically says that if an event occurs with *yesterday* more than 0.2% of the time, we will assume that the event lasts less than a day.

5.2.2 Fine-Grained Prediction

As with the coarse-grained task, our fine-grained approach begins by collecting counts using the three fine-grained patterns discussed above. Since each fine-grained pattern has both an <event> and a <bucket> slot to be filled, for a single event and a single pattern, we end up making 8 queries to cover each of the 8 buckets: *seconds*, *minutes*, *hours*, *days*, *weeks*, *months*, *years* and *decades*. After these queries, we have a pattern-specific distribution of counts over the various buckets, a coarse measure of the types of durations that might be appropriate to this event. Figure 1(a) shows an example of such a distribution.

As can be seen in Figure 1(a), this initial distribution can be skewed in various ways – in this case, *years* is given far too much mass. This is because in addition to the single event interpretation of words like "saying", there are iterative or habitual interpretations (Moens and Steedman, 1988; Frawley, 1992). Iterative events occur repeatedly over a period of time, e.g., "he's been saying for years that..." The two interpretations are apparent in the raw distributions of *smile* and *run* in Figure 2. The large peak at *years* for *run* shows that it is common to say someone "was running for years." Conversely, it is less common to say someone "was smiling for years," so the distribution for *smile* is less biased towards *years*.

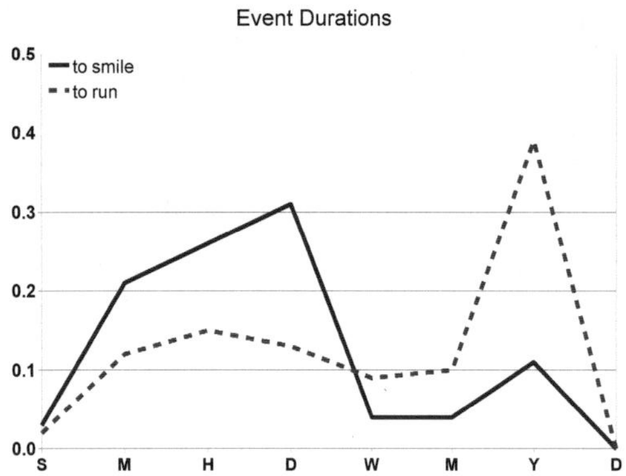

Figure 2: Two double peaked distributions.

Coverage of Fine-Grained Query Patterns

Number of Patterns	Total Events	Precision
At least one	1359 (81.7%)	57.3
At least two	1142 (68.6%)	58.6
All three	428 (25.7%)	65.7

Figure 3: The number of events that match n fine-grained patterns and the pattern precision on these events. The training set consists of 1664 events.

While the problem of distinguishing single events from iterative events is out of the scope of this paper (though an interesting avenue for future research), we can partially address the problem by recognizing that some buckets are simply more frequent in text than others. For example, Figure 1(b) shows that it is by far more common to see "for <bucket>" filled with *years* than with any other duration unit. Thus, for each bucket, we divide the counts collected with the event patterns by the counts we get for the pattern without the event[3]. Essentially, this gives us for each bucket the probability of the event given that bucket. Figure 1(c) shows that the resulting normalized distribution fits our intution of how long "saying" should last much better than the raw counts: *seconds* and *minutes* have much more of the mass now.

After normalizing an event's counts for each pattern, we combine the distributions from the three different patterns if their hit counts pass certain confidence thresholds. The total hit count for each pattern must exceed a minimum threshold $t_{min} = 100$ and not exceed a maximum threshold $t_{max} = 100,000$ (both thresholds were optimized on the training data). The former avoids building distributions from a sparse number of hits, and the latter avoids classifying generic and polysemous events like 'to make' that return a large number of hits. We found such events to produce generic distributions that do not help in classification. If all three patterns pass our confidence thresholds, we merge the pattern distributions by summing them bucket-wise together and renormalizing the resulting distribution to sum to 1. Merging the patterns mitigates the noise from any single pattern.

To predict the event's duration, we then select the bucket with the highest *smoothed* score:

$$score(b_i) = b_{i-1} + b_i + b_{i+1}$$

where b_i is a duration bucket and $0 < i < 9$. We define $b_0 = b_9 = 0$. In other words, the score of the *minute* bucket is the sum of three buckets: *second*, *minute* and *hour*. This parallels the smoothing of the evaluation metric introduced by (Pan et al., 2006) which we also adopt for evaluation in Section 7.

In the case that fewer than three of our patterns matched, we backoff to the majority class (*months* for fine-grained, and *more-than-a-day* for coarse-grained). We experimented with only requiring one or two patterns to match, but found the best results on training when requiring all three. Figure 3 shows the large jump in precision when all three are required. The evaluation is discussed in Section 7.

5.2.3 Coarse-Grained Prediction via Fine-Grained Prediction

We can also use the distributions collected from the fine-grained task to predict coarse-grained labels. We use the above approach and return *less than a day* if the selected fine-grained bucket was *seconds, minutes* or *hours*, and *more than a day* otherwise. We also tried summing over the duration buckets: p(seconds) + p(minutes) + p(hours) for *less than day* and p(days) + p(weeks) + p(months) + p(years) + p(decades) for *more than a day*, but the simpler approach outperformed these summations in training.

[3]We also explored normalizing not by the global distribution on the Web, but by the average of the distributions of all the events in our dataset. However, on the training data, using the global distribution performed better.

6 Datasets

6.1 Timebank Duration

As described in Section 3, Pan et al. (2006) labeled 58 documents with event durations. We follow their method of isolating the 10 WSJ articles as a separate test set which we call *TestWSJ* (147 events). For the remaining 48 documents, they split the 2132 event instances into a *Train* and *Test* set with 1705 and 427 events respectively. Their split was conducted over the bag of events, so their train and test sets may include events that came from the same document. Their particular split was unavailable.

We instead use a document-split that divides the two sets into bins of documents. Each document's entire set of events is assigned to either the training set or the test set, so we do not mix events across sets. Since documents often repeat mentions of events, this split is more conservative by not mixing test mentions with the training set. Train, Test, and TestWSJ contain 1664 events (714 unique verbs), 471 events (274 unique), and 147 events (84 unique) respectively. For each base verb, we created queries as described in Section 5.1.2. The train/test split is available at *http://cs.stanford.edu/people/agusev/durations/*.

6.2 Mechanical Turk Dataset

We also collected event durations from Amazon's Mechanical Turk (MTurk), an online marketplace from Amazon where requesters can find workers to solve Human Intelligence Tasks (HITs) for small amounts of money. Prior work has shown that human judgments from MTurk can often be as reliable as trained annotators (Snow et al., 2008) or subjects in controlled lab studies (Munro et al., 2010), particularly when judgments are aggregated over many MTurk workers ("Turkers"). Our motivation for using Turkers is to better analyze system errors. For example, if we give humans an event in isolation (no sentence context), how well can they guess the durations assigned by the Pan et. al. annotators? This measures how big the gap is between a system that looks only at the event, and a system that integrates all available context.

To collect event durations from MTurk, we presented Turkers with an event from the TimeBank (a superset of the events annotated by Pan et al. (2006)) and asked them to decide whether the event was most likely to take *seconds*, *minutes*, *hours*, *days*, *weeks*, *months*, *years* or *decades*. We had events annotated in two different contexts: in isolation, where only the event itself was given (e.g., "allocated"), and in subject-object context, where a minimal phrase including the event and its subject and object was given (e.g., "the mayor allocated funds"). In both types of tasks, we asked 10 Turkers to label each event, and they were paid \$0.0025 for each annotation (\$0.05 for a block of 20 events). To filter out obvious spammers, we added a test item randomly to each block, e.g., adding the event "minutes" and rejecting work from Turkers who labeled this anything other than the duration *minutes*.

The resulting annotations give duration distributions for each of our events. For example, when presented the event "remodeling", 1 Turker responded with *days*, 6 with *weeks*, 2 with *months* and 1 with *years*. These annotations suggest that we generally expect "remodeling" to take weeks, but it may sometimes take more or less. To produce a single fine-grained label from these distributions, we take the duration bin with the largest number of Turker annotations, e.g. for "remodeling", we would produce the label *weeks*. To produce a single coarse-grained label, we use the label *less-than-a-day* if the fine-grained label was *seconds*, *minutes* or *hours* and *more-than-a-day* otherwise.

7 Experiment Setup

As discussed in Section 3, we convert the minimum and maximum duration annotations into labels by converting each to seconds using ISO standards and calculating the arithmetic mean. If the mean is ≤ 86400 seconds, it is considered *less-than-a-day* for the coarse-grained task. The fine-grained buckets are similarly calculated, e.g., X is labeled *days* if $86400 < X \leq 604800$. The Pan et al. (2006) evaluation does not include a *decades* bucket, but our system still uses "decades" in its queries.

We optimized all parameters of both the supervised and unsupervised systems on the training set, only running on test after selecting our best performing model. We compare to the majority class as a baseline,

Coarse-Grained

	Test	TestWSJ
Supervised, Pan	**73.3**	73.5
Supervised, all	73.0	**74.8**

Fine-Grained

	Test	TestWSJ
Supervised, Pan	62.2	61.9
Supervised, all	**62.4**	**66.0**

Figure 4: Accuracies of the supervised maximum entropy classifiers with two different feature sets.

Coarse-Grained

	Test	TestWSJ
Majority class	62.4	57.1
Supervised, all	**73.0***	**74.8***
Web counts, yesterday	70.7*	**74.8***
Web counts, buckets	72.4*	73.5*

Fine-Grained

	Test	TestWSJ
Majority class	59.2	52.4
Supervised, all	62.4	66.0†
Web counts, buckets	**66.5***	**68.7***

Figure 5: System accuracy compared against supervised and majority class. * indicates statistical significance (McNemar's Test, two-tailed) against majority class at the $p < 0.01$ level, † at $p < 0.05$

tagging all events as *more-than-a-day* in the coarse-grained task and *months* in the fine-grained task.

To evaluate our models, we use simple accuracy on the coarse-grained task, and approximate agreement matching as in Pan et al. (2006) on the fine-grained task. In this approximate agreement, a guess is considered correct if it chooses either the gold label or its immediate neighbor (e.g., *hours* is correct if *minutes*, *hours* or *days* is the gold class). Pan et al. use this approach since human labeling agreement is low (44.4%) on the exact agreement fine-grained task.

8 Results

Figure 4 compares the performance of our two supervised models; the reimplementation of Pan et al. (2006) (**Supervised, Pan**), and our improved model with new features (**Supervised, all**). The new model performs similarily to the Pan model on the in-domain **Test** set, but better on the out-of-domain financial news articles in the **TestWSJ** test. On the latter, the new model improves over Pan et al. by 1.3% absolute on the coarse-grained task, and by 4.1% absolute on the fine-grained task. We report results from the maximum entropy model as it slightly outperformed the naive bayes and support vector machine models[4].

We compare these supervised results against our web-based unsupervised systems in Figure 5. For the coarse-grained task, we have two web count systems described in Section 5: one based on the *yesterday* patterns (**Web counts, yesterday**), and one based on first gathering the fine-grained bucket counts and then converting those to coarse-grained labels (**Web counts, buckets**). Generally, these models perform within 1-2% of the supervised model on the coarse-grained task, though the *yesterday*-based classifier exactly matches the supervised system's performance on the TestWSJ data. The supervised system's higher results are not statistically significant against our web-based systems.

For the fine-grained task, Figure 5 compares our web counts algorithm based on duration distributions (Section 5) to the baseline and supervised systems. Our web counts approach outperforms the best supervised system by 4.1% absolute on the Test set and by 2.7% absolute on the out-of-domain TestWSJ.

To get an idea of how much the subject/object context could help predict event duration if integrated perfectly, we evaluated the Mechanical Turk annotations against the Pan et. al. annotated dataset using approximate agreement as described in Section 7. Figure 6 gives the performance of the Turkers given two types of context: just the event itself (**Event only**), and the event plus its subject and/or object (**Event and args**). Turkers performed below the majority class baseline when given only the event, but generally above the baseline when given the subject and object, improving up to 20% over the event-only condition.

Figure 7 shows examples of events with different learned durations.

[4]This differs from Pan et al. who found support vector machines to be the best classifier.

Mechanical Turk Accuracy

	Coarse		Fine	
	Test	WSJ	Test	WSJ
Majority class	62.4	57.1	**59.2**	52.4
Event only	52.0	49.4	42.1	43.8
Event and args	**65.0**	**70.1**	56.7	**59.9**

Figure 6: Accuracy of Mechanical Turkers against Pan et. al. annotations.

Learned Examples

talk to tourism leaders	minutes
driving	hours
shut down the supply route	days
travel	weeks
the downturn across Asia	months
build a museum	years

Figure 7: Examples of web query durations.

9 Discussion

Our novel approach to learning event durations showed 4.1% and 2.7% absolute gains over a state-of-the-art supervised classifier. Although the gain is not statistically significant, these results nonetheless suggest that we are learning as much about event durations from the web counts as we are currently able to learn with our improvements to Pan et al.'s (2006) supervised system. This is encouraging because it indicates that we may not need extensive manual annotations to acquire event durations. Further, our final query system achieves these results with only the event word, and without considering the subject, object or other types of context.

Despite the fact that we saw little gains in performance when including subjects and objects in our query patterns, the Mechanical Turk evaluation suggests that more information may still be gleaned from the additional context. Giving Turkers the subject and object improved their label accuracy by 10-20% absolute. This suggests that finding a way to include subjects and objects in the web queries, for example by using thesauri to generate related queries, is a valuable line of research for future work.

Finally, these MTurk experiments suggest that classifying events for duration *out of context* is a difficult task. Pan et al. (2006) reported 0.88 annotator agreement on the coarse-grained task when given the entire document context. Out of context, given just the event word, our Turkers only achieved 52% and 49% accuracy. Not surprisingly, the task is more difficult without the document. Our system, however, was also only given the event word, but it was able achieve over 70% in accuracy. This suggests that rich language understanding is often needed to correctly label an event for duration, but in the absence of such understanding, modeling the duration by web counts appears to be a practical and useful alternative.

10 A Database of Event Durations

Given the strong performance of our model on duration classification, we are releasing a database of events and their normalized duration distributions, as predicted by our bucket-based fine-grained model. We extracted the 1000 most frequent verbs from a newspaper corpus (the NYT portion of Gigaword Graff (2002)) with the 10 most frequent grammatical objects of each verb. These 10,000 events and their duration distributions are available at *http://cs.stanford.edu/people/agusev/durations/*.

Acknowledgements

Thanks to Chris Manning and the anonymous reviewers for insightful comments and feedback. This research draws on data provided by Yahoo!, Inc., through its Yahoo! Search Services offering. We gratefully acknowledge the support of the Defense Advanced Research Projects Agency (DARPA) Machine Reading Program under Air Force Research Laboratory (AFRL) prime contract no. FA8750-09-C-0181. Any opinions, findings, and conclusion or recommendations expressed in this material are those of the author(s) and do not necessarily reflect the view of DARPA, AFRL, or the US government.

References

Bergsma, S. (2005). Automatic acquisition of gender information for anaphora resolution. In *Advances in Artificial Intelligence*, Volume 3501 of *Lecture Notes in Computer Science*, pp. 342–353. Springer Berlin / Heidelberg.

Chen, Z. and H. Ji (2009). Graph-based event coreference resolution. In *Proceedings of the Workshop on Graph-based Methods for Natural Language Processing (TextGraphs-4)*, Singapore, pp. 54–57. ACL.

Chklovski, T. and P. Pantel (2004). Verbocean: Mining the web for fine-grained semantic verb relations. In D. Lin and D. Wu (Eds.), *Proceedings of EMNLP 2004*, Barcelona, Spain, pp. 33–40.

Dowty, D. R. (1979). *Word Meaning and Montague Grammar*. Kluwer Academic Publishers.

Frawley, W. (1992). *Linguistic Semantics*. Routledge.

Graff, D. (2002). English Gigaword. *Linguistic Data Consortium*.

Haghighi, A. and D. Klein (2009). Simple coreference resolution with rich syntactic and semantic features. In *Proceedings of EMNLP-2009*, Singapore, pp. 1152–1161.

Hearst, M. A. (1998). Automated discovery of wordnet relations. In *WordNet: An Electronic Lexical Database*. MIT Press.

Ji, H. and D. Lin (2009). Gender and animacy knowledge discovery from web-scale n-grams for unsupervised person mention detection. In *Proceedings of the Pacific Asia Conference on Language, Information and Computation*.

Klein, D. and C. D. Manning (2003). Accurate unlexicalized parsing. In *Proceedings of the 41st Annual Meeting of the Association for Computational Linguistics*, Sapporo, Japan, pp. 423–430.

Moens, M. and M. Steedman (1988). Temporal ontology in natural language. *Computational Linguistics 2*(14), 15–21.

Munro, R., S. Bethard, V. Kuperman, V. T. Lai, R. Melnick, C. Potts, T. Schnoebelen, and H. Tily (2010). Crowdsourcing and language studies: the new generation of linguistic data. In *Proceedings of the NAACL HLT 2010 Workshop on Creating Speech and Language Data with Amazon's Mechanical Turk*, Los Angeles, pp. 122–130.

Pan, F., R. Mulkar, and J. Hobbs (2006). Learning event durations from event descriptions. In *Proceedings of COLING-ACL*.

Pustejovsky, J., P. Hanks, R. Sauri, A. See, D. Day, L. Ferro, R. Gaizauskas, M. Lazo, A. Setzer, and B. Sundheim (2003). The timebank corpus. *Corpus Linguistics*, 647–656.

Pustejovsky, J. and M. Verhagen (2009). Semeval-2010 task 13: Evaluating events, time expressions, and temporal relations (tempeval-2). In *Proceedings of the Workshop on Semantic Evaluations: Recent Achievements and Future Directions (SEW-2009)*, Boulder, Colorado, pp. 112–116.

Siegel, E. V. and K. R. McKeown (2000). Learning methods to combine linguistic indicators: improving aspectual classification and revealing linguistic insights. *Computational Linguistics 26*(4), 595–628.

Snow, R., B. O'Connor, D. Jurafsky, and A. Ng (2008). Cheap and fast – but is it good? evaluating non-expert annotations for natural language tasks. In *Proceedings of EMNLP-2008*, Hawaii.

Vendler, Z. (1976). Verbs and times. *Linguistics in Philosophy*, 97–121.

Verhagen, M., R. Gaizauskas, F. Schilder, M. Hepple, G. Katz, and J. Pustejovsky (2007). Semeval-2007 task 15: Tempeval temporal relation identification. In *Proceedings of the Fourth International Workshop on Semantic Evaluations (SemEval-2007)*, Prague, Czech Republic, pp. 75–80.

A Representation Framework for Cross-lingual/Interlingual Lexical Semantic Correspondences

Yoshihiko Hayashi
Osaka University, Japan
hayashi@lang.osaka-u.ac.jp

Abstract

This paper proposes a framework for representing cross-lingual/interlingual lexical semantic correspondences that are expected to be recovered through a series of on-demand/on-the-fly invocations of a lexical semantic matching process. One of the central notions of the proposed framework is a *pseudo synset*, which is introduced to represent a cross-lingual/multilingual lexical concept, jointly denoted by word senses in more than one language. Another important ingredient of the proposed framework is a framework for *semantifying bilingual lexical resource entries*. This is a necessary substep when associating and representing corresponding lexical concepts in different languages by using bilingual lexical resources. Based on these devices, this paper further discusses possible extensions to the ISO standard lexical markup framework (LMF). These extensions would enable recovered correspondences to be organized as a dynamic *secondary language resource*, while keeping the existing primary language resources intact.

1 Introduction

As the world goes more global, the demand for multilingual lexical semantic resources has increased. A central approach to realize such a multilingual resource has been nicely demonstrated by the EuroWordNet (Vossen 2004) and the succeeding it, Global WordNet Grid project[1]. In these projects, the goal is to build a worldwide grid of wordnets by means of interlingual pivots. While we may assume that the grid is static and stable in its nature, *dynamic lexical resources* (Calzolari 2008) are possible, provided a variety of language resources are wrapped as Web services[2] and are accessible on a service infrastructure. For example, a virtually *combined lexicon*[3] can be evolutionarily realized by opportunistically associating semantically corresponding entries in the relevant lexical resources.

However, existing frameworks for modeling and representing lexical resources are not applicable to this new type of lexical resource in their current configurations. For example, while the ISO lexical markup framework (LMF)[4] provides useful constructs to represent a range of lexicons, it still concentrates on modeling one lexical resource at a time, and does not provide effective devices to integrate different types of lexical resources into a single combined resource. This has motivated us to develop a framework for representing cross-lingual/interlingual lexical semantic correspondences that may be recovered through a series of on-demand/on-the-fly invocations of a lexical semantic matching process that underlies combined lexicon access services.

The central concept of the framework is the notion of *pseudo synset*, which is introduced to represent a cross-lingual/multilingual lexical concept, jointly denoted by words in more than one language. As the name implies, it inherits and extends the constituting principle of wordnets: a lexical concept is

[1] http://www.globalwordnet.org/gwa/gwa_grid.htm

[2] We use the term *servicize* to mean the wrapping of a static language resource as a dynamic Web service, which provides a standardized application program interface (API).

[3] Hartmann(2005) discusses a range of *hybrid dictionaries*, which includes, for example, *monolingual cum interlingual dictionary*.

[4] Standardized as ISO 24613:2008.

defined as a set of synonymous word senses. Another component of the proposed framework is a framework for *semantifying* bilingual lexical resource entries, which is a necessary substep for associating and representing corresponding lexical concepts in different languages by using bilingual lexical resources.

This paper starts with a motivating example and a look at how to represent the abovementioned components in the example. This paper then discusses possible extensions to the ISO LMF, which would enable recovered cross-lingual/interlingual correspondences to be organized as a *dynamic* language resource. This dynamic resource is *secondary*, because it is created on top of the existing *primary* language resources. Here it should be noted that this secondary language resource can be enriched and expanded, gradually *evolving* in a collaborative Web service environment.

2 A Motivating Example and Representations

Figure 1 shows our motivating example, depicting five direct cross-lingual lexical semantic correspondences: a Japanese word *kawa* can be translated into either *river* or *stream* in English; *river* is associated with either of *rivière* or *fleuve* in French, depending on where the river flows into; *stream* is associated only with *rivière* in French.

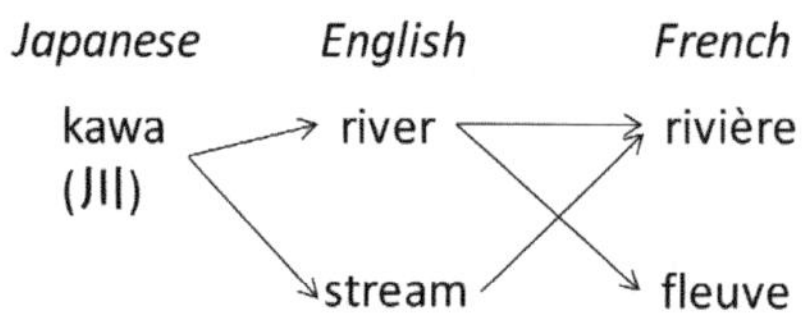

Figure 1: Motivating Example.

Situations similar to this one would be brought about, for example, by invoking a lexical access service on a Web-based linguistic service infrastructure. More specifically, think of a dictionary service that implements a virtually combined dictionary. One user of this service might like to find the meaning of the Japanese word *kawa* (by consulting a Japanese lexical semantic resource) and then want to know the equivalents in English (by consulting a bilingual dictionary); another user may want to look for French counterparts of *river*. To fulfill these requirements, a computational lexical semantic matching process behind the dictionary service should be invoked in an on-demand and on-the-fly manner, if the relevant cross-lingual semantic correspondences are unknown to it. These invocations of the matching process can induce possible indirect lexical semantic correspondences: for example, between *kawa* and *rivière*, via *river*.

2.1 Problems with a Possible LMF Representation

The LMF *NLP multilingual notation extension* (Francopoulo et al. 2009) is devised to model and represent lexical semantic correspondences across languages. We can use this device to model and represent the situation in the motivating example, as shown in Fig. 2, which makes use of the `Sense Axis` construct. Actually, this figure has been created from a figure presented in (Francopoulo et al. 2009) by adding the following: a Japanese `Sense` node associated with *kawa*; an English `Sense` node associated with *stream*; and a `Sense Axis` node that links the Japanese `Sense` node to the two English `Sense` nodes. Although this configuration seems to be natural, several questions may arise, including:

- How can we represent an indirect correspondence that could be dynamically derived or inferred from a combination of direct correspondences? For example, should the derivable indirect correspondence between *kawa* and *fleuve* also be represented by adding the `Sense Axis` and `Sense Axis Relation` constructs? Or should we introduce another `Sense Axis` node, which, as an interlingual pivot, aggregates all the corresponding senses?

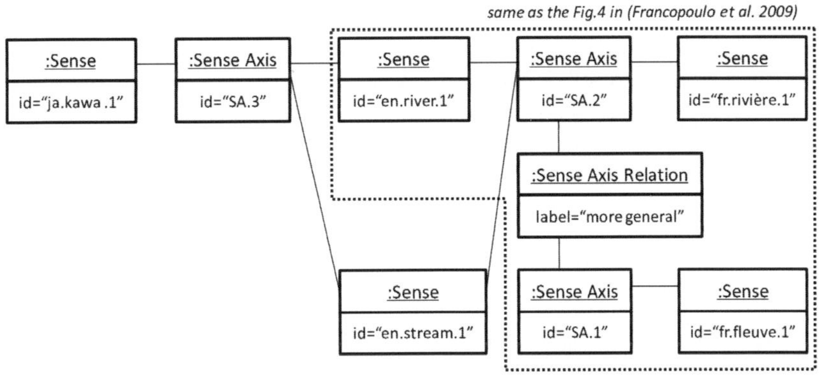

Figure 2: Straightforward LMF Representation of the Motivating Example.

- How and where should the details of a matching process be encoded? This is particularly crucial for a dynamic resource, so that the potential user is able to assess the reliability of the resource.
- Is the introduction of the `Sense Axis Relation` instance with the label "more general" necessary or adequate? The LMF specification states that a `Sense Axis Relation` instance should be introduced if the correspondence is not direct (partially equivalent). However, in our scenario, it is reasonable to expect that the lexical semantic relation between *rivière* and *fleuve* has already been encoded somewhere in an existing French lexical semantic resource. This suggests that the introduction of the `Sense Axis Relation` might be redundant.

2.2 Proposed Representation: Overview

Figure 3 shows the conceptual overview of the proposed representation for the motivating example in consideration of these questions. In this representation, we have eight nodes, each depicted by a shaded round rectangle node. Each of these nodes is classified as a *cross-lingual pseudo synset* (`CP_Synset`) node (marked by a number) or a *multilingual pseudo synset* (`MP_Synset`) node (marked by a Greek letter). While the former represents a directed cross-lingual correspondence between two senses, the latter shows a set of multilingual word senses that may share an intersectional concept across the languages. For example, the `CP_Synset` node labeled "1" represents a concept denoted by senses of *kawa* and *stream*, along with the depicted direction. The node marked α indicates a concept jointly denoted by the multilingual sense set: $\{$*kawa*, *stream*, *rivière*$\}$.

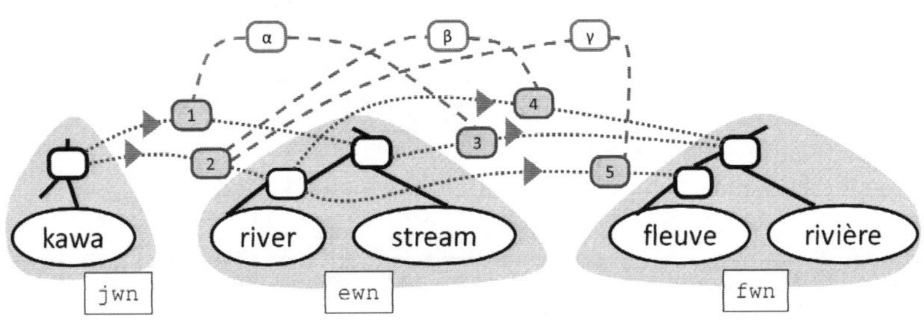

Figure 3: Conceptual Overview of the Proposed Representation for the Motivating Example.

Given the previously mentioned use case scenario, we presuppose that two types of lexical resources already exist, and that they are made accessible by appropriate Web service interfaces:

- Three WordNet-type monolingual lexical semantic resources for Japanese (`jwn`), English (`ewn`) and French (`fwn`) are assumed. We assume that they are modeled and represented using the LMF NLP semantics extension.

- Although not explicitly depicted in this figure, two bilingual lexical resources for Japanese-to-English (`j-to-e`) and English-to-French (`e-to-f`) are assumed. They are assumed to be modeled and represented by employing the LMF machine readable dictionary (MRD) extension. However these resources would be augmented externally by the semantification mechanism described in the next section.

As we will see later in this paper, derived correspondences between/among the existing lexical resource elements should be organized as a kind of secondary language resource in order to be reused.

3 Semantifying Bilingual Lexical Resource Entries

The semantification of a bilingual lexical resource entry is a necessary substep when associating possibly corresponding lexical concepts in different languages. In principle, the source language (SL) expression (entry word) is first associated with a sense in an SL lexical semantic resource. Then, we seek a possible corresponding sense for the target language (TL) expression (translation equivalent) in a TL lexical semantic resource. This process enriches the bilingual lexical resource by grounding it in the lexical semantic resources in the SL and TL.

3.1 Necessity of Semantification

Bilingual dictionaries provide lexical items in one language with counterparts in another language that are similar in meaning and usage. However, although this definition is fairly straightforward, bilingual dictionaries do exhibit problems that need to be addressed, mainly owing to differences in concept formation in different languages (Svensén 2009). Although the idea of using bilingual lexical resources to integrate semantic resources is not new, as demonstrated by Daudé (1999) or Chen (2002), bilingual dictionaries, in general, have attracted less attention than monolingual dictionaries. As pointed out by Fontenelle (1997), this may, in part, be owing to their less structured machine-readable data format, making it harder for a researcher to mine useful information from bilingual resources. However, a standardized modeling framework such as the ISO LMF can enable more bilingual lexical resources to be disseminated in a well-structured format. The LMF introduces the MRD extension to provide a metamodel to represent monolingual/bilingual dictionaries that are primarily compiled for human use.

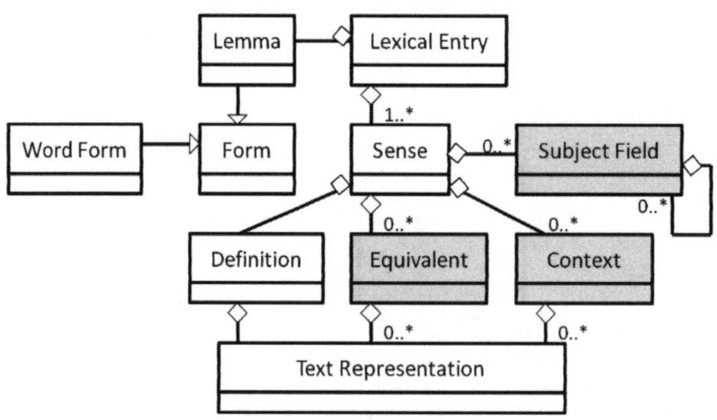

Figure 4: LMF MRD Class Model.

Figure 4 provides an overview of the LMF MRD extension in a UML diagram. It shows that the translation equivalents in the TL for an entry word in the SL are represented by using `Equivalent` nodes, each of which is associated with a `Sense` node of the `Lexical Entry` node. The figure also shows that a translation equivalent is represented by an instance of `Text Representation` class, which basically carries a text string that may be annotated with linguistic data categories. This simple and somewhat unstructured configuration is reasonable and can be acceptable, given the fact that most bilingual resources are structurally messy. However, the configuration may be insufficient if we are to exploit a bilingual dictionary as a kind of semantic resource and leverage it as a bridge to associate potentially corresponding lexical concepts in different languages. This motivated us to develop a framework to semantify bilingual lexical resources.

3.2 Framework of Semantification

Figure 5 shows the process of semantification. It is noteworthy that before the semantification, the bilingual lexical entry is represented according to the definition in the LMF MRD extension.

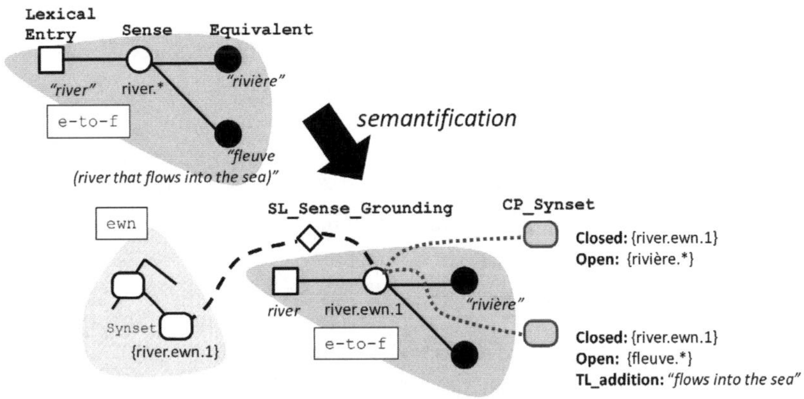

Figure 5: Example of Semantification of a Bilingual Dictionary Entry.

The semantification is as follows:

1. We first perform *SL sense grounding* to associate the `Sense` node in the bilingual lexical resource `e-to-f` with a `Sense` node in the SL lexical semantic resource `ewn`. To accomplish this, a computational lexical semantic matching process first looks for possibly corresponding `Sense` nodes in `ewn`. This process[5], is never decisive, even if it makes full use of the information, such as the entry word itself, a gloss description, or additional semantic markers, provided in the lexical resources. Therefore, a human judgment is then necessary to choose among the candidates and establish a correspondence. Once the correspondence has been established, the formerly underspecified word sense `river.*` in `e-to-f` is disambiguated as `river.ewn.1`. Here `ewn.1` is an identifier[6] of the `Sense` node in `ewn`. At the same time, these two `Sense` nodes are interlinked by an `SL_Sense_Grounding` node, as shown in the Fig. 5.

2. Two `CP_Synset` nodes are then created. For example, the cross-lingual pseudo synset {`river.ewn.1`, `rivière.*`} is associated with the upper `CP_Synset` node, indicating that the intersection of these two senses denotes a multilingual lexical concept across individual languages. However, note that the sense `rivière.*` indicates that it is not yet grounded to a French lexical semantic resource, and so the `CP_synset` node is still underspecified. In the figure, the set marked **Closed** represents the set of grounded senses, whereas the set marked **Open** denotes the still underspecified senses. These two sets together define the current status of the multilingual pseudo synset. It should be noted that the `Sense` node in the `e-to-f` dictionary is associated with two `CP_Synset` nodes. This is different from the original LMF specification, in which a `Sense` node can only be associated with one `Synset` node. It does not matter, however, as the associations are accomplished only externally, thereby keeping the existing LMF-modeled resource intact.

3. The additional description of the second translation equivalent "fleuve," which is a "river that flows into the sea," is encoded as the value of the `TL_addition` feature and is stored in the

[5]We are now developing the process, which basically relies on textual overlap (Banerjee and Pedersen 2003).

[6]A rigorous specification has not yet been determined.

CP_synset node. As discussed in the next subsection, additional descriptions in a bilingual lexical resource offer useful information to fill the semantic gap between an entry word and the translation equivalents. This information includes semantic restrictions on the translation equivalents, as well as collocational or phrasal equivalents that detail the semantic range of an entry word. However, to extract the information from an additional description, we need to analyze the presented translation equivalent appropriately. This process would be highly resource-dependent, owning to lack of a standardized presentation format. Nevertheless, a technique to extract differentia (O'hara and Wiebe 2004) can be applied, as some of the translation equivalents are given in the so-called *genus-differentia* expression pattern.

4. Although it is not depicted in Fig. 5, if necessary, two underspecified TL senses, will eventually be grounded to the corresponding Sense nodes in a French lexical semantic resource. This sub-process is called *TL sense grounding* and is organized in a similar way to that of SL sense grounding, requiring a computational lexical semantic matching process with human intervention. However it may be a more difficult process, because, in general, translation equivalents provided in a bilingual resource are not well structured and tend to lack rich semantic descriptions.

3.3 Dealing with Partial Equivalences

The method used for creating a CP_Synset node should consider the nature of the translation equivalents given in a variety of bilingual resources. Translation equivalence can be classified into full equivalence, partial equivalence or zero equivalence (Svensén 2009). He points out that this classification is rough, but important, in the sense that it may determine the way in which a translation equivalent is presented. Among these, partial equivalence is the most noteworthy, because *equivalent differentiation* has to be implemented in the dictionary description in some way, and the relevant information should be extracted and encoded in the computational representation. The cases of partial equivalence can be further divided into *convergence* (*neutralization*) or *divergence*.

The English-to-French correspondences in the motivating example can be classified as an instance of divergence. Another example of divergence is presented by the Japanese word *shujin*, which, in English, corresponds to *host* or *hostess*, depending on the gender of the person[7]. This example can be represented in a similar way to Fig. 5: a CP_synset node for {shujin.jwn.1, host.*}, with TL_addition "male", and another CP_synset for {shujin.jwn.1, hostess.*}, with TL_addition "female." These examples show that in cases of divergence, an SL sense is divided into a set of finer-grained concepts. Generally, a divergence instance is signalled by the additional description that specifies the sense or semantic range of a translation equivalent.

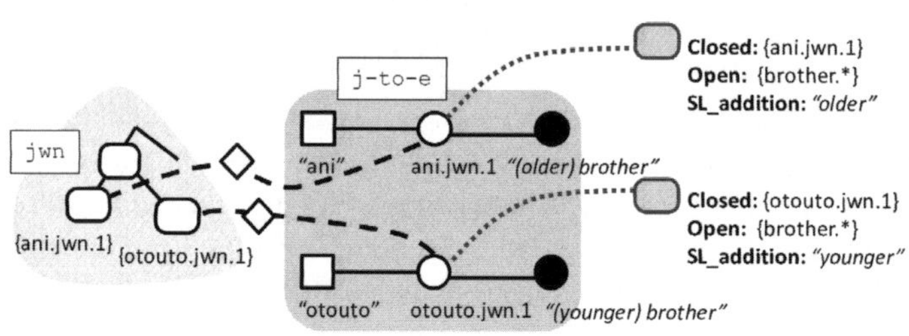

Figure 6: Sample Representation of Conversion-type Partial Equivalence.

Convergence can be illustrated by the example schematized in Figure 6, in which the Japanese word *ani* (elder brother) and *otouto* (younger brother) are jointly associated with the English word *brother*, in the sense of blood brother. Contrary to the divergence cases, a convergence instance may be indicated by a phrasal translation equivalent that preserves, or tries to convey, the finer-grained SL meaning.

[7]Actually, the EDR bilingual dictionary (http://www2.nict.go.jp/r/r312/EDR/) presents: "⟨⟨*male*⟩⟩ host" and "⟨⟨*female*⟩⟩ hostess," respectively.

To encode the semantic restriction to the entry word in the SL, we introduce the `SL_addition` feature, as shown in Fig. 6. It should be noted that the two underspecified `CP_synset` nodes would eventually be grounded to the same `Sense` node in an English semantic resource and hence disambiguated and *converged*.

4 Modeling Cross-lingual/Interlingual Correspondences for Reuse

4.1 *Overall Picture*

Figure 7 shows almost the entire representation of the motivating example, providing more detail than the brief sketch shown in Fig. 3. Note that the numbered `CP_Synset` nodes are placed at logically identical positions to those in Fig. 3. In Fig. 7, we introduce instances of the class `TL_Sense_Grounding` (shaded diamonds): a `TL_Sense_Grounding` node is created when the open translation equivalent of an `MP_Synset` node is closed by being grounded to a `Synset` node in the TL lexical semantic resource. With this grounding, together with the `SL_Sense_grounding`, an entry in a bilingual lexical resource works as a bridge from an SL lexical concept to the corresponding TL lexical concept via the `MP_Synset` node.

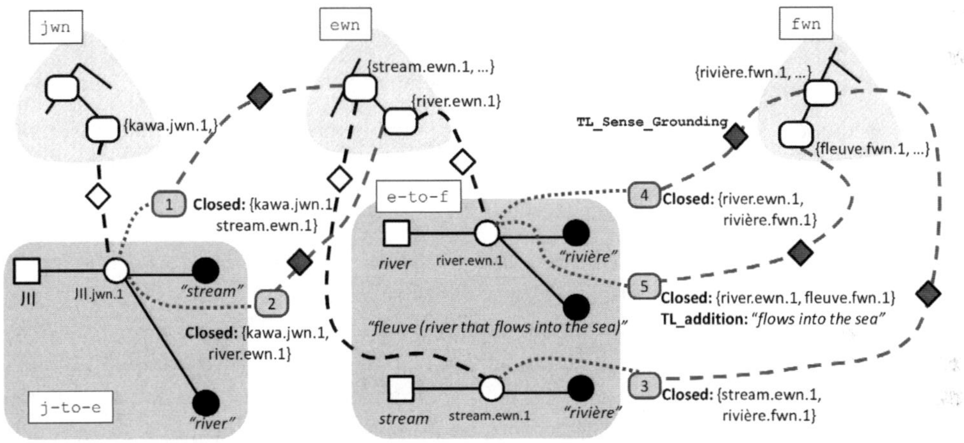

Figure 7: Proposed Representation of the Motivating Example.

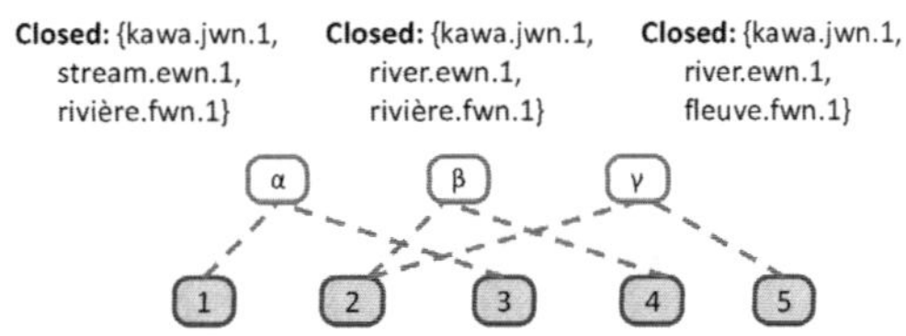

Figure 8: Resulted Lattice-like Structure.

To avoid an unnecessarily complicated diagram, Fig. 8 shows an extra part of the configuration shown in Fig. 7. In this figure, three `MP_Synset` nodes (indicated by Greek letters) are introduced, and linked to the associated `CP_Synset` nodes. At the time of writing this paper, the underlying computational process for deriving the indirect correspondences was still under investigation. However, it is however obvious that the process has to properly filter out inappropriate transitivities to avoid the semantic drift across languages. Again, this would need human intervention, but this may require that the person has competence for all the relevant languages. Therefore an effective machinery to assist him/her to make judgments will be necessary.

Incremental creation of the `MP_Synset` nodes gradually forms a lattice-like multilingual concept structure. This suggests that our proposed framework is similar to SIM*u*LLDA (Janssen 2004), which applies formal concept analysis (FCA) to derive a concept lattice with the words and formal concepts. However, our framework is clearly different in the sense that we propose an LMF-based representation framework, while considering an incremental formulation of a distributed network structure, as discussed.

4.2 Specifications of the Proposed Constructs

All in all, we have proposed four classes in this paper: `CP_Synset`, `MP_Synset`, `SL_Sense_Grounding`, and `TL_Sense_Grounding`. These classes, which could extend the current ISO LMF, are specified as follows.

- A `CP_Synset` node is initiated when a lexical entry in a bilingual lexical resource is activated.
- An `MP_Synset` node is introduced when `CP_Synset`/`MP_Synset` nodes are combined to define a multilingual pseudo synset.
- An instance node of the `SL_Sense_Grounding` class associates a `Sense` node of an existing bilingual lexical resource entry with the corresponding `Synset` node in an SL lexical semantic resource. In the original LMF, `Sense`-to-`Synset` association is direct and does not require an intermediate node. However, the insertion of an `SL_Sense_Grounding` node is necessary to record the detail of the lexical semantic matching process.
- An instance node of the `TL_Sense_Grounding` class associates the translation equivalent of a bilingual lexical resource entry with the corresponding TL `Synset` node, closing the formerly open translation equivalent.

Central to our framework is the `CP_Synset` and `MP_Synset` classes, which are similar to the LMF `Synset` class in the sense that an instance of these classes represents a set of synonymous senses. However, the `CP_Synset` and `MP_Synset` classes differ from the LMF `Synset` class, because an instance node of the classes gathers synonymous senses across the languages. The LMF `Sense Axis` class is another LMF construct that has something in common with the `MP_Synset` class is. However, we strongly expect that with the `MP_Synset` class, multilingual correspondences will be incrementally recovered and established, while also pointing to the `Sense` nodes in bilingual lexical resources.

4.3 Toward Reusing Recovered Correspondences

Recovered and established cross-lingual/interlingual correspondences should be made persistent somewhere on the Web-based linguistic service infrastructure, so that they can be reused. In other words, these correspondences should be converted into a sort of secondary language resource. Just like the `Sense Axis` class in the original LMF, instances of the `CP_Synset` and `MP_Synset` classes can be aggregated in an instance of the `Lexical Resource`. In this way, the `Lexical Resource` instance can indirectly associate the involved `Lexicon` instances, which are existing primary resources.

However, to make this scenario work, the following issues have to be addressed.

- All the nodes and links external to the existing language resources have to be properly stored somewhere in the infrastructure and made retrievable. This means that standardized Web APIs that enable the search and retrieval of the storage have to be provided.
- At the same time, relevant elements of the existing language resources, such as `Synset` nodes or `Sense` nodes, have to be indexed and be retrievable externally. Assigning global identifiers (URIs) to the elements may be a feasible way to do this. This may also facilitate the servicization of language resources as exemplified in (Savas et al. 2010).

5 Related Work

This paper discusses a framework for representing a global and distributed lexical semantic network, while presupposing an environment in which a number of lexical resources have been Web-servicized. Given such an environment, (Calzolari 2008) has pointed out the possibility of creating new resources on the basis of existing resources, and some work in this direction has been published, such as Soria et al. (2009) and Savas et al. (2010). This line of work is expected to improve further and increase, as Web-based linguistic service infrastructures evolve and gain popularity.

Obviously, another related area of research is lexicon modeling. Although the ISO LMF will undoubtedly be used as a solid and shared framework, requirements to its revisions/extensions continue to emerge. Among them, Maks et al. (2008) pointed out that LMF should more explicitly represent language-dependent usage and contrasts, and they proposes a model that compromises between the MRD extension and the multilingual extension. This solution might be reasonable, if we are to represent an existing bilingual dictionary precisely. Nevertheless, the solution may not be sufficient to model and represent an evolving distributed lexical semantic network, which is a prerequisite for this paper. The problem raised up by Maks et al. (2008) is closely related to the issue posed by Trippel (2010), in which he states: *LMF provides the container for combining such resources of different types, but does not merge them into one formalism.* Given this motivation, he presented a formal lexicon model called *Lexicon Graph*, arguing that the lossless combination of lexical resources could be accomplished.

6 Conclusions

Presupposing a highly servicized language resources environment, this paper proposed a representation framework for cross-lingual/interlingual lexical semantic correspondences that would be recovered incrementally on a Web-based linguistic service infrastructure. The main contribution of this paper is twofold: (1) the notion of *pseudo synset*, which is introduced to represent pseudo lexical concepts shared by more than one language; (2) the framework for *semantifying bilingual lexical resources*, which allows bilingual lexical resources to be used as a bridge to associate lexical concepts in different languages. This paper also discussed how the recovered correspondences can be organized as a dynamic *secondary language resource*, while examining a set of possible extensions to the ISO LMF.

For future work, several items need to be pursued. First we have to extend the representation framework to appropriately accommodate verb and adjective concepts, in which more complicated relationships among linguistic elements have to be organized. Second, we plan to work further on the semantification of bilingual lexical resources. In particular, we intend to devise a formalism and mechanism to represent multi-word lexical entries and complicated translation equivalents. Multi-word expressions are more frequently observed in bilingual resources compared to monolingual resources; they are useful to describe the lexical semantic gaps between the languages. Last but not least, we intend to implement prototype services around some existing lexical resources. To do this, along with the basic semantic matching processes, we have to establish an effective workflow that involves human assessors to approve the recovered cross-lingual correspondences and the inferred multilingual correspondences. In this regard, the notion of a *sense pool* and the verification process proposed by Yu et al. (2007) should be highly relevant as a reference.

Acknowledgments

The author greatly appreciates anonymous reviewers for their thoughtful and informative comments. The presented work supported by KAKENHI (21520401) and the Strategic Information and Communications R&D Promotion Programme (SCOPE) of the Ministry of Internal Affairs and Communications of Japan.

References

[Banerjee and Pedersen 2003] Banerjee, S., and Pedersen, J. (2003). Extended Gloss Overlaps as a Measure of Semantic Relatedness. In: *IJCAI 2003*, pp.805–810.

[Calzolari 2008] Calzolari, N. (2008). Approaches towards a 'Lexical Web': the Role of Interoperability. In: *ICGL2008*, pp.34–42.

[Chen 2002] Chen, H.H., Lin, C.C., and Lin, W.C. (2002). Building a Chinese-English WordNet for Translingual Application. In: *ACM Transactions on Asian Language Information Processing*, Vol.1, No.2, pp.103–122.

[Daudé 1999] Daudé, J., Padró, L., and Rigau, G. (1999). Mapping Multilingual Hierarchies Using Relaxation Labeling. In: *EMNLP/VLC-99*.

[Fontenelle 1997] Fontenelle, T. (1997). Using a Bilingual Dictionary to Create Semantic Networks. In: *International Journal of Lexicography*, Vol.10, No.4, pp.275–303.

[Francopoulo et al. 2009] Francopoulo, G., Bel, N. et al. (2009). Multilingual Resources for NLP in the Lexical Markup Framework (LMF). In: *Language Resources and Evaluation*, Vol.43, No.1, pp. 57–70.

[Hartmann 2005] Pure or Hybrid? The Development of Mixed Dictionary Genres. In: *Linguistics and Literature*, Vol.3, No.2, pp.192–208.

[Janssen 2004] Janssen, M. (2004). Multilingual Lexical Databases, Lexical Gaps, and SIM*u*LLDA. In: *International Journal of Lexicography*, Vol.17, Vol.2, pp.138–154.

[Maks et al. 2008] Maks, I., Tibeius, C., and van Veenendaal R. (2008). Standardising Bilingual Lexical Resources according to the Lexicon Markup Framework. In: *LREC 2008*, pp.1723–1727.

[O'hara and Wiebe 2004] O'hara, T., and Wiebe, J. (2004). Empirical Acquisition of Differentiating Relations from Definitions. In: *COLING 2004 Workshop on Enhancing and Using Electronic Dictionaries*, pp.77–80.

[Savas et al. 2010] Savas, B., Hayashi, Y., Monachini, M., Soria, C., and Calzolari, N. (2010). An LMF-based Web Service for Accessing WordNet-type Semantic Lexicons. In: *LREC2010*, pp.507–513.

[Soria et al. 2009] Soria, C., Monachini, M., Bertagna, F., Calzolari, N., Huan, C.R., Hsieh, S.K., Marchetti, A., and Tesconi, M. (2009). Exploring Interoperability of Language Resources: The Case of Cross-Lingual Semi-automatic Enrichment of Wordnets. In: *Language Resources and Evaluation*, Vol.43, pp.87–96.

[Svensén 2009] Svensén, B. (2009). Equivalents in Bilingual Dictionaries. In: Svensén, B. *A Handbook of Lexicography*, Cambridge University Press, pp.253–280.

[Trippel 2010] Trippel, T. (2010). Representation Formats and Models for Lexicons. In: Witt, A., and Metzing, D. (Eds.), *Linguistic Modeling of Information and Markup Languages*, Springer, pp.165–184.

[Vossen 2004] Vossen, P. (2004). EuroWordNet: A Multilingual Database of Autonomous and Language-Specific Wordnets Connected via an Inter-lingual Index. In: *International Journal of Lexicography*, Vol.17, No.2, pp.161–173.

[Yu et al. 2007] Yu, L.C., Wu, C.H., Philpet, A., and Hovy, E. (2007). OntoNotes: Sense Pool Verification Using Google N-gram and Statistical Tests. In: *OntoLex 2007*.

Formalising and specifying underquantification

Aurelie Herbelot
University of Cambridge
ah433@cam.ac.uk

Ann Copestake
University of Cambridge
aac@cl.cam.ac.uk

Abstract

This paper argues that *all* subject noun phrases can be given a quantified formalisation in terms of the intersection between their denotation set and the denotation set of their verbal predicate. The majority of subject noun phrases, however, are only implicitely quantified and the task of retrieving the most plausible quantifier for a given NP is non-trivial. We propose a formalisation which captures the underspecification of the quantifier in subject NPs and we show that this formalisation is widely applicable, including in statements involving kinds. We then present a baseline for a quantification resolution system using syntactic features as basis for classification. Although the syntactic baseline provides a respectable 78% precision, our error analysis shows that obtaining true performance on the task requires information beyond syntax.

1 Quantification resolution

Most subject noun phrases in English are not explicitly quantified. Still, humans are able to give them quantificational interpretations in context:

1. Cats are mammals = *All* cats...
2. Cats have four legs = *Most* cats...
3. Cats were sleeping by the fire = *Some* cats...
4. The beans spilt out of the bag = *Most/All of the* beans...
5. Water was dripping through the ceiling = *Some* water...

We refer to this process as **quantification resolution**, that is, the process of giving an implicitely quantified NP a formalisation which expresses a *unique* set relation appropriate to the semantics of the utterance. For instance, the most plausible resolution of 1 can be expressed as:

6. All cats are mammals.
   $|\phi \cap \psi| = |\phi|$ where ϕ is the set of all cats and ψ the set of all mammals.

Resolving the quantification value of NPs is important for many NLP tasks, in particular for inference. We would like to be able to automatically perform the type of interpretations shown in 1 to 5. It will allow us to draw conclusions such as *If (all) cats are mammals and Tom is a cat, then Tom is a mammal* and *If (some) cats are in my garden, then (some) animals are in my garden.*[1]

The task of quantification resolution involves finding a semantic representation that goes beyond what is directly obtainable from a sentence's syntactic composition. We can write $the(x, \text{cat'}(x), \text{sleep'}(x))$ as we would write $some(x, \text{cat'}(x), \text{sleep'}(x))$[2], but while the quantification semantics of *some* can be

[1]The type of entailment relying on word substitution is dependent on quantification: *(All) cats are mammals* doesn't imply that *(All) animals are mammals.*

[2]We use here a generalised quantifier notation were the first argument of the quantifier is the bound variable.

fully defined (given a singular NP, we are talking of one entity only), that of *the* cannot: in a singular NP introduced by *the*, the referent can either be a single entity or a plurality with various possible quantificational interpretations (cf *The cat is sleeping* vs *The cat is a mammal*).

This paper is an attempt to provide a formal semantics for implicitely quantified NPs which a) supports the type of inferences required by NLP, b) has good empirical coverage (beyond 'standard' linguistic examples), c) lends itself to evaluation by human annotation and d) can be derived automatically. We draw on work in formal linguistics, but by formulating the problem as quantification resolution, we obtain an account which is more tractable from an NLP perspective. We also present preliminary experiments that automate quantification resolution using a syntax-driven classifier.

2 Under(specified) quantification

The phenomenon of ambiguous quantification overlaps with **genericity**. Generic NPs have traditionally been described as referring to **kinds** (Krifka et al., 1995) and one of their most frequent syntactic expressions is the bare plural, although they occur in definite and indefinite singulars too, as well as bare singulars. There are many views on the semantics of generics (e.g. Carlson, 1995; Pelletier and Asher, 1997; Heyer, 1990; Leslie, 2008) but one of them is that they quantify (Cohen, 1996), although, puzzlingly enough, not always with the same quantifier:

7. Dogs are in my garden = *Some* dogs...
8. Frenchmen eat horsemeat = *Some/Relatively-many* Frenchmen... (For the *relatively many* reading, see Cohen, 2001.)
9. Cars have four wheels = *Most* cars...

This behaviour has so far prevented linguists from agreeing on a single formalisation for all generics. Note that relegating the various readings to a matter of pragmatics, formalising all bare plurals using an existential, is no solution as we are then unable to explain the semantic difference between, for instance, *Mosquitoes carry malaria* and *Some mosquitoes carry malaria*. The only accepted assumption is that an operator GEN exists, which acts as a silent quantifier over the restrictor (subject) and matrix (verbal predicate) of the generic statement.

In this paper, we take an approach which sidesteps some of the intractable problems associated with the literature on generics and which also extends to definite plurals, as discussed below. Instead of talking of ambiguous quantification, we will talk of **underspecified quantification**, or **underquantification**. By this, we mean that the bare plural, rather than exhibiting a silent, GEN quantifier, simply features a placeholder in the logical form which must be filled with the appropriate quantifier (e.g., $uq(x, \text{cat'}(x), \text{sleep'}(x))$, where uq is the placeholder quantifier). This account caters for the facts that so-called generics can so easily be quantified via traditional quantifiers, that GEN is silent in all known languages, and it explains also why it is the bare form which has the highest productivity, and can denote a range of quantified entities, from existentials to universals. Using the underquantification hypothesis, we can paraphrase any generic of the form 'X does Y' as 'there is a set of things X, *a certain number of which* do Y' (note the partitive construction).

We now turn to definite plurals which have traditionally been thought to be outside of the genericity phenomenon and associated with universals (e.g., Lyons, 1999). Definite plurals do exhibit a range of quantificational behaviour and thus we argue that they should be studied as underquantified forms too. Consider the following, from Dowty (1987):

10. At the end of the press conference, the reporters asked the president questions.

Dowty remarks that it is not necessary that all reporters ask questions for the sentence to be true. In fact, it is only necessary that *some of them* did. Dowty says: "The question of how many members of the group referent of a definite NP must have the distributive property is in part lexically determined and in part determined by the context, and only rarely is every member required to have these properties."

Following the existential reading, we can write:

11. $some(x, \text{reporter'}(x), \text{askQuestion'}(x))$

The problem is that for Dowty, the NP refers to a 'group', i.e., to the reporters as a whole, and not to specific reporters. We don't want to say 'there is a small set of reporters, each of which asked a question'; we want to say 'there is a large set of reporters – all those present at the press conference – and some of them asked a question', i.e., we want to use a partitive construction. We follow Brogaard's (2007) account of definite plurals as partitive constructions, where she examines the following:

12. The students asked questions.

Brogaard argues that, given X, the denotation of *the students*, a subset Y of X is selected via the quantifier *some* and that the verbal predicate applies (distributively) to Y. A similar account can be given of (10): there is a set of reporters, and a certain number of elements in that set (some reporters) asked questions — which is our desired reading. Note that all definite plurals can have this interpretation (e.g., possessives and demonstratives also).

We will next argue that the partitive construct observed in definite plurals can be generally applied to subject NPs and we will propose a single formalisation for all underquantified statements.

3 Formalisation

3.1 Link's notation (1983)

In what follows, we briefly define each item of notation used in this work, as taken from Link (1983). We illustrate the main points via examples over a closed world W containing three cats (Kitty, Sylvester and Bagpuss).

The background assumption for our formalisation is that, following Link, plurals can be represented as lattices. The star sign * generates all individual sums of members of the extension of predicate P. So if P is cat$'$, the extension of $^*P$ is a join-semilattice representing all possible sums of cats in the world under consideration. The join-semilattice of cats in world W is shown in Fig 1.

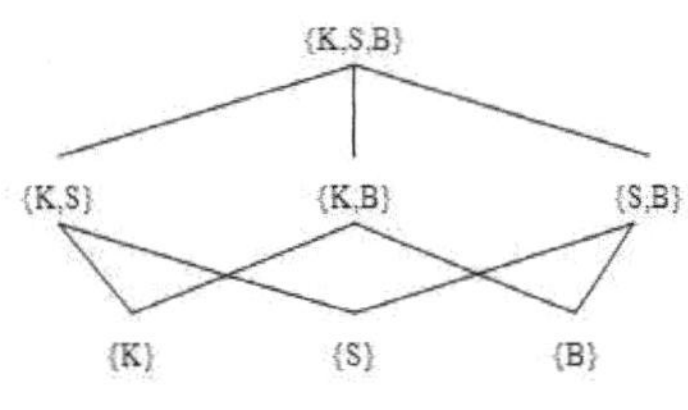

Figure 1: Join-semilattice of all cats in world W

The sign σ is the sum operator. $\sigma x Px$ represents the sum, or supremum, of all objects that are $^*P$. $\sigma^* x Px$ represents the **proper sum** of Ps, that is, the supremum of all objects that are proper plural predicates of P. The sum includes (non-plural) individuals such as K or S while the proper sum doesn't. In worlds where there is more than one object in the extension of $^*P$, $\sigma x Px = \sigma^* x Px$: e.g., in Fig 1, the sum of all cats is the same as the proper sum of all cats, i.e., the set $\{\text{K,S,B}\}$. (Compare this with a world where there is only one cat, say Kitty: then $\sigma x Px = \{K\}$ while $\sigma^* x Px = \emptyset$).

The product sign $\prod$ expresses an **individual-part** relation. The $\cdot$ sign in combination with $\prod$ indicates **atomic part**. Following Chierchia (1998), we assume the same underlying lattice for both mass terms and count nouns, so we use the $\prod$ and $\cdot$ operators for formalising quantification over mass entities.

3.2 Collective and distributive predicates

Some predicates are collective: they refer to a group as a whole and not to its instances (13). Other predicates are always distributive (14):

13. Antelopes gather near water holes (*Andy the antelope gathers near water holes.)
14. Three soldiers were asleep (Tom was asleep, Bill was asleep, Cornelia was asleep.)

Most verbal phrases, though, are 'mixed predicates' that accept both readings:

15. Three soldiers stole wine from the canteen.

(Tom, Bill and Cornelia went together to the canteen to steal wine or Tom, Bill and Cornelia each stole wine from the canteen.)

Collective predicates can be a source of confusion when trying to directly apply quantification to an ambiguously quantified NP:

16. (*Some/Most/All) Americans elect a new president every five years.

Quantifying 16 seems initially impossible in shallow form: we cannot write $all(x,\text{american}'(x),\text{electPres}'(x))$ as it seems to imply distributivity. However, we refer to the reporter example (10) and the latent partitive construct that we suggested existed in that (distributive) sentence. By similarity, we can say that there is a set X of Americans able to vote, and a subset Y of those — which in this case is selected by the quantifier *all* and is therefore equal to X — collectively elects the president.

3.3 Formalising the partitive construct

Following Link (1998) for the formalisation of collective and distributive predicates, we can write, for 10 and 16:

17. $X = \sigma^*x\ \text{reporterAtPressConference}'(x) \wedge \exists Y[Y \prod X \wedge \forall z[z \cdot \prod Y \rightarrow \text{askques}'(z)]]$
18. $X = \sigma^*x\text{votingAmerican}'(x) \wedge \exists Y[Y \prod X \wedge \text{electPresident}'(Y)]$[3]

For the collective case, we just apply the verbal predicate collectively.

We can then add the quantifier resolution. We assume a three-fold partitioning of the quantificational space, corresponding to the natural language quantifiers *some*, *most* and *all* (in addition to *one*, for the description of singular, unique entities). The corresponding set relations are:

19. if $some(\phi, \psi)$ then $0 < |\phi \cap \psi|$
20. if $most(\phi, \psi)$ then $|\phi - \psi| \leq |\phi \cap \psi|$
21. if $all(\phi, \psi)$ then $|\phi - \psi| = 0$

These set relations can be expressed in terms of the sets involved in the partitive construction: in 16, if X is the set of all Americans able to vote, Y the subset of X selected by the quantifier, and Z the set of all things that elect the president, then Y actually represents the intersection $X \cap Z$. We can thus write:

22. $X = \sigma^*x\ \text{reporterAtPressConference}'(x) \wedge \exists Y[Y \prod X \wedge \forall z[z \cdot \prod Y \rightarrow \text{askques}'(z)] \wedge (0 < |Y|)]$
23. $X = \sigma^*x\ \text{votingAmerican}'(x) \wedge \exists Y[Y \prod X \wedge \text{electPresident}'(Y) \wedge (|X - Y| = 0)]$

The same principle applies to mass nouns. We show below a distributive example.

24. Water was dripping through the ceiling.
$X = \sigma^*x\ \text{water}'(x) \wedge \exists Y[Y \prod X \wedge \forall z[z \cdot \prod Y \rightarrow \text{dripThroughCeiling}'(z)] \wedge (0 < |Y|)]$

We thus write the underspecified quantifier as:

25. $X = \sigma^*x\ P'(x) \wedge \exists Y[Y \prod X \wedge Q(Y)] \wedge quantConstraint(X, Y)]$

where the quantConstraint ensures the correct cardinality of Y for various quantifiers and the predicate Q applies distributively or collectively depending on the semantics of the sentence. X and Y respectively denote the Nbar and NP referents in the quantified paraphrase of the statement.

[3] Note that in the two examples, we have restricted X to the relevant set of entities. We will not investigate here how this particular reference resolution takes place.

4 Kinds

In order to argue that our formalisation is applicable to all subject noun phrases, we must briefly come back to the case of generics which, in some linguistic accounts, are not seen as quantified (Carlson, 1977).[4] According to those accounts, the subject NP in sentences such as *The cat is a mammal* (the **kind**) can be regarded as an entity similar to proper nouns. The generic reading of the sentence then takes a straightforward subject/predicate formalisation of the type mammal'(cat'). The main argument in favour of such a representation is the existence of sentences where the verbal predicate seems to only be applicable to a species rather than to its instances:

26. The dodo is extinct.

Such cases, we claim, do not preclude quantification. We use the accounts of Chierchia (1998) and Krifka (2004), where a kind is defined as a function that returns the greatest element of the extension of the property relevant to that kind: $Kind(X) = \sigma^*x\ X'(x)$. This gives us the following for 26:

27. $X = \sigma^*x\ dodo'(x) \wedge \exists Y[Y \prod X \wedge extinct'(Y) \wedge (|Y - X| = 0)]$

We stress however that we do not deny the validity of representations that involve a simple subject/predicate structure. It should be clear that the sentence *The cat is a mammal* has an interpretation where the species 'cat' is attributed the property of being a mammal. What we argue is simply that the meaning of the sentence also includes a quantificational aspect. We want, after all, to be able to make natural inferences about individual cats: if the cat is a mammal then Tom the cat is a mammal. We believe that both quantification and a subject/predicate formalisation are necessary to fully render the semantics of such sentences. We will also argue in Section 7 that for the purposes of computational linguistics, it is actually desirable to formalise the quantificational aspect separately, as part of the full semantics.

We should also note that the genericity phenomenon is usually seen as encompassing habitual constructions (Krifka et al., 1995). Our quantificational account of kinds will not necessarily be applicable to quantification of events and we do not wish to make any claims with regard to habituality in this paper. For completeness, we will however point out that, following Chierchia (1995) on indefinites, we see quantification adverbs as able to bind, and therefore quantify over individuals: according to this view, the most felicitous reading of *Mosquitoes sometimes carry malaria* is *Some mosquitoes carry malaria*, formalisable with 25.

5 Automatic quantification: first attempts

To our knowledge, no attempt at the automatic specification of quantification has been made before. In consequence, we start our investigation with the simplest possible type of machine learning algorithm, using as determining features the direct syntactic context of the statement to be quantified. The general idea of such a system is that grammatical information such as the number of a subject noun phrase and the tense of its verbal predicate may be statistically related to its classification.

5.1 Gold standard

We built a gold standard by re-using and expanding the quantification annotations we produced in Herbelot and Copestake (2010). This small corpus, which contains randomly extracted Wikipedia[5] sentences, provides 300 instances of triply annotated subject noun phrases. The categories used for annotation are the natural language quantifiers ONE, SOME, MOST, ALL and the label QUANT (for noun phrases of the type *some cats*, *most turtles* or *more than 37 unicorns* which, being explicitly quantified, do not enter our underquantification account and must be marked with a separate label). In order to convert the multiple

[4]A more comprehensive discussion can be found in Herbelot (2010).

[5]http://www.wikipedia.org/

annotations to a gold standard, we used majority opinion when it was available and negotiation in cases of complete disagreement. There were only 14 cases where a majority opinion cannot be obtained.

The main issue with the resulting gold standard is its relatively small size. The 300 data points it provides are clearly insufficient for machine learning, but the annotation process is time-consuming and we do not have the resources to set up a large-scale annotation effort. As a trade-off, the first author of this paper annotated a further 300 noun phrases, thus doubling the size of the gold standard. As a precaution, we ran the classifier presented later in this section over the original gold standard and over the new annotations; no substantial difference in performance between the two runs was found.

Table 1 shows the class distribution of our five quantification labels over the 600 instances of the extended gold standard.

Class	Number of instances	Percentage of corpus
ONE	367	61%
SOME	53	9%
MOST	34	6%
ALL	102	17%
QUANT	44	7%

Table 1: Class distribution over 600 instances

We note, first, that the number of explicitly quantified noun phrases amounts to only 7% of the annotation set. This shows that the resolution of underquantification has potentially high value for NLP systems. Next, we remark that 61% of all instances simply denote a single entity, leaving 32% to underquantified plurals — 189 instances. This imbalance is problematic for the machine learning task that we set out to achieve. First, it means that the training data available for SOME, MOST and ALL annotations is comparably sparse. Secondly, it implies that the baseline for our future classifier is relatively high: assuming a most frequent class baseline, we must beat 61% precision.

5.2 Quantifying with syntax

Most of the remarks that can be found in the literature on the relation between syntax and quantification have been written with respect to the generic versus non-generic distinction. Although we have moved away from the terminology on genericity, the two following examples show the potential promises — and hurdles — of using syntax to induce quantification annotations.

- Noun phrases which act as subjects of simple past tense verbs are usually non-generic: *A cow says 'moo' / A cow said 'moo'* (Gelman, 2004). However, the so-called 'historic past' is an exception to this rule: *The woolly mammoth roamed the earth many years ago.*
- The combination of a bare plural and present tense is a prototypical indication of genericity: *Tigers are massive* (Cimpian and Markman, 2008). But news headlines behave differently: *Cambridge students steal cow.*

We informally investigate the distribution of various grammatical constructions with respect to quantification, as obtained from our gold standard. Although some constructions give a clear majority to one or another label, that majority is not always overwhelming. For instance, consistently annotating bare plurals followed by a past tense as SOME would result in a precision of only 54%. It is therefore unclear how accurate a classifier based only on syntax can be. (Note that the quantification phenomenon is understood to be semantically complex and that syntax is only one of many features used in the annotation guidelines produced in Herbelot and Copestake, 2010.)

5.3 Features

We give the system article and number information for the noun phrase to be quantified, as well as the tense of the verbal predicate following it. In order to cater for proper nouns, we also indicate whether the head of the noun phrase is capitalised or not. Article, number and capitalisation information is similarly provided for the object of the verb. All features are automatically extracted from the Robust Minimal Recursion Semantics (RMRS, Copestake, 2004) representation of the sentence in which the noun phrase appears (obtained via a RASP parse, Briscoe et al., 2006). The following shows an example of a feature line for a particular noun phrase (the sentence in which the noun phrase appears is also given):

```
ORIGINAL: [His early blues influences] included artists such as Robert
          Johnson, Bukka White, Skip James and Sleepy John Estes.
FEATURES: past,possessive,plural,nocap,bare,plural,nocap
```

Note that articles belonging to the same class are labelled according to that class: all possessive articles, for instance, are simply marked as 'possessive'. This is the same for demonstrative articles.

5.4 Experiments and results

The aim of this work is not only to produce an automatic quantification system, but also, if possible, to learn about the linguistic phenomena surrounding the underspecification of quantification. Because of this, we choose a tree-based classifier which has the advantage of letting us see the rules that are created by the system and thereby may allow us to make some linguistic observations with regard to the cooccurrence of certain quantification classes with certain grammatical constructions. We use an off-the-shelf implementation of the C4.5 classifier (Quinlan, 1993) included in the Weka data mining software.[6] We perform a 6-fold cross-validation on the gold standard and report class precision, recall and F-score.

Class	Precision	Recall	F-score
ONE	86% (362/422)	99% (362/367)	92%
SOME	60% (25/42)	47% (25/53)	53%
MOST	33% (2/6)	6% (2/34)	10%
ALL	53% (57/108)	56% (57/102)	54%
QUANT	100% (22/22)	50% (22/44)	67%

Table 2: Class precision and recall for the quantification task

The C4.5 classifier gives 78% overall precision to the quantification task. Tables 2 shows per class results for the three tasks. The figures in brackets indicate the number of true positives for a particular class, followed by the total number of instances annotated by the system as instances of that class. The classifier performs extremely well with the ONE class, reaching 92% F-score. Already quantified noun phrases yield perfect precision and mediocre recall, as might be expected since we do not provide the system with a list of quantifiers. The system performs less well with the labels SOME, MOST and ALL.

In order to understand the distribution of errors, we perform a detailed analysis on the first fold of our data. Out of 100 instances, the classifier assigns 25 to an incorrect class. The majority of those errors (44%) are due to the fact that the classifier labels all singulars as ONE, missing out on generic interpretations and in particular on the plural reading of mass terms: out of 11 errors, 5 are linked to a bare singular). The next most frequent type of error, covering another 16% of incorrectly classified instances, comes from already quantified noun phrases being labelled as another class. These errors affect the recall of the QUANT class and the precision of the SOME, MOST and ALL labels in particular (most of those errors occur in plural noun phrases). The coarseness of the rules is again to blame for the remaining errors: looking at the decision tree produced by the classifier, we observe that all bare

[6]http://www.cs.waikato.ac.nz/ml/weka/

plurals followed by a present tense, as well as all definite plurals, are labelled as universals, while all bare plurals followed by a past tense are labelled as SOME. This accounts for a further 7 errors. The last three incorrect assignments are due to a dubious capitalisation rule.

5.5 Correspondence with linguistics

We observe that most definite plurals (including demonstratives and possessives) are classified as either MOST or ALL. This fits the linguistic notion of a definite as being essentially universal (Lyons, 1999) but also misses out on the correct quantification of statements such as 10.

We note also that non-capitalised bare plurals followed by a present tense are similarly classed as ALL. This echoes the observation that the combination of bare plural and present is a typical manifestation of genericity (if one understands genericity as a quantification phenomenon close to universality). When followed by past or perfect tenses, an existential quantification with SOME is however preferred.

One of the puzzles opened by the classifier's decision trees is the use of the direct object feature to distinguish between MOST and ALL in the case of some definite plurals. Given Sentences 28 and 29, our classifier would label the first one as ALL and the second one as MOST.

28. *My cats* like the armchair. ALL
29. *My cats* like the armchairs. MOST

At first glance, the rule seems to be a mere statistical effect of our data. We will however remark that statements like 29 are reserved a special section in Link (1998), where they are introduced as 'relational plural sentences'. One of Link's claims is that those sentences warrant four collective/distributive combinations — as opposed to two only in the case where the object is an individual. So we can say in Sentence 29 that a collective of cats likes a collective of armchairs, or that this collective of cats likes each armchair individually, etc. This proliferation of interpretations makes uncertainties more likely with regard to who likes what, and to the quantification of the subject and object.

For now, we will simply conclude that, although a simple syntax-based classifier is able to classify certain constructs with high precision, other constructs are beyond its capabilities. Further, it is difficult to see how improvements can be made to the current classification without venturing outside of the grammatical context. For instance, it seems practically impossible to improve on the high-precision rule specifying that every singular noun phrase should be classified as ONE. Due to space constraints, we will not report any further experiments in this paper. However, preliminary investigations into the use of lexical similarity to resolve quantification ambiguity can be found in Herbelot (2010).

6 Previous work

The general framework of this proposal is an underspecification account close to that described in Pinkal (1996) or Egg (2010). Computational approaches to underspecified quantification have so far focused on the genericity phenomenon. Leaving aside the question of annotation, which is treated in Herbelot and Copestake (2010), research on genericity can be classified within two strands: theoretical research on defeasible reasoning and extraction of common sense knowledge. Attempts to model defeasible reasoning were made in the 1980s with, for instance, the developments of default logic (Reiter, 1980) and non-monotonic logic (McDermott and Doyle, 1982). With information extraction as aim, Suh et al. (2006) attempt to retrieve 'common sense' statements from Wikipedia. They posit that common sense is contained in generic sentences. Their system, however, makes simplifying assumptions with regard to syntax: in particular, all bare plurals (and bare plurals only) are considered generic. In general, common sense extraction systems tend to restrict the data they mine to avoid the problem of identifying genericity (e.g., Voelker et al., 2007).

7 Conclusion, with some remarks on semantics

We have shown in this paper that subject noun phrases that are not explicitly quantified could be represented in an underspecified form. We have also argued that this formalisation is applicable to all constructs, including so-called generics. We have introduced a syntax-based classifier for quantification resolution and discussed the limits of an approach relying on compositional information only.

We acknowledge that our quantificational account of noun phrases, and especially of generics, does not satisfy the common requirement that a formalisation be a full description of the semantic particularities of a linguistic phenomenon. We think, however, that this requirement has led to over-restrictive approaches. One of the debates surrounding generics, for instance, relates to whether they should be given a 'rules and regulations' or an inductivist truth condition (Carlson, 1995). Our view is that it would be a mistake to exclude either interpretation. Burton-Roberts' (1977) *A gentleman opens doors for ladies* clearly has normative force and without doubt, also allows the hearer to make their own conclusions with regard to the intersection between the set of all gentlemen and the set of people opening doors for ladies.

Our view of semantics is that it is a layered system and that specifying the quantification semantics of a noun phrase does not mean providing the full semantics of that noun phrase. It may be argued that the ideal semantics of generics should be unified and integrate all possible aspects of meaning. But such a theory is yet to be developed for genericity and, from a computational point of view, may not even be desirable: a modular representation of meaning allows us to only formalise the aspects that we are interested in for a particular task, leaving the rest out.

The approach presented here can be said to implement the idea of 'slacker' semantics (Copestake, 2009) in that a) our experiments try to derive a specification from compositional information only and b) we only attempt to specify one aspect of the meaning of noun phrases (quantification), leaving other aspects unspecified. In the future, we would like to take away some of the slack in a) by using lexical semantics in the specification of quantification. In order to do this, a much larger corpus should be created for the training and testing of the system, and this will be our next task.

References

Briscoe, T., J. Carroll, and R. Watson (2006). The second release of the RASP system. In *Proceedings of the COLING/ACL on Interactive presentation sessions*, Morristown, NJ, USA, pp. 77–80.

Brogaard, B. (2007). The But Not All: A Partitive Account of Plural Definite Descriptions. *Mind & Language 22*(4), 402–426.

Burton-Roberts, N. (1977). Generic sentences and analyticity. *Studies in Language 1*, 155–196.

Carlson, G. N. (1977). *Reference to Kinds in English.* Ph. D. thesis, University of Massachusetts at Amherst.

Carlson, G. N. (1995). Truth-Conditions of Generic Sentences: Two Contrasting Views. In G. N. Carlson and F. J. Pelletier (Eds.), *The Generic Book*, pp. 224–237. Chicago: University of Chicago Press.

Chierchia, G. (1995). Individual-level predicates as inherent generics. In G. N. Carlson and F. J. Pelletier (Eds.), *The Generic Book*, pp. 176–223. Chicago: University of Chicago Press.

Chierchia, G. (1998). Reference to kinds across languages. *Natural Language Semantics 6*, 339–405.

Cimpian, A. and E. M. Markman (2008). Preschool children's use of cues to generic meaning. *Cognition 107*(1), 19–53.

Cohen, A. (1996). *Think Generic: The Meaning and Use of Generic Sentences.* Ph. D. thesis, Carnegie-Mellon University at Pittsburgh.

Copestake, A. (2004). Robust Minimal Recursion Semantics. http://www.cl.cam.ac.uk/~aac10/papers/rmrsdraft.pdf.

Copestake, A. (2009). Slacker semantics : why superficiality , dependency and avoidance of commitment can be the right way to go. In *Proceedings of the 12th Conference of the European Chapter of the Association for Computational Linguistics*, Athens, Greece, pp. 1–9.

Dowty, D. (1987). Collective predicates, distributive predicates and all. In F. Marshall, A. Miller, and Z.-s. Zhang (Eds.), *The Third Eastern States Conference on Linguistics*, Columbus, pp. 97–115. The Ohio State University, Department of Linguistics.

Egg, M. (2010). Semantic Underspecification. *Language and Linguistics Compass 4*(3), 166–181.

Gelman, S. A. (2004). Learning words for kinds: Generic noun phrases in acquisition. In D. Hall and S. Waxman (Eds.), *Weaving a lexicon*. Cambridge, MA: MIT Press.

Herbelot, A. (2010). *Underspecified quantification*. Ph. D. thesis, University of Cambridge.

Herbelot, A. and A. Copestake (2010). Annotating underquantification. In *Proceedings of the Fourth Linguistic Annotation Workshop*, Uppsala, Sweden, pp. 73–81.

Heyer, G. (1990). Semantics and Knowledge Representation in the Analysis of Generic Descriptions. *Journal of Semantics 7*(1), 93–110.

Krifka, M. (2004). Bare NPs: Kind-referring, Indefinites, Both, or Neither? In O. Bonami and P. Cabredo Hofherr (Eds.), *Empirical Issues in Formal Syntax and Semantics*, pp. 111–132.

Krifka, M., F. J. Pelletier, G. N. Carlson, A. ter Meulen, G. Chierchia, and G. Link (1995). Genericity: An Introduction. In G. N. Carlson and F. J. Pelletier (Eds.), *The Generic Book*, pp. 1–125. Chicago: Chicago University Press.

Leslie, S.-J. (2008). Generics: Cognition and Acquisition. *Philosophical Review 117*(1), 1–47.

Link, G. (1983). The Logical Analysis of Plurals and Mass Terms: a Lattice-Theoretical Approach. In R. Bauerle, C. Schwarze, and A. von Stechow (Eds.), *Meaning, Use, and Interpretation of Language*, pp. 302–323. Berlin: de Gruyter.

Link, G. (1998). Plural. In *Algebraic Semantics in Language and Philosophy*. Stanford: CSLI Publications.

Lyons, C. (1999). *Definiteness*. Cambridge: Cambridge University Press.

McDermott, D. and J. Doyle (1982). Non-monotonic Logic I. *Artificial Intelligence 13*, 41–72.

Pelletier, F. J. and N. Asher (1997). Generics and Defaults. In J. van Bethem and A. ter Meulen (Eds.), *Handbook of Logic and Language*, pp. 1125–1177. Amsterdam: Elsevier.

Pinkal, M. (1996). Radical Underspecification. In P. Dekker and M. Stokhof (Eds.), *Proceedings of the 10th Amsterdam Colloquium*, Amsterdam, pp. 479–498. de Gruyter.

Quinlan, J. (1993). *Programs for Machine Learning*. San Francisco, CA: Morgan Kaufmann.

Reiter, R. (1980). A logic for default reasoning. *Artificial Intelligence 13*(1-2), 81–132.

Suh, S., H. Halpin, and E. Klein (2006). Extracting Common Sense Knowledge from Wikipedia. In *Proceedings of the International Semantic Web Conference (ISWC-06). Workshop on Web Content Mining with Human Language Technology*, Athens, GA.

Voelker, J., P. Hitzler, and P. Cimiano (2007). Acquisition of OWL DL Axioms from Lexical Resources. In *Proceedings of the Fourth European conference on The Semantic Web: Research and Applications*, Innsbruck, Austria, pp. 670–685. Springer Verlag.

The Exploitation of Spatial Information in Narrative Discourse

Blake Stephen Howald
Georgetown University
bsh25@georgetown.edu

E. Graham Katz
Georgetown University
egk7@georgetown.edu

Abstract

We present the results of several machine learning tasks that exploit explicit spatial language to classify rhetorical relations and the spatial information of narrative events. Three corpora are annotated with figure and ground (granularity) relationships, mereotopologically classified verbs and prepositions, and frames of reference. For rhetorical relations, Naïve Bayesian models achieve 84.90% and 57.87% accuracy in classifying NARRATION and BACKGROUND / ELABORATION relations respectively (16% and 23% above baseline). For the spatial information of narrative events, K* models achieve 55.68% average accuracy (12% above baseline) for all spatial information types. This result is boosted to 71.85% (28% above baseline) when inertial spatial reference and text sequence information are considered. Overall, spatial information is shown to be central to narrative discourse structure and prediction tasks.

1 Introduction

Clauses in discourse are related to one another in a number of semantic and pragmatic ways. Some of the most prominent are temporal relations that hold among the times of events and states described (Partee, 1984; Pustejovsky et al., 2003) and the rhetorical relations that hold between a pair of clauses (Mann and Thompson, 1987; Asher and Lascarides, 2003). For example, (1) illustrates the NARRATION relation which obtains between (1a-b) and between (1b-c).

(1) a. Klose was sitting with his teammates.
b. He walked to the sidelines.
c. Then he entered the game.

Because of the temporal properties of NARRATION (Asher and Lascarides 2003, p. 462), the event described in (1a) is taken to precede that described in (1b) and (1b)'s event to precede (1c)'s. As Asher and Lascarides show, there is a close tie between the rhetorical structure of a discourse and its temporal structure. In (2), for example, the fact that the clauses are related by ELABORATION entails that the temporal relation between (2a) and (2b) is inclusion.

(2) a. Klose scored a goal.
b. He headed the ball into the upper corner.

We observe that the spatial relations among the locations of the events described in these discourses are also highly determined by the rhetorical relations between the clauses used to describe them. In the NARRATION-related discourse (1), there is a spatial progression: Klose is located relative to his teammates (1a), he then moves from the bench to the sidelines (1b), and then he moves from the sidelines into the game (1c). In the ELABORATION-related discourse (2), there is no such progression.

In this paper, we investigate the degree to which the spatial structure of discourse and its rhetorical structure are co-determined. Using supervised machine learning techniques (Witten and Frank, 2002), we evaluate two hypotheses: (a) spatial information encoded in adjacent clauses is highly predictive of the rhetorical relations that hold between them and (b) spatial information is highly predictable based on associated spatial information within narrative event clauses. To do this, we build a corpus of narrative texts which are annotated both for spatial information (figure and ground (granularity) relationships, mereotopologically classified verbs and prepositions, and frames of reference) and rhetorical relations (a binary NARRATION vs. ELABORATION/BACKGROUND distinction discussed in Section 3.2). This corpus is then used to train two types of classifiers - one type that classifies the rhetorical relations holding between clauses on the basis of spatial information, and another type that classifies spatial relationships within clauses where the NARRATION relation holds. The results support both hypotheses and indicate the centrality of spatial information to narrative discourse structure and associated classification tasks.

2 Background and Related Research

2.1 Rhetorical Relations

Rhetorical relations describe the role that one clause plays with respect to another in a text and contributes to a text's coherence (Hobbs, 1985). As such, these relations are pragmatic features of a text. In NLP generally, classifying rhetorical relations has been an important area of research (Marcu, 2000; Sporleder and Lascarides, 2005) and has been shown to be useful for tasks such as text summarization (Marcu, 1998). The inventory of rhetorical relations in Segmented Discourse Representation Theory (SDRT) (Asher and Lascarides, 2003) is widely used in these applications. This inventory includes the following relations, illustrated by example: NARRATION: *Klose got up. He entered the game.* ELABORATION: *Klose pushed the Serbian midfielder. He knew him from school.* BACKGROUND: *Klose entered the game. The pitch was very wet.* EXPLANATION: *Klose received a red card. He pushed the Serbian midfielder.* CONSEQUENCE: *If Klose received a red card, then he pushed the Serbian midfielder.* RESULT: *Klose pushed the Serbian midfielder. He received a red card.* ALTERNATION: *Klose received a red card or he received a yellow card.* CONTINUATION: *Klose received a red card. Ronaldo received a yellow card.*

In previous work, rhetorical relations have been predicted based on a range of features including discourse connectives, relation location, clause length, part-of-speech, content and function words, and syntactic features (Marcu and Echihabi, 2002; Lapata and Lascarides, 2004). These systems have a wide range of average accuracies for all relations sought to be predicted - e.g. 33.96% (Marcu and Echihabi, 2002) to 70.70% (Lapata and Lascarides, 2004) - and individual relations - e.g. RESULT - 16.21% and EXPLANATION - 75.39% (Marcu and Echihabi, 2002) and CONTRAST - 43.64% and CONTINUATION - 83.35% (Sporleder and Lascarides, 2005). Our focus is on the NARRATION, BACKGROUND and ELABORATION relations, which account for over 90% of the discourses in our corpus.

2.2 Spatial Language and Discourse

Spatial language has been discussed in a number of NLP contexts. For example, linking natural language with physical locations via semantic mark-up (e.g. SpatialML (MITRE, 2009)); spatial description and wayfinding tasks (e.g. Anderson et al., 1991); and dialogue systems (e.g. Coventry et al., 2009), just to name a very few. Perspectives on spatial language are similarly varied in terms of their focus and theoretical background (e.g. cognitive, semantic and syntactic); however, common threads do emerge. First, all physical spatial references are reducible to figure and ground relationships (Talmy, 2000). In English, these are triggered by a deictic verb or adverb (e.g. *went, here*) (3a); a spatial preposition (e.g. *in, at*) (3b); a particle verb (e.g. *put on, got out*) (3c); or a motion verb (e.g. *drive, follow*) (3d).

(3) a. [Ronaldo]$_{figure}$ is [here]$_{ground}$.
b. [Ronaldo]$_{figure}$ is in [the park]$_{ground}$.
c. [Ronaldo]$_{figure}$ rolled over [Ø]$_{ground}$.
d. [Ronaldo]$_{figure}$ ran to [the park]$_{ground}$.

Second, figure and ground relationships qualitatively vary by the type of verb and preposition creating the relationship. These differences can be modeled in mereotopology, which defines spatial relationships in terms of regions and connections (e.g. RCC-8 (Randell et al., 1992)). We follow Asher and Sablayrolles (1995) who classify prepositions based on the position (Position - *at*, Initial Direction - *from*, Medial Position - *through*, Final Position - *to*) and contact (Inner - *in*, Contact - *against*, Outer

- *along*, and Outer-Most - *beyond*) of two regions (figure and ground). For verbs, Muller (2002) proposes six mereotopological classes: Reach, Leave, Internal, External, Hit, and Cross. Pustejovsky and Moszkowicz (2008) mapped Muller's classes to FrameNet and VerbNet and propose ten general classes of motion (Move, Move-External, Move-Internal, Leave, Reach, Detach, Hit, Follow, Deviate, Stay).

Third, figure and ground relationships vary by the perspective used to describe the relationship. For this discussion, perspective takes two forms, granularity of spatial description (following Montello (1993)) and frames of reference (following Levinson (1996)). Granularity refers to the level of detail in a given spatial description. Montello (1993, p. 315) indicates four spatial granularities based on the cognitive organization of spatial knowledge (summarized in (4)).

(4)
a. Ronaldo jumped on the ball.
b. Ronaldo is in the corner.
c. Ronaldo is running around the field.
d. Ronaldo is in Cape Town.

(4a) is a **Figural** granularity which describes space smaller than the human body. (4b) is a **Vista** granularity which describes space from a single point of view. (4c) is an **Environmental** granularity which describes space larger than the body with multiple (scanning) point(s) of view. (4d) is a **Geographic** granularity which describes space even larger than the body and is learned by symbolic representation.

Frames of reference provide different ways of describing the same spatial relationships. For example, given a static scene of Ronaldo sitting on a bench next to his coach, each utterance in (5) would be an accurate spatial description.

(5)
a. **Deictic**: *Ronaldo is there.*
b. **Contiguity**: *Ronaldo is on the bench.*
c. **Named Location**: *Ronaldo is at the sideline.*
d. **Relative**: *Ronaldo is in front of me.*
e. **Intrinsic**: *Ronaldo is behind his coach.*
f. **Absolute**: *Ronaldo is north of his coach.*

(5a-c) are non-coordinated as they relate just the figure and ground. Coordinated information, relating the figure to an additional entity within the ground, occurs in (5d-f). Frames of reference apply to both static and dynamic relationships (Levinson, 1996, p. 360).

In terms of attending to spatial information in discourse, Herman (2001) argues that spatial information patterns in narrative discourse carve out spatially defined domains that group narrative actions. In particular, the emergence and change in different types of spatial reference to physical location (discourse cues) create maps of the narrative actions. These discourse cues include figure, ground and path (motion) relationships (3); frames of reference (5); and deictic shifts - *here* vs. *there*. Herman's demonstration is based on ghost story narratives that are rich in spatial reference.

Howald (2010) showed in a corpus of serial killer first person narratives, also rich in spatial reference, that these spatial narrative domains, in the form of abstract Pre-Crime, Crime and Post-Crime events, were predicted to a 90% accuracy from three spatial features (figure, ground, and spatial verb) and discourse sequence. Overall, research by Herman (2001) and Howald (2010) demonstrates some level of dependency between spatial information and discourse structure. The present research addresses the specific question of whether there is a systematic relationship between spatial information and temporal information via rhetorical relations and the spatial architecture of narrative events.

3 Data and Annotation

3.1 Data

Three corpora of narrative discourse were annotated with rhetorical and spatial information. These corpora were then used to train and test machine learning systems. Summarized in Table 1, the three different narrative corpora selected for analysis were: (1) narratives from serial criminals (CRI) - oral and written confession statements and guilty pleas; (2) American National Corpus Charlotte Narrative and Conversation Collection (Ide and Suderman, 2007) (ANC) - oral narratives in conversations collected in a sociolinguistic interview format; and (3) The Degree Confluence Project (DEG) - this project, which seeks to map all possible latitude-longitude intersections on Earth, requires that participants who visit these intersections provide written narratives of the visit for inclusion on the project's website.

Table 1: Relation and Spatial Clause Distribution

Corpus	ANC (n=20)	DEG (n=20)	CRI (n=20)	Total (N=60)
Total Clauses	588	611	1,710	2,909
Spatial Clauses	260	354	932	1,546
Average	44.21	57.93	54.50	53.14
Total Rhetorical	568	591	1,690	2,848
Spatial Rhetorical	259	345	929	1,533
Average	45.59	58.37	55.00	53.82

20 narratives from each corpus were selected. There was a total of 2,909 (independent) clauses with 1,546 of those clauses containing spatial information - spatial clauses (53.14% on average). There was a total of 2,848 relations with 1,533 of those relations where *both* clauses contained spatial information - spatial rhetorical (53.82% on average).

3.2 Spatial Information and Rhetorical Relation Annotation

We developed a coding scheme for spatial information that consolidates the insights on spatial langauge discussed in Section 2.2.

- FIGURE is an indication of grammatical person or a non-person entity (**1** = *I, my*; **2** = *you, your*; **3** = *he, she, it, his, her*; **4** = *we, our*; **5** = *you, your*; **6** = *they, their*; **NP** = *the purse, a bench, three cars*);
- VERB is one of the four mereotopological classes - a consolidation of Pustejovsky and Moszkowicz's (2008) ten classifications (**State** = *was, stay, was sitting*; **Move** = *run, go, jump*; **Outside** = *follow, pass, track*; **Hit** = *attach, detach, strike*);
- PREPOSITION is one of four mereotopological classes based on Asher and Sablayrolles (1995) (**Positional** = *in, on*; **Initial** = *from* ; **Medial** = *through*; **Final** = *to*);
- GROUND is one of four granularities (**Figural**, **Environmental**, **Vista**, **Geographic**) (see (4) above);
- FRAME is one of six frames of reference (**Deictic**, **Contiguity**, **Named Location**, **Relative**, **Intrinsic**, **Absolute**) (see (5) above).

The three corpora were annotated by one of the authors. Annotation occurred one narrative at a time and any information from that narrative could be used to resolve rhetorical relations and spatial information. A reference sheet including several examples of each coding element was available to the annotator. The annotation happened in two phases. First, each pair of clauses was annotated with an SDRT relation. Second, each clause that contained a physical figure and ground relationship was identified. The figure, ground, preposition and verb were annotated with a **Figure**, **Verb**, **Preposition**, **Ground**, and **Frame**. We illustrate with (6) where the NARRATION relation obtains between (6a-b).

(6) a. Kaka kicked the ball into the goal.
    b. Then he ran to the left side of the bench.

The spatial annotation of (6a) is: FIGURE = **NP**, *the ball*; VERB = **Hit (H)**, *kicked*; PREPOSITION = **Final (F)**, *into*; GROUND = **Environmental (E)**, *the goal*; and FRAME = **Contiguity (C)**. The spatial annotation of (6b) is: FIGURE = **3**, *he*; VERB = **Move (M)**, *ran*; PREPOSITION = **Final (F)**, *to the left side of*; GROUND = **Environmental (E)**, *the bench*; and FRAME = **Intrinsic (INT)**. The distribution of spatial rhetorical relations is summarized in Table 2.

Table 2: Spatial Rhetorical Relation Distribution per Corpus

Relation	**ANC**	**DEG**	**CRI**	**Total**
NARRATION	133	124	654	911
BACKGROUND	74	87	238	399
ELABORATION	34	63	17	114
CONTINUATION	14	27	10	51
RESULT	3	22	0	25
EXPLANATION	0	16	1	17
ALTERNATION	0	0	9	9
CONSEQUENCE	1	6	0	7
Total	259	345	929	1,533

An additional individual was queried for inter-rater reliability against the author annotation. The rater was given roughly one-third of the data (10 narratives (4 ANC, 4 DEG, 2 CRI) accounting for 510 spatial clause pairs), the same example sheet used by the author, and as much time as needed to complete the task. Average agreement and Cohen's kappa statistics (Cohen, 1960) were computed between the inter-rater and the author for the spatial annotations and NARRATION, BACKGROUND, and ELABORATION codings. Individually, BACKGROUND and ELABORATION have low interannotator agreement (κ = 32.92 and 54.20 respectively), but these two relations were often confused (26% of BACKGROUND relations coded as ELABORATION and 12% of ELABORATION relations coded as BACKGROUND). As illustrated in (7-8), both BACKGROUND and ELABORATION add information to the surrounding state of affairs.

(7) a. Klose entered the game.
    b. The pitch was very wet.

(8) a. Klose pushed the Serbian midfielder.
    b. He knew him from school.

As evidenced by the annotation confusions, the difference between these relations is difficult to distinguish and the distinction made by Asher and Lascarides (2003) is subtle - BACKGROUND's temporal consequence is one of *overlap* and ELABORATION, a subordinating relation, is one of *part-of*. However collapsing these relations resulted in a fairly reliably distinguished category. Average agreement and kappa statistics are summarized in Table 3.

Table 3: Agreement and Kappa Statistics for Relation and Spatial Codings

Coding	**Agreement (%)**	**Kappa (κ)**
All Rhetorical Relations	71.97	60.27
NARRATION	86.32	74.36
BACKGROUND / ELABORATION	73.40	62.20
Figure	94.91	89.92
Verb	90.90	81.80
Preposition	78.35	56.70
Granularity	87.87	75.74
Frame	69.38	38.76

For rhetorical relations, the average agreement and kappa statistic are consistent with previously reported performances (e.g. Agreement = 71.25 / κ = 61.00 (Sporleder and Lascarides, 2005)). We have not been able to find previously reported performance accuracies for NARRATION, ELABORATION and BACKGROUND relations specifically. However, κ statistics from 60.00 to 75.00 and above are considered acceptable (e.g. Landis and Koch, 1977). For the spatial codings, the average agreements are relatively high with **Preposition** and **Frame** falling lowest. There is no basis for direct comparison of these numbers to other research as the coding scheme is novel.

4 Machine Learning Experiments

We constructed two machine learning tasks to exploit the annotated spatial information to determine what contributions the information is making to narrative structure. The first task evaluates the prediction of NARRATION and BACKGROUND/ ELABORATION relations based on pairs of spatial clauses. The second task evaluates the prediction of spatial information types, based on the other spatial information types in that clause, in individual clauses where the NARRATION relation holds.

4.1 Rhetorical Relation Prediction

4.1.1 Methods and Results

Task 1 builds a 2-way classifier for the NARRATION and BACKGROUND/ ELABORATION relations. Clause pairs were coded as vectors (n = 1,424) - for example, the vector for (6) is **NP3**, **HM**, **FF**, **EE**, **CINT**. These vectors were used to train and test (10-fold cross-validation) a number of classifiers. The Naïve Bayes classifier performed the best. Results are reported in Table 4.

Table 4: Naïve Bayes Classification Accuracy and F-Measures for Task 1

NARRATION	**Accuracy (% / baseline)**	**Precision**	**Recall**	**F-Score**
ANC	63.29 / 58	.676	.633	.654
DEG	75.71 / 61	.803	.757	.779
CRI	90.12 / 73	.822	.901	.860
TOTAL	84.90 / 68	.808	.841	.824
BACK/ ELAB	**Accuracy (% / baseline)**	**Precision**	**Recall**	**F-Score**
ANC	57.89 / 41	.532	.579	.555
DEG	70.11 / 38	.642	.701	.670
CRI	45.63 / 26	.624	.456	.527
TOTAL	57.87 / 35	.622	.567	.593

For all corpora combined, the majority class ("baseline") for NARRATION is 68% and 26% for BACKGROUND / ELABORATION; the classifier performs 16% and 22% above baseline respectively. The difference between the NARRATION and BACKGROUND / ELABORATION relations and baselines is statistically significant for each corpus and all corpora combined - ANC: χ^2 = 25.64, d.f. = 1, p $\leq$ .001; DEG: χ^2 = 33.86, d.f. = 1, p $\leq$ .001; CRI: χ^2 = 22.69, d.f. = 1, p $\leq$ .001; and TOTAL:χ^2 = 34.09, d.f. = 1, p $\leq$ .001.

4.1.2 Discussion

Again, we have not been able to find reported results for a direct comparison of NARRATION and BACKGROUND/ ELABORATION. However, the 84.90% and 57.87% (at 16% and 22% over baseline) performance of our Naïve Bayesian model is consistent with results reported in similar tasks. For example, Marcu and Echihabi (2002) report an average accuracy of 33.96% (5-way classifier) and 49.70% (6-way classifier) based on training with very large data sets. Sporleder and Lascarides (2005) report a 57.55% average accuracy, based on training with large data sets, which is 20% over Marcu and Echihabi's 5-way classifier and almost 40% over a random 20% baseline. Lapata and Lascarides (2004) report an average accuracy of 70.70% for inferring temporal relations based on training.

We ran an additional set of experiments to determine the relative contribution of spatial features to predict NARRATION and BACKGROUND / ELABORATION relations. As shown in Table 5, **Figure** and **Verb** outperform **Ground**, **Preposition** and **Frame** in accuracy. **Figure** performs at a 71% average accuracy (85% for NARRATION and 40% for BACKGROUND/ ELABORATION) and **Verb** performs at a 74% average accuracy (84% for NARRATION and 54% for BACKGROUND/ ELABORATION). **Figure** and **Verb** appear to be most discriminating. Note that we are not suggesting that *subject* and *verb* generally are similarly discriminatory - **Figure** and **Verb** in this task are overtly spatial. Despite the performance of **Figure** and **Verb**, different subsets of spatial information worked better (we ran all permutations of spatial features - the top five are listed in Table 5). However, the difference in performance is negligible. For example, the best subset of **Figure**, **Verb** and **Ground** (85% and 58%) only performed 1% above NARRATION and BACKGROUND/ ELABORATION prediction based on all five features combined.

Table 5: Single and Combined Spatial Feature Performance

Feature	NARRATION	BACK/ ELAB	Features	NARRATION	BACK/ ELAB
Figure (F)	85.58	40.33	**FVG**	85.24	58.33
Verb (V)	84.59	54.97	**VGP**	84.34	58.33
Prepostion (P)	97.34	1.00	**FVGR**	86.33	56.45
Ground (G)	97.33	1.00	**FV**	86.56	56.90
Frame (R)	98.02	2.00	**VG**	85.37	57.33

These results tell us several things about the relationship between spatial information and rhetorical structure as it applies to narrative discourse. First, spatial information predicts rhetorical structure as good as non-spatial types of linguistic information reported in other investigations and with many fewer features. For example, Sporleder and Lascarides (2005) rely on 72 different features falling into nine classes whereas we rely on 14 features in five classes. This suggests that spatial information is not only central to rhetorical stucture, like temporal components, but central to the task of prediction. Second, while the type of spatial information that predicts rhetorical structure is based on the primary figure and ground relationship, it is the qualitative semantic variations within these elements that is providing the discrimination. It is the organization of spatial relationships - (**Verb** and **Preposition**) and the perspective provided by the narrator (**Figure**, **Ground** and **Frame**) combined - rather than any individual elements.

4.2 Spatial Information Prediction

4.2.1 Methods and Results

Task 2 is a series of five experiments. Each experiment builds a classifier for each type of spatial information: a 6-way classifier for **Frame**; a 5-way classifier for **Figure** (**Figure** types **2** and **5** did not occur in our corpus); and 4-way classifiers for **Ground**, **Preposition** and **Verb**. Single clauses that contribute to the NARRATION relation were coded as vectors (n = 911) - for example, the single vectors for (6a) and (6b) are **NP**, **H**, **F**, **E**, **C** and **3**, **M**, **F**, **E**, **INT**. These vectors were used to train and test (10-fold cross-validation) a number of classifiers to predict one of the five spatial features given the remaining four. The K* classifier performed the best. Results are reported in Table 6. For all corpora combined, the K* classifier performs above baseline for all spatial information (**Figure** = 9%, **Verb** = 17%, **Preposition** = 9%, **Ground** = 19%, **Frame** = 8%) (χ^2 = 20.95, d.f. = 4, p $\leq$ .001).

4.2.2 Discussion

Even though the accuracies of predicting spatial information are significantly above baseline, we sought ways to boost performance by considering implicit spatial information. For those clauses without explicit spatial information, we extended the annotation of the previous clause's coding based on the inertia of

Table 6: K* Classification Accuracy and F-Measures for Task 2

Spatial Information	Accuracy (% / baseline)	Precision	Recall	F-Score
Figure	47.97 / 38	.464	.480	.428
Verb	67.32 / 50	.635	.673	.640
Preposition	53.69 / 46	.492	.537	.499
Ground	53.59 / 34	.530	.536	.519
Frame	55.67 / 47	.507	.557	.511

narrative texts. Rapaport, et al. (1994) discuss the temporal inertia of narrative texts - time moves forward through narrative events. In the absence of updating, information is maintained. We suggest that inertia applies to spatial information as well. For example, given the clauses - *John entered the room. He sat down.* - we make the assumption that John sat down in the room that he entered. We illustrate with (9).

(9) a. Kaka kicked the ball into the goal.
NP, H, F, E, C, .33
b. The goaltender yelled in frustration.
NP, H, F, E, C, .66
c. Then Kaka ran to the left side of the bench.
3, M, F, E, INT, 1

No explicit spatial information exists in (9b). We took the coding from the explicit spatial information in (9a) and maintained it for (9b). New explicit spatial information occurs in (9c) and the coding is updated. Further, we included explicit sequence information as a measure of a given clause's proportional position within the text (**.33**, **.66** and **1**). In the absence of overt temporal specification (occuring in only 10% of the clauses in our corpus), the sequence information, a textual feature, parallels the temporal progression (and inertia) of narrative events. This added 560 additional vectors (n = 1,471). The K* classifier still performed the best. The results are summarized in Table 7.

Table 7: K* Classification Accuracy and F-Measures for Task 2 Boosted Vectors

SPATIAL INERTIA	Accuracy (% / baseline)	Precision	Recall	F-Score
Figure	51.73 / 41	.509	.517	.473
Verb	70.22 / 48	.673	.700	.679
Preposition	57.30 / 47	.571	.573	.540
Ground	62.61 / 35	.636	.626	.611
Frame	59.82 / 44	.574	.598	.564
SPATIAL INERTIA + SEQUENCE	**Accuracy (% / baseline)**	**Precision**	**Recall**	**F-Score**
Figure	70.56 / 41	.702	.706	.699
Verb	79.33 / 48	.789	.793	.790
Preposition	67.91 / 47	.676	.679	.674
Ground	72.39 / 35	.721	.724	.721
Frame	69.06 / 44	.678	.691	.681

Inclusion of the spatial inertia values improves performance of the K* classifier in all cases (χ^2 = 40.59, d.f. = 4, p $\leq$ .001). Inclusion of sequence information improves performance even further (χ^2 = 102.36, d.f. = 4, p $\leq$ .001). Note that, despite the increase in performance, sequencing information alone does not do as well, indicating that spatial information still plays a discriminatory role. Using sequence information alone as a baseline (**Figure** = 47%, **Verb** = 52%, **Preposition** = 47%, **Ground** = 44%, **Frame** = 48%;), the normalized performance values above sequence baseline become **Figure** = 23%, **Verb** = 27%, **Preposition** = 28%, **Ground** = 20%, and **Frame** = 21%.

The ability to predict spatial features appears to be dependent both on a patterned distribution of the per-clause spatial information (increased by spatial inertia) and on the textual feature of sequence (temporal inertia). This seems to hold despite the specific subject matter or spatial characteristics of a given narrative. Considering the complete spatiotemporal picture for narrative clauses yields the best prediction results and suggests that the spatial information structure of narrative discourse represents some type of organization akin to what Herman (2001) and Howald (2010) have evaluated in spatially-rich narratives. Based on the tasks presented here, this organization appears to be fundamental and relative to formal temporally-informed discourse structure.

5 Conclusion

Exploration of the spatial dimension in narrative discourse provides interesting and robust possibilities for computational discourse analysis. We have described two machine learning tasks which exploit spatial linguistic features. In addition to improving on existing prediction systems, both tasks empirically demonstrate that, when available, certain types of spatial information are predictors of the rhetorical structure of narrative discourse and the spatial information of narrative event sequences. Based on these results, we indicate that spatial structure is related to temporal structure in narrative discourse.

The coding scheme proposed here models complex and interrelated properties of spatial relationships and perspectives and should be generalizeable to other non-narrative discourses. Future research will focus on different discourse corpora to determine how spatial information is related to rhetorical structure. Additional future research will also focus on automation of the annotation process. The ambiguity of spatial language makes automatic extraction of spatial features infeasible at the current state of the art. Fortunately, average agreement and kappa statistics for coding of the spatial information and rhetorical relations are within acceptable ranges. The annotated spatial features are semantically deep and useful for not only computational discourse systems, but tasks that involve the semantic modeling of spatial relations and spatial reasoning.

Acknowledgments

Thank you to David Herman and James Pustejovsky for productive comments and discussion and to Jerry Hobbs for suggesting the Degree Confluence Project as a source of spatially rich narratives. Thank you also to four anonymous reviewers for very helpful insights.

References

[1] Anne Anderson, Miles Bader, Ellen Bard, Elizabeth Boyle, Gwyneth Doherty, Simon Garrod, Stephen Isard, Jacqueline Kowtko, Jan McAllister, Jim Miller, Catherine Sotillo, Henry Thompson, and Regina Weinert. 1991. The HCRC Map Task Corpus. *Language and Speech*, 34:351–366.

[2] Nicholas Asher and Alex Lascarides. 2003. *Logics of Conversation.* Cambridge University Press, Cambridge, UK.

[3] Nicholas Asher and Pierre Sablayrolles. 1995. A Typology and Discourse Semantics for Motion Verbs and Spatial PPs in French. *Journal of Semantics*, 12(2):163–209.

[4] Jacob Cohen. 1960. A Coefficient of Agreement for Nominal Scales. *Educational and Psychological Measurement*, 20(1):37–46.

[5] Kenny Coventry, Thora Tenbrink, and John Bateman. 2009. *Spatial Language and Dialogue*. Oxford University Press, Oxford, UK.

[6] David Herman. 2001. Spatial Reference in Narrative Domains. *Text*, 21(4):515–541.

[7] Jerry R. Hobbs. 1985. On The Coherence and Structure of Discourse. CSLI Technical Report, 85-37.

[8] Blake Howald. 2010. Linguistic Spatial Classifications of Event Domains in Narratives of Crime. *Journal of Spatial Information Science*, 1.75–93.

[9] Nancy Ide and Keith Suderman. 2007. The Open American National Corpus (OANC), available at http://www.AmericanNationalCorpus.org/OANC.

[10] Richard Landis and Gary Koch. 1977. The Measurement of Observer Agreement for Categorical Data. Biometrics, 33(1):159–174.

[11] Mirella Lapata and Alex Lascarides. 2004. Inferring sentence internal temporal relations. In Proceedings of NAACL-04, 153–160.

[12] Stephen C. Levinson. 1996. Language and Space. *Annual Review of Anthropology*, 25(1):353–382.

[13] William Mann and Sandra Thompson. 1987. Rhetorical Structure Theory: A Framework for The Analysis of Texts. *International Pragmatics Association Papers in Pragmatics*, 1:79–105.

[14] Daniel Marcu. 1998. Improving Summarization Through Rhetorical Parsing Tuning. In *The 6th Workshop on Very Large Corpora*, 206–215.

[15] Daniel Marcu. 2000. The Rhetorical Parsing of Unrestricted Texts: A Surface-Based Approach. *Computational Linguistics*, 26(3):395–448.

[16] Daniel Marcu and Abdessamad Echihabi. 2002. An Unsupervised Approach to Recognizing Discourse Relations. In *Proceedings of ACL-02*, 368–375.

[17] MITRE. 2009. SpatialML: Annotation Scheme for Marking Spatial Expressions in Natural Language, Version 3.0. April 3, 2009.

[18] Daniel R. Montello. 1993. Scale and Multiple Psychologies of Space. In A. Frank and I. Campari (eds.), *Spatial Information Theory: A Theoretical Basis for GIS* (LNCS 716), 312–321. Springer-Verlag, Berlin.

[19] Philippe Muller. 2002. Topological Spatio-temporal Reasoning and Representation. *Computational Intelligence*, 18(3):420–450.

[20] Barbara Partee. 1984. Nominal and Temporal Anaphora. *Linguistics and Philosophy*, 7(3):243–286.

[21] James Pustejovsky and Jessica Moszkowicz. 2008. Integrating motion predicate classes with spatial and temporal annotations. *COLING 2008*:95–98.

[22] James Pustejovsky, José Castaño, Robert Ingria, Roser Saur, Robert Gaizauskas, Andrea Setzer, and Graham Katz. 2003. TimeML: Robust Specification of Event and Temporal Expressions in Text. *In Proceedings of the IWCS-5, Fifth International Workshop on Computational Semantics.*

[23] David Randell, Zhan Cui, and Anthony Cohn. 1992. A Spatial Logic Based on Regions and Connection. *Proceedings of KR92*, 394–398. Los Altos, CA: Morgan Kaufmann.

[24] William Rapaport, Erwin Segal, Stuart Shapiro, David Zubin, Gail Bruder, Judith Duchan, Michael Almeida, Joyce Daniels, Mary Galbraith, Janyce Wiebe and Albert Yuhan. 1994. Deictic Centers and the Cognitive Structure of Narrative Comprehension. Technical Report No. 89-01. Buffalo, NY: SUNY Buffalo Department of Computer Science.

[25] Caroline Sporleder and Alex Lascarides. 2005. Exploiting Linguistic Cues to Classify Rhetorical Relations. *Proceedings of Recent Advances in Natural Language Processing (RANLP-05)*, 532–539.

[26] Leonard Talmy. 2000. *Toward a Cognitive Semantics, Volume 2*. The MIT Press, Cambridge, MA.

[27] Ian Witten and Eibe Frank. 2002. *Data Mining Practical Machine Learning Tools and Techniques with Java Implementation*. Morgan Kaufmann.

Measuring the semantic relatedness between words and images

Chee Wee Leong and Rada Mihalcea
Department of Computer Science and Engineering
University of North Texas
cheeweeleong@my.unt.edu, rada@cs.unt.edu

Abstract

Measures of similarity have traditionally focused on computing the semantic relatedness between pairs of words and texts. In this paper, we construct an evaluation framework to quantify cross-modal semantic relationships that exist between arbitrary pairs of words and images. We study the effectiveness of a corpus-based approach to automatically derive the semantic relatedness between words and images, and perform empirical evaluations by measuring its correlation with human annotators.

1 Introduction

Traditionally, a large body of research in natural language processing has focused on formalizing word meanings. Several resources developed to date (e.g., WordNet (Miller, 1995)) have enabled a systematic encoding of the semantics of words and exemplify their usage in different linguistic frameworks. As a result of this formalization, computing semantic relatedness between words has been possible and has been used in applications such as information extraction and retrieval, query reformulation, word sense disambiguation, plagiarism detection and textual entailment.

In contrast, while research has shown that the human cognitive system is sensitive to visual information and incorporating a dual linguistic-and-pictorial representation of information can actually enhance knowledge acquisition (Potter and Faulconer, 1975), the *meaning* of an image in isolation is not well-defined and it is mostly task-specific. A given image, for instance, may be simultaneously labeled by a set of words using an automatic image annotation algorithm, or classified under a different set of semantic tags in the image classification task, or simply draw its meaning from a few representative regions following image segmentation performed in an object localization framework.

Given that word meanings can be acquired and disambiguated using dictionaries, we can perhaps express the meaning of an image in terms of the words that can be suitably used to describe it. Specifically, we are interested to bridge the *semantic gap* (Smeulders et al., 2000) between words and images by exploring ways to harvest the information extracted from visual data in a general framework. While a large body of work has focused on measuring the semantic similarity of words (e.g., (Miller and Charles, 1998)), or the similarity between images based on image content (e.g., (Goldberger et al., 2003)), very few researchers have considered the measure of semantic relatedness[1] between words and images.

But, how exactly is an image related to a given word? In reality, quantification of such a cross-modal semantic relation is impossible without supplying it with a proper definition. Our work seeks to address this challenge by constructing a standard evaluation framework to derive a semantic relatedness metric for arbitrary pairs of words and images. In our work, we explore methods to build a representation model consisting of a joint semantic space of images and words by combining techniques widely adopted in computer vision and natural language processing, and we evaluate the hypothesis that we can automatically derive a semantic relatedness score using this joint semantic space.

Importantly, we acknowledge that it is significantly harder to decode the semantics of an image, as its interpretation relies on a subjective and perceptual understanding of its visual components (Biederman,

[1]In our paper, we are concerned with semantic *relatedness*, which is a more general concept than semantic *similarity*. Similarity is concerned with entities related by virtues of their likeness, e.g., *bank-trust company*, but dissimilar entities may also be related, e.g., *hot-cold*. A full treatment of the topic can be found in Budanitsky and Hirst (2005).

1987). Despite this challenge, we believe this is a worthy research direction, as many important problems can benefit from the association of image content in relation to word meanings, such as automatic image annotation, image retrieval and classification (e.g., (Leong et al., 2010)) as well as tasks in the domains of of text-to-image synthesis, image harvesting and augmentative and alternative communication.

2 Related Work

Despite the large amount of work in computing semantic relatedness between words or similarity between images, there are only a few studies in the literature that associate the meaning of words and pictures in a joint semantic space. The work most similar to ours was done by Westerveld (2000), who employed LSA to combine textual words with simple visual features extracted from news images using colors and textures. Although it was concluded that such a joint textual-visual representation model was promising for image retrieval, no intensive evaluation was performed on datasets on a large scale, or datasets other than the news domain. Similarly, Hare et al. (2008) compared different methods such as LSA and probabilistic LSA to construct joint semantic spaces in order to study their effects on automatic image annotation and semantic image retrieval, but their evaluation was restricted exclusively to the Corel dataset, which is somewhat idealistic and not reflective of the challenges presented by real-world, noisy images.

Another related line of work by Barnard and Forsyth (2001) used a generative hierarchical model to learn the associative semantics of words and images for improving information retrieval tasks. Their approach was supervised and evaluated again only on the Corel dataset.

More recently, Feng and Lapata (2010) showed that it is possible to combine visual representations of word meanings into a joint bimodal representation constructed by using latent topics. While their work focused on unifying meanings from visual and textual data via supervised techniques, no effort was made to compare the semantic relatedness between arbitrary pairs of word and image.

3 Bag of Visual Codewords

Inspired by the bag-of-words approach employed in information retrieval, the "bag of visual codewords" is a similar technique used mainly for scene classification (Yang et al., 2007). Starting with an image collection, visual features are first extracted as data points from each image, characterizing its appearance. By projecting data points from all the images into a common space and grouping them into a large number of clusters such that similar data points are assigned to the same cluster, we can treat each cluster as a "visual codeword" and express every image in the collection as a "bag of visual codewords". This representation enables the application of methods used in text retrieval to tasks in image processing and computer vision.

Typically, the type of visual features selected can be *global* – suitable for representation in all images, or *local* – specific to a given image type and task requirement. Global features are often described using a continuous feature space, such as color histogram in three different color spaces (RGB, HSV and LAB), or textures using Gabor and Haar wavelets (Makadia et al., 2008). In comparison, local features such as key points (Fei-Fei and Perona, 2005) are often distinct across different objects or scenes. Regardless of the features used, visual codeword generation involves the following three important phases.

1. **Feature Detection**: The image is divided into partitions of varying degrees of granularity from which features can be extracted and represented. Typically, we can employ normalized cuts to divide an image into irregular regions, or apply uniform segmentation to break it into smaller but fixed grids, or simply locate information-rich local patches on the image using interest point detectors.
2. **Feature Description**: A descriptor is selected to represent the features that are being extracted from the image. Typically, feature descriptors (global or local) are represented as numerical vectors, with each vector describing the feature extracted in each region. This way, an image is represented by a set of vectors from its constituent regions.

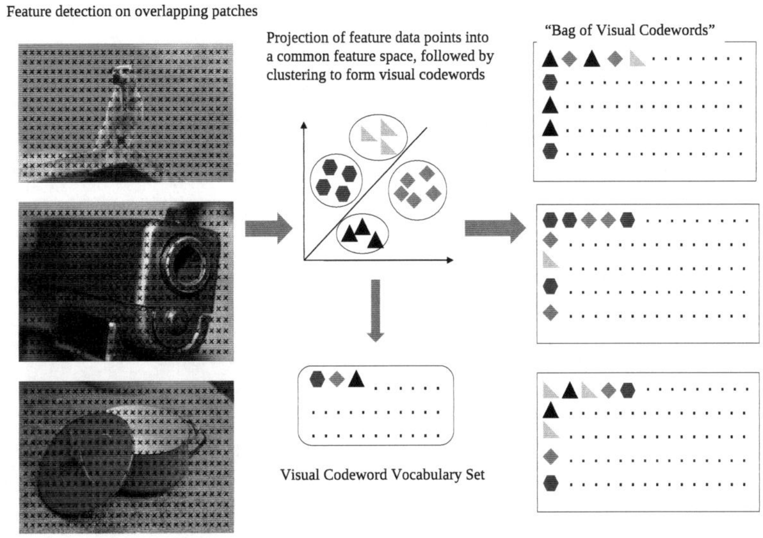

Figure 1: An illustration of the process of generating "Bag of Visual Codewords"

3. **Visual Codeword Generation**: Clustering methods are applied to group vectors into clusters, where the center of each cluster is defined as a visual codeword, and the entire collection of clusters defines the visual vocabulary for that image collection. Each image region or patch abstracted in feature detection is now represented by the visual codeword mapped from its corresponding feature vector.

The process of visual codeword generation is illustrated in Figure 1. Fei-Fei and Perona (2005) has shown that, unlike most previous work on object or scene classification that focused on adopting global features, local features are in fact extremely powerful cues. In our work, we use the Scale-Invariant Feature Transform (SIFT) introduced by Lowe (2004) to describe distinctive local features of an image in the feature description phase. SIFT descriptors are selected for their invariance to image scale, rotation, differences in 3D viewpoints, addition of noise, and change in illumination. They are also robust across affine distortions.

4 Semantic Vector Models

The underlying idea behind semantic vector models is that concepts can be represented as points in a mathematical space, and this representation is learned from a collection of documents such that concepts related in their meanings are near to one another in that space. In the past, semantic vector models have been widely adopted by natural language processing researchers for tasks ranging from information retrieval and lexical acquisition, to word sense disambiguation and document segmentation. Several variants have been proposed, including the original vector space model (Salton et al., 1997) and the Latent Semantic Analysis (Landauer and Dumais, 1997). Generally, vector models are attractive because they can be constructed using unsupervised methods of distributional corpus analysis and assume little language-specific requirements as long as texts can be reliably tokenized. Furthermore, various studies (Kanerva, 1998) have shown that by using collaborative, distributive memory units to represent semantic vectors, a closer correspondence to human cognition can be achieved.

While vector-space models typically require nontrivial algebraic machinery, reducing dimensions is often key to uncover the hidden (latent) features of the terms distribution in the corpus, and to circumvent the sparseness issue. There are a number of methods that have been developed to reduce dimensions – see e.g., Widdows and Ferraro (2008) for an overview. Here, we briefly describe one commonly used technique, namely the Latent Semantic Analysis (LSA), noted for its effectiveness in previous works for reducing dimensions.

In LSA, term co-occurrences in a corpus are captured by means of a dimensionality reduction operated by a **Singular Value Decomposition (SVD)** on the term-by-document matrix **T** representing the corpus. SVD is a well-known operation in linear algebra, which can be applied to any rectangular matrix in order to find correlations among its rows and columns. SVD decomposes the term-by-document matrix **T** into three matrices $\mathbf{T} = \mathbf{U}\Sigma_k\mathbf{V}^T$ where Σ_k is the diagonal $k \times k$ matrix containing the singular k values of **T**, $\sigma_1 \geq \sigma_2 \geq ... \geq \sigma_k$ and **U** and **V** are column-orthogonal matrices. When the three matrices are multiplied together the original term-by-document matrix is re-composed. Typically we can choose $k' \ll k$ obtaining the approximation $\mathbf{T} \simeq \mathbf{U}\Sigma_{k'}\mathbf{V}^T$.

5 Semantic Relatedness between Words and Images

Although the bag of visual codewords has been extensively used in image classification and retrieval tasks, and vector-space models are well explored in natural language processing, there has been little connection between the two streams of research. Specifically, to our knowledge, there is no research work that combines the two techniques to model multimodal meaning relatedness. Since we are exploring new grounds, it is important to clarify what we mean by computing the semantic relatedness between a word and an image, and how the nature of this task impacts our hypothesis. The assumptions below are necessary to validate our findings:

1. Computing semantic relatedness between a word and an image involves comparing the concepts invoked by the word and the salient objects in the image as well as their interaction. This goes beyond simply identifying the presence or absence of specific objects indicated by a given word. For instance, we expect a degree of relatedness between an image showing a soccer ball and the word "jersey," since both invoke concepts like {sports, soccer, teamwork} and so on.
2. The semantics of an image is dependent on the focus, size and position of distinct objects identified through image segmentation. During labeling, we expect this segmentation to be performed implicitly by the annotators. Although it is possible to focus one's attention on specific objects via bounding boxes, we are interested to harvest the meaning of an image using a holistic approach.
3. In the case of measuring the relatedness of a word that has multiple senses with a given image, humans are naturally inclined to choose the sense that provides the highest relatedness inside the pair. For example, an image of a river bank expectedly calls upon the "river bank" sense of the word "bank" (and not "financial bank" or other alternative word senses).
4. A degree of semantic relatedness can exist between any arbitrary word and image, on a scale ranging from being totally unrelated to perfectly synonymous with each other. This is trivially true, as the same property holds when measuring similarity between words and texts.

Next, we evaluate our hypothesis that we can measure the relatedness between a word and an image empirically, using a parallel corpus of words and images as our dataset.

5.1 ImageNet

We use the ImageNet database (Deng et al., 2009), which is a large-scale ontology of images developed for advancing content-based image search algorithms, and serving as a benchmarking standard for various image processing and computer vision tasks. ImageNet exploits the hierarchical structure of WordNet by attaching relevant images to each synonym set (known as "synset"), hence providing pictorial illustrations of the concept associated with the synset. On average, each synset contains 500-1000 images that are carefully audited through a stringent quality control mechanism.

Compared to other image databases with keyword annotations, we believe that ImageNet is suitable for evaluating our hypothesis for three reasons. First, by leveraging on reliable keyword annotations in WordNet (i.e., words in the synset and their gloss naturally serve as annotations for the corresponding images), we can effectively circumvent the propagation of errors caused by unreliable annotations, and consequently hope to reach more conclusive results for this study. Second, unlike other image databases,

ImageNet consists of millions of images, and it is a growing resource with more images added on a regular basis. This aligns with our long-term goal of building a large-scale joint semantic space of images and words. Finally, third, although we can search for relevant images using keywords in ImageNet,[2] there is currently no method to query it in the reverse direction. Given a test image, we must search through millions of images in the database to find the most similar image and its corresponding synset. A joint semantic model can hopefully augment this shortcoming by allowing queries to be made in both directions. Figure 2 shows an example of a synset and the corresponding images in ImageNet.

(a)

(b)

Joint Semantic Space of Words and Images		
Synsets		167
Images		230,864
Words		1144
	Nouns	783
	Verbs	140
	Adjectives	221
Image:Words ratio		202:1

Figure 2: (a) A subset of images associated with a node in ImageNet. The WordNet synset illustrated here is {*Dog, domestic dog, Canis familiaris*} with the gloss: *A member of the genus Canis (probably descended from the common wolf) that has been domesticated by man since prehistoric times; occurs in many breeds; "the dog barked all night"* (b) A table showing statistical information on our joint semantic space model

5.2 Dataset

For our experiments, we randomly select 167 synsets[3] from ImageNet, covering a wide range of concepts such as plants, mammals, fish, tools, vehicles etc. We perform a simple pre-processing step using Tree Tagger (Schmid, 1994) and extract only the nouns. Multiwords are explicitly recognized as collocations or named entities in the synset. Not considering part-of-speech distinctions, the vocabulary for synset words is 352. The vocabulary for gloss words is 777. The shared vocabulary between them is 251.

There are a total of 230,864 images associated with the 167 synsets, with an average of 1383 images per synset. We randomly select an image for each synset, thus obtaining a set of 167 test images in total. The technique explained in Section 3 is used to generate visual codewords for each image in this dataset.[4] Each image is first pre-processed to have a maximum side length of 300 pixels. Next, SIFT descriptors are obtained by densely sampling the image on 20x20 overlapping patches spaced 10 pixels apart. K-means clustering is applied on a random subset of 10 million SIFT descriptors to derive a visual vocabulary of 1,000 codewords. Each descriptor is then quantized into a visual codeword by assigning it to the nearest cluster.

To create the gold-standard relatedness annotation, for each test image, six nouns are randomly selected from its associated synset and gloss words, and six other nouns are again randomly selected from the shared vocabulary words.[5] In all, we have 167 x 12 = 2004 word-image pairs as our test dataset. Similar to previous word similarity evaluations (Miller and Charles, 1998), we ask human annotators to rate each pair on a scale of 0 to 10 to indicate their degree of semantic relatedness using the evaluation framework outlined below, with 0 being totally unrelated and 10 being perfectly synonymous with each other. To ensure quality ratings, for each word-image pair we used 15 annotators from Amazon Mechanical

[2]http://www.image-net.org/

[3]Not all synsets in ImageNet are annotated with images. We obtain our dataset from the Spring 2010 version of ImageNet built around Wordnet 3.0.

[4]For our experiments, we obtained the visual codewords computed a priori from ImageNet. Test images are not used to construct the model

[5]12 data points are generally considered sufficient for reliable correlation measures (Vania Kovic, p.c.).

		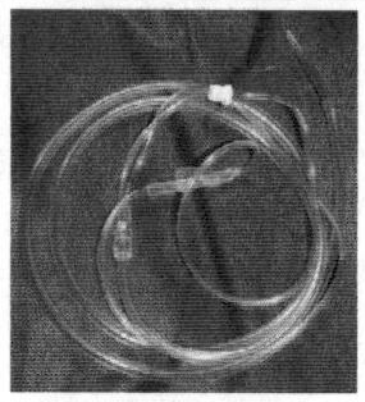			
Synset {sunflower, helianthus}		**Synset** {oxygen-mask}		**Synset** {submarine , pigboat , sub , U-boat}	
Gloss any plant of the genus Helianthus having large flower heads with dark disk florets and showy yellow rays		**Gloss** a breathing device that is placed over the mouth and nose; supplies oxygen from an attached storage tank		**Gloss** a submersible warship usually armed with torpedoes	
Relatedness Scores		**Relatedness Scores**		**Relatedness Scores**	
color (5.13)	dog (0.53)	basketball (0.20)	central (1.53)	africa (0.80)	brass (1.73)
floret (6.53)	flower (9.67)	device (5.47)	family (0.80)	door (1.67)	good (2.40)
freshwater (2.40)	hair (1.00)	iron-tree (0.47)	mouth (5.13)	pacific (2.40)	pigboat (6.47)
garden (6.60)	head (3.80)	oxygen-mask (7.73)	tank (4.47)	sub (8.20)	submarine (9.67)
plant (8.47)	ray (3.67)	storage (3.07)	supply (5.20)	tail (0.93)	torpedo (7.60)
sunflower (9.80)	reed (2.27)	nose (6.20)	time (1.13)	u-boat (7.47)	warship (8.73)

Table 1: A sample of test images with their synset words and glosses : The number in parenthesis represents the numerical association of the word with the image (0-10). Human annotations reveal different degree of semantic relatedness between the image and words in the synset or gloss.

Turk.[6] Finally, the average of all 15 annotations for each word-image pair is taken as its gold-standard relatedness score[7]. Note that only the pairs of images and words are provided to the annotators, and not their synsets and gloss definitions.

The set of standard criteria underlying the cross-modal similarity evaluation framework shown here is inspired by the semantic relations defined in Wordnet. These criteria were provided to the human annotators, to help them decide whether a word and an image are related to each other.

1. **Instance of itself**: Does the image contain an entity that is represented by the word itself (e.g. an image of "Obama" vs the word "Obama") ?
2. **Member-of Relation**: Does the image contain an entity that is a member of the class suggested by the word or vice versa (e.g. an image of an "apple" vs the word "fruits") ?
3. **Part-of Relation**: Does the image contain an entity that is a part of a larger entity represented by the word or vice versa (e.g. an image of a "tree" vs the word "forest") ?
4. **Semantically Related**: Do both the word and the image suggest concepts that are related (e.g. an image of troops at war vs the word "peace") ?
5. **Semantically Close**: Do both the word and the image suggest concepts that are not only related but also close in meaning? (e.g. an image of troops at war vs the word "gun") ?

Criterion (1) basically tests for synonym relation. Criteria (2) and (3) are modeled after the hyponym-hypernym and meronym-holonym relations in WordNet, which are prevalent among nouns. Note that none of the criteria is preemptive over the others. Rather, we provide these criteria as guidelines in a *subjective* evaluation framework, similar to the word semantic similarity task in Miller and Charles (1998). Importantly, criterion (4) models dissimilar but related concepts, or any other relation that indicates frequent association, while criterion (5) serves to provide additional distinction for pairs of words and images on a higher level of relatedness toward similarity. In Table 1, we show sample images from our test dataset, along with the annotations provided by the human annotators.

[6]We only allowed annotators with an approval rating of 97% or higher. Here, we expect some variance in the degree of relatedness between the candidate words and images, hence annotations marked with all 10s or 0s are discarded due to lack of distinctions in similarity relatedness

[7]Annotation guidelines and dataset can be downloaded at http://lit.csci.unt.edu/index.php/Downloads

5.3 Experiments

Following Erk and McCarthy (2009), who argued that word meanings are graded over their senses, we believe that the meaning of an image is not limited to a set of "best fitting" tags, but rather it exists as a distribution over arbitrary words with varying degrees of association. Specifically, the focus of our experiments is to investigate the correlation between automatic measures of such relatedness scores with respect to human judgments.

To construct the joint semantic space of words and images, we use the SVD described in Section 4 to reduce the number of dimensions. To build each model, we use the 167 synsets from ImageNet and their associated images (minus the held out test data), hence accounting for 167 latent dimensions. We first represent the synsets as a collection of documents D, each document containing visual codewords used to describe their associated images as well as textual words extracted from their gloss and synset words. Thus, computing a cross-modal relatedness distance amounts to comparing the cosine similarity of vectors representing an image to the vector representing a word in the term-document vector space. Note that, unlike textual words, an image is represented by multiple visual codewords. Prior to computing the actual cosine distance, we perform a weighted addition of vectors representing each visual codeword for that image.

To illustrate, consider a single document d_i, representing the synset "snail," which consists of {cw0, cw555, cw23, cw124, cw876, snail, freshwater, mollusk, spiral, shell}, where cwX represents a particular visual codeword indexed from 0-999[8], and the textual words are nouns extracted from the associated synset and gloss. Given a test image I, it can be expressed as a bag of visual codewords $\{cw_1, ..., cw_k\}$. We first represent each visual codeword in I as a vector of length $|D|$ using term-frequency inverse-document-frequency ($tfidf$) weighting, e.g., cw_k=<0.4*d_1, 0.2*d_2, ... , 0.9*d_m>, where m=167, and perform an addition of k such vectors to form a final vector v_i. To measure the semantic relatedness between image I and a word w, e.g., "snail," we simply compute the cosine similarity between v_i and v_w, where v_w is also a vector of length $|D|$ calculated using $tfidf$.

This paper seeks answers to the following questions. First, what is the relation between the discriminability of the visual codewords and their ability to capture semantic relatedness between a word and an image, as compared to the gold-standard annotation by humans? Second, given the unbalanced dataset of images and words, can we use a relatively small number of visual codewords to derive such semantic relatedness measures reliably? Third, what is the efficiency of an unsupervised vector semantic model in measuring such relatedness, and is it applicable to large datasets?

Analogous to text-retrieval methods, we measure the discriminability of the visual codewords using two weighting factors. The first is *term-frequency (tf)*, which measures the number of times a codeword appears in all images for a particular synset, while the second, *image-term-frequency (itf)*, captures the number of images using the codeword in a synset. For the two weighting schemes, we apply normalization by using the total number of codewords for a synset (for *tf* weighting) and the total number of images in a synset (for *itf* weighting).

We are interested to quantify the relatedness for pairs of words and images under two scenarios. By ranking the 12 words associated with an image in reverse order of their relatedness to the image, we can determine the ability of our models to identify the most related words for a given image (**image-centered**). In the second scenario, we measure the relatedness of words and images regardless of the synset they belong to, thus evaluating the ability of our methods to capture the relatedness between any word and any image. This allows us to capture the correlation in an (**arbitrary-image**) scenario. For the evaluations, we use the Spearman's Rank correlation.

To place our results in perspective, we implemented two baselines and an upper bound for each of the two scenarios above. The *Random* baseline randomly assigns ratings to each word-image pair on the same 0 to 10 scale, and then measures the correlation to the human gold-standard. The *Vector-Based (VB)* method is a stronger baseline aimed to study the correlation performance in the absence of dimensionality reduction. As an upper bound, the *Inter-Human-Agreement (IHA)* measures the correlation of the rating by each annotator against the average of the ratings of the rest of the annotators, averaged over the 167 synsets (for the image-centered scenario) and over the 2004 word-image pairs (for the arbitrary-image scenario).

[8]For simplicity, we only show the top 5 visual codewords

	Spearman's Rank Coefficient (image-centered)									
Top K codewords	100	200	300	400	500	600	700	800	900	1000
LSA tf	0.228	**0.325**	0.273	0.242	0.185	0.181	0.107	0.043	-0.018	0.000
LSA tf (norm)	0.233	**0.339**	0.293	0.254	0.202	0.180	0.124	0.047	-0.012	0.000
*LSA tf*itf*	0.268	**0.317**	0.256	0.248	0.219	0.166	0.081	-0.004	-0.037	0.000
*LSA tf*itf (norm)*	0.252	**0.327**	0.257	0.246	0.211	0.153	0.097	0.002	-0.042	0.000
VB tf	**0.243**	0.168	0.101	0.055	-0.021	-0.084	-0.157	-0.210	-0.236	-0.332
VB tf (norm)	**0.240**	0.181	0.110	0.062	-0.010	-0.082	-0.152	-0.204	-0.235	-0.332
*VB tf*itf*	**0.262**	0.181	0.107	0.065	-0.019	-0.081	-0.156	-0.211	-0.241	-0.332
*VB tf*itf (norm)*	**0.257**	0.180	0.116	0.068	-0.014	-0.079	-0.150	-0.250	-0.237	-0.332
Random	0.001	0.018	0.016	-0.008	0.008	0.005	-0.001	0.014	-0.035	0.012
IHA	0.687									
	Spearman's Rank Coefficient (arbitrary-image)									
Top K codewords	100	200	300	400	500	600	700	800	900	1000
LSA tf	0.236	**0.341**	0.291	0.249	0.208	0.183	0.106	0.033	-0.039	0.000
LSA tf (norm)	0.230	**0.353**	0.301	0.271	0.220	0.186	0.115	0.032	-0.029	0.000
*LSA tf*itf*	0.291	**0.332**	0.289	0.262	0.235	0.172	0.092	0.008	-0.041	0.000
*LSA tf*itf (norm)*	0.277	**0.345**	0.292	0.269	0.234	0.164	0.098	0.015	-0.046	0.000
VB tf	**0.272**	0.195	0.119	0.059	-0.012	-0.088	-0.164	-0.218	-0.240	-0.339
VB tf (norm)	**0.277**	0.207	0.130	0.069	-0.003	-0.083	-0.160	-0.215	-0.242	-0.339
*VB tf*itf*	**0.287**	0.206	0.127	0.062	-0.008	-0.085	-0.161	-0.214	-0.241	-0.339
*VB tf*itf (norm)*	**0.286**	0.212	0.132	0.071	-0.005	-0.081	-0.158	-0.214	-0.241	-0.339
Random	-0.024	-0.014	0.015	-0.015	-0.004	-0.014	0.024	-0.009	-0.007	0.007
IHA	0.764									

Table 2: Correlation of automatically generated scores with human annotations on cross-modal semantic relatedness, as performed on the ImageNet test dataset of 2004 pairs of word and image. Correlation figures scoring the highest within a weighting scheme are marked in bold, while those scoring the highest across weighting schemes and within a visual vocabulary size are underlined.

6 Discussion

Our experimental results are shown in Table 2. A somewhat surprising observation is the consistency of correlation figures between the two scenarios. In both scenarios, a representative set of 200 visual codewords is sufficient to consistently score the highest correlation ratings across the 8 weighting schemes. Intuitively, based on the experimental results, automatically choosing the top 10% or 20% of the visual codewords seems to suffice and gives optimal correlation figures, but requires further justification. Conversely, the relatively simple weighting scheme using *tf (normalized)* produces the highest correlation in six visual codeword sizes (K=200,300,400,700,800,900) for the image-centered scenario, as well as in another six visual codeword sizes (K=200,300,400,600,700,900) for the arbitrary-image scenario. Unlike stopwords in text retrieval accounting for most of the highest *tf* scores, visual codewords weighted by the same scheme *tf* and a similar *tf (normalized)* scheme seem to be the most discriminative. The correlation for including the entire visual vocabulary set (1000) produces identical results for all vector-based and LSA weighting schemes, as images across synsets are now encoded by the same set of visual codewords without discrimination between them.

Dimensionality reduction using SVD gains an advantage over the vector-based method for both scenarios, with the highest correlation rating in LSA (200 visual codeword, *tf(norm)*) achieving 0.077 points better than the corresponding highest correlation in Vector-based (100 visual codeword, *tf*itf*) for the image-centered scenario, representing a 29.3% improvement. Similarly, in the arbitrary-image scenario, the increase in correlation from 0.287 (VB *tf*itf* at 100 visual codeword) to 0.353 (LSA *tf(norm)* at 200 visual codeword) underlines a gain of approximately 23.0%. Overall, the arbitrary-image scenario also scores consistently higher than the image-centered scenario under similar experimental conditions. For instance, for the top 200 visual words, the same weighting schemes produce consistently lower correlation figures for the image-centered scenario. This is also true for the Inter-Human-Agreement score, which is higher in the arbitrary-image scenario (0.764) compared to the image-centered scenario (0.687). Note that for all the experiments, the semantic relatedness scores generated from the semantic vector space are significantly more correlated with the human gold-standard than the random baselines.

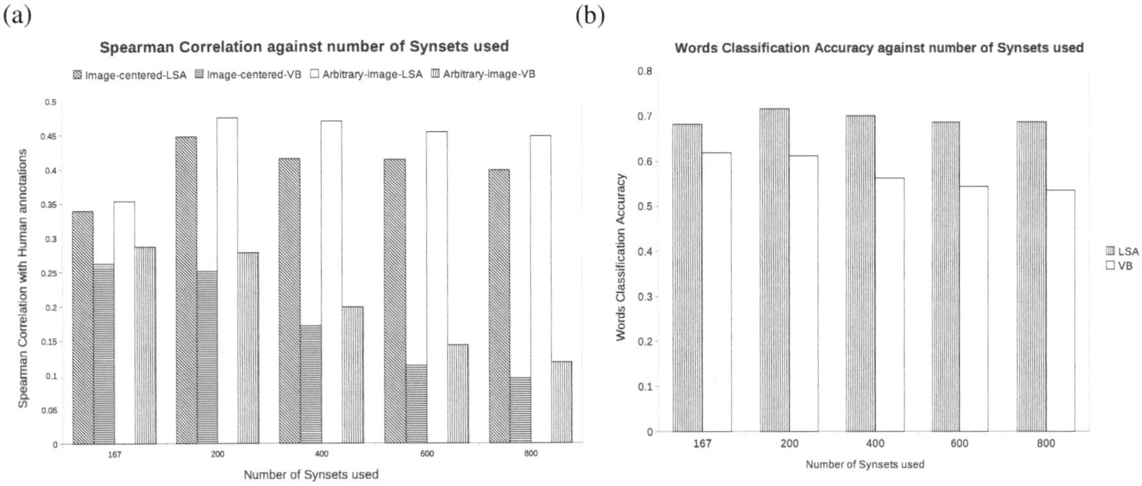

Figure 3: (a) Correlation performance, and (b) Classification accuracy, as more data is added to construct the semantic space model.

To investigate the effectiveness of the model when scaling up to large datasets, we employ the best combination of weighting scheme and vocabulary size shown in Table 2, i.e., a visual vocabulary size of 200 and *tf (normalized)* weighting for LSA, and vocabulary size of 100 and *tf*itf* weighting for the vector-based model, and incrementally construct models ranging from 167 synsets to 800 synsets (all randomly selected from ImageNet). We then measure the correlation of relatedness scores generated using the same test dataset with respect to human annotations. The dataset was randomly selected to increase by approximately five times, from a total of 230,864 images with 878 words to a total of 1,014,528 images with 3887 words. Furthermore, for each unseen test image taken from Synset S_i and the associated 12 candidate words, we evaluate the ability of the model to identify which of the candidate words actually appear in the gloss or the synset of S_i, in a task we term as word classification. Here, the top six words are predictably classified as those appearing in S_i while the last six are classified as outside of S_i , after all 12 words are ranked in reverse order of their relatedness to the test image. We measure the accuracy of the word classification task using $\frac{TP+TN}{2004}$, where TP is the number of words correctly classified as synset or gloss words, and TN is the number of words correctly classified as outside of synset or gloss, both summed over the 2004 pairs of words and images.

As shown in Figure 3, when a small number of synsets (33) was added to the original semantic space, correlation with human ratings increased steeply to around 0.45 and higher for LSA in both scenarios, while the vector-based method suffers a slight decrease in correlation ratings from 0.262 to 0.251 (image-centered) and from 0.287 to 0.278 (arbitrary-image). As more images and words are added, correlation for the vector-based model continues to decrease markedly. Comparatively, LSA is less sensitive to data scaling, as correlation figures for both scenarios decreases slightly but stays within a 0.40 to 0.45 range. Additionally, we infer that LSA is consistently more effective than the vector-based model in the words classification task (as also seen in Figure 3). Even with more data added to the semantic space, word classification accuracy stays consistently at 0.7 for LSA, while it drops to 0.535 for the vector-based model at a synset size of 800.

7 Conclusion

In this paper, we provided a proof of concept in quantifying the semantic relatedness between words and images through the use of visual codewords and textual words in constructing a joint semantic vector space. Our experiments showed that the relatedness scores have a positive correlation to human gold-standards, as measured using a standard evaluation framework.

We believe many aspects of this work can be explored further. For instance, other visual codeword attributes, such as pixel coordinates, can be employed in a structured vector space along with the existing model for improving vector similarity measures. To improve textual words coverage, a potentially effective way would be to create mappings from WordNet synsets to Wikipedia entries, where the concepts represented by the synsets are discussed in detail. We also plan to study the applicability of the joint semantic representation model to tasks such as automatic image annotation and image classification.

Acknowledgments

This material is based in part upon work supported by the National Science Foundation CAREER award #0747340 and IIS award #1018613. Any opinions, findings, and conclusions or recommendations expressed in this material are those of the authors and do not necessarily reflect the views of the National Science Foundation.

References

Barnard, K. and D. Forsyth (2001). Learning the semantics of words and pictures. In *Proceedings of International Conference on Computer Vision*.

Biederman, I. (1987). Recognition-by-components: A theory of human image understanding. In *Psychological Review*, Volume 94, pp. 115–147.

Budanitsky, A. and G. Hirst (2005). Evaluating wordnet-based measures of lexical semantic relatedness. In *Computational Linguistics*, Volume 32.

Deng, J., W. Dong, R. Socher, L.-J. Li, K. Li, and L. Fei-Fei (2009). ImageNet: A Large-Scale Hierarchical Image Database. In *Proceedings of the IEEE Conference on Computer Vision and Pattern Recognition*.

Erk, K. and D. McCarthy (2009). Graded word sense assignment. In *Proceedings of Empirical Methods in Natural Language Processing*.

Fei-Fei, L. and P. Perona (2005). A bayesian hierarchical model for learning natural scene categories. In *Proceedings of the IEEE Conference on Computer Vision and Pattern Recognition*.

Feng, Y. and M. Lapata (2010). Visual information in semantic representation. In *Proceedings of the Annual Conference of the North American Chapter of the ACL*.

Goldberger, J., S. Gordon, and H. Greenspan (2003). An efficient image similarity measure based on approximations of kl-divergence between two gaussian mixtures. In *Proceedings of IEEE International Conference on Computer Vision*.

Hare, J. S., S. Samangooei, P. H. Lewis, and M. S. Nixon (2008). Investigating the performance of auto-annotation and semantic retrieval using semantic spaces. In *Proceedings of the international conference on content-based image and video retrieval*.

Kanerva, P. (1998). Sparse distributed memory. In *MIT Press*.

Landauer, T. and S. Dumais (1997). A solution to platos problem: The latent semantic analysis theory of acquisition. In *Psychological Review*, Volume 104, pp. 211–240.

Leong, C. W., R. Mihalcea, and S. Hassan (2010). Text mining for automatic image tagging. In *Proceedings of the International Conference on Computational Linguistics*.

Lowe, D. (2004). Distinctive image features from scale-invariant keypoints. In *International Journal of Computer Vision*.

Makadia, A., V. Pavlovic, and S. Kumar (2008). A new baseline for image annotation. In *Proceedings of European Conference on Computer Vision*.

Miller, G. (1995). Wordnet: A lexical database for english. In *Communications of the ACM*, Volume 38, pp. 39–41.

Miller, G. and W. Charles (1998). Contextual correlates of semantic similarity. *Language and Cognitive Processes 6*(1).

Potter, M. C. and B. A. Faulconer (1975). Time to understand pictures and words. In *Nature*, Volume 253, pp. 437–438.

Salton, G., A. Wong, and C. Yang (1997). A vector space model for automatic indexing. In *Readings in Information Retrieval*, pp. 273–280. San Francisco, CA: Morgan Kaufmann Publishers.

Schmid, H. (1994). Probabilistic part-of-speech tagging using decision trees. In *Proceedings of the International Conference on New Methods in Language Processing*.

Smeulders, A. W., M. Worring, S. Santini, A. Gupta, and R. Jain (2000). Content-based image retrieval at the end of the early years. In *IEEE Transactions on Pattern Analysis and Machine Intelligence*, Volume 22, pp. 1349–1380.

Westerveld, T. (2000). Image retrieval: Context versus context. In *Content-Based Multimedia Information Access*.

Widdows, D. and K. Ferraro (2008). Semantic vectors: a scalable open source package and online technology management application. In *Proceedings of the Sixth International Language Resources and Evaluation (LREC'08)*.

Yang, J., Y.-G. Jiang, A. G. Hauptmann, and C.-W. Ngo (2007). Evaluating bag-of-visual-words representations in scene classification. In *ACM Multimedia Information Retrieval Workshop*.

Elaborating a Knowledge Base for Deep Lexical Semantics

Niloofar Montazeri and Jerry R. Hobbs
Information Sciences Institute
University of Southern California
Marina del Rey, California

Abstract

We describe the methodology for constructing axioms defining event-related words, anchored in core theories of change of state and causality. We first derive from WordNet senses a smaller set of abstract, general "supersenses". We encode axioms for these, and we test them on textual entailment pairs. We look at two specific examples in detail to illustrate both the power of the method and the holes in the knowledge base that it exposes. Then we address the problem of holes more systematically, asking, for example, what kinds of "pairwise interactions" are possible for core theory predicates like `change` and `cause`.[1]

1 Introduction

From the sentence

> Russia is blocking oil from entering Ukraine.

we would like to be able to conclude

> Oil can not be delivered to Ukraine.

But doing this requires fairly complex inference, because the words "block", "enter", "can", "not" and "deliver" carve up the world in different ways. Our approach is to define words such as these by means of axioms that link with underlying core theories[2] explicating such very basic concepts as change of state and causality. Given the logical form of sentences like these two, we apply these axioms to express the meaning of the sentences in more fundamental predicates, and do a certain amount of defeasible reasoning in the core theories to determine that the second follows from the first.

More generally, we are engaged in an enterprise we call "deep lexical semantics" (Hobbs, 2008), in which we develop various core theories of fundamental commonsense phenomena and define English word senses by means of axioms using predicates explicated in these theories. Among the core theories are cognition, microsociology, and the structure of events. The last of these is the focus of this paper. We use textual entailment pairs like the above to test out subsets of related axioms. This process enforces a

[1]This research was supported in part by the Defense Advanced Research Projects Agency (DARPA) Machine Reading Program under Air Force Research Laboratory (AFRL) prime contract no. FA8750-09-C-0172, and in part by the Office of Naval Research under contract no. N00014-09-1-1029.. Any opinions, findings, and conclusion or recommendations expressed in this material are those of the author(s) and do not necessarily reflect the view of the DARPA, AFRL, ONR, or the US government.

[2]`http://www.isi.edu/ hobbs/csk.html`.

uniformity in the way axioms are constructed, and also exposes missing inferences in the core theories. The latter is a major issue in this paper.

In Section 2 we describe three aspects of the framework we are working in—the logical form we use, abductive interpretation and defeasibility, and the core theories of change of state and causality. In Section 3 we describe the methodology we use for constructing axioms, deriving from WordNet senses a smaller set of abstract, general "supersenses", encoding axioms for these, and testing them on textual entailment pairs. In Section 4 we look at two specific examples to illustrate both the power of the method and the holes in the knowledge base that it exposes. In Section 5 we address the problem of holes more systematically, specifically asking, for example, what kinds of "pairwise interactions" are possible for core theory predicates like `change` and `cause`.

2 Framework

We use a logical notation in which states and events (eventualities) are reified. Specifically, if the expression `(p x)` says that `p` is true of `x`, then `(p' e x)` says that `e` is the eventuality of `p` being true of `x`. Eventuality `e` may exist in the real world (`Rexist`), in which case `(p x)` holds, or it may only exist in some modal context, in which case that is expressed simply as another property of the possible individual `e`. (In this paper we use a subset of Common Logic[3] for the syntax of our notation.)

The logical form of a sentence is a flat conjunction of existentially quantified postive literals, with about one literal per morpheme. (For example, logical words like "not" and "or" are treated as expressing predications about possible eventualities.) We have developed software[4] to translate Penn TreeBank-style trees (as well as other syntactic formalisms) into this notation. The underlying core theories are expressed as axioms in this notation (Hobbs, 1985).

The interpretation of a text is taken to be the lowest-cost abductive proof of the logical form of the text, given the knowledge base. That is, to interpret a text we prove the logical form, allowing for assumptions at cost, and pick the lowest-cost proof. Factors involved in computing costs include, besides the number of assumptions, the salience of axioms, the plausibility of axioms expressing defeasible knowledge, and consiliance or the degree to which the pervasive implicit redundancy of natural language texts is exploited. We have demonstrated that many interpretation problems are solved as a by-product of finding the lowest-cost proof. This method has been implemented in an abductive theorem-prover called Mini-Tacitus[5] that has been used in a number of applications (Hobbs et al., 1993; Mulkar et al., 2007), and is used in the textual entailment problems described here. We are also working toward a probabilistic semantics for the cost of proofs (Blythe et al., 2011). Abductive interpretation accounts for script-like understanding of text—a script predicate provides the most economical interpretation (Hobbs et al., 1993)—but also enables interpretation of novel texts.

Most commonsense knowledge is defeasible, i.e., it can be defeated. This is represented in our framework by having a unique "et cetera" proposition in the antecedent of Horn clauses that cannot be proved but can be assumed at a cost corresponding to the likeliehood that the conclusion is true. For example, the axiom

```
(forall (x) (if (and (bird x)(etc-i x))(fly x)))
```

would say that if `x` is a bird and other unspecified conditions hold, `(etc-i)`, then `x` flies. No other axioms enable proving `(etc-i x)`, but it can be assumed, and hence participate in the lowest cost

[3]http://common-logic.org/.

[4]http://www.rutumulkar.com/download/NL-Pipeline/NL-Pipeline.php.

[5]http://rutumulkar.com/download/TACITUS/tacitus.php.

proof. The index `i` is unique to this axiom. In this paper rather than invent new indices for each axiom, we will use the abbreviation `(etc)` to indicate the defeasibility of the rule. (This approach to defeasibility is similar to circumscription (McCarthy, 1980).)

We have articulated a number of core theories[6]. The two most relevant to this paper are the theory of change of state and the theory of causality. The predication `(change' e e1 e2)` says that `e` is a change of state whose initial state is `e1` and whose final state is `e2`. The chief properties of `change` are that there is some entity whose state is undergoing change, that `change` is defeasibly transitive, that `e1` and `e2` cannot be the same unless there has been an intermediate state that is different, and that `change` is consistent with the `before` relation from our core theory of time. Since many lexical items focus only on the initial or the final state of a change, we introduce for convenience the predications `(changeFrom' e e1)` and `(changeTo' e e2)`, defined in terms of `change`.

The chief distinction in our core theory of causality is between the notions of `causalComplex` and `cause`. A causal complex includes all the states and events that have to happen or hold in order for the effect to happen. A cause is that contextually relevant element of the causal complex that is somehow central to the effect, whether because it is an action the agent performs, because it is not normally true, or for some other reason. Most of our knowledge about causality is expressed in terms of the predicate `cause`, rather than in terms of causal complexes, because we rarely if ever know the complete causal complex. Typically planning, explanation, and the interpretation of texts (though not diagnosis) involves reasoning about `cause`. Among the principal properties of `cause` are that it is defeasibly transitive, that events defeasibly have causes, and that `cause` is consistent with `before`.

We also have a core theory of time, and the times of states and events can be represented as temporal properties of the reified eventualities. The theory of time has an essential function in axioms for words explicitly referencing time, such as "schedule" and "delay". But for most of the words we are explicating in this effort, we base our approach to the dynamic aspects of the world on the cognitively more basic theory of change of state. For example, the word "enter" is axiomatized as a change of state from being outside to being inside, and the fact that being outside comes *before* being inside follows from the axiom relating the predicates `change` and `before`.

We find that reifying states and events as eventualities and treating them as first-class individuals is preferable to employing the event calculus (Gruninger and Menzel, 2010; Mueller, 2006) which makes a sharp distinction between the two, because language makes no distinction in where they can appear and we can give them a uniform treatment.

3 Methodology

Our methodology consists of three steps.

1. Analyzing the structure of a word's WordNet senses.
2. Writing axioms for the most general senses
3. Testing the axioms on textual entailment pairs.

Our focus in this paper is on words involving the concepts of change of state and causality, or event words, such as "block", "delay", "deliver", "destroy", "enter", "escape", "give", "hit", "manage", and "provide". For each word, we analyze the structure of its WordNet senses. Typically, there will be pairs that differ only in, for example, constraints on their arguments or in that one is inchoative and the other

[6] `http://www.isi.edu/ hobbs/csk.html`.

causative. This analysis generally leads to a radial structure indicating how one sense leads by increments, logically and perhaps chronologically, to another word sense (Lakoff, 1987). The analysis also leads us to posit "supersenses" that cover two or more WordNet senses. (Frequently, these supersenses correspond to senses in FrameNet (Baker et al., 2003) or VerbNet (Kipper et al., 2006), which tend to be coarser grained; sometimes the desired senses are in WordNet itself.)

For example, for the verb "enter", three WordNet senses involve a change into a state:

V2: become a participant
V4: play a part in
V9: set out on an enterprise

Call this supersense S1. Two other senses add a causal role to this:

V5: make a record of
V8: put or introduce into something

Two more senses specialize supersense S1 by restricting the target state to be in a physical location:

V1: come or go into
V6: come on stage

One other sense specializes S1 by restricting the target state to be membership in a group.

V3: register formally as a participant or member

Knowing this radial structure of the senses helps enforce uniformity in the construction of the axioms. If the senses are close, their axioms should be almost the same.

We are currently only constructing axioms for the most general or abstract senses or supersenses. In this way, although we are missing some of the implications of the more specialized senses, we are capturing the most basic topological structure in the meanings of the words. Moreover, the specialized senses usually tap into some specialized domain that needs to be axiomatized before the axioms for these senses can be written.

In constructing the axioms in the event domain, we are very much informed by the long tradition of work on lexical decomposition in linguistics (e.g., Gruber, 1965; Jackendoff, 1972). Our work differs from this in that our decompositions are done as logical inferences and not as tree transformations as in the earliest linguistic work, they are not obligatory but only inferences that may or may not be part of the lowest-cost abductive proof, and the "primitives" into which we decompose the words are explicated in theories that enable reasoning about the concepts.

Figure 1 shows the radial structure of the senses for the word "enter", together with the axioms that characterize each sense. A link between two word senses means an incremental change in the axiom for one gives the axiom for the other. For example, the axiom for `enter-S2` says that if `x1` enters `x2` in `x3`, then `x1` causes a change to the eventuality `i1` in which `x2` is in `x3`; and the expanded axiom for `enter-S1.1` states that if `x1` enters `x2`, then there is a change to a state `e1` in which `x1` is in `x2`. So `enter-S2` and `enter-S1.1` are closely related and thus linked together.

Abstraction is a special incremental change where one sense S1.1 specializes another sense S1 either by adding more predicates to or specializing some of the predicates in S1's axiom. We represent abstractions via arrows pointing from the subsenses to the supersenses. In Figure 1, `enter-S1.1` and `enter-S1.2` both specialize `enter-S1`. The predicate `enter-S1.1` adds an extra predicate describing `e1` as an `in` eventuality and `enter-S1.2` specializes `e1` to membership in `x2`, where `x2` is a group.

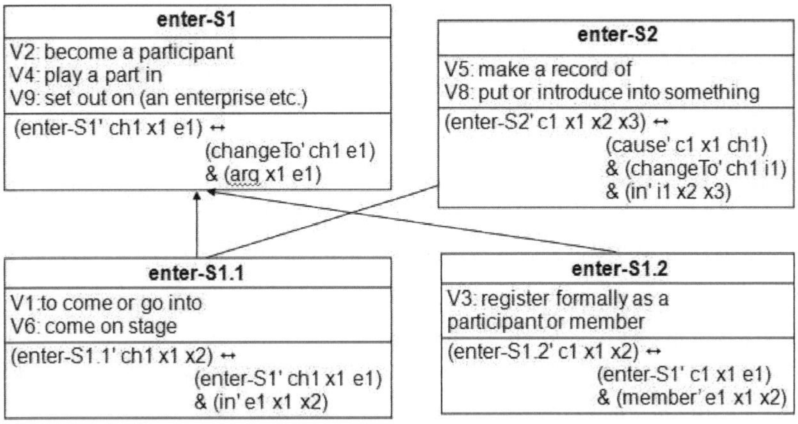

Figure 1: Senses of and axioms for the verb "enter"

The supersenses capture the basic topology of the senses they subsume. The extra information that the subsenses convey are typically the types and properties of the arguments, such as being a place or a process, or qualities of the causing event, such as being sudden or forceful.

For each set of inferentially related words we construct textual entailment pairs, where the hypothesis (H) intuitively follows from text (T), and use these for testing and evaluation. The person writing the axioms does not know what the pairs are, and the person constructing the pairs does not know what the axioms look like.

The ideal test then is whether given a knowledge base K consisting of all the axioms, H cannot be proven from K alone, but H can be proven from the union of K and the best intepretation of T. This is often too stringent a condition, since H may contain irrelevant material that doesn't follow from T, so an alternative is to determine whether the lowest cost abductive proof of H given K plus T is substantially lower than the lowest cost abductive proof of H given K alone, where "substantially lower" is defined by a threshold that can be trained (Ovchinnikova et al., 2011).

4 Two Examples

Here we work through two examples to illustrate how textual entailment problems are handled in our framework. In these examples, given a text T and a hypothesis H, we ask if H can be proven from T, perhaps with a small number of low-cost assumptions.

Because the examples we deal with involve a great deal of embedding, we need to use the primed predicates, keeping the eventuality arguments explicit.

We also assume in these examples that lexical disambiguation has been done correctly. With more context, lexical disambiguation should fall out of the best interpretation, but it is unreasonable to expect that in these short examples. In practice we run the examples both with disambiguated and with nondisambiguated predicates.

In these examples we do not show the costs, although they are used by our system.

The first example is the pair

T: Russia is blocking oil from entering Ukraine.

H: Oil cannot be delivered to Ukraine.

The relevant part of the logical form of the text is

```
(and (block-V3' b1 x1 e1)(enter-S2' e1 o1 u1))
```

That is, there is a blocking event `b1` in which Russia `x1` blocks eventuality `e1` from occurring, and `e1` is the eventuality of oil `o1` entering Ukraine `u1`. The `-V3` on `block` indicates that it is the third WordNet sense of the verb "block" and the `-S2` suffix on `enter` indicates that it is the second supersense of "enter".

The relevant part of the logical form of the hypothesis is

```
(and (not' n2 c2) (can-S1' c2 x2 d2) (deliver-S2' d2 x2 o2 u2))
```

That is, `n2` is the eventuality that `c2` is not the case, where `c2` is some `x2`'s being able to do `d2`, where `d2` is `x2`'s delivering oil `o2` to Ukraine `u2`. Note that we don't know yet that the oil and Ukraine in the two sentences are coreferential.

The axiom relating the third verb sense of "block" to the underlying core theories is

```
AX4: (forall (c1 x1 e1)
        (if (block-V3' c1 x1 e1)
            (exist (n1 p1)
               (and (cause' c1 x1 n1)(not' n1 p1)(possible' p1 e1)))))
```

This rule says that for `x1` to block some eventuality `e1` is for `x1` to cause `e1` not to be possible. (In this example, for expositional simplicity, we have allowed the eventuality `c1` of blocking be the same as the eventuality of causing, where properly they should be closely related but not identical.)

The other axioms needed in this example are

```
AX1: (forall (c1 e1)
        (if (and (possible' c1 e1)(etc))
            (exist (x1)(can-S1' c1 x1 e1))))

AX2: (forall (d1 x1 c1 r1 x2 x3)
        (if (and (cause' d1 x1 c1)(changeTo' c1 r1)(rel' r1 x2 x3)
            (deliver-S2' d1 x1 x2 x3))))

AX3: (forall (c1 x1 x2)
        (if (enter-S2' c1 x1 x2)
            (exist (i1)(and changeTo' c1 i1)(in' i1 x1 x2))))
```

AX1 says that defeasibly, if an eventuality `e1` is possible, then someone can do it. AX2 says that if `x1` causes a change to a situation `r1` in which `x2` in in some relation to `x3`, then in a very general sense (`S2`), `x1` has delivered `x2` to `x3`. AX3 says that if `c1` is the eventuality of `x1` entering `x2`, then `c1` is the change into a state `i1` in which `x1` is in `x2`.

Starting with the logical form of H as the initial interpretation and applying axioms AX1 and AX2, we get interpretation H1:

```
H1: (and (not' n2 c2) (possible' c2 d2) (cause' d2 x2 c1)
          (changeTo' c1 r1)(rel' r1 o2 u2))
```

At this point we are stuck in our effort to back-chain to T. An axiom is missing, namely, one that says that "in" is a relation between two entities.

```
AX5:  (forall (r x1 x2) (if (in' r1 x1 x2)(rel' r1 x1 x2)))
```

Using AX5, we can back-chain from H1 and derive interpretation H2:

```
H2: (and (not' n2 c2)(possible' c2 d2)(cause' d2 x2 c1)
          (changeTo' c1 r1)(in' r1 o2 u2))
```

We can then further back-chain with AX3 to interpretation H3:

```
H3: (and (not' n2 c2)(possible' c2 d2)(cause' d2 x2 c1)
         (enter-S2' c1  o2 u2))
```

Again, we need a missing axiom, AX6, to get closer to the logical form of T:

```
AX6:   (forall (p e1)
         (if (and (possible' p,e1)(etc))
             (exist (c x1) (and (possible' p c)(cause' c x1 e1)))))
```

That is, if something is possible, it is possible for something to cause it. Using this axiom, we can derive

```
H4: (and (not' n2 c2)(possible' c2 c1)(enter-S2' c1  o2 u2))
```

The final missing axiom, AX7, says that if `x1` causes eventuality `c2` not to occur, then `c2` doesn't occur.

```
AX7:   (forall (n x1 n1 c2)
         (if (and (cause' n x1 n1)(not' n1 c2))( not' n c2)))
```

Using this we derive interpretation H5.

```
H5: (and (cause' n2 x3 n)(not' n c2)(possible' c2 c1)(enter-S2' c1 o2 u2))
```

We can now apply the rule for "block", identifying `b1` and `n2`, `x1` and `x3`, `e1` and `c1`, `o1` and `o2`, and `u1` and `u2`, yielding H6 and establishing the entailment relation between H and T.

```
H6: (and (block-V3' n2 x3 c1)(enter-S2' c1 o2 u2))
```

Our second example is the text-hypothesis pair

T: The plane managed to escape the attack.
H: The plane was not captured.

The relevant parts of the logical forms of T and H are as follows:

```
T: (and (manage-V1' m1 p1 e1)(escape-S1' e1 p1 a1))

H: (and (not' n2 c2)(capture-S1' c2 x2 p2))
```

The axioms relating these words to the core theories are as follows:

```
AX1: (forall (cp c x2 n chf a y1 x3 y0 x2)
       (if (and (changeTo' cp c)(cause' c x2 n)(not' n chf)
                (changeFrom' chf a)(at' a y1 x3)(arg' y0 x2))
           (capture' cp y0 y1)))

AX2: (forall (es x0 x1)
       (if (escape' es x0 x1)
           (exist (ch a)
              (and (cause' es x0 ch)(changeFrom' ch a)(at' a x0 x1)))))

AX3: (forall (m y0 e1)
       (if (manage' m y0 e1) (Rexist (m e1))))
```

The first says that a change to a situation in which x2 is causing y1 not to change location is a capturing by some y0 of y1. The second says that escaping implies causing a change from being at a location. The third says that if you manage to do e1, then e1 occurs.

Using these axioms, we would like to establish the entailment relation from T to H. However, in order for this reasoning to go through, we need several more axioms—saying that if an eventuality does not hold, there has been no change to that eventuality, and nothing has caused it to occur; that double negation cancels out; and that if something is caused, it occurs.

It may seem at first blush that any new text-hypothesis pair will reveal new axioms that must be encoded, and that therefore it is hopeless ever to achieve completeness in the theories. But a closer examination reveals that the missing axioms all involve relations among the most fundamental predicates, like cause, change, not, and possible. These are axioms that should be a part of the core theories of change and causality. They are not a random collection of facts, any one of which may turn out to be necessary for any given example. Rather we can investigate the possibilities systematically. That investigation is what we describe in the following section.

5 Relations among Fundamental Predicates

For completeness in the core theories, we need to look at pairs of fundamental predicates and ask what relations hold between them, what their composition yields, and for each such axiom whether it is defeasible or indefeasible. The predicates we consider are possible, Rexist, not, cause, changeFrom, and changeTo.

The first type of axiom formulates the relationship between two predicates. For example, the rule relating cause and Rexist is

```
(forall (x e) (if (cause x e)(Rexist e)))
```

That is, if something is caused, then it actually occurs. Other rules of this type are as follows:

```
(forall (x e) (if (Rexist e)(possible e)))

(forall (e) (if (and (Rexist e)(etc))(exist (x)(cause x e))))

(forall (e2)
   (if (changeTo e2)
       (exist (e1)(and (changeFrom e1)(not' e1 e2)))))

(forall (e1)
   (if (changeFrom e1)
       (exist (e2)(and (changeTo e2)(not' e2 e1)))))

(forall (e) (if (changeTo e)(Rexist e)))

(forall (e) (if (changeFrom e)(not e)))

(forall (e) (if (and (Rexist e)(etc))(changeTo e)))
```

That is, if something occurs, it is possible and, defeasibly, something causes it. If there is a change to some state obtaining, then there is a change from its not obtaining, and vice versa. If there is a change to something, then it obtains, and if there is a change from something, then it no longer obtains. If some state obtains, then defeasibly there was a change from something else to that state obtaining.

The second type of axiom involves the composition of predicates, and gives us rules of the form

```
(forall (e1 e2 x) (if (and (p' e1 e2)(q' e2 x)) (r' e1 x)))
```

That is, when `p` is applied to `q`, what relation `r` do we get?

Figure 2 shows the axioms encoding these compositions. The rows correspond to the `(p' e1 e2)`'s and the columns correspond to the `(q' e2 x)`'s, and the cell contains the consequents `(r' e1 x)`. If the rule is defeasible, the cell indicates that by adding `(etc)` to the antecedent. The consequents in italics are derivable from other rules.

	(possible' e2 e3)	**(Rexist' e2 e3)**	**(not' e2 e3)**	**(cause' e2 x2 e3)**	**(changeFrom' e2 e3)**	**(changeTo' e2 e3)**
(possible'e1 e2)	(possible' e1 e3)	(possible' e1 e3)		*(possible'e1 e3)*		*(possible'e1 e3)*
(Rexist' e1 e2)	(possible' e1 e3)	(Rexist' e1 e3)	(not' e1 e3)	*(Rexist' e1 e3)*	*(not' e1 e3)*	*(Rexist' e1 e3)*
(not' e1 e2)	(not' e1 e3)	(not' e1 e3)	(Rexist' e1 e3)	(etc) ->(not' e1 e3)	(Rexist' e1 e3)	(etc) ->(not' e1 e3)
(cause' e1 x1 e2)	*(possible' e1 e3)*	(cause' e1 x1 e3) *(Rexist' e1 e3)*	*(not' e1 e3)*	(cause' e1 x1 e3) *(Rexist' e1 e3)*	*(not' e1 e3)* *(changeFrom' e1 e3)*	*(cause' e1 x1 e3)* *(changeTo' e1 e3)*
(changeFrom' e1 e2)		(changeFrom' e1 e3)	(changeTo' e1 e3) *(Rexist' e1 e3)*	(etc) -> (changeFrom' e1 e3) *(etc) -> (not' e1 e3)*	*(Rexist' e1 e3)*	*(etc) ->(not' e1 e3)*
(changeTo' e1 e2)	*(possible' e1 e3)*	(changeTo' e1 e3) *(Rexist' e1 e3)*	(changeFrom' e1 e3) *(not' e1 e3)*	(etc) -> (changeTo' e1 e3) *(Rexist' e1 e3)* *(cause' e1 x1 e3)*	*(not' e1 e3)* *(changeFrom' e1 e3)*	*(Rexist' e1 e3)* *(changeTo' e1 e3)*

Figure 2: Axioms expressing compositions of fundamental predicates

For example, in the `possible-possible` cell, the rule says that if it is possible that something is possible, then it is possible. To take a more complex example, the `changeFrom-cause` cell says that if there is a change from some entity causing (or maintaining) a state, then defeasibly there will be a change from that state. So if a glass is released, it will fall.

We have also looked at axioms whose pattern is the converse of those in Figure 2. For example, if something does not hold, then it was not caused. Many of the axioms used in the examples are of this sort.

6 Conclusion

If we are ever to have sophisticated natural language understanding, our systems will have to be able to draw inferences like the ones illustrated here, and therefore they will need axioms of this complexity or something equivalent. Because of their complexity, we cannot expect to be able to acquire the axioms automatically by statistical methods. But that does not mean the situation is bleak. We have shown in this paper that there is a systematic methodology for developing axioms characterizing the meanings of words in a way that enforces uniformity and for elaborating the core theories these axioms are anchored in. Doing this for several thousand of the most common words in English would produce a huge gain in the inferential power of our systems, as illustrated by the textual entailment examples in this paper, and would be an enterprise no greater in scope than the manual construction of other widely used resources such as WordNet and FrameNet.

References

[1] Baker, C., Fillmore, C., Cronin, B.: The Structure of the Framenet Database, International Journal of Lexicography, Volume 16.3: (2003) 281-296.

[2] J. Blythe, J. Hobbs, P. Domingos, R. Kate, and R. Mooney, 2011. "Implementing Weighted Abduction in Markov Logic", *Proceedings of the 9th International Conference on Computational Semantics*, Oxford, United Kingdom.

[3] Gruber, Jeffrey C., 1965. *Studies in Lexical Relations*, unpublished Ph.D. dissertation, Massachusetts Institute of Technology, Cambridge, Massachusetts.

[4] Gruninger, Michael, and Christopher Menzel, 2010. "The Process Specification Language (PSL) Theory and Applications", *AI Magazine*, Vol 24, No 3.

[5] Hobbs, Jerry R. 1985. "Ontological Promiscuity." *Proceedings, 23rd Annual Meeting of the Association for Computational Linguistics*, pp. 61-69. Chicago, Illinois, July 1985.

[6] Hobbs, Jerry R., 2008. "Deep Lexical Semantics", *Proceedings*, 9th International Conference on Intelligent Text Processing and Computational Linguistics (CICLing-2008), Haifa, Israel, February 2008.

[7] Hobbs, Jerry R., Mark Stickel, Douglas Appelt, and Paul Martin, 1993. "Interpretation as Abduction", *Artificial Intelligence*, Vol. 63, Nos. 1-2, pp. 69-142.

[8] Jackendoff, Ray S. 1972. *Semantic interpretation in generative grammar*. Cambridge, MA: The MIT Press.

[9] Kipper, Karin, Anna Korhonen, Neville Ryant, and Martha Palmer (2006) Extensive Classifications of English verbs. *Proceedings*, 12th EURALEX International Congress. Turin, Italy. September, 2006.

[10] Lakoff, George, 1987. *Women, Fire, and Dangerous Things: What Categories Reveal About the Mind*, University of Chicago Press, Chicago.

[11] McCarthy, John, 1980. "Circumscription: A Form of Nonmonotonic Reasoning", *Artificial Intelligence*, 13: 27-39.

[12] Mueller, Erik T., 2006. *Commonsense Reasoning*, Morgan Kaufmann Publishers, Inc., San Mateo, California.

[13] R. Mulkar, J.R. Hobbs, and E. Hovy, 2007. "Learning from Reading Syntactically Complex Biology Texts", *Proceedings of the AAAI Spring Symposium Commonsense'07*. Stanford University, CA, 2007.

[14] E. Ovchinnikova, N. Montazeri, T. Alexandrov, J. Hobbs, M. McCord, and R. Mulkar-Mehta, 2011. "Abductive Reasoning with a Large Knowledge Base for Discourse Processing", *Proceedings of the 9th International Conference on Computational Semantics*, Oxford, United Kingdom.

The People's Web meets Linguistic Knowledge: Automatic Sense Alignment of Wikipedia and WordNet

Elisabeth Niemann and **Iryna Gurevych**
Ubiquitous Knowledge Processing Lab
Technische Universität Darmstadt
Hochschulstraße 10
D-64289 Darmstadt, Germany
http://www.ukp.tu-darmstadt.de

Abstract

We propose a method to automatically align WordNet synsets and Wikipedia articles to obtain a sense inventory of higher coverage and quality. For each WordNet synset, we first extract a set of Wikipedia articles as alignment candidates; in a second step, we determine which article (if any) is a valid alignment, i.e. is about the same sense or concept. In this paper, we go significantly beyond state-of-the-art word overlap approaches, and apply a threshold-based Personalized PageRank method for the disambiguation step. We show that WordNet synsets can be aligned to Wikipedia articles with a performance of up to 0.78 F_1-Measure based on a comprehensive, well-balanced reference dataset consisting of 1,815 manually annotated sense alignment candidates. The fully-aligned resource as well as the reference dataset is publicly available.[1]

1 Introduction

Lexical semantic resources often used as sense inventories are a prerequisite in automatic processing of human language. In the last few years, there has been a rise in research aligning different resources to overcome the knowledge acquisition bottleneck and coverage problems pertinent to any single resource. In this paper, we address the task of aligning WordNet noun synsets and Wikipedia articles to obtain a sense inventory of higher coverage and quality. WordNet, a lexical database for English, is extensively used in the NLP community and is a de-facto standard resource in many NLP tasks, especially in current WSD research (Fellbaum, 1998). WordNet's manually defined comprehensive taxonomy motivates many researchers to utilize it. However, as WordNet is maintained by only a small group of experts, it is hard to cope with neologisms, named entities, or rare usages on a large scale (Agirre and Edmonds, 2006; Meyer and Gurevych, 2010). In order to compensate for WordNet's lack of coverage, Wikipedia has turned out to be a valuable resource in the NLP community. Wikipedia has the advantage of being constantly updated by thousands of voluntary contributors. It is multilingual and freely available containing a tremendous amount of encyclopedic knowledge enriched with hyperlink information.

In the past, researchers have explored the alignment of Wikipedia categories and WordNet synsets (e.g., Toral et al. (2008); Ponzetto and Navigli (2009)). However, using the categories instead of the articles causes three limitations: First, the number of Wikipedia categories (about 0.5 million in the English edition) is much smaller compared to the number of articles (about 3.35 million). Secondly, the category system in Wikipedia is not structured consistently (Ponzetto and Navigli, 2009). And finally, disregarding the article level neglects the huge amount of textual content provided by the articles.

Therefore, attempts to align WordNet synsets and Wikipedia articles (instead of categories) have been recently made. This has three major benefits. First of all, as WordNet and Wikipedia were found to be partly complementary on the word sense level, an aligned resource would increase the coverage of

[1] http://www.ukp.tu-darmstadt.de/data/sense-alignment

senses (Wolf and Gurevych, 2010). Second, word senses contained in both resources can then be represented by relational information from WordNet and encyclopedic information from Wikipedia in a multilingual manner yielding an enriched knowledge representation. And finally, the third major benefit of the alignment is the ability to automatically acquire sense-tagged corpora in a mono- and multilingual fashion. For each WordNet synset, the text of the aligned Wikipedia article (or all sentences or paragraphs in Wikipedia that contain a link to the article) can be automatically extracted similar to the approach proposed by Mihalcea (2007). Automatically generated sense-tagged corpora can be used to, e.g., counter the bottleneck of supervised WSD methods that rely on such sense-tagged text collections, which are rare. Further, due to the cross-lingual links in Wikipedia, also corpora in different languages can be constructed easily.

Our contribution to this paper is two-fold. First, we propose a novel two-step approach to align WordNet synsets and Wikipedia articles. We model the task as a word sense disambiguation problem applying the Personalized PageRank algorithm proposed by Agirre and Soroa (2009) as it is state-of-the-art in WSD and combine it with a word overlap measure, which increases the overall performance. Second, we generate and introduce a well-balanced reference dataset for evaluation consisting of 1,815 manually annotated sense alignment candidates. WordNet synsets and their corresponding Wikipedia article candidates are sampled along their distinctive properties such as synset size, domain, or the location in the WordNet taxonomy. An evaluation on this dataset let us generalize the performance to a full alignment between WordNet and Wikipedia, which is publicly available for further research activities.

2 Related work

The alignment of WordNet and Wikipedia has been an active area of research for several years with the goal of creating an enriched ontology. One of the first attempts proposed a new resource YAGO integrating WordNet and Wikipedia consisting of more than 1 million entities and 5 million facts (Suchanek et al., 2007). The set of entities contains all WordNet synsets and Wikipedia articles with titles that are not represented as terms in WordNet. Thus, they ignore ambiguous entities, e.g., the British rock band *Queen* is not covered as the term *queen* is already contained in WordNet.

Other approaches automatically align WordNet with the categories of Wikipedia instead of the articles. Toral et al. (2008) enrich WordNet with named entities mined from Wikipedia. Therefore, the noun *is-a* hierarchy of WordNet is mapped to the Wikipedia categories determining the overlap of articles belonging to the category and the instances for each of the senses of a polysemous word in WordNet.

Ponzetto and Navigli (2009) applied a knowledge-rich method which maximizes the structural overlap between the WordNet taxonomy and the category graph extracted from Wikipedia. Based on the mapping information, the taxonomy automatically generated from the Wikipedia category graph is restructured to enhance the quality. Toral et al. (2009) disambiguate WordNet noun synsets and Wikipedia categories using multiple text similarity measures similar to our approach. A Wikipedia category is thereby represented by its main article or an article, which has the same title string as the category. Wu and Weld (2008) integrate the Wikipedia's infobox information with WordNet to build a rich ontology using statistical-relational learning.

Ruiz-Casado et al. (2005) proposed a method to align WordNet synsets and Wikipedia articles (instead of categories). They align articles of the *Simple* English Wikipedia to their most similar WordNet synsets depending on the vector-based similarity of the synset's gloss and the article text. Recently, Ponzetto and Navigli (2010) presented a method based on a conditional probability $p(s|w)$ of selecting the WordNet sense s given the Wikipedia article w, whereas the conditional probability relies on a normalized word overlap measure of the textual sense representation. Both approaches, however, have the following two major drawbacks: first, the algorithms are modeled such that they always assume a counterpart in WordNet for a given Wikipedia article, which does not hold for the English Wikipedia (see Section 4). Second, the algorithms always assign the most likely WordNet synset to a Wikipedia article, not allowing multiple alignments. However, due to the different sense granularities in WordNet and Wikipedia, some Wikipedia articles might be assigned to more than one WordNet synset. Based on these observations, there is a need for a better approach yielding none, one, or more than one alignment for a given synset or article. We will describe a novel idea to tackle this in the next section.

3 Methodology

Automatic sense alignment aims to match senses of different resources that have the same meaning.[2] In general, one sense is given and the task is to find a correspondent within another resource, in case one exists. Thereby, automatic sense alignment meets two subgoals. At first, all potential alignment candidate senses for a given sense have to be extracted. Secondly, these extracted candidates have to be scored to select the sense(s) that match in meaning. For example, given the WordNet synset wn =<*schooner: sailing vessel used in former times*> and the two Wikipedia alignment candidate articles wp_1 =<*Schooner: A schooner is a type of sailing vessel ...*> and wp_2 =<*Schooner (glass): A schooner is a type of glass used for ...*>; the article wp_1 should be aligned with the synset wn, while the second should not be aligned. The recall of the extraction step can highly influence the performance of the whole alignment process. If a sense is not extracted in the first step, it cannot be selected in the alignment step either.
In Section 3.1, we state how we extract Wikipedia alignment candidate articles for a given synset. In the subsequent Section 3.2, we describe how we determine the article that is aligned to the synset (if any at all). As almost all Wikipedia articles refer to nouns, we focus on this part-of-speech.

3.1 Candidate extraction

In order to extract Wikipedia articles for a given WordNet synset, we follow the procedure introduced by Wolf and Gurevych (2010). We shortly summarize this method here: Let wn be a WordNet synset with a set of synonyms $\{s_1, \cdots, s_n\}$ of size n. For each synonym $s \in wn$, we extract all Wikipedia articles $wp \in WP_{wn}$ that match one of the following constraints:

a) the article title matches s, e.g., the article *Window* is retrieved for the synonym term *Window*,
b) the article title is of the form *s_(description tag)*, e.g., *Window_(computing)*,
c) the article has a redirect that matches s or is of the form *s_(description tag)*, e.g., *Chaff_(countermeasure)* has a redirect *Window_(codename)* and, thus, is retrieved for the synonym term *Window*,
d) the article is linked in a hyperlink, in which the link anchor text matches s, e.g., the article *Bandwagon effect* is retrieved for the term *bandwagon*, as there exist a hyperlink of the form [[*Bandwagon effect*|*bandwagon*]]. Only hyperlinks that occur in at least 3 different articles are taken into account in order to reduce noise.

3.2 Candidate alignment

Given the set of Wikipedia candidates WP_{wn} extracted for synset wn, we have to classify each Wikipedia article $wp \in WP_{wn}$ as being a valid alignment or not with respect to wn. Therefore, we first calculate similarities between synset–article pairs of a given training set. In a second step, we learn a threshold corresponding to the minimum similarity a sense pair should have to be aligned. This threshold is then used to fully align WordNet and Wikipedia.

Sense similarity. The basis of our new approach for sense alignment is the PageRank algorithm (Brin and Page, 1998) relying on a lexical-semantic knowledge base, which is modeled as a graph $G = (V, E)$. As knowledge base we use WordNet 3.0 extended with manually disambiguated glosses from the "Princeton Annotated Gloss Corpus"[3]. The vertices $v \in V$ represent the synsets; the edges (undirected and unweighted) represent semantic relations between synsets, such as hyponym and hypernym relations.

[2]We do not differentiate between the terms *sense* and *concept* in this paper as they both refer to the same 'artifact' and only differ in representation. Concepts in WordNet are described by the entire synset, e.g. the synset <*design, plan*>. Senses, however, are words tagged with a sense number, e.g. *design_N_#2*, which means the word *check* as a noun in its second sense.

[3]`http://wordnet.princeton.edu/glosstag.shtml`

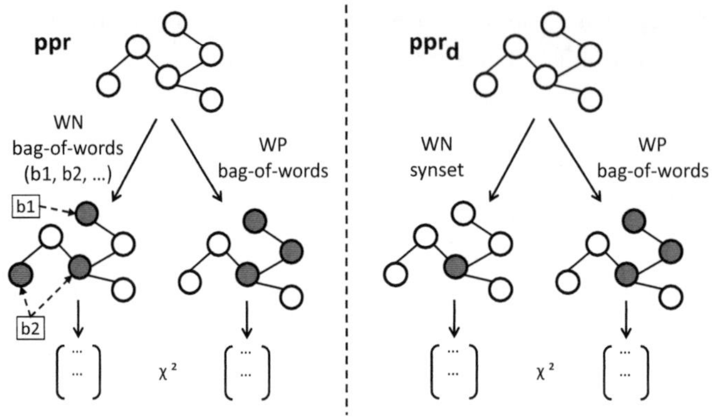

Figure 1: Schematic illustration of the basic ppr (left) and direct $\mathtt{ppr}_d$ (right) approach.

The PageRank algorithm ranks the vertices in a graph according to their importance within the set. Let M be a $(n \times n)$ transition probability matrix, where $M_{ji} = \frac{1}{\text{outdegree}_i}$, if there exist a link from vertex i to vertex j. Then, the PageRank vector **pr** over the graph G is equivalent to resolve:

$$\mathbf{pr} = cM\mathbf{pr} + (1 - c)v\,, \tag{1}$$

whereas c is a damping factor between 0 and 1, and v is an n-dimensional vector whose elements are $\frac{1}{n}$. An element of the PageRank vector denotes the probability for the corresponding vertex that a jumper, randomly following the edges in the graph, ends at that vertex, i.e. the importance of that vertex.
Now, vector v can be *personalized* by assigning stronger initial probabilities to certain vertices in the graph. This personalized version of the PageRank algorithm (Agirre and Soroa, 2009) is used in our approach in two different ways (see Figure 1):
In the *basic* version **ppr** , we represent both, Wikipedia articles and WordNet synsets as bag-of-words (abbreviated as b in the following). The textual representation is tokenized and lemmatized using the TreeTagger (Schmid, 1994); standard stopword removal is applied. For a given synset–article pair, we calculate two Personalized PageRank vectors. For each Personalized PageRank vector, we initialize vector v depending on the terms occurring in b:

$$v_i = \begin{cases} \frac{1}{m} & \text{if} \quad \text{a synonymous word of synset}_i \text{ in WordNet occurs in } b \\ 0 & \text{else}\,, \end{cases} \tag{2}$$

where m is the number of synsets with a synonymous word occurring in b. For example, given the WordNet synset <*payment, defrayal, defrayment: the act of paying money*> with its bag-of-words *(payment, defrayal, defrayment, act, paying, money)*, we assign each synset, i.e. vertex in the graph, a weight, for which at least one of its synonymous words occurs in the bag-of-words. Then, the PageRank vector is a semantic representation over all WordNet synsets for the given bag-of-words.
In the *direct* version **ppr** $_\mathbf{d}$, the WordNet synset is directly represented in v by assigning a weight of 1 to the corresponding vector element. It induces that the WordNet synset is already disambiguated and thus, motivates the use of the Personalized PageRank algorithm on the WordNet graph. Only for the Wikipedia article, the vector v is built up according to Eq. 2.
Given two Personalized PageRank vectors $\mathtt{ppr}_{wn}$ and $\mathtt{ppr}_{wp}$ for the WordNet synset wn and the Wikipedia article wp, we calculate their similarity using the χ^2 measure.[4]

$$sim_{ppr}(wn, wp) = 1 - \chi^2(ppr_{wn}, ppr_{wp}) = 1 - \sum_i \frac{(ppr_{wn_i} - ppr_{wp_i})^2}{ppr_{wn_i} + ppr_{wp_i}} \tag{3}$$

[4]This vector distance measure has shown the best overall performance compared to the cosine and euclidean distance in our experiments.

Learning classifier. Based on the similarity, the sense pair has to be classified as alignment (class 1) or non-alignment (class 0) formally defined as:

$$c(wn, wp) = \begin{cases} 1 & \text{if} \quad sim(wn, wp) > t \\ 0 & \text{else}, \end{cases} \tag{4}$$

where $sim(wn, wp)$ is the similarity of a WordNet synset and a Wikipedia article, and t is a real valued threshold. We apply 10-fold cross-validation to determine the threshold. We measure the performance of classification by means of F_1-Measure (see Section 5) and iteratively search (from 0 to 1 in 0.001 steps) for a threshold that maximizes the performance on the training fold. A threshold-based classification scheme induces that a WordNet synset can be aligned to none, one, or more than one Wikipedia article, which is the main potential of our approach compared to existing methods. However, in the scope of this paper, we assign at most one Wikipedia article (if any) to a WordNet synset (the one with the highest similarity above the threshold) as this yields the best performance (see Section 5).

Word overlap measure. For comparison, we also applied the standard cosine word overlap similarity measure **`cos`** used in existing sense alignment approaches (e.g., Ruiz-Casado et al. (2005)). We determine the similarity of the bag-of-words vectors of the WordNet synset and Wikipedia article calculating the cosine between them. According to Eq. 4 we also learn a classifier based on the cosine similarity.

Combination of the classifiers' output. Finally, we experiment with a heuristic, classifying only those synset–article pairs as alignment, for which the Personalized PageRank-based classifier and the cosine-based classifier, i.e. c_{ppr} and c_{cos}, or c_{ppr_d} and c_{cos}, return an alignment to further increase the precision.

Baselines. We implemented two different baselines. The baseline **`rand`** randomly selects a Wikipedia article from the extracted candidate set for each synset. The baseline **`mfs`** (most frequent sense) assigns always the most frequently linked Wikipedia article of the candidate set defined as the article with the highest number of incoming links. For example, for the synset wn =<*tree: a tall perennial woody plant having a main trunk* [...]> suppose we extract the two Wikipedia articles, namely wp_1 =<*Tree: A tree is a perennial woody plant.*> and wp_2 =<*Tree (data structure)*>. In this case, the sense wp_1 is aligned to the synset wn as it has 4,339 inlinks, about 4,000 more than the article wp_2. Both, the `rand` and `mfs` baseline always return a one-to-one alignment.

4 Well-balanced reference dataset

Publicly available evaluation datasets as provided by Fernando and Stevenson (2010) and Wolf and Gurevych (2010), are either quite small or follow a different annotation scheme. Others consist of randomly sampled synsets, which do not properly represent the distribution of synsets in WordNet following specific properties. For example, the dataset used in (Ponzetto and Navigli, 2010) consists of only 2 sense pairs, whose lemmas are monosemous in WordNet and Wikipedia (e.g. the lemma *specifier* corresponds to one synset in WordNet and one article in Wikipedia). As this property holds for one-third of all WordNet noun synsets, it is crucial for the choice of the alignment method and thus, should be represented in the evaluation dataset adequately. Therefore, our goal in this paper is to compile a well-balanced dataset to cover different domains and properties.

Synsets can be characterized with respect to their so-called assigned *Unique Beginner*, their synset size, and their location within the WordNet taxonomy. The *Unique Beginners* group synsets in semantically related fields (Fellbaum, 1998) such as *entity* (subsuming animals, persons, plants, artifacts, body and food related synsets), *abstraction*, *psychological features*, *shapes*, *states*, and *locations*. The synset size refers to the number of synonymous word senses in the synset. A synset can further be characterized by its location within the WordNet taxonomy defined as the shortest path between the given synset and the synset *entity*, which is the root element of all noun synsets. In addition, we distinguish between

Property		# synsets in WordNet	# sampled synsets	# manually aligned synsets
Synset size	=1	42,054	160	110
	> 1	40,061	160	111
Path length to root	0-5	8,586	60	33
	6-10	67,082	200	143
	11-16	6,447	60	45
Unique Beginner	*Entity*	47,330	160	118
	Non-Entity	34,785	160	103
# extracted WP candidates	=1	23,991	160	108
	> 1	46,569	160	113
Total #		82,115	320	221

Table 1: Sampling by properties and # manual alignments

Annotator	*A*	*B*	*C*	majority
# non-alignments	1,586	1,571	1,605	1,588
# alignments	229	244	210	227

Table 2: Annotations per class

	A–B	*A–C*	*B–C*
A_O	.9697	.9741	.9724
κ	.8663	.8782	.8742

Table 3: Inter-annotator agreement

synsets for which more than one Wikipedia candidate article is returned. In summary, for example, the synset <*article, clause: a separate section of a legal document*> has a synset size of 2, is assigned to the Unique Beginner *communication*, has a shortest path to the root element of length 6, and has 5 extracted Wikipedia candidate articles.

Based on these distinctive properties, we sampled 320 noun synsets yielding 1,815 sense pairs to be annotated, i.e. 5.7 Wikipedia articles per synset on average. The exact proportion of synsets with respect to their properties is detailed in Table 1 in the first four columns.

The manual sense alignment is performed by three human annotators. The annotators were provided sense alignment candidate pairs, each consisting of a WordNet synset and a Wikipedia article. The annotation task was to label each sense pair either as alignment or not. Table 2 outlines the class distribution for three annotators and the majority decision.

The most sense alignment candidates were annotated as non-alignments; only between 210 and 244 sense pairs were considered as alignments (extracted for 320 WordNet synsets). To assess the reliability of the annotators' decision, we computed the pairwise observed inter-annotator agreement A_O and the chance-corrected agreement κ (Artstein and Poesio, 2008)[5]. The agreement values are shown in Table 3. The average observed agreement A_O is 0.9721, while the multi-κ is 0.8727 indicating high reliability. The final dataset was compiled by means of a majority decision. Given 1,815 sense alignment candidate pairs, 1,588 were annotated as non-alignments, while 227 were annotated as alignments. 215 synsets were aligned with one article, while 6 synsets were aligned with two articles. Interesting to note is that the aligned samples are uniformly distributed among the different sampling dimensions as shown in Table 1 (right column). It demonstrates that WordNet synsets of different properties are contained in Wikipedia. On the other side, 99 synsets, i.e. approx. 1/3 of the sampled synsets, could not be aligned. Most of them are not contained in Wikipedia at all, e.g. the synset <*dream (someone or something wonderful)*> or <*outside, exterior (the region that is outside of something)*>. Others are not explicitly encoded on the article level such as the synset <*quatercentennial, quatercentenary (the 400th anniversary (or the celebration of it))*>, which is part of the more general Wikipedia article <*Anniversary*>.

5 Experiments

In our experiments, we represent a WordNet synset either by itself (in the direct version $\texttt{ppr}_d$) or by its set of synonymous word senses and its gloss and examples (in the basic version `ppr`). Optionally, we include hyponym and hypernym synsets to extend the sense representation of a synset: (SYN): the

[5]Note: "As the class distribution is highly skewed, the test for reliability in such cases is the ability to agree on the rare categories [...]" (Artstein and Poesio, 2008). This, in fact, is the category/class, in which we are most interested in.

WordNet	Wikipedia	`cos`		$\texttt{ppr}_d$		$\texttt{ppr}_d$ + `cos`		`ppr`		`ppr` + `cos`	
		F_1	Acc	F_1	Acc	F_1	Acc	F_1	Acc	F_1	Acc
SYN	P+T	.691	.907	.719	.921	.726	.923	.707	.914	.727	.927
+HYPO	P+T	.694	.908	.701	.916	.716	.931	.700	.912	.718	.926
+HYPER	P+T	.726	.921	.708	.918	.737	.935	.756	.928	.774	.940
+HYP2	P+T	.725	.927	.713	.920	.720	.937	.741	.923	.756	.940
SYN	P+T+R	.684	.907	.721	.921	.738	.936	.707	.913	.725	.926
+HYPO	P+T+R	.689	.910	.711	.918	.729	.936	.698	.910	.721	.927
+HYPER	P+T+R	.719	.917	.724	.928	.748	.937	.762	.938	.755	.940
+HYP2	P+T+R	.727	.920	.729	.929	.739	.937	.747	.932	.761	.940
SYN	P+T+C	.698	.909	**.754**	**.930**	**.756**	**.937**	.726	.918	.743	.931
+HYPO	P+T+C	.702	.910	.739	.927	.747	.938	.722	.917	.740	.930
+HYPER	P+T+C	**.738**	**.925**	**.752**	**.931**	.765	.943	.765	.935	**.781**	**.945**
+HYP2	P+T+C	.732	.923	.739	.928	.757	.942	.746	.930	.769	.942
SYN	P+T+R+C	.699	.912	.736	.926	.752	.939	.719	.916	.734	.929
+HYPO	P+T+R+C	.695	.911	.736	.926	.735	.936	.711	.914	.727	.928
+HYPER	P+T+R+C	.718	.917	.744	.930	.758	.940	**.776**	**.940**	.772	.943
+HYP2	P+T+R+C	.724	.918	.751	.932	.756	.939	.762	.936	.769	.942
`rand`	–	.527	.857								
`mfs`	–	.534	.860								

Table 4: Results for the automatic alignment

given synset; (HYPER): all hypernym synsets of the given synset; (HYPO): all hyponym synsets of the given synset; (HYP2): all hypernym and hyponym synsets of the given synset.
A Wikipedia article is represented by either its first paragraph[6] as it usually contains a compact description of the article or its whole article text. The article title and additional assigned information such as categories or redirects can also be taken into account: (P): first paragraph of Wikipedia article (with a minimum length of 200 characters[7]); (TXT): the whole article text; (T): article title; (C): all categories assigned to the article; (R): all redirects assigned to the article.
Table 4 lists the performance of our approach for different experimental settings.[8] We evaluate our approach in terms of F_1-Measure ($F_1 = \frac{2*P*R}{P+R}$), where P is the precision and R the recall. The precision P determines the ratio of correct alignments to all alignments assigned by the algorithm. The recall R identifies the number of correct alignments to the total number of correct alignments in the gold standard. Further, we provide an accuracy measure Acc, which denotes the percentage of the correctly identified alignments and non-alignments.

Similarity measure. Overall, the Personalized PageRank approach outperforms the cosine similarity. `cos` achieves an F_1-Measure of 0.738, while $\texttt{ppr}_d$ reaches 0.754 and `ppr` even 0.776, which is a performance gain of 2.1% and 5.1%, respectively. This, in fact, strengthens our motivation to employ semantic relatedness based approaches instead of a simple word overlap approach. For example, the synset *<Johannesburg>* and its corresponding Wikipedia article is not aligned based on the cosine approach as only three terms overlap. However, the `ppr` and $\texttt{ppr}_d$ approach classify the synset–article pair as alignment as there exists semantic relatedness between "large economy" and "commercial center" occurring in the textual sense representations.
The performance differences between $\texttt{ppr}_d$ and `ppr` correlate with the synset representation. On the one hand, utilizing the SYN representation, $\texttt{ppr}_d$ outperforms the `ppr` approach. This shows the effect of disambiguating the WordNet synset beforehand. On the other hand, when presenting the synset together with its hypernym or both, hypernyms and hyponyms, `ppr` yields the best performance. This might be due to the fact that a Wikipedia article often contains more general terms, i.e. hypernym concepts, especially within the first paragraph of a Wikipedia article.
All combinations yield higher performance compared to the stand-alone classifiers. For example, for the setting SYN+HYPER and P+T+C, `cos` yields 0.738, `ppr` 0.765, and the combination of both 0.781

[6]Extracted with JWPL (Zesch et al., 2008) and some additional post-processing steps.
[7]We have not optimized this value for this task.
[8]As all experimental settings, in which the Wikipedia article was represented with its first paragraph instead of the whole article text, yield higher performance, we report only these numbers here.

Measure	A	B	C
`cos`	.688	**.692**	.676
$\texttt{ppr}_d$	**.711**	**.711**	.690
$\texttt{ppr}_d$ + `cos`	**.724**	. 714	.716
`ppr`	**.737**	.718	.716
`ppr` + `cos`	**.740**	.730	.728

Table 5: Agreement (κ) between automatic and human annotators

		automatic	
		alignment	non-alignment
manual	alignment	178	**49**
	non-alignment	**51**	1,537

Table 6: Confusion matrix (Setting: `ppr` + `cos` , SYN+HYPER, P+T+C)

performance, which is an improvement of 5.8% and 2.1% compared to the `cos` and `ppr` approach, respectively. The performance gain originates from higher precision.

Sense representation. All similarity measures yield better performance representing the WordNet synset together with their hypernym synsets regardless of the representation of the Wikipedia article. As stated before, this might be due to the fact that Wikipedia articles often contain hypernym concepts in their textual representation. Further, each synset has exactly one direct hypernym concept, while the number of hyponym concepts is not limited. This can cause a very noisy description of a synset, not focusing on the textual representation of the actual sense. When representing the Wikipedia sense, the categories always boost the performance, while redirects are not helpful and can yield even a performance drop. The reason might be that redirects contain much noisy information, e.g. spelling variations.

Baselines. The `rand` and the `mfs` baselines achieve an F_1-Measure of 0.527 and 0.534, respectively. They always assign a sense even only 221 of 320 synsets can be aligned to Wikipedia. If we only consider the 221 synsets for which an alignment exist, the `mfs` baseline achieves an F_1-Measure of 0.76, i.e. for 146 out of 221 synsets the aligned Wikipedia article is the most frequent sense as we defined it in Section 3.2.

Upper bound. The human annotators show a pairwise agreement κ between 0.866 and 0.878, which serves as an upper bound for this task. For each measure and its best performing experimental setting as listed in Table 4, we calculate the agreement with the annotators' alignments (see Table 5). The combined approach `ppr` + `cos` achieves the highest agreement values κ, between 0.728 and 0.740. These values show that the automatic annotation is fairly reliable.

5.1 Error analysis

We manually analyzed the alignments generated by the best performing experimental setup (`ppr` + `cos`, SYN+HYPER, P+T+C). For synsets corresponding to more than one extracted Wikipedia candidate, the average number of Wikipedia candidates is around 10, which, indeed, makes the alignment step very challenging for some synsets. For example, for the synset *<mission, military mission (an operation that is assigned by a higher headquarters)>* 30 Wikipedia candidates were extracted in total, whereas only the article with the title *<Military operation>* was aligned manually. 10 out of the 30 are articles about space flight missions and Christian missionary. Most of the remaining 19 refer to city names, song titles, and other named entities. Our approach returns the highest similarity for the article *<Military operation>*, which demonstrates that the alignment works well in this example.

As listed in Table 6, the best performing experimental setup correctly aligned 178 of the 227 manual alignments. The remaining 49 manual alignments were not assigned. Instead, 51 additional sense can-

didate pairs were incorrectly considered as alignment. It is noticeable that the errors are almost equally distributed among the distinctive properties a synset can have as defined in Section 4. We could not observe that a specific synset property causes the majority of errors.
Most of the 51 false positives are due to highly related sense alignment candidates, e.g. *(cottonseed, cottonseed oil)*, *(electroretinogram, electroretrinography)*, or *(insulin shock, insulin shock therapy)*. These sense alignment candidates have either the same stem but different suffixes or one part is a holonym or meronym of the other part. This knowledge can be used to apply additional post-processing steps to boost the performance. Further, even if they are non-aligned manually as they do not describe the same sense, the concepts are highly related, and thus, the alignment might be useful in specific tasks.
Most of the 49 manual alignments that could not be aligned automatically are due to the differences how senses are defined in WordNet and Wikipedia. For example, the WordNet synset *<payment, defrayal, defrayment: the act of paying money>* and the manually aligned Wikipedia article *<Payment: A payment is the transfer of wealth from one party (such as person or company) to another ...>* could not be aligned automatically. In this example, the textual similarity or relatedness is not sufficient to classify them as a valid alignment. This fact shows that other types of knowledge should be additionally integrated in the alignment approach, such as structural or taxonomic knowledge.

6 Conclusions

We have presented a novel two-step approach to automatically align English Wikipedia articles and WordNet synsets. We have shown that a threshold-based method models the task properly yielding none, one, or more than one alignment of a Wikipedia article for a given WordNet synset. This is different to previous sense alignment approaches. Further, we have shown that it is important to employ semantic relatedness measuring the similarity of textual sense representations. Our approach to the automatic alignment shows an encouraging performance of 0.78 F_1-Measure and 94.5% accuracy based on a comprehensive, well-balanced reference dataset consisting of 1,815 manually annotated sense alignment candidates.
We have created a fully-aligned resource with our best performing setting (`ppr` + `cos`, SYN+HYPER, P+T+C, threshold: 0.439 for `ppr`, 0.048 for `cos`), in which two-thirds of all WordNet noun synsets are aligned with one article from the English Wikipedia. On the one hand, this fact supports our assumption and overall motivation that both resources are partly complementary at the sense level (one-third of all noun synsets are not in Wikipedia). On the other hand, for the two-thirds of WordNet noun synsets, the alignment yields relational information from WordNet and encyclopedic information from Wikipedia.
We believe that this new resource and the enhanced knowledge therein can boost the performance of various NLP systems that previously had to rely on a single resource only. We already started research on integrating the aligned resource in WSD and semantic relatedness tasks. The fully-aligned resource as well as the reference dataset are publicly available at `http://www.ukp.tu-darmstadt.de/data/sense-alignment` for further research activities.

Acknowledgments

This work has been supported by the Emmy Noether Program of the German Research Foundation (DFG) under the grant No. GU 798/3-1, and by the Volkswagen Foundation as part of the Lichtenberg-Professorship Program under the grant No. I/82806. We thank our colleague Christian M. Meyer for many fruitful discussions during the work on this paper and our students Yevgen Chebotar and Christian Kirschner for their help on the experiments. Further, we thank the IXA group at the University of the Basque Country for making their code on the Personalized PageRank method based on WordNet available online.[9]

[9] `http://ixa2.si.ehu.es/ukb`

References

Agirre, E. and P. G. Edmonds (2006). *Word Sense Disambiguation: Algorithms and Applications.* Springer.

Agirre, E. and A. Soroa (2009). Personalizing PageRank for Word Sense Disambiguation. In *Proceedings of the 12th Conference of the European Chapter of the Association for Computational Linguistics*, Athens, Greece, pp. 33–41.

Artstein, R. and M. Poesio (2008). Inter-Coder Agreement for Computational Linguistics. *Computational Linguistics 34*(4), 555–596.

Brin, S. and L. Page (1998). The Anatomy of a Large-Scale Hypertextual Web Search Engine. *Computer Networks 30*(1-7), 107–117.

Fellbaum, C. (1998). *WordNet: An Electronic Lexical Database (Language, Speech, and Communication).* Cambridge, MA: MIT Press.

Fernando, S. and M. Stevenson (2010). Aligning WordNet Synsets and Wikipedia Articles. In *Proceedings of the AAAI Workshop on Collaboratively-built Knowledge Sources and Artificial Intelligence*, Atlanta, GA, USA.

Meyer, C. M. and I. Gurevych (2010). How Web Communities Analyze Human Language: Word Senses in Wiktionary. In *Proceedings of the Second Web Science Conference*, Raleigh, NC, USA.

Mihalcea, R. (2007). Using Wikipedia for Automatic Word Sense Disambiguation. In *Proceedings of the North American Chapter of the Association for Computational Linguistics*, Rochester, NY, USA, pp. 196–203.

Ponzetto, S. P. and R. Navigli (2009). Large-Scale Taxonomy Mapping for Restructuring and Integrating Wikipedia. In *Proceedings of the 21th International Joint Conference on Artificial Intelligence*, Pasadena, CA, USA, pp. 2083–2088.

Ponzetto, S. P. and R. Navigli (2010). Knowledge-rich Word Sense Disambiguation rivaling supervised system. In *Proceedings of the 48th Annual Meeting of the Association for Computational Linguistics*, Uppsala, Sweden, pp. 1522–1531.

Ruiz-Casado, M., E. Alfonseca, and P. Castells (2005). Automatic Assignment of Wikipedia Encyclopedic Entries to WordNet Synsets. In *Advances in Web Intelligence*, Volume 3528 of *LNCS*, pp. 380–386. Springer Verlag.

Schmid, H. (1994). Probabilistic Part-of-Speech Tagging Using Decision Trees. In *Proceedings of the International Conference on New Methods in Language Processing*, Manchester, United Kingdom, pp. 44–49.

Suchanek, F. M., G. Kasneci, and G. Weikum (2007). Yago: A Core of Semantic Knowledge. In *Proceedings of the 16th International World Wide Web Conference*, Banff, Canada, pp. 697–706.

Toral, A., O. Ferrandez, E. Agirre, and R. Munoz (2009). A study on Linking Wikipedia categories to Wordnet using text similarity. In *Proceedings of Recent Advances in Natural Language Processing*, Borovets, Bulgaria, pp. 449–454.

Toral, A., R. Munoz, and M. Monachini (2008). Named Entity WordNet. In *Proceedings of the 6th International Conference on Language Resources and Evaluation*, Marrakech, Marocco, pp. 741–747.

Wolf, E. and I. Gurevych (2010). Aligning Sense Inventories in Wikipedia and WordNet. In *Proceedings of the 1st Workshop on Automated Knowledge Base Construction*, Grenoble, France, pp. 24–28.

Wu, F. and D. S. Weld (2008). Automatically Refining the Wikipedia Infobox Ontology. In *Proceedings of the 17th International Conference on World Wide Web*, Beijing, China, pp. 635–644.

Zesch, T., C. Müller, and I. Gurevych (2008). Extracting Lexical Semantic Knowledge from Wikipedia and Wiktionary. In *Proceedings of the 6th International Conference on Language Resources and Evaluation*, Marrakech, Marocco, pp. 1646–1652.

Recognizing Confinement in Web Texts

Megumi Ohki†
Suguru Matsuyoshi†
Junta Mizuno‡
Kentaro Inui‡
Nara Insutitute of Science and Technology†

Eric Nichols‡
Koji Murakami†*
Shouko Masuda†
Yuji Matsumoto†
Tohoku University‡

{megumi-o, shouko, matuyosi, matsu}@is.naist.jp
{eric, junta-m, inui}@tohoku.ac.jp
koji.murakami@mail.rakuten.co.jp

Abstract

In the Recognizing Textual Entailment (RTE) task, sentence pairs are classified into one of three semantic relations: ENTAILMENT, CONTRADICTION or UNKNOWN. While we find some sentence pairs hold full entailments or contradictions, there are a number of pairs that partially entail or contradict one another depending on a specific situation. These partial contradiction sentence pairs contain useful information for opinion mining and other such tasks, but it is difficult for Internet users to access this knowledge because current frameworks do not differentiate between full contradictions and partial contradictions. In this paper, under current approaches to semantic relation recognition, we define a new semantic relation known as CONFINEMENT in order to recognize this useful information. This information is classified as either CONTRADICTION or ENTAILMENT. We provide a series of *semantic templates* to recognize CONFINEMENT relations in Web texts, and then implement a system for recognizing CONFINEMENT between sentence pairs. We show that our proposed system can obtains a F-score of 61% for recognizing CONFINEMENT in Japanese-language Web texts, and it outperforms a baseline which does not use a manually compiled list of lexico-syntactic patterns to instantiate the semantic templates.

1 Introduction

On the Internet, there are various kinds of documents, and they often include conflicting opinions or differing information on a single topic. Collecting and organizing this diverse information is an important part of multi-document summarization.

When searching with a particular query on the Internet, we want information that tells us what other people think about the query: e.g. do they believe it is true or not; what are the necessary conditions for it to apply. For example, consider the hypothetical search results for the query given in (1). You get opinion (2a), which supports the query, and opinion (2b) which opposes it.

(1) *Xylitol is effective at preventing tooth decay.*

(2) a. *Xylitol can prevent tooth decay.*
    b. *Xylitol is not effective at all at preventing tooth decay.*

A major task in the Recognizing Textual Entailment (RTE) Challenge (Giampiccolo et al. (2007)) is classifying the semantic relation between a Text and a Hypothesis into ENTAILMENT, CONTRADICTION, or UNKNOWN. Murakami et al. (2009) report on the STATEMENT MAP project, the goal of which is to help Internet users evaluate the credibility of information sources by analyzing supporting evidence from a variety of viewpoints on their topics of interest and presenting them to users together with the supporting evidence in a way that makes it clear how they are related. A variety of techniques have been successfully employed in the RTE Challenge in order to recognize instances of textual entailment.

*Current affiication: Rakuten Institute of Technology

However, as far as we know, there have been no studies on recognizing sentences which specify conditions under which a query applies, despite the fact that these relations are useful information for Internet users. Such useful sentences are plentiful on the Web. Consider the following examples of CONTRADICTION and ENTAILMENT.

(3) a. *Xylitol can not prevent tooth decay* ***if it not at least 50%***.
b. *The effect of Xylitol on preventing tooth decay is* ***limited***.

In example (3a), the necessary condition to prevent tooth decay by Xylitol is "it contains at least fifty percent Xylitol". That condition is expressed by the phrase in bold in (3a). This sentence informs users that if they want to prevent tooth decay, the products they use must contain a certain amount of Xylitol to be effective. In example (3b), we obtain information on uncertainty of Xylitol's tooth decay prevention effectiveness from the phrase "*is limited*". It tells that Xylitol is not necessarily effective at preventing tooth decay, and thus it is not completely in agreement with or contradiction to the original sentence (1).

It is important to recognize the semantic relation shown in (3) because it provides more specific information about the query or specifies the conditions under which the statement holds or does not. This is valuable information for Internet users and needs to be distinguished from fully contradicting or agreeing opinions.

We call this semantic relation CONFINEMENT because it confines the situation under which a query applies. In this paper, we give a language independent definition of the CONFINEMENT relation in predicate logic and provide a framework for detecting the relation through a series of *semantic templates* that take logical and semantic features as input. We implement a system that detects CONFINEMENT relations between sentence pairs in Japanese by instantiating the semantic templates using rules and a list of lexico-semantic patterns. Finally, we conduct empirical evaluation of recognition of the CONFINEMENT relation between queries and sentences in Japanese-language Web texts.

2 Related Work

In RTE research, only three types of relations are defined: ENTAILMENT, CONTRADICTION, and UNKNOWN. RTE is an important task and has been the target of much research (Szpektor et al. (2007); Sammons et al. (2009)). However, none of the previous research has introduced relations corresponding to CONFINEMENT.

Cross-document Structure Theory (CST, Radev (2000)) is another approach to recognizing semantic relations between sentences. CST is an extended rhetorical structure analysis based on Rhetorical Structure Theory (RST). It attempts to describe the semantic relations between two or more sentences from different source documents that are related to the same topic. It defines 18 kinds of semantic relations between sentences. Etoh and Okumura (2005) constructed a Japanese Cross-document Relation Corpus and defined 14 kinds of semantic relations. It is difficult to consider CONFINEMENT relations in the CST categorical semantic relations because it focuses on comparing sentences in terms of equivalence and difference between sentences. At first glance, CONFINEMENT may seem to be defined in terms of difference between sentences, but this approach does not capture the idea of restriction on a sentence's applicability. Thus, it is beyond the scope of CST.

In the field of linguistics, Nakagawa and Mori (1995) discussed restrictions as represented in the four Japanese subordinate clause patterns. Abe (1996) researched the role of quantifiers in quantitative restrictions and the role of "だけ (only)." There is much other researches on expressions representing "confinement" in a sentence in linguistics. These expressions are useful in order to recognize phrases which contradict each other. However, as far as we know, there is no research on the relation of CONFINEMENT *between two sentences* in the linguistics literature. The absence of related research makes defining and recognizing CONFINEMENT a very challenging task.

3 The CONFINEMENT Relation

We present the definition of the CONFINEMENT relation and describe its differences from ENTAILMENT and CONTRADICTION. In essence, a pair of sentences is in the CONFINEMENT relation if either the premise or consequent of the second sentence has a certain condition or restriction, and without such condition or restriction the pair is equivalent to either ENTAILMENT or CONTRADICTION.

Consider an example of CONFINEMENT setence pair: (2a) and (3a). The statement "it (Xylitol) is not at least 50%" is a condition of the statement "Xylitol can not prevent tooth decay." It is a CONTRADICTION if the conditional statement is satisfied. Because the truth value of the whole statement depends on various conditions to be satisfied, it is important to properly define a framework to define them.

3.1 A Logical Definition of CONFINEMENT

We present a definition of CONFINEMENT in predicate logic. We define CONFINEMENT as a semantic relation between two sentences, where the first sentence corresponds to RTE's *Hypothesis*, or the user Query, and the second sentence corresponds to RTE's Text that has some semantic relation with the Query, which we want to identify.

Here we consider sentence pairs where the Query matches the logical pattern $\forall x(P(x) \rightarrow C(x))$, where we call $P(x)$ the Premise and $C(x)$ the Consequence. There are many ways of representing sentences as logical expressions, and we think that the logical pattern $(\forall(P(x) \rightarrow C(x)))$ can cover a variety of queries. For example, the sentence "*Xylitol is effective at preventing tooth decay.*" can be represented as $\forall x(\text{isXylitol}(x) \rightarrow \text{effectiveAtPreventingToothDecay}(x))$. Consider the case where one sentence contains only a Consequence. This case can be regarded as a special case of the above formula. We write such a sentence as $\forall x(T \rightarrow C(x))$ showing that the Premise is always True.

In this paper, we limit discussion of the CONFINEMENT relation to the Query matching to the above logical pattern. Recognizing CONFINEMENT between the Text and the Query having more complex semantic patterns is an area of future work. Here, we split the definition of CONFINEMENT into subtypes according to: (i) conditions to satisfy in addition to the Premise, and (ii) limitations on the degree of the Consequence.

Premise side Additional conditions for achieving the Consequence

Explicit constraint

Some conditional sentences use an expression correspoinding to logical "only if," which explicitly means two way conditions as the following formula.

$$\begin{aligned}\forall x((P(x) \land AdditionalCondition(x) \rightarrow C(x)) \\ \land(P(x) \land \neg AdditionalCondition(x) \rightarrow \neg C(x)))\end{aligned} \tag{1}$$

For example, S_1 in Table 1, "*Xylitol is effective at preventing cavities only when it is 100%*", explicitly specify that Xylitol is effective if it is 100% and is not effective if it is not 100%. So, we assume the form of the above formula for this type of statement.

Implicit constraint

This type of sentence specifies an additional condition on the Premise and is represented by the following formula. The Premise needs to be satisfied for the consequence to be achieved.

$$\forall x((P(x) \land AdditionalCondition(x) \rightarrow C(x)) \tag{2}$$

Example S_5 in Table 1 says "Xylitol is effective at preventing tooth decay if it is 100%", which is assumed by Formula (2). S_5 does not contain an expression such as "only (だけ)", which explicitly specifies that $C(x)$ does not hold when an additional condition is not satisfied. One may understand that it implicitly means "Xylitol is not effective at preventing tooth decay if it is not 100%," but S_5 does not structly require this.

Consequence side Constraints on the degree of achieving the Consequence

There are sentences in partial entailment or contradiction where the degree of achieving of the Consequence is limited. To represent these limitations on the Consequence side, we define a CONFINEMENT relation where the degrees of the Consequence are limited as in Example (3b). We define the following formula to represent these limitations on the Consequence side.

$$\forall x((P(x) \rightarrow C_r(x)) \tag{3}$$

$C_r(x)$ represents $C(x)$ with additional restriction. For example, S_3 in Table 1 says that Xylitol is somewhat effective at preventing tooth decay, which means that there are cases in which Xylitol can not prevent tooth decay. In the case of S_3, $C_r(x)$ is "is a bit effective". This type of CONFINEMENT provides valuable information about Xylitol's limited ability to promote dental hygiene in S_3.

All CONFINEMENTs on the Consequence side are of type EXPLICIT CONFINEMENT, because they explicitly mean that a part of the Consequence is achieved but no other parts are achieved.

3.2 Semantic Templates

We propose a series of semantic templates to classify sentence pairs into one of the CONFINEMENT relation subtypes we define. The semantic templates take a set of features as input and use their values to categorize the sentence pair. In Section 4, we evaluate the coverage of the semantic templates by classifying a small set of sentence pairs using manually set feature values. In Section 6, we provide more realistic evaluation by using a proposed system to set the feature values automatically and classify sentence pairs as ENTAILMENT / CONTRADICTION, or CONFINEMENT.

We assume that each sentence consists of a Premise and Consequence, and that each sentence pair which has a CONFINEMENT relation contains at least one additional condition or one additional limitation as defined in Section 3.1.

We know that there are a variety of expressions that indicate the presence of a CONFINEMENT relation. For example, both "*Only 100% pure Xylitol is effective at preventing tooth decay.*" and "*Xylitol is not effective at preventing tooth decay unless it is 100% pure.*" are CONFINEMENTs of "*Xylitol is effective at preventing tooth decay.*" Since it is impossible to handle all possible expressions that indicate CONFINEMENT, we focus on covering as many as possible with three features: (1) the type of constraint, (2) the type of Premise, and (3) the type of Consequence. The features are defined in more detail below.

IF-Constraint This feature indicates the type of logical constraint in the Text sentence. Its values can be "IF," "ONLY-IF."

Premise This feature indicates the type of Premise in the Text sentence. The value "P+A" or "notP+A" means there is an Additional Condition on the Premise. The value "P" or "notP" means there is just a Premise. "not" represents the Premise have a negation.

Consequence This feature indicates the type of Consequence. Its possible values are "C" (just a Consequence), "notC" (negated Consequence), "C_r" or "notC_r" (certain partial Consequence).

Semantic templates consist of a tuple of four feature values and a mapping to the confinement type they indicate. A full list of templates is given in Table 1. In the templates, a wildcard asterisk "*" indicates that any feature value can match in that slot of the template. The abbreviations ENT, CONT and CONF stand for ENTAILMENT, CONFINEMENT and CONFINEMENT respectively.

Semantic templates are applied in turn from top pattern by determining the value of each feature and looking up the corresponding relation type in Table 1. We give a classification examples below. The user query is sentence S_0. Sentences S_1 are Web texts.

Query : S_0. Xylitol is effective at preventing tooth decay.

Text [*ONLY-IF* $P(x) \wedge AC(x)$ *then* $C(x)$]: S_1. Xylitol is effective at preventing tooth decay when you take it every day without fail.

In Example, *IF-Constraint* is "ONLY-IF", *Premise* is "P+A", and the type of *Consequence* is "C". This instance has an additional condition and the Consequence matches the Query, so it is identified as an EXPLICIT CONFINEMENT.

4 Verifying Semantic Templates

In this section, we verify the effectiveness of semantic templates in recognizing CONFINEMENT relations by testing them on real-world data in Japanese. To directly evaluate the quality of the templates, we construct a small data set of sentence pairs and manually annotate them with the correct values for each of the features defined in Section 3.2.

4.1 Data

We constructed the Development set and the Open-test set of sample Japanese user queries and Internet text pairs following the methodology of Murakami et al. (2009). However, Murakami et al. (2009) annotated Query-Text pairs with coarse-grained AGREEMENT and CONFLICT relations that subsume the

Table 1: Semantic templates for recognizing CONFINEMENT

Semantic features			Relation	Number of positive example	Number of negative example	Example
IF-constraint	*Premise*	*Consequence*				S_0:キシリトールは虫歯予防に効果がある. Xylitol is effective at preventing tooth decay.
ONLY-IF	P+A	*	EXPLICIT CONF	8	0	S_1:キシリトールは 100%の時にだけ虫歯予防に効果があります. Xylitol is effective at preventing tooth decay only when it is 100%.
ONLY-IF	notP+A	*	EXPLICIT CONF	0	0	S_2:キシリトールは 50%未満でない時にしか虫歯予防に効果がありません. Xylitol is effective at preventing tooth decay only when it is not under 50%.
*	*	C_r	EXPLICIT CONF	11	0	S_3:キシリトールは虫歯予防に僅かに効果があります. Xylitol is a bit effective at preventing tooth decay.
*	*	notC_r	EXPLICIT CONF	12	0	S_4:キシリトールは虫歯予防にほとんど効果がありません. Xylitol is not almost of effective at preventing tooth decay.
IF	P+A	*	IMPLICT CONF	62	0	S_5:キシリトールは 100%ならば虫歯予防に効果があります. Xylitol is effective at preventing tooth decay if it is 100%.
IF	notP+A	*	IMPLICIT CONF	1	0	S_6:キシリトールは 100%でないならば虫歯予防に効果がありません. Xylitol is not effective at preventing tooth decay if it is not 100%
IF	P	C	ENT	279	0	S_7:キシリトールを食べると虫歯予防に効果があります. Xylitol is effective at preventing tooth decay if it is eaten.
IF	notP	C	CONT	0	0	S_8:キシリトールを食べないと虫歯予防に効果があります. Xylitol is effective at preventing tooth decay if it is not eaten.
IF	P	notC	CONT	13	0	S_9:キシリトールを食べると虫歯予防に効果がありません. Xylitol is not effective at preventing tooth decay if it is eaten.
IF	notP	notC	ENT	0	0	S_{10}:キシリトールを食べないと虫歯予防に効果がありせん. Xylitol is not effective at preventing tooth decay if it is not eaten.
ONLY-IF	P	C	ENT	3	0	S_{11}:キシリトールを食べたときだけ虫歯予防に効果があります. Xylitol is effective at preventing tooth decay only when it is eaten.
ONLY-IF	notP	C	CONT	0	0	S_{12}:キシリトールを食べなかったときだけ虫歯予防に効果があります. Xylitol is effective at preventing tooth decay only when it is not eaten.
ONLY-IF	P	notC	CONT	0	0	S_{13}:キシリトールを食べたときだけ虫歯予防に効果がありせん. Xylitol is effective at preventing tooth decay only when it is eaten.
ONLY-IF	notP	notC	ENT	0	0	S_{14}:キシリトールを食べなかったときだけ虫歯予防に効果がありせん. Xylitol is not effective at preventing tooth decay only when it is not eaten.

Table 2: Data set (Counts of sentences out of parenthesis and statements in parentheses)

	Entailment	Contradiction	Confinement	All
Development	258 (282)	8 (13)	79 (94)	345 (389)
Open-test	230	170	200	600

RTE relations of ENTAILMENT and CONTRADICTION. As our task is to discriminate between CONFINEMENT and RTE relations, we annotate each sentence pair or each statement[1] pair with one of the following relations instead: ENTAILMENT, CONTRADICTION, or CONFINEMENT. In the case of CONFINEMENT, we annotate Query-Text pairs which are not full ENTAILMENT or CONTRADICTION but these Text partially agrees and disagrees with the Query. Annotations were checked by two native speakers of Japanese, and any sentence pair where annotation agreement is not reached was discarded. Table 2 shows that how many sentences or statements are in each data set. Annotated statements counts are written in parentheses. We use the Development set for evaluation of verifying semantic templates and develop list of lexical and syntactic patterns for semantic features extraction, and the Open-test set for evaluation in Section 6.

4.2 Verification Result

After the data was prepared, we annotated it with the correct feature values for use with the semantic templates. This was done by manually checking for words or phrases in the sentences that indicated one of the features in Table 1. Once the features were set, we used them to classify each sentence pair.

We give the numbers of instances that we could confirm for each pattern in the sixth column of Table 1 and the numbers of negative instances in the seventh column, which satisfy semantic template but does not agree Relation values in the fifth column. As a result we find that there were no statement pairs that could not be successfully classified. We grasp CONFINEMENT relation with semantic templates for the most part. This verification data does not cover all combinations of patterns in our semantic templates, so we can not rule out the possibility of existence of an exception that cannot be classified by the semantic templates. However, we find these results to be an encouraging indication of the usefulness of semantic templates. Here are some example classifications found in the verification data.

Coordinate clauses Combining multiple of IMPLICIT CONFINEMENTs results in an EXPLICIT CONFINEMENT relation

(4)S_0. ステロイドは副作用がある.

Steroid has side-effects.

S_1. ステロイドの副作用はステロイド剤を長期に使用した場合におこることが多いですが短

[1]Murakami et al. define a "statement" as the smallest unit that can convey a complete thought or viewpoint. In practice, this can be a sentence or something smaller such as a clause.

期間の使用では副作用の心配はありません.

Long-term use of steroid causes side-effects, but there is no need to worry about side-effects in short-term usage.

In Example (4), S_1 is an EXPLICIT CONFINEMENT for S_0. This is derived from the combination of CONFINEMENT of the two coordinate clauses of S_1: the former phrase "Long-term use of steroid causes side-effects" of S_1 is an IMPLICIT CONFINEMENT for S_0 by our semantic templates and the latter phrase is an IMPLICIT CONFINEMENT for S_0.

Additional information for whole Query Combining of a CONTRADICTION and an IMPLICIT CONFINEMENT result in an EXPLICIT CONFINEMENT

(5) S_0. キシリトールは虫歯予防に効果的だ.

Xylitol is effective at preventing tooth decay.

S_1. 虫歯予防はキシリトールだけで済むわけではなく,基本的には規則正しい食生活とキシリトールを毎食後とることで虫歯の予防ができます.

Tooth decay can not be prevented with Xylitol alone, but it can be fundamentally prevented with an appropriate diet and by taking Xylitol after every meal.

The first clause before the comma in S_1 of Example (5) corresponds to the entire sentence of S_0. The second clause after the comma helps us recognize that it is a CONFINEMENT relation. This instance is also a combination of semantic templates, so we need to recognize negation of each statement and adversative conjunction but we do not need to add new features to Table 1.

5 Proposed System

We propose a system which uses semantic templates for recognizing CONFINEMENT consists of six steps: (I) linguistic analysis, (II) structural alignment, (III) Premise and Consequence identification, (IV) semantic feature extraction, (V) adversative conjunction identification, and (VI) semantic template application. Figure 1 shows the work flow of the system. This system takes as input corresponding to S_0 and S_1, and return a semantic relation.

5.1 I. Linguistic Analysis

In linguistic analysis, we conduct word segmentation, POS tagging, dependency parsing, and extended modality analysis. This linguistic analysis acts as the basis for alignment and semantic feature extraction. For syntactic analysis, we identify words and POS tags with the Japanese morphological analyser Mecab[2], and we use the Japanese dependency parser CaboCha (Kudo and Matsumoto (2002)) to produce dependency trees. We also conduct extended modality analysis using the resources provided by Matsuyoshi et al. (2010).

5.2 II. Structural Alignment

To identify the consequence of S_0 in S_1, we use Structural Alignment (Mizuno et al. (2010)). In Structural Alignment, dependency parent-child links are aligned across sentences using a variety of resources to ensure semantic relatedness.

5.3 III. Premise and Consequence identification

In this step, we identify the Premise and the Consequence in S_1. When a sentence pair satisfies all items is satisfying, we can identify a focused chunk as the Consequence in S_1:

1. A chunk's modality in S_0 is assertion, this chunk is the Consequence in S_0
2. A chunk in S_1 align with the Consequence in S_0

We identify the Premise in S_1 when a sentence pair satisfies first, and either second or third item of the following conditions:

1. A case particle of chunks in S_0 is either "が (agent marker)" or "は (topic marker)" and these chunks are children of the Consequence in S_0's dependency tree
2. The subject in S_0 aligns with the subject of S_1
3. All of the dependants of the expression "には (to, for)" have alignments in S_0 dependency tree

[2] http://chasen.org/taku/ software/mecab/.

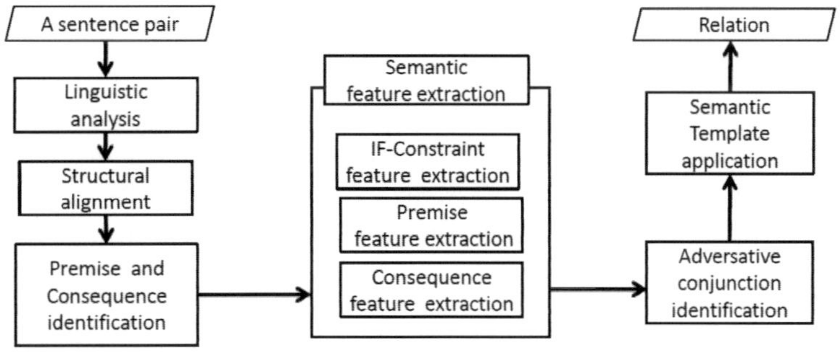

Figure 1: An overview of a proposal system to recognize CONFINEMENT

5.4 IV. Semantic Feature Extraction

We extract features for the semantic templates using a list of lexical and syntactic patterns. These patterns were manually compiled using the development data set introduced in Section 4. Features for the semantic templates are then automatically extracted by applying these patterns to input sentence pairs. The following overviews our extraction approach for each feature.

5.4.1 IF-Constraint Feature Extraction

Using CaboCha, we manually constructed lists of words and their POS that are indicators of the semantic condition under which a Premise occurs. We extract as features any words in the input sentences that appear in the list with the corresponding POS. The "IF" lexical type lists conjunctions that are the results of a conditional chunk or noun phrases that indicate a case or situation. The "ONLY-IF" lexical type is used to represent the most constraining situations. The following is our list of expressions.

⋆ **IF:** 場合 (in case), 時/とき/と (when), ば/なら/たら (if), で (with)

⋆ **ONLY-IF:** 限り/かぎり (for this time), だけ/しか/こそ (only), 初めて (for the first time), には (to, for)

5.4.2 Premise Feature Extraction

We treat the words or phrases which are extracted from the constraint as conditions, and need to decide whether a given condition is the Premise or an additional condition for the Premise. The *Premise* is set to "P" when first step and either the second or third step of the following conditions are satisfied, and it is set to "P+A" otherwise:

1. ⋆ The condition have children in the S_1's dependency tree or the condition's children are not aligned to chunks in S_0
2. ⋆ The condition's parent in S_0's dependency tree has any chunk with a child aligned with the Consequence in S_0, or the condition's parent is not aligned with chunks in S_0
3. ⋆ The condition's parent does not have any expression with the meaning of "use" in the S_0's dependency tree

When these step are satisfied and negation exists in conditional chunks, *Premise* is set to "notP+A," if these step are not satisfied, *Premise* is set to "notP." In the third step, we identify expressions with the meaning of "use" with our lexical list. For example 使う (use), 食べる (eat), 摂取 (take) and so on. If the condition's parent has words in our lexical list, we identify that "Xylitol" and "eating Xylitol" and "using Xylitol" are equivalent.

5.4.3 Consequence Feature Extraction

This feature is used to indicate the semantic relationship between Consequences of the sentences pair. Sentences with Consequences that share a certain amount of similarity in polarity and syntax are judged to have ENTAILMENT, otherwise they are in CONTRADICTION. In order to be judged as ENTAILMENT, the following conditions must all be true:

1. The modality of the Consequences must be identical.
2. The polarity of the Consequences must be identical as indicated by the resources in (Sumida et al. (2008))
3. The Premises of both sentences must align with each other

4. ⋆ The sentences must not contain expressions that limit range or degree such as "ほとんど (almost)" or "程度 (degree)"

When all item are satisfied, the *Consequence* is set to "C", otherwise it is set to "notC." We identify whether the consequence has expressions which limit the degree or not. The *Consequence* is set to "C_r" or "notC_r" when the following all conditions is satisfied:

1. Any of the children of the Consequence align with a chunk in S_0's dependency tree.
2. ⋆ There are expressions limiting the degree of the Consequence or the siblings in S_1's dependency tree

When this two steps are satisfied and the all four steps to judge whether sentence pairs is ENTAILMENT or not are not satisfied, *Consequence* is set to "notC_r."

5.5 V. Adversative Conjunction Identification

We manually compiled a list of target expressions including conjunctions such as "が (but)." When a S_1 chunk containing an adversative conjunction that aligns with the Premise of S_0 or the S_0's Premise depends on S_1 chunk containing an adversative conjunction, we set each feature set in a chunk before an adversative conjunction and after an adversative conjunction to semantic templates.

5.6 VI. Semantic Template Application

We apply semantic feature extracted in Step IV to semantic templates. If S_1 matches multiple semantic templates with an adversative conjunction from Step V, we combine the semantic templates. We get a relation for a sentence pair in this step.

5.7 Example of Semantic Features Extraction

Feature extraction is illustrated in greater detail in the examples S_0 which is the query and S_1 in Table 1. First, we identify words represented *IF-Constraint* is "ONLY-IF": "時 (when)" is in S_1 and the conditional chunk has a word "だけ (only)." Next, we evaluate each the type of Premise of each chunk to determine if it is a premise or an additional condition. The subject word "Xylitol" align between S_0 and S_1, and the conditional chunk's sibling in dependency tree of S_1 is a chunk which has the subject. And the conditional chunk have a child which is not aligned any chunk in S_0, it is "100%の (100%)." And the conditional chunk has no negations. So, *Premise* is set to "P+A." Finally, we check if the consequences to the conditions are aligned to the verbs and nouns indicating consequences in S_0: "prevent" and "is effective" are aligned, the modality and polarity of the Consequence are identical, these depended on by the condition, and the Consequence has no expressions which limited range or degree. *Consequence* is set to "C." We set the semantic template features and get a result which the sentences relation is EXPLICIT CONFINEMENT. Ideally patterns for setting semantic feature for semantic templates should be learned automatically, but this remains an area of future work. Nonetheless, our current experiment gives a good measure of the effectiveness of semantic templates in recognizing CONFINEMENT relations.

6 Evaluation

In Section 4, we verified that the semantic templates defined in Section 3.2 can successfully classify semantic relations as CONFINEMENT given the correct feature values. In this Section, we present the results of an experiment in a more realistic setting by using semantic templates together with the features automatically extracted as described with our proposed system in Section 5 to determine whether or not a sentence pair has a CONFINEMENT relation.

6.1 Setting up Evaluation

While more research on recognizing ENTAILMENT or CONTRADICTION between sentences pairs is necessary, it is important to recognize new relations that cannot be analysed in existing frameworks in order to provide Internet users with the information they need. Thus, We assume that unrelated sentence pairs will be discarded before classification, in this experiment we focus only on the recognition of CONFINEMENT relations. So our goal in this experiment is to classify between CONFINEMENT and NOT CONFINEMENT. We will evaluate determining whether CONFINEMENT sentence pairs are Explicit or Implicit in future. In our experiment, we used a gold data for structural alignment to evaluate semantic feature extraction.

Table 3: Results of recognizing confinement relations with our proposal system

	Recall	Precision	F-Score
proposed system	0.65(129/200)	0.57(129/225)	0.61
baseline system	0.96(192/200)	0.34(192/562)	0.50

Table 4: Instances of incorrect classification

		S_0	S_1
False Negative	A	イソフラボンで健康を回復できる. A person can regain their health with isoflavon.	イソフラボンの健康への効果に期待しすぎての過剰摂取は禁物です. Excess intake of isoflavon to boost its health effects is prohibited.
	B	キシリトールは虫歯予防に効果がある. Xylitol has effects on preventing tooth decay.	歯を磨く・規則正しい食生活を送る等がきちんと行われている上でキシリトールを用いることが虫歯予防に効果的となるのです. The use of xylitol is effective at preventing tooth decay when done while eating properly and brushing one's teeth regularly.
False Positive	C	キシリトールは虫歯を予防することができる. Xylitol can prevent tooth decay.	キシリトールを口にしていれば、虫歯を予防できると考えるのは大きな間違いです. It is a big mistake to think that one can prevent tooth decay if they put Xylitol in their mouth.
	D	ステロイドで病気は改善できる. Steroids can cure illnesses.	アトピー性皮膚炎は、ステロイドの使用を止めれば完治する. Atrophic dermatitis will heal completely if steroid use is stopped.
	E	ステロイドは副作用が懸念される. Side effects are a worry for steroids.	ステロイドの副作用は、どのくらいの量でどのくらいの期間使い続ければ現れるかは人それぞれです. The amount of steroids or period of time that causes side effects differs from person to person.

6.2 Baseline System

We developed a baseline system that does not use our manually-compiled lexico-syntactic patterns in order to act as a point of comparison for the proposed system in evaluating their contribution to CONFINEMENT recognition.

The baseline system consists of performing all of the steps from of our proposed system that do not rely on manually compiled lexico-syntactic patterns. Step relying on these resources are marked with a $\star$ in Section 5 and are skipped in the baseline. Essentially, we conduct Steps I, II, and III, the parts of Step IV that can be done without manually-compiled patterns, and, finally, Step VI.

In Step IV, we determine if there are any limitations on the Consequence in the Consequence Feature subset, but we do not judge whether the Consequence is ENTAILMENT or CONTRADICTION in the baseline system.

6.3 Result and Error Analysis

The results are given in Table 3. We find that our system has much higher precision than the baseline, improving by over 20%. In our system, the list of semantic patterns is effective at recognizing CONFINEMENT. On the other hand recall has gone down compared to the baseline. The baseline judged that almost sentences are CONFINEMENT, so the list of semantic patterns employed in our rule-based system is useful at eliminating false positives. Table 4 shows some instances of incorrect classification. Each instance is a pair (S_0, S_1).

Example A-S_1 means "Excess intake of isoflavon can not boost one's health" and "excess intake" is an additional condition for A-S_1. In this case "excess" is a lexical specifier of the specific condition and is indicated by the particle "は". The particle "は (topic marker)" is not currently used as a feature in the semantic templates since it is very noisy, so this instance can not be detected. We need to expand our method of acquiring semantic patterns to better handle such cases.

The additional condition phrase in Example B-S_1 modifies "The use of Xylitol" instead of "is effective at preventing tooth decay", preventing us from properly recognizing the limiting condition in this case. We need to conduct deeper scopal analysis to determine when the modifier of an embedded chunk should be considered as an additional condition.

Example C-S_1 is an instance where the system fails to recognize that "put in their mouth" is an expression meaning "use" since our lists of lexical words for features did not have it. We should increase our ability to recognize synonyms of "to use" by automatically mining data for paraphrases or approaching it as a machine learning task in order to handle examples like C-S_1. On the other hands "if steroid use is stopped" in example D-S_1 is the premise which should indicate an IF condition and Negation exists, however we can not recognize it correctly since the phrase lacks negation. We will make a list of words and phrases that are antonyms of "use" in order to recognize such instances.

The condition in example E-S_1 is about how side-effects appear, and not a condition for the other sentence example E-S_0. This instance requires detailed semantic analysis and cannot be solved with alignment-based approaches. It represents a very difficult class of problems.

7 Conclusion

On the Web, much of the information and opinions we encounter indicates the conditions or limitations under which a statement is true. This information is important to Internet users who are interested in determining the validity of a query of interest, but such information cannot be represented under the prevalent RTE framework containing only ENTAILMENT and CONTRADICTION.

In this paper, we provided a logical definition of the CONFINEMENT relation and showed how it could be used to represent important information that is omitted under an RTE framework. We also proposed a set of semantic templates that use set of features extracted from sentences pairs to recognize CONFINEMENT relations between two sentences. Preliminary investigations showed that given correct feature input, semantic templates could effectively recognize CONFINEMENT relations.

In addition, we presented empirical evaluation of the effectiveness of semantic templates and automatically-extracted features at recognizing CONFINEMENT between user queries and Web text pairs, and conducted error analysis of the results. Currently, our system does not deal with unknown instances well since it extracts features for semantic template using manually constructed lexical patterns. In future work, we will learn features for the semantic templates directly from data to better handle unknown instances.

Acknowledgment

This work is supported by the National Institute of Information and Communications Technology Japan.

References

Abe, T. (1996). Restriction with ‘dake’ and modification with quantifier. *Tsukuba Japanese Research 1*, 4–20. in Japanese.

Etoh, J. and M. Okumura (2005). Cross-document relationship between sentences corpus. In *Proceedings of the 14th Annual Meeting of the Association for Natural Language Processing*, pp. 482–485. (in Japanese).

Giampiccolo, D., B. Magnini, I. Dagan, and B. Dolan (2007). The third pascal recognizing textual entailment challenge. In *Proceedings of the ACL-PASCAL Workshop on Textual Entailment and Paraphrasing*, RTE '07, Morristown, NJ, USA, pp. 1–9. Association for Computational Linguistics.

Kudo, T. and Y. Matsumoto (2002). Japanese dependency analysis using cascaded chunking. In *CoNLL 2002: In Proceedings of the 6th Conference on Natural Language Learning 2002 (COLING 2002 Post-Conference Workshops)*, pp. 63–69.

Matsuyoshi, S., M. Eguchi, C. Sao, K. Murakami, K. Inui, and Y. Matsumoto (2010). Annotating event mentions in text with modality, focus, and source information. In *Proceedings of the 7th International Language Resources and Evaluation (LREC'10)*.

Mizuno, J., H. Goto, Y. Watanabe, K. Murakami, K. Inui, and Y. Matsumoto (2010). Local Structural Alignment for Recognizing Semantic Relations between Sentences. In *Proceedings of IPSJ-NL196*. (in Japanese).

Murakami, K., S. Matsuyoshi, K. Inui, and Y. Matsumoto (2009). A corpus of statement pairs with semantic relations in Japanese. In *Proceedings of the 15th Annual Meeting of the Association for Natural Language Processing*.

Murakami, K., E. Nichols, S. Matsuyoshi, A. Sumida, S. Masuda, K. Inui, and Y. Matsumoto (2009). Statement map: Assisting information credibility analysis by visualizing arguments. In *Proceedings of the 3rd ACM Workshop on Information Credibility on the Web (WICOW 2009)*, pp. 43–50.

Nakagawa, H. and T. Mori (1995). Pragmatic analysis of aspect morphemes in manual sentences in Japanese. *The Association for Natural Language Processing* 2(4), 19 – 36. in Japanese.

Radev, D. R. (2000). Common theory of information fusion from multiple text sources step one: Cross-document structure. In *Proceedings of the 1st SIGdial workshop on Discourse and dialogue*, pp. 74–83.

Sammons, M., V. G. V. Vydiswaran, T. Vieira, N. Johri, M.-W. Chang, D. Goldwasser, V. Srikumar, G. Kundu, Y. Tu, K. Small, J. Rule, Q. Do, and D. Roth (2009). Relation alignment for textual entailment recognition. In *Proceedings of Recognizing Textual Entailment 2009*.

Sumida, A., N. Yoshinaga, and K. Torisawa (2008). Boosting precision and recall of hyponymy relation acquisition from hierarchical layouts in Wikipedia. In *Proceedings of the 6th International Language Resources and Evaluation (LREC'08)*.

Szpektor, I., E. Shnarch, and I. Dagan (2007). Instance-based evaluation of entailment rule acquisition. In *Proceedings of the 45th Annual Meeting of the Association of Computational Linguistics*, pp. 456–463.

Abductive Reasoning with a Large Knowledge Base for Discourse Processing

Ekaterina Ovchinnikova
University of Osnabrück
eovchinn@uos.de

Niloofar Montazeri
USC ISI
niloofar@isi.edu

Theodore Alexandrov
University of Bremen
theodore@uni-bremen.de

Jerry R. Hobbs
USC ISI
hobbs@isi.edu

Michael C. McCord
IBM Research
mcmccord@us.ibm.com

Rutu Mulkar-Mehta
USC ISI
me@rutumulkar.com

Abstract

This paper presents a discourse processing framework based on weighted abduction. We elaborate on ideas described in Hobbs et al. (1993) and implement the abductive inference procedure in a system called Mini-TACITUS. Particular attention is paid to constructing a large and reliable knowledge base for supporting inferences. For this purpose we exploit such lexical-semantic resources as WordNet and FrameNet. We test the proposed procedure and the obtained knowledge base on the Recognizing Textual Entailment task using the data sets from the RTE-2 challenge for evaluation. In addition, we provide an evaluation of the semantic role labeling produced by the system taking the Frame-Annotated Corpus for Textual Entailment as a gold standard.

1 Introduction

In this paper, we elaborate on a semantic processing framework based on a mode of inference called *abduction*, or inference to the best explanation. In logics, abduction is a kind of inference which arrives at an explanatory hypothesis given an observation. Hobbs et al. (1993) describe how abductive reasoning can be applied to the discourse processing problem viewing the process of interpreting sentences in discourse as the process of providing the best explanation of why the sentence would be true. In this framework, interpreting a sentence means 1) proving its logical form, 2) merging redundancies where possible, and 3) making assumptions where necessary. As the reader will see later in this paper, abductive reasoning as a discourse processing technique helps to solve many pragmatic problems such as reference resolution, the interpretation of noun compounds, the resolution of some kinds of syntactic, and semantic ambiguity as a by-product. We adopt this approach. Specifically, we use a system we have built called *Mini-TACITUS*[1] (Mulkar et al., 2007) that provides the expressivity of logical inference but also allows probabilistic, fuzzy, or defeasible inference and includes measures of the "goodness" of abductive proofs and hence of interpretations of texts and other situations.

The success of a discourse processing system based on inferences heavily depends on a knowledge base. The main contribution of this paper is in showing how a large and reliable knowledge base can be obtained by exploiting existing lexical semantic resources and can be successfully applied to reasoning tasks on a large scale. In particular, we experiment with axioms extracted from WordNet, see Fellbaum (1998), and FrameNet, see Ruppenhofer et al. (2006). In axiomatizing FrameNet we rely on the study described in Ovchinnikova et al. (2010).

We evaluate our inference system and the obtained knowledge base in recognizing textual entailment (RTE). As the reader will see in the following sections, inferences carried out by Mini-TACITUS are fairly general and not tuned for a particular application. We decided to test our approach on RTE because this is a well-defined task that captures major semantic inference needs across many natural language

[1] *http://www.rutumulkar.com/download/TACITUS/tacitus.php*

processing applications, such as question answering, information retrieval, information extraction, and document summarization. For evaluation, we have chosen the RTE-2 data set (Bar-Haim et al., 2006), because besides providing text-hypothesis pairs and a gold standard this data set has been annotated with FrameNet frame and role labels (Burchardt and Pennacchiotti, 2008) which gives us the possibility of evaluating our frame and role labeling based on the axioms extracted from FrameNet.

2 NL Pipeline and Abductive Reasoning

Our natural language pipeline produces interpretations of texts given the appropriate knowledge base. A text is first input to the English Slot Grammar (ESG) parser (McCord, 1990, 2010). For each segment, the parse produced by ESG is a dependency tree that shows both surface and deep structure. The deep structure is exhibited via a word sense predication for each node, with logical arguments. These logical predications form a good start on a logical form (LF) for the whole segment. An add-on to ESG converts the parse tree into a LF in the style of Hobbs (1985). The LF is a conjunction of predications, which have generalized entity arguments that can be used for showing relationships among the predications. These LFs are used by the downstream components.

The interpretation of the text is carried out by an inference system called Mini-TACITUS using weighted abduction as described in detail in Hobbs et al. (1993). Mini-TACITUS tries to prove the logical form of the text, allowing assumptions where necessary. Where the system is able to prove parts of the LF, it is anchoring it in what is already known from the overall discourse or from a knowledge base. Where assumptions are necessary, it is gaining new information. Obviously, there are many possible proofs in this procedure. A cost function on proofs enables the system to chose the "best" (the cheapest) interpretation. The key factors involved in assigning a cost are the following: 1) proofs with fewer assumptions are favored, 2) short proofs are favored over long ones, 3) plausible axioms are favored over less plausible axioms, and 4) proofs are favored that exploit the inherent implicit redundancy in text.

Let us illustrate the procedure with a simple example. Suppose that we want to construct the best interpretation of the sentence *John composed a sonata*. As a by-product, the procedure will disambiguate between two readings of *compose*, namely between the "form" reading instantiated for example in the sentence *Three representatives composed a committee*, and the "create art" meaning instantiated in the given sentence. After being processed by the parser, the sentence will be assigned the following logical form where the numbers (20) after every proposition correspond to the default costs of these propositions.[2] The total cost of this logical form is equal to 60.

John(x1):20 & *compose*(e1,x1,x2):20 & *sonata*(x2):20

Suppose our knowledge base contains the following axioms:
1) *form*(e0,x1,x2):90 $\rightarrow$ *compose*(e0,x1,x2)
2) *create_art*(e0,x1,x2):50 & *art_piece*(x2):40 $\rightarrow$ *compose*(e0,x1,x2)
3) *art_piece*(x1):90 $\rightarrow$ *sonata*(x1)

Unlike deductive axioms, abductive axioms should be read "right to left". Thus, the propositions on the right hand side (*compose*, *sonata*) correspond to an input, whereas the left hand side propositions will be assumed given the input. The number assigned to each proposition on the left hand side shows what percentage of the total input cost the assumption of this proposition will cost.[3] For example, if the proposition *compose* costs 20 then the assumption of *form* will cost 18.

Two interpretations can be constructed for the given logical form. The first one is the result of the application of axioms 1 and 3. Note that the costs of the backchained propositions (*compose*, *sonata*) are

[2]The actual value of the default costs of the input propositions does not matter, because, as the reader will see in this section, the axiom weights which affect the costs of the resulting interpretations are given as *percentages* of the input proposition costs. The only heuristic we use here concerns setting all costs of the input propositions to be equal (all propositions cost 20 in the discussed example). This heuristic needs a further investigation to be approved or modified.

[3]The axiom weights in the given example are arbitrary.

set to 0, because their costs are now carried by the newly introduces assumptions (*form*, *art_piece*). The total cost of the first interpretation **I1** is equal to 56.

I1: *John*(x1):20 & *compose*(e1,x1,x2):0 & *sonata*(x2):0 & *form*(e1,x1,x2):18 & *art_piece*(x2):18

The second interpretation is constructed in two steps. First, axioms 2 and 3 are applied as follows.

I2$_1$: *John*(x1):20 & *compose*(e1,x1,x2):0 & *sonata*(x2):0 &
create_art(e1,x1,x2):10 & *art_piece*(x2):8 & *art_piece*(x2):18

The total cost of **I2**$_1$ is equal to 56. This interpretation is redundant, because it contains the proposition *art_piece* twice. The procedure will merge propositions with the same predicate, setting the corresponding arguments of these propositions to be equal and assigning the minimum of the costs to the result of merging. The idea behind such mergings is that if an assumption has already been made then there is no need to make it again. The final form of the second interpretation **I2**$_2$ with the cost of 38 is as follows. The "create art" meaning of *compose* has been brought forward because of the implicit redundancy in the sentence which facilitated the disambiguation.

I2$_2$: *John*(x1):20 & *compose*(e1,x1,x2):0 & *sonata*(x2):0 & *create_art*(e1,x1,x2):10 &
art_piece(x2):8

Thus, on each reasoning step the procedure 1) applies axioms to propositions with non-zero costs and 2) merges propositions with the same predicate, assigning the lowest cost to the result of merging. Reasoning terminates when no more axioms can be applied.[4] The procedure favors the cheapest interpretations. Among them, the shortest proofs are favored, i.e. if two interpretations have the same cost then the one which has been constructed with fewer axiom application steps is considered to be "better".

It is easy to see that changing weights of axioms can crucially influence the reasoning process. Axiom weights can help to propagate more frequent and reliable inferences and to distinguish between "real" abduction and deduction. For example, an axiom backchaining from *dog* to *animal* should in the general case have a weight below 100, because it is cheap to assume that there is an animal if there is a dog; it is a reliable deduction. On the contrary, assuming *dog* given *animal* should have a weight above 100.

In order to avoid undesirable mergings, we introduce non-merge constraints. For example, in the sentence *John reads a book and Bill reads a book* the two *read* propositions should not be merged because they refer to different actions. This is ensured by the following non-merge constraint: if not all arguments of two propositions (which are not nouns) with the same predicate can be merged, then these propositions cannot be merged. The constraint implies that in the sentence above two *read* propositions cannot be merged, because *John* being the first argument of the first *read* cannot be merged with *Bill*.[5] This constraint is a heuristic; it corresponds to the intuition that it is unlikely that the same noun refers to different objects in a short discourse, while for other parts of speech it is possible. An additional corpus study is needed in order to prove or disprove it.

The described procedure provides solutions to a whole range of natural language pragmatics problems, such as resolving ambiguity, discovering implicit relations in nouns compounds, prepositional phrases, or discourse structure. Moreover, this account of interpretation solves the problem of where to stop drawing inferences, which could easily be unlimited in number; an inference is appropriate if it is part of the lowest-cost proof of the logical form.

Adapting Mini-TACITUS to a Large-Scale Knowledge Base

Mini-TACITUS (Mulkar et al., 2007) began as a simple backchaining theorem-prover intended to be a more transparent version of the original TACITUS system, which was based on Stickel's PTTP system (Stickel, 1988). Originally, Mini-TACITUS was not designed for treating large amounts of data. A clear and clean reasoning procedure rather than efficiency was in the focus of its developers. In order to make the system work with the large-scale knowledge base, we had to perform several optimization steps and add a couple of new features.

[4]In practice, we use the depth parameter *d* and do not allow an inference chain with more that *d* steps.

[5]Recall that only propositions with the same predicate can be merged, therefore *John* and *Bill* cannot be merged.

For avoiding the reasoning complexity problem, we have introduced two parameters. The time parameter t is used to restrict the processing time. After the processing time exceeds t the reasoning terminates and the best interpretation so far is output. The time parameter ensures that an interpretation will be always returned by the procedure even if reasoning could not be completed in a reasonable time. The depth parameter d restricts the depth of the inference chain. Suppose that a proposition p occurring in the input has been backchained and a proposition p' has been introduced as a result. Then, p' will be backchained and so on. The number of such iterations cannot exceed d. The depth parameter reduces the number of reasoning steps.

Since Mini-TACITUS processing time increases exponentially with the input size (sentence length and number of axioms), making such a large set of axioms work was an additional issue. For speeding up reasoning it was necessary to reduce both the number of the input propositions and the number of axioms. In order to reduce the number of axioms, a two-step reduction of the axiom set is performed. First, only the axioms which could be evoked by the input propositions or as a result of backchaining from the input are selected for each reasoning task. Second, the axioms which could never lead to any merging are filtered out. Concerning the input propositions, those which could never be merged with the others (even after backchaining) are excluded from the reasoning process.

3 Knowledge Base

As described in the previous section, the Mini-TACITUS inferences are based on a knowledge base (KB) consisting of a set of axioms. In order to obtain a reliable KB with a sufficient coverage we have exploited existing lexical-semantic resources.

First, we have extracted axioms from WordNet (Fellbaum, 1998), version 3.0, which has already proved itself to be useful in knowledge-intensive NLP applications. The central entity in WordNet is called a *synset*. Synsets correspond to word senses, so that every lexeme can participate in several synsets. For every word sense, WordNet indicates the frequency of this particular word sense in the WordNet annotated corpora. We have used the lexeme-synset mapping for generating axioms, with the corresponding frequencies of word senses converted into the axiom weights. For example, in the axioms below, the verb *compose* is mapped to its sense 2 in WordNet which participates in *synset-X*.

compose-2(e1,x1,x2):80 $\rightarrow$ *compose*(e1,x1,x2)
synset-X(e0,e1):100 $\rightarrow$ *compose-2*(e1,x1,x2)

Moreover, we have converted the following WordNet relations defined on synsets into axioms: hypernymy, instantiation, entailment, similarity, meronymy. Hypernymy and instantiation relations presuppose that the related synsets refer to the same entity (the first axiom below), whereas other types of relations relate synsets referring to different entities (the second axiom below). All axioms based on WordNet relations have the weights equal to 100.

synset-1(e0,e1):100 $\rightarrow$ *synset-2*(e0,e1)
synset-1(e0,e1):100 $\rightarrow$ *synset-2*(e2,e3)

WordNet also provides morphosemantic relations which relate verbs and nouns, e.g., *buy-buyer*. WordNet distinguishes between 14 types of such relations.We use relation types in order to define the direction of the entailment and map the arguments. For example, the "agent" relation (*buy-buyer*) stands for a bi-directional entailment such that the noun is the first (agentive) argument of the verb:

buy-1(e0,x1,x2):100 $\rightarrow$ *buyer-1*(x1)
buyer-1(x1):100 $\rightarrow$ *buy-1*(e0,x1,x2)

Additionally, we have exploited the WordNet synset definitions. In WordNet the definitions are given in natural language form. We have used the extended WordNet resource[6] which provides logical forms for the definition in WordNet version 2.0. We have adapted logical forms from extended WordNet to our

[6] *http://xwn.hlt.utdallas.edu/*

representation format and converted them into axioms; for example the following axiom represents the meaning of the synset containing such lexemes as *horseback*. These axioms have the total weight of 100.

on(e2,e1,x2):25 & *back*(e3,x2):25 & *of*(e4,x2,x1):25 & *horse*(e5,x1):25 → *synset-X*(e0,x0)

The second resource which we have used as a source of axioms is FrameNet, release 1.5, see Ruppenhofer et al. (2006). FrameNet has a shorter history in NLP applications than WordNet, but lately more and more researchers have been demonstrating its potential to improve the quality of question answering (Shen and Lapata, 2007) and recognizing textual entailment (Burchardt et al., 2009). The lexical meaning of predicates in FrameNet is represented in terms of frames which describe prototypical situations spoken about in natural language. Every frame contains a set of roles corresponding to the participants of the described situation. Predicates with similar semantics are assigned to the same frame; e.g. both *give* and *hand over* refer to the GIVING frame. For most of the lexical elements FrameNet provides syntactic patterns showing the surface realization of these lexical elements and their arguments. Syntactic patterns also contain information about their frequency in the FrameNet annotated corpora. We have used the patterns and the frequencies for deriving axioms such as for example the following.

GIVING(e1,x1,x2,x3):70 & DONOR(e1,x1):0 & RECIPIENT(e1,x2):0 & THEME(e1,x3):0 →
give(e1,x1,x3) & *to*(e2,e1,x2)
HIRING(e1,x1,x3):90 & EMPLOYER(e1,x1) & EMPLOYEE(e1,x3) →
give(e1,x1,x2,x3):10 & *job*(x2)

The first pattern above corresponds to the phrases like *John gave a book to Mary* and the second – less frequent – to phrases like *John gave Mary a job*. It is interesting to note that application of such axioms provides a solution to the problem of semantic role labeling as a by-product. As in the statistical approaches, more frequent patterns will be favored. Moreover, patterns helping to detect implicit redundancy will be brought forward.

FrameNet also introduces semantic relations defined on frames such as inheritance, causation or precedence; for example the GIVING and GETTING frames are connected with the causation relation. Roles of the connected frames are also linked, e.g. DONOR in GIVING is linked with SOURCE in GETTING. Frame relations have no formal semantics in FrameNet. In order to generate corresponding axioms, we have used the previous work on axiomatizing frame relations and extracting new relations from corpora (Ovchinnikova et al., 2010). Weights of the axioms derived from frame relations depend on corpus-based similarity of the lexical items assigned to the corresponding frames. An example of an axiomatized relation is given below.[7]

GIVING(e0,x1,x2,x3):120 & DONOR(e0,x1):0 & RECIPIENT(e0,x2):0 & THEME(e0,x3):0 &
causes(e0,e1):0 → GETTING(e1,x2,x3,x1) & SOURCE(e1,x1) & RECIPIENT(e1,x2) & THEME(e1,x3)

Both WordNet and FrameNet are manually created resources which ensures a relatively high quality of the resulting axioms as well as the possibility of exploiting the linguistic information provided for structuring the axioms. Although manual creation of resources is a very time-consuming task, WordNet and FrameNet, being long-term projects, have an extensive coverage of English vocabulary. The coverage of WordNet is currently larger than that of FrameNet (155 000 vs. 12 000 lexemes). However, the fact that FrameNet introduces complex argument structures (roles) for frames and provides mappings of these structures makes FrameNet especially valuable for reasoning.

The complete list of axioms we have extracted from these resources is given in table 1.

4 Recognizing Textual Entailment

As the reader can see from the previous sections, the discourse processing procedure we have presented is fairly general and not tuned for any particular type of inferences. We have evaluated the procedure and

[7]The "causes" predicate is supposed to be linked to an underlying causation theory, see for example *http://www.isi.edu/~hobbs/bgt-cause.text*. However, in the described experimental settings we have left the abstract theories out and evaluated only the axioms extracted from the lexical-semantic resources.

Table 1: Statistics for extracted axioms

Axiom type	Source	Numb. of axioms
Lexeme-synset mappings	WN 3.0	422,000
Lexeme-synset mappings	WN 2.0	406,000
Synset relations	WN 3.0	141,000
Derivational relations	WN 3.0 (annotated)	35,000
Synset definitions	WN 2.0 (parsed, annotated)	120,500
Lexeme-frame mappings	FN 1.5	50,000
Frame relations	FN 1.5 + corpora	6,000

the KB derived from WordNet and FrameNet on the Recognizing Textual Entailment (RTE) task, which is a generic task that seems to capture major semantic inference needs across many natural language processing applications. In this task, the system is given a text and a hypothesis and must decide whether the hypothesis is entailed by the text plus commonsense knowledge.

Our approach is to interpret both the text and the hypothesis using Mini-TACITUS, and then see whether adding information derived from the text to the knowledge base will reduce the cost of the best abductive proof of the hypothesis as compared to using the original knowledge base only. If the cost reduction exceeds a threshold determined from a training set, then we predict entailment.

A simple example would be the text *John gave a book to Mary* and the hypothesis *Mary got a book*. Our pipeline constructs the following logical forms for these two sentences.

T: *John*(x1):20 & *give*(e1,x1,x2):20 & *book*(x3):20 & *to*(e2,e1,x3):20 & *Mary*(x3):20
H: *Mary*(x1):20 & *get*(e1,x1,x2):20 & *book*(x2):20

These logical forms constitute the Mini-TACITUS input. Mini-TACITUS applies the axioms from the knowledge base to the input logical forms in order to reduce the overall cost of the interpretations. Suppose that we have three FrameNet axioms in our knowledge base. The first one maps *give to* to the GIVING frame, the second one maps *get* to GETTING and the third one relates GIVING and GETTING with the causation relation. The first two axioms have the weights of 90 and the third 120. As a result of the application of the axioms the following best interpretations will be constructed for T and H.

I(T): *John*(x1):20 & *give*(e1,x1,x2):0 & *book*(x3):20 & *to*(e2,e1,x3):0 & *Mary*(x3):20 & GIVING(e0,x1,x2,x3):18
I(H): *Mary*(x1):20 & *get*(e1,x1,x2):0 & *book*(x2):20 & GETTING(e0,x1,x2):18

The total cost of the best interpretation for H is equal to 58. Now the best interpretation of T will be added to H with the zero costs (as if T has been totally proven) and we will try to prove H once again. First of all, merging of the propositions with the same names will result in reducing costs of the propositions *Mary* and *book* to 0, because they occur in T:

I(T+H): *John*(x1):0 & *give*(e1,x1,x2):0 & *book*(x3):0 & *to*(e2,e1,x3):0 & *Mary*(x3):0 & GIVING(e0,x1,x2,x3):0 & *get*(e1,x1,x2):0 & GETTING(e0,x1,x2):18

The only proposition left to be proved is GETTING. Using the GETTING-GIVING relation as described in the previous section, this proposition can be backchained on to GIVING which will merge with GIVING coming from the T sentence. H appears to be proven completely with respect to T; the total cost of its best interpretation given T is equal to 0. Thus, using knowledge from T helped to reduce the cost of the best interpretation of H from 58 to 0.

The approach presented does not have any special account for logical connectors such as *if*, *not*, *or* etc. Given a text *If A then B* and a hypothesis *A and B* our procedure will most likely predict entailment. At the moment our RTE procedure mainly accounts for the informational content of texts, being able to detect the "aboutness" overlap of T and H. In our framework, a fuller treatment of the logical structure of the natural language would presuppose a more complicated strategy of merging redundancies.

5 Evaluation Results

We have evaluated our procedure on the RTE-2 dataset [8], see Bar-Haim et al. (2006) . The RTE-2 dataset contains the development and the test set, both including 800 text-hypothesis pairs. Each dataset consists of four subsets, which correspond to typical success and failure settings in different applications: information extraction (IE), information retrieval (IR), question answering (QA), and summarization (SUM). In total, 200 pairs were collected for each application in each dataset.

As a baseline we have processed the datasets with an empty knowledge base. Then we have done 2 runs, first, using axioms extracted from WordNet 3.0 plus FrameNet, and, second, using axioms extracted from the WordNet 2.0 definitions. In both runs the depth parameter was set to 3. The development set was used to train the threshold as described in the previous section.[9] Table 2 contains results of our experiments.[10] Accuracy was calculated as the percentage of pairs correctly judged. The results suggest that the proposed method seems to be promising as compared to the other systems evaluated on the same task. Our best run gives 63% accuracy. Two systems participating the RTE-2 Challenge had 73% and 75% accuracy, two systems achieved 62% and 63%, while most of the systems achieved 55%-61%, cf. Bar-Haim et al. (2006). For our best run (WN 3.0 + FN), we present the accuracy data for each application separately (table 2). The distribution of the performance of Mini-TACITUS on the four datasets corresponds to the average performance of systems participating in RTE-2 as reported by Garoufi (2007). The most challenging task in RTE-2 appeared to be IE. QA and IR follow, and finally, SUM was titled the "easiest" task, with a performance significantly higher than that of any other task.[11]

It is worth noting that the performance of Mini-TACITUS increases with the increasing time of processing. This is not surprising. We use the time parameter t for restricting the processing time. The smaller t is, the fewer chances Mini-TACITUS has for applying all relevant axioms. The experiments carried out suggest that optimizing the system computationally could lead to producing significantly better results. Tracing the reasoning process, we found out that given a long sentence and a short processing time Mini-TACITUS had time to construct only a few interpretations, and the real best interpretation was not always among them.

The lower performance of the system using the KB based on axioms extracted from extended WordNet can be easily explained. At the moment we define non-merge constraints (see section 2) for the input propositions only. The axioms extracted from the synset definitions introduce a lot of new lexemes into the logical form, since these axioms define words with the help of other words rather than abstract concepts. These new lexemes, especially those which are frequent in English, result in undesired mergings (e.g., mergings of frequent prepositions), since no non-merge constraints are defined for them. In order to fix this problem, we will need to implement dynamic non-merge constraints which will be added on the fly if a new lexeme is introduced during reasoning. The WN 3.0 + FN axiom set does not fall into this problem, because these axioms operate on frames and synsets rather than on lexemes.

In addition, for the run using axioms derived from FrameNet, we have evaluated how well we do in assigning frames and frame roles. For Mini-TACITUS, semantic role labeling is a by-product of constructing the best interpretation. But since this task is considered to be important as such in the NLP community, we provide an additional evaluation for it. As a gold standard we have used the Frame-Annotated Corpus for Textual Entailment, FATE, see Burchardt and Pennacchiotti (2008). This corpus provides frame and semantic role label annotations for the RTE-2 challenge test set.[12] It is important to

[8] *http://pascallin.ecs.soton.ac.uk/Challenges/RTE2/*

[9] Interpretation costs were normalized to the number of propositions in the input.

[10] "Time" stands for the value of the time parameter – processing time per sentence, in minutes; "Numb. of ax." stands for the average number of axioms per sentence.

[11] In order to get a better understanding of which parts of our KB are useful for computing entailment and for which types of entailment, in future, we are planning to use the detailed annotation of the RTE-2 dataset describing the source of the entailment which was produced by Garoufi (2007). We would like to thank one of our reviewers for giving us this idea.

[12] FATE was annotated with the FrameNet 1.3 labels, while we have been using 1.5 version for extracting axioms. However,

Table 2: Evaluation results for the RTE-2 test set

KB	Accuracy	Time	Numb. of ax. T	Numb. of ax. H
No KB	57%	1	0	0
WN 3.0 + FN	62%	20	533	237
WN 3.0 + FN	63%	30	533	237
Ext. WN 2.0	60%	20	3700	1720
Ext. WN 2.0	61%	30	3700	1720

Task	Accuracy
SUM	75%
IR	64%
QA	62%
IE	50%

Table 3: Evaluation of frames/roles labeling towards FATE

System	Frame match	Role match	
	Recall	Precision	Recall
Shalmaneser	0.55	0.54	0.37
Shalmaneser + Detour	0.85	0.52	0.36
Mini-TACITUS	0.65	0.55	0.30

note that FATE annotates only those frames which are relevant for computing entailment. Since Mini-TACITUS makes all possible frame assignments for a sentence, we provide only the recall measure for the frame match and leave the precision out.

The FATE corpus was also used as a gold standard for evaluating the Shalmaneser system (Erk and Pado, 2006) which is a state-of-the-art system for assigning FrameNet frames and roles. In table 2 we replicate results for Shalmaneser alone and Shalmaneser boosted with the WordNet Detour to FrameNet (Burchardt et al., 2005). The WN-FN Detour extended the frame labels assigned by Shalmaneser with the labels related via the FrameNet hierarchy or by the WordNet inheritance relation, cf. Burchardt et al. (2009). In frame matching, the number of frame labels in the gold standard annotation that can also be found in the system annotation (recall) was counted. Role matching was evaluated only on the frames that are correctly annotated by the system. The number of role labels in the gold standard annotation that can also be found in the system annotation (recall) as well as the number of role labels found by the system which also occur in the gold standard (precision) were counted.[13] Table 3 shows that given FrameNet axioms, the performance of Mini-TACITUS on semantic role labeling is compatible with those of the system specially designed to solve this task.

6 Conclusion and Future Work

This paper presents a discourse processing framework underlying the abductive reasoner called *Mini-TACITUS*. We have shown that interpreting texts using weighted abduction helps solve pragmatic problems in discourse processing as a by-product. In this paper, particular attention was paid to the construction of a large and reliable knowledge base populated with axioms extracted from such lexical-semantic resources as WordNet and FrameNet. The reasoning procedure as well as the knowledge base were evaluated in the Recognizing Textual Entailment task. The data for evaluation were taken from the RTE-2 Challenge. First, we have evaluated the accuracy of the entailment prediction. Second, we have eval-

in the new FN version the number of frames and roles increases and there is no message about removed frames in the General Release Notes R1.5, see *http://framenet.icsi.berkeley.edu*. Therefore we suppose that most of the frames and roles used for the FATE annotation are still present in FN 1.5.

[13]We do not compare filler matching, because the FATE syntactic annotation follows different standards as the one produced by the ESG parser, which makes aligning fillers non-trivial.

uated frame and role labeling using the Frame-Annotated Corpora for Textual Entailment as the gold standard. In both tasks our system showed performance compatible with those of the state-of-the art systems. Since the inference procedure and the axiom set are general and not tuned for a particular task, we consider the results of our experiments to be promising concerning possible manifold applications of Mini-TACITUS.

The experiments we have carried out have shown that there is still a lot of space for improving the procedure. First, for successful application of Mini-TACITUS on a large scale the system needs to be computationally optimized. In its current state, Mini-TACITUS requires too much time for producing satisfactory results. As our experiments suggest (cf. table 2), speeding up reasoning may lead to significant improvements in the system performance. Since Mini-TACITUS was not originally designed for large-scale processing, its implementation is in many aspects not effective enough. We hope to improve it by changing the data structure and re-implementing some of the main algorithms.

Second, in the future we plan to elaborate our treatment of natural language expressions standing for logical connectors such as implication *if*, negation *not*, disjunction *or* and others. Quantifiers such as *all*, *each*, *some* also require a special treatment. This advance is needed in order to achieve more precise entailment inferences, which are at the moment based in our approach on the core information content ("aboutness") of texts. Concerning the heuristic non-merge constraints preventing undesired mergings as well as the heuristic for assigning default costs (see section 2), in the future we would like to perform a corpus study for evaluating and possibly changing these heuristics.

Another future direction concerns the enlargement of the knowledge base. Hand-crafted lexical-semantic resources such as WordNet and FrameNet provide both an extensive lexical coverage and a high-value semantic labeling. However, such resources still lack certain features essential for capturing some of the knowledge required for linguistic inferences. First of all, manually created resources are static; updating them with new information is a slow and time-consuming process. By contrast, commonsense knowledge and the lexicon undergo daily updates. In order to accommodate dynamic knowledge, we plan to make use of the distributional similarities of words in a large Web-corpus such as for example Wikipedia. Many researchers working on RTE have already been using word similarity for computing similarity between texts and hypotheses, e.g., Mehdad et al. (2010). In our approach, we plan to incorporate word similarities into the reasoning procedure making them affect proposition costs so that propositions implied by the context (similar to other words in the context) will become cheaper to prove. This extension might give us a performance improvement in RTE, because it will help to relate those propositions from H for which there are no appropriate axioms in the KB to propositions in T.

Lexical-semantic resources as knowledge sources for reasoning have another shortcoming: They imply too little structure. WordNet and FrameNet enable some argument mappings of related synsets or frames, but they cannot provide a more detailed concept axiomatization. We are engaged in two types of efforts to obtain more structured knowledge. The first effort is the manual encoding of abstract theories explicating concepts that pervade natural language discourse, such as causality, change of state, and scales, and the manual encoding of axioms linking lexical items to these theories. A selection of the core theories can be found at *http://www.isi.edu/ hobbs/csk.html*. The second effort concerns making use of the existing ontologies. The recent progress of the Semantic Web technologies has stimulated extensive development of the domain-specific ontologies as well as development of inference machines specially designed to reason with these ontologies.[14] In practice, domain-specific ontologies usually represent detailed and structured knowledge about particular domains (e.g. geography, medicine etc.). We intend to make Mini-TACITUS able to use this knowledge through querying an externally stored ontology with the help of an existing reasoner. This extension will give us a possibility to access elaborated domain-specific knowledge which might be crucial for interpretation of domain-specific texts.

We believe that implementation of the mentioned improvements and extensions will make Mini-TACITUS a powerful reasoning system equipped with enough knowledge to solve manifold NLP tasks on a large scale. In our view, the experiments with the axioms extracted from the lexical-semantic resources presented in this paper show the potential of weighted abduction for natural language reasoning and open

[14] *www.w3.org/2001/sw/,http://www.cs.man.ac.uk/ sattler/reasoners.html*

new ways for its application.

References

Bar-Haim, R., I. Dagan, B. Dolan, L. Ferro, D. Giampiccolo, B. Magnini, and I. Szpektor (2006). The second PASCAL recognising textual entailment challenge. In *Proc. of the Second PASCAL Challenges Workshop on Recognising Textual Entailment.*

Burchardt, A., K. Erk, and A. Frank (2005). A WordNet Detour to FrameNet. In *Sprachtechnologie, mobile Kommunikation und linguistische Resourcen*, Volume 8.

Burchardt, A. and M. Pennacchiotti (2008). FATE: a FrameNet-Annotated Corpus for Textual Entailment. In *Proc. of LREC'08.*

Burchardt, A., M. Pennacchiotti, S. Thater, and M. Pinkal (2009). Assessing the impact of frame semantics on textual entailment. *Natural Language Engineering 15*(4), 527–550.

Erk, K. and S. Pado (2006). Shalmaneser - a flexible toolbox for semantic role assignment. In *Proc. of LREC'06*, Genoa, Italy.

Fellbaum, C. (Ed.) (1998). *WordNet: An Electronic Lexical Database* (First ed.). MIT Press.

Garoufi, K. (2007). Towards a better understanding of applied textual entailment: Annotation and evaluation of the rte-2 dataset. Master's thesis, Saarland University.

Hobbs, J. R. (1985). Ontological promiscuity. In *Proceedings, 23rd Annual Meeting of the Association for Computational Linguistics*, Chicago, Illinois, pp. 61–69.

Hobbs, J. R., M. Stickel, and P. Martin (1993). Interpretation as abduction. *Artificial Intelligence 63*, 69–142.

McCord, M. C. (1990). Slot grammar: A system for simpler construction of practical natural language grammars. In *Natural Language and Logic: International Scientific Symposium, Lecture Notes in Computer Science*, pp. 118–145. Springer Verlag.

McCord, M. C. (2010). Using Slot Grammar. Technical report, IBM T. J. Watson Research Center. RC 23978Revised.

Mehdad, Y., A. Moschitti, and F. M. Zanzotto (2010). Syntactic/semantic structures for textual entailment recognition. In *Proc. of HLT '10: The 2010 Annual Conference of the North American Chapter of the Association for Computational Linguistics*, pp. 1020–1028.

Mulkar, R., J. R. Hobbs, and E. Hovy (2007). Learning from Reading Syntactically Complex Biology Texts. In *Proc.of the 8th International Symposium on Logical Formalizations of Commonsense Reasoning. Palo Alto.*

Ovchinnikova, E., L. Vieu, A. Oltramari, S. Borgo, and T. Alexandrov (2010). Data-Driven and Ontological Analysis of FrameNet for Natural Language Reasoning. In *Proc. of LREC'10*, Valletta, Malta.

Ruppenhofer, J., M. Ellsworth, M. Petruck, C. Johnson, and J. Scheffczyk (2006). FrameNet II: Extended Theory and Practice. *International Computer Science Institute.*

Shen, D. and M. Lapata (2007). Using Semantic Roles to Improve Question Answering. In *Proc. of EMNLP-CoNLL*, pp. 12–21.

Stickel, M. E. (1988). A prolog technology theorem prover: Implementation by an extended prolog compiler. *Journal of Automated Reasoning 4*(4), 353–380.

Incremental dialogue act understanding

Volha Petukhova
Tilburg Center for Creative Computing
Tilburg University, The Netherlands,
v.petukhova@uvt.nl

Harry Bunt
Tilburg Center for Creative Computing
Tilburg University, The Netherlands,
harry.bunt@uvt.nl

Abstract

This paper presents a machine learning-based approach to the incremental understanding of dialogue utterances, with a focus on the recognition of their communicative functions. A token-based approach combining the use of local classifiers, which exploit local utterance features, and global classifiers which use the outputs of local classifiers applied to previous and subsequent tokens, is shown to result in excellent dialogue act recognition scores for unsegmented spoken dialogue. This can be seen as a significant step forward towards the development of fully incremental, on-line methods for computing the meaning of utterances in spoken dialogue.

1 Introduction

When reading a sentence in a text, a human language understander obviously does not wait trying to understand what he is reading until he has come to the end of the sentence. Similarly for participants in a spoken conversation. There is overwhelming psycholinguistic evidence that human understanders construct syntactic, semantic, and pragmatic hypotheses on the fly, while receiving the written or spoken input. Dialogue phenomena such as backchannelling (providing feedback while someone else is speaking), the completion of a partner utterance, and requests for clarification that overlap the utterance of the main speaker, illustrate this. Evidence from the analysis of nonverbal behaviour in multimodal dialogue lends further support to the claim that human understanding works incrementally, as input is being received. Dialogue participants start to perform certain body movements and facial expressions that are perceived and interpreted by others as dialogue acts (such as head nods, smiles, frowns) while another participant is speaking, see e.g. Petukhova and Bunt (2009). As another kind of evidence, eye-tracking experiments by Tanenhaus et al. (1995), Sedivy et al. (1999) and Sedivy (2003) showed that definite descriptions are resolved incrementally when the referent is visually accessible.

Traditional models of language understanding for dialogue systems, by contrast, are pipelined, modular, and operate on complete utterances. Typically, such a system has an automatic speech recognition module, a language understanding module responsible for syntactic and semantic analysis, an interpretation manager, a dialogue manager, a natural language generation module, and a module for speech synthesis. The output of each module is the input for another. The language understanding module typically performs the following tasks: (1) *segmentation*: identification of relevant segments in the input, such as sentences;(2) *lexical analysis*: lexical lookup, possibly supported by morphological processing, and by additional resources such as WordNet, VerbNet, or lexical ontologies; (3) *parsing*: construction of syntactic interpretations; (4) *semantic analysis*: computation of propositional, referential, or action-related content; and (5) *pragmatic analysis*: determination of speaker intentions.

Of these tasks, lexical analysis, being concerned with local information at word level, can be done for each word as soon as it has been recognized, and is naturally performed as an incremental part of utterance processing, but syntactic, semantic and pragmatic analysis are traditionally performed on complete utterances. Tomita's pioneering work in left-to-right syntactic parsing has shown that incremental parsing can be much more efficient and of equal quality as the parsing of complete utterances (Tomita (1986)). Computational approaches to incremental semantic and pragmatic interpretation have been less successful (see e.g. Haddock (1989); Milward and Cooper (2009)), but work in computational semantics on the design of underspecified representation formalisms has shown that such formalisms, developed originally for the underspecified representation of quantifier scopes, can also be applied in situations where incomplete input information is available (see e.g. Bos (2002); Bunt (2007), Hobbs (1985), Pinkal (1999)) and as such hold a promise for incremental semantic interpretation.

Pragmatic interpretation, in particular the recognition of a speaker's intentions in incoming dialogue utterances, is another major aspect of language understanding for dialogue systems. Computational modelling of dialogue behaviour in terms of dialogue acts aims to capture speaker intentions in the communicative functions of dialogue acts, and offers an effective integration with semantic content analysis through the information state update approach (Poesio and Traum (1998)). In this approach, a dialogue act is viewed as having as its main components a communicative function and a semantic content, where the semantic content is the referential, propositional, or action-related information that the dialogue act addresses, and the communicative function defines how an understander's information state is to be updated with that information.

Evaluation of a non-incremental dialogue system and its incremental counterpart reported in Aist et al. (2007) showed that the latter is faster overall than the former due to the incorporation of pragmatic information in early stages of the understanding process. Since users formulate utterances incrementally, partial utterances may be available for a substantial amount of time and may be interpreted by the system. An incremental interpretation strategy may allow the system to respond more quickly, by minimizing the delay between the time the user finishes and the time the utterance is interpreted DeVault and Stone (2003).

This suggests that a dialogue system performance may benefit from reliable partial processing of input. This paper is concerned with the automatic recognition of dialogue acts based on partially available input and shows that in order to arrive at the best output prediction two different classification strategies are needed: (1) local classification that is based on features observed in dialogue behaviour and that can be extracted from the annotated data; and (2) global classification that takes the locally predicted context into account.

This paper is structured as follows. In Section 2 we will outline performed experiments describing the data, tagset, features, algorithms and evaluation metrics that have been used. Section 3 reports on the experimental results, applying a variety of machine learning techniques and feature selection algorithms, to assess the automatic recognition and classification of dialogue acts using simultaneous incremental segmentation and dialogue act classification. In Section 4 we discuss strategies in management and correction of the output of local classifies. Section 5 concludes.

2 Incremental understanding experiments

2.1 Related work

Nakano et al. (Nakano et al. (1999)) proposed a method for the incremental understanding of utterances whose boundaries are not known. The *Incremental Sentence Sequence Search* (ISSS) algorithm finds plausible boundaries of utterances, called significant utterances (SUs), which can be a full sentence or a subsentential phrase, such as a noun phrase or a verb phrase. Any phrase that can change the belief state is defined as a SU. In this sense an SU corresponds more or less with what we call a 'functional segment', which is defined as a minimal stretch of behaviour that has a communicative function (see Bunt et al. (2010)). ISSS maintains multiple possible belief states, and updates these each time a word hypothesis is input. The ISSS approach does not deal with the multifunctionality of segments, however, and does not allow segments to overlap.

Lendvai and Geertzen (Lendvai and Geertzen (2007)) proposed *token-based* dialogue act segmentation and classification, which was worked out in more detail in Geertzen (2009). This approach takes dialogue data that is not segmented into syntactic or semantic units, but operates on the transcribed speech as a stream of words and other vocal signs (e.g. laughs), including disfluent elements (e.g. abandoned

Dimension	Frequency	General-purpose function	Frequency
Task	31.8	PropositionalQuestion	5.8
Auto-Feedback	20.5	Set Question	2.3
Allo-Feedback	0.7	Check Question	3.3
Turn Management	50.2	Propositional Answer	9.8
Social Obligation Management	0.5	Set Answer	3.9
Discourse Structuring	2.8	Inform	11.7
Own Communication Management	10.3	InformRhetorical	21.9
Time Management	26.7	Instruct	0.3
Partner Communication Management	0.3	Suggest	10.1
Contact Management	0.1	Request	5.6

Table 1: *Distribution of functional tags across dimensions and general-purpose functions for the AMI corpus (in %).*

or interrupted words). Segmentation and classification of dialogue acts are performed simultaneously in one step. Geertzen (2009) reports on classifier performance on this task for the DIAMOND data[1] using DIT^{++} labels. The success scores in terms of F-scores range from 47.7 to 81.7. It was shown that performing segmentation and classification together results in better segmentation, but affects the dialogue act classification negatively.

The incremental dialogue act recognition system proposed here takes the token-based approach for building classifiers for the recognition (segmentation and classification) of multiple dialogue acts for each input token, and adopts the ISSS idea for information-state updates based on partial input interpretation.

2.2 Tagset

The data selected for the experiments was annotated with the DIT^{++} tagset Release 4[2]. The DIT taxonomy distinguishes 10 dimensions, addressing information about: the domain or task (*Task*), feedback on communicative behaviour of the speaker (*Auto-feedback*) or other interlocutors (*Allo-feedback*), managing difficulties in the speaker's contributions (*Own-Communication Management*) or those of other interlocutors (*Partner Communication Management*), the speaker's need for time to continue the dialogue (*Time Management*), establishing and maintaining contact (*Contact Management*), about who should have the next turn (*Turn Management*), the way the speaker is planning to structure the dialogue, introducing, changing or closing a topic (*Dialogue Structuring*), and conditions that trigger dialogue acts by social convention (*Social Obligations Management*), see Table 1.

For each dimension, at most one communicative function can be assigned, which is either a function that can occur in this dimension alone (a *dimension-specific* (DS) function) or a function that can occur in any dimension (a *general-purpose* (GP) function). Dialogue acts with a DS communicative function are always concerned with a particular type of information, such as a Turn Grabbing act, which is concerned with the allocation of the speaker role, or a Stalling act, which is concerned with the timing of utterance production. GP functions, by contrast, are not specifically related to any dimension in particular, e.g. one can ask a question about any type of semantic content, provide an answer about any type of content, or request the performance of any type of action (such as *Could you please close the door* or *Could you please repeat that*). These communicative functions include Question, Answer, Request, Offer, Inform, and many other familiar core speech acts.

The tagset used in these studies contains 38 dimension-specific functions and 44 general-purpose functions. A tag consists either of a pair consisting of a communicative function (CF) and the addressed dimension (D).

[1]For more information see Geertzen,J., Girard,Y., and Morante,R. 2004. The DIAMOND project. Poster at the 8th Workshop on the Semantics and Pragmatics of Dialogue (CATALOG 2004).

[2]For more information about the tagset and the dimensions that are identified, please visit:`http://dit.uvt.nl/` or see Bunt (2009).

Speaker	Token	Task	Auto-F.	Allo-F.	TurnM.	TimeM.	ContactM.	DS	OCM	PCM	SOM
B	it	B;inf	O	O	O	O	O	O	O	O	O
B	has	I:inf	O	O	O	O	O	O	O	O	O
B	to	I:inf	O	O	O	O	O	O	O	O	O
B	look	I:inf	O	O	O	O	O	O	O	O	O
B	you	O	O	B:check	O	O	O	O	O	O	O
B	know	O	O	E:check	O	O	O	O	O	O	O
B	cool	I:inf	O	O	O	O	O	O	O	O	O
D	mmhmm	O	BE:positive	O	O	O	O	O	O	O	O
B	and	I:inf	O	O	BE:t_keep	O	O	O	O	O	O
B	gimmicky	E:inf	O	O	O	O	O	O	O	O	O

Figure 1: *Segment boundaries and dialogue act label encoding in different dimensions.*

2.3 Features and data encoding

In the recognition experiments we used data from the AMI meeting corpus[3]. For training we used three annotated AMI meetings that contain 17,335 tokens forming 3,897 functional segments. The distribution of functional tags across dimensions is given in Table 1.

Features extracted from the data considered here relate to *dialogue history*: functional tags of the 10 previous turns; *timing*: token *duration* and *floor-transfer offset*[4] computed in milliseconds; *prosody*: minimum, maximum, mean, and standard deviation for pitch (F0 in Hz), energy (RMS), voicing (fraction of locally unvoiced frames and number of voice breaks) and speaking rate (number of syllables per second)[5]; and *lexical information*: token occurrence, bi- and trigram of those tokens. In total, 1,668 features are used for the AMI data.

To be able to identify segment boundaries, we assign to each token its communicative function label and indicate whether a token starts a segment (B), is inside a segment (I), ends a segment (E), is outside a segment (O), or forms a functional segment on its own (BE). Thus, the class labels consist of a segmentation prefix (IBOE) and a communicative function label, see example in Figure 1.

2.4 Classifiers and evaluation metrics

A wide variety of machine-learning techniques has been used for NLP tasks with various instantiations of feature sets and target class encodings. For dialogue processing, it is still an open issue which techniques are the most suitable for which task. We used two different types of classifiers to test their performance on our dialogue data: a probabilistic one and a rule inducer.

As a probabilistic classifier we used *Bayes Nets*. This classifier estimates probabilities rather than produce predictions, which is often more useful because this allows us to rank predictions. Bayes Nets estimate the conditional probability distribution on the values of the class attributes given the values of the other attributes.

As a rule induction algorithm we chose *Ripper* (Cohen (1995)). The advantage of a rule inducer is that the regularities discovered in the data are represented as human-readable rules.

The results of all experiments were obtained using 10-fold cross-validation.[7] As a baseline it is common practice to use the majority class tag, but for our data sets such a baseline is not very useful because of the relatively low frequencies of the tags in some dimensions. Instead, we use a baseline

[3]The Augmented Multi-party Interaction meeting corpus consists of multimodal task-oriented human-human multi-party dialogues in English, for more information visit (`http://www.amiproject.org/`

[4]Difference between the time that a turn starts and the moment the previous turn ends.

[5]These features were computed using the PRAAT tool[6]. We examined both raw and normalized versions of these features. Speaker-normalized features were obtained by computing z-scores (z = (X-mean)/standard deviation) for the feature, where mean and standard deviation were calculated from all functional segments produced by the same speaker in the dialogues. We also used normalizations by first speaker turn and by previous speaker turn.

[7]In order to reduce the effect of imbalances in the data, it is partitioned ten times. Each time a different 10% of the data is used as test set and the remaining 90% as training set. The procedure is repeated ten times so that in the end, every instance has been used exactly once for testing and the scores are averaged. The cross-validation was stratified, i.e. the 10 folds contained approximately the same proportions of instances with relevant tags as in the entire dataset.

that is based on a single feature, namely, the tag of the previous dialogue utterance (see Lendvai et al. (2003))).

Several metrics have been proposed for the evaluation of a classifier's performance: error metrics and performance metrics. The word-based error rate metric, introduced in Ang et al. (2005), measures the percentage of words that were placed in a segment perfectly identical to that in the reference. The dialogue act based metric (DER) was proposed in Zimmermann et al. (2005). In this metric a word is considered to be correctly classified if and only if it has been assigned the correct dialogue act type and it lies in exactly the same segment as the corresponding word of the reference. We will use the combined DER_{sc} error metric to evaluate joint segmentation (s) and classification (c):

$$DER_{sc} = \frac{Tokens\ with\ wrong\ boundaries\ and/or\ function\ class}{total\ number\ of\ tokens} \times 100$$

To assess the quality of classification results, the standard F-score metric is used, which represents the balance between precision and recall.

3 Classification results

Dialogue utterances are often multifunctional, having a function in more than one dimension (see e.g. Bunt (2010)). This makes dialogue act recognition a complex task. Splitting up the output structure may make the task more manageable; for instance, a popular strategy is to split a multi-class learning task into several binary learning tasks. Sometimes, however, learning of multiple classes allows a learning algorithm to exploit the interactions among classes. We will combine these two strategies. We have built in total 64 classifiers for dialogue act recognition for the AMI data. Some of the tasks were defined as binary ones, e.g. the dimension recognition task, others are multi-class learning tasks.

We first trained classifiers to recognize the boundaries of a segment and its communicative functions (joint multi-class learning task) per dimension, see Table 2.

	BL		BayesNet		Ripper	
Dimensions	F_1	DER_{sc}	F_1	DER_{sc}	F_1	DER_{sc}
Task	32.7	51.2	52.1	48.7	**66.7**	42.6
Auto-Feedback	43.2	84.4	**62.7**	33.9	60.1	45.6
Allo-Feedback	70.2	59.5	**73.7**	35.1	71.3	49.1
Turn Management:initial	34.2	95.2	**57.0**	58.4	54.3	81.3
Turn Management:close	33.3	92.7	**54.2**	46.9	49.3	87.3
Time Management	43.7	96.5	**64.5**	46.1	61.4	53.1
Discourse Structuring	41.2	35.1	**72.7**	19.9	50.2	30.9
Contact Management	59.9	53.2	71.4	49.9	**83.3**	37.2
Own Communication Management	36.5	87.9	**68.3**	51.3	58.3	76.8
Partner Communication Management	49.5	59.0	**58.5**	45.5	51.4	58.7
Social Obligation Management	34.5	47.5	**86.5**	35.9	83.3	44.3

Table 2: Overview of F-scores and DER_{sc} for the baseline (BL) and the classifiers for joint segmentation and classification for each DIT^{++} dimension, for the data of the AMI corpus.

The results show that both classifiers outperform the baseline by a broad margin. The Bayes Nets classifier marginally outperforms the Ripper rule inducer, but shows no significant differences in overall performance. Though the results obtained are quite encouraging, the performance on the joint segmentation and classification task does not outperforms the two-step segmentation and classification task reported in Geertzen et al. (2007). There is a drop in F-scores compared to the results reported by Geertzen et al. (2007), which is explained by the fact that recall was quite low. This means that the classifiers missed a lot of relevant cases. Looking more closely at the predictions made by the classifiers, we noticed that beginnings and endings of many segments were not found. For example, the beginnings of Set Questions are identified with perfect precision (100%), but about 60% of the segment beginnings were not found. The reason that the classifiers still show a reasonable performance is that most tokens occur *inside* segments and are better classified, e.g. the inside-tokens of Set Questions are classified with high precision (83%) and reasonably high recall scores (76%). Still, this is rather worrying, since the correct identification of, in particular, the start of a relevant segment is crucial for future decisions. These observations led us to the conclusion that the search space and the number of initially generated hypotheses for classifiers should be reduced, and we split the classification task in such a way that a classifier needs to learn one particular type of communicative function.

We trained a classifier for each general-purpose and dimension-specific function defined in the DIT^{++} taxonomy, and observed that this has the effect that the various classifiers perform significantly better. These functions were learned (1) in isolation; (2) as semantically related functions together, e.g. all information-seeking functions (all types of questions) or all information-providing functions (all answers and all informs). Both the recognition of communicative functions and that of segment boundaries improves significantly. Table 3 gives an overview of the overall performance (best obtained scores) of the trained classifiers after splitting the learning task.

	BL		BayesNet		Ripper	
Classification task	F_1	DER_{sc}	F_1	DER_{sc}	F_1	DER_{sc}
General-purpose functions						
Propositional Questions	47.0	39.1	**94.9**	3.9	75.8	23.5
Check Questions	43.8	56.4	**68.5**	19.6	61.3	33.1
Set Questions	44.8	52.1	74.1	18.6	**76.3**	17.7
Inform	45.8	39.9	**79.8**	18.7	66.5	30.5
Inform Rhetorical	37.2	38.9	**69.1**	13.4	68.7	23.9
Agreement	41.3	79.1	**72.1**	12.6	71.6	60.2
Propositional Answer	32.0	77.8	**66.8**	26.1	52.2	53.8
Set Answer	44.3	54.2	**77.5**	13.2	57.3	44.1
Suggest	45.8	38.4	**65.6**	17.3	48.8	35.6
Request	45.8	49.3	**75.8**	14.5	50.3	36.9
Instruct	46.3	49.3	**60.5**	14.5	46.3	36.9
Dimension-specific functions						
Auto-Feedback	57.1	23.5	**78.8**	13.2	66.7	15.5
Allo-Feedback	89.3	4.4	**95.1**	2.9	94.3	3.9
Turn Management:initial	24.8	21.9	**72.8**	7.4	46.3	10.7
Turn Management:close	30.7	64.9	**62.0**	22.5	54.7	39.6
Time management	68.3	32.3	82.4	13.7	**92.8**	11.4
Discourse Structuring	40.7	13.6	72.6	2.5	**74.5**	1.7
Contact Management	21.4	48.6	89.2	5.7	**92.3**	3.6
Own Communication Management	26.7	48.6	**78.0**	11.6	68.1	20.0
Partner Communication Management	33.4	18.2	77.8	8.5	**88.9**	6.5
Social Obligation Management	60.0	18.7	88.9	8.3	**90.1**	5.5

Table 3: Overview of F-scores and DER_{sc} for the baseline (BL) and the classifiers upon joint segmentation and classification task for each DIT^{++} communicative function or cluster of functions. (Best scores indicated by numbers in bold face.)

Segments having a general-purpose functions may address any of the ten DIT dimensions. The task of dimension recognition can be approached in two ways. One approach is to learn segment boundaries, communicative function label and dimension in one step (e.g. the class label *B:task;inform*). This task is very complicated, however. First, it leads to data which are high dimensional and sparse, which will have a negative influence on the performance of the trained classifiers. Second, in many cases the dimension can be recognized reliably only with some delay; for the first few segment tokens it is often impossible to say what the segment is about. For example:

(1) 1. What do you think who we're aiming this at?
    2. What do you think we are doing next?
    3. What do you think Craig?

The three Set Questions in (1) start with exactly the same words, but they address different dimensions: Question 1 is about the Task (in AMI - the design the television remote control); Question 2 serves the purpose of Discourse Structuring; and Question 3 elicits feedback.

Another approach is to first recognize segment boundaries and communicative function, and define dimension recognition as a separate classification task.

Tokens	SetQuestion		Task		Auto-F.		TurnM.		Complex label (BIOE:D;CF)	
	label	p	label	p	label	p	label	p	label	p
what	B:setQ	0.85	O	0.71	O	1	O	0.68	O	0.933
you	I:setQ	1	task	0.985	O	1	B:give	0.64	O	0.869
guys	I:setQ	1	task	0.998	O	1	E:give	0.66	O	0.937
have	I:setQ	1	task	0.997	O	1	O	1	I:task;setQ	0.989
already	I:setQ	1	task	0.996	O	1	O	0.99	I:task;setQ	0.903
received	I:setQ	1	task	0.987	O	1	O	1	I:task;setQ	0.813
um	O	0.93	O	0.89	O	1	BE:keep	0.99	O	0.982
in	I:setQ	1	task	0.826	O	1	O	0.89	I:task;setQ	0.875
your	I:setQ	1	task	0.996	O	1	O	0.99	I:task;setQ	0.948
mails	E:setQ	0.99	task	0.987	O	1	O	1	E:task;setQ	0.948

Figure 2: *Predictions with indication of confidence scores (highest* p *class probability selected) for each token assigned by five trained classifiers simultaneously.*

We tested both strategies. The F-scores for the joint learning of complex class labels range from 23.0 (DER_{sc} = 68.3) to 45.3 (DER_{sc} = 63.8). For dimension recognition as a separate learning task the F-scores are significantly higher, ranging from 70.6 to 97.7. The scores for joint segmentation and function recognition in the latter case are those listed in Table 3. Figure 2 gives an example of predictions made by five classifiers for the input *what you guys have already received um in your mails*.

4 Managing local classifiers

4.1 Global classification and global search

As shown in the previous section, given a certain input we obtain all possible output predictions (hypotheses) from local classifiers. Some predictions are false, but once a local classifier has made a decision it is never revisited. It is therefore important to base the decision on dialogue act labels not only on local features of the input, but to take other parts of the output into account as well. For example, the partial output predicted so far, i.e. the history of previous predictions, may be taken as features for the next classification step, and helps to discover and correct errors. This is known as 'recurrent sliding window strategy' (see Dietterich (2002)) when the true values of previous predictions are used as features. This approach suffers from the label bias problem, however, when a classifier overestimates the importance of certain features, and moreover does not apply in a realistic situation, since the true values of previous predictions are not available to a classifier in real time. A solution proposed by Van den Bosch (1997) is to apply adaptive training using the *predicted* output of previous steps as features.

We trained higher-level classifiers (often referred to as 'global') that have, along with features extracted locally from the input data as described above, the partial output predicted so far from all local classifiers. We used five previously predicted class labels, assuming that long distance dependencies may be important, and taking into account that the average length of a functional segment in our data is 4.4 tokens. Table 4 gives an overview of the results of applying these global classifiers. We see that the global classifiers make more accurate predictions than the local classifiers, showing an improvement of about 10% on average. The classifiers still make some incorrect predictions, because the decision is sometimes based on incorrect previous predictions. An optimized global search strategy may lead to further improvements of these results.

A strategy to optimize the use of output hypotheses, is to perform a global search in the output space looking for best predictions. Our classifiers do not just predict the most likely class for an instance, but also generate a distribution of output classes. Class distributions can be seen as confidence scores of all predictions that led to a certain state. Our confidence models are constructed based on token level information given the dialogue left-context (i.e. dialogue history, wording of the previous and

Classification task	BayesNet		Ripper	
	F_1	DER_{sc}	F_1	DER_{sc}
Task	65.3	14.9	**79.1**	21.8
Auto-Feedback	72.9	8.1	**77.8**	7.2
Allo-Feedback	67.7	10.9	**74.2**	9.5
Turn Management:initial	**72.2**	11.5	69.5	11.4
Turn Management:close	82.7	5.0	**83.0**	4.9
Time Management	70.0	3.0	**73.5**	2.1
Discourse Structuring	**72.3**	4.9	63.7	3.6
Contact Management	79.1	4.5	**84.3**	4.6
Own Communication Management	66.0	2.4	**68.3**	2.3
Partner Communication Management	**63.2**	7.8	59.5	11.4
Social Obligation Management	**88.4**	0.9	81.6	1.7

Table 4: Overview of F-scores and DER_{sc} of the global classifiers for the AMI data based on added previous predictions of local classifiers.

currently produced functional segment). This is particular useful for dialogue act recognition because the recognition of intentions should be based on the system's understanding of discourse and not just on the interpretation of an isolated utterance. Searching the (partial) output space for the best predictions is not always the best strategy, however, since the highest-ranking predictions are not always correct in a given context. A possible solution to this is to postpone the prediction until some (or all) future predictions have been made for the rest of the segment. For training, the classifier then uses not only previous predictions as additional features, but also some or all future predictions of local classifiers (till the end of the current segment or to the beginning of the next segment, depending on what is recognized). This forces the classifier to not immediately select the highest-ranking predictions, but to also consider lower-ranking predictions that could be better in the context of the rest of the sequence.

Classification task	BayesNet		Ripper	
	F_1	DER_{sc}	F_1	DER_{sc}
Task	82.6	9.5	**86.1**	8.3
Auto-Feedback	81.9	1.9	**95.1**	0.6
Allo-Feedback	**96.3**	0.6	95.7	0.5
Turn Management:initial	**85.7**	1.5	81.5	1.6
Turn Management:close	90.9	3.8	**91.2**	3.6
Time management	90.4	2.4	**93.4**	1.7
Discourse Structuring	**82.1**	1.7	78.3	1.8
Contact Management	87.9	1.2	**94.3**	0.6
Own Communication Management	78.4	2.2	**81.6**	2.0
Partner Communication Management	**71.8**	2.4	70.0	4.6
Social Obligation Management	98.6	0.4	98.6	0.5

Table 5: Overview of F-scores and DER_{sc} of global classifiers for the AMI data per DIT^{++} dimension.

The results show the importance of optimal global classification for finding the best output prediction.

We performed similar experiments on the English MapTask data[8] and obtained comparable results, where F-scores on the global classification task range from 66.7 for Partner Communication Management and Discourse Structuring to 79.7 for Task and 91.2 for Allo-Feedback. For the MapTask corpus the performance of human annotators on segmentation and classification has been assessed; standard kappa scores reported in Bunt et al. (2007) range between 0.92 and 1.00, indicating near perfect agreement between two expert annotators[9].

[8]For more information about the MapTask corpus see `http://www.hcrc.ed.ac.uk/maptask/`

[9]Note, however, that a slightly simplified version of the DIT^{++} tagset has been used here, called the LIRICS tagset, in which the five DIT levels of processing in the Auto- and Allo-Feedback dimensions were collapsed into one.

5 Conclusions and future research

The incremental construction of input interpretation hypotheses is useful in a language understanding system, since it has the effect that the understanding of a relevant input segment is already nearly ready when the last token of the segment is received; when a dialogue act is viewed semantically as a recipe for updating an information state, this means that the specification of the update operation is almost ready at that moment, thus allowing an instantaneous response from the system. It may even happen that the confidence score of a partially processed input segment is that high, that the system may decide to go forward and update its information state without waiting until the end of the segment, and prepare or produce a response based on that update. Of course, full incremental understanding of dialogue utterances includes not only the recognition of communicative functions, but also that of semantic content. However, many dialogue acts have no or only marginal semantic content, such as turn-taking acts, backchannels (*m-hm*) and other feedback acts (*okay*), time management acts (*Just a moment*), apologies and thankings and other social obligation management acts, and in general dialogue acts with a dimension-specific function; for these acts the proposed strategy can work well without semantic content analysis, and will increase the system's interactivity significantly. Moreover, given that the average length of a functional segment in our data is no more than 4.4 tokens, the semantic content of such a segment tends not to be very complex, and its construction therefore does not seem to require very sophisticated computational semantic methods, applied either in an incremental fashion (see e.g. Aist et al. (2007) and DeVault and Stone (2003)) or to a complete segment.

Interactivity is however not the sole motivation for incremental interpretation. The integration of pragmatic information obtained from the dialogue act recognition module, as proposed here, at early processing stage can be beneficially used by the incremental semantic parser (but also syntactic parser module). For instance, information about the communicative function of the incoming segment at early processing stage can defuse a number of ambiguous interpretations, e.g. used for the resolution of many anaphoric expressions. A challenge for future work is to integrate the incremental recognition of communicative functions with incremental syntactic and semantic parsing, and to exploit the interaction of syntactic, semantic and pragmatic hypotheses in order to understand incoming dialogue segments incrementally in an optimally efficient manner.

Acknowledgments

This research was conducted within the project 'Multidimensional Dialogue Modelling', sponsored by the Netherlands Organisation for Scientific Research (NWO), under grant reference 017.003.090. We are also very thankful to anonymous reviewers for their valuable comments.

References

Aist, G., J. Allen, E. Campana, C. Gomez Gallo, S. Stoness, M. Swift, and M. K. Tanenhaus (2007). Incremental understanding in human-computer dialogue and experimental evidence for advantages over nonincremental methods. In *Proceedings of the 11th Workshop on the Semantics and Pragmatics of Dialogue*, Trento, Italy, pp. 149–154.

Ang, J., Y. Liu, and E. Shriberg (2005). Automatic dialog act segmentation and classification in multiparty meetings. In *Proceedings of the ICASSP*, Volume vol. 1, Philadelphia, USA, pp. 10611064.

Bos, J. (2002). *Underspecification and resolution in discourse semantics. PhD Thesis.* Saarbrücken: Saarland University.

Bunt, H. (2007). Semantic underspecification: which techniques for what purpose? In *Computing Meaning, Vol. 3*, pp. 55–85. Dordrecht: Springer.

Bunt, H. (2009). The DIT++ taxonomy for functional dialogue markup. In *Proceedings of the AAMAS 2009 Workshop 'Towards a Standard Markup Language for Embodied Dialogue Acts' (EDAML 2009)*, Budapest.

Bunt, H. (2010). Multifunctionality in dialogue and its interpretation. *Computer, Speech and Language, Special issue on dialogue modeling.*

Bunt, H., J. Alexandersson, J. Carletta, J.-W. Choe, A. Fang, K. Hasida, K. Lee, V. Petukhova, A. Popescu-Belis, L. Romary, C. Soria, and D. Traum (2010). *Language resource management – Semantic annotation framework – Part 2: Dialogue acts. ISO DIS 24617-2*. Geneva: ISO Central Secretariat.

Bunt, H., V. Petukhova, and A. Schiffrin (2007). Lirics deliverable d4.4. multilingual test suites for semantically annotated data. Available at `http://lirics.loria.fr`.

Cohen, W. (1995). Fast effective rule induction. In *Proceedings of the 12th International Conference on Machine Learning (ICML'95)*, pp. 115–123.

DeVault, D. and M. Stone (2003). Domain inference in incremental interpretation. In *Proceedings of the Workshop on Inference in Computational Semantics*, INRIA Lorraine, Nancy, France.

Dietterich, T. (2002). Machine learning for sequential data: a review. In *Proceedings of the Joint IAPR International Workshop on Structural, Syntactic, and Statistical Pattern Recognition*, pp. 15–30.

Geertzen, J. (2009). *Dialogue act recognition and prediction: exploration in computational dialogue modelling*. The Netherlands: Tilburg University.

Geertzen, J., V. Petukhova, and H. Bunt (2007, September). A multidimensional approach to utterance segmentation and dialogue act classification. In *Proceedings of the 8th SIGdial Workshop on Discourse and Dialogue*, Antwerp, Belgium, pp. 140–149. Association for Computational Linguistics.

Haddock, N. (1989). Computational models of incremental semantic interpretation. *Language and Cognitive Processes Vol. 14 (3)*, SI337–SI380.

Hobbs, J. (1985). Ontological promiscuity. In *Proceedings 23rd Annual Meeting of the ACL*, Chicago, pp. 61–69.

Lendvai, P., v. d. A. Bosch, and E. Krahmer (2003). Machine learning for shallow interpretation of user utterances in spoken dialogue systems. In *Proceedings of EACL-03 Workshop on Dialogue Systems: interaction, adaptation and styles of management*, Budapest.

Lendvai, P. and J. Geertzen (2007). Token-based chunking of turn-internal dialogue act sequences. In *Proceedings of the 8th SIGdial Workshop on Discourse and Dialogue*, Antwerp, Belgium, pp. 174–181.

Milward, D. and R. Cooper (2009). Incremental interpretation: applications, theory, and relationship to dynamic semantics. In *Proceedings COLING 2009, Kyoto, Japan*, pp. 748–754.

Nakano, M., N. Miyazaki, J. Hirasawa, K. Dohsaka, and T. Kawabata (1999). Understanding unsegmented user utterances in real-time spoken dialogue systems. In *Proceedings of the 37th Annual Conference of the Association of Computational Linguistics, ACL*, pp. 200–207.

Petukhova, V. and H. Bunt (2009). Who's next? speaker-selection mechanisms in multiparty dialogue. In *Proceedings of the Workshop on the Semantics and Pragmatics of Dialogue*, Stockholm,, pp. 19–26.

Pinkal, M. (1999). On semantic underspecification. In *Computing Meaning, Vol. 1*, pp. 33–56. Dordrecht: Kluwer.

Poesio, M. and D. Traum (1998). Towards an Axiomatization of Dialogue Acts. In *Proceedings of the Twente Workshop on the Formal Semantics and Pragmatics of Dialogue*, Twente, pp. 309–347.

Sedivy, J. (2003). Pragmatic versus form-based accounts of referential contrast: Evidence for effects of informativity expectations. *Journal of Psycolinguistic Research 32(1)*, 3–23.

Sedivy, J., M. Tanenhaus, C. Chambers, and G. Carlson (1999). Achieving incremental semantic interpretation through contextual representation. *Cognition 71*, 109–147.

Tanenhaus, M., M. Spivey-Knowlton, K. Eberhard, and J. Sedivy (1995). Intergration of visual and linguistic information in spoken language comprehension. *Science 268*, 1632–1634.

Tomita, M. (1986). *Efficient parsing for natural language*. Dordrecht: Kluwer.

Van den Bosch, A. (1997). *Learning to pronounce written words: A study in inductive language learning. PhD thesis*. The Netherlands: Maastricht University.

Zimmermann, M., Y. Lui, E. Shriberg, and A. Stolcke (2005). Toward joint segmentation and classification of dialog acts in multiparty meetings. In *Proceedings of the Multimodal Interaction and Related Machine Learning Algorithms Workshop (MLMI05)*, pp. 187–193. Springer.

Extracting aspects of determiner meaning from dialogue in a virtual world environment

Hilke Reckman, Jeff Orkin, and Deb Roy
MIT Media Lab
{reckman,jorkin,dkroy}@media.mit.edu

Abstract

We use data from a virtual world game for automated learning of words and grammatical constructions and their meanings. The language data are an integral part of the social interaction in the game and consist of chat dialogue, which is only constrained by the cultural context, as set by the nature of the provided virtual environment. Building on previous work, where we extracted a vocabulary for concrete objects in the game by making use of the non-linguistic context, we now target NP/DP grammar, in particular determiners. We assume that we have captured the meanings of a set of determiners if we can predict which determiner will be used in a particular context. To this end we train a classifier that predicts the choice of a determiner on the basis of features from the linguistic and non-linguistic context.

1 Introduction

Determiners are among those words whose meanings are hardest to define in a dictionary. In NLP, determiners are often considered 'stop words' that are not relevant for understanding the content of a document and should be removed before any interesting processing is done. On the other hand, it has been shown that children are sensitive to determiner choice already at a very early age, using these function words in figuring out what content nouns are intended to refer to. Meanings of determiners have been argued to include important pragmatic and discourse-related functions.

We have a corpus of dialogue that is grounded in a virtual environment. This means that in our data there is a relation between what people are saying and what they are doing, providing cues as to what they mean by the words and constructions they use. We have chosen to use a virtual world environment to collect data in, rather than a real world environment, because relatively rich virtual worlds are by now available that are able to provide an interesting level of grounding, whereas making sense of real world scenes using computer vision is still very challenging. In addition, this choice allows us to conveniently collect data online[1].

Although there exists a rich body of computational linguistics research on learning from corpus data, these corpora usually consist of text only. Only recently corpora that include non-linguistic context have started to be collected and used for grounded learning of semantics (Chen et al., 2010; Frank et al., 2009; Fleischman and Roy, 2005; Gorniak and Roy, 2005). This kind of work offers new and insightful perspectives on learning meanings of natural language words and constructions, based on the idea that our own knowledge of natural language meanings is grounded in action and perception (Roy, 2005), and that language is a complex adaptive system which evolves in a community through grounded interaction (e.g. Steels, 2003). So far the language in virtually grounded datasets has often been restricted to either descriptions or directives, so utterances can be paired fairly directly with the actions they describe. The interaction in our data is much freer. That means that it is more representative for the data that human learners get, and that our methods can be applied to a wider variety of data, possibly also to datasets

[1] Von Ahn and Dabbish (2004) were among the first to realize the potential of collecting human knowledge data online, in a game setup, collecting a large image-labeling corpus.

that have not been collected specifically for this purpose. A related project is KomParse (Klüwer et al., 2010). Piantadosi et al. (2008) developed a Bayesian model that learns compositional semantic meanings of different kinds of words, including quantifiers, but from completely artificial data.

Our research focuses on learning from data, rather than through interaction, though the latter may be possible in a later stage of the project. An example of a virtual world project where language is learned through interaction is 'Wubble World' (Hewlett et al., 2007). In the Give Challenge (Byron et al., 2009) a virtual world setup is used to evaluate natural language generation systems.

In previous work we have extracted words and multi-word expressions that refer to a range of objects that are prominent in our virtual environment (Reckman et al., 2010). Now we investigate if aspects of determiner meaning can be learned from this dataset. The extracted knowledge of nouns makes the learning of determiners possible. We study what factors contribute to the choice of the determiner and how they relate to each other, by training a decision tree classifier using these factors as features. The decision tree provides insight in which features are actually used, in which order, and to which effect. The accuracy of the resulting classifier on a test set should give us an impression of how well we understand the use of the different determiners. Although one may argue that this study is about use rather than about meaning, we take it that meaning can only be learned through use, and it is meaning that we are ultimately interested in. One of the overarching questions we are concerned with is what knowledge about language and how it works is needed to extract knowledge about constructions and their meanings from grounded data. Practically, a computational understanding of determiners will contribute to determining the reference of referential expressions, particularly in situated dialogue, and to generating felicitous referential expressions (cf. Belz et al., 2010).

We first introduce our dataset. Then we discuss the automated extraction of determiners. Subsequently, we motivate the features we use, present our classifier experiments, and discuss the results.

2 Data: The Restaurant Game

Orkin and Roy (2007) showed in The Restaurant Game project that current computer game technology allows for simulating a restaurant at a high level-of-detail, and exploiting the game-play experiences of thousands of players to capture a wider coverage of knowledge than what could be handcrafted by a team of researchers. The restaurant theme was inspired by the idea of Schank and Abelson (1977), who argued that the understanding of language requires the representation of common ground for everyday scenarios. The goal is automating characters with learned behavior and dialogue. The ongoing Restaurant Game project has provided a rich dataset for linguistic and AI research. In an online two-player game humans are anonymously paired to play the roles of customers and waitresses in a virtual restaurant (http://theRestaurantGame.net). Players can chat with open-ended typed text, move around the 3D environment, and manipulate 47 types of interactive objects through a point-and-click interface (see figure 1). Every object provides the same interaction options: pick up, put down, give, inspect, sit on, eat, and touch, but objects respond to these actions in different ways. The chef and bartender are hard-coded to produce food items based on keywords in chat text. A game takes about 10-15 minutes to play. Everything players say and do is logged in time-coded text files on our servers. Although player interactions vary greatly, we have demonstrated that enough people do engage in common behavior that it is possible for an automatic system to learn statistical models of typical behavior and language that correlate highly with human judgment of typicality (Orkin and Roy, 2007).

Over 10.000 games have been collected. The dialogue is grounded in two (partially overlapping) ways. Not only is there a simulated physical environment with objects that can be manipulated in various ways, but also social patterns of recurring events provide an anchor for making sense of the dialogue. Previous research results include a first implementation of a planner that drives AI characters playing the game (Orkin and Roy, 2009).

The intuition is that a human student of English starting from scratch (but with some common sense knowledge about restaurants), could learn quite a bit of English from studying the Restaurant Game episodes; possibly enough to play the game. We try to computationally simulate such a learning process.

Figure 1: Screen-shots from The Restaurant Game, from left to right: third-person perspective, waitress's perspective with dialogue, menu for interacting with objects.

3 Extracting nouns

Previously, we extracted a vocabulary of referring expressions for a set of concrete objects, based on which words and phrases have the highest relative frequency in the contexts in which the objects are used (see figure 2). We extracted words and phrases that can refer to the food and drink items on the restaurant's menu, the menu, and the bill, and some other items. These expressions represent the core nominal phrases in the game. We will use these expressions as a starting point to extract determiners and nominal modifiers. We restrict ourselves to the ordered food and drink items, the menu and the bill, expecting that these show a somewhat uniform and interesting behavior, as they are the objects that can appear and disappear during the course of a game.

food type	referring expressions
SOUP	'soup' 'vegetable soup' 'soup du jour' 'soup de jour'
SALAD	'salad' 'cobb salad'
SPAGHETTI	'spaghetti' 'spaghetti marinara'
FILET	'steak' 'filet' 'filet mignon'
SALMON	'salmon' 'grilled salmon'
LOBSTER	'lobster' 'lobster thermador'
CHEESECAKE	'cheesecake' 'cheese' 'cake' 'cherry cheesecake' 'cheese cake'
PIE	'pie' 'berry pie'
TART	'tart' 'nectarine tart'

drink type	referring expressions
WATER	'water'
TEA	'tea'
COFFEE	'coffee'
BEER	'beer'
REDWINE	'red' 'wine' 'red wine'
WHITEWINE	'white' 'white wine'

item type	referring expressions
MENU	'menu'
BILL	'bill' 'check'

Figure 2: Extracted referring expressions for relevant items.

The referring expressions for these object types have been extracted in an unsupervised manner making use of the relative frequency of words and phrases in the context of the objects being used. Words, bigrams and trigrams were validated against each other with the use of one threshold. For more detail see (Reckman et al., 2010).

4 Extracting determiners

Extracting determiners totally unsupervised is a non-trivial task. Attempts to use the existing fully unsupervised grammar induction algorithm ADIOS (Solan et al., 2005) did not give us the results we were hoping for. Instead, we decided to make use of the knowledge of nouns that we already have and target determiners directly, rather than having to induce a full grammar. In future work we will look into using alternative grammar induction systems, for a wider range of learning tasks.

We first narrowed down our search space by collecting words that are positively associated with the position directly to the left of the nominal expression above a high recall, low precision threshold (phi=0.01)[2]. This should favor determiners and other nominal modifiers over, for example, verbs.

We expect determiners to appear with a wider range of different nouns than adjectival modifiers do. Especially in this restricted domain, adjectives are more likely to be restricted to specific object types. We consider pre-nominal terms that are general enough to appear with more than 5 different objects (out of 17) to be determiner candidates. We also check that our candidates can be preceded by an utterance boundary.

The word *the* is most strongly associated with the relevant position, combines with most different nouns, and can occur as only element between a boundary and a noun. We therefore assume that at least *the* is a determiner. We order the other candidates according to their similarity to *the*, measured as the cosine distance in a vector-space, with their two words to the left and to the right as dimensions. We accept words as determiners in order of similarity to *the*, starting with the most similar word, after checking that they are in complementary distribution with all of the already accepted words, i.e. that the word does not occur adjacent to any of those. This gives us the following determiners: *the*, *my*, *your*, *some*, *a*, *another*, *our*, *one*, *ur*, *two*, *2*.[3]

We can then identify adjectival modifiers by looking at what occurs between determiners and nouns. By checking what else these modifiers can be preceded by (that is also in complementary distribution with known determiners), we can do another round of determiner search, and that lets us add *any* to our list. As nouns can also be immediately preceded by an utterance boundary, we establish that the determiner position is not obligatorily filled.

Of course this is not a complete set of determiners, but they appear to be the most prominent ones in the game. Real quantifiers are relatively rare and that is to be expected, given the setting. Perhaps more surprisingly, *this* and *that* are not associated with the left-of-noun position. It turns out that they are not used very frequently as determiners in the game, and much more as pronouns. In future work we will extract pronouns, by looking for single words that have a distribution that is similar to the distribution of full noun phrases with a determiner.

In the process of extracting determiners, we also extract adjectives and modifiers such as *glass of*. With little extra effort we can build a vocabulary of these as well, including information as to which nouns they are associated with. Their meanings, however, are in most cases not sufficiently grounded in the game to be understood. We may in a more advanced stage of the project be able to figure out that the adjective *free* makes the item less likely to appear on the bill, but the meaning of *hot* will always remain unclear, as temperature is not modeled in the game. Finding words associated with the position to the left of specific nouns can also help us further improve our vocabulary of referring expressions, for example by identifying *veg* and *veggie* as alternatives for *vegetable* in *vegetable soup*[4].

We took a shortcut by directly targeting the position left of the noun. This involves language-specific knowledge about English. To make this method applicable to different languages and only use very general knowledge at the start, we would first have to find out what the position of the determiner is. This may be to the right of the noun or affixed to it. Not all languages have articles, but we can expect determiners like *my*, *your*, *another* etc. to occur either adjacent to[5], or morphologically expressed on the noun[6]. In previous work we have shown how a construction for coordination can be extracted (Reckman

[2]The phi-score is a chi-square based association metric. Manning and Schütze (2000) argue that such metrics are suitable to quantify collocational effects. We also used it in extracting the referring expressions.

[3]For the experiments we replace *ur* by *your*, and *2* by *two*. We assume this could in principle be done automatically, although especially in the latter case this is not trivial.

[4]We do already have a list of spelling variants for all the terms, but *veg* and *veggie* were too different from the canonical form to get through the edit-distance filter

[5]Obviously we do not catch floating quantifiers this way. We might catch their non-floating counterparts and then discover that they occur in other positions as well.

[6]Several unsupervised morphological analyzers have been developed, which should in principle be run in an early stage of learning. For English however, the only interesting morphology at play here is plural formation.

et al., 2010). Coordination, to our knowledge, occurs in all languages and this is probably a feature of general human cognition, so it makes sense to assume it exists in a language and look for it in the data. It can then be used as a probe on structure. Categories that are grammatically intimately connected to nouns are more likely to be repeated in a coordination involving two nouns. If we look at our English data, for example, we see that a lot more material tends to occur between *and* and the second noun-conjunct, than between the first noun-conjunct and *and*, which suggests that things that are grammatically close to the noun occur to the left of it.

5 Features

In this section we motivate the features we will use. To capture the full meaning of determiners, we would probably have to model the mental states of the players. However, what we aim at here is a preliminary understanding of determiners as a step towards the understanding of full sentences, and the resolution of NP reference and co-reference, which would be prerequisites for any serious modeling of mental states. So we are interested in what can be learned from directly observable features. The features are theoretically motivated, and reflect the nature of the referent, whether the referent has been mentioned before, whether the referent is present, and who the speaker and addressee are.

The first feature is object type. There are 17 different objects that we take into account: BEER, BILL, CHEESECAKE, COFFEE, FILET, LOBSTER, MENU, PIE, REDWINE, SALAD, SALMON, SOUP, SPAGHETTI, TART, TEA, WATER, and WHITEWINE. We expect this feature to matter, because in a restaurant situation one usually orders '*the* spaghetti', but '*a* beer'. This may be to some extent dependent on what is on the menu, but not completely. Regardless of what is on the menu, ordering '*the* Heineken' seems to be more unusual than ordering '*the* Merlot'. This may mean that our data is not entirely representative of the general case, because of our restaurant setting. However, it cannot be excluded that similar effects play a role in other settings, too. There is of course the effect of mass versus count nouns, too, but this may be a bit masked, because of unit expressions like *glass of*. We chose to not include these unit expressions as a feature, because the decision to use such modifiers can be considered part of the decision on which determiner to use. So using the modifier as a feature, would be giving away part of the solution to the determiner-choice problem.

The second feature captures the notion of discourse-old versus discourse-new. We distinguish between cases where an object of a particular type is mentioned for the first time, and where it has already been mentioned before. In the latter case, we take it that the discourse referent has already been introduced. The expected effect is that first mentions tend to be indefinite.[7] This is only an approximation, because sometimes a second object of the same type is introduced and we do not resolve the reference of our instances.

The third and fourth features incorporate present versus future presence of the object, plus the position of the utterance with respect to the central action involving the object. We keep track of the previous and following action in which the object is involved. Actions of interest are restricted to the appearance of the object and and its central action: 'eating' for food and drink items, 'looking at' for the menu, and 'paying' for the bill. Being involved in such an action also implies presence. Other intervening actions are ignored. The features are 'preceding_action' and 'following_action', and the values are 'appearance', 'main_action', and 'none'. We expect indefinites before appearance, when the object is not yet present. Note that these features rely entirely on non-linguistic context.

The fifth and sixth features identify speaker and addressee. The speaker can be the customer or the waitress. For the addressee the relevant distinction is whether the staff (chef and bartender) are addressed or not. We expect a tendency of the waitress using *your* when talking to the customer, and of the customer using *my* more often. We expect more indefinites or absence of a determiner when the staff is spoken to. These features are central to dialogue, and may reveal differences between the roles.

[7]This is a typical feature for languages that have articles, and may be expressed through other means in other languages.

6 Experiments

We use the decision tree classifier from the Natural Language ToolKit for Python (Loper and Bird, 2002) and train and test it through 10-fold cross-validation on 74304 noun phrases from 5000 games, 23776 of which actually have determiners. The noun phrases used all contain nouns that can refer to the selected objects, though we cannot guarantee that they were intended to do so in all cases. In fact, we have seen examples where this is clearly not the case, and for example *filet*, which normally refers to the FILET object, is used in the context of salmon. This means that there is a level of noise in our data.

The instances where the determiner is absent are very dominant, and this part of the data is necessarily noisy, because of rare determiners that we've missed[8], and possibly rather heterogeneous, as there are many reasons why people may choose to not type a determiner in chat. Therefore we focus on the experiments where we have excluded these cases, as the results are more interesting. We will refer to the data that excludes instances with no determiner as the **restricted dataset**. When instances with no determiner are included, we will talk about the **full dataset**.

6.1 Baselines

In the experiments we compare the results of using the features to two different baselines. The simplest baseline is to always choose the most frequent determiner. For the instances that have overt determiners, the most frequent one is *the*. Always choosing *the* gives us a mean accuracy of 0.364. If we include the instances with no overt determiners, that gives us a much higher baseline of 0.680, when the no determiner option is always chosen. We call this the **simple baseline**.

The second baseline is the result of using only the object feature, and forms the basis of our experiments. We call this the **object-only baseline**. On the restricted dataset the resulting classifier assigns the determiner *a* to the objects BEER, COFFEE, PIE, REDWINE, SALAD, TEA, WATER, and WHITEWINE, and the determiner *the* to BILL, CHEESECAKE, FILET, LOBSTER, MENU, SALMON, SOUP, SPAGHETTI, and TART. This yields a mean accuracy of 0.520, which is a considerable improvement over the simple baseline that is relevant for this part of the data. If we look at the confusion matrix in figure 3 that summarizes the results of all 10 object-only runs we see that the objects' preferences for definite versus indefinite determiners are also visible in the way instances with determiners other than *the* and *a* are misclassified. Instances with definite determiners are more often classified as *the*, and indefinites as *a*.

	a	another	any	my	one	our	some	the	two	your
a	<4984>	.	.	.	.	.	.	2912	.	.
another	608	<.>	.	.	.	.	.	76	.	.
any	56	.	<.>	.	.	.	.	24	.	.
my	238	.	.	<.>	.	.	.	742	.	.
one	354	.	.	.	<.>	.	.	241	.	.
our	28	.	.	.	.	<.>	.	178	.	.
some	1109	.	.	.	.	.	<.>	438	.	.
the	1270	.	.	.	.	.	.	<7383>	.	.
two	191	.	.	.	.	.	.	58	<.>	.
your	805	.	.	.	.	.	.	2075	.	<.>

Figure 3: Confusion matrix for the object-only baseline.

On the full dataset, the classifier assigns *the* to instances of BILL and MENU and no determiner to everything else, reflecting the count/mass distinction, and resulting in a mean accuracy of 0.707. This is also a statistically significant improvement over its baseline, but much less spectacular. The definite/indefinite distinction that we saw with the restricted dataset, does not really emerge here.

[8]It is also hard to reliably recognize misspelled determiners as determiners tend to be very short words.

6.2 Adding the other features

In the core experiments of this paper we always use the object feature as a basis and measure the effect of adding the other features, separately and in combination. All differences reported are significant, unless stated otherwise. The table in figure 5 at the end of the section summarizes the results.

If we add the feature of whether the item has been mentioned before or not, we get more indefinites, as was to be expected. On the restricted dataset, the MENU, PIE, and TART objects get *a* if not mentioned previously, and *the* otherwise. The mean accuracy is 0.527, which is a statistically significant improvement over the object-only baseline (the improvement is consistent over all 10 runs), but it seems rather small, nevertheless. (Using the discourse feature without the object feature gives a score of 0.377.) Adding information as to whether the customer has seen the menu does not make any difference. On the full dataset the discourse feature matters only for MENU, which gets *a* if not previously mentioned. The mean accuracy is 0.709.

If, instead, we add the action features we get a somewhat more substantial improvement for the restricted dataset; a mean accuracy of 0.561. We also get a wider range of determiners: *your* tends to be chosen after appearing and before eating, *another* after eating, and *a* between no action and appearing. The order in which the following and preceding action features are applied by the classifier differs per object. (The action features without the object feature give a mean accuracy score of 0.427.) For the full dataset the mean accuracy is 0.714, again a consistent, but marginal improvement. However, *a*, *the* and *your* are the only determiners used, in addition to the no determiner option.

Adding the speaker and addressee features to the object feature base gives the classifier a better grip on *your*. More indefinites are used when the staff is addressed, *your* when the customer is spoken to. However, *my* is still not picked up. The speaker and addressee features are used in both orders. The mean accuracy is 0.540, which is better than with the discourse feature, but worse than with the action features. (The speaker and addressee features without the object feature give a mean accuracy score of 0.424.) In the case of the full dataset, the new features are barely used, and there is no consistent improvement over the different runs. The mean accuracy is 0.711.

If we combine the action features and speaker/addressee features on top of the object feature basis, we see a substantial improvement again for the restricted dataset. The mean accuracy is 0.592. Finally, we get some cases of *my* being correctly classified, and also *your* is correctly classified significantly more often than in the previous experiments. The object feature always comes first in the decision tree. For the other features, all relative orders are attested. Adding the 'previously-mentioned' feature to this combination (see also figure 4) improves this result a little bit more, to a mean accuracy of 0.594, although we can expect the information contained in it to have a large overlap with the information in other features, for example, items mentioned for the first time will typically not have appeared yet.

	a	another	any	my	one	our	some	the	two	your
a	<5732>	163	1	11	20	.	70	1773	1	125
another	175	<350>	.	2	.	.	48	70	.	39
any	44	4	<.>	.	.	.	2	29	.	1
my	154	19	.	<9>	.	.	20	765	.	13
one	437	20	.	2	<16>	.	4	70	.	46
our	29	1	.	.	.	<.>	1	161	.	14
some	881	48	.	6	3	.	<114>	421	.	74
the	1332	74	.	33	8	.	34	<6131>	.	1040
two	191	10	.	2	.	.	1	45	<.>	.
your	218	88	.	.	.	.	20	781	.	<1773>

(row = reference; col = test)

Figure 4: Confusion matrix for the object, action, speaker/addressee and discourse features combined.

6.3 Linguistic context and dialogue acts

It will be part of future research to distinguish the different dialogue acts that the nominal phrases that we studied can be part of. Identifying the 'task' that an expression is part of may have a similar effect. Tasks of the type 'customer gets seated', 'waitress serves food', 'customer eats meal', etc. are annotated for supervised learning, and may consist of several actions and utterances (Orkin et al., 2010).

To give an indication that the dialogue act that an expression is part of may be informative as to the correct choice of the determiner, we have done an extra experiment, where we have used the word before and the word after the DP as features. This gives a tremendous amount of feature values, which are not very insightful, due to the lack of generalization, and are a near guarantee for over-fitting. However, it does yield an improvement over using the object-only baseline. Moreover, the preceding word and following word features are now applied before the object feature. The mean accuracy in this experiment was 0.562, which is comparable to the experiment with object and action features. At the same time we get a wider range of determiners than we have had before, including some correctly classified instances of *our*. On the full dataset we even get a higher accuracy score than in any of the other experiments: 0.769, also with a much wider range of determiners. We suspect that this local linguistic context gives quite good cues as to whether the expression is part of a proper sentence or not, and that in the former case an overt determiner is much more likely[9]. The results of all experiments are summarized in figure 5.

	restricted	full
simple baseline	0.364	0.680
object-only baseline	0.520	0.707
object + discourse	0.527	0.709
object + action	0.561	0.714
object + speaker	0.540	0.711
object + action + speaker	0.592	0.721
object + action + speaker + discourse	**0.594**	0.721
object + surrounding words	0.562	**0.769**

Figure 5: Summary of the testing results.

7 Discussion

Maybe the most surprising outcome is that the object type turns out to be the main factor in choosing the determiner in this virtual restaurant setting. It would beinteresting to see this reproduced on the data of two new games that are currently being developed, with novel scenarios, locations and objects. At the same time, it is a strength of our approach, that we can simulate a specific setting and capture its ideosyncrasies, learning domain-specific aspects of language, and hopefully eventually learn what generalizes across different scenarios.

For the restricted dataset we see that, consistently, indefinites are mostly misclassified as *a*, and definites mostly as *the*. If we evaluate only for definiteness, we get a mean accuracy of 0.800 for the case with all features combined. We could distinguish these two classes of determiners on the basis of the similarity of each determiner to the two dominant types. It is, however, the object feature that seems to be mainly responsible for the gain in definiteness accuracy with respect to the simple baseline.

It is unsurprising that we haven't learned much about *one* and *two*, except that they pattern with indefinites, as we haven't included features that have to do with the number of objects. There actually are more numerals that appear in the game, but did not make it into our list of determiners, because they did not occur with enough different objects. In the general case, we are doubtful that numerals are sufficiently grounded in this game for their exact meanings to be learned. It may however be possible to learn a one-two-many kind of distinction. This would also involve looking into plural morphology, and remains for future research.

[9]We have observed that in several games people tend to just sum up food items, without embedding them in a sentence.

We also haven't learned anything about *our*, except that it patterns with definites. It is not quite clear what kind of features would be relevant to *our* in this setting.

For the possessive pronouns *your* and *my* we have learned that one tends to be linked to the waitress as a speaker (and the customer as addressee) and the other to the customer. It will be challenging to reach an understanding that goes deeper than this[10]. The range of interactions in the game may be too limited to learn the meanings of all determiners in their full generality.

While we have treated *a* and *another* as different determiners, we have included cases of *some more* under *some*. It may be worthwhile to include *some more* (and perhaps *any more* and *one more* as well) as a separate determiner. However, our best classifier so far still cannot distinguish between *a* and *another* very well.

The experiments with linguistic context suggest that dialogue act may make for an additional, powerful, albeit indirect, feature. The fact that it helps to know when the main action involving the object took place, rather than just its appearance, may also be taken to point in the same direction, as people tend to say different kinds of things about an object before and after the main action.

Using a classifier seems to be a reasonable way of testing how well we understand determiners, as long as our features provide insight. Although there is still a lot of room for improvement, there is likely to be a ceiling effect at some point, because sometimes more than one option is felicitous. We also have to keep in mind that chat is likely to be more variable than normal written or spoken language.

8 Conclusion

We have carried out an exploratory series of experiments, to see if meanings of determiners, a very abstract linguistic category, could be learned from virtually grounded dialogue data. We have trained a classifier on a set of theoretically motivated features, and used the testing phase to evaluate how well these features predict the choice of the determiner.

Altogether, the results are encouraging. If we exclude instances with no determiner we reach an accuracy of 0.594 over a baseline of 0.364. The features that identify the dialogue participants and surrounding actions, including appearance, play an important role in this result, even though the object type remains the main factor. A clear dichotomy between definite and indefinite determiners emerges. The results for the complete dataset are a bit messier, and need more work.

In future work we will identify utterance types, or dialogue acts, that also rely on surrounding actions and on the speaker and addressee. We will also look into resolving reference and co-reference.

Acknowledgments

This research was funded by a Rubicon grant from the Netherlands Organisation for Scientific Research (NWO), project nr. 446-09-011.

References

Belz, A., E. Kow, J. Viethen, and A. Gatt (2010). Generating referring expressions in context: The GREC task evaluation challenges. In *Empirical Methods in Natural Language Generation*, pp. 294–327. Springer.

Byron, D., A. Koller, K. Striegnitz, J. Cassell, R. Dale, J. Moore, and J. Oberlander (2009). Report on the First NLG Challenge on Generating Instructions in Virtual Environments (GIVE). In *Proceedings of the 12th European Workshop on Natural Language Generation*, pp. 165–173. ACL.

Chen, D., J. Kim, and R. Mooney (2010). Training a Multilingual Sportscaster: Using Perceptual Context to Learn Language. *Journal of Artificial Intelligence Research 37*, 397–435.

[10] For their personal pronoun counterparts *you* and *I* we might stand a better chance.

Fleischman, M. and D. Roy (2005). Why verbs are harder to learn than nouns: Initial insights from a computational model of intention recognition in situated word learning. In *27th Annual Meeting of the Cognitive Science Society, Stresa, Italy*.

Frank, M., N. Goodman, and J. Tenenbaum (2009). Using speakers' referential intentions to model early cross-situational word learning. *Psychological Science 20*(5), 578.

Gorniak, P. and D. Roy (2005). Probabilistic grounding of situated speech using plan recognition and reference resolution. In *Proceedings of the 7th international conference on Multimodal interfaces*, pp. 143. ACM.

Hewlett, D., S. Hoversten, W. Kerr, P. Cohen, and Y. Chang (2007). Wubble world. In *Proceedings of the 3rd Conference on Artificial Intelligence and Interactive Entertainment*.

Klüwer, T., P. Adolphs, F. Xu, H. Uszkoreit, and X. Cheng (2010). Talking NPCs in a virtual game world. In *Proceedings of the ACL 2010 System Demonstrations*, pp. 36–41. ACL.

Loper, E. and S. Bird (2002). NLTK: The natural language toolkit. In *Proceedings of the ACL-02 Workshop on Effective tools and methodologies for teaching natural language processing and computational linguistics-Volume 1*, pp. 70. ACL.

Manning, C. and H. Schütze (2000). *Foundations of statistical natural language processing*. MIT Press.

Orkin, J. and D. Roy (2007). The restaurant game: Learning social behavior and language from thousands of players online. *Journal of Game Development 3*(1), 39–60.

Orkin, J. and D. Roy (2009). Automatic learning and generation of social behavior from collective human gameplay. In *Proceedings of The 8th International Conference on Autonomous Agents and Multiagent Systems-Volume 1*, pp. 385–392. International Foundation for Autonomous Agents and Multiagent Systems.

Orkin, J., T. Smith, H. Reckman, and D. Roy (2010). Semi-Automatic Task Recognition for Interactive Narratives with EAT & RUN. In *Proceedings of the 3rd Intelligent Narrative Technologies Workshop at the 5th International Conference on Foundations of Digital Games (FDG)*.

Piantadosi, S., N. Goodman, B. Ellis, and J. Tenenbaum (2008). A Bayesian model of the acquisition of compositional semantics. In *Proceedings of the Thirtieth Annual Conference of the Cognitive Science Society*. Citeseer.

Reckman, H., J. Orkin, and D. Roy (2010). Learning meanings of words and constructions, grounded in a virtual game. In *Proceedings of the 10th Conference on Natural Language Processing (KONVENS)*.

Roy, D. (2005). Semiotic schemas: A framework for grounding language in action and perception. *Artificial Intelligence 167*(1-2), 170–205.

Schank, R. and R. Abelson (1977). *Scripts, plans, goals and understanding: An inquiry into human knowledge structures*. Lawrence Erlbaum Associates Hillsdale, NJ.

Solan, Z., D. Horn, E. Ruppin, and S. Edelman (2005). Unsupervised learning of natural languages. *Proceedings of the National Academy of Sciences of the United States of America 102*(33), 11629.

Steels, L. (2003). Evolving grounded communication for robots. *Trends in cognitive sciences 7*(7), 308–312.

Von Ahn, L. and L. Dabbish (2004). Labeling images with a computer game. In *Proceedings of the SIGCHI conference on Human factors in computing systems*, pp. 319–326. ACM.

On the Maximalization of the Witness sets in Independent Set readings

Livio Robaldo
Department of Computer Science, University of Turin,
robaldo@di.unito.it

1 Pre - Introduction

Before starting, I would like to ask reader's opinion about the truth/falsity of certain NL statements. The statements are about figures depicting dots connected to stars. In the figures, we distinguish between dots and stars that are connected, i.e. such that every dot is connected with at least one star and every star is connected with at least one dot, and dots and stars that are *totally* connected, i.e. such that every dot is connected to every star. For instance, in (1), the dots d_1, d_2, and d_3 are connected with the stars s_1, s_2, and s_3 (on the left) while d_4 and d_5 are *totally* connected with s_4, s_5, and s_6 (on the right).

(1)

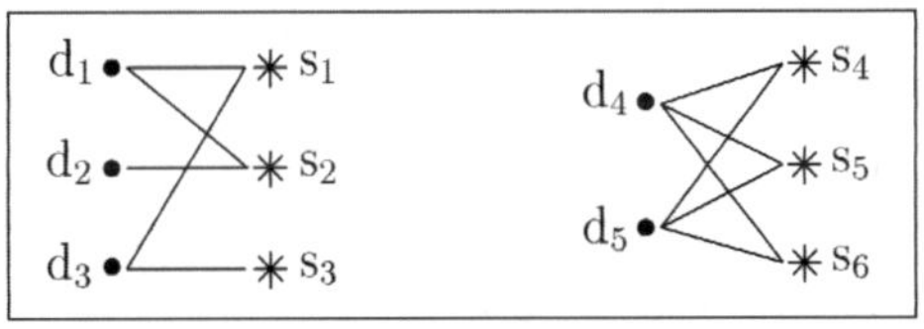

given these premises, is it true that in the next figure *Less than half of the dots are totally connected with exactly three stars*? (do not read below before answering)

(2)

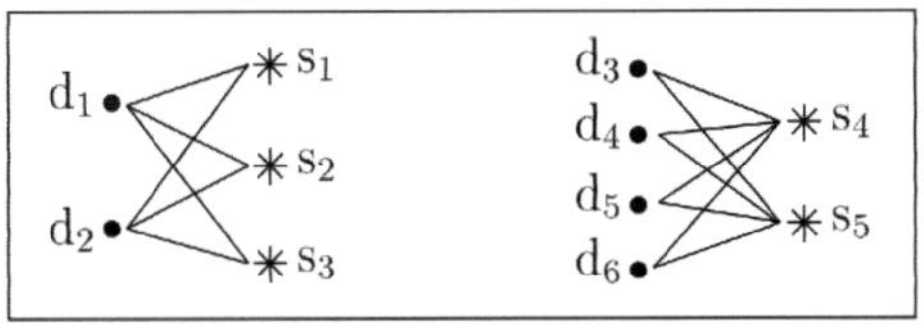

I do think that the answer is yes. The same answer has been given by several friends/colleagues that were asked to judge the example. In fact, the figure does contain two dots d_1 and d_2, which are less than half of all the dots in the figure, and they are both connected with three same stars s_1, s_2, and s_3.
Now, is it true in (3) that *Few dots are totally connected with few stars?*

(3)

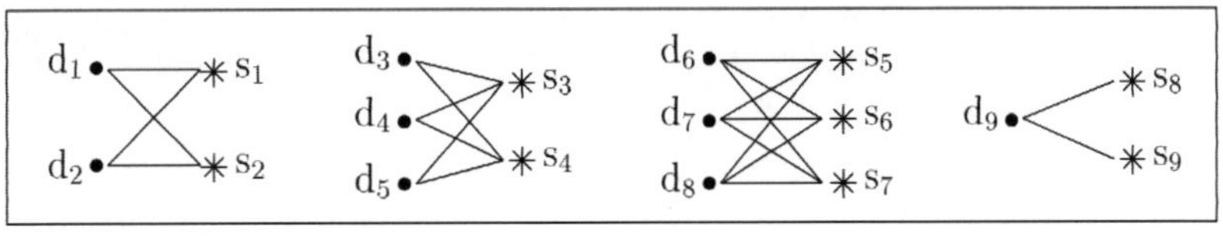

It is somehow harder to provide an answer to this second question. At first sight, it seems the sentence is false, or at least 'strange': no English speaker would ever utter that sentence in that context, whatever he wants to describe.

We are ready now to explore the proposals that aimed at formally defining the truth conditions of sentences as the two ones above. In the literature, most logical approaches to the problem state that the two sentences are both false in contexts (2) and (3). In (Robaldo, 2009a), drawing from (Sher, 1997), I proposed a new alternative where they are both evaluated as true. It seems then that neither proposals is completely satisfatory. The present paper proposes a "pragmatic" revision of (Robaldo, 2009a) that achieves – what are claimed to be – the proper truth values of such sentences.

2 Introduction

In the Pre-Introduction, it has been asked to judge the truth values of two NL sentences according to their 'Scopeless interpretation', termed in (Robaldo, 2009a) as 'Independent Set (IS) reading'. In constrast, in a linear reading one of the sets may vary on the entities in the other one. An example is *Each boy ate two apples*, whose preferred reading is a linear reading where *Each* outscopes *Two*, i.e. where each boy ate two *different* apples. Four kinds of IS readings have been identified in the literature, from (Scha, 1981).

(4) a. **Branching Quantifier readings**, e.g. *Two students of mine have seen three drug-dealers in front of the school.* (Robaldo, 2009a)

b. **Collective readings**, e.g. *Three boys made a chair yesterday.* (Nakanishi, 2007)

c. **Cumulative readings**, e.g. *Three boys invited four girls.* (Landman, 2000)

d. **Cover readings**, e.g. *Twenty children ate ten pizzas.* (Kratzer, 2007)

The preferred reading of (4.a) is the one where there are exactly two[1] students and exacly three drug-dealers and each of the students saw each of the drug-dealers. Note that these are the truth values assigned to (1)-(3) when dots and stars are asked to be *totally* connected. (4.b) may be true in case three boys cooperated in the construction of a single chair. In the preferred reading of (4.c), there are three boys and four girls such that each of the boys invited at least one girl, and each of the girls was invited by at least one boy. These are the truth values assigned to (1) when dots and stars are asked to be connected, possibly not totally. Finally, (4.d) allows for any sharing of ten pizzas between twenty children. In Cumulative readings, the single actions are carried out by *atomic*[2] individuals only, while in (4.d) it is likely that the pizzas are shared among subgroups of children. For instance, *Three children ate five pizzas* is satisfied by the following extension of ate' ('$\oplus$' is the standard sum operator (Link, 1983)):

(5) $$\|ate'\|^M \equiv \{\langle c_1 \oplus c_2 \oplus c_3, p_1 \oplus p_2\rangle, \langle c_2 \oplus c_3, p_3 \oplus p_4\rangle, \langle c_3, p_5\rangle\}$$

In (5), children c_1, c_2, and c_3 (cut into slices and) share pizzas p_1 and p_2, c_2 and c_3 (cut into slices and) share p_3 and p_4, and c_3 also ate pizza p_5 on his own.

Branching Quantifier readings have been the more controversial (cf. (Beghelli et al., 1997) and (Gierasimczuk and Szymanik, 2009)). Many authors claim that those readings are always subcases of Cumulative readings, and they often co-occur with certain adverbs (May, 1989), (Schein, 1993). In fact, in the Pre-Introduction, in order to force such a reading on (1)-(3), it was necessary to add the adverb *totally* to the verb *connected.* Collective and Cumulative readings have been largely studied; see (Scha, 1981), (Link, 1983), (Beck and Sauerland, 2000), and (Ben-Avi and Winter, 2003).

However, the focus here is on Cover readings. This paper assumes – following (van der Does, 1993), (van der Does and Verkuyl, 1996), (Schwarzschild, 1996), (Kratzer, 2007) – that they are *the* IS readings, of which the three kinds exemplified in (4.a-c) are merely special cases. The name "Cover readings" comes from the fact that their truth values are traditionally captured in terms of Covers. A Cover is a mathematical structure defined with respect to one or more sets. With respect to two sets S_1 and S_2, a Cover Cov is formally defined as:

[1] In (4.a-d) "two/three/ten/etc." are interpreted as "*exactly* two/three/ten/etc." as in (Scha, 1981). That is actually a pragmatic implicature, as noted in (Landman, 2000), pp.224-238.

[2] In line with (Landman, 2000), pp.129, and (Beck and Sauerland, 2000), def.(3), that explicitly define Cumulative readings as statements among atomic individuals only.

(6) A Cover Cov is a subset of $Cov_1 \times Cov_2$, where $Cov_1 \subseteq \wp(S_1)$ and $Cov_2 \subseteq \wp(S_2)$ s.t.

a. $\forall s_1 \in S_1, \exists cov_1 \in Cov_1$ s.t. $s_1 \in cov_1$, and $\forall s_2 \in S_2, \exists cov_2 \in Cov_2$ s.t. $s_2 \in cov_2$.

b. $\forall cov_1 \in Cov_1, \exists cov_2 \in Cov_2$ s.t. $\langle cov_1, cov_2 \rangle \in Cov$.

c. $\forall cov_2 \in Cov_2, \exists cov_1 \in Cov_1$ s.t. $\langle cov_1, cov_2 \rangle \in Cov$.

Covers may be denoted by 2-order variables called "Cover variables". We may then define a meta-predicate $Cover$ that, taken a Cover variable C and two unary predicates P_1 and P_2, asserts that the extension of the former is a Cover of the extensions of the latter:

(7) $$\begin{aligned} &Cover(C, P_1, P_2) \Leftrightarrow \\ &\quad \forall_{X_1 X_2}[C(X_1, X_2) \rightarrow \forall_{x_1 x_2}[((x_1 \subset X_1) \wedge (x_2 \subset X_2)) \rightarrow (P_1(x_1) \wedge P_2(x_2))]] \wedge \\ &\quad \forall_{x_1}[\, P_1(x_1) \rightarrow \exists_{X_1 X_2}[\, (x_1 \subset X_1) \wedge C(X_1, X_2)\,]\,] \wedge \\ &\quad \forall_{x_2}[\, P_2(x_2) \rightarrow \exists_{X_1 X_2}[\, (x_2 \subset X_2) \wedge C(X_1, X_2)\,]\,] \end{aligned}$$

Thus, it is possible to decouple the quantifications from the predications. This is done by introducing two relational variables whose extensions include the *atomic* individuals involved. Another relational variable that covers them describes how the actions are actually done. For instance, in (5), in order to evaluate as true the variant of (4.d), we may introduce three variables P_1, P_2, and C such that:

$$\|P_1\|^M = \{c_1, c_2, c_3\} \qquad \|P_2\|^M = \{p_1, p_2, p_3, p_4, p_5\}$$
$$\|C\|^M = \{\ \langle c_1 \oplus c_2 \oplus c_3,\ p_1 \oplus p_2 \rangle,\ \langle c_2 \oplus c_3,\ p_3 \oplus p_4 \rangle,\ \langle c_3,\ p_5 \rangle\ \}$$

The above extensions of P_1, P_2, and C satisfy $Cover(C, P_1, P_2)$.

Among the Cover approaches mentioned above, an interesting one is (Schwarzschild, 1996). Schwarzschild discusses numerous NL sentences where the identification of Covers appears to be pragmatically determined, rather than existentially quantified. In other words, in the formulae the value of the Cover variables ought to be provided by an assignment g. One of the examples mostly discussed in (Schwarzschild, 1996) is:

(8) a. The cows and the pigs were separated.

b. The cows and the pigs were separated *according to color.*

The preferred reading of (8.a) is the one where the cows were separated from the pigs. However, that is actually an implicature that may be rewritten as in (8.b), where the separation is not done by race. Examples like (8) are used by (Schwarzschild, 1996) in order to argue against the existence of groups and the overgeneration of readings, extensively advocated by (Landman, 2000). Schwarzschild claims that the NP in (8.a) must correspond to a unary predicate whose extension is the set of *individual* cows and pigs, while the precise separation is described by a contextually-dependent Cover variable. Similarly, in (4.c) the Cumulative interpretation is preferred as in real contexts invitations are usually thought as actions among pairs of persons. But it may be the case that two or more boys *collectively* invited two or more girls. On the other hand, in (4.a) the fact that each student saw each drug-dealer seems to be favoured by the low value of the numerals. If the sentence were *Almost all of my students have seen several drug-dealers in front of the school*, the preferred reading appears to be Cumulative.

The next section illustrates a final component needed to build whole formulae for representing Cover readings. This is the requirement of Maximal participancy of the witness sets, e.g. the Maximal participancy of P_1 and P_2's extension in the formula representing the meaning of the variant of (4.d). It will be also shown that there are two possible ways to maximize the witness sets: *Locally* and *Globally*. The former predicts that both examples in (2) and (3) are true, while the latter predicts that they are both false.

3 The Maximality requirement

The previous section showed that, for representing IS readings, it is necessary to reify the witness sets into relational variables as P_1 and P_2. Separately, the elements of these sets are combined as described by the Cover variables, in order to assert the predicates on the correct pairs of (possibly plural) individuals. Conversely, it is not possible to represent an IS reading by nesting quantifiers into the scope of other quantifiers, as it is done in the standard Generalized Quantifier (GQ) approach (Keenan and Westerståhl, 1997), because the set of entities quantified by the narrow-scope quantifier would vary on each entity quantified by the wide-scope one.
As argued by (van Benthem, 1986), (Kadmon, 1987), (Sher, 1990), (Sher, 1997), (Spaan, 1996), (Steedman, 2007), (Robaldo, 2009a), and (Robaldo, 2009b) the relational variables must, however, be *Maximized* in order to achieve the proper truth values with any quantifier, regardless to its monotonicity. To see why, let us consider sentences in (9), taken from (Robaldo, 2009a), that involve a single quantifier.

(9) a. At least two men walk.

b. At most two men walk.

c. Exactly two men walk.

In terms of reified relational variables, it seems that the meaning of (9.a-c) may represented via (10.a-c), where $^{\geq}2$, $^{\leq}2$, and $^{=}2$ are, respectively, an M↑, an M↓, and a non-M Generalized Quantifier.

(10) a. $\exists P[\,^{\geq}2_x(\text{man'}(x), P(x)) \wedge \forall_x[P(x) \rightarrow \text{walk'}(x)]\,]$

b. $\exists P[\,^{\leq}2_x(\text{man'}(x), P(x)) \wedge \forall_x[P(x) \rightarrow \text{walk'}(x)]\,]$

c. $\exists P[\,^{=}2_x(\text{man'}(x), P(x)) \wedge \forall_x[P(x) \rightarrow \text{walk'}(x)]\,]$

Only (10.a) correctly yields the truth values of the corresponding sentence. To see why, consider a model in which three men walk. In such a model, (10.a) is true, while (10.b-c) are false. Conversely, all formulae in (10) evaluate to true, as all of them allow to choose P such that $\|P\|^M$ is a set of two walking men. Therefore, we cannot allow a free choice of P. Instead, P must denote the Maximal set of individuals satisfying the predicates, i.e. the Maximal set of walking men, in (10). This is achieved by changing (10.b-c) to (11.a-b) respectively.

(11) a. $\exists P[\,^{\leq}2_x(\text{man'}(x), P(x)) \wedge \forall_x[P(x) \rightarrow \text{walk'}(x)] \wedge$
$\forall'_P[(\forall_x[P(x) \rightarrow P'(x)] \wedge \forall_x[P'(x) \rightarrow \text{walk'}(x)]) \rightarrow \forall_x[P'(x) \rightarrow P(x)]\,]\,]$

b. $\exists P[\,^{=}2_x(\text{man'}(x), P(x)) \wedge \forall_x[P(x) \rightarrow \text{walk'}(x)] \wedge$
$\forall'_P[(\forall_x[P(x) \rightarrow P'(x)] \wedge \forall_x[P'(x) \rightarrow \text{walk'}(x)]) \rightarrow \forall_x[P'(x) \rightarrow P(x)]\,]\,]$

The clauses $\forall'_P[\,\ldots\,]$ in the second rows are Maximality Conditions asserting the non-existence of a superset P' of P that also satisfies the predication. There is a single choice for P in (11.a-b): it must denote the set of *all* walking men. Note that, for the sake of uniformity, the Maximality condition may be added in (10.a) as well: in case of M↑ quantifiers, it does not affect the truth values.

3.1 Local Maximalization

Let me term the kind of Maximalization done in (11) as *Local* Maximalization. The Maximality conditions in (11) require the non-existence of a set $\|P'\|^M$ of walkers *that includes* $\|P\|^M$. In (Robaldo, 2009a) and (Robaldo, 2009b), I proposed a logical framework for representing Branching Quantifier based on Local Maximalization. For instance, in (Robaldo, 2009a), the *two* witness sets of students and drug-dealers in (4.a) are respectively reified into two variables P_1 and P_2, and the Maximality condition requires the non-existence of a *Cartesian Product* $\|P'_1\|^M \times \|P'_2\|^M$, that also satisfies the main predication and *that includes* $\|P_1\|^M \times \|P_2\|^M$:

(12) $$\exists P_1 P_2[\,{}^{=}2_x(\text{stud'}(x), P_1(x)) \wedge {}^{=}3_x(\text{drugD'}(y), P_2(y)) \wedge \forall_{xy}[(P_1(x) \wedge P_2(y)) \rightarrow \text{saw'}(x, y)] \wedge \forall_{P'_1 P'_2}[\,(\forall_{xy}[(P_1(x) \wedge P_2(y)) \rightarrow (P'_1(x) \wedge P'_2(y))] \wedge \forall_{xy}[(P'_1(x) \wedge P'_2(y)) \rightarrow \text{saw'}(x, y)]\,) \rightarrow \forall_{xy}[(P'_1(x) \wedge P'_2(y)) \rightarrow (P_1(x) \wedge P_2(y))]\,]\,]$$

In order to extend (Robaldo, 2009a) to Cover readings, which are assumed to be the most general cases of IS readings, we cannot simply require the inclusion of $||P_1||^M \times ||P_2||^M$ into the main predicate's extension. Rather, we require the inclusion therein of a pragmatically-determined Cover $||C||^{M,g}$ of $||P_1||^M$ and $||P_2||^M$. Furthermore, the (local) Maximality condition must require the non-existence of a superset of either $||P_1||^M$ or $||P_2||^M$ whose corresponding Cover is a superset of $||C||^{M,g}$ that is also included in the main predicate's extension. Thus, (4.d) is represented as[3]:

(13) $$\exists P_1 P_2[\,{}^{=}20_x(\text{child'}(x), P_1(x)) \wedge {}^{=}10_y(\text{pizza'}(y), P_2(y)) \wedge Cover(C, P_1, P_2) \wedge \forall_{xy}[C(x, y) \rightarrow \text{ate'}(x, y)] \wedge \forall_{P'_1}[(\forall_x[P_1(x) \rightarrow P'_1(x)] \wedge \exists_{C'}[Cover(C', P'_1, P_2) \wedge \forall_{xy}[C(x,y) \rightarrow C'(x,y)] \wedge \forall_{xy}[C'(x,y) \rightarrow \text{ate'}(x, y)]]) \rightarrow \forall_x[P'_1(x) \rightarrow P_1(x)]\,]\,] \wedge \forall_{P'_2}[(\forall_y[P_2(y) \rightarrow P'_2(y)] \wedge \exists_{C'}[Cover(C', P_1, P'_2) \wedge \forall_{xy}[C(x,y) \rightarrow C'(x,y)] \wedge \forall_{xy}[C'(x,y) \rightarrow \text{ate'}(x, y)]]) \rightarrow \forall_y[P'_2(y) \rightarrow P_2(y)]\,]\,]\,]$$

Note that there are two Maximality conditions: $\forall_{P'_1}[\ \dots\ ]$ and $\forall_{P'_2}[\ \dots\ ]$. In fact, contrary to what is done with Cartesian Products, in Cover readings P_1 and P_2 must be Maximized independently, as it is no longer required that *every* member of the former is related with *every* member of the latter. Note also that the inner Cover variable C' is existentially quantified. Of course, it would make no sense to pragmatically interpret it as it is done with C.

3.2 Global Maximalization

The other kind of Maximalization of the witness sets, termed here as 'Global Maximalization' has been advocated by (Schein, 1993), and formalized in most formal theories of Cumulativity, e.g. (Landman, 2000), (Hackl, 2000), and (Ben-Avi and Winter, 2003). With respect to IS readings involving two witness sets $||P_1||^M$ and $||P_2||^M$, Global Maximalization requires the non-existence of other two witness sets that also satisfy the predication but *that do not necessarily include* $||P_1||^M$ *and* $||P_2||^M$. For instance, the event-based logic defined by (Landman, 2000) represents the Cumulative reading of (4.c) as:

(14) $$\exists e \in {}^*\text{INVITE}: \exists x \in {}^*\text{BOY}: |x|=3 \wedge {}^*\text{Ag}(e)=x \wedge \exists y \in {}^*\text{GIRL}: |y|=4 \wedge {}^*\text{Th}(e)=y \wedge$$
$$\mathbf{|{}^*Ag(\bigcup\{\mathit{e} \in INVITE: Ag(\mathit{e}) \in BOY \wedge Th(\mathit{e}) \in GIRL\})| = 3} \wedge$$
$$\mathbf{|{}^*Th(\bigcup\{\mathit{e} \in INVITE: Ag(\mathit{e}) \in BOY \wedge Th(\mathit{e}) \in GIRL\})| = 4}$$

Formula in (14) asserts the existence of a plural event e whose Agent is a plural individual made up of three boys and whose Theme is a plural individual made up of four girls. The two final conjuncts, in boldface, are Maximality conditions *asserted on pragmatic grounds* (see footnote 1 above). Taken e_x as the plural sum of all inviting events having a boy as agent and a girl as theme, i.e.

$$e_x = \bigcup\{e \in \text{INVITE}: \text{Ag}(e) \in \text{BOY} \wedge \text{Th}(e) \in \text{GIRL}\}$$

the cardinality of its agent $^*\text{Ag}(e_x)$ is exactly three while the one of its theme $^*\text{Th}(e_x)$ is exactly four. Therefore, Landman's Maximality conditions in (14) do not refer to the same events and actors quantified in the first row. Rather, they require that the number of the boys who invited a girl *in the whole model* is exactly three and the number of girls who were invited by a boy *in the whole model* is exactly four.

[3]Without going down into further details, I simply stipulate that the GQs used in the article are Conservative (Barwise and Cooper, 1981), (Keenan and Stavi, 1986). In other words, for every quantifier Q_x, we require $||P^B_x||^M \subseteq ||P^R_x||^M$.

4 Local Maximalization VS Global Maximalization

We are ready now to compare the two kinds of Maximalization. Global Maximalization appears to be more problematic than Local one. Since Branching Quantifier readings are special cases of Cumulative readings, and it has been discussed above that many authors, e.g. (Beghelli et al., 1997), argue that this is even a good reason to avoid an explicit representation of them, sentence (15.a) entails (15.b).

(15) a. Less than half of the dots are totally connected with exactly three stars.

b. Less than half of the dots are connected with exactly three stars.

Nevertheless, Global Maximalization predicts that (15.b) is false in figure (2). The number of all dots in the model connected to a star is six, while the number of all stars in the model connected to a dot is five, not exactly three. On the contrary, once the witness sets have been identified as in (16), Local Maximalization predicts (15.b) as true, in that no other star is connected to a dot *occurring in* $||P_1||^M$, and no other dot is connected to a star *occurring in* $||P_2||^M$.

(16)

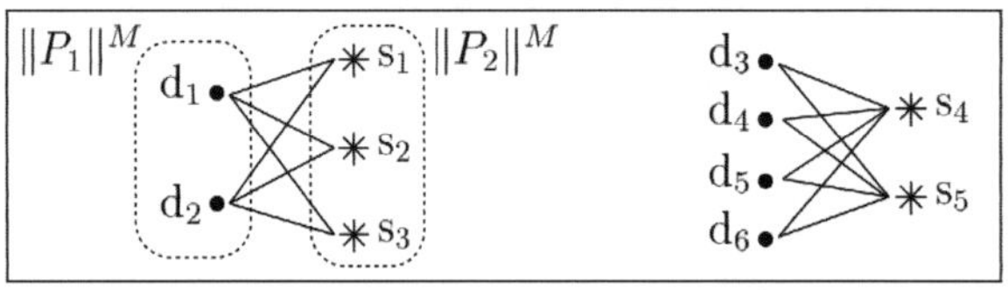

Another scenario where Global Maximalization predicts presumably wrong truth values, with respect to formula (14) and sentence (4.c), is shown in (17):

(17)

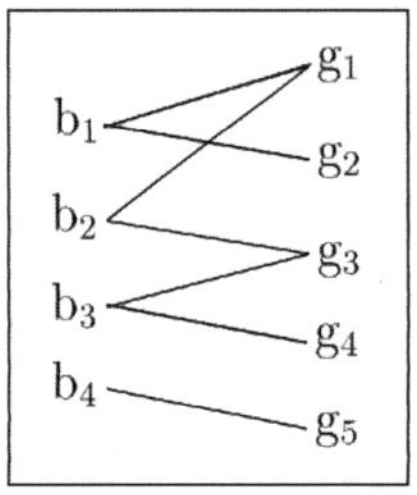

In (17), the Cumulative readings of all (18.a-c) appear to be true provided that numerals N are still interpreted as exactly-N.

(18) a. Three boys invited four girls.

b. One boy invited one girl.

c. Four boys invited five girls.

Global Maximalization states that only (18.c) is true in (17). Local Maximalization evaluates all (18.a-c) as true; the witness sets are obviously identified.

Landman does not discuss the evaluation of his formulae in contexts like (17). This is done instead by (Ferreira, 2007) and (Brasoveanu, 2009). However, the latter do not provide strong linguistic motivations: they simply claim that (18.a-b) are false in (17), as the present paper claims they are not. A comparison between Local and Global Maximalization is found in (Schein, 1993), even if no formalization is presented. (Schein, 1993), §12, reasonably argues, contra (Sher, 1997), that (19.a-b) are false in contexts like (20) (or (3)), while (19.c) is true. Local Maximalization predicts all (19.a-c) as true.

(19) a. Few dots are totally connected with few stars.

b. Exactly two dots are totally connected with exactly two stars.

c. At least two dots are totally connected with at least two stars.

(20)

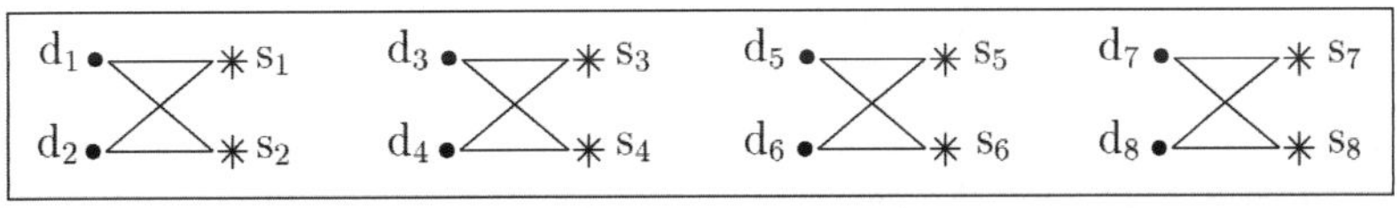

From these observations, Schein concludes that (Sher, 1997)'s Local Maximalization, which is defined for any kind of quantifier, with any monotonicity, is incorrect. A proper semantics for NL quantification should instead stipulate two *different* semantics depending on the monotonicity: one for M↑ quantifiers, e.g. *At least two*, and one for M↓ quantifiers, e.g. *Few*, and non-M quantifiers, e.g. *Exactly two*. The truth conditions of the former should be defined in terms of Local Maximalization, while those of the latter in terms of Global Maximalization.

While I accept the truth values attested by Schein for sentences (19.a-c) in (20), I do not share his conclusions. On the one hand, there are several cases, particularly mixed cases, that are quite hard to reconcile in Schein's view. An example is the sentence evaluated in (2), which include a M↓ quantifier (*Less than half*) and a non-M one (*Exactly three*). Global Maximalization, contrary to Local Maximalization, evaluates the sentence as false in (2), as pointed out above. Also (21.a), which includes an M↓ quantifier and an M↑ one (*More than half*), and sentence (21.b), which is not a mixed case as it includes two M↓ quantifiers, seems to be true in (2), contra Schein's predictions.

(21) a. Less than half of the dots are connected with more than half of the stars.

b. Less than half of the dots are connected with less than five stars.

On the other hand, all sentences in (19.a-c) seems to be true in (22), while in Schein's view they should have the same truth values they have in (20).

(22)

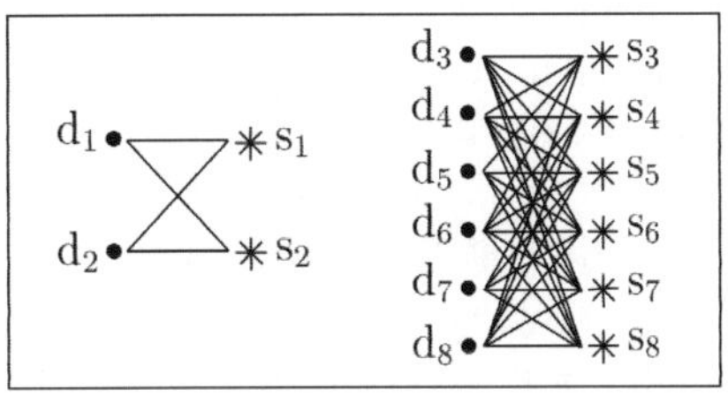

These considerations lead to conclude that the oddity of sentences (19) in contexts (20) or (3) does not depend on the monotonicity of the quantifiers involved.

The present paper suggests instead that such an oddity stems from Pragmatics. No English speaker would ever utter those sentences in those contexts, as they would not be informative enough, and so they would violate a Gricean Maxim. From the examples above, it seems that sentences involving non-M↑ quantifiers sound odd in contexts where more pairs of witness sets are available. For instance, the reader gets confused when he tries to evaluate (19.a) in (20), as multiple pairs of (witness) sets of dots and stars are available, i.e. $\langle\{d_1, d_2\}, \{s_1, s_2\}\rangle$, $\langle\{d_3, d_4\}, \{s_3, s_4\}\rangle$, etc., and he does not have enough information to prefer one of them upon the others. This does not arises in (3) or (22), where the witness sets are immediatly and uncontroversially identified.

The multiple availability of witness sets does not seem to confuse the reader for sentences involving M↑ quantifiers, perhaps because they are simpler to interpret (cf. (Geurts and van der Silk, 2005)). However, several cognitive experimental results showed that many other factors besides monotonicity, e.g. expressivity/computability, fuzzyness, the fact that quantifiers are cardinal rather than proportional, etc., may affect the accuracy and reaction time of the interpretation of IS readings (cf. (Sanford and Paterson, 1994), (Bott and Radó, 2009), (Musolino, 2009), and (Szymanik and Zajenkowski, 2009)).

As it is clear to understand, however, extra-linguistic factors seem the ones that mainly affect the interpretation of quantifiers. For instance, in (17), if the boys b_1, b_2, b_3 are friends who decided to go to a party with some girls, and b_4 wants to go there with his girlfriend (g_5) only, the witness sets are most likely identified for (18.a-b) rather than for (18.c), as the two groups of persons are not related. Conversely, if the four boys belong to the same group of friends hanging out together, the identification of the witness sets most likely fails in (18.a-b). That is probably the assumption done by (Ferreira, 2007) and (Brasoveanu, 2009) for claiming that sentences like (18.a-b) are false in contexts like (17). Analogously, in the children-pizza example in (4.d), the arrangement of the children among the tables of the pizzeria, their mutual friendship, and so on, may affect the identification of the witness sets. Similar discussions may be found in (Fintel, 1994) and (Winter, 2000).

Of course, an exhaustive study of all factors involved in the pragmatic identification of the witness sets goes much beyond the goal of the present paper. The aim of this paper is to argue that, once witness sets are identified, Local Maximalization applies to them. In order to formally obtain this result, a final modification of the formulae is needed: it is necessary to pragmatically interpret the relational variables denoting the witness sets, besides those denoting the Covers. Formula (13) is then revised as in (23).

(23)
$$
\begin{aligned}
&{}^{=}20_x(\text{child'}(x),\, P_1(x)) \wedge {}^{=}10_y(\text{pizza'}(y),\, P_2(y)) \wedge \\
&Cover(C, P_1, P_2) \wedge \forall_{xy}[C(x,y)) \rightarrow \text{ate'}(x,y)] \wedge \\
&\forall_{P_1'}[(\forall_x[P_1(x) \rightarrow P_1'(x)] \wedge \exists_{C'}[Cover(C', P_1', P_2) \wedge \forall_{xy}[C(x,y) \rightarrow C'(x,y)] \wedge \\
&\quad \forall_{xy}[C'(x,y) \rightarrow \text{ate'}(x,y)]]) \rightarrow \forall_x[P_1'(x) \rightarrow P_1(x)]\,]\,] \wedge \\
&\forall_{P_2'}[(\forall_y[P_2(y) \rightarrow P_2'(y)] \wedge \exists_{C'}[Cover(C', P_1, P_2') \wedge \forall_{xy}[C(x,y) \rightarrow C'(x,y)] \wedge \\
&\quad \forall_{xy}[C'(x,y) \rightarrow \text{ate'}(x,y)]]) \rightarrow \forall_y[P_2'(y) \rightarrow P_2(y)]\,]\,]
\end{aligned}
$$

The only difference between (23) and (13) is that the value of P_1 and P_2 is provided by an assignment g, as it is done for the Cover variable C. g must obey to all (extra-)linguistic pragmatic constraints briefly listed above. The reader could start thinking that, in the new version of the formulae, we may avoid Maximality conditions, either Local or Global. In fact, Maximalization could be simply implemented as a constraint on the assignment function g. In other words, we could simply impose g to select only Maximal witness sets. If g is unable to do so, the intepretation fails as in the cases discussed above. Such a solution has been actually proposed in (Steedman, 2007) and (Brasoveanu, 2009). Conversely, in (Robaldo, 2009b) I explained that we do need to explicitly represent the Maximality conditions. In other words, those are not only seen as necessary conditions needed to determine if a sentence is true or false in a certain context. Rather, in (Robaldo, 2009b), it is extensively argued that they are part of the knowledge needed to draw the appropriate inferences from the sentences' meaning.

5 Conclusions

This paper compared the two kind of Maximalization proposed in the literature for handling the proper truth values of Independent Set readings. They have been termed as Local and Global Maximalization. The former requires the non-existence of any tuple of supersets of the witness sets that also satisfy the predication. The latter requires the witness sets to be the only tuple of sets that satisfy the predication. The present paper argues in favour of Local Maximalization, and claims that the motivations that led to the definition of Global Maximalitation, and its incorporation within most current formal approaches to NL quantification, do not appear to be justified enough. These claims are supported by showing that, for many NL sentences, Global Maximalization predicts counter-intuitive truth conditions.
Also several examples are hard to reconcile in a logical framework based on Local Maximalization. It seems, however, that the oddity of such examples depends upon pragmatic grounds.

Based on these assumptions, the solution presented here still adopts Local Maximalization, but advocates a pragmatic interpretation of all relational variables. Drawing from (Schwarzschild, 1996), the present paper evolves the formulae in (Robaldo, 2009a) and (Robaldo, 2009b), making them able to handle Cover readings, which are assumed to be the more general cases of Independent Set readings.

In the resulting formulae, the witness sets are firstly pragmatically identified, as it is done with Cover variables, then they are locally Maximized. In other words, Pragmatics is responsible for identifying both the (atomic) individuals involved, and the way they sub-combine to carry out the singular actions.

The result is able to predict the suitable truth values of Cover readings in all examples considered, and seems to mirror the correct interplay between the Semantics and the Pragmatics of NL quantifiers.

References

Barwise, J. and R. Cooper (1981). Generalized quantifiers and natural language. *Linguistics and Philosophy 4*(2), 159–219.

Beck, S. and U. Sauerland (2000). Cumulation is needed: A reply to winter (2000). *Natural Language Semantics 8*(4), 349–371.

Beghelli, F., D. Ben-Shalom, and A. Szabolski (1997). Variation, distributivity, and the illusion of branching. In *Ways of Scope Taking*, pp. 29–69. Dordrecht: Kluwer Academic Publishers.

Ben-Avi, G. and Y. Winter (2003). Monotonicity and collective quantification. *Journal of Logic, Language and Information 12*, 127–151.

Bott, O. and J. Radó (2009). How to provide exactly one interpretation for every sentence, or what eye movements reveal about quantifier scope. In *The fruits of empirical linguistics*. Berlin: de Gruyter.

Brasoveanu, A. (2009). Modified numerals as post-suppositions. In *Proc. of the 17th Amsterdam Colloquium.*

Ferreira, M. (2007). Scope splitting and cumulativity. In *Proc. of the Workshop on quantifier modification, ESSLLI 2007.*

Fintel, K. (1994). *Restrictions on quantifiers domains.* Amherst, University of Massachusetts.

Geurts, B. and F. van der Silk (2005). Monotonicity and processing load. *The Journal of Semantics 22(17).*

Gierasimczuk, N. and J. Szymanik (2009). Branching quantification vs. two-way quantification. *The Journal of Semantics. 26(4)*, 367–392.

Hackl, M. (2000). *Comparative quantifiers.* Ph. D. thesis, Massachusetts Institute of Technology.

Kadmon, N. (1987). *On unique and non-unique reference and asymmetric quantification.* Ph. D. thesis, University of Massachusetts, Amherst.

Keenan, E. and D. Westerståhl (1997). Generalized quantifiers in linguistics and logic. In *Handbook of Logic and Language*, pp. 837–893. Cambridge: MIT Press.

Keenan, E. L. and J. Stavi (1986). A semantic characterization of natural language determiners. *Linguistics and Philosophy 9*(3), 253–326.

Kratzer, A. (2007). On the plurality of verbs. In *Event Structures in Linguistic Form and Interpretation.* Berlin: Mouton de Gruyter.

Landman, F. (2000). *Events and Plurality: The Jerusalem Lectures.* Kluwer Academic Publishers.

Link, G. (1983). The logical analysis of plurals and mass terms. In *Meaning, Use, and Interpretation in Language*, pp. 302–323. Berlin: de Gruyter.

May, R. (1989). Interpreting logical form. *Linguistics and Philosophy 12*(4), 387–437.

Musolino, J. (2009). The logical syntax of number words: Theory, acquisition and processing. *Cognition 111.*

Nakanishi, K. (2007). Event quantification and distributivity. In *Event Structures in Linguistic Form and Interpretation*. Mouton de Gruyter.

Robaldo, L. (2009a). Independent set readings and generalized quantifiers. *The Journal of Philosophical Logic 39(1)*, 23–58.

Robaldo, L. (2009b). Interpretation and inference with maximal referential terms. *The Journal of Computer and System Sciences. 76(5)*, 373–388.

Sanford, A. J., M. L. M. and K. Paterson (1994). Psychological studies of quantifiers. *The Journal of Semantics 11*(3), 153170.

Scha, R. (1981). Distributive, collective and cumulative quantification. In *Formal Methods in the Study of Language, Part 2*. Amsterdam: Mathematisch Centrum.

Schein, B. (1993). *Plurals and Events*. MIT Press, Cambridge, MA, USA.

Schwarzschild, R. (1996). *Pluralities*. Dordrecht: Kluwer.

Sher, G. (1990). Ways of branching quantifiers. *Linguistics and Philosophy 13*, 393–422.

Sher, G. (1997). Partially-ordered (branching) generalized quantifiers: a general definition. *The Journal of Philosophical Logic 26*, 1–43.

Spaan, M. (1996). Parallel quantification. In *Quantifiers, Logic, and Language*, Volume 54, pp. 281–309. Stanford: CSLI Publications.

Steedman, M. (2007). *The Grammar of Scope*. forthcoming. See 'Surface-Compositional Scope-Alternation Without Existential Quantifiers'. Draft 5.2, Sept 2007. Retrieved September 25, 2007 from ftp://ftp.cogsci.ed.ac.uk/pub/steedman/quantifiers/journal6.pdf.

Szymanik, J. and M. Zajenkowski (2009). Comprehension of simple quantifiers empirical evaluation of a computational model. *Cognitive Science: A Multidisciplinary Journal*.

van Benthem, J. (1986). *Essays in logical semantics*. Dordrecht, Reidel.

van der Does, J. (1993). Sums and quantifiers. *Linguistics and Philosophy 16*, 509–550.

van der Does, J. and H. Verkuyl (1996). The semantics of plural noun phrases. In *Quantifiers, Logic and Language*. CSLI.

Winter, Y. (2000). Distributivity and dependency. *Natural Language Semantics 8*, 27–69.

Ontology-based Distinction between Polysemy and Homonymy

Jason Utt
Institut für Maschinelle Sprachverarbeitung
Universität Stuttgart
uttjn@ims.uni-stuttgart.de

Sebastian Padó
Seminar für Computerlinguistik
Universität Heidelberg
pado@cl.uni-heidelberg.de

Abstract

We consider the problem of distinguishing polysemous from homonymous nouns. This distinction is often taken for granted, but is seldom operationalized in the shape of an empirical model. We present a first step towards such a model, based on WordNet augmented with ontological classes provided by CoreLex. This model provides a *polysemy index* for each noun which (a), accurately distinguishes between polysemy and homonymy; (b), supports the analysis that polysemy can be grounded in the frequency of the meaning shifts shown by nouns; and (c), improves a regression model that predicts when the "one-sense-per-discourse" hypothesis fails.

1 Introduction

Linguistic studies of word meaning generally divide ambiguity into homonymy and polysemy. Homonymous words exhibit idiosyncratic variation, with essentially unrelated senses, e.g. *bank* as FINANCIAL INSTITUTION versus as NATURAL OBJECT. In polysemy, meanwhile, sense variation is systematic, i.e., appears for whole sets of words. E.g., *lamb*, *chicken* and *salmon* have ANIMAL and FOOD senses.

It is exactly this systematicity that represents a challenge for lexical semantics. While homonymy is assumed to be encoded in the lexicon for each lemma, there is a substantial body of work on dealing with general polysemy patterns (cf. Nunberg and Zaenen (1992); Copestake and Briscoe (1995); Pustejovsky (1995); Nunberg (1995)). This work is predominantly theoretical in nature. Examples of questions addressed are the conditions under which polysemy arises, the representation of polysemy in the semantic lexicon, disambiguation mechanisms in the syntax-semantics interface, and subcategories of polysemy.

The distinction between polysemy and homonymy also has important potential ramifications for computational linguistics, in particular for Word Sense Disambiguation (WSD). Notably, Ide and Wilks (2006) argue that WSD should focus on modeling homonymous sense distinctions, which are easy to make and provide most benefit. Another case in point is the *one-sense-per-discourse hypothesis* (Gale et al., 1992), which claims that within a discourse, instances of a word will strongly tend towards realizing the same sense. This hypothesis seems to apply primarily to homonyms, as pointed out by Krovetz (1998).

Unfortunately, the distinction between polysemy and homonymy is still very much an unsolved question. The discussion in the theoretical literature focuses mostly on clear-cut examples and avoids the broader issue. Work on WSD, and in computational linguistics more generally, almost exclusively builds on the WordNet (Fellbaum, 1998) word sense inventory, which lists an unstructured set of senses for each word and does not indicate in which way these senses are semantically related. Diachronic linguistics proposes etymological criteria; however, these are neither undisputed nor easy to operationalize. Consequently, there are currently no broad-coverage lexicons that indicate the polysemy status of words, nor even, to our knowledge, precise, automatizable criteria.

Our goal in this paper is to take a first step towards an automatic polysemy classification. Our approach is based on the aforementioned intuition that meaning variation is systematic in polysemy, but not in homonymy. This approach is described in Section 2. We assess systematicity by mapping WordNet senses onto *basic types*, a set of 39 ontological categories defined by the CoreLex resource (Buitelaar, 1998), and looking at the prevalence of pairs of basic types (such as {FINANCIAL INSTITUTION, NATURAL

OBJECT} above) across the lexicon. We evaluate this model on two tasks. In Section 3, we apply the measure to the classification of a set of typical polysemy and homonymy lemmas, mostly drawn from the literature. In Section 4, we apply it to the one-sense-per-discourse hypothesis and show that polysemous words tend to violate this hypothesis more than homonyms. Section 5 concludes.

2 Modeling Polysemy

Our goal is to take the first steps towards an empirical model of polysemy, that is, a computational model which makes predictions for – in principle – arbitrary words on the basis of their semantic behavior.

The basis of our approach mirrors the focus of much linguistic work on polysemy, namely the fact that polysemy is *systematic*: There is a whole set of words which show the same variation between two (or more) ontological categories, cf. the "universal grinder" (Copestake and Briscoe, 1995). There are different ways of grounding this notion of systematicity empirically. An obvious choice would be to use a corpus. However, this would introduce a number of problems. First, while corpora provide frequency information, the role of frequency with respect to systematicity is unclear: should acceptable but rare senses play a role, or not? We side with the theoretical literature in assuming that they do. Another problem with corpora is the actual observation of sense variation. Few sense-tagged corpora exist, and those that do are typically small. Interpreting context variation in untagged corpora, on the other hand, corresponds to unsupervised WSD, a serious research problem in itself – see, e.g., Navigli (2009).

We therefore decided to adopt a knowledge-based approach that uses the structure of the WordNet ontology to calculate how systematically the senses of a word vary. The resulting model sets all senses of a word on equal footing. It is thus vulnerable to shortcomings in the architecture of WordNet, but this danger is alleviated in practice by our use of a "coarsened" version of WordNet (see below).

2.1 WordNet, CoreLex and Basic Types

WordNet provides only a flat list of senses for each word. This list does not indicate the nature of the sense variation among the senses. However, building on the generative lexicon theory by Pustejovsky (1995), Buitelaar (1998) has developed the "CoreLex" resource. It defines a set of 39 so-called *basic types* which correspond to coarse-grained ontological categories. Each basic type is linked to one or more WordNet *anchor nodes*, which define a complete mapping between WordNet synsets and basic types by dominance.[1] Table 1 shows the set of basic types and their main anchors; Table 2 shows example lemmas for some basic types.

Ambiguous lemmas are often associated with two or more basic types. CoreLex therefore further assigns each lemma to what Buitelaar calls a *polysemy class*, the set of all basic types its synsets belong to; a class with multiple representatives is considered *systematic*. These classes subsume both idiosyncratic and systematic patterns, and thus, despite their name, provide no clue about the nature of the ambiguity.

CoreLex makes it possible to represent the meaning of a lemma not through a set of synsets, but instead in terms of a set of basic types. This constitutes an important step forward. Our working hypothesis is that these basic types approximate the ontological categories that are used in the literature on polysemy to define polysemy patterns. That is, we can define a meaning shift to mean that a lemma possesses one sense in one basic type, while another sense belongs to another basic type. Naturally, this correspondence is not perfect: systematic polysemy did not play a role in the design of the WordNet ontology. Nevertheless, there is a fairly good approximation that allows us to recover many prominent polysemy patterns. Table 3 shows three polysemy patterns characterized in terms of basic types. The first class was already mentioned before. The second class contains a subset of "transparent nouns" which can denote a container or a quantity. The last class contains words which describe a place or a group of people.

[1] Note that not all of CoreLex anchor nodes are disjoint; therefore a given WordNet synset may be dominated by two CoreLex anchor nodes. We assign each synset to the basic type corresponding to the most specific dominating anchor node.

BT	WordNet anchor	BT	WordNet anchor	BT	WordNet anchor
abs	ABSTRACTION	loc	LOCATION	pho	PHYSICAL OBJECT
act	ACTION	log	GEOGRAPHICAL AREA	plt	PLANT
agt	AGENT	mea	MEASURE	pos	POSSESSION
anm	ANIMAL	mic	MICROORGANISM	pro	PROCESS
art	ARTIFACT	nat	NATURAL OBJECT	prt	PART
atr	ATTRIBUTE	phm	PHENOMENON	psy	PSYCHOLOGICAL FEATURE
cel	CELL	frm	FORM	qud	DEFINITE QUANTITY
chm	CHEMICAL ELEMENT	grb	BIOLOGICAL GROUP	qui	INDEFINITE QUANTITY
com	COMMUNICATION	grp	GROUP	rel	RELATION
con	CONSEQUENCE	grs	SOCIAL GROUP	spc	SPACE
ent	ENTITY	hum	PERSON	sta	STATE
evt	EVENT	lfr	LIVING THING	sub	SUBSTANCE
fod	FOOD	lme	LINEAR MEASURE	tme	TIME

Table 1: The 39 CoreLex basic types (BTs) and their WordNet anchor nodes

Basic type	WordNet anchor	Examples
agt	AGENT	*driver, menace, power, proxy, ...*
grs	SOCIAL GROUP	*city, government, people, state, ...*
pho	PHENOMENON	*life, pressure, trade, work, ...*
pos	POSSESSION	*figure, land, money, right, ...*
qui	INDEFINITE QUANTITY	*bit, glass, lot, step, ...*
rel	RELATION	*function, part, position, series, ...*

Table 2: Basic types with example words

Pattern (Basic types)	Examples
ANIMAL, FOOD	*fowl, hare, lobster, octopus, snail, ...*
ARTIFACT, INDEFINITE QUANTITY	*bottle, jug, keg, spoon, tub, ...*
ARTIFACT, SOCIAL GROUP	*academy, embassy, headquarters, ...*

Table 3: Examples of polysemous meaning variation patterns

2.2 Polysemy as Systematicity

Given the intuitions developed in the previous section, we define a *basic ambiguity* as a pair of basic types, both of which are associated with a given lemma. The *variation spectrum* of a word is then the set of all its basic ambiguities. For example, *bottle* would have the variation spectrum {{art qui} } (cf. Table 3); the word *course* with the three basic types act, art, grs would have the variation spectrum {{act art}; {act grs}; {art grs} }.

There are 39 basic types and thus $39 \cdot 38/2 = 741$ possible basic ambiguities. In practice, only 663 basic ambiguities are attested in WordNet. We can quantify each basic ambiguity by the number of words that exhibit it. For the moment, we simply interpret frequency as systematicity.[2] Thus, we interpret the high-frequency (systematic) basic ambiguities as polysemous, and low-frequency (idiosyncratic) basic ambiguities as homonymous. Table 4 shows the most frequent basic ambiguities, all of which apply to several hundred lemmas and can safely be interpreted as polysemous. At the other end, 56 of the 663 basic ambiguities are singletons, i.e. are attested by only a single lemma.

In a second step, we extend this classification from basic ambiguities to lemmas. The intuition is again fairly straightforward: A word whose basic ambiguities are systematic will be perceived as polysemous, and as homonymous otherwise. This is clearly an oversimplification, both practically, since we depend on WordNet/CoreLex having made the correct design decisions in defining the ontology and the basic types; as well as conceptually, since not all polysemy patterns will presumably show the same degree of systematicity. Nevertheless, we believe that basic types provide an informative level of abstraction, and that our model is in principle even able to account for conventionalized metaphor, to the extent that the corresponding senses are encoded in WordNet.

[2]Note that this is strictly a type-based notion of frequency: corpus (token) frequencies do not enter into our model.

Basic ambiguity	Examples
{act com}	*construction, consultation, draft, estimation, refusal, ...*
{act art}	*press, review, staging, tackle, ...*
{com hum}	*egyptian, esquimau, kazakh, mojave, thai, ...*
{act sta}	*domination, excitement, failure, marriage, matrimony, ...*
{art hum}	*dip, driver, mouth, pawn, watch, wing, ...*

Table 4: Top five basic ambiguities with example lemmas

Noun	Basic types	Noun	Basic types
chicken	anm fod evt hum	*lamb*	anm fod hum
salmon	anm fod atr nat	*duck*	anm fod art qud

Table 5: Words exhibiting the "grinding" (animal – food) pattern

The exact manner in which the systematicity of the individual basic ambiguities of one lemma are combined is not a priori clear. We have chosen the following method. Let P be a basic ambiguity, $\mathcal{P}(w)$ the variation spectrum of a lemma w, and freq(P) the number of WordNet lemmas with basic ambiguity P. We define the set of *polysemous basic ambiguities* $\mathcal{P}_N$ as the N-most frequent bins of basic ambiguities: $\mathcal{P}_N = \{[P_1], ..., [P_N]\}$, where $[P_i] = \{P_j | \text{freq}(P_i) = \text{freq}(P_j)\}$ and $\text{freq}(P_k) > \text{freq}(P_l)$ for $k < l$. We call non-polysemous basic ambiguities *idiosyncratic*. The *polysemy index of a lemma* w, $\pi_N(w)$, is:

$$\pi_N(w) = \frac{|\mathcal{P}_N \cap \mathcal{P}(w)|}{|\mathcal{P}(w)|} \tag{1}$$

π_N simply measures the ratio of w's basic ambiguities which are polysemous, i.e., high-frequency basic ambiguities. π_N ranges between 0 and 1, and can be interpreted analogously to the intuition that we have developed on the level of basic ambiguities: high values of π (close to 1) mean that the majority of a lemma's basic ambiguities are polysemous, and therefore the lemma is perceived as polysemous. In contrast, low values of π (close to 0) mean that the lemma's basic ambiguities are predominantly idiosyncratic, and thus the lemma counts as homonymous. Again, note that we consider basic ambiguities at the type level, and that corpus frequency does not enter into the model.

This model of polysemy relies crucially on the distinction between systematic and idiosyncratic basic ambiguities, and therefore in turn on the parameter N. N corresponds to the sharp cutoff that our model assumes. At the N-th most frequent basic ambiguity, polysemy turns into homonymy. Since frequency is our only criterion, we have to lump together all basic ambiguities with the same frequency into 135 bins. If we set $N = 0$, none of the bins count as polysemous, so $\pi_0(w) = 0$ for all w – all lemmas are homonymous. In the other extreme, we can set N to 135, the total number of frequency bins, which makes all basic ambiguities polysemous, and thus all lemmas: $\pi_{135}(w) = 1$ for all w. The optimization of N will be discussed in Section 3.

2.3 Gradience between Homonymy and Polysemy

We assign each lemma a polysemy index between 0 and 1. We thus abandon the dichotomy that is usually made in the literature between two distinct categories of polysemy and homonymy. Instead, we consider polysemy and homonymy the two end points on a gradient, where words in the middle show elements of both. This type of behavior can be seen even for prototypical examples of either category, such as the homonym *bank*, which shows a variation between SOCIAL GROUP and ARTIFACT:

(1) a. The bill would force **banks** [...] to report such property. (grs)
b. The coin **bank** was empty. (art)

Note that this is the same basic ambiguity that is often cited as a typical example of polysemous sense variation, for example for words like *newspaper*.

On the other hand, many lemmas which are presumably polysemous show rather unsystematic basic ambiguities. Table 5 shows four lemmas which are instances of the meaning variation between ANIMAL

Homonymous nouns	*ball, bank, board, chapter, china, degree, fall, fame, plane, plant, pole, post, present, rest, score, sentence, spring, staff, stage, table, term, tie, tip, tongue*
Polysemous nouns	*bottle, chicken, church, classification, construction, cup, development, fish, glass, improvement, increase, instruction, judgment, lamb, management, newspaper, painting, paper, picture, pool, school, state, story, university*

Table 6: Experimental items for the two classes *hom* and *poly*

(`anm`) and FOOD (`fod`), a popular example of a regular and productive sense extension. Yet each of the nouns exhibits additional basic types. The noun *chicken* also has the highly idiosyncratic meaning of a person who lacks confidence. A *lamb* can mean a gullible person, *salmon* is the name of a color and a river, and a *duck* a score in the game of cricket. There is thus an obvious unsystematic variety in the words' sense variations – a single word can show both homonymic as well as polysemous sense alternation.

3 Evaluating the Polysemy Model

To identify an optimal cutoff value N for our polysemy index, we use a simple supervised approach: we optimize the quality with which our polysemy index models a small, manually created dataset. More specifically, we created a two-class, 48-word dataset with 24 homonymous nouns (class *hom*) and 24 polysemous nouns (class *poly*) drawn from the literature. The dataset is shown in Table 6.

We now rank these items according to π_N for different values of N and observe the ability of π_N to distinguish the two classes. We measure this ability with the Mann-Whitney U test, a nonparametric counterpart of the t-test.[3] In our case, the U statistic is defined as

$$U(N) = \sum_{i=1}^{m} \sum_{j=1}^{n} \mathbf{1}(\pi_N(\text{hom}_i) < \pi_N(\text{poly}_i))$$

where $\mathbf{1}$ is the function function that returns the truth value of its argument (1 for "true"). Informally, $U(N)$ counts the number of correctly ranked pairs of a homonymous and a polysemous noun.

The maximum for U is the number of item pairs from the classes ($24 \cdot 24 = 576$). A score of $U = 576$ would mean that every π_N-value of a homonym is smaller than every polysemous value. $U = 0$ means that there are no homonyms with smaller π-scores. So U can be directly interpreted as the quality of separation between the two classes. The null hypothesis of this test is that the ranking is essentially random, i.e., half the rankings are correct[4]. We can reject the null hypothesis if U is significantly larger.

Figure 1(a) shows the U-statistic for all values of N (between 0 and 135). The left end shows the quality of separation (i.e. U) for few basic ambiguities (i.e. small N) which is very small. As soon as we start considering the most frequent basic ambiguities as systematic and thus as evidence for polysemy, *hom* and *poly* become much more distinct. We see a clear global maximum of U for $N = 81$ ($U = 436.5$). This U value is highly significant at $p < 0.005$, which means that even on our fairly small dataset, we can reject the null hypothesis that the ranking is random. π_{81} indeed separates the classes with high confidence: 436.5 of 576 or roughly 75% of all pairwise rankings in the dataset are correct. For $N > 81$, performance degrades again: apparently these settings include too many basic ambiguities in the "systematic" category, and homonymous words start to be misclassified as polysemous.

The separation between the two classes is visualized in the box-and-whiskers plot in Figure 1(b). We find that more than 75% of the polysemous words have $\pi_{81} > .6$. The median value for *poly* is 1, thus for more than half of the class $\pi_{81} = 1$, which can be seen in Figure 2(b) as well. This is a very positive result, since our hope is that highly polysemous words get high scores. Figure 2(a) shows that homonyms are concentrated in the mid-range while exhibiting a small number of π_{81}-values at both extremes.

We take the fact that there is indeed an N which clearly maximizes U as a very positive result that validates our choice of introducing a sharp cutoff between polysemous and idiosyncratic basic ambiguities.

[3]The advantage of U over t is that t assumes comparable variance in the two samples, which we cannot guarantee.

[4]Provided that, like in this case, the classes are of equal size.

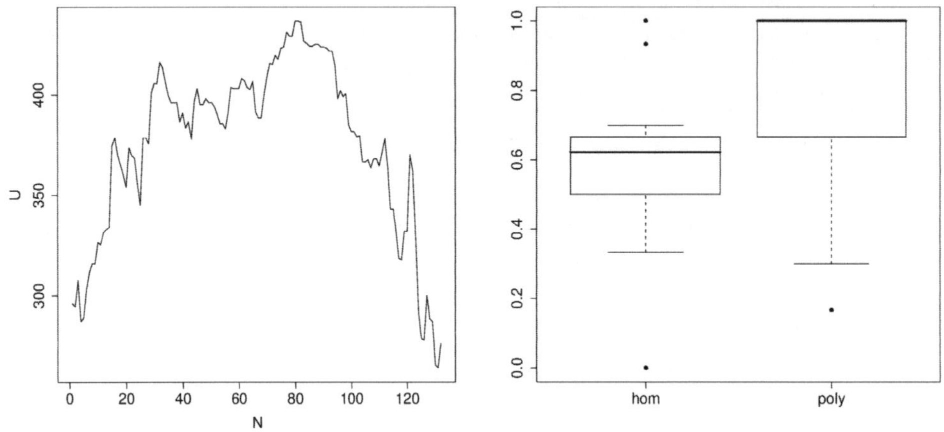

(a) The U statistic for different values of the cutoff N (b) Distribution of π_{81} values by class

Figure 1: Separation of the *hom* and *poly* classes in our dataset

These 81 frequency bins contain roughly 20% of the most frequent basic ambiguities. This corresponds to the assumption that basic ambiguities are polysemous if they occur with a minimum of about 50 lemmas.

If we look more closely at those polysemous words that obtain low scores (*school, glass* and *cup*), we observe that they also show idiosyncratic variation as discussed in Section 2.3. In the case of *school*, we have the senses *schooltime* of type `tme` and *group of fish* of type `grb` which one would not expect to alternate regularly with `grs` and `art`, the rest of its variation spectrum. The word *glass* has the unusual type `agt` due to its use as a slang term for crystal methamphetamine. Finally, *cup* is unique in that means both an indefinite quantity as well as the definite measurement equal to half a pint. Only 10 other words have this variation in WordNet, including such words as *million* and *billion*, which are often used to describe an indefinite but large number.

On the other hand, those homonyms that have a high score (e.g. *tie, staff* and *china*) have somewhat unexpected regularities due to obscure senses. Both *tie* and *staff* are terms used in musical notation. This leads to basic ambiguities with the `com` type, something that is very common. Finally, the obviously unrelated senses for *china*, *China* and *porcelain*, are less idiosyncratic when abstracted to their types, `log` and `art`, respectively. There are 117 words that can mean a location as well as an artifact, (e.g. *fireguard, bath, resort, front, ...*) which are clearly polysemous in that the location is where the artifact is located.

In conclusion, those examples which are most grossly miscategorized by π_{81} contain unexpected sense variations, a number of which have been ignored in previous studies.

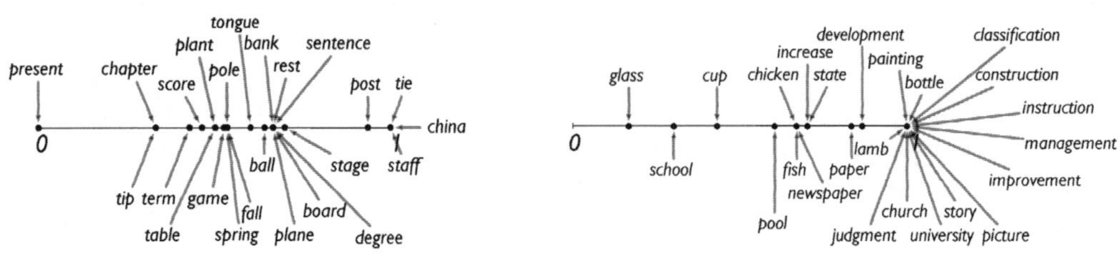

(a) Class *hom* (b) Class *poly*

Figure 2: Words and their π_{81}-scores

4 The One-Sense-Per-Discourse Hypothesis

The second evaluation that we propose for our polysemy index concerns a broader question on word sense, namely the so-called *one-sense-per-discourse (1spd)* hypothesis. This hypothesis was introduced by Gale et al. (1992) and claims that "[...] if a word such as *sentence* appears two or more times in a well-written discourse, it is extremely likely that they will all share the same sense". The authors verified their hypothesis on a small experiment with encouraging results (only 4% of discourses broke the hypothesis). Indeed, if this hypothesis were unreservedly true, then it would represent a very strong global constraint that could serve to improve word sense disambiguation – and in fact, a follow-up paper by Yarowsky (1995) exploited the hypothesis for this benefit.

Unfortunately, it seems that *1spd* does not apply universally. At the time (1992), WordNet had not yet emerged as a widely used sense inventory, and the sense labels used by Gale et al. were fairly coarse-grained ones, motivated by translation pairs (e.g., English *duty* translated as French *droit (tax)* vs. *devoir (obligation)*), which correspond mostly to homonymous sense distinctions.[5] Current WSD, in contrast, uses the much more fine-grained WordNet sense inventory which conflates homonymous and polysemous sense distinctions. Now, *1spd* seems intuitively plausible for homonyms, where the senses describe different entities that are unlikely to occur in the same discourse (or if they do, different words will be used). However, the situation is different for polysemous words: In a discourse about a party, *bottle* might felicitously occur both as an object and a measure word. A study by Krovetz (1998) confirmed this intuition on two sense-tagged corpora, where he found 33% of discourses to break *1spd*. He suggests that knowledge about polysemy classes can be useful as global biases for WSD.

In this section, we analyze the sense-tagged SemCor corpus in terms of the basic type-based framework of polysemy that we have developed in Section 2 both qualitatively and quantitatively to demonstrate that basic types, and our polysemy index π, help us better understand the *1spd* hypothesis.

4.1 Analysis by Basic Types and One-Basic-Type-Per-Discourse

The first step in our analysis looks specifically at the basic types and basic ambiguities we observe in discourses that break *1spd*. Our study reanalyses SemCor, a subset of the Brown corpus annotated exhaustively with WordNet senses (Fellbaum, 1998). SemCor contains a total of 186 discourses, paragraphs of between 645 and 1023 words. These 186 discourses, in combination with 1088 nouns, give rise to 7520 *lemma-discourse pairs*, that is, cases where a sense-tagged lemma occurs more than once within a discourse.[6] These 7520 lemma-discourse pairs form the basis of our analysis. We started by looking at the relative frequency of *1spd*. We found that the hypothesis holds for 69% of the lemma-discourse pairs, but not for the remaining 31%. This is a good match with Krovetz' findings, and indicates that there are many discourses where there lemmas are used in different senses.

In accordance with our approach to modeling meaning variation at the level of basic types, we implemented a "coarsened" version of *1spd*, namely *one-basic-type-per-discourse (1btpd)*. This hypothesis is parallel to the original, claiming that it is extremely likely that all words in a discourse share the same *basic type*. As we have argued before, the basic-type level is a fairly good approximation to the most important ontological categories, while smoothing over some of the most fine-grained (and most troublesome) sense distinctions in WordNet. In this vein, *1btpd* should get rid of "spurious" ambiguity, but preserve meaningful ambiguity, be it homonymous or polysemous. In fact, the basic type with most of these "within-basic-type" ambiguities is PSYCHOLOGICAL FEATURE, which contains many subtle distinctions such as the following senses of *perception*:

a. a way of conceiving something
b. the process of perceiving
c. knowledge gained by perceiving
d. becoming aware of something via the senses

Such distinctions are collapsed in *1btpd*. In consequence, we expect a noticeable, but limited, reduction in

[5] Note that Gale et al. use the term "polysemy" synonymously with "ambiguous".

[6] We exclude cases where a lemma occurs once in a discourse, since *1spd* holds trivially.

Basic ambiguity	most common breaking words	freq(P breaks *1btpd*)	freq(P)	N
{com psy}	evidence, sense, literature, meaning, style, ...	89	365	13
{act psy}	study, education, pattern, attention, process, ...	88	588	7
{psy sta}	need, feeling, difficulty, hope, fact, ...	79	338	14
{act atr}	role, look, influence, assistance, interest, ...	79	491	9
{act art}	church, way, case, thing, design, ...	67	753	2
{act sta}	operation, interest, trouble, employment, absence, ...	60	615	4
{act com}	thing, art, production, music, literature, ...	59	755	1
{atr sta}	life, level, desire, area, unity, ...	58	594	6

Table 7: Most frequent basic ambiguities that break the *1btpd* hypothesis in SemCor

the cases that break the hypothesis. Indeed, *1btpd* holds for 76% of all lemma-discourse pairs, i.e., for 7% more than *1spd*. For the remainder of this analysis, we will test the *1btpd* hypothesis instead of *1spd*.

The basic type level also provides a good basis to analyze the lemma-discourse pairs where the hypothesis breaks down. Table 7 shows the basic ambiguities that break the hypothesis in SemCor most often. The WordNet frequencies are high throughout, which means that these basic ambiguities are polysemous according to our framework. It is noticeable that the two basic types PSYCHOLOGICAL FEATURE and ACTION participate in almost all of these basic ambiguities. This observation can be explained straightforwardly through polysemous sense extension as sketched above: Actions are associated, among other things, with attributes, states, and communications, and discussion of an action in a discourse can fairly effortlessly switch to these other basic types. A very similar situation applies to psychological features, which are also associated with many of the other categories. In sum, we find that the data bears out our hypothesis: almost all of the most frequent cases of several-basic-types-per-discourse clearly correspond to basic ambiguities that we have classified as polysemous rather than homonymous.

4.2 Analysis by Regression Modeling

This section complements the qualitative analysis of the previous section with a quantitative analysis which predicts specifically for which lemma-discourse pairs *1btpd* breaks down. To do so, we fit a logit mixed effects model (Breslow and Clayton, 1993) to the SemCor data. Logit mixed effects models can be seen as a generalization of logistic regression models. They explain a binary *response variable* y in terms of a set of *fixed effects* x, but also include a set of *random effects* x'. Fixed effects correspond to "ordinary" predictors as in traditional logistic regression, while random effects account for correlations in the data introduced by groups (such as items or subjects) without ascribing these random effects the same causal power as fixed effects – see, e.g., Jaeger (2008) for details.

The contribution of each factor is modelled by a coefficient β, and their sum is interpreted as the logit-transformed probability of a positive outcome for the response variable:

$$p(y = 1) = \frac{1}{1 + e^{-z}} \text{ with } z = \sum \beta_i x_i + \sum \beta'_j x'_j \qquad (2)$$

Model estimation is usually performed using numeric approximations. The coefficients β' of the random effects are drawn from a multivariate normal distribution, centered around 0, which ensures that the majority of random effects are ascribed very small coefficients.

From a linguistic perspective, a desirable property of regression models is that they describe the importance of the different effects. First of all, each coefficient can be tested for significant difference to zero, which indicates whether the corresponding effect contributes significantly to modeling the data. Furthermore, the absolute value of each β_i can be interpreted as the *log odds* – that is, as the (logarithmized) change in the probability of the response variable being positive depending on x_i being positive.

In our experiment, each datapoint corresponds to one of the 7520 lemma-discourse pair from SemCor (cf. Section 4.1). The response variable is binary: whether *1btpd* holds for the lemma-discourse pair or not. We include in the model five predictors which we expect to affect the response variable: three fixed effects and two random ones. The first fixed effect is the ambiguity of the lemma as measured by the

Predictor	Coefficient	Odds (95% confidence interval)	Significance
Number of basic types	-0.50	0.61 (0.59–0.63)	***
Log length of discourse (words)	0.60	1.83 (1.14–2.93)	–
Polysemy index (π_{81})	-0.91	0.40 (0.35–0.46)	***

Table 8: Logit mixed effects model for the response variable "one-basic-type-per-discourse (*1btpd*) holds" (SemCor; random effects: discourse and lemma; significances: –: $p > 0.05$; ***: $p < 0.001$)

number of its basic types, i.e. the size of its variation spectrum. We expect that the more ambiguous a noun, the smaller the chance for *1btpd*. We expect the same effect for the (logarithmized) length of the discourse in words: longer discourses run a higher risk for violating the hypothesis. Our third fixed effect is the polysemy index π_{81}, for which we also expect a negative effect. The two random effects are the identity of the discourse and the noun. Both of these can influence the outcome, but should not be used as full explanatory variables.

We build the model in the R statistical environment, using the `lme4`[7] package. The main results are shown in Table 8. We find that the number of basic types has a highly significant negative effect on the *1btpd* hypothesis ($p < 0.001$) . Each additional basic type lowers the odds for the hypothesis by a factor of $e^{-0.50} \approx 0.61$. The confidence interval is small; the effect is very consistent. This was to be expected – it would have been highly suspicious if we had not found this basic frequency effect. Our expectations are not met for the discourse length predictor, though. We expected a negative coefficient, but find a positive one. The size of the confidence interval shows the effect to be insignificant. Thus, we have to assume that there is no significant relationship between the length of the discourse and the *1btpd* hypothesis. Note that this outcome might result from the limited variation of discourse lengths in SemCor: recall that no discourse contains less than 645 or more than 1023 words.

However, we find a second highly significant negative effect ($p < 0.001$) in our polysemy index π_{81}. With a coefficient of -0.91, this means that a word with a polysemy index of 1 is only 40% as likely to preserve *1btpd* than a word with a polysemy index of 0. The confidence interval is larger than for the number of basic types, but still fairly small. To bolster this finding, we estimated a second mixed effects model which was identical to the first one but did not contain π_{81} as predictor. We tested the difference between the models with a likelihood ratio test and found that the model that includes π_{81} is highly preferred ($p < 0.0001; D = -2\Delta LL = 40; df = 1$).

These findings establish that our polysemy index π can indeed serve a purpose beyond the direct modeling of polysemy vs. homonymy, namely to explain the distribution of word senses in discourse better than obvious predictors like the overall ambiguity of the word and the length of the discourse can. This further validates the polysemy index as a contribution to the study of the behavior of word senses.

5 Conclusion

In this paper, we have approached the problem of distinguishing empirically two different kinds of word sense ambiguity, namely homonymy and polysemy. To avoid sparse data problems inherent in corpus work on sense distributions, our framework is based on WordNet, augmented with the ontological categories provided by the CoreLex lexicon. We first classify the basic ambiguities (i.e., the pairs of ontological categories) shown by a lemma as either polysemous or homonymous, and then assign the ratio of polysemous basic ambiguities to each word as its polysemy index.

We have evaluated this framework on two tasks. The first was distinguishing polysemous from homonymous lemmas on the basis of their polysemy index, where it gets 76% of all pairwise rankings correct. We also used this task to identify an optimal value for the threshold between polysemous and homonymous basic ambiguities. We located it at around 20% of all basic ambiguities (113 of 663 in the top 81 frequency bins), which apparently corresponds to human intuitions. The second task was an analysis of the one-sense-per-discourse heuristic, which showed that this hypothesis breaks down

[7] `http://cran.r-project.org/web/packages/lme4/index.html`

frequently in the face of polysemy, and that the polysemy index can be used within a regression model to predict the instances within a discourse where this happens.

It may seem strange that our continuous index assumes a gradient between homonymy and polysemy. Our analyses indicate that on the level of actual examples, the two classes are indeed not separated by a clear boundary: many words contain basic ambiguities of either type. Nevertheless, even in the linguistic literature, words are often considered as either polysemous or homonymous. Our interpretation of this contradiction is that some basic types (or some basic ambiguities) are more prominent than others. The present study has ignored this level, modeling the polysemy index simply on the ratio of polysemous patterns without any weighting. In future work, we will investigate human judgments of polysemy vs. homonymy more closely, and assess other correlates of these judgments (e.g., corpus counts).

A second area of future work is more practical. The logistic regression incorporating our polysemous index predicts, for each lemma-discourse pair, the probability that the one-sense-per-discourse hypothesis is violated. We will use this information as a global prior on an "all-words" WSD task, where all occurrences of a word in a discourse need to be disambiguated. Finally, Stokoe (2005) demonstrates the chances for improvement in information retrieval systems if we can reliably distinguish between homonymous and polysemous senses of a word.

References

Breslow, N. and D. Clayton (1993). Approximate inference in generalized linear mixed models. *Journal of the American Statistical Society 88*(421), 9–25.

Buitelaar, P. (1998). CoreLex: An ontology of systematic polysemous classes. In *Proceedings of FOIS*, Amsterdam, Netherlands, pp. 221–235.

Copestake, A. and T. Briscoe (1995). Semi-productive polysemy and sense extension. *Journal of Semantics 12*, 15–67.

Fellbaum, C. (1998). *WordNet: An Electronic Lexical Database*. MIT Press.

Gale, W. A., K. W. Church, and D. Yarowsky (1992). One sense per discourse. In *Proceedings of HLT*, Harriman, NY, pp. 233–237.

Ide, N. and Y. Wilks (2006). Making sense about sense. In E. Agirre and P. Edmonds (Eds.), *Word Sense Disambiguation: Algorithms and Applications*, pp. 47–74. Springer.

Jaeger, T. (2008). Categorical data analysis: Away from ANOVAs and toward Logit Mixed Models. *Journal of Memory and Language 59*(4), 434–446.

Krovetz, R. (1998). More than one sense per discourse. In *Proceedings of SENSEVAL*, Herstmonceux Castle, England.

Navigli, R. (2009). Word Sense Disambiguation: a survey. *ACM Computing Surveys 41*(2), 1–69.

Nunberg, G. (1995). Transfers of meaning. *Journal of Semantics 12*(2), 109–132.

Nunberg, G. and A. Zaenen (1992). Systematic polysemy in lexicology and lexicography. In *Proceedings of Euralex II*, Tampere, Finland, pp. 387–395.

Pustejovsky, J. (1995). *The Generative Lexicon*. Cambridge MA: MIT Press.

Stokoe, C. (2005). Differentiating homonymy and polysemy in information retrieval. In *Proceedings of the conference on Human Language Technology and Empirical Methods in NLP*, Morristown, NJ, pp. 403–410.

Yarowsky, D. (1995). Unsupervised word sense disambiguation rivaling supervised methods. In *Proceedings of ACL*, Cambridge, MA, pp. 189–196.

Towards semi-automatic methods for improving WordNet

Nervo Verdezoto
University of Trento &
LOA-ISTC-CNR, Trento
nverdezoto@gmail.com

Laure Vieu
IRIT-CNRS, Toulouse &
LOA-ISTC-CNR, Trento
vieu@irit.fr

Abstract

WordNet is extensively used as a major lexical resource in NLP. However, its quality is far from perfect, and this alters the results of applications using it. We propose here to complement previous efforts for "cleaning up" the top-level of its taxonomy with semi-automatic methods based on the detection of errors at the lower levels. The methods we propose test the coherence of two sources of knowledge, exploiting ontological principles and semantic constraints.

1 Introduction

WordNet (Princeton WordNet (Fellbaum, 1998), henceforth WN) is a lexical resource widely used in a host of applications in which language or linguistic concepts play a role. For instance, it is a central resource for the quantification of semantic relatedness (Budanitsky and Hirst, 2006), in turn often exploited in applications. The quality of this resource therefore is very important for NLP as a whole, and beyond, in several AI applications. Neel and Garzon (2010) show that the quality of a knowledge resource like WN affects the performance in recognizing textual entailment (RTE) and word-sense disambiguation (WSD) tasks. They observe that the new version of WN induced improvements in recent RTE challenges, but conclude that WN currently is not rich enough to resolve such a task. What is more, its quality may be too low to even be useful at all. Bentivogli et al. (2009) discuss the results[1] of 20 "ablation tests" on systems submitted to the main RTE-5 task in which WN (alone) was ablated: 11 of these tests demonstrated that the use of this resource has a positive impact (up to 4%) on the performance of the systems but 9 showed a negative (up to 2% improvement when ablated) or null impact.

In the area of automatic recognition of part-whole relations, Girju and Badulescu (2006) proposed a learning method relying on WN's taxonomy. Analyzing the classification rules obtained, we could see that WN taxonomical errors lead to absurd rules, which can explain wrong recognition results. For instance, the authors obtain pairs such as ⟨*shape*, *physical_phenomenon*⟩ and ⟨*atmospheric_phenomenon*, *communication*⟩ as positive constraints for part-whole recognition, while sentences like *a curved shape is part of the electromagnetic radiation* or *rain is part of this document* would make no sense.

Some semantic problems of WN are well-known: confusion between concepts and individuals (in principle solved since WN 2.1), heterogeneous levels of generality, inappropriate use of multiple inheritance, confounding and missing senses, and unclear glosses (Kaplan and Schubert, 2001; Gangemi et al., 2003; Clark et al., 2006). Nevertheless, the number of applications where WN is used as an ontology has been increasing. In fact, apart from the synonymy relation on which synsets are defined, the hyponymy/hypernymy relation is WN's semantic relation most exploited in applications; it generates WN's taxonomy, which can be seen as a lightweight ontology, something it was never designed for, though. Several works tried to address these shortcomings. Gangemi et al. (2003) proposed a manual restructuring through the alignment of WN's taxonomy and the foundational ontology DOLCE[2], but this restructuring just focused on the upper levels of the taxonomy. Applying formal ontology principles

[1] http://www.aclweb.org/aclwiki/index.php?title=RTE5_-_Ablation_Tests
[2] See (Masolo et al., 2003) and http://www.loa-cnr.it/DOLCE.html

(Guarino, 1998) and the OntoClean methodology (Guarino and Welty, 2004) have also been suggested for manually "cleaning up" the whole resource. This however is extremely demanding, because the philosophical principles involved require a deep analysis of each concept, and as a result, is unlikely to be achieved in a near future. Clark et al. (2006) also gave some general suggestions as design criteria for a new WN-like knowledge base and recommended that WN should be cleaned up to make it logically correct, but did not provide any practical method for doing so. Two other more extensive works rely on manual interventions, either the mapping of each synset in WN to a particular concept in the SUMO ontology (Pease and Fellbaum, 2009), or the tagging of each synset in WN with "features" from the Top Concept Ontology (Alvez et al., 2008) to substitute or contrast the original WN taxonomy. Such approaches are clearly very costly, as each synset needs to be examined. In addition, the ontological value of these additional resources themselves remains to be proven. The method used in (Alvez et al., 2008) has though helped pointing out a large number of errors in WN 1.6.

Our purpose in this paper is to show that automatic methods to spot errors, especially in the lower levels of WN's taxonomy, can be developed. Spotting errors can then efficiently direct the manual correction task. Such methods could be used to complement a manual top-level restructuring and could be seen as an alternative to fully manual approaches, which are very demanding and in principle require validation between experts. Here, we explore methods based on internal coherence checks within WN, or on checking the coherence between WN and annotated corpora such as those of Semeval-2007 Task 4 (Girju et al., 2007).

The paper is structured as follows: Section 2 presents the data used and the methodology; Section 3 discusses the results; Section 4 concludes, exploring how the method could be extended and applied.

2 Methodology

To spot errors in WN, our basic idea is to contrast two sources of knowledge and automatically check their coherence. Here, we contrast part-whole data with WN taxonomy structure, on the basis of constraints stemming from the semantics of the part-whole relations and ontological principles. The part-whole data used is taken either from the meronymy/holonymy relations of WN or from available annotated corpora.

An incoherence between two sources of knowledge may be caused by an error in either one (or both). Contrasting part-whole data with the taxonomy will indeed help detecting errors in the taxonomy —the most numerous— but errors are also found in the part-whole data itself (see Section 3.3).

2.1 Extracting the Dataset

We started extracting WN taxonomy from the hypernym relations in the current version of WN (3.0), a network of 117,798 nouns grouped in 82,155 synsets. We also extracted WN meronymy relations, i.e., 22,187 synset pairs, split into 12,293 "member", 9,097 "part" and 797 "substance", to constitute the first part-whole dataset. In order to replicate our methodology, we also extracted 89 part-whole relation word pairs annotated with WN senses from the SemEval-2007 Task 4 datasets (Girju et al., 2007). We kept the positive examples from the training and test datasets,[3] excluding redundant pairs, and correcting a couple of errors. This data is also annotated with the meronymy sub-relations inspired from the classification of Winston et al. (1987), but five subtypes instead of WN's three, although "member-collection" can safely be assumed to correspond to WN's "member" meronymy. We will call this sub-relation `Member`, be it from WN or from SemEval.

We also tried to get similar datasets from the SemEval-2010 Task 8 but, not being annotated with WN senses, they are useless for our purposes. Figure 1 illustrates a WN-extracted meronymy pair from our corpus[4], encoded in our own xml format. Synsets are presented with the standard WN sense keys for each word, the recommended reference for stability from one WN release to another.[5]

[3] `http://nlp.cs.swarthmore.edu/semeval/tasks/task04/data.shtml`

[4] Available at `http://www.loa-cnr.it/corpus/corpus.tar.gz`

[5] A sense key combines a lemma field and several codes like the synset type and the lexicographer id. See `http://`

```
<pair relationOrder="(e1, e2)" comment="meronym_part" source="WordNet-3.0">
    <e1 synset="head%1:06:04" isInstance="No">
        <hypernym>
            {obverse%1:06:00}...{surface%1:06:00}...{artifact%1:03:00 }...{physical_object%1:03:00}{entity%1:03:00}
        </hypernym>
    </e1>
    <e2 synset="coin%1:21:02" isInstance="No">
        <hypernym>
            ...{metal_money%1:21:00}{currency%1:21:00}...{quantity%1:03:00}{abstract_entity%1:03:00}{entity%1:03:00}
        </hypernym>
    </e2>
</pair>
```

Figure 1: Example pair from the annotated dataset

2.2 The Tests

2.2.1 Ontological constraints

The semantics of the part-whole relation on which the meronymy/holonymy relations are founded involves ontological constraints: in short, the part and the whole should be of a similar nature. Studies in Mereology show that part-whole relations occur on all sub-domains of reality, concrete or abstract (Simons, 1987; Casati and Varzi, 1999). As a few cognitively oriented works explicitly state, the part and the whole should nevertheless belong to the same subdomain (Masolo et al., 2003; Vieu and Aurnague, 2007). Other work, e.g., the influential (Winston et al., 1987), more or less implicitly exploit this homogeneity constraint. Our tests examine and compare the nature of the part and the whole in attested examples of meronymy, looking for incoherences. Here we use only a few basic ontological distinctions, namely, the distinction between:

- endurants (ED) or physical entities (like a dog, a table, a cave, smoke),
- perdurants (PD) or eventualities (like a lecture, a sleep, a downpour), and
- abstract entities (AB — like a number, the content of a text, or a time).

These are only three of the four topmost distinctions in DOLCE (Masolo et al., 2003), that is, we actually group qualities (Q, the fourth top-level category) into abstract entities here.

Tests 1–3 are directly aimed at detecting ontological heterogeneity in meronymy pairs that mix the three categories ED, PD and AB, as just explained. The tests are queries on our corpus to extract and count meronymy pairs (pairs of synsets of the form $\langle e1,e2\rangle$ where *e1* is the part and *e2* is the whole) that involve an ontological heterogeneity. **Test 1** focuses on pairs mixing endurants and abstract entities (pairs of type $\langle$ED,AB$\rangle$ or $\langle$AB,ED$\rangle$), **Test 2** on endurants and perdurants ($\langle$ED,PD$\rangle$ or $\langle$PD,ED$\rangle$) and **Test 3** on perdurants and abstract entities ($\langle$PD,AB$\rangle$ or $\langle$AB,PD$\rangle$).

However, WN 3.0's top-level is not as simple as DOLCE's, so to recover the three basic categories we had to group several classes from different WN branches. In particular perdurants are found both under *physical_entity%1:03:00* (*process%1:03:00*) and under *abstraction%1:03:00* (*event%1:03:00* and *state%1:03:00*). The map we first established was then as follows:

- ED = *physical entity%1:03:00* $\setminus$ *process%1:03:00*;
- PD = *process%1:03:00* $\cup$ *event%1:03:00* $\cup$ *state%1:03:00*;
- AB = *abstraction%1:03:00* $\setminus$ (*event%1:03:00* $\cup$ *state%1:03:00*).

Since all groups in WordNet are under *abstraction%1:03:00* irrespective of the nature of the members, it was obvious from the start that most "member" meronymy pairs would be caught by Tests 1 or 3. This is the reason why groups were actually removed from AB so the final map posited:

- AB = *abstraction%1:03:00* $\setminus$ (*event%1:03:00* $\cup$ *state%1:03:00* $\cup$ *group%1:03:00*).

wordnet.princeton.edu/wordnet/documentation/

2.2.2 Semantic constraints

Two more tests were designed to check basic semantic constraints involved in meronymy relations.

Test 0 is related to the problem of confusion between classes and individuals evoked above and checks for meronymy pairs between an individual and a class. Meronymy in WN applies to pairs of classes and to pairs of individuals, but mixed pairs are also found, either between a class and an individual or between an individual and a class. The semantics of WN meronymy is not precisely described in Fellbaum (1998), but observing the data, the following appears to fit the semantics of "is a meronym of" between two classes A and B: the disjunction of the formulas "for all/most instances a of A, there is an instance b of B such that $P(a, b)$" and "for all/most instances b of B, there is an instance a of A such that $P(a, b)$", where P is the individual-level part-whole relation. On this basis, a meronymy between a class A and an individual b would simply mean: "for all/most instances a of A, $P(a, b)$", while a meronymy between an individual a and a class B would mean: "for all/most instances b of B, $P(a, b)$". The former can make sense, cf. ⟨*sura%1:10:00, koran%1:10:00*⟩ (all suras are part of the Koran). However, the latter would imply that all (most) instances of the class would share a same part, i.e., they would overlap. That the instances of a given class all overlap is of course not logically impossible, but it is highly unlikely for lexical classes. The purpose of Test 0 is to check for such cases, expected to reveal confusion between individuals and classes, that is, errors remaining after the introduction of the distinction in WN 2.1.[6]

Test 4 is dedicated to the large number of `Member` pairs in WN and SemEval data, somehow disregarded by the removal of groups from `AB` above. The semantics of this special case of meronymy clearly indicates that the whole denotes some kind of group, e.g., a collection or an organization, and that the part is a member of this group (Winston et al., 1987; Vieu and Aurnague, 2007). Group concepts in WN are hyponyms of *group%1:03:00*. A last coherence check, done by Test 4, thus extracts the `Member` pairs in which the whole is not considered a group because it is not an hyponym (or instance) of *group%1:03:00*.

3 Results, Analysis and Discussion

Table 1: Number of pairs extracted by the tests

Error Category	Test	WordNet		SemEval	
Semantic	0	349	1.57%	0	0%
	4	550	4.47%	7	7.87%
Ontological	1	163	1.62%	2	2.78%
	2	45	0.45%	2	2.78%
	3	108	1.07%	0	0%

The number of pairs extracted by our queries are summarized on Table1. The error rates are quite low, ranging from 0 to 7.87% depending on the data set of meronymy pairs (WN or SemEval). The highest error rate is provided by Test 4: 550 (4.47%) of the 12,293 WN `Member` pairs and 7 (7.87%) of 19 `Member` pairs in SemEval dataset were identified as semantic errors because the whole is not a group in WN taxonomy. Test 0 has the lowest rate, just 349 (1.57%) of 22,187 WN meronymy pairs are suspected of confusing classes and individuals. More important than the error rate is that the tests achieved maximal precision. After manual inspection of all the suspect pairs extracted, it turns out all the pairs indeed suffered from some sort of error or another. Of course, the few tests proposed here cannot aim at spotting all the taxonomy errors in WN, i.e., recall surely is low, but their precision is a proof of the effectiveness of the method proposed, which can be extended by further tests to uncover more errors.

For Tests 1–3, since the three categories `ED`, `PD` and `AB` are large and diverse, the analysis of the errors started with looking for regularities among the taxonomic chains of hypernyms of the synsets in

[6] Another, very simple and superficial test could be to check synsets for names with capital letters. This of course doesn't rely on ontological knowledge.

the pairs. In particular, we looked for taxonomic generalizations of sets of pairs to divide the results in meaningful small sets. These sets were manually examined in order to check the intended meaning of the meronymy relations and determine the possible problems, either in the taxonomy or in the meronymy; for this we used all the information provided by WordNet as synset, synonymy, taxonomy, and glosses. For Tests 0 and 4, similar regularities could be observed. Several regularities denote a few systematic errors relatively easily solved using standard ontological analysis, described in the Sections 3.1–3.5.

3.1 Confusion between class and group

Several individual collections e.g., *new_testament%1:10:00* , organizations e.g., *palestine_liberation_organization%1:14:00*, and genera e.g., *genus_australopithecus%1:05:00* are considered as classes in WN instead of groups (errors extracted with Test 0). The first example, *new_testament%1:10:00*, is glossed as "the collection of books ...", but is not considered as an instance of group, it is a subclass of *document%1:10:00*.[7] The latter two are seen as subclasses instead of instances of group; this would mean that all instances of *palestine_liberation_organization%1:14:00* (whatever these could be) and all instances of *genus_australopithecus%1:05:00* (which makes more sense) actually are groups. But if there are instances of the genus Australopithecus at all, these are individual hominids, not groups. In fact, the hesitation of the lexicographer is visible here, since *lucy%1:05:00* is both a `Member` of *genus_australopithecus%1:05:00* and an instance of *australopithecus_afarensis%1:05:00*, a subclass of *hominid%1:05:00* (not of group). To show further the confusion here, *australopithecus_afarensis%1:05:00* itself also is a `Member` of *genus_australopithecus%1:05:00*, which, with the semantics of `Member` between classes, would mean that instances of *australopithecus_afarensis%1:05:00* are members of instances of *genus_australopithecus%1:05:00*, which is clearly not adequate.

Despite this confusion, dealing with collections, organizations and groups as individuals poses no real problem. The `Member` meronymy is adequately used elsewhere in WN to relate individuals (e.g., *balthazar%1:18:00*, an instance of *sage%1:18:00*, is a `Member` of *magi%1:14:00*, an instance of *collection%1:14:00*). Dealing with biological genera is arguably more complex, as one can see them both as classes whose instances are the individual organisms, and as individuals which are instances of the class *genus%1:14:00*. A first-order solution to this dilemma, which applies more generally to socially defined concepts, proposes to consider concepts (and genera) as individuals, and to introduce another sort of instance relation for them (Masolo et al., 2004). Beyond genera, related problems occur with the classification of biological orders, divisions, phylums, and families, most of which are correctly considered as groups (e.g., *chordata%1:05:00*), except for a few, pointed out by Test 4 (e.g., *amniota%1:05:00*, *arenaviridae%1:05:00*). All these though should be group individuals, not group classes as now in WN.

3.2 Confusion between class and individual which is a specific instance of the class

Test 0 also points at a few errors where a class is confused with a specific instance of this class. This error corresponds to a missing sense of the word, used with a specific sense. Examples include the individual-class pairs ⟨*great_divide%1:15:00*, *continental_divide%1:15:00*⟩,[8] ⟨*saturn%1:17:00*, *solar_system%1:17:00*⟩, ⟨*renaissance%1:28:00*, *history%1:28:00*⟩, in which the continental divide at stake is not any one but that of North America, the solar system, ours, and the history, the history of mankind. Sometimes the gloss itself makes it clear that the lexicographer wanted to do two things at a time; cf. for *continental_divide%1:15:00*: "the watershed of a continent (especially the watershed of North America formed by a series of mountain ridges extending from Alaska to Mexico)".

[7]This particular error doesn't show again with Test 4 because the meronyms of *new_testament%1:10:00* are "part" meronyms, not `Member` meronyms.

[8]WN has chosen a restrictive sense for the Great Divide, making it a proper part of the Continental Divide. In other interpretations these two names are synonyms.

3.3 Confusion between meronymy and other relations

The meronymy relation itself can be wrong, that is, it is confused with other relations, especially "is located in" ⟨*balkan_wars%1:04:00, balkan_peninsula%1:15:00*⟩ (Test 2), ⟨*nessie%1:18:00, loch_ness%1:17:00*⟩ (Test 1); "participates in" ⟨*feminist%1:18:00, feminist_movement%1:04:00*⟩, ⟨*air%1:27:00, wind%1:19:00*⟩ (Test 2); "is a quality of" ⟨*personality%1:07:00, person%1:03:00*⟩, ⟨*regulation_time%1:28:00, athletic_game%1:04:00*⟩ (Test 3); or still other dependence relations such as in ⟨*operating_system%1:10:00, platform%1:06:03*⟩ (Test 1). Diseases and other conditions regularly give rise to a confusion with "participates in" or its inverse, as with ⟨*cancer_cell%1:08:00, malignancy%1:26:00*⟩, ⟨*knock-knee%1:26:00, leg%1:08:01*⟩, and ⟨*acardia%1:26:00, monster%1:05:00*⟩ (Test 2).

3.4 Confusion between property (`AB`) and an entity (`ED` or `PD`) having that property

A regular confusion occurs between an entity and a property of that entity, for instance a shape, a quantity or measure, or a location. Similarly, confusions occur between a relation and an `ED` or `PD` being an argument of that relation. Examples are extracted mostly with Tests 1 and 3, but a few examples are also found with Tests 2 and 4, when several problems co-occurred. Such confusions lead to wrong taxonomic positions: *coin%1:21:02, haymow%1:23:00* and *tear%1:08:01* are attached under *quantity%1:03:00* (`AB`), while the intuition as well as the glosses make it clear that a coin is a flat metal piece and a haymow a mass of hay, that is, concrete physical entities under `ED`; similarly, *corolla%1:20:00* and *mothball%1:06:00* are attached under *shape%1:03:00* (`AB`), while there are clearly `ED`.

Regularities group together some cases, e.g., many hyponyms of *helping%1:13:00* (*drumstick, fillet, sangria...*) are spotted because *helping%1:13:00* is under *small_indefinite_quantity%1:23:00* (`AB`). It turns out that *small_indefinite_quantity%1:23:00* and its direct hypernym *indefinite_quantity%1:23:00* cover more physical entities of a certain quantity rather than quantities themselves. The tests reveal similar errors at higher levels in the hierarchy: *possession%1:03:00* "anything owned or possessed" is attached under *relation%1:03:00* "an abstraction belonging to or characteristic of two entities or parts together" (`AB`), that is, the object possessed is confused with the relation of possession. Test 1 points at this error 16 times (e.g., *credit_card%1:21:00* and *hacienda%1:21:00*, clearly not abstracts, are spotted this way). Another important mid-level error of this kind is that *part%1:24:00*, while glossed "something determined in relation to something that includes it", is attached under *relation%1:03:00* (`AB`) as well. As a result, all its hyponyms, for instance, *news_item%1:10:00*, and notably, *substance%1:03:00* "the real physical matter of which a person or thing consists" and all its hyponyms (e.g., *dust%1:27:00, beverage%1:13:00*) are considered abstract entities.[9]

3.5 Confusion between two senses of a word

All the tests yield errors denoting missing senses of some words in WN. Test 4 shows that `Member` is systematically used between a national of a country and that individual country, e.g. ⟨*ethiopian%1:18:00, ethiopia%1:15:00*⟩, thus referring to the sense of *country* as "people of that nation". But while the word *country* has both the "location" and the "people" senses (among others) in WN, individual countries do not have multiple senses and are all instances of *country%1:15:00*, the "location" sense.

Similarly, hyponyms of *natural_phenomenon%1:19:00* (`PD`) are often confused with the object (`ED`) involved, i.e., the participant to the process, revealing missing senses (examples extracted with Test 2). *Precipitation* has (among others) two senses, *precipitation%1:23:00* "the quantity of water falling to earth" (a quantity, `AB`), and *precipitation%1:19:00* "the falling to earth of any form of water" (a natural phenomenon, `PD`). The actual water fallen (`ED`), is missing, as revealed by the pair ⟨*ice_crystal%1:19:00, precipitation%1:19:00*⟩ (from Test 2).

Other errors of this kind are more sporadic, as with ⟨*golf_hole%1:06:00, golf_course%1:06:00*⟩ (*golf hole* has only a "playing period" sense, its "location" sense is missing, from Test 1), and ⟨*coma%1:17:00,*

[9] *substance%1:03:00* acquires though a physical entity character through multiple inheritance, since it also has matter and physical entity as hypernyms. It not not obvious why multiple inheritance has been used here.

comet%1:17:00⟩ (*coma* has only a "process" sense, its "physical entity" sense is missing, from Test 2).

3.6 Polysemy in WordNet

The last two types of error, 3.4 and 3.5, point at polysemy issues, as well as the few cases of 3.2. There are two strategies to address polysemy in WN. The main one is the distinction of several synsets for the different senses of a word, but there is also the use of multiple inheritance that gives several facets to a single synset. The literature on WN doesn't make it clear why and when to use multiple inheritance rather than multiple synsets, and it appears that lexicographers have not been methodical is its use. Some cases of "dot objects" (Pustejovsky, 1995) have been accounted this way. For instance, *letter%1:10:00* inherits both its abstract content from its hypernym *text%1:10:00* (`AB`) and its physical aspect from its hypernym *document%1:06:00* (`ED`). However, the polysemy of *book*, the classical similar case, is not accounted for in this way: *book%1:10:00* only is `ED`. And while *document* has two separate senses, *document%1:10:00* (`AB`) and *document%1:06:00* (`ED`), there is no separate abstract sense for *book*. Test 1 points at this problem with the pair ⟨*book_of_psalms%1:10:01*, *book_of_common_prayer%1:10:00*⟩, where the part is a sub-class (rather than an instance, but this is an additional problem pointed by Test 0) of *book%1:10:00* (`ED`), while the whole is an instance of *sacred_text%1:10:00*, a *communication%1:03:00* (`AB`).

As far as polysemy standardly accounted with multiple senses goes, our tests point at a need for a more principled use there as well. In particular, the polysemy accounted for at a given level is often not reproduced at lower levels, as just observed for *document* and *book*. We also have seen above that the polysemy of the word *country* is not "inherited" by individual countries. Similarly the polysemy of *precipitation* has no repercussion on that of *rain*, which has a sense *rain%1:19:00* under *precipitation%1:19:00*, and none under *precipitation%1:23:00* (on the other hand, the material sense of *rain*, *rain%1:27:00* "drops of fresh water that fall", an `ED`, lacks for *precipitation*).

A few pairs extracted with Test 4 show the hesitation of the lexicographer between the classification of a collection as a group, and a classification that accounts for the nature of the collection elements. For instance *constellation%1:17:00* and *archipelago%1:17:00* have members but are `ED`, while *galaxy%1:14:00* is a group. This could be properly addressed by splitting the group category, erroneously situated among abstract entities anyway, into different group categories (e.g., one for each of `ED`, `PD` and `AB`), or exploit multiple inheritance if compatible with its regimentation.

3.7 Difficult ontological issues

Although all the pairs retrieved by our tests point at (one or several) errors, in a few cases, these are not solved easily. In particular, difficult ontological issues are faced with fictional entities. WN classifies most of these under *psychological_feature%1:03:00* (`AB`). However, these fictional entities often show very similar properties to those of concrete entities. As a result, some of them are classified as `ED` or `PD`, e.g., *acheron%1:17:00* is an instance of *river%1:17:00* (`ED`), while being somehow recognized as fictional since it is a meronym of *hades%1:09:00*, a subclass (here again, not an instance, an additional problem) of *psychological_feature%1:03:00* (`AB`), something pointed out by Test 1. Others have concrete parts, e.g. we find the pair ⟨*wing%1:05:00*, *angel%1:18:00*⟩ among the cases of ⟨`ED`,`AB`⟩, i.e. Test 1 results. Angel wings (and feathers, etc.) are of course of a different nature than bird wings, and hellish rivers are not real rivers, but how to distinguish them without duplicating most concrete concepts under *psychological_feature%1:03:00* (`AB`) is unclear.[10]

Another regular anomaly is found with roles and relations, e.g., with pairs like ⟨*customer%1:18:00*, *business_relation%1:24:00*⟩, an ⟨`ED`,`AB`⟩ case (Test 1). A straightforward analysis saying that meronymy has been confused with participation (cf. 3.3) would overlook the fact that the customer role is defined by the business relation itself, i.e., that the dependence is even tighter. Since currently in WN, *customer%1:18:00* simply is a sub-class of *person%1:03:00* (`ED`), in any case the classical issues related to

[10] Although the ontological nature of fictional entities is discussed in metaphysics (see, e.g., (Thomasson, 1999)), how to deal with their "concrete" aspects is not a central issue.

the representation of roles are not addressed, and a more general solution should be looked for, perhaps along the lines of (Masolo et al., 2004).

3.8 Small errors

Finally, our tests identify a few isolated WN errors, which can be seen as small slips, such as for instance a wrong sense selected in the meronymy, e.g., ⟨*seat%1:06:01*, *seating_area%1:06:00*⟩ where *seat%1:15:01* (the area, not the chair) should have been selected,[11] or a wrong taxonomical attachment, that is, a wrong sense selected for an hypernym, e.g., *infrastructure%1:06:01* is an hyponym of *structure%1:07:00*, a property, instead of *structure%1:06:00*, an artifact (from the pair ⟨*infrastructure%1:06:01*, *system%1:06:00*⟩ extracted with Test 1).

3.9 Types of solutions

As can be observed, tests do not all point at a unique type of problem, nor suggest a unique type of solution. Basically, there are five kinds of formal issues underlying the types of errors analyzed above, each calling for different modifications of WN:

- a synset is considered as a class but should be an individual (3.1): need to change its direct hypernym link into an instance-of link, possibly changing as well the attachment point in the taxonomy;
- a synset is not attached to the right place in the taxonomy (3.4, 3.8): need to move it in the taxonomy;
- a synset mixes two senses (3.2, 3.5): need to introduce a missing sense, either attached elsewhere in the taxonomy or as instance of the synset at hand;
- the meronymy relation is confused with another one (3.3): need to remove it (or change it for another sort of relation when this is introduced in WN);
- the meronomy relation is established between the wrong synsets (3.8): need to change one of the two synsets related by another sense of a same word.

In some cases, the problems should be addressed through more general cures, at a higher level in the taxonomy (3.4) or by imposing more systematic modeling choices (3.6, 3.7).

4 Looking forward

We showed in this paper that automatic methods can be developed to spot errors in WN, especially in the hyperonymy relations in the lower levels of the taxonomy. The query system based on ontological principles and semantic constraints we proposed was very effective, as all the items retrieved did point to one or more errors. With such generic tests though, a manual analysis of the extracted examples by lexicographers, domain or ontological experts is necessary to decide on how the error should be solved. However, this same analysis showed many regularities pointing at standard ontological errors, which suggested that the tests can be much refined to limit the variety of issues caught by a single test and that simple repair guidelines can be written.

This work can therefore be developed in several directions. On the one hand, the same tests can be exploited further by expanding the meronymy datasets, for instance if some annotated corpus similar to the SemEval2007 datasets becomes available. The range of tests can be extended as well. For instance, one can make further coherence tests exploiting meronymy data, refining or complementing the Tests 0–4 presented here. The class of abstract entities `AB` groups a variety of concepts, so incompatible combinations of subclasses are certainly present in ⟨`AB`,`AB`⟩ pairs (e.g., across *relation%1:03:00*, *psychological_feature%1:03:00*, or *measure%1:03:00*), suggesting new tests. Without considering to remove groups from abstract entities, cases of incoherence involving groups could also be addressed by checking

[11] This is extracted with Test 1, because an additional problem appears with *seating_area%1:06:00* (or rather with its direct hypernym *room%1:23:00*), which is under *spatial_relation%1:07:00* (`AB`) rather than area and location (`ED`). This shows that the error in the meronomy relation would in principle require finer-grained tests to be found.

the compatibility of the ontological categories of their members. Among the class of physical entities ED, we disregarded the presence of location entities, so new tests could also examine incompatible combinations of subclasses of ED. Finally, we could check whether the "substance" meronym relation indeed involves substances, in a similar way as Test 4 for groups. Additional tests can be considered using other knowledge sources than meronymy data. Within WN, we could exploit the semantics of tagged glosses (cf. Princeton WordNet Gloss Corpus) in order to check the coherence with the taxonomy. And since WN is more than a network of nouns, others relations can be exploited, for instance between nouns and verbs. Similarly, SemEval datasets deal with other relations than the one exploited here: from other subtypes of meronymy (e.g., "place-area"), to any of the semantic relations analyzed in the literature (e.g., "instrument-agency"). In particular, relations involving thematic roles are quite easily associated with ontological constraints and so can constitute the basis for further tests.

On the other hand, methods aiming at improving the quality of WN can be concretely built on the basis of these tests. A semi-automatic tool for "cleaning-up" WN could be fully developed, which could contribute to the next, improved, version of WN. The analysis of regular errors made in WN could simply lead to *guidelines* to help lexicographers avoid classical ontological mistakes. Such guidelines could be used for the extension of Princeton WN, e.g., for new domains. They could be used also during the creation of new WordNets for other languages, suggesting at the same time to abandon the common practice of simply importing the taxonomy of Princeton WN, importing also its errors. These two ideas could be combined in creating a tool to assist the development of WordNets by automatically checking errors and pointing out them in the development phase. This could well complement the TMEO methodology, based on ontological distinctions, used during the creation of the Sensocomune computational lexicon (Oltramari et al., 2010).

Acknowledgements

We wish to thank Alessandro Oltramari for his contribution to the initial stages of this work, Laurent Prévot for fruitful discussions on this topic and comments on a previous draft, Emanuele Pianta and three anonymous reviewers for their comments. This work has been supported by the LOA-ISTC-CNR and the ILIKS joint European laboratory.

References

Alvez, J., J. Atserias, J. Carrera, S. Climent, E. Laparra, A. Oliver, and G. Rigau (2008). Complete and consistent annotation of WordNet using the Top Concept Ontology. In *Proceedings of LREC2008*, pp. 1529–1534.

Bentivogli, L., I. Dagan, H. T. Dang, D. Giampiccolo, and B. Magnini (2009). The Fifth PASCAL Recognizing Textual Entailment Challenge. In *Proceedings of TAC 2009 Workshop*, Gaithersburg, Maryland, USA.

Budanitsky, A. and G. Hirst (2006). Evaluating WordNet-based Measures of Lexical Semantic Relatedness. *Computational Linguistics 32*(1), 13–47.

Casati, R. and A. Varzi (1999). *Parts and Places - The Structures of Spatial Representation.* Cambridge, MA: MIT Press.

Clark, P., P. Harrison, T. Jenkins, J. Thompson, and R. Wojcik (2006). From WordNet to a Knowlege Base. In C. Baral (Ed.), *Formalizing and Compiling Background Knowledge and Its Applications to Knowledge Representation and Question Answering. Papers from the 2006 AAAI Spring Symposium*, pp. 10–15. AAAI Press.

Fellbaum, C. (Ed.) (1998). *WordNet. An Electronic Lexical Database.* Cambridge (MA): MIT Press.

Gangemi, A., N. Guarino, C. Masolo, and A. Oltramari (2003). Sweetening WordNet with DOLCE. *AI Magazine 24*(3), 13–24.

Girju, R. and A. Badulescu (2006). Automatic Discovery of Part-Whole Relations. *Computational Linguistics 32*(1), 83–135.

Girju, R., V. Nastase, and P. Turney (2007). SemEval-2007 Task 04: Classification of Semantic Relations between Nominals. In *Proceedings of the 4th International Workshop on Semantic Evaluations (SemEval-2007)*, pp. 13–18. Association for Computational Linguistics.

Guarino, N. (1998). Some ontological principles for designing upper level lexical resources. In A. Rubio, N. Gallardo, R. Castro, and A. Tejada (Eds.), *First International Conference on Language Resources and Evaluation*, pp. 527–534. European Language Resources Association.

Guarino, N. and C. Welty (2004). An overview of OntoClean. In S. Staab and R. Studer (Eds.), *Handbook on Ontologies*, pp. 151–159. Springer-Verlag.

Kaplan, A. N. and L. K. Schubert (2001). Measuring and Improving the Quality of World Knowledge Extracted From WordNet. Technical Report 751, University of Rochester.

Masolo, C., S. Borgo, A. Gangemi, N. Guarino, and A. Oltramari (2003). The WonderWeb library of foundational ontologies and the DOLCE ontology. WonderWeb (EU IST project 2001-33052) deliverable D18, LOA-ISTC-CNR.

Masolo, C., L. Vieu, E. Bottazzi, C. Catenacci, R. Ferrario, A. Gangemi, and N. Guarino (2004). Social roles and their descriptions. In D. Dubois and C. Welty (Eds.), *Proceedings of the 9th Int. Conf. on Principles of Knowledge Representation and Reasoning (KR 2004)*, pp. 267–277. Menlo Park (CA): AAAI Press. Whistler June, 2-5, 2004.

Neel, A. and M. Garzon (2010). Semantic Methods for Textual Entailment: How Much World Knowledge is Enough? In *Proceedings of FLAIRS 2010*, pp. 253–258.

Oltramari, A., G. Vetere, M. Lenzerini, A. Gangemi, and N. Guarino (2010). Senso comune. In N. Calzolari, K. Choukri, B. Maegaard, J. Mariani, J. Odijk, S. Piperidis, M. Rosner, and D. Tapias (Eds.), *Proceedings of the Seventh conference on International Language Resources and Evaluation (LREC'10)*, Valletta, Malta, pp. 3873–3877. European Language Resources Association (ELRA).

Pease, A. and C. Fellbaum (2009). Formal ontology as interlingua: the SUMO and WordNet linking project and Global WordNet. In C.-R. Huang, N. Calzolari, A. Gangemi, A. Lenci, A. Oltramari, and L. Prévot (Eds.), *Ontology and the Lexicon. A Natural Language Processing Perspective*, pp. 31–45. Cambridge University Press.

Pustejovsky, J. (1995). *The generative lexicon.* Cambridge (MA): MIT Press.

Simons, P. (1987). *Parts - A study in ontology.* Oxford: Clarendon Press.

Thomasson, A. (1999). *Fiction and Metaphysics.* Cambridge University Press.

Vieu, L. and M. Aurnague (2007). Part-of relations, functionality and dependence. In M. Aurnague, M. Hickmann, and L. Vieu (Eds.), *The Categorization of Spatial Entities in Language and Cognition*, pp. 307–336. Amsterdam: John Benjamins.

Winston, M., R. Chaffin, and D. Herrmann (1987). A taxonomy of part-whole relations. *Cognitive Science 11*(4), 417–444.

Compositional Expectation: A Purely Distributional Model of Compositional Semantics

Justin Washtell
University of Leeds, UK
washtell@comp.leeds.ac.uk

The past year has witnessed a surge of interest in the issue of compositional semantics: modelling the meaning of complex phrases. To date, distributional approaches have successfully dealt only with the meaning of individual words in context. Recent attempts to address the more general case of compositional meaning have tended to focus either on mathematical models, which have yet to be demonstrated useful in a linguistic setting, or on syntactically-motivated approaches which do not yet permit application to unconstrained text. We present a purely distributional compositional model, based on the simple addition of expectation vectors. Expectation vectors (Washtell, 2010) are particularly appealing from a compositional standpoint as they are naturally sensitive to word-order alterations whilst being insensitive to the substitution of distributionally similar words. We explore the properties of these and two baseline models using datasets based upon human judgements of phrasal similarity. Whilst far from solving the problem of compositionality, our findings raise interesting questions and provide some useful ideas and benchmarks for those tackling this very current problem.

1. Introduction and motivation

The distributional hypothesis has enjoyed great success over the past decade in the field of empirical lexical semantics, with distributional models performing competitively in tasks which would once have been considered the province of knowledge-driven systems. Many of these successes have been based upon geometric/vector representations and have dealt with the classification of individual words in generalised or specific contexts, in which the unstructured content of those contexts has proven sufficient to enable useful inferences regarding the semantics of the word in question. Such purely distributional models of semantics are particularly attractive from a cognitive perspective as they presuppose little language-specific knowledge, and thus can also be construed as models of language acquisition[1]. This also represents a practical benefit for applications-oriented research as such models can be applied to various languages and registers with little modification.

However if distributional models, or indeed semantic models in general, are to describe language adequately and continue their success, then the issue of compositional meaning remains to be addressed (Pustejovsky, 1995). Baroni (2010) observes that a *"long tradition of scholars unsympathetic to statistical* [i.e. distributional] *approaches to language have argued that they are doomed to fail because they cannot capture compositionality"*. As limits are being reached regarding what can be accomplished with existing (i.e. non-compositional) models, and the growing volume of un-annotated digital content continues to motivate a search for ever more sophisticated ways of making sense of it, the importance of Baroni's scholars' challenge is beginning to become acutely felt in the research community. 2010 saw the introduction of the ESSLLI workshop on Compositionality and Distributional Semantic Models (DistComp), conceived specifically to address this problem. At the same time, over half of the papers at the ACL 2010 workshop on Geometrical Models of Natural Language Semantics (GEMS'10) dealt explicitly with the issue of compositionality (in contrast with just a single paper the previous year).

In this paper we present a purely distributional vector model of semantic compositionality. The model is based on work inspired by principles in semiotics (Washtell, 2010), a field which traditionally has philosophical and sociolinguistic leanings. However, the main idea exploited – that of the central role of expectation in meaning – has begun to receive attention elsewhere in the lexical

[1] In reality nearly all present models incorporate *some* language or task specific knowledge; the most pervasive is the need to define what constitutes a lexical unit (token), without which distributional analysis is problematic. The fact that distributional regularities can be observed on many scales suggest that this is an uneasy solution.

semantics literature (Erk & Padó, 2008, 2009; Yuret, 2007, 2010) and has support in both psycholinguistics and information theory (Attneave, 1959; Brouwer *et al*, 2010; Mitchell *et al*, 2010).

2. Background

Frege's *principle of compositionality* asserts that the meaning of a complex expression is determined by the *meanings of its parts* and the *way in which those parts are combined*. This seems somewhat at odds with the distributional hypothesis; whereas the latter links the meaning of an utterance to its external context, the former focuses on the internal; together these create an apparently circular delegation of responsibility concerning the residence of meaning[2]. In empirical lexical semantics, it is the distributional hypothesis which has received the most attention. This accords with the fact that most attempts to model meaning have focused on atomic units (i.e. words or lemmas), this either being seen as a necessary step towards conquering compositional meaning, or having provided sufficient gains in its own right to distract from what is generally considered a harder problem.

Perhaps one of the simplest geometric model of phrase meaning found in the literature is the bag-of-vectors (more generally the "bag-of-words") in which a vector model of word meaning is elevated to the phrase or document level by summing (or alternatively performing component-wise multiplication[3]) of word vectors (Schütze, 1998). This has the advantage that it is immediately applicable to any model in which word meaning can be expressed as a vector. The principle limitation of course is that this takes no account of word order. Therefore, while it has proven effective in the context of document retrieval and coarse-grained classification tasks, it is generally considered insufficient for fine-grained semantic tasks such as lexical entailment and question answering in which structure tends to play a dominant role. One major line of investigation therefore has been into vector models which are capable of encoding word order information. Vector representations, despite their convenience, seem to present something of a hurdle in this respect. One obvious approach is to use a non-commutative vector operator, such as the tensor product (Smolensky, 1990). Alas, as the product of two tensors results in a tensor of higher order (e.g. a matrix from a vector), the dimensionality of the representation increases exponentially with each term added. This obviously presents a problem for the meaningful comparison of phrases of different lengths, not to mention scalability.

Circular convolution has been proposed as a non-commutative vector operator which does not suffer from the problem of dimensionality explosion (Plate, 1995; Jones & Mewhort, 2007). Sahlgren *et al* (2008) describe an alternative vector-based approach to combining words-in-context with word-order information which does not focus on a specific operator. Rather, a vector for a given word is "contextualized" by merging it with permuted forms of the vectors representing its neighbouring words. After this, simple vector addition is used[4]. The number of times a vector is permuted depends on its distance from the word of interest. Owing to this explicit dependence on word positions, the method is only proposed as a way of comparing individual words in context, not arbitrary passages (i.e. such that context words are imbued with meaningful positions relative to the headword slot). Both convolution and permutation seem like somewhat heavy-handed ways of encoding structure for semantic applications: while structures having similar words at identical positions may be compositionally similar under these approaches (depending on how those words' vectors are formed), structures having similar or even identical words at slightly different positions will not be, as any similarities will have been obfuscated by the permutation or convolution process. Convolutions in particular were designed to operate upon periodic functions and time-series data; the manner in which they discard information in a linguistic context seems rather arbitrary. Unsurprisingly, Mitchell & Lapata (2010) find compositional models built upon convolution to perform very poorly.

Rudolph & Giesbrecht (2010) have proposed square matrices as an alternative to vectors for building compositional models. Standard matrix multiplication is both non-commutative and will take

[2] Some citations of Frege's principle bring the distributional and compositional hypotheses into even starker conflict, observing that the meaning of a part is the *contribution* it makes to the phrase *to which it belongs*.

[3] In vectors comprising positive non-zero elements, these operators are equivalent: adding components such as PMI which incorporates a log function, is equivalent to multiplying them in the absence of the log. The preferred function is therefore dependent upon the nature of the vector components (see Mitchell & Lapata, 2010).

[4] Although Sahlgren *et al*'s model is not cast in terms of operators, it can be thought of as involving a non-commutative operator which entails a permutation and an addition, so making it comparable to a convolution.

two square matrices and produce another matrix of the same dimensions. The authors show that such a matrix representation is able to subsume various existing vector models (e.g. circular convolution) by varying the manner in which vectors are encoded into matrices. Nonetheless, it is not yet clear how this approach can be used to transcend the existing limitations of these models.

Specifically, while the various approaches described attempt to address the issue of differing linguistic forms requiring different representations, it is not clear how any of them might usefully capture structural synonymy, in which markedly different forms have very similar meanings (e.g. *[noun1][passive verb] [noun2]* versus *[noun2][active verb][noun1]*), or differentiate either case from those in which word order is relatively unimportant (e.g. *"they researched it thoroughly"* versus *"they thoroughly researched it"*). Also, while going to lengths to compose words in a way that is non-commutative, these methods largely assume *associativity*. While in some cases this may seem inconsequential: *dogs (chase cats)* $\approx$ *(dogs chase) cats*. In other, especially less compositional (more lexicalised) cases, it seems unsatisfactory: *(new york) skyline* $\neq$ *new (york skyline)*. Arguably what is needed are models which contend intelligently with varying degrees of compositionality. This would seem to favour something more sophisticated than can be captured by a mathematical operator.

The limitations of mathematical approaches to "compositionalising" distributional models are perhaps one reason why many researchers have eschewed a purely distributional approach in favour of more linguistically informed models, incorporating notions of word or relationship *type* (Padó & Lapata, 2007; Clark *et al* 2008). A full review of these is beyond the scope of this paper, suffice to say that some of these models have demonstrated promise under restricted experimental conditions. Of particular relevance to us are the approaches taken by Erk & Padó (2008, 2009) and Thater *et al* (2010) in which a component word is represented by combining a vector describing its type with one describing the selectional preferences (or expectations) of one of its dependent terms, in parsed text. In this way, words provide context for each other, and the two newly contextualized words define the meaning of the whole: an idea known as *co-compositionality* (Putsejovsky, 1995; Baroni, 2010; Gamallo *et al,* 2004). Gayral *et al* (2000) argue that this type of compositionality alone (see also Kintsch & Mangalath, 2010) is insufficient, and that compositional meaning is dependent on features which go beyond immediate arguments. Erk & Padó acknowledge that the generalisation of their approach to multi-word contexts is an open problem. Baroni (2010) speculates that some form of "recursive" compositionality to this end ought to be achievable, providing that the principles governing when and how words influence each other's meaning can be resolved.

3. Expectation vectors

Expectation Vectors were introduced by Washtell (2010) as an intuitive way of modelling the meaning of a word-in-context. An expectation vector for any context or word-in-context can be formed by applying a predictive language model to that context and generating a distribution over word types in the lexicon which reflects the likelihood of each word occurring in the headword-slot. This distribution can then be treated as a vector, and similarity comparisons performed using standard wordspace techniques. The attraction of these vectors lies in perhaps three key features. The first is the intuitive way in which word meaning is modelled: not in terms of a set of context features, but rather the set of words which can be substituted in a given context. It is reasoned that abstracting away from context features in this manner allows for similarity metrics which more directly capture phenomena such as polysemy and synonymy. Secondly, this separation allows for the leveraging of arbitrarily sophisticated language models, such as are able to capture complex interdependencies between words in use and incorporate broader contextual information without the need to complicate the resultant vector space. Thirdly, this can result in markedly denser vectors than using surface features directly. Washtell (2010) and Yuret (2007, 2010) both found approaches based on expectation to perform well in word sense disambiguation tasks, hypothesizing that data-density plays a key role in this setting.

Another, as yet unexplored, advantage of methods based on expectation is that they seem to lend themselves particularly well to modelling compositional meaning. It is this benefit which is the focus of the present work. The key observation is that, providing a non-trivial language model is employed, expectation vectors are naturally word-order dependent. Thus, unlike previously proposed approaches such as that of Sahlgren (2008), which hinge upon the post-hoc manipulation or contextualization of word-type vectors, a word-instance and its context are much more fundamentally intertwined.

In this work we compute a *compositional* vector for an arbitrary fragment of text by generating an expectation vector **e** for every word position in that text (using the remaining words as context in each case) and then simply summing. For generating expectations, we take the approach described in Washtell (2010), in which a structural similarity metric compares the candidate context **c** to the context of every word position o in a large corpus O:

$$\mathbf{e}_j = P(j|c) \sim \max_{o_j^k \in O_j} \text{sim}(o_j^k, c)$$

Where O_j represents the set of contexts for word type j in the corpus, and k is a specific instance of j. The maximum similarity score across all instances of a word type in the corpus therefore forms that word type's corresponding vector component. In this way the similarity metric constitutes a general language model and, along with a raw corpus, a specific language model. This is a computationally expensive approach. Washtell (2010) presents a cumbersome similarity metric based on distance ratios. Here we take a simpler and more efficient approach. First, we form context vectors by summing the negative exponents of each word type's occurrence positions relative to the context head. That is to say that in the context *"the cat sat on the _"*, *the* will have a value of $b^{-1} + b^{-5}$, *on* will have a value of b^{-2}, and so on, with the base b constituting a distance falloff parameter. Similarity is then computed by simply taking the square of the dot product of the two vectors. When $b>1$, this product will never exceed a constant value, irrespective of the context size, thus avoiding the need for normalization. As well as giving an intuitive measure of similarity (effectively computing a "structural" correlation), this approach has the advantage that similarities can be calculated incrementally as we pass through the corpus. The complexity of calculating an expectation vector is therefore more-or-less linear with the size of the corpus, irrespective of the size of the supplied context. Further optimizations can be made if we observe that, for $b>=2$, matching a single pair of words at a given distance from the head always results in a greater similarity than matching any number of words further away.

For the evaluations performed herein we use the British National Corpus and a value of $b=2$. This was found to generate subjectively coherent and cohesive text when recursively extending a context by selecting one of its higher-ranking expectations: a promising trait for the generation of meaningful expectation vectors. The remaining details differentiating our approach from that in Washtell (2010) lie in the handling of the vector components. First, the vectors are normalized so that their components sum to one, giving a pseudo-probabilistic distribution. We then divide each component by its respective word type's prior probability (i.e. its frequency in the corpus) to give a set of probability ratios. Practically speaking these steps prevent function words, and vague expectations which comprise many equally likely words, from routinely dominating our compositional vectors.

4. Evaluation

Distributional wordspace models are often evaluated on their ability to capture meaning by comparing the predictions of their similarity metrics with datasets encapsulating human judgements of word similarity. Achananuparp *et al* (2008) and Mitchell & Lapata (2010) have extended this philosophy to evaluating a variety of phrasal similarity measures. The former rely on human-annotated paraphrase and entailment datasets. Arguably these datasets concern themselves with a much narrower notion of similarity than do word-oriented studies: that of a kind of logical or truth-conditional equivalence. This binary concept does not sit particularly well with vector models, in which meaning is considered to occupying a continuum. Nor does it allow for, say, analogous meanings, or statements of fact re-expressed as questions or opinions. As we cannot say *a priori* that any particular type of relationship plays a dominant role in human intuitions of meaning, it seems unreasonable to exclude any from our investigations; from a application-oriented perspective, if we can first establish *what* it is that our compositional approaches capture, then we will be better placed to pursue specific types of meaning.

Mitchell & Lapata (2010) build a dataset from the ground up which is arguably better suited to this task (hereafter the "M&L dataset"), using phrases extracted from the BNC with the aid of heuristics conceived to capture a range and variety of semantic similarities. We adopt their dataset here, as we believe it provides a sound starting point for evaluating compositional models. We then go on to describe a complementary evaluation in which we attempt to address some of the weaknesses inherent in the M&L dataset in order to provide a more holistic picture. We compare three similarity measures across these evaluations: our proposed expectation-oriented approach and two baselines, each outlined below. In keeping with our purely distributional interests, no language-specific pre-processing steps such as lemmatisation, POS-tagging or parsing were used with any of the measures in either of the evaluations.

Bigram overlap (BIGRAM) is simply the total number of character bigrams that two phrases have in common, normalized by the total number of bigrams they collectively possess (i.e. the Jaccard coefficient). Identical strings achieve a similarity score of 1, with less similar strings having scores that tend towards zero. The main advantages of this approach in the settings herein is that it is forgiving of small changes in word or clause order, and in the inflected forms of words, which in many cases may not significantly affect meaning. By the same token however, it is insensitive to significant shifts in meaning which can sometimes be induced in this way (for example, by the swapping of subject and object). The other main disadvantage of the character bigram model is that, being a simple string similarity measure, it is fundamentally incapable of acknowledging similarities in meaning between completely different forms (i.e. synonymy).

Bag-of-vectors (VECTORBAG) entails summing co-occurrence vectors for the component words of a phrase, where those vectors are derived from a large corpus containing examples of the words in context. Summed vectors are then compared using cosine similarity, which ignores the vector size (effectively factoring out phrase length), focusing instead on the relative balance of components present. This is comparable to the higher-order approaches taken by Schütze (1998) and Landauer & Dumais (1997). Note however that we use a distance-based association measure *co-dispesion* to construct word vectors (Washtell & Markert, 2010). As well as avoiding the thorny issue of window-size and arguably providing a better exploitation of the data in general, this provides a more meaningful baseline for our expectation model which uses a distance-based language model. The principle advantage of working with co-occurrence vectors is that distributionally similar words become comparable by virtue of their vectors being similar. As word-type vectors are the centroids of all occurrences in a corpus, senses are conflated, so synonymy is not modelled particularly cleanly, and polysemy arguably not at all. However the thinking is that when combined in a phrase, the common semantic components of the words dominate, with incidental senses being relegated to some acceptable level of noise. The major disadvantage with such a "bagged" approach is that word order is entirely discarded; whereas under the bigram model switching subject and object would at least incur a small penalty, here the two resultant phrases appear entirely equivalent.

As with VECTORBAG, in compositional expectation (COMPEXP) phrase vectors are formed by summing the vectors of their component words, and then compared using cosine similarity. Rather than the component vectors being based upon word-types however, we use expectation vectors (see section 3) which are unique to the phrasal context in which each word occurs.

4.1. Evaluation 1: Simple Phrase Similarity

Our first method of evaluation is against the M&L phrase similarity dataset (see section 4). This consists of around 200 short phrase pairs rated by human subjects on a scale of 1-7 for their semantic similarity. Each phrase is comprised of two words in the form verb-object, noun-noun, or adjective-noun, extracted from the BNC. The authors applied quite sophisticated heuristics based on phrase frequency and WordNet word similarity (Lesk, 1986) in an attempt to produce a set which exhibits an even spread of subjective similarities, from near-synonymy to near-total unrelatedness. Their analysis of human ratings confirmed that they were reasonably successful in this.

Table 1 shows the performance of the models upon the M&L dataset, in terms of Spearman's rank correlation. Two additional columns are included for reference: the inter-annotator agreement reported by M&L (which in this experiment serves as an upper-bound), calculated using leave-one-out sampling, and the results from the best-performing model reported by M&L for each phrase class. Our additive distance-based model performs fairly competitively on this task, and is superior to all methods on verb-object combinations. Interestingly, compositional expectation fairs relatively poorly, turning in a respectable performance only for noun-noun combinations and performing particularly poorly on verb-object combinations. This last observation is at odds with the surprisingly good performance on verb sense disambiguation previously observed using expectation vectors (Washtell, 2010), leading us to speculate whether this was rather a symptom of the distance-based approach used in that work (although it should be noted that there are many confounding differences separating the tasks and models in these works). Unsurprisingly, the bigram measure performs very poorly across the board. When interpreting these figures it is worth bearing in mind that, differences in our approaches to composition aside, unlike Mitchell & Lapata we are operating on unlemmatized data.

	Human	M&L BEST (various)	BIGRAM	VECTORBAG	COMPEXP
ADJ-NOUN	0.52	**0.46** (multiplicative)	0.2	0.27	0.28
NOUN-NOUN	0.49	**0.49** (multiplicative)	-0.11	0.47	0.41
VERB-OBJ	0.55	0.41 ("dilated" LDA)	0.11	**0.45**	0.2

Table 1: Spearman's rank correlation between human and computational similarity ratings for M&L dataset.

While the form of the M&L dataset makes it suitable for use as a Gold Standard, it does come with certain limitations. Most notably, the phrases comprise only two words. While this is a logical starting point for assessing compositional models, it gives little scope for testing the ability to capture structural aspects of composition (as M&L anyway restrict phrase pairs to identically structured phrase types, this point is all but moot). Related to this is the fact that while the heuristics applied in generating the M&L dataset attempt to generate superficially different yet synonymous phrases (e.g *"reduce amount", "cut cost"*), there are very few cases of polysemy or superficial similarity (e.g. *"stout Russian", "Russian stout"* or *"arresting music", "arresting criminals"*) which is an important confounding issue for compositional models. In the next section we outline a complementary evaluation approach with which we attempt to address some of these issues.

4.2. Evaluation 2: Unconstrained Phrase Similarity

A restricted register of about 300 noun, verb and adjective lemmas was selected with the aid of Wordnet and BNC frequency information. Sentences were then automatically selected from the BNC with the constraint that each sentence was at least 3 words in length and a certain minimum proportion of its lemmas belonged to the restricted register. This minimum proportion was tweaked such that the entire BNC generated approximately 1000 qualifying sentences. The aim was to produce a manageably sized collection of real-world phrases wherein a range of similarities and similarity types (both semantic and superficial) existed between a proportion of the phrases. In selecting the register, the purpose was therefore to find a compact set of words which exhibited both a high degree of ambiguity (polysemy) and interchangeability (synonymy). Because words satisfying the former requirement tend to be very frequent (e.g. the auxiliary verbs), while those satisfying the latter tend to be very rare, this task was difficult. An additional complication was that the types of phrase selected from the corpus were found to be highly sensitive to the specific words in the register, with certain words resulting in a disproportionate contingent of highly synonymous idiomatic phrases being selected (*"let's take the following", "consider the following", "look at the following"* etc), which was considered undesirable. In the end a lot of judgement was exercised in selecting the register.

For each phrase in the dataset, the two most similar candidate phrases also in the dataset were identified according to each of our three similarity measures. An additional two candidate phrases were selected at random to act as a control. This resulted in at most eight candidate sentences for each source sentence, and less where different methods selected the same phrases. Agreement between BIGRAM and VECTORBAG was 19.7% (which is both surprising and reassuring, considering the size of the dataset and how different these approaches are). Agreement between these and the novel COMPEXP method was markedly less, at 12.7% and 9.1% respectively. Agreement between the random control and each of the methods was in keeping with chance (<0.4%). To aid annotation, further steps were taken to reduce the size of the dataset and increase the proportion of subjectively similar phrases expressed. For each method, the top candidate phrase attributed to each source phrase was ranked amongst those attributed to all source phrases (according to the actual similarity score attributed). The source phrases were then ordered according to the minimum of these ranks, and the lower 50% were discarded. This resulted in a set of 500 source sentences to which at least one of the methods had attributed a candidate sentence with relatively high confidence. Agreement between methods after this step was 28.6%, 18.6% and 13.9% respectively (a uniform 50% increase).

English-speaking subjects were invited to participate in an annotation process via a website. Upon visiting the site subjects were presented with a source sentence, and its set of "similar" candidate sentences as chosen by the four approaches, presented in a random order. In cases where methods had agreed, fewer than eight sentences were displayed (i.e. there were no visible repetitions). The annotators were asked to identify the *two* candidate sentences which were "*most similar in meaning*" to the source sentence, and to award an explicit first and second place accordingly. Upon completing a question, participants progressed onto another selected at random from those having received the fewest annotations so far. Participants were required to identify two sentences in every case, no matter how relevant they thought their meanings were in absolute terms, but were free to cease answering questions at any point. No knowledge of the methods used to generate or select the sentences, or of the purpose of the study, was made available to the annotators.

Approximately 90 mostly native English speakers participated in the annotation process. The number of questions answered by each annotator followed a roughly geometric distribution, with maximum, median and minimum of 266, 8 and 1 respectively. The median time taken to answer each question was 24 seconds. Average Kappa for random pairs of responses was 0.25 for annotators' first choices alone, and 0.39 when first and second choices are treated equally. As we are gathering psycholinguistic data, and not developing a gold standard for a supposed underlying objective classification, such moderate levels of agreement are not problematic. What is important for our purposes is that, given the number of annotators involved, the observed levels of agreement are highly significant. The distribution of agreement levels was more-or-less uniform, with a slight dip in the mid-range. Interestingly there was negligible correlation between inter-annotator agreement and the average time taken to answer each question, indicating that seemingly "hard" questions did not take appreciably longer to answer than "easier" questions.

Table 2 presents a summary the agreement between each of the phrasal similarity methods and the votes of the human annotators. Results are separated into annotators' first choices only, and their combined first and second choices. The figures in parentheses are the raw percentage of votes awarded to each method. As there was some corroboration between the methods themselves, these total more than 100% across methods. The figures outside of the parentheses are agreements expressed as a proportion of chance, taking any such corroboration into account. There was only slight variation in the relative balance of scores when stratified according to annotator agreement: the random control unsurprisingly showed an increase at the lowest agreement levels, with BIGRAM and VECTORBAG increasing slightly with agreement, and COMPEXP peaking in the midrange.

	BIGRAM	VECTORBAG	COMPEXP	RANDOM
1st choices only	3.14 (47%)	**3.29** (49%)	2.29 (35%)	0.60 (8%)
All votes	2.87 (43%)	**3.03** (45%)	2.21 (33%)	0.74 (11%)

Table 2: Agreement between computational phrasal similarity measures and human annotations

Despite its ignorance of word order and context, the most successful method in this experiment is the bag of vectors. Arguably more remarkable is the success of the relatively naïve string similarity measure. The fact that these methods also show a surprisingly high degree of agreement with each other (28.6%), suggests that a fair proportion of the phrase similarities present in our dataset can be adequately identified simply by the word forms that comprise them, without recourse to distributional information. Our compositional expectation model is less successful overall, though still receiving several times as many votes as the random control. The fact that its agreement with the two baselines is comparatively low would suggest that it is identifying a different kind of similarity. Given that the mechanisms of compositional expectation are least understood, some kind of qualitative analysis may provide useful insight. To this end, tables 3 and 4 show a selection of 10 phrases deemed *most* similar by the COMPEXP model, that were unanimously awarded first place by the human annotators or unanimously rejected respectively. Rejected phrases are only shown for cases where there was a clear favourite phrase which had been selected by one of the competing models (also shown). The examples were hand-picked for illustrative purposes from qualifying lists of two to three times the size.

The phrase pairs in table 3 can be broadly categorized in terms of their structural and semantic similarities. While one can observe cases of phrases which have near-synonymous meanings in spite of markedly different wording or structure (B, D, F, G, I, J), there also seem to exist pairs which have essentially equivalent structures, yet are somewhat more loosely related in meaning (A, C, E, H). Note that this is a very informal analysis and a lot of overlap between these classes can be acknowledged.

	Source phrase	**Selected phrase**
A	She moved cautiously into the room	She looked slowly around the room
B	She's an exceptionally nice woman	She's really a nice person
C	It was a desperately lonely time	It was a really bad time
D	Of course I take it seriously	I took it terribly seriously
E	He went into the sitting room	He entered the throne room
F	I left the room	I ran back out of the room
G	He held desperately onto her arm	He held her tightly
H	She hurried towards the white van	She ran straight out of the house
I	I'd hardly made a sound	I could manage only a whisper
J	He made his reasons absolutely clear	He certainly made his point

Table 3: Phrases uniquely selected by compositional expectation model and unanimously selected by annotators.

	Source phrase	**Rejected phrase**	**Most strongly selected phrase**
A	Good, good, good	Sweet and beautiful and good	Good good good
B	It was a really good night	It makes a good story	I thought it was really good
C	He moved slowly along the beach	He moved vaguely around the room	He moved slowly and quietly
D	It was peaceful by the river	It was dark in the room	They even took to the river
E	The event went smoothly and pleasantly	The house was dark and quiet	It was a good time really
F	They took it very badly	Obviously they'd lost it	My family took it badly
G	He really should have won it	He took it personally	It's good we won
H	I take the left	I ran back out of the room	Take a big left turn
I	He's made a good marriage	He's probably making a mistake	He made a good world
J	Isobel moved restlessly around the room	Gaily moved it nearer the counter	She looked slowly around the room

Table 4: Phrases uniquely selected by compositional expectation model, but unanimously rejected by annotators.

Compared to table 3, those phrases in table 4 which exhibit similar structure relate more loosely in their subject matter (C, D, E, J); nonetheless, parts-of-speech and aspects of semantic category do seem to be largely preserved (*dark-peaceful, room-river-beach, in-by, along-around slowly-vaguely, Isobel-Gaily*) resulting in some cases in what might better be described as analogy than synonymy. Where phrases do deviate in structure, their similarities are much less prescriptive; in many cases they seem to imply an almost rhetorical relationship (B, F, G, I).

These observations seem to indicate that compositional expectation is capable of capturing both structural and semantic aspects of similarity, with a leaning towards the former. With some notable exceptions (E), the phrases chosen by the competing methods - and preferred by the annotators - tend to exhibit a more literal or topical relationship with the source phrase (in keeping with how these methods are formulated). We should point out though that while the qualitative observations made here do seem to hold in some measure across the dataset, it is very difficult - and necessarily left to future work - to objectify them; it remains possible that the some of the patterns identified are due to chance and the limited set of phrases comprising our dataset.

5. Discussion

We have presented a novel approach to purely distributional semantic composition, called compositional expectation. By employing a language model and representing phrase constituents in terms of the expectations evoked in their stead, it is possible to represent phrase meaning in a way that is sensitive to word order without recourse to problematic vector operations. While there is evidence to suggest that this approach is able to usefully capture compositional meaning in certain cases – and in a manner that is complementary to more naive methods - its overall performance as measured against the two human-annotated datasets in this study suggests a lot of room for improvement. At present it is unclear to what extent this is a reflection of limitations of these datasets (whether either of them accurately models the problem), deficiencies in the specific formulation of our model (the language model employed, the vector handling etc), or fundamental shortcomings of this approach to capturing semantic similarity.

A qualitative analysis seems to suggest that compositional expectation is capable of capturing some quite complex structural similarities, as well as broad semantic correspondences between dissimilarly structured phrases. While some capacity to encode structure was presupposed owing to the strong dependence of expectation vectors upon the context in which words appear, it does not obviously follow that similar-meaning but structurally-unlike phrases should have comparable vectors. Our vectors are simply calculated on a token-by-token basis, without consideration of any hierarchical structure present - a generally assumed requirement of compositional models (Padó & Lapata, 2007; Mitchell & Lapata, 2010). While we can speculate that the expectations generated at the terminal positions of synonymous phrases (and therefore sub-phrases) ought to be similar, it is hard to imagine that the strong internal expectations within idiomatic expressions, say, are anything but obstructive to compositional meaning. Perhaps we will find that, as with Schütze's (1998) second-order vectors, the information associated with the most pertinent interpretation tends to dominate the sum. If this is so then the fact that simple vector addition is both associative and commutative - and therefore agnostic of any structure present - may actually play an important role in these models. Given this commutative operator, there would seem to be no means of determining retrospectively to which constituents of a phrase any portion of a compositional vector belongs; this would appear to be a fundamental limitation with respect to the encoding of structure. However, we can speculate that in practice the overwhelming contingent of possible factorizations will tend to be syntactically or semantically implausible. The most plausible interpretations may therefore tend to be those formed by the original word vectors, or very similar ones. Because under an expectation model, jumbling the word order tends to result in *different* component vectors, most ordered interpretations of such factorizations will also tend to be implausible (unless perhaps they actually constitute a valid paraphrase). As this kind of plausibility is information which the language user has, it need not be encoded.

Such lines of thought suggest another problem which needs to be addressed if any of the models considered herein are to be claimed as cognitively plausible takes on compositional meaning: the re-encoding of vector representations into natural language. This would seem to be a straightforward but computationally hard search problem, analogous to that which lies at the heart of machine translation: simultaneously maximizing the plausibility and the faithfulness of a linguistic realisation. Indeed, this might be the acid-test for any proposed compositional representation of meaning. If such "language-meaning codecs" are attainable, then it would pave the way for a host of applications that work natively with meaning, and could revolutionize the way search engines, dialogue agents and machine translation systems are engineered.

Acknowledgements

Sincerest thanks are extended to Jeff Mitchell and Mirella Lapata for the use of their dataset, and as ever to Eric Atwell and Katja Markert for their constructive criticism and support.

Bibliography

Palakorn Achananuparp (2008), "The Evaluation of Sentence Similarity Measures", Proceedings of the 10th International Conference on Data Warehousing and Knowledge Discovery

F. Attneave (1959), "Applications of Information Theory to Psychology: A summary of basic concepts, methods, and results". Holt, Rinehart and Winston.

Baroni (2010) "Distributional semantics IV: Is distributional semantics really 'semantics'?", UPF Computational Semantics Course

Harm Brouwer, Hartmut Fitz & John C. J. Hoeks (2010), "Modeling the Noun Phrase versus Sentence Coordination Ambiguity in Dutch: Evidence from Surprisal Theory" Proceedings of the 2010 Workshop on Cognitive Modeling and Computational Linguistics, ACL 2010, pages 72–80,

Stephen Clark, Bob Coecke & Mehrnoosh Sadrzadeh (2008), "A Compositional Distributional Model of Meaning", Proceedings of the Second Symposium on Quantum Interaction (QI-2008), pp.133-140

Katrin Erk & Sebastian Padó (2008), "A structured vector space model for word meaning in context", Proceedings of EMNLP 2008.

Katrin Erk & Sebastian Padó (2009). "Paraphrase assessment in structured vector space: Exploring parameters and datasets". Proceedings of the EACL Workshop on Geometrical Methods for Natural Language Semantics

Pablo Gamallo, Gabriel P Lopes & Alexandre Agustini (2004) "The Role of Optional Co-composition to Solve Lexical and Syntactic Ambiguity", Procesamiento del Lenguaje Natural, volume 33, pages 73-80

Francoise Gayral, Nathalie Pernellel & Patrick Saint-Dizier Gayral (2000), "On Verb Selectional Restrictions: Advantages and Limitations", NLP 2000, LNCS 1835, pages. 57-68

Thomas K Landauer & Susan T Dumais (1997), "A solution to Plato's problem: the latent semantic analysis theory of acquisition, induction and representation of knowledge." Psychological Review CIV/2. 211-240.

M. Lesk. (1986). "Automatic sense disambiguation using machine readable dictionaries: how to tell a pine cone from and ice cream cone". In Proceedings of the ACM SIGDOC Conference, pages 24–26, Toronto, Canada.

Jones & Mewhort (2007), "Representing word meaning and order information in a composite holographic lexicon." Psychological Review, 114, 3 1–37.

Walter Kintsch & Praful Mangalath (2010), "The Construction of Meaning", Topics in Cognitive Science

Jeff Mitchell, Mirella Lapata, Vera Demberg & Frank Keller (2010), "Syntactic and Semantic Factors in Processing Difficulty: An Integrated Measure" Proceedings of ACL 2010

Jeff Mitchell & Mirella Lapata (2008), "Vector-based models of semantic composition". Proceedings of the 46th Annual Meeting of the Association for Computational Linguistics: Human Language Technologies. 236-244.

Jeff Mitchell & Mirella Lapata (2010). "Composition in Distributional Models of Semantics". Cognitive Science (to appear).

Sebastian Padó & Mirella Lapata (2007). "Dependency-based construction of semantic space models". Computational Linguistics XXXIII/2. 161-199.

Plate (1995),"Holographic reduced representations". IEEE Transactions on Neural Networks, 6, 623–641.

James Putsejovsky (1995), "The Generative Lexicon." Cambridge, MA: MIT Press.

Sebastian Rudolph & eugenie Giesbrecht (2010), "Compositional Matrix-Space Models of Language", Proceedings of the 48th Annual Meeting of the Association for Computational Linguistics, pages 907-916

Magnus Sahlgren, Anders Holst, & Pentti Kanerva (2008), "Permutations as a means to encode order in word space". Proceedings of Cognitive Science 2008, pages 1300–1305.

Hinrich Schütze (1998). "Automatic word sense discrimination". Computational Linguistics, 24(1):97–124.

Paul Smolensky (1990). "Tensor product variable binding and the representation of symbolic structures in connectionist networks". Artificial Intelligence, 46, 159–216.

Stefan Thater, Hagen Fürstenau & Manfred Pinkal (2010). "Contextualizing Semantic Represenations Using Syntactically Enriched Vector Models". Proceedings of ACL2010

Justin Washtell (2009). "Co-dispersion: A windowless approach to lexical association." Proceedings EACL'09.

Justin Washtell (2010). "Expectation Vectors: A Semiotics-Inspired Approach to Geometric Lexical-Semantic Representation", GEMS-2010

Justin Washtell & Katja Markert (2009). "Comparing windowless and window-based computational association measures as predictors of syntagmatic human associations". In Proceedings of EMNLP-2009, pages 628-637.

Deniz Yuret (2007), "KU: Word Sense Disambiguation by Substitution", Proceedings of SemEval-2007

Deniz Yuret (2010), "The Noisy Channel Model for Unsupervised Word Sense Disambiguation, Computational Linguistics", Volume 31, Number 1

Structured Composition of Semantic Vectors

Stephen Wu
Mayo Clinic
wu.stephen@mayo.edu

William Schuler
The Ohio State University
schuler@ling.ohio-state.edu

Abstract

Distributed models of semantics assume that word meanings can be discovered from "the company they keep." Many such approaches learn semantics from large corpora, with each document considered to be unstructured bags of words, ignoring syntax and compositionality within a document. In contrast, this paper proposes a *structured* vectorial semantic framework, in which semantic vectors are defined and composed in syntactic context. As such, syntax and semantics are fully interactive; composition of semantic vectors necessarily produces a hypothetical syntactic parse. Evaluations show that using relationally-clustered headwords as a semantic space in this framework improves on a syntax-only model in perplexity and parsing accuracy.

1 Introduction

Distributed semantic representations like Latent Semantic Analysis (Deerwester et al., 1990), probabilistic LSA (Hofmann, 2001), Latent Dirichlet Allocation (Blei et al., 2003), or relational clustering (Taskar et al., 2001) have garnered widespread interest because of their ability to quantitatively capture 'gist' semantic content.

Two modeling assumptions underlie most of these models. First, the typical assumption is that words in the same document are an unstructured *bag of words*. This means that word order and syntactic structure are ignored in the resulting vectorial representations of meaning, and the only relevant relationship between words is the 'same-document' relationship. Second, these semantic models are not *compositional* in and of themselves. They require some external process to aggregate the meaning representations of words to form phrasal or sentential meaning; at best, they can jointly represent whole strings of words without the internal relationships.

This paper introduces *structured vectorial semantics* (SVS) as a principled response to these weaknesses of vector space models. In this framework, the syntax–semantics interface is fully interactive: semantic vectors exist in syntactic context, and any composition of semantic vectors necessarily produces a hypothetical syntactic parse. Since semantic information is used in syntactic disambiguation (MacDonald et al., 1994), we would expect practical improvements in parsing accuracy by accounting for the interactive interpretation process.

Others have incorporated syntactic information with vector-space semantics, challenging the bag-of-words assumption. Syntax and semantics may be jointly generated with Bayesian methods (Griffiths et al., 2005); syntactic structure may be coupled to the basis elements of a semantic space (Padó and Lapata, 2007); clustered semantics may be used as a pre-processing step (Koo et al., 2008); or, semantics may be learned in some defined syntactic context (Lin, 1998). These techniques are interactive, but their semantic models are not syntactically compositional (Frege, 1892). SVS is a generative model of sentences that uses a variant of the last strategy to incorporate syntax at preterminal tree nodes, but is inherently compositional.

Mitchell and Lapata (2008) provide a general framework for semantic vector composition:

$$\mathbf{p} = f(\mathbf{u}, \mathbf{v}, R, K) \tag{1}$$

where $\mathbf{u}$ and $\mathbf{v}$ are the vectors to be composed, R is syntactic context, K is a semantic knowledge base, and $\mathbf{p}$ is a resulting composed vector (or tensor). In this initial work of theirs, they leave out any notion of syntactic context, focusing on additive and multiplicative vector composition (with some variations):

$$\text{Add: } \mathbf{p}[i] = \mathbf{u}[i] + \mathbf{v}[i] \qquad\qquad \text{Mult: } \mathbf{p}[i] = \mathbf{u}[i] \cdot \mathbf{v}[i] \tag{2}$$

Since the structured vectorial semantics proposed here may be viewed within this framework, our discussion will begin from their definition in Section 2.1.

Erk and Padó's (2008) model also fits inside Mitchell and Lapata's framework, and like SVS, it includes syntactic context. Their semantic vectors use syntactic information as relations between multiple vectors in arriving at a final meaning representation. The emphasis, however, is on selectional preferences of individual words; resulting representations are similar to word-sense disambiguation output, and do not construct phrase-level meaning from word meaning. Mitchell and Lapata's more recent work (2009) combines syntactic parses with distributional semantics; but the underlying compositional model requires (as other existing models would) an interpolation of the vector composition results with a separate parser. It is thus not fully interactive.

Though the proposed structured vectorial semantics may be defined within Equation 1, the end output necessarily includes not only a semantic vector, but a full parse hypothesis. This slightly shifts the focus from the semantically-centered Equation 1 to an accounting of meaning that is necessarily interactive (between syntax and semantics); vector composition and parsing are then twin lenses by which the process may be viewed. Thus, unlike previous models, a unique *phrasal* vectorial semantic representation is composed during decoding.

Due to the novelty of phrasal vector semantics and lack of existing evaluative measures, we have chosen to report results on the well-understood dual problem of parsing. The structured vectorial semantic framework subsumes variants of several common parsing algorithms, two of which will be discussed: lexicalized parsing (Charniak, 1996; Collins, 1997, etc.) and relational clustering (akin to latent annotations (Matsuzaki et al., 2005; Petrov et al., 2006; Gesmundo et al., 2009)). Because previous work has shown that linguistically-motivated syntactic state-splitting already improves parses (Klein and Manning, 2003), syntactic states are split as thoroughly as possible into subcategorization classes (e.g., transitive and intransitive verbs). This pessimistically isolates the contribution of semantics on parsing accuracy — it will only show parsing gains where semantic information does not overlap with distributional syntactic information. Evaluations show that interactively considering semantic information with syntax has the predicted positive impact on parsing accuracy over syntax alone; it also lowers per-word perplexity.

The remainder of this paper is organized as follows: Section 2 describes SVS as both vector composition and parsing; Section 3 shows how relational-clustering SVS subsumes PCFG-LAs; and Section 4 evaluates modeling assumptions and empirical performance.

2 Structured Vectorial Semantics

2.1 Vector Composition

We begin with some notation. This paper will use boldfaced uppercase letters to indicate matrices (e.g., $\mathbf{L}$), boldfaced lowercase letters to indicate vectors (e.g., $\mathbf{e}$), and no boldface to indicate any single-valued variable (e.g. i). Indices of vectors and matrices will be associated with semantic concepts (e.g., $\mathrm{i}_1, \mathrm{i}_2, \ldots$); variables over those indices are single-value (scalar) variables (e.g., i); the contents of vectors and matrices can be accessed by index (e.g., $\mathbf{e}[\mathrm{i}_1]$ for a constant, $\mathbf{e}[i]$ for a variable). We will also define an operation $d(\cdot)$, which lists the elements of a column vector on the diagonal of a diagonal matrix, i.e., $d(\mathbf{e})[i,i]$=$\mathbf{e}[i]$. Often, these variables will technically be functions with arguments written in parentheses, producing vectors or matrices (e.g., $\mathbf{L}(l)$ produces a matrix based on the value of l).

As Mitchell and Lapata (2008) did, let us temporarily suspend discussion on what semantics populate our vectors for now. We can rewrite their equation (Equation 1) in SVS notation by following several conventions. All semantic vectors have a fixed dimensionality and are denoted $\mathbf{e}$; source vectors and the

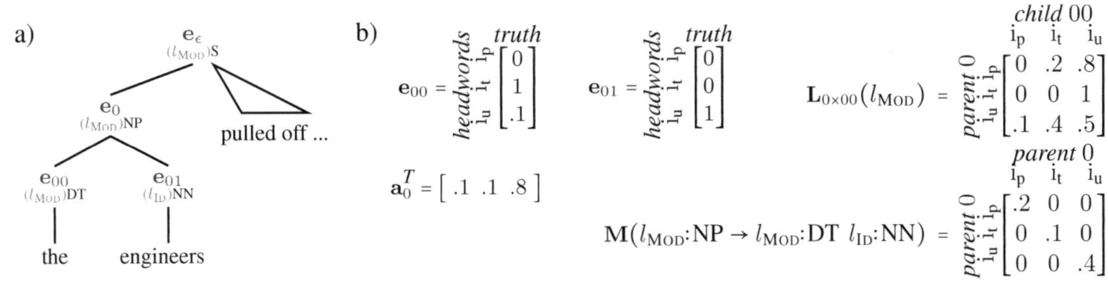

Figure 1: a) Syntax and semantics on a tree during decoding. Semantic vectors $\mathbf{e}$ are subscripted with the node's address. Relations l and syntactic categories c are constants for the example. b) Example vectors and matrices needed for the composition of a vector at address 0 (Section 2.2.1).

target vector are differentiated by subscript; instead of context variables R and K we will use M and L:

$$\mathbf{e}_\gamma = f(\mathbf{e}_\alpha, \mathbf{e}_\beta, M, L) \tag{3}$$

Syntactic context is in the form of grammar rules M that are aware of semantic concepts; semantic knowledge is in the form of labeled dependency relationships between semantic concepts, L. Both of these are present and explicitly modeled as matrices in SVS's canonical form of vector composition:

$$\mathbf{e}_\gamma = \mathbf{M} \cdot d(\mathbf{L}_{\gamma\times\alpha} \cdot \mathbf{e}_\alpha) \cdot d(\mathbf{L}_{\gamma\times\beta} \cdot \mathbf{e}_\beta) \cdot \mathbf{1} \tag{4}$$

Here, $\mathbf{M}$ is a diagonal matrix that encapsulates probabilistic syntactic information, where the syntactic probabilities depend on the semantic concept being considered. The $\mathbf{L}$ matrices are linear transformations that capture how semantically relevant source vectors are to the resulting vector (e.g., $\mathbf{L}_{\gamma\times\alpha}$ defines the the relevance of $\mathbf{e}_\alpha$ to $\mathbf{e}_\gamma$), with the intuition that two 1D vectors are under consideration and require a 2D matrix to relate them. $\mathbf{1}$ is a vector of ones — this takes a diagonal matrix and returns a column vector corresponding to the diagonal elements.

Of note in this definition of $f(\cdot)$ is the presence of matrices that operate on distributed semantic vectors. While it is widely understood that matrices can represent transformations, relatively few have used matrices to represent the distributed, dynamic nature of meaning composition (see Rudolph and Giesbrecht (2010) for a counterexample).

2.2 Syntax–Semantics Interface

This section aims to more thoroughly define the way in which the syntax and semantics interact during structured vectorial semantic composition. SVS will specify this interface such that the composition of semantic vectors is probabilistically consistent and subsumes parsing under various frameworks. Parsing has at times added semantic annotations that unwittingly carry some semantic value: headwords (Collins, 1997) are one-word concepts that subsume the words below them; latent annotations (Matsuzaki et al., 2005) are clustered concepts that touch on both syntactic and semantic information at a node. Of course, other annotations (Ge and Mooney, 2005) carry more explicit forms of semantics. In this light, semantic concepts (vector indices i) and relation labels (matrix arguments l) may also be seen as annotations on grammar trees.

Let us introduce notation to make the connection with parsing and syntax explicit. This paper will denote syntactic categories as c and string yields as x. The location of these variables in phrase structure will be identified using subscripts that describe the path from the root to the constituent.[1] Paths consist of left and/or right branches (indicated by '0's and '1's, respectively, as in Figure 1a). Variables α, β, and ι stand for whole paths; γ is the path of a composed vector; and ϵ is the empty path at the root. The yield x_γ is the observed (sub)string that eventually results from the progeny of c_γ. Multiple trees τ_γ can be constructed at γ by stringing together grammar rules that are consistent with observed text.

[1]For simplicity, trees are assumed to be compiled into strictly binary-branching form.

2.2.1 Lexicalized Parsing

To illustrate the definitions and operations presented in this section, we start with the concrete 'semantic' space of headwords (i.e., bilexical parsing) before moving on to a formal definition. Our example here corresponds to the best parse of the first two words in Figure 1a. In this example domain, assume that the semantic space of concept headwords is $\{\mathrm{i}_{\text{pulled}}, \mathrm{i}_{\text{the}}, \mathrm{i}_{\text{unk}}\}$, abbreviated as $\{\mathrm{i}_{\text{p}}, \mathrm{i}_{\text{t}}, \mathrm{i}_{\text{u}}\}$ where the last concept is a constant for infrequently-observed words. This semantic space becomes the indices of semantic vectors; complete vectors $\mathbf{e}$ at each node of Figure 1a are shown in Figure 1b.

The tree in Figure 1a contains complete concept vectors $\mathbf{e}$ at each node, with corresponding indices i. Values in these vectors (see Figure 1b) are probabilities, indicating the likelihood that a particular concept summarizes the meaning below a node. For example, consider $\mathbf{e}_{00}$: i_{t} produces the yield below address 00 ('the') with probability 1, and i_{u} may also produce 'the' with probability 0.1.

Not shown on the tree are the matrices in Figure 1b. In the parametrized matrix $\mathbf{M}(l_{\text{MOD}}\text{:NP} \to l_{\text{MOD}}\text{:DT}\ l_{\text{ID}}\text{:NN})$, each diagonal element corresponds to the hypothesized grammar rule's probability, given a headword. Similarly, the matrix $\mathbf{L}_{0\times00}(l_{\text{MOD}})$ is parametrized by the semantic context l_{MOD} — here, l_{MOD} represents a generalized 'modifier' semantic role. For the semantic concept i_{p} at address 0, the left-child modifier (address 00) could be semantic concept i_{t} with probability 0.2, or concept i_{u} with probability 0.8. Finally, by adding an identity matrix for $\mathbf{L}_{0\times01}(l_{\text{ID}})$ (a 'head' semantic role) to the quantities in Figure 1b, we would have all the components to construct the vector at address 0:

$$\mathbf{e}_0 = \underbrace{\begin{bmatrix} .2 & 0 & 0 \\ 0 & .1 & 0 \\ 0 & 0 & .4 \end{bmatrix}}_{\mathbf{M}} \cdot d\left(\underbrace{\begin{bmatrix} 0 & .2 & .8 \\ 0 & 0 & 1 \\ .1 & .4 & .5 \end{bmatrix}}_{\mathbf{L}_{0\times01}} \underbrace{\begin{bmatrix} 0 \\ 1 \\ .1 \end{bmatrix}}_{\mathbf{e}_{00}} \right) \cdot d\left(\underbrace{\begin{bmatrix} 1 & 0 & 0 \\ 0 & 1 & 0 \\ 0 & 0 & 1 \end{bmatrix}}_{\mathbf{L}_{0\times01}} \underbrace{\begin{bmatrix} 0 \\ 0 \\ 1 \end{bmatrix}}_{\mathbf{e}_{01}} \right) \cdot \underbrace{\begin{bmatrix} 1 \\ 1 \\ 1 \end{bmatrix}}_{\mathbf{1}} = \begin{matrix} \mathrm{i}_{\text{p}}: \\ \mathrm{i}_{\text{t}}: \\ \mathrm{i}_{\text{u}}: \end{matrix} \underbrace{\overset{\textit{truth}}{\begin{bmatrix} 0 \\ 0 \\ 0.036 \end{bmatrix}}}_{\mathbf{e}_0}$$

Since the vector was constructed in syntactic and semantic context, the tree structure shown (including semantic relationships l) is implied by the context.

2.2.2 Probabilities in vectors and matrices

Formally defining the probabilities in Figure 1, SVS populates vectors and matrices by means of 5 probability models (models are denoted by θ), along with the process of composition:

$$\begin{aligned}
&\text{Syntactic model} && \mathbf{M}(lc_\gamma \to lc_\alpha\, lc_\beta)[i_\gamma, i_\gamma] = \mathsf{P}_{\theta_{\text{M}}}(lci_\gamma \to lc_\alpha\, lc_\beta) \\
&\text{Semantic model} && \mathbf{L}_{\gamma\times\iota}(l_\iota)[i_\gamma, i_\iota] = \mathsf{P}_{\theta_{\text{L}}}(i_\iota \mid i_\gamma, l_\iota) \\
&\text{Preterminal model} && \mathbf{e}_\gamma[i_\gamma] = \mathsf{P}_{\theta_{\text{P-Vit(G)}}}(x_\gamma \mid lci_\gamma), \quad \text{for preterm } \gamma \qquad (5) \\
&\text{Root const. model} && \mathbf{a}^T_\epsilon[i_\epsilon] = \mathsf{P}_{\pi_{\text{G}\epsilon}}(lci_\epsilon) \\
&\text{Any const. model} && \mathbf{a}^T_\gamma[i_\gamma] = \mathsf{P}_{\pi_{\text{G}}}(lci_\gamma)
\end{aligned}$$

These probabilities are encapsulated into vectors and matrices using a convention: column indices of vectors or matrices represent *conditioned* semantic variables, row indices represent *modeled* variables.

As an example, from Figure 1b, elements of $\mathbf{L}_{0\times00}(l_{\text{MOD}})$ represent the probability $\mathsf{P}_{\theta_{\text{L}}}(i_{00} \mid i_0, l_{00})$. Thus, the conditioned variable i_{00} is shown in the figure as column indices, and the modeled i_0 as row indices. This convention applies to the $\mathbf{M}$ matrix as well. Recall that $\mathbf{M}$ is a diagonal matrix — its rows and columns model the same variable. Thus, we could rewrite $\mathsf{P}_{\theta_{\text{M}}}(lci_\gamma \to lc_\alpha\, lc_\beta)$ as $\mathsf{P}_{\theta_{\text{M}}}(lci_\gamma \to lc_\alpha\, lc_\beta, i_\gamma)$ to make a consistent probabilistic interpretation.

We have intentionally left out the probabilistic definition of normal (non-preterminal) nonterminals $\mathsf{P}_{\theta_{\text{Vit(G)}}}$, and the rationale for $\mathbf{a}^T$ vectors. These are both best understood in the dual problem of parsing.

2.2.3 Vector Composition for Parsing

The vector composition of Equation 4 can be rewritten with all arguments and syntactic information as:

$$\mathbf{e}_\gamma = \mathbf{M}(lc_\gamma \to lc_\alpha\, lc_\beta) \cdot d(\mathbf{L}_{\gamma\times\alpha}(l_\alpha) \cdot \mathbf{e}_\alpha) \cdot d(\mathbf{L}_{\gamma\times\beta}(l_\beta) \cdot \mathbf{e}_\beta) \cdot \mathbf{1} \qquad (4')$$

a compact representation that masks the underlying consistent probability operations. This section will expand the vector composition equation to show its equivalence to standard statistical parsing methods.

Let us say that $\mathbf{e}_\gamma[i_\gamma] = \mathsf{P}(x_\gamma \,|\, lci_\gamma)$, the probability of giving a particular yield given the present distributed semantics. Recall that in matrix multiplication, there is a summation over the inner dimensions of the multiplied objects; replacing matrices and vectors with their probabilistic interpretations and summing in the appropriate places, each element of $\mathbf{e}_\gamma$ is then:

$$\mathbf{e}_\gamma[i_\gamma] = \mathsf{P}_{\theta_\mathrm{M}}(lci_\gamma \rightarrow lc_\alpha\; lc_\beta) \cdot \sum_{i_\alpha} \mathsf{P}_{\theta_\mathrm{L}}(i_\alpha \,|\, i_\gamma, l_\alpha) \cdot \mathsf{P}_{\theta_{\mathrm{Vit(G)}}}(x_\alpha \,|\, lci_\alpha) \cdot \sum_{i_\beta} \mathsf{P}_{\theta_\mathrm{L}}(i_\beta \,|\, i_\gamma, l_\beta) \cdot \mathsf{P}_{\theta_{\mathrm{Vit(G)}}}(x_\beta \,|\, lci_\beta) \quad (6)$$

This can be loosely considered the multiplication of the syntax (θ_M term), left-child semantics (first sum), and right-child semantics (second sum). The only summations are between $\mathbf{L}$ and e, since all other multiplications are between diagonal matrices (similar to pointwise multiplication).

We can simplify this probability expression by grouping θ_M and θ_L into a grammar rule $\mathsf{P}_{\theta_\mathrm{G}}(lci_\gamma \rightarrow lci_\alpha\; lci_\beta) \stackrel{\mathrm{def}}{=} \mathsf{P}_{\theta_\mathrm{M}}(lci_\gamma \rightarrow lc_\alpha\; lc_\beta) \cdot \mathsf{P}_{\theta_\mathrm{L}}(i_\alpha \,|\, i_\gamma, l_\alpha) \cdot \mathsf{P}_{\theta_\mathrm{L}}(i_\beta \,|\, i_\gamma, l_\beta)$, since they deal with everything except the yield of the two child nodes. The summations are then pushed to the front:

$$\mathbf{e}_\gamma[i_\gamma] = \sum_{i_\alpha, i_\beta} \mathsf{P}_{\theta_\mathrm{G}}(lci_\gamma \rightarrow lci_\alpha\; lci_\beta) \cdot \mathsf{P}_{\theta_{\mathrm{Vit(G)}}}(x_\alpha \,|\, lci_\alpha) \cdot \mathsf{P}_{\theta_{\mathrm{Vit(G)}}}(x_\beta \,|\, lci_\beta) \quad (7)$$

Thus, we have a standard chart-parsing probability $\mathsf{P}(x_\gamma \,|\, lci_\gamma)$ — with distributed semantic concepts — in each vector element.

The use of grammar rules necessarily builds a hypothetical subtree τ_γ. In a typical CKY algorithm, the tree corresponding to the highest probability would be chosen; however, we have not defined how to make this choice for vectorial semantics.

We will choose the best tree with probability 1.0, so we define a deterministic Viterbi probability over candidate *vectors* (not concepts) and context variables:

$$\mathsf{P}_{\theta_{\mathrm{Vit(G)}}}(x_\gamma \,|\, lc\mathbf{e}_\gamma) \stackrel{\mathrm{def}}{=} [\![\, \mathbf{e}_\gamma = \operatorname*{arg\,max}_{lc\mathbf{e}_\iota} \left(\mathbf{a}_\iota^T \mathbf{e}_\iota \cdot \mathsf{P}_{\pi_\mathrm{G}}(lc\mathbf{a}_\iota^T) \cdot \mathsf{P}_{\theta_{\mathrm{Vit(G)}}}(x \,|\, lc\mathbf{e}_\iota) \right)]\!] \quad (8)$$

where $[\![\cdot]\!]$ is an indicator function such that $[\![\phi]\!] = 1$ if ϕ is true, 0 otherwise. Intuitively, the process is as follows: we construct the vector $\mathbf{e}_\iota$ at a node, according to Eqn. 4′; we then weight this vector against prior knowledge about the context $\mathbf{a}_\iota^T$; the best vector in context will be chosen (the argmax). Also, the vector at a node comes with assumptions of what structure produced it. Thus, the last two terms in the parentheses are deterministic models ensuring that the best subtree τ_ι is indeed the one generated.

Determining the root constituent of the Viterbi tree is the same process as choosing any other Viterbi constituent, except that prior contextual knowledge gets its own probability model in $\mathbf{a}_\epsilon^T$. As before, the most likely tree $\hat{\tau}_\epsilon$ is the tree that maximizes the probability at the root, and can be constructed recursively from the best child trees. Importantly, $\hat{\tau}_\epsilon$ has an associated, *sentential* semantic vector which may be construed as the composed semantic information for the whole parsed sentence. Similar *phrasal* semantic vectors can be obtained anywhere on the parse chart.

These equations complete the linear algebraic definition of structured vectorial semantics.

3 SVS with Relational Clusters

3.1 Inducing Relational Clusters

Unlike many vector space models that are based on the frequencies of terms in documents, we may consider frequencies of terms that occur in similar semantic relations (e.g., head l_ID or modifier l_MOD). Reducing the dimensionality of terms in a term–context matrix will result in relationally-clustered concepts. From a parsing perspective, this amounts to latent annotations (Matsuzaki et al., 2005) in l-context.

Let us re-notate the headword-lexicalized version of SVS (the example in Section 2.2.1) using h for headword semantics, and reserve i for relationally-clustered concepts. Treebank trees can be deterministically annotated with headwords h and relations l by using head rules (Magerman, 1995). The 5 SVS models θ_{M}, θ_{L}, $\theta_{\text{P-Vit(G)}}$, $\pi_{\text{G}\epsilon}$, and π_{G} can thus be obtained by counting instances and normalizing. Empirical probabilities of this kind are denoted with a tilde, whereas estimated models have a hat.

Concepts i in a distributed semantic representation, however, cannot be found from annotated trees (see example concepts in Figure 2). Therefore, we use Expectation Maximization (EM) in a variant of the inside-outside algorithm (Baker, 1979) to learn distributed-concept behavior. In the M-step, the data-informed result of the E-step is used to update the estimates of θ_{M}, θ_{L}, and θ_{H} (where θ_{H} is a generlization of $\theta_{\text{P-Vit(G)}}$ to any nonterminal). These updated estimates are then plugged back in to the next E-step. The two steps continually alternate until convergence or a maximum number of iterations.

E-step:

$$\hat{\mathsf{P}}(i_\gamma, i_\alpha, i_\beta \,|\, lc_\gamma, lc_\alpha, lc_\beta) = \frac{\hat{\mathsf{P}}_{\theta_{\text{Out}}}(lci_\gamma, lch_\epsilon - lch_\gamma) \cdot \hat{\mathsf{P}}_{\theta_{\text{Ins}}}(lch_\gamma \,|\, lci_\gamma)}{\hat{\mathsf{P}}(lch_\epsilon)} \tag{9}$$

$$\mathsf{E}(lci_\gamma, lci_\alpha, lci_\beta) = \hat{\mathsf{P}}(i_\gamma, i_\alpha, i_\beta | lc_\gamma, lc_\alpha, lc_\beta) \cdot \tilde{\mathsf{P}}(lc_\gamma, lc_\alpha, lc_\beta)$$

M-step:

$$\hat{\mathsf{P}}_{\theta_{\text{M}}}(lci_\gamma \to lc_\alpha, lc_\beta) = \frac{\sum_{i_\alpha, i_\beta} \mathsf{E}(lci_\gamma, lci_\alpha, lci_\beta)}{\sum_{lci_\alpha, lci_\beta} \mathsf{E}(lci_\gamma, lci_\alpha, lci_\beta)}$$

$$\hat{\mathsf{P}}_{\theta_{\text{L}}}(i_\alpha \,|\, i_\gamma; l_\alpha) = \frac{\sum_{lc_\gamma, c_\alpha, lci_\beta} \mathsf{E}(lci_\gamma, lci_\alpha, lci_\beta)}{\sum_{lc_\gamma, ci_\alpha, lci_\beta} \mathsf{E}(lci_\gamma, lci_\alpha, lci_\beta)} \tag{10}$$

$$\hat{\mathsf{P}}_{\theta_{\text{H}}}(h_\gamma \,|\, lci_\gamma) = \frac{\mathsf{E}(lci_\gamma, -, -)}{\sum_{h_\gamma} \mathsf{E}(lci_\gamma, -, -)}$$

Inside probabilities can be recursively calculated on training trees from the bottom up. These are simply probability sums of all subsumed subtrees (Viterbi probabilities with sums instead of maxes).

Outside probabilities can also be recursively calculated from training trees, here from parent probabilities. For a left child (the right-child case is similar):

$$\hat{\mathsf{P}}_{\theta_{\text{Out}}}(lci_\alpha, lch_\epsilon - lch_\alpha) = \hat{\mathsf{P}}_{\theta_{\text{Out}}}(lci_\gamma, lch_\epsilon - lch_\gamma) \cdot \hat{\mathsf{P}}_{\theta_{\text{M}}}(lci_\gamma \to lc_\alpha, lc_\beta) \cdot \sum_{i_\beta} \hat{\mathsf{P}}_{\theta_{\text{L}}}(i_\beta \,|\, i_\gamma, l_\beta) \cdot \hat{\mathsf{P}}_{\theta_{\text{Ins}}}(lch_\beta \,|\, lci_\beta) \cdot \hat{\mathsf{P}}_{\theta_{\text{L}}}(i_\alpha \,|\, i_\gamma, l_\alpha) \tag{11}$$

Since outside probabilities signify everything *but* what is subsumed by the node, they carry a complementary set of information to inside probabilities. Thus, inside and outside probabilities together are a natural way to produce parent and child clustered concepts.

3.2 Relational Semantic Clusters in Parsing

Section 2.2.2 listed the five probability models necessary for SVS. To define SVS with relational clusters, the estimates in Equation 10 can be used for θ_{M} and θ_{L}.

The preterminal model is based on θ_{H}, but it also includes some backoff for words that have not been used as headwords. The other two models also fall out nicely from the algorithm, though they are not explicitly estimated in EM. The prior probability at the root is just the base case for outside probabilities:

$$\hat{\mathsf{P}}_{\pi_{\text{G}\epsilon}}(lci_\epsilon) \stackrel{\text{def}}{=} \hat{\mathsf{P}}_{\theta_{\text{Out}}}(lci_\epsilon, lch_\epsilon - lch_\epsilon) \tag{12}$$

Prior probabilities at non-root constituents are estimated from the empirically-weighted joint probability.

$$\hat{\mathsf{P}}_{\pi_{\text{G}}}(lci_\gamma) \stackrel{\text{def}}{=} \sum_{lci_\alpha, lci_\beta} \tilde{\mathsf{P}}(lci_\gamma, lci_\alpha, lci_\beta) \tag{13}$$

With these models, a relationally-clustered SVS parser is now defined.

Cluster i_1 'announcement'		Cluster i_5 'change in value'		Cluster i_7 'change possession'	
unk	0.362	rose	0.137	unk	0.381
was	0.173	fell	0.124	had	0.065
reported	0.097	unk	0.116	was	0.062
posted	0.036	gained	0.063	took	0.036
earned	0.029	dropped	0.051	bought	0.027
filed	0.024	attributed	0.051	completed	0.025
were	0.022	jumped	0.046	received	0.024
had	0.020	added	0.041	were	0.023
told	0.013	lost	0.039	got	0.018
approved	0.013	advanced	0.022	made	0.018
				acquired	0.016

Figure 2: Example θ_H clusters from 1,000 headwords clustered into 10 referents, after 10 EM iterations, for transitive past-tense verbs (VBD-argNP).

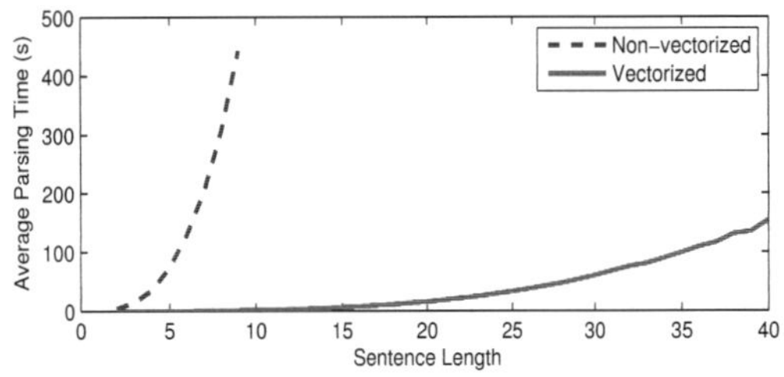

Figure 3: Speed of relationally-clustered SVS parsers, with and without vectorization.

4 Evaluation

Sections 02–21 of the Wall Street Journal (WSJ) corpus were used as training data; Section 23 was used as test data with reported parsing results on sentences greater than length 40. Punctuation was left in for all reported evaluations. Trees were binarized, and syntactic states were thoroughly split into subcategorization classes. As previously discussed, unlike tests on state-of-the-art automatically state-splitting parsers, this isolates the contribution of semantics. The baseline 83.57 F-measure is comparable to Klein and Manning (2003) before the inclusion of head annotations.

Subsequently, each branch was annotated with a head relation l_{ID} or a modifier relation l_{MOD} according to a binarized version of headword percolation rules (Magerman, 1995; Collins, 1997), and the headword was propagated up from its head constituent. The most frequent headwords (e.g., $h_1, \ldots, h_{50}$) were stored, and the rest were assigned a constant, 'unk' headword category.

From counts on the binary rules of these annotated trees, the θ_{M}, θ_{L}, $\theta_{\text{P-Vit(G)}}$, $\pi_{\text{G}\epsilon}$, and π_{G} probabilities for headword-lexicalization SVS were obtained. Modifier relations l_{MOD} were deterministically augmented with their syntactic context; both c and l symbols appearing fewer than 10 times in the whole corpus were assigned 'unknown' categories.

These lexicalized models served as a baseline, but the augmented trees from which they were derived were also inputs to the EM algorithm in Section 3.1. Each parameter in the model or training algorithm was examined, with $|I| = \{1, 5, 10, 15, 20\}$ clusters, random initialization from reproducible seeds, and a varying numbers of EM iterations.

The implemented parser had few adjustments from a plain CKY parser other than these vectors. No approximate inference was used, with no beam for candidate parses and no re-ranking.

4.1 Interpretable relational clusters

Figure 2 shows example clusters for one of the headword models used, where EM clustered 1,000 headwords into 10 concepts in 10 iterations. The lists are parts of the $\hat{\mathsf{P}}_{\theta_{\text{H}}}(h_\gamma \mid lci_\gamma)$ model. As such, each of the 10 clusters will only produce headwords in light of some syntactic constituent. The figure shows how distributed concepts produce headwords for transitive past-tense verbs. Note that the probability distributions for different headwords are quite uneven, again confirming that some clusters are more specific, and others are more general.

Each cluster has been given a heading of its approximate meaning — i_5, for example, mostly picks verbs that are 'change in value' events. With 10 clusters, we might not expect such fine-grained clusters, since pLSA-related approaches typically use several hundred for such tasks. The syntactic context of transitive (and therefore state-split) past-tense verbs allows for much finer-grained distinctions, which are then predominantly semantic in nature.

a)

Sec. 23, length < 40 wds	LR	LP	F
syntax-only baseline:	83.32	83.83	83.57
headword-lex. 10hw:	83.10	83.61	83.35
headword-lex. 50hw:	83.09	83.40	83.24
rel'n clust. 50hw→10 clust:	83.67	84.13	**83.90**

b)

Sec. 23, length < 40 wds	LR	LP	F
baseline→1 clust	83.34	83.90	83.62
1000 hw→5 clust, avg	83.85	84.23	84.04
1000 hw→10 clust, avg	84.04	84.40	84.21
1000 hw→15 clust, avg	84.15	84.38	84.26
1000 hw→20 clust, avg	**84.21**	**84.42**	**84.31**

Table 1: a) Unsmoothed lexicalized CKY parsers versus 10 semantic clusters. Evaluations were run with EM trained to 10 iterations. b) Average dependence of parsing performance on number of semantic clusters. Averages are taken over different random seeds, with EM running 4 or 10 iterations.

4.2 Engineering considerations

We should note that relationally-clustered SVS is feasible with respect to random initialization and speed.

Four relationally-clustered SVS models (with 500 headwords clustered into 5 concepts) were trained, each having a different random initialization. We found that the parsing F-score had a mean of 83.98 and a standard deviation of 0.21 across different initializations of the model. This indicates that though there are significant difference between the models, they still outperform models without SVS (see next section).

Also, it may seem slow to consider the set of semantic concepts and relations alongside syntax, at least with respect to normal parsing. The definition of SVS in terms of vectors actually mitigates this effect on WSJ Section 23, according to Figure 3. Since SVS is probabilistically consistent, the parser could be defined without vectors, but this would have the 'non-vectorized' speed curve. The contiguous storage and access of information in the 'vectorized' version leads to an efficient implementation.

4.3 Comparison to Lexicalization

One important comparison to draw here is between the effectiveness of semantic clusters versus headword-lexicalization. For fair head-to-head comparison on WSJ Section 23, both models were vectorized and included no smoothing or backoff. Neither relational clusters nor lexicalization were optimized with backoff or smoothing.

Table 1a shows precision, recall, and F-score for lexicalized models and for clustered semantic models. First, note that the 10-cluster model (in bold) improves on a syntax-only parser (top line), showing that the semantic model is contributing useful information to the parsing task.

Next, compare the 50-headword, 10-cluster model (in bold) to the line above it. It is natural to compare this model to the headword-lexicalized model with 50 headwords, since the same information from the trees is available to both models. The relationally-clustered model outperforms the headword-lexicalized model, showing that clustering the headwords actually improves their usefulness, despite the fact that fewer referents are used in the actual vectors.

It is also interesting, then, to compare this 50-headword, 10-cluster model to a headword-lexicalized model with 10 headwords. In this case, the possible size of the grammar is equal. Again, the relationally-clustered model outperforms plain lexicalization. This indicates that the 10 clustered referents are much more meaningful than 10 headword referents for the disambiguating of syntax.

4.4 Effect of Number of clusters

The final experiment on relational-clustering SVS was to determine whether performance would vary with the number of clusters. Table 1b compares average performance (over different random initializations) for numbers of clusters from 1 (a syntax-equivalent case) to 20.

First, it should be noted that all of the relationally clustered models improved on the baseline. Random initializations did not vary enough for these models to do worse than syntax alone. For each vector/domain size, in fact, the gains over syntax-only are substantial.

In addition, the table shows that average performance increases with the number of clusters. This loosely positive slope means that EM is still finding useful parts of the semantic space to explore and cluster, so that the clusters remain meaningful. However, the increase in performance with number of clusters is likely to eventually plateau.

Maximum-accuracy models were also evaluated, since each model is a full-fledged parser. The best 20-referent model obtained an F score of 84.60%, beating the syntactic baseline by almost a full absolute point. Thus, finding relationally-clustered semantic output also contributes to some significant parsing benefit.

4.5 Perplexity

Finally, per-word perplexities were calculated for a syntactic model and for a 5-concept relationally-clustered model. Specific to this evaluation, following Mitchell and Lapata (2009), only the top 20,000 words in WSJ Sections 02-21 were kept in training or test sentences, and the rest replaced with 'unk'; numbers were replaced with 'num.'

Sec. 23, 'unk'+'num'	Perplexity
syntax only baseline	428.94
rel'n clust. 1khw→005e	371.76

Table 2: Model fit as measured by perplexity.

Table 2 shows that adding semantic information greatly reduces perplexity. Since as much syntactic information as possible (such as argument structure) has been pre-annotated onto trees, the isolated contribution of interactive semantics improves on a syntax-only model model.

5 Conclusion

This paper has introduced a structured vectorial semantic (SVS) framework in which vector composition and syntactic parsing are a single, interactive process. The framework thus fully integrates distributional semantics with traditional syntactic models of language.

Two standard parsing techniques were defined within SVS and evaluated: headword-lexicalization SVS (bilexical parsing) and relational-clustering SVS (latent annotations). It was found that relationally-clustered SVS outperformed the simpler lexicalized model and syntax-only models, and that additional clusters had a mildly positive effect. Additionally, perplexity results showed that the integration of distributed semantics in relationally-clustered SVS improved the model over a non-interactive baseline.

It is hoped that this flexible framework will enable new generations of interactive interpretation models that deal with the syntax–semantics interface in a plausible manner.

References

Baker, J. (1979). Trainable grammars for speech recognition. In D. Klatt and J. Wolf (Eds.), *Speech Communication Papers for the 97th Meeting of the Acoustical Society of America*, pp. 547–550.

Blei, D. M., A. Y. Ng, and M. I. Jordan (2003). Latent dirichlet allocation. *Journal of Machine Learning Research 3*, 993–1022.

Charniak, E. (1996). Tree-bank grammars. In *Proceedings of the National Conference on Artificial Intelligence*, pp. 1031–1036.

Collins, M. (1997). Three generative, lexicalised models for statistical parsing. In *Proceedings of the 35th Annual Meeting of the Association for Computational Linguistics (ACL '97)*.

Deerwester, S., S. Dumais, G. W. Furnas, T. K. Landauer, and R. Harshman (1990). Indexing by latent semantic analysis. *Journal of the American Society for Information Science 41*(6), 391–407.

Erk, K. and S. Padó (2008). A structured vector space model for word meaning in context. In *Proceedings of EMNLP 2008.*

Frege, G. (1892). Uber sinn und bedeutung. *Zeitschrift fur Philosophie und Philosophischekritik 100*, 25–50.

Ge, R. and R. J. Mooney (2005). A statistical semantic parser that integrates syntax and semantics. In *Ninth Conference on Computational Natural Language Learning*, pp. 9–16.

Gesmundo, A., J. Henderson, P. Merlo, and I. Titov (2009). A latent variable model of synchronous syntactic-semantic parsing for multiple languages. In *Proceedings of CoNLL*, pp. 37–42. Association for Computational Linguistics.

Griffiths, T. L., M. Steyvers, D. M. Blei, and J. B. Tenenbaum (2005). Integrating topics and syntax. *Advances in neural information processing systems 17*, 537–544.

Hofmann, T. (2001). Unsupervised learning by probabilistic latent semantic analysis. *Machine Learning 42*(1), 177–196.

Klein, D. and C. D. Manning (2003). Accurate unlexicalized parsing. In *Proceedings of the 41st Annual Meeting of the Association for Computational Linguistics*, Sapporo, Japan, pp. 423–430.

Koo, T., X. Carreras, and M. Collins (2008). Simple semi-supervised dependency parsing. In *Proceedings of the 46th Annual Meeting of the ACL*, Volume 8. Citeseer.

Lin, D. (1998). An information-theoretic definition of similarity. In *Proceedings of the 15th International Conference on Machine Learning*, Volume 296304.

MacDonald, M. C., N. J. Pearlmutter, and M. S. Seidenberg (1994). The lexical nature of syntactic ambiguity resolution. *Psychological Review 101*(4), 676–703.

Magerman, D. (1995). Statistical decision-tree models for parsing. In *Proceedings of the 33rd Annual Meeting of the Association for Computational Linguistics (ACL'95)*, Cambridge, MA, pp. 276–283.

Matsuzaki, T., Y. Miyao, and J. Tsujii (2005). Probabilistic CFG with latent annotations. In *Proceedings of the 43rd Annual Meeting on Association for Computational Linguistics*, pp. 75–82. Association for Computational Linguistics.

Mitchell, J. and M. Lapata (2008). Vector-based models of semantic composition. In *Proceedings of ACL-08: HLT*, Columbus, OH, pp. 236–244.

Mitchell, J. and M. Lapata (2009). Language Models Based on Semantic Composition. In *Proceedings of the 2009 Conference on Empirical Methods in Natural Language Processing*, pp. 430–439.

Padó, S. and M. Lapata (2007). Dependency-based construction of semantic space models. *Computational Linguistics 33*(2), 161–199.

Petrov, S., L. Barrett, R. Thibaux, and D. Klein (2006). Learning accurate, compact, and interpretable tree annotation. In *Proceedings of the 44th Annual Meeting of the Association for Computational Linguistics (COLING/ACL'06).*

Rudolph, S. and E. Giesbrecht (2010). Compositional matrix-space models of language. In *Proceedings of ACL 2010.* Association for Computational Linguistics.

Taskar, B., E. Segal, and D. Koller (2001). Probabilistic classification and clustering in relational data. In *IJCAI'01: Proceedings of the 17th international joint conference on Artificial intelligence*, San Francisco, CA, USA, pp. 870–876. Morgan Kaufmann Publishers Inc.

Discovering Semantic Classes for Urdu N-V Complex Predicates

Tafseer Ahmed
Universität Konstanz
tafseer.khan@uni-konstanz.de

Miriam Butt
Universität Konstanz
miriam.butt@uni-konstanz.de

Abstract

This paper reports on an exploratory investigation as to whether classes of Urdu N-V complex predicates can be identified on the basis syntactic patterns and lexical choices associated with the N-V complex predicates. Working with data from a POS annotated corpus, we show that choices with respect to the number of arguments, case marking on subjects and which light verbs are felicitous with which nouns depend heavily on the semantics of the noun in the N-V complex predicate. This initial work represents an important step towards identifying semantic criteria relevant for complex predicate formation. Identifying the semantic criteria and being able to systematically code them in turn represents a first step towards building up a lexical resource for nouns as part of developing natural language processing tools for the underresourced South Asian language Urdu.

1 Introduction

Urdu is an Indo-Aryan South Asian language spoken primarily in Pakistan and India. It is structurally almost identical to Hindi and together Urdu and Hindi consitute the third-most spoken language (Graddol, 2004). At the same time, Urdu/Hindi is a severely underresourced language. We are currently engaged in building a broad-coverage, robust computational ParGram grammar for Urdu (Butt and King, 2007; Butt et al., 2009) and one of the major bottlenecks for development is the lack of lexical resources, which are needed, for example, for the development of a verb lexicon with subcategorization frames or lists of argument taking nouns and verbs.

Urdu actually has only about 700 simple verbs (Humayoun, 2006), so the task of finding the range of possible subcategorization frames could be done mostly manually in a reasonable amount of time. However, as is characteristic of South Asian languages in general, Urdu employs wide variety of different types of complex predicates (Butt, 1995; Mohanan, 1994) to express its full range of verbal predication. The complex predicates can be V-V, Adj-V, PP-V or N-V combinations. In this paper, we focus on the highly productive N-V complex predicates in order to try to identify: 1) possible constraints on the range of combinatory possibilities; 2) possible systematic semantic groupings/classes of the nouns involved.

The paper is organized as follows. In section 2 we first describe the basic phenomenon. In section 3 we describe the corpus-based study we performed to see if we can identify systematic semantic classes for nouns. The results are presented in section 4 and the paper is concluded by section 5.

2 Combinatory Possibilities for N-V Complex Predicates

Urdu makes use of only about 700 simple verbs. The bulk of verbal predication in Urdu is effected by complex predicates of various types. The complex predicates are highly productive and different types can be stacked on top of one another (Butt and Ramchand, 2005), so capturing their use computationally in a systematic, generalizable and efficient manner is a challenge. One cannot just trawl a corpus to extract and then list various possibilities as there are potentially infinitely many combinations (though one can choose to list the 100 or so most frequently occurring ones, as done in the Hindi WordNet, for example; Bhattacharyya 2010).

In this paper, we focus on the combinatorial possibilities in N-V complex predicates. In N-V complex predicates the noun contains the main predicational content. The verb, usually referred to as the *light verb*, dictates the case marking of the subject, determines agreement patterns, carries information about tense/aspect and adds information about agentivity vs. experiencer subjects and makes some further subtle semantic contributions. We illustrate the basics of the construction with respect to the noun *yad* 'memory' and the light verbs *kar* 'do' and *ho* 'be'. Other light verbs may be used as well, but these are two of the most basic ones.

(1) a. nadya=ne kahani yad k-i
Nadya.F.Sg=Erg story.F.Sg.Nom memory do-Perf.F.Sg
'Nadya remembered a/the story.' (lit.: 'Nadya did memory of the story.')

b. nadya=ko kahani yad hɛ
Nadya.F.Sg=Dat story.F.Sg.Nom memory be.Pres.3.Sg
'Nadya remembers/knows a/the story.' (lit.: 'Memory of the story is at Nadya.')

c. nadya=ko kahani yad hu-i
Nadya.F.Sg=Dat story.F.Sg.Nom memory be.Part-Perf.F.Sg
'Nadya came to remember a/the story.' (lit.: 'Memory of the story became to be at Nadya.')

In all of the examples in (1), it is evident that the noun and the verb form a single predicational element. The object *kahani* 'story' is thematically licensed by the noun *yad* 'memory', but it is not realized as a genitive, as would be typical for arguments of nouns (and as in the English translations). Rather, *kahani* 'story' functions as the syntactic object of the joint predication (see Mohanan 1994 for details on the argument structure and agreement patterns).

In (1a) the noun *yad* 'memory' is combined with the light verb *kar* 'do'. In this case the subject must be ergative and overall reading is one of an agentive, deliberate remembering. In (1b), in contrast, Nadya is already taken to be in the state of remembering the story. The difference between (1b) and (1c) is one of eventive vs. stative, so that in (1b), Nadya is already taken to be in the state of remembering the story (and not actively entering a state of remembering the story). In (1c) the light verb is the participial form of *ho* 'be' and essentially means 'become'.

A superficial look at Urdu patterns shows that not all nouns are as versatile as *yad* 'memory'. That is, certain nouns are only compatible with a subset of the potentially available light verbs. What has not so far been explored, however, is what the semantic constraints on N-V complex predicate formation are. In order to achieve a first understanding of the relevant patterns, we follow Levin (1993)'s classic assumption that semantic predicational classes can be identified on the basis of a study of the syntactic contexts the predicates occur in (cf. also Schulte im Walde 2009). Our main aim is therefore to identify semantic classes of nouns on the basis of their syntactic patterns with respect to complex predicates.

3 Corpus Study

According to the best of our knowledge there is no systematic inventory of which types of nouns are allowed to combine with which types of light verbs in Urdu, though the basic problem has been recognized for Hindi by Hwang et al. (2010), who are developing annotation guidelines for complex predicate constructions. We used a small Part-of-Speech (POS) tagged corpus to extract a number of N-V complex predicates and then used native speaker judgements to further manually explore their ability to appear with each of the light verbs *kar* 'do', *ho* 'be', *hu-* 'become'.[1] The manual exploration was necessary due to a data sparseness problem, since the available tagged corpora for Urdu are of a limited size.

3.1 Corpus

We used an Urdu POS tagged corpus compiled by the Center for Research in Urdu Language Processing (CRULP) in Lahore, Pakistan (available at http://www.crulp.org/software/ling_resources/UrduNepali-EnglishParallelCorpus.htm). The corpus consists of 100 000 words from the English Penn Treebank that have been (manually) translated into Urdu. The corpus consists of three files and the tag-set contains a specialized POS tag called VBL for the light verbs that are used in N-V complex predicates.

3.2 Method

We manually collected N-V complex predicates starting from the beginning of each of the corpus files. Given that we were interested in conducting an initial feasibility study, we stopped going through the files once we had collected 45 distinct nouns that appeared in N-V complex predicates containing the light verbs *kar* 'do', *ho* 'be' *hu-* 'become'. We compiled a full set of combinatorial (im)possibilities of these 45 nouns with the three light verbs by taking the instances identified in the corpora and supplementing the "missing cells", so to speak, via native speaker judgements as to whether the combination is possible.

An analysis of the resulting patterns did allow an identification of several distinct semantically coherent classes. Pertinent semantic factors appear to be stative vs. eventive nouns, agentivity vs. experiencer verbs (psych predications) and the licensing of a dative recipient.

4 Results

4.1 Class A: Full Range

4 out of 45 nouns allowed the full range of patterns shown in (1). The complex predicates these nouns appear in are psych verbs and include the nouns *yad* 'memory' and *yaqin* 'belief'.

4.2 Class B: Exclusion of Dative Subjects

The bulk of the nouns, namely 38 out of the 45, allow an agentive (ergative) subject, but this subject does not alternate with a dative subject, as shown in (2).

(2) a. bɪlal=ne makan tamir ki-ya
Bilal.M.Sg=Erg house.M.Sg.Nom construction.F.Sg do-Perf.M.Sg
'Bilal built a/the house.'

[1] Further common light verbs are *de* 'give' and *a* 'come'. These light verbs have a more complex distribution and so we chose to concentrate initially on just three basic and very common light verbs. Further light verbs could be investigated in an extension of this work.

b. *bɪlal=ko mɑkan tɑmir hɛ/hu-a
Bilal.M.Sg=Dat house.M.Sg.Nom construction.F.Sg be.Pres.3.Sg/be.Part-Perf.M.Sg
'Bilal built a/the house.'

The nouns here are eventive nouns which presuppose an agent. As such, a non-agentive dative subject N-V complex predicate cannot be formed with this version of the noun. As shown in (3), grammatical combinations of these nouns with the light verb *hu-* 'become' do exist — this has an intransitivizing effect. Semantically, these are resultative state readings that are straightforwardly related to (2).

(3) mɑkan tɑmir hu-a/*hɛ
house.M.Sg.Nom construction.F.Sg be.Part-Perf.M.Sg
'A/The house was/*is built.'

One noun in our set patterns essentially as shown in (2) and (3) with the difference that the noun licenses a dative recipient rather than a direct object (which can be marked as nominative or accusative, depending on the definiteness of the object in a well-known pattern of object alternation). In (3) the nominative object of (2a) is realized as a nominative subject. Similarly, as shown in (4), a dative object in a complex predicate with *kar* 'do' is realized as a dative subject when the light verb is *hu-* 'become'. Other nouns in Urdu which display this pattern are: *ɪʃara* 'signal', *xabɑr* 'news' and *ɪnkar* 'refusal'.

(4) a. nadya=ne bɪlal=ko ɪʃara ki-ya
Nadya.F.Sg=Erg Bilal.M.Sg=Dat signal.M.Sg do-Perf.M.Sg
'Nadya signaled Bilal.'

b. bɪlal=ko ɪʃara hu-a
Bilal.M.Sg=Dat signal.M.Sg be.Part-Perf.M.Sg
'Bilal was signaled.' (lit.: A signal came to be at Bilal.')

4.3 Class C: Exclusion of Light Verb *hu-* 'become'

Another class (2 nouns in our set) allows for combinations with the light verbs *kar* 'do' and *ho* 'be', but not with *hu-* 'become', as illustrated in (5) for the noun *ɪntɪzar* 'wait'. Other nouns like this are *taslim* 'acceptance' and *bardaʃt* 'tolerance'. Presumably the *hu-* 'become' does not work with these nouns because the subject is too agentive to be felicitous as the undergoer of a 'become' predication.

(5) a. bɪlal=ne nadya=ka ɪntɪzar ki-ya
Bilal.M.Sg=Erg Nadya.F.Sg=Gen.M.Sg wait.M.Sg do-Perf.M.Sg
'Bilal waited for Nadya.'

b. bɪlal=ko nadya=ka ɪntɪzar hɛ/*hu-a
Bilal.M.Sg=Dat Nadya.F.Sg=Gen.M.Sg wait.M.Sg be.Pres.3.Sg
'Bilal is waiting/*waited for Nadya.'

5 Discussion and Conclusions

Our corpus study showed that one can identify at least 3 different classes of nouns with one class consisting of at least two subclasses (Class B). The identification of classes was based on an investigation of their syntactic distribution in N-V complex predicates with respect to the light verbs *kar* 'do', *hu-* 'become' and *hɛ* 'be'. A follow up study could include an extension of the set of light verbs. Another follow up study could look at the N-V complex predicates in relation to another set of light verbs which occur with V-V complex predicates. The N-V complex predicate is predicationally equivalent to a simple verb and as such can further combine with light verbs. Initial investigations have shown that the semantics of the noun governs the choice of this further light verb, so that the phenomenon of complex predicate stacking could provide further clues as to a semantic basis for the classification of Urdu nouns.[2]

The semantic factors identified so far include the eventive vs. statitivity of the nouns, the agentivity vs. experience of the action and whether the noun licenses a dative recipient. The first identification of noun classes in terms of systematic syntactic and semantic differences achieved in this paper represents a step towards overcoming the lack of lexical resources for natural language processing of Urdu.

References

Bhattacharyya, P. (2010). IndoWordNet. In *Proceedings of LREC2010.* Malta, May.

Butt, M. (1995). *The Structure of Complex Predicates in Urdu.* Stanford: CSLI Publications.

Butt, M., T. Bögel, A. Hautli, and S. Sulger (2009). Urdu and the modular architecture of ParGram. In *Proceedings of the Conference on Language and Technology 2009 (CLT09)*, pp. 1–7.

Butt, M. and T. H. King (2007). Urdu in a parallel grammar development environment. *Language Resources and Evaluation 41*, 191–207.

Butt, M. and G. Ramchand (2005). Complex aspectual structure in Hindi/Urdu. In N. Ertischik-Shir and T. Rapoport (Eds.), *The Syntax of Aspect*, pp. 117–153. Oxford: Oxford University Press.

Graddol, D. (2004). The future of language. *Science 303*, 1329–1331.

Humayoun, M. (2006). Urdu morphology, orthography and lexicon extraction. MSc Thesis, Department of Computing Science, Chalmers University of Technology.

Hwang, J. D., A. Bhatia, C. Bonial, A. Mansouri, A. Vaidya, N. Xue, and M. Palmer (2010). Propbank annotation of multilingual light verb constructions. In *Proceedings of the Fourth Linguistic Annotation Workshop (LAW), ACL 2010*, Uppsala, Sweden, pp. 82–90.

Levin, B. (1993). *English Verb Classes and Alternations. A Preliminary Investigation.* Chicago: The University of Chicago Press.

Mohanan, T. (1994). *Argument Structure in Hindi.* Stanford: CSLI Publications.

Schulte im Walde, S. (2009). The induction of verb frames and verb classes from corpora. In A. Lüdeling and M. Kytö (Eds.), *Corpus Linguistics. An International Handbook.* Berlin: Mouton de Gruyter.

[2]A reviewer asks whether our method could scale up for larger corpora and whether resources such as WordNet could be used to assist the investigation. We here are faced with a lack of resources. We would first need a larger POS tagged corpora with a more differentiated POS tag set. However, in order to achieve this larger and more differentiated tagging, more information about the language is needed. We see our paper as contributing to this effort. With respect to WordNet, we face the problem that the classes provided for the English WordNet do not always match what we find in Urdu. In our Class B, nouns of communication form an identifiable subclass in Urdu and are also found to be related in English. However, the members of our Class C do not form a related net in English WordNet. With respect to Hindi WordNet, the ontology provided is not deep enough as yet to be able to provide useful information for investigations of this type.

DISCUSS: A dialogue move taxonomy layered over semantic representations

Lee Becker[1] Wayne H. Ward[1,2] Sarel van Vuuren[1] Martha Palmer[1]
{lee.becker, martha.palmer, sarel.vanvuuren}@colorado.edu,
wward@bltek.com

[1]University of Colorado at Boulder, [2]Boulder Language Technologies

Abstract

In this paper we describe DISCUSS, a dialogue move taxonomy layered over semantic representations. We designed this scheme to enable development of computational models of tutorial dialogues and to provide an intermediate representation suitable for question and tutorial act generation. As such, DISCUSS captures semantic and pragmatic elements across four dimensions: Dialogue Act, Rhetorical Form, Predicate Type, Semantic Roles. Together these dimensions provide a summary of an utterance's propositional content and how it may change the underlying information state of the conversation. This taxonomy builds on previous work in both general dialogue act taxonomies as well as work in tutorial act and tutorial question categorization. The types and values found within our taxonomy are based on preliminary observations and on-going annotation from our corpus of multimodal tutorial dialogues for elementary school science education.

1 Introduction

Past successes with conversational Intelligent Tutoring Systems (ITS) (Graesser et al., 2001), have helped to demonstrate the efficacy of computer-led, tutorial dialogue. However, ITS will not reach their full potential until they can overcome current limitations in spoken dialogue technologies. Producing systems capable of leading open-ended, Socratic-style tutorials will likely require more sophisticated models to automate analysis and generation of dialogue. A well defined tutorial dialogue annotation scheme can serve as a stepping stone towards these goals. Such a scheme should account for differences in tutoring style and question scaffolding techniques and should capture the subtle distinctions between different question types. To do this, requires a representation that connects a turn's communicative and rhetorical functions to its underlying semantic content.

While efforts such as DAMSL (Core and Allen, 1997) and DIT++ (Bunt, 2009) have helped to make dialogue act annotation more uniform and applicable to a wider audience, and while tutoring-specific initiatives (Tsovaltzi and Karagjosova, 2004; Buckley and Wolska, 2008) have helped to bring dialogue acts to tutorial dialogue, the move granularity in these schemas is too coarse to capture the differences in tutorial questioning styles exhibited in our corpus of Socratic-style tutorial dialogues. Conversely, question type categories (Graesser and Person, 1994; Nielsen et al., 2008) have been designed with education in mind, but they largely ignore how the student and tutor may work together to construct meaning. The DISCOUNT scheme's (Pilkington, 1999) combination of dialogue acts and rhetorical functions enabled it to better capture tutoring moves, but its omission of shallow semantics prevents it from capturing how content influences behavior.

Our long-term goals of automatic dialogue characterization, tutorial move prediction and question generation led us to design our own dialogue representation called DISCUSS (Dialogue Scheme for Unifying Speech and Semantics). Design of this dialogue move taxonomy was based on preliminary observations from our corpus of tutorial dialogues, and was influenced by the aforementioned research. We hope that undertaking this ambitious endeavor to capture not only a turn's pragmatic interpretation, but also its rhetorical and semantic functions will enable us to better model the complexity of open-ended, tutorial dialogue.

The remainder of the this paper is organized as follows. In the next section we describe our tutorial dialogue setting and our data. Section 3 discusses the organization of the DISCUSS annotation scheme. Section 4 briefly explains the current status of our annotation. Lastly section 5 outlines our future plans and conclusions.

2 Tutorial Dialogue Setting and Data

My Science Tutor (MyST) (Ward et al., 2010) is a conversational virtual tutor designed to improve science learning and understanding for students in grades 3-5. Students using MyST investigate and discuss science through natural spoken dialogues and multimedia interactions with a virtual tutor named Marni. The MyST dialogue design and tutoring style is based on a pedagogy called Questioning the Author (QtA) (Beck et al., 1996), wherein the teacher facilitates discovery by challenging students with open-ended questions and by directly keying in on ideas expressed in the student's language.

To gather data for MyST system coverage and dialogue analysis, we ran Wizard-of-Oz (WoZ) experiments that allowed a human tutor to be inserted into the interaction loop. Project tutors trained in QtA served as Wizards and were responsible for accepting and overriding system actions. Over the past three years we have accumulated over five-hundred, 15-minute WoZ sessions across four modules Magnetism and Electricity, Measurement, Variables, and Water, each with 16 lessons. Student speech from these sessions was professionally transcribed at the word level.

3 The DISCUSS Annotation Scheme

The Dialogue Scheme for Unifying Speech and Semantics (DISCUSS) is a multifaceted dialogue move taxonomy intended to capture both the pragmatic and semantic interpretations of an utterance. A DISCUSS move is a tuple composed of values from four dimensions: *Dialogue Act*, *Rhetorical Form*, *Predicate Type*, and *Semantic Roles*. Together these dimensions convey the communicative action, surface form, and meaning of an utterance independent of the original utterance text.

We designed DISCUSS to serve as an intermediate representation that will enable future work in dialogue session characterization, dialogue strategy optimization, and automatic question generation. To facilitate these goals, we have endeavored to create a taxonomy that is both descriptive and curriculum-independent while allowing for expansion as necessary. A complete listing of all the DISCUSS moves and dimensions can be found in our forthcoming technical report.

In the following subsection we will describe the different DISCUSS move categories. Descriptions of the *Semantic Role* and *Predicate Type* are found in the subsection about semantic dimensions, while discussion about the *dialogue act* and *rhetorical form* has been placed in the pragmatic dimensions subsection. Throughout the rest of this paper we denote DISCUSS tuples using the following notation: Dialogue Act/Rhetorical Form/Predicate Type ⟨Semantic Role⟩.

3.1 Move Categories

DISCUSS moves are dictated by the dialogue act dimension and may belong to one of three broad categories: *Dialogue Control*, *Information Exchange*, and *Attention Management*. Dialogue Control moves are largely concerned with maintaining and enabling the flow of information. This includes dialogue acts such as *Acknowledge, Open, Close, Repeat, and RequestRepeat*. The Information Exchange moves relay content (often lesson-specific) between speakers using moves such as *Assert, Ask, Answer, Mark, Revoice*. For tutorial dialogue the bulk of student-tutor interactions reside in this category. Lastly, Attention Management moves indicate how a speaker exercises initiative over other speakers or topics. Dialogue acts found in the attention category are *Focus, Defer, Elicit, and Direct*.

3.2 Semantic Dimensions

The semantic dimensions define the objects, events, properties and relations contained within an utterance. The semantic roles at the lowest level of the DISCUSS hierarchy directly capture the propositional entities. Predicate Types summarize the interactions between all of the semantic roles found within an utterance.

Semantic Roles: The MyST system models a lesson's key concepts as propositions which are realized as semantic frames. For MyST natural language understanding, these frames serve as the top-level nodes for a manually written semantic grammar used by the Phoenix parser (Ward, 1994). Two example concepts/frames and Phoenix parses are shown below. Although these semantic frames form the basis of MyST dialogues, for DISCUSS annotation we sought a more domain-independent representation that would generalize across a wide range of subjects. We began with VerbNet (Schuler, 2005) for defining our set of semantic roles because of its intuitive balance between descriptiveness and portability. While we used a majority of the labels as is, we found that the definition of some roles needed to be modified or extended to properly cover our set of concepts. For example, many concepts that express proportionality relationships can not be easily represented using predicate argument structure, and are more easily decomposed into *cause* and *effect* roles. We also added the catch-all *keyword* label to reflect terms that may relate to the proposition, but are not part of the core representation.

For our annotation project, rather than manually tagging all of the utterances with VerbNet labels, we created a mapping layer between the Phoenix frame roles and the VerbNet roles. The table below shows two frames along with their role mappings. We envision that in future projects, the hand-tuned semantic grammars could be replaced with a statistically trained semantic role labeler.

Frame:	BatteryFunction	Frame:	MagnetsAttract
Description:	*The DCell is the source of electricity.*	Description:	*Magnets attract to certain objects.*
⟨Instrument⟩:	[Battery]	⟨Instrument⟩:	[Magnet]
⟨Predicate⟩:	[Source]	⟨Predicate⟩:	[Attract]
⟨Theme⟩:	[Electricity]	⟨Theme⟩:	[Object]

Predicate Type: Simply knowing an utterance's propositional content is insufficient for inferring what was stated. Consider the two exchanges shown in the table below. The mixture of semantic roles in both students' responses are identical. Additionally, we can not differentiate between the exchanges based solely on dialogue act or rhetorical form. We need additional information to know the first scenario seeks to elicit discussion about observations while the second scenario focuses on procedures. One can also imagine such information would be useful for identifying communication breakdowns. For example, responding with a description of a procedure to a request about a process may indicate that the student did not understand the question or that the student is unwilling or unable to address the question.

T12:	*Tell me about what's going on here in this picture.* Ask/Describe/**Observation**
S13:	*The wires connect the battery and the light bulb and then then light bulb lights up.* Answer/Describe/**Observation** ⟨Instrument⟩.*wires* ⟨Predicate⟩.*connect* ⟨Theme1⟩.*battery* ⟨Theme2⟩.*light bulb* ⟨Effect⟩.*bulb lights up*
T7:	*Tell me about how you got the bulb to light up.* Ask/Describe/**Procedure**
S8:	*To make the light go we connected the wires to the battery and the bulb.* Answer/Describe/**Procedure** ⟨Effect⟩.*light go* ⟨Predicate⟩.*connected* ⟨Instrument⟩.*wires* ⟨Theme1⟩.*battery* ⟨Theme2⟩.*bulb*

To address this need, we created the *Predicate Type* based partly on the rhetorical predicates used in the DISCOUNT (Pilkington, 1999) scheme. While DISCOUNT included discourse relations in the set of predicate types, we restrict predicate types to those that encapsulate or summarize the collection of semantic roles in an utterance. Example predicate types include *procedure*, *observation* and *purpose*. A complete list of predicate types can be found in our forthcoming technical report.

3.3 Pragmatic Dimensions

The pragmatic dimensions are composed of the dialogue act dimension and the rhetorical form dimension. The dialogue act expresses the communicative function of a move and is the most general dimension in DISCUSS. The rhetorical form expresses attributes of the utterance's surface realization and can be thought of as refining the intent of the coarser dialogue act.

Dialogue Act: The dialogue act dimension is the top-level dimension in DISCUSS with the values of all other dimensions depending on the value of this dimension. Like with the majority of dialogue act taxonomies, DISCUSS dialogue acts have a grounding in speech act theory with a focus on what action the utterance performs. While most of the dialogue acts in the Dialogue Control and Information Exchange move categories have direct corollaries to those found in other taxonomies like DIT++ or DAMSL, we needed to supplement them with two frequently used Questioning the Author discussion moves: *marking* and *revoicing*. In marking, the tutor highlights parts of the student's language to emphasize important points and to steer the conversation towards key concepts. Revoicing serves a similar purpose, but instead of highlighting, the tutor rephrases student speech to clarify ideas they may have been struggling with. Examples of these acts are shown below.

S5:	*that when you stick a magnet to a rusty nail and then you stick it to a paper clip it sticks* Answer/Describe/Process
T6:	*I think I heard you say something about magnets sticking or attracting. Tell me more about that.* **Mark**/None/None, Ask/Elaborate/Process
S33:	*well when you scrub the the paperclip to the magnet the paperclip is starting to be a magnet* Answer/Describe/Process
T34:	*very good, so if the magnet gets close to the paperclip it picks it up* Feedback/Positive/None, **Revoice**/None/None

Dialogue acts in the Attention Management move category also reflect many of the actions regularly seen in tutorial dialogue. *Focus* and *Defer* acts are often used to move to or away from lesson-specific topics. In our corpus *Direct* is typically used to give instructions related to the multimedia (e.g. "Click on the box" or "Look at this animation.").

Rhetorical Form: The DISCUSS *Rhetorical Form* dimension provides another mechanism for differentiating between utterances with identical semantic content. While the dialogue act dimension is useful for providing an utterance's pragmatic interpretation and for determining what sequences are licensed, by itself it provides no indication of how a speaker is advancing the topic under discussion. Additional information is needed to create an utterance's surface form. Consider the two transactions in the table below. The semantic parses in both scenarios would be identical, however the tutor's questions and the resulting student response serve very different functions. In the first, the tutor is asking for a description and in the second, identification. Selection of the DISCUSS rhetorical forms found in the Information Exchange move category were inspired by the sixteen top-level tags used in Rhetorical Structure Theory (RST) (Mann and Thompson, 1988). While RST uses a rhetorical relation to link clauses and to show the development of an argument, DISCUSS uses the rhetorical form to refine the dialogue act. A sequence of dialogue acts paired with rhetorical forms can show progressions in the dialogue and tutoring process such as a shift from open-ended to directed questioning.

T1: *Can you tell which one is the battery?* Ask/**Describe**/Visual	T1: *Can you describe what is going on with the battery?* Ask/**Identify**/None
S2: *The battery is putting out electricity.* Answer/**Describe**/Process	S2: *The battery is the one putting out the electricity.* Answer/**Identify**/None

4 Annotation Status

We are still in the early stages of this ambitious annotation project. We currently have approximately 60 transcripts singly-annotated with DISCUSS moves. Each of these transcripts represents roughly 15 minutes of conversation and 50 turns on average. The DISCUSS taxonomy is a work in progress. Though we have created the tags for each dimension based on a wide body of prior research and on preliminary studies of our transcripts, we expect that future analysis of our annotation reliability and consistency will likely lead us to add, modify, and combine tags. We anticipate that DISCUSS's multidimensional nature will likely raise issues for inter-annotator reliability, and the ability to add multiple tags per turn will further complicate the process of evaluating agreement.

5 Future Work and Conclusions

We plan to use our corpus of DISCUSS annotated tutorial dialogues to build dialogue models for a variety of applications including assessment of tutorial quality and dialogue move prediction. This annotation will allow us to investigate what features of tutorial dialogue correlate with increased learning gains and what types of questions encourage greater student interaction. Data-driven dialogue characterization will also allow us to explore how tutorial tactics vary across domains and tutors. We envision this work as an important first step towards automatic question generation.

In this paper we introduced the DISCUSS dialogue move taxonomy. This scheme overlays dialogue act and rhetorical annotation over semantic representations. We believe this combination of pragmatic interpretations and semantic representations provide an intermediate representation rich enough to analyze the interactions in a complex task-oriented domain like tutorial dialogue. Furthermore, we think DISCUSS moves can succinctly summarize the actions of a speaker's turn, while still providing sufficient information for natural language generation of dialogue moves.

Acknowledgments This work was supported by grants from the NSF (DRL-0733322, DRL-0733323) and the IES (R3053070434). Any findings, recommendations, or conclusions are those of the author and do not necessarily represent the views of NSF or IES.

References

Beck, I. L., M. G. McKeown, J. Worthy, C. A. Sandora, and L. Kucan (1996). Questioning the author: A year-long classroom implementation to engage students with text. *The Elementary School Journal 96*(4), 387–416.

Buckley, M. and M. Wolska (2008). A classification of dialogue actions in tutorial dialogue. In *Proc. COLING*, pp. 73–80. ACL.

Bunt, H. (2009). The dit++ taxonomy for functional dialogue markup. In *Proc. EDAML 2009*.

Core, M. and J. Allen (1997). Coding dialogs with the damsl annotation scheme. In *AAAI Fall Symposium on Comm. Action in Humans and Machines*, pp. 28–35.

Graesser, A., X. Hu, S. Susarla, D. Harter, N. Person, M. Louwerse, B. Olde, and the Tutoring Research Group (2001). Autotutor: An intelligent tutor and conversational tutoring scaffold. In *Proc. AIED'01*, pp. 47–49.

Graesser, A. and N. Person (1994). Question asking during tutoring. *American Educational Research Journal 31*, 104–137.

Mann, W. C. and S. A. Thompson (1988). Rhetorical structure theory: Toward a functional theory of text organization. *Text 8*(3), 243–281.

Nielsen, R. D., J. Buckingham, G. Knoll, B. Marsh, and L. Palen (2008, September). A taxonomy of questions for question generation. In *Proc. WS on the Question Generation STEC*.

Pilkington, R. M. (1999). Analysing educational discourse: The discount scheme. Technical Report 99/2, Computer Based Learning Unit, University of Leeds.

Schuler, K. K. (2005). *VerbNet: A broad-coverage, comprehensive verb lexicon*. Ph. D. thesis, University of Pennsylvania.

Tsovaltzi, D. and E. Karagjosova (2004). A view on dialogue move taxonomies for tutorial dialogues. In *Proc. SIGDial*, pp. 35–38. ACL.

Ward, W. (1994). Extracting information from spontaneous speech. In *Proc. ICSLP*.

Ward, W., R. Cole, D. Bolanos, C. Buchenroth-Martin, E. Svirsky, S. Van Vuuren, T. Weston, J. Zheng, and L. Becker (2010). My science tutor: A conversational multi-media virtual tutor for elementary school science. *ACM TSLP: Special Issue on Speech and Language Processing of Children's Speech for Child-machine Interaction Applications*.

Using Topic Salience and Connotational Drifts to Detect Candidates to Semantic Change

Armelle Boussidan
L2C2, Institut des Sciences Cognitives - CNRS, Université de Lyon, Bron, France
armelle.boussidan@isc.cnrs.fr

Sabine Ploux
L2C2, Institut des Sciences Cognitives - CNRS, Université de Lyon, Bron, France
sploux@isc.cnrs.fr

Abstract

Semantic change has mostly been studied by historical linguists and typically at the scale of centuries. Here we study semantic change at a finer-grained level, the decade, making use of recent newspaper corpora. We detect semantic change candidates by observing context shifts which can be triggered by topic salience or may be independent from it. To discriminate these phenomena with accuracy, we combine variation filters with a series of indices which enable building a coherent and flexible semantic change detection model. The indices include widely adaptable tools such as frequency counts, co-occurrence patterns and networks, ranks, as well as model-specific items such as a variability and cohesion measure and graphical representations. The research uses ACOM, a co-occurrence based geometrical model, which is an extension of the Semantic Atlas. Compared to other models of semantic representation, it allows for extremely detailed analysis and provides insight as to how connotational drift processes unfold.

1 Introduction

Semantic change has long been analyzed and theorized upon in historical linguistics. Its abstract and ungraspable nature made its detection a difficult task for computational semantics, despite the many tools available from various models of lexical treatment. Most extant theories are based on manual analysis of century long semantic drifts. From these works we inherit various typologies and repertories of causes of change (e.g., Bloomfield (1933)). However these types of analyses may not be suited to the large scale production of text in our societies. Not only has the quantity of produced text rocketed but its diffusion and speed of transmission has radically increased. In this context, recent studies have yielded promising results, showing that computational models of semantics can deal with assessed semantic change examples as well as detect candidates in corpora. Among them, some include topic salience as an index and others do not, as they rather try to quantify semantic change with reliable measures. In an era of information overflow, topic change takes on a new linguistic value, as it may be responsible for extremely quick paced semantic change, which can be ephemeral or become fixed. Topic salience might as well be a sociologically induced or press phenomenon with no semantic impact at all. However when both topic salience and connotational drift take place, a semantic phenomenon may be at stake. Our analysis is anchored in this process. We shall briefly introduce other approaches, explain our methods and the structure of our detection prototype (in progress) as well as give preliminary results before concluding with a discussion.

2 Measuring semantic change : previous work

To measure semantic change, one has to evaluate the semantics of a lexical item at a given point. To do so, semantic similarity measures in vector spaces or geometrical spaces may be used to compare the

item with its own occurrences at later points. This method has been applied in Sagi et al. (2009), where semantic *density* was calculated as the average angle between vectors in a semantic space. The *variability* of that density was observed for the same lexical item at different points in time. Density measures were applied to a series of acknowledged semantic change cases, in the *Project Gutenberg* Corpus, a historical corpus of English organized by documents. Results mostly include broadening and narrowing cases. The same method yielded results on the difference between nominal and verbal types of change, showing that verbs were more likely to change than nouns (Sagi (2010)).
Cook and Stevenson (2010) also used assessed cases from the historical linguistics literature. They detected changes in the semantic orientation of words (or polarity shifts) namely amelioration and pejoration. They then applied this methodology to detect possible un-assessed candidates. They used three English corpora as corpus slices, covering approximately a four century time-span.
Volatility has also been assessed by Holz and Teresniak (2010), who adapted a measure from econometrics to quantify semantic change in a time sliced corpus. The volatility measure relied on the computation of the rank series for every co-occurent term and on the coefficient of variation of all co-occurrent terms (Holz and Teresniak (2010)). The method was applied to search words in modern corpora in German and English (the *Wortschatz* and *the New York Times*). The strong point of this measure is that it is independent from word frequency, however it does not provide detailed analysis about the underlying semantic processes.

3 Methods

Of the three cited works, our approach is closer to that of Holz and Teresniak (2010) in that both their work and ours are conducted on very recent corpora. We are currently conducting short diachrony detection, analysis and representation on a modern press corpus in French (the newspapers *Le Monde*, 1997-2007). We use the ACOM model (Ji et al. (2003)) an extension of the Semantic Atlas Model (Ploux et al. (2010)) that uses factor analysis to provide geometrical representations of word co-occurrence in corpus (both models are freely available on `http://dico.isc.cnrs.fr/eng/index.html`). The model relies on *cliques*, which are organized subsets of co-occurrent words, from which clustering can be made. To extract co-occurrent words, we apply ACOM on a time-sliced corpus. For each slice t, a word-association table is constructed using all headwords (see Ploux et al. (2010) for a complete methodological description). Each headword $W_t^i(1 \leq i \leq N$, where N is the total number of types in the corpus slice) has children ($c_j s$) that are arranged in descending order of co-occurrence with W_t^i [1]:

$$W_t^i : c1; c2; \ldots ; cn$$

We apply two factors to filter this table: α where $0 \leq \alpha \leq 1$ to eliminate the rarely co-occurring children of W_n^i :

$$W_t^i : c1; c2; \ldots ; ck$$

where $k = n\alpha$ and n is the original number of children of W_t^i, and β where $\beta(0 \leq \beta \leq 1)$ to cut off rarely co-occurring of children of c_j:

$$(c_j^m : g1; g2; \ldots ; gl(1 \leq j \leq k; l = m\beta))$$

On the basis of that table, cliques are calculated. The notion of clique is taken from graph theory (on graph therory see for ex. Golumbic (2004)). Mathematically, cliques are maximum connected subgraphs. In our case, the nodes are contexonyms. Then, correspondence factor analysis is applied (Benzécri (1980)) and the χ^2 distance is calculated between pairs of cliques to obtain a multidimensional space. A hierarchical clustering algorithm clusters cliques in thematic sets at several degrees of detail. Clusters show broad topic shifts whereas the cliques show fine-grained sub-organisation. Therefore the model allows for very detailed analysis as well as topical analysis. It also provides a graphic visualization for the semantics of a word. With the time-sliced corpus, we may extract maps for each subpart of the

[1] Children with co-occurrences under a 10,000th of the global frequency of the headword W_t^i are removed to reduce noise.

corpus and compare the spaces generated for the same word at different points in time, to complete the analysis.

3.1 Structure of the detection prototype

Currently our model is structured as follows: the corpus is transformed into a time-sliced ACOM database, with word frequencies and co-occurence frequencies. We apply an adjustable standard deviation filter to extract significant frequency and co-occurrence frequency variations as well as co-occurrence network variations. (The co-occurrence window is adjustable to the sentence, paragraph or other window sizes). If we only detect frequency variation, there is a suspicion that the headword might undergo context variation later, but it could also be an ephemeral press or fashion phenomenon with no semantic impact. However if we detect both significant frequency variations and co-occurrence variations, there is a higher chance that the context variations are a reflection of semantic variation. At this stage we apply indices based on rank variation, clique analysis and clique-term variation analysis (described in Boussidan et al. (2010)) as well as manual analysis to determine the nature of the change. The next step to verify that the item has undergone semantic change is its stabilization over time. This detection path highlights short diachronic change. We may also detect significant co-occurence variations with no significant headword frequency variation, in which case we may apply directly the indices to check whether the context shifts reveal an anchored meaning shift. If the indices highlight a meaning shift, the former is necessarily much more subtle than the short diachronic change that we detected previously. It might be the reflection of a longer term process of which the trigger might not be contained in the given corpus.

4 Preliminary results

4.1 Testing examples

To conceive a detection model, we first conducted experiments using attested examples or using words that we selected after manually observing that a shift was taking place. By testing these examples, we could extract data about how the model would render them so as to use it to create detection indices and parameters. Among these was the French word *malbouffe* (literally "bad grub" or "junk food"), a neology selected from a previously established list of new dictionary entries (Martinez (2009)). The corpus showed how the different spellings of the words alternated before yielding the current one. Analysis of the co-occurrence networks showed that one of the most important co-occurrent words, *Bové*, the name of a French political actor, had almost the same co-occurrence network as *malbouffe*. From this observation and after comparing definitions and previous contexts of use, we could infer that this person gave the word *malbouffe* its new meaning, by superimposing political values on it, on top of its dietetic values. Co-occurrence networks therefore allowed us to analyse the process of meaning shift. The full analysis of this example may be found in Boussidan et al. (2009).
We also tested a more subtle connotational drift with the word *mondialisation* ("globalization"), which undergoes clear contextual change in the corpus. The word first appeared in contexts defined by the political, economical and intellectual positions it brings about, with strong co-occurrents such as *défi* ("challenge"), *progrès* ("progress") or *menace* ("threat"). It then drifted into a complete network of words related to one single French political movement of anti-globalization in 2001. Therefore the use of *mondialisation* gained a new connotation, whereas its synonym *globalisation* ("globalization") remained quite neutral politically. The analysis of this example revealed that some terms were used as pivots, providing linkage between the existing cliques and the new ones. Pivots therefore provided a good tool to observe meaning re-organisation. The full analysis of this example may be found in Boussidan et al. (2010) and the corresponding dynamic representation on `http://dico.isc.cnrs.fr/en/diachro.html`.

4.2 Semantic change detection

On the basis of these preliminary examples, we designed a semantic change detection prototype. Testing examples brought to light the difficulty of discriminating press-related topic salience with no semantic impact from topic salience with a semantic impact. Detection is conducted in three stages. The first stage relies on frequency variation to extract topic variations of context in the corpus. For instance by setting the filter to retain words for which the coefficient of variation[2] is higher than 0.5, we obtain a list of words that may be classified into three loose semantic sets and a fourth set grouping all independent items. These semantic sets include words related to:

- war, terrorism and violence
- technology
- illness

By adjusting the settings we mayalso include more subtle topic variations if needed or conversely, looser ones. The second stage involves co-occurrence variation so as to extract the changes in semantic networks and thus in connation, for a lexical item. For instance, we detected that the word *logiciel* ("software") underwent a frequency co-occurrence peak with *libre* ("free") in January 2001. The expression *logiciel libre* stands for "freeware" and has been renamed *gratuiciel* or *graticiel* (a blending of *gratuit*, "free" with *logiciel*, "software") in Quebec. We therefore detect a new compositional expression that coins a French equivalent to the word *freeware* used until then.

Another example of connotational drift is the word *navigation* ("navigation") which is only attested in the TLFI[3] and the Dictionnaire Historique de la Langue Française (Rey et al. (1998)), under the meaning relating to transport, firstly on seas and rivers and then via plane or spaceship. However, between 1997 and 2001 the word takes on a new major meaning in internet search, meaning "browsing". This is aparent when looking at the co-occurrence patterns of *navigation* with words related to technology and comparing them with co-occurrences of words related to transport. The technology words show peaks between 1997 and 2001 and then lower frequencies until 2007, whereas the transport words show stable use all the way through the corpus. The new use of *navigation*, however is almost obsolete now in spoken speech -or at least it has gone out of fashion- but the semantics of *navigation* have clearly integrated an additional domain and broadened. A simple search of French results on Google provides 5,500,000 documents for *navigation internet*, among which are a lot of recent ones. However the meaning *to search the internet* grew from the name of a specific web navigator: the *Netscape Navigator* which was widespread in the 1990s but is no longer supported nowadays.

Both previous stages provide us with candidates to semantic change. The last stage is the stabilization of a connotational drift, whether it is a broadening, a narrowing, a domain shift or other. We are currently working on this last index. We often find that when a word undergoes semantic change, it goes through a phase of onomasiological competition in which other possible candidates may in turn become the new bearers of certain meanings. For *navigation* for instance, the word *surf* was a competitor, however both words now sound obsolete. It may be that none of them wins the competition, in which case the concept has become so deeply anchored in language and society that it does not need naming any more.

5 Discussion and Future Work

Since semantic phenomena, whether synchronic or diachronic, are very much corpus specific, it is difficult to conceive of a large scale universal detection method for them. However, tools may be built to be highly flexible in order to allow users to adjust settings to adapt to the corpus they deal with. This flexibility may encompass genre and stylistic variations when working with the same language as well as adaptation to a completely different language. We are considering global evaluations of the corpora's stylistics to avoid the detection of corpus specfic phenomena instead of broader language phenomena.

[2]The coefficient of variation is the ratio of the standard deviation to the mean

[3]`http://atilf.atilf.fr/tlf.htm`

Ideally the model should also be able to deal with timescale differences.The precise adjustment of these settings is part of our future research avenues along with incorporating an index for stabilization. This last filter is particularly difficult to create when dealing with ongoing phenomena. We may sometimes need to wait a few years to be able to establish whether a semantic change has stabilized.
To summarize, we are currently developing a filtering tool to extract candidates to semantic change on the basis of topic salience variation in corpus and co-occurrence network variation. Our approach shed light on the emergence of these phenomena at a very detailed level. Preliminary results showed that the tool was succesful at extracting those candidates; however it is not yet advanced enough to discriminate between context changes that affect a word without semantic impact and those that do have a semantic impact. This aspect constitutes our current research perspective.

6 Acknowledgements

This research is supported by the Région Rhône-Alpes, via the Cible Project 2009. Many thanks to Sylvain Lupone, previously engineer at the L2c2 for the tools he developed in this research's framework.

References

Benzécri, J.-P. (1980). *L'analyse des données : l'analyse des correspondances.* Paris: Bordas.

Bloomfield, L. (1933). *Language.* New York: Allen and Unwin.

Boussidan, A., S. Lupone, and S. Ploux (2009). La malbouffe : un cas de néologie et de glissement sémantique fulgurants. In *"Du thème au terme, émergence et lexicalisation des connaissances"*, Toulouse, France. 8 ème conférence internationale Terminologie et Intelligence Artificielle.

Boussidan, A., A.-L. Renon, C. Franco, S. Lupone, and S. Ploux (2010). Vers une méthode de visualisation graphique de la diachronie des néologies. Tubingen, Germany. Colloque Néologie sémantique et Corpus. in press.

Cook, P. and S. Stevenson (2010). Automatically identifying changes in the semantic orientation of words. In *Proceedings of the Seventh conference on International Language Resources and Evaluation*, Valletta,Malta. LREC 2010.

Golumbic, M. (2004). *Algorithmic graph theory and perfect graphs.* North-Holland.

Holz, F. and S. Teresniak (2010). Towards automatic detection and tracking of topic change. *Computational Linguistics and Intelligent Text Processing*, 327–339.

Ji, H., S. Ploux, and E. Wehrli (2003). Lexical knowledge representation with contexonyms. *Proceedings of the 9th Machine Translation Summit*, 194–201.

Martinez, C. (2009). *L'évolution de l'orthographe dans les Petit Larousse et les Petit Robert 1997-2008: une approche généalogique du texte lexicographique.* Ph. D. thesis, Université de Cergy-Pontoise.

Ploux, S., A. Boussidan, and H. Ji (2010). The semantic atlas: an interactive model of lexical representation. In *Proceedings of the Seventh conference on International Language Resources and Evaluation*, Valletta, Malta. LREC 2010.

Rey, A., T. Hordé, and L. Robert (1998). *Dictionnaire historique de la langue française : contenant les mots français en usage et quelques autres délaissés, avec leur origine proche et lointaine.* Paris.

Sagi, E. (2010). Nouns are more stable than verbs: Patterns of semantic change in 19th century english. Portland, OR. 32nd AnnualConference of the Cognitive Science Society. to be published.

Sagi, E., S. Kaufmann, and B. Clark (2009). Semantic density analysis: Comparing word meaning across time and phonetic space. In *GEMS: GEometrical Models of Natural Language Semantics.* EACL.

Towards Component-Based Textual Entailment

Elena Cabrio[1,2] and Bernardo Magnini[1]
[1]FBK-irst, Trento, Italy
[2]University of Trento, Italy
{cabrio,magnini}@fbk.eu

Abstract

In the Textual Entailment community, a shared effort towards a deeper understanding of the core phenomena involved in textual inference is recently arose. To analyse how the common intuition that decomposing TE would allow a better comprehension of the problem from both a linguistic and a computational viewpoint, we propose a definition for *strong component-based TE*, where each component is in itself a complete TE system, able to address a TE task on a specific phenomenon in isolation. We review the literature according to our definition, trying to position relevant work as more or less close to our idea of strong component-based TE. Several dimensions of the problem are discussed: *i)* the implementation of system components to address specific inference types, *ii)* the analysis of the phenomena relevant to component-based TE, and *iii)* the development of evaluation methodologies to assess TE systems capabilities to address single phenomena in a pair.

1 Introduction

The Recognizing Textual Entailment (RTE) task (Dagan et al. (2009)) aims at capturing a broad range of inferences that are relevant for several Natural Language Processing applications, and consists of deciding, given two text fragments, whether the meaning of one text (the *hypothesis H*) is entailed, *i.e.* can be inferred, from another text (the *text T*).

Although several approaches to face this task have been experimented, and progresses in TE technologies have been shown in RTE evaluation campaigns, a renewed interest is rising in the TE community towards a deeper and better understanding of the core phenomena involved in textual inference. In line with this direction, we are convinced that crucial progress may derive from a focus on decomposing the complexity of the TE task into basic phenomena and on their combination. This belief demonstrated to be shared by the RTE community, and a number of recently published works (e.g. Sammons et al. (2010), Bentivogli et al. (2010)) agree that incremental advances in local entailment phenomena are needed to make significant progress in the main task, which is perceived as omnicomprehensive and not fully understood yet. According to this premise, the aim of this work is to systematize and delve into the work done so far in component-based TE, focusing on the aspects that contribute to highlight a common framework and to define a clear research direction that deserves further investigation.

Basing on the original definition of TE, that allows to fomulate textual inferences in an application independent way and to take advantage of available datasets for training provided in the RTE evaluation campaigns, we intend to analyse how the common intuition of decomposing TE would allow a better comprehension of the problem from both a linguistic and a computational viewpoint. Aspects related to meaning compositionality, which are absent in the original proposal, could potentially be introduced into TE and may bring new light into textual inference.

In this direction, we propose a definition for "strong" component-based TE, where each component is in itself a complete TE system, able to address a TE task on a specific phenomenon in isolation. Then, we review the literature in the TE field according to our definition, trying to position relevant work as more or less close to our idea of strong component-based TE. We have analysed and carried out research on several dimensions of the problem, including: *i)* the definition and implementation of system components able to address specific inference types (Section 2); *ii)* the analysis of the phenomena relevant to component-based TE (Section 3); *iii)* the development of methodologies for the analysis of component-based TE systems, providing a number of qualitative indicators to assess the capabilities that systems have to address single phenomena in a pair and to combine them (Section 4).

2 Component-based TE framework

We define a component-based TE architecture as a set of clearly identifiable TE modules that can be singly used on specific entailment sub-problems and can be then combined to produce a global entailment judgement. Each component receives a certain example pair as input, and outputs an entailment judgment concerning the inference type it is built to address. In other words, each component is in turn a TE system, that performs the same task focusing only on a certain sub-aspect of entailment. According to our proposal the following requirements need to be fulfilled in component-based TE architecture: *i)* each compenent must provide a 3-way judgment (i.e. entailment, contradiction, unknown) on a specific aspect underlying entailment, where the unknown judgement might be interpreted as the absence of the phenomenon in the TE pair; *ii)* in a component-based architecure, the same inference type (e.g. temporal, spatial inferences) can not be covered by more than one component; this is because in the combination phase we do not want that the same phenomen is counted more than one time.

No specific constraints are defined with respect to how such components should be implemented, i.e. they can be either a set of classifiers or rule-based modules. In addition, linguistic processing and annotation of the input data (e.g. parsing, NER, semantic role labeling) can be required by a component according to the phenomenon it considers. An algorithm is then applied to judge the entailment relation between T and H with respect to that specific aspect. Unlike similarity algorithms, with whom algorithms performing entailment are often associated in the literature, the latter are characterized by the fact that the relation on which they are asked to judge is directional. According to such definition, the nature of the TE task is not modified, since each sub-task independently performed by the system components keeps on being an entailment task. Suitable composition mechanisms should then be applied to combine the output of each single module to obtain a global judgment for a pair.

The definition presented above provides a strong interpretation of the compositional framework for TE, that can be described as a continuum that tends towards systems developed combining identifiable and separable components addressing specific inference types. A number of works in the literature can be placed along this continuum, according to how much they get closer to this interpretation.

Systems addressing TE exploiting machine learning techniques with a variety of features, including lexical-syntactic and semantic features (e.g. Kozareva and Montoyo (2006), Zanzotto et al. (2007)) tend towards the opposite extreme of this framework, since even if linguistic features are used, they bring information about a specific aspect relevant to the inference task but they do not provide an independent judgment on it. These systems are not modular, and it is difficult to assess the contribution of a certain feature in providing the correct overall judgment for a pair. A step closer towards the direction of component-based TE is done by Bar-Haim et al. (2008), that model semantic inference as application of entailment rules specifying the generation of entailed sentences from a source sentence. Such rules capture semantic knowledge about linguistic phenomena (e.g. paraphrases, synonyms), and are applied in a transformation-based framework. Even if these rules are clearly identifiable, their application per se does not provide any judgment about an existing entailment relation between T and H.

A component-based system has been developed by Wang and Neumann (2008), based on three specialized RTE-modules: (i) to tackle temporal expressions; (ii) to deal with other types of NEs; (iii) to deal with cases with two arguments for each event. Besides these precision-oriented modules, two robust but less accurate backup strategies are considered, to deal with not yet covered cases. In the final stage, the results of all specialized and backup modules are joint together, applying a weighted voting mechanism.

Getting closer to the definition of component-based TE presented at the beginning of this Section, in Magnini and Cabrio (2009) we propose a framework for the definition and combination of specialized entailment engines, each of which able to deal with a certain aspect of language variability. A distance-based framework is assumed, where the distance d between T and H is inversely proportional to the entailment relation in the pair. We assume an edit distance approach (Kouylekov and Magnini (2005)), where d is estimated as the sum of the costs of the edit operations (i.e. insertion, deletion, substitution), which are necessary to transform T into H. Issues underlying the combination of the specialized entailment engines are discussed, i.e. the order of application and the combination of individual results in order to produce a global result.

3 Linguistic analysis and resources for component-based TE

The idea underlying component-based TE is that each component should independently solve the entailment relation on a specific phenomenon relevant to inference, and then the judgments provided by all the modules are combined to obtain an overall judgment for a pair. Our definition abstracts from the different theories underlying the categorization of linguistic phenomena, so a straightforward relation between TE component and linguistic phenomena cannot be defined a priori. Some work has already been done in investigating in depth sub-aspects of entailment, and in developing *ad hoc* resources to assess the impact of systems components created to address specific inference types. Earlier works in the field (e.g. Vanderwende et al. (2005), Clark et al. (2007)) carried out partial analysis of the data sets in order to evaluate how many entailment examples could be accurately predicted relying only on lexical, syntactic or world knowledge. Bar-Haim et al. (2005) defined two intermediate models of textual entailment, corresponding to lexical and lexical-syntactic levels of representation, and a sample from RTE-1 data set was annotated according to each model.

A step further, other RTE groups have developed focused data sets with the aim of investigating and experimenting on specific phenomena underlying language variability. For instance, to evaluate a contradiction detection module Marneffe et al. (2008) created a corpus where contradictions arise from negation, by adding negative markers to the RTE-2 test data. Kirk (2009) describes his work of building an inference corpus for spatial inference about motion, while Akhmatova and Dras (2009) experiment current approaches on hypernymy acquisition to improve entailment classification.

The first systematic work of annotation of TE data sets is done by Garoufi (2007), that propose a scheme for manual annotation of textual entailment data sets (ARTE). The aim is to highlight a wide variety of entailment phenomena in the data, in relation to three levels, i.e. *Alignment*, *Context* and *Coreference*. 23 different features are extracted for positive entailment annotation, while for the negative pairs a more basic scheme is conceived. The ARTE scheme has been applied to the complete positive entailment RTE-2 Test Set (400 pairs), and to a random 25% portion of the negative entailment Test Set.

More recently, in Bentivogli et al. (2010) we present a methodology for the creation of specialized TE data sets, made of *monothematic T-H pairs*, i.e. pairs in which a certain phenomenon relevant to the entailment relation is highlighted and isolated (Magnini and Cabrio (2009)). Such monothematic pairs are created basing on the phenomena that are actually present in the RTE pairs, so that the distribution of the linguistic phenomena involved in the entailment relation emerges. A number of steps are carried out manually, starting from a T-H pair taken from one of the RTE data sets, and decomposing it in a number of monothematic pairs T-H_i, where T is the original text and H_i are the hypotheses created for each linguistic phenomenon relevant for judging the entailment relation in T-H. Phenomena are grouped using both fine-grained and broader categories (e.g. *lexical*, *syntactic*, *lexical-syntactic*, *discourse* and *reasoning*). After applying the proposed methodology, all the monothematic pairs T-H_i relative to the same phenomenon i are grouped together, resulting in several data sets specialized for phenomenon i. Unlike previous work of analysis of RTE data, the result of this study is a resource that allows evaluation of TE systems on specific phenomena relevant to inference, both when isolated and when interacting with the others (the annotation of RTE data with the linguistic phenomena underlying the entailment/contradiction relations in the pairs is also provided). A pilot study has been carried out on 90 pairs from RTE-5 data set.[1]

Highlighting the need of resources for solving textual inference problems in the context of RTE, Sammons et al. (2010) challenge the NLP community to contribute to a joint, long term effort in this

[1]The resulting data sets are freely available at `http://hlt.fbk.eu/en/Technology/TE_Specialized_Data`

direction, making progress both in the analysis of relevant linguistic phenomena and their interaction, and developing resources and approaches that allow more detailed assessment of RTE systems. The authors propose a linguistically-motivated analysis of entailment data based on a step-wise procedure to resolve entailment decision, by first identifying parts of T that match parts of H, and then identifying connecting structure. Their inherent assumption is that the meanings of T and H could be represented as sets of n-ary relations, where relations could be connected to other relations (i.e. could take other relations as arguments). The authors carried out a feasibility study applying the procedure to 210 examples from RTE-5, marking for each example the entailment phenomena that are required for the inference.

4 Evaluation in component-based TE

The evaluation measure adopted in the RTE challenges is accuracy, i.e. the percentage of pairs correctly judged by a TE system. In the last RTE-5 and RTE-6 campaigns, participating groups were asked to run ablation tests, to evaluate the contribution of publicly available knowledge resources to the systems' performances. Such ablation tests consist of removing one module at a time from a system, and rerunning the system on the test set with the other modules, except the one tested. The results obtained were not satisfactory, since the impact of a certain resource on system performances is really dependent on how it is used by the system. In some cases, resources like WordNet demonstrated to be very useful, while for other systems their contribution is limited or even damaging, as observed also in Sammons et al. (2010).

To provide a more detailed evaluation of the capabilities of a TE system to address specific inference types, in Cabrio and Magnini (2010) we propose a methodology for a qualitative evaluation of TE systems, that takes advantage of the decomposition of T-H pairs into *monothematic pairs* (described in Section 3). The assumption is that the more a system is able to correctly solve the linguistic phenomena underlying the entailment relation separately, the more the system should be able to correctly judge more complex pairs, in which different phenomena are present and interact in a complex way. According to such assumption, the higher the accuracy of a system on the monothematic pairs and the compositional strategy, the better its performances on the original RTE pairs. The precision a system gains on single phenomena should be maintained over the general data set, thanks to suitable mechanisms of meaning combination. A number of quantitative and qualitative indicators about strength and weaknesses of TE systems result from the application of this methodology. Comparing the qualitative analysis obtained for two TE systems, the authors show that several systems' behaviors can be explained in terms of the correlation between the accuracy on monothematic pairs and the accuracy on the corresponding original pairs. In a component based framework, such analysis would allow a separate evaluation of TE modules, focusing on their ability to correctly address the inference types they are built to deal with.

5 Conclusions

This paper provides a definition for strong component-based TE framework, exploiting the common intuition that decomposing the complexity of TE would allow a better comprehension of the problem from both a linguistic and a computational viewpoint. We have reviewed the literature according to our definition, trying to position relevant works as more or less close to our idea of strong component-based TE. We hope that the analysis of the different dimensions of the problem we provided may bring interesting elements for future research works. In this direction, we propose a research program in which for different applications (e.g. domain, genre) specific TE component-based architectures could be optimized, i.e. composed by modules that meet the requirements of that specific genre/domain.

References

Akhmatova, E. and M. Dras (2009). Using hypernymy acquisition to tackle (part of) textual entailment. In *Proceedings of TextInfer 2009*, Singapore. 6 August.

Bar-Haim, R., J. Berant, I. Dagan, I. Greental, S. Mirkin, E. Shnarch, and I. Szpektor (2008). Efficient semantic deduction and approximate matching over compact parse forests. In *Proceedings of the TAC 2008 Workshop on TE*, Gaithersburg, Maryland, USA. 17 November.

Bar-Haim, R., I. Szpektor, and O. Glickman (2005). Definition and analysis of intermediate entailment levels. In *Proceedings of the ACL 2005 Workshop on Empirical Modeling of Semantic Equivalence and Entailment*, Ann Arbor, Michigan. 30 June.

Bentivogli, L., E. Cabrio, I. Dagan, D. Giampiccolo, M. L. Leggio, and B. Magnini (2010). Building textual entailment specialized data sets: a methodology for isolating linguistic phenomena relevant to inference. In *Proceedings of LREC 2010*, Valletta, Malta. 19-21 May.

Bentivogli, L., B. Magnini, I. Dagan, H. Dang, and D. Giampiccolo (2009). The fifth pascal recognizing textual entailment challenge. In *Proceedings of the TAC 2009 Workshop on TE*, Gaithersburg, Maryland. 17 November.

Cabrio, E. and B. Magnini (2010). Toward qualitative evaluation of textual entailment systems. In *Proceedings of COLING 2010: Posters*, Beijing, China. 23-27 August.

Clark, P., P. Harrison, J. Thompson, W. Murray, J. Hobbs, and C. Fellbaum (2007). On the role of lexical and world knowledge in rte3. In *Proceedings of the ACL-07 Workshop on TE and Paraphrasing*, Prague, Czech Republic. 28-29 June.

Dagan, I., B. Dolan, B. Magnini, and D. Roth (2009). Recognizing textual entailment: Rational, evaluation and approaches. *Natural Language Engineering (JNLE) 15*(Special Issue 04), i–xvii.

Garoufi, K. (2007). Towards a better understanding of applied textual entailment. In *Master Thesis*, Saarland University. Saarbrücken, Germany.

Kirk, R. (2009). Building an annotated textual inference corpus for motion and space. In *Proceedings of TextInfer 2009*, Singapore. 6 August.

Kouylekov, M. and B. Magnini (2005). Tree edit distance for textual entailment. In *Proceedings of RALNP-2005*, Borovets, Bulgaria. 21-23 September.

Kozareva, Z. and A. Montoyo (2006). Mlent: The machine learning entailment system of the university of alicante. In *Proc. of the second PASCAL Challenge Workshop on RTE*, Venice, Italy. 10 April.

Magnini, B. and E. Cabrio (2009). Combining specialized entailment engines. In *Proceedings of LTC'09*, Poznan, Poland. 6-8 November.

Marneffe, M. D., A. Rafferty, and C. Manning (2008). Finding contradictions in text. In *Proceedings of ACL-08*, Columbus, OH, 15-20 June.

Sammons, M., V. Vydiswaran, and D. Roth (2010). Ask not what textual entailment can do for you... In *Proceedings of ACL-10*, Uppsala, Sweden. 11-16 July.

Vanderwende, L., D. Coughlin, and B. Dolan (2005). What syntax can contribute in entailment task. In *Proceedings of the First PASCAL Challenges Workshop on RTE*, Southampton, U.K., 11-13 April.

Wang, R. and G. Neumann (2008). An accuracy-oriented divide-and-conquer strategy. In *Proceedings of the TAC 2008 Workshop on TE*, Gaithersburg, Maryland. 17 November.

Zanzotto, F., M. Pennacchiotti, and A. Moschitti (2007). Shallow semantics in fast textual entailment rule learners. In *Proceedings of the ACL-PASCAL Workshop on TE and Paraphrasing*, Prague, Czech Republic. 23-30 June.

Algebraic Approaches to Compositional Distributional Semantics

Daoud Clarke
University of Hertfordshire
daoud@metrica.net

David Weir
University of Sussex
davidw@sussex.ac.uk

Rudi Lutz
University of Sussex
rudil@sussex.ac.uk

Abstract

The question of how to compose meaning in distributional representations of meaning has recently been recognised as a central issue in computational linguistics. In this paper we describe three general and powerful tools that can be used to describe composition in distributional semantics: quotient algebras, learning of finite dimensional algebras, and the construction of algebras from semigroups.

1 Introduction

Vector based representations of meaning have wide application in natural language processing. While these techniques work well at the word level, for longer strings, data becomes extremely sparse. The question of how the principle of compositionality might apply for such representations has thus been recognised as an important one (Widdows, 2008; Clark et al., 2008).

Context-theoretic semantics (Clarke, 2007) is a framework for composing meanings in vector based semantics, in which the composition of the meaning of strings is described by a multiplication on a real vector space $\mathcal{A}$ that is bilinear with respect to the addition of the vector space, i.e.

$$x(y+z) = xy + xz \quad (x+y)z = xz + yz \quad (\alpha x)(\beta y) = \alpha\beta xy$$

where $x, y, z \in \mathcal{A}$ and $\alpha, \beta \in \mathbb{R}$. It is assumed that the multiplication is associative, but *not* commutative. The resulting structure is an associative algebra over a field — or simply an algebra when there is no ambiguity. Clarke (2007) gives a mathematical model of meaning as context, and shows that under this model, the meaning of natural language expressions can be described by an algebra. The framework is also applied to models of textual entailment, and logical and ontological representations of natural language meaning.

In this paper, we identify three general techniques for constructing algebras.

- Using quotient algebras to impose relations on a free algebra, as described in (Clarke et al., 2010).
- Defining finite-dimensional algebras using matrices. Any finite-dimensional algebra can be described in this way; we have investigated the possibility of learning such algebras using least squares regression.
- Constructing algebras from a semigroup to give it vector space properties. We sketch a possible method of using this technique, identified by Clarke (2007), to endow logical semantics with a vector space nature.

This paper presents a preliminary consideration of these general techniques, and our goal is simply to show that they are worthy of further exploration.

	apple	*big apple*	*red apple*	*city*	*big city*	*red city*	*book*	*big book*	*red book*
apple	1.0	0.26	0.24	0.52	0.13	0.12	0.33	0.086	0.080
big apple		1.0	0.33	0.13	0.52	0.17	0.086	0.33	0.11
red apple			1.0	0.12	0.17	0.52	0.080	0.11	0.33
city				1.0	0.26	0.24	0.0	0.0	0.0
big city					1.0	0.33	0.0	0.0	0.0
red city						1.0	0.0	0.0	0.0
book							1.0	0.26	0.24
big book								1.0	0.33
red book									1.0

Figure 1: Cosine similarity values between phrases

see red apple
buy apple
read big book
throw old small red book
buy large new book
see big city
visit big apple
modernise city
see modern city

Figure 2: The corpus used to compute the vectors that formed the generating set for the ideal.

2 Quotient Algebras

One commonly used bilinear multiplication operator on vector spaces is the tensor product (denoted $\otimes$), whose use as a method of combining meaning was first proposed by Smolensky (1990), and has been considered more recently by Clark and Pulman (2007) and Widdows (2008), who also looked at the direct sum (which Widdows calls the direct product, denoted $\oplus$).

The tensor algebra on a vector space V (where V is a space of context features) is defined as:

$$T(V) = \mathbb{R} \oplus V \oplus (V \otimes V) \oplus (V \otimes V \otimes V) \oplus \cdots$$

Any element of $T(V)$ can be described as a sum of components with each in a different tensor power of V. Multiplication is defined as the tensor product on these components, and extended linearly to the whole of $T(V)$.

Previous work has not made full use of the tensor product space; only tensor products are used, not sums of tensor products, giving us the equivalent of the product states of quantum mechanics. Our approach imposes relations on the vectors of the tensor product space that causes some product states to become equivalent to entangled states, containing sums of tensor products of different degrees. This allows strings of different lengths to share components. We achieve this by constructing a quotient algebra.

An ideal I of an algebra A is a sub-vector space of A such that $xa \in I$ and $ax \in I$ for all $a \in A$ and all $x \in I$. An ideal introduces a congruence $\equiv$ on A defined by $x \equiv y$ if and only if $x - y \in I$. For any set of elements $\Lambda \subseteq A$ there is a unique minimal ideal I_Λ containing all elements of Λ; this is called the ideal generated by Λ. The quotient algebra A/I is the set of all equivalence classes defined by this congruence. Multiplication is defined on A/I by the multiplication on A, since $\equiv$ is a congruence.

Elements that are congruent with respect to the ideal have equivalence classes that are equal in the quotient algebra. The construction is thus a way of imposing relations between vector elements: we simply choose a set of pairs that we wish to be equal, and put their difference in the generating set Λ.

Clarke et al. (2010), showed how an inner product can be computed for elements of the quotient algebra by taking the quotient of a finite dimensional subspace of the ideal and how a treebank could be used to identify suitable elements to put into the generating set for the ideal in such a way that strings of different lengths become comparable. Figure 1 shows similarities between adjective phrases computed using vectors derived from the corpus in figure 2. The construction allows many properties of the tensor product to carry over into the quotient algebra, for example the similarity of *red book* to *red apple* is the same as the similarity of *book* to *apple*, as we would expect from the tensor product. Unlike the tensor product, strings of different length are comparable, so for example, the similarity of *apple* to *red apple* is non-zero. The benefit of using quotient algebras for compositional distributional semantics lies in this ability to extend the favourable properties of the tensor product by imposing linguistically plausible relations between vectors.

3 Learning Finite-dimensional Algebras

Quotient algebras are useful constructions when we have a small number of relations which we wish to impose on the tensor algebra. In highly lexicalised grammars, the number of relations we wish to impose may become so large that the ideal generates the whole vector space, and is thus useless, since the resulting quotient space will be trivial. An alternative to this is to restrict the space of exploration to finite-dimensional algebras. In this case, we can explore the space of possible products in relation to the set of relations we wish to hold; in other words, we can view this as an optimisation problem in which we want to find the best possible product given the required relations.

We apply this to the situation where we obtain a vector $\hat{x}$ for each individual word and pair of words in sequence. We then find the product that best fits these observed vectors. Given a set $W = \{w_1, w_2 \ldots w_m\}$ of words, we want to define a product $\odot$ to minimise the difference between $\hat{w}_i \odot \hat{w}_j$ and $\widehat{w_i w_j}$, for $1 \leq i, j \leq m$. Specifically, we can define this as minimising

$$\sum_{i,j} \|\widehat{w_i w_j} - \hat{w}_i \odot \hat{w}_j\|$$

If word vectors have n dimensions, then $\odot$ is defined by an n^3 dimensional vector, which we denote f_{rst} for $1 \leq r, s, t \leq n$, where $(e_r \odot e_s)_t = f_{rst}$ and e is the vector with 1 in every component, and v_t is the tth component of v.

We can view this as a linear model:

$$(\widehat{w_i w_j})_t = \epsilon_{ijt} + \sum_{r,s=1}^{n} (\hat{w}_i)_r (\hat{w}_j)_s f_{rst}$$

where we have m^2 statistical units to learn n^2 parameters relating to the tth component of the vector space. Since these parameters are independent for each value of t, each set of n^2 parameters can be learnt in parallel. We are currently exploring ways of learning these parameters. The form of the equation above suggests the use of least squares, and we have performed some experiments using this method using a corpus extracted from the ukWaC corpus (Ferraresi et al., 2008). We extracted a list of $verb$ $adjective^* noun$ sequences, and used latent semantic analysis (Deerwester et al., 1990) to generate n-dimensional vectors for the 160 most common adjectives and nouns, and pairs of these adjectives and nouns. Our initial results indicate that the learnt parameters tend to get very large when using least squares to find the parameters, leading to poor results; we plan to investigate other methods such as linear optimisation.

Guevara (2010) proposed a related method of learning composition which used linear regression to learn how components compose. His model is however much more restrictive than ours in that the value of a component in the product depends only on that same component in the composed vectors, whereas in our model, the value of the component can depend on all components in the composed vectors.

Baroni and Zamparelli (2010) took a similar approach, in which adjectives are modelled as matrices acting on the space of nouns, and the matrices are learnt using least squares regression. The algebra products we propose learning are more general than matrix products; in addition we do not need to distinguish between words which are represented as matrices and words which are represented as vectors.

4 Constructing Algebras from Semigroups

Whilst the previous two techniques we have discussed are very general, and allow corpus data to be easily incorporated into the composition definition, our implementations are currently a long way from being able to represent the complexities of natural language semantics that is currently possible with logical semantics. This has become the standard method of representing natural language meaning, originating in the work of Montague (1973), however there is currently no way to incorporate statistical features of meaning that are described by the distributional hypothesis of Harris (1968).

Term	Context vector
fish	$(0, 0, 1)$
big	$(1, 2, 0)$

Figure 3: Example context vectors for terms.

$$n_i = (N, \lambda x \, \text{noun}_i(x))$$
$$a_i = (N/N, \lambda p \lambda y \, \text{adj}_i(y) \wedge p.y)$$

Figure 4: Equations describing syntax and semantics of adjectives and nouns.

In related work, Clark et al. (2008) described a method of composing meanings which they noted was a generalisation of Montague semantics. However, their version of Montague semantics assumed a particular model, and thus effectively mapped sentences to truth values. This omits much of the power of Montague semantics in which sentences are mapped to logical forms which then provide restrictions on the set of allowable models, allowing, for example, entailments to be computed between sentences.

We will sketch a method by which Montague semantics can be described within the context-theoretic framework. We follow a standard method of representing logic in language, but instead of representing words using logic, we represent an individual dimension of meaning of a word by a logical form — we call this dimension a "aspect". The general scheme is to represent aspects as elements of a semigroup, from which we form an algebra. Words are then represented as weighted sums over individual aspects.

We define a set S of all aspects as the set of pairs (s, σ), where s is the syntactic type of an aspect (for example in the Lambek calculus) and σ is the semantics of the aspect (for example described in the lambda calculus). We can extend S by defining a product on such pairs reducing each element to a normal form. This defines a semigroup: the Lambek calculus can be described in terms of a residuated lattice, which is a partially ordered semigroup (Lambek, 1958), and the lambda calculus is equivalent to a Cartesian closed category under β-equivalence (Lambek, 1985), which can be considered as a semigroup with additional structure.

Given any semigroup S we can construct an algebra $L^1(S)$ of real-valued functions on S which are finite under the L^1 norm with multiplication defined by convolution:

$$(u \cdot v)(x) = \sum_{y,z \in S: yz = x} u(y)v(z).$$

For example, suppose we have context vectors for the terms *big* and *fish* as described in Figure 3. We represent the syntax and semantics of adjectives and nouns by elements a_i and n_i respectively of a semigroup S (Figure 4), where we assume equivalence under β-reduction is accounted for. The predicates adj_i and noun_j correspond to aspects, in this case each dimension i of the three dimensions in the context vectors has a corresponding adj_i and noun_i. We may then represent the vectors for these terms as elements of the algebra $\widehat{big} = a_1 + 2a_2$ and $\widehat{fish} = n_3$, where we equate an element u of the semigroup with the function in the algebra $L^1(S)$ which maps u to 1 and every other element to zero. Then $\widehat{big}\,\widehat{fish} = a_1 n_3 + 2a_2 n_3$, where

$$a_i n_j = (N, \lambda x(\text{noun}_j(x) \wedge \text{adj}_i(x))).$$

Note that the elements a_i form a commutative, idempotent subsemigroup of S, so they have a semilattice structure. In order for this structure to carry over to the vector structure in the algebra, we would need a more sophisticated construction, such as a C* enveloping algebra; we leave the investigation of this possibility to further work.

5 Discussion

We have presented our initial investigations into the application of three powerful methods of constructing algebras to representing natural language semantics. Each of these approaches has potential use in representing meaning; here we have only touched the surface of what is possible with each technique. We hope that with further work, these methods will lead to a true synthesis between logical and distributional approaches to natural language semantics.

6 Acknowledgments

We are grateful to Peter Hines, Stephen Clark and Peter Lane for useful discussions. The first author also wishes to thank Metrica for supporting this research.

References

Baroni, M. and R. Zamparelli (2010). Nouns are vectors, adjectives are matrices: Representing adjective-noun constructions in semantic space. In *Proceedings of the Conference on Empirical Methods in Natural Language Processing (EMNLP 2010), East Stroudsburg PA: ACL*, pp. 1183–1193.

Clark, S., B. Coecke, and M. Sadrzadeh (2008). A compositional distributional model of meaning. In *Proceedings of the Second Quantum Interaction Symposium (QI-2008)*, Oxford, UK, pp. 133–140.

Clark, S. and S. Pulman (2007). Combining symbolic and distributional models of meaning. In *Proceedings of the AAAI Spring Symposium on Quantum Interaction*, Stanford, CA, pp. 52–55.

Clarke, D. (2007). *Context-theoretic Semantics for Natural Language: an Algebraic Framework*. Ph. D. thesis, Department of Informatics, University of Sussex.

Clarke, D., R. Lutz, and D. Weir (2010, July). Semantic composition with quotient algebras. In *Proceedings of the 2010 Workshop on GEometrical Models of Natural Language Semantics*, Uppsala, Sweden, pp. 38–44. Association for Computational Linguistics.

Deerwester, S., S. Dumais, G. Furnas, T. Landauer, and R. Harshman (1990). Indexing by latent semantic analysis. *Journal of the American Society for Information Science 41*(6), 391–407.

Ferraresi, A., E. Zanchetta, M. Baroni, and S. Bernardini (2008). Introducing and evaluating ukwac, a very large web-derived corpus of english. In *Workshop Programme*, pp. 47.

Guevara, E. (2010). A Regression Model of Adjective-Noun Compositionality in Distributional Semantics. *ACL 2010*, 33.

Harris, Z. (1968). *Mathematical Structures of Language*. Wiley, New York.

Lambek, J. (1958). The mathematics of sentence structure. *American Mathematical Monthly 65*, 154–169.

Lambek, J. (1985, May). Cartesian closed categories and typed lambda-calculi. In G. Cousineau, P.-L. Curien, and B. Robinet (Eds.), *Combinators and Functional Programming Languages*, Lecture Notes in Computer Science. Springer-Verlag.

Montague, R. (1973). *The proper treatment of quantification in ordinary English*. Dordrecht, Holland: D. Reidel Publishing Co.

Smolensky, P. (1990, November). Tensor product variable binding and the representation of symbolic structures in connectionist systems. *Artificial Intelligence 46*(1-2), 159–216.

Widdows, D. (2008). Semantic vector products: Some initial investigations. In *Proceedings of the Second Symposium on Quantum Interaction, Oxford, UK*.

Question Classification for Email*

Rachel Cotterill
University of Sheffield
r.cotterill@sheffield.ac.uk

Abstract

Question classifiers are used within Question Answering to predict the expected answer type for a given question. This paper describes the first steps towards applying a similar methodology to identifying question classes in dialogue contexts, beginning with a study of questions drawn from the Enron email corpus. Human-annotated data is used as a gold standard for assessing the output from an existing, open-source question classifier (QA-SYS). Problem areas are identified and potential solutions discussed.

1 Introduction and Motivation

In information retrieval, question classification is an important first stage of the question answering task. A question classification module typically takes a question as input and returns the class of answer which is anticipated. In an IR context, this enables candidate answers to be identified within a set of documents, and further methods can then be applied to find the most likely candidate.

The present work is motivated by a desire to identify questions and their answers in the context of written dialogue such as email, with the goal of improving inbox management and search. Reconstruction of meaning in a single email may often be impossible without reference to earlier messages in the thread, and automated systems are not yet equipped to deal with this distribution of meaning, as text mining techniques developed from document-based corpora such as newswire do not translate naturally into the dialogue-based world of email. Take the following hypothetical exchange:

From: john@example.com **To:** jane@example.com

```
Jane,
Can you let me know the name of your lawyer?  Thanks.
John
```

From: jane@example.com **To:** john@example.com

```
Ally McBeal.
-- Jane
```

This is an extreme example, but it serves to illustrate the "separate document problem" in email processing. Context is critical to pragmatic analysis, but with email and related media the context (and consequently, a single piece of information) may be spread across more than one document. In this case the second message in isolation gives no information concerning "Ally McBeal" as we do not have any context to put her in. However, by considering the question and answer pair together, we can discover that she is a lawyer (or, at the very least, that Jane believes or claims that to be the case; a philosophical distinction best left aside for the time being).

It is anticipated that questions in a dialogue context will exhibit a somewhat different range of types to typical IR questions, but that some will indeed be seeking the kind of factual information for which QA classifiers are currently designed. If this subset of fact-seeking questions can be reliably identified

*The author would like to thank GCHQ for supporting this research.

by an automated process, then existing question classifiers could be used to identify the expected answer type. Candidate answers could then be sought within the text of replies to the message in which the question is asked.

This paper briefly describes the gold standard data (Section 2), compares human annotation to the output of Ng & Kan's (2010) QA-SYS question classifier (Section 3), and proposes some future directions for research (Section 4).

2 The Data

In order to investigate question types in email, a suitable set of questions was required. To this end questions were automatically extracted from CMU's deduplicated copy of the Enron corpus (Klimt & Yang 2004). Of the 39,530 unique question strings identified in Enron outboxes, a random sample of 1147 were manually examined and annotated with the expected question type.

A number of taxonomies have been proposed for classifying answer types, of which Li & Roth's (2002) two-tier hierarchy is a reasonably comprehensive and widely-adopted example. Their coarse classes are Abbreviation (ABBR), Description (DESC), Entity (ENTY), Human (HUM), Location (LOC), and Numeric (NUM), and they then define a set of 50 subclasses. Table 1 shows how Li & Roth's taxonomy was mapped to the category labels adopted for the current work.

Cotterill 2010	**Li & Roth 2002**	**%**
Person(s)	HUM{individual,title}	2.53
Group or Organisation	HUM{group}	0.17
Descriptive text	HUM{description} DESC{manner, definition, description}	11.51
Reason	DESC{reason}	1.57
Date or Time	NUM{date, period}	3.57
Numeric	NUM{weight, volume/size, ordinal, percentage, count, speed, money, temperature, distance, other}	1.92
Phone	NUM{code}[1]	0.40
URL		0.17
Email		0.17
Place	LOC{country, state, city, mountain, other}	0.96
Animal	ENTY{animal}	0.00
Physical Object	ENTY{instrument, plant, body part, vehicle, food, product, substance}	0.30
Concept	ENTY{language, religion, letter, color, creative/artwork, disease/medical, currency}	0.40
Event or Activity	ENTY{event, sport, technique/method}	0.87
Other	ENTY{symbol, term, word, other} ABBR{abbreviation, expression}	0.00
Yes/No		41.33
Action Request		8.98
Rhetorical		5.23
Multiple		3.23
Non-Question		16.74

Table 1: The new dialogue taxonomy, with mappings to Li & Roth where applicable, and percentage distribution in the Enron sample

[1]Phone number is actually a subset of the NUM:code category, but it accounts for all instances in the Enron sample.

"Are you guys still thinking of maybe joining us skiing?"	Yes/No
"Did you know Moller was going to be on TV or were you just channel surfing?" "Do you stock those wheels and tires or would I have to order them?"	Multiple choice
"Will it ever end???"	Rhetorical
"Would you please handle this?" "Also, could you check for reservations at the Georgian hotel in Santa Monica?"	Action Request

Table 2: Examples of questions in dialogue-specific categories

A number of extra categories were added to account for the nature of the data, as identified by preliminary experiments. Examples of questions falling into some of the new categories are presented in Table 2.

It is important to observe that a massive 75.5% of questions in the Enron sample do not fall into any of the categories defined by Li & Roth. Assuming that this is a fair representation of the distribution across the Enron corpus (if not email as a whole) then we are clearly justified in stating that some further work will be required before question classification can be meaningfully applied to the email task.

The most common category is Yes/No, giving a "most common class" baseline of 41.3%. That is to say, a classification system which classified every question as a Yes/No question would expect to see accuracy in this region, and any results must be considered in this context.

The most common of the IR-derived categories is Description, representing 11.51% of questions overall, or 46.2% of those falling into IR categories. This compares to 26.6% reported across the equivalent categories in Li & Roth's analysis of TREC questions.

Full details of the Enron question dataset will be published in due course.

3 Performance of QA-SYS

QANUS (Ng & Kan 2010) is an open-source question answering framework which uses the Li & Roth categories in its question classification module. The framework is designed to be extensible, which makes it a good candidate for further work. However, the results presented in this section deal only with the output of the QA-SYS default question processing module as supplied with QANUS v26Jan2010. The question classification component of QA-SYS is an instance of the Stanford classifier, a supervised learning module trained on a dataset of information retrieval questions.

Ng & Kan do not report their question classification accuracy, providing figures only for the "factoid accuracy" of the end-to-end question answering system, which makes it difficult to compare their results to the present study. However Huang, Thint & Cellikyilmaz (2009) publish results for a maximum entropy classifier trained on similar IR data, reporting an encouragingly high accuracy of 89.0%.

QA-SYS question classification was used to provide an automatic classification for each of the questions extracted from the Enron dataset. In order to assess the performance of the system, the results were compared to the hand-annotated examples.

QA-SYS output agreed with human annotation in only 13.4% of cases overall – much lower than the "most common class" baseline defined above. However, this figure is artificially low as QA-SYS supplies a result in all circumstances, without any associated level of confidence. The system will therefore provide an incorrect result in cases where it does not have an appropriate category (even when faced with a nonsense string).

This may be acceptable behaviour within information retrieval, particularly for participating in competitions when there is a high expectation of the question falling into one of Li & Roth's categories, but for dialogue questions it produces a number of undesirable effects. Any competent end-to-end system would need (at a minimum) to filter out nonsense strings, and direct questions to appropriate classifiers

"Remind me when your wedding date is?"	NUM:date	DateTime
"Also, who is following up on the VA license?"	HUM:ind	Person
"What is our strategy/plan in agricultural commodities training?"	DESC:desc	Description

Table 3: Examples of questions correctly classified

Category	Recall	Precision	F-measure
Description	62.8	28.6	39.3
DateTime	53.7	28.6	37.3
Numeric	40.9	15.5	22.5
Reason	61.1	10.2	17.5
Person	65.5	6.7	12.2
Place	45.5	5.2	9.3
Event	10.0	2.9	4.6

Table 4: Recall and precision by category

based on language (therefore removing the need to attempt an intelligent classification of texts in multiple languages). Considering the proportion of questions in our sample which fell into the new categories of our extended taxonomy, the framework should also be extended to include a number of classifiers to handle these data types specifically.

We are therefore justified in considering what might happen if a pre-classifier fed to QA-SYS only those questions which it may stand some chance of categorising correctly. Including only those questions falling into categories on which QA-SYS has been trained, output agrees with human annotation in 55.0% of cases. Table 3 presents a small number of examples where the QA-SYS annotation agreed with human assessment.

It may also be instructive to consider the recall and precision on a per-category basis, as there is a strong variation between the success rates for different QA-SYS categories. Table 4 gives the figures for those classes with at least 10 examples in the current dataset, and which QA-SYS claims to address.

This shows that some categories with the highest recall (e.g. Person, Reason) suffer from low precision, but examination of the full confusion matrix shows that the incorrect categorisation is largely accounted for by the categories for which QA-SYS is not trained (particularly Yes/No questions). If reliable classifiers could be trained to filter out these question types at an earlier stage, the validity of QA-SYS results would be significantly improved.

However, there are some features of QA-SYS question classification which cannot be resolved by simply adding additional categories to the classifier framework.

Most notably, the system exhibits a high degree of case sensitivity. For example, the two strings "What do you think?" and "what do you think?" are both present in the Enron corpus. To a human eye the lack of capitalisation is unlikely to affect the meaning, but QA-SYS categorises these two sentences differently: the former as DESC:desc, the latter as ENTY:term.

A further example of case-sensitivity is found in the response of QA-SYS to questions written entirely in uppercase. Of the eleven examples in the dataset which contain only uppercase letters, all are classified as ABBR:exp. The 'uppercase' feature seems to overwhelm any other considerations (such as question word) which may be present. For instance "WHAT?" is classified as ABBR:exp, whereas "What?" and "what?" are (correctly) classified as DESC:desc.

Certain words also have a significant impact on the classification, regardless of the syntax of the question. For example, a question containing the word 'percent' is likely to be classified as NUM:perc, a question containing the word 'week' is likely to be classified as NUM:date, and a question containing the word 'state' is likely to be classifed as some subtype of LOCATION.

Other lexical effects were surprising by their absence. For instance, of 111 questions (in the entire Enron question-set) beginning "What time..." only eleven are classified as requiring the NUM:date response.

"How many kids are in the class and who is the instructor?"	NUM:count
"do you want to get together on friday or saturday and where?"	LOC:other
"How (and when) do you plan to get there?"	DESC:manner

Table 5: Examples of compound questions

Another small but important set of questions, which are barely represented in the current dataset, are compound questions. These are cases, such as the examples in Table 5, in which more than one answer is expected. In all of these examples, the category generated by QA-SYS can hardly be called incorrect, however it is not the whole story. Presently QA-SYS does not allow for multiple answer types. This is worthy of further study.

4 Future Work

The present work should be extended using a larger dataset to train additional classifiers for the answer types which are beyond the scope of IR classifiers such as QA-SYS. A larger dataset will also enable further analysis, for example to identify any common features of questions which prove particularly hard to categorise. Specific work to identify further examples in the very small categories (including a representative sample of compound questions) would also be beneficial.

The next step is to extend the QANUS framework with additional classifiers trained on Enron data, and this work should be thoroughly tested to ensure it is not over-fitted to Enron. There is a wealth of public dialogue data on the web, available from textual media such as web forums and Twitter, which may be reasonably expected to have some characteristics in common with email and which could be used for testing the classifiers.

Recent work on email has considered the task of highlighting messages within an inbox which require action (e.g Bennett & Carbonell 2005, achieving 81.7% accuracy). This is an interesting result for us as the set of actions intersects with the set of questions: some questions have the pragmatic force of an action request. It would be interesting to examine the size of this intersection.

5 References

Bennett, Paul and Carbonell, Jaime. 2005. 'Detecting Action-Items in Email' in proceedings of *SIGIR '05.*

Huang, Zhiheng, Thint, Marcus, and Celikyilmaz, Asli. 2009. 'Investigation of Question Classifier in Question Answering' in proceedings of *EMNLP '09.*

Klimt, Bryan and Yang, Yiming. 2004. 'Introducing the Enron Corpus' in proceedings of *First Conference on Email and Anti-Spam.*

Li, Xin and Roth, Dan. 2002. 'Learning Question Classifiers' in proceedings of *COLING 2002.*

Ng, Jun-Ping and Kan, Min-Yen. 2010. *QANUS: An Open-source Question-Answering Platform*, from http://www.comp.nus.edu.sg/~junping/docs/qanus.pdf

Towards a More Natural Multilingual Controlled Language Interface to OWL

Normunds Gruzitis and Guntis Barzdins
Institute of Mathematics and Computer Science, University of Latvia
normundsg@ailab.lv, guntis@latnet.lv

Abstract

The paper presents an ongoing research that aims at OWL ontology authoring and verbalization using a deterministic controlled natural language (CNL) that would be as natural and intuitive as possible. Moreover, we focus on a multilingual CNL interface to OWL by considering both highly analytical and highly synthetic languages (namely, English and Latvian). We propose a flexible two-level translation approach that is enabled by the Grammatical Framework and that has allowed us to develop a more natural, but still predictable multilingual CNL on top of the widely used Attempto Controlled English (its subset for OWL, ACE-OWL). This has also allowed us to exploit the readily available ACE parser and verbalizer not only for the modified and extended version of ACE-OWL, but also for the corresponding controlled Latvian.

1 Introduction

Several notations are widely used to make the formal OWL ontologies more intelligible for both domain experts and knowledge engineers. They can be divided in several groups: graphical notations, like UML and its profiles (Barzdins et al., 2010), controlled natural languages (CNL), like Attempto Controlled English or ACE (Kaljurand and Fuchs, 2007), and human-readable formal syntaxes, like the Manchester OWL Syntax (Horridge et al., 2006). The latter kind of notation explicitly follows the underlying formalism and therefore requires substantial training to obtain acceptable reading and writing skills. CNL, in contrast, provides the most informal and intuitive means for knowledge representation and has been successfully used in ontology authoring, where involvement of domain experts is crucial (Dimitrova et al., 2008). Graphical notations are in between and provide a complementary view, unveiling the high-level structure of the ontology in a more comprehensible way. In this paper we focus on untrained domain experts and end-users, and, thus, on CNL that has to be as natural and grammatical as possible. Moreover, we focus on multilingual ontology verbalization to facilitate ontology localization and reuse.

Note that CNL has to ensure deterministic interpretation of its statements, and bidirectional mapping to OWL, so that the CNL user could easily predict or grasp the precise meaning of the specification that is being written or read, and so that the roundtrip from OWL to CNL and back would not introduce any semantic changes in the ontology (if the user has not made changes in the verbalization). In addition to the highly restricted syntactic subset of full natural language, this is typically achieved by a small set of interpretation rules and a monosemous (domain-specific) lexicon.

The state of the art CNLs for OWL (Schwitter et al., 2008) are based on English — a highly analytical language (strict word order, simple morphology, systematic use of determiners) that facilitates the rather straightforward translation of CNL sentences into their semantic representation (axioms in description logic). Regardless of the chosen notation, English is often used also as a meta-language for naming the logical symbols (class and property names) at the ontology level.

Angelov and Ranta (2010) have recently shown that the Grammatical Framework (GF), a formalism and a resource grammar library that provide means for developing parallel grammars, is a convenient framework for rapid implementation of multilingual CNLs. Such seamless cross-translation capability allows easy reuse of the tools developed for existing CNLs — in this way we will reuse the ACE to OWL and OWL to ACE translators.

However, in the case of highly synthetic languages (like Slavic and Baltic) that have rich morphology and relatively free word order, the bidirectional translation to English (i.e., ACE or some other CNL) is not straightforward, especially if we are dealing with statements that represent not only axioms[1] but also rules. For rules (such as SWRL), anaphoric noun phrases (NP) are frequently used: in English they are marked by the definite article, while in Baltic and in most of the Slavic languages such markers are generally not explicitly used and are not encoded even in noun endings. Thus, one of the central problems during the semantically precise translation is how to distinguish between axioms and rules, and how to convey, which information is new (potential antecedents) and which is already given (anaphors).

In this paper we primarily consider Latvian — a member of the Baltic language group. In Section 2 we briefly describe its design and coverage. In Section 3 we illustrate the proposed two-level approach that is used to translate controlled Latvian to (and from) OWL via ACE as an interlingua[2]. We show that this approach allows also for flexible and independent development of an extended and/or modified (adjusted) controlled English interface at the end-user side, if compared to ACE, especially its subset for OWL (ACE-OWL). We conclude the paper with a brief discussion on the current results and future tasks.

2 Grammar

The information structure of a sentence indicates what we are talking about (the topic) and what we are saying about it (the focus) (Hajicova, 2008). In (controlled) English, changes in the information structure typically are reflected by the use of different syntactic constructions, for instance, by using the passive voice instead of the active voice. In Latvian, this is typically reflected by a different word order, for instance, by changing a subject-verb-object (SVO) sentence into OVS or SOV sentence. Thus, in languages like Latvian the word order is syntactically (rather) free, but semantically bound.

Although the topic and focus parts of a sentence, in general, are not reflected by systematic (deterministic) changes in the word order, it has been shown (Gruzitis, 2010) that, in the case of controlled Latvian, the information structure of a sentence can be systematically and reliably conveyed by relying on simplified analysis of the topic-focus articulation (TFA), i.e., on simple word order patterns: if the object comes after the verb (the neutral word order) it belongs to the focus part of the sentence (new information), but if it precedes the verb — to the topic part (given information). As the initial evaluation shows (Gruzitis et al., 2010), the "correct" word order is both intuitively satisfiable by a native speaker and enables the automatic detection of anaphoric NPs in controlled Baltic languages (Latvian and Lithuanian). The simplified TFA method can be adjusted also to controlled Slavic languages.

It should be noted that in Latvian it could be theoretically possible to impose the mandatory use of artificial determiners, by using, for example, indefinite and demonstrative pronouns, however, such "articles" would be unnatural in most cases. Lack of articles is even more apparent in Lithuanian, which, in contrast to Latvian, has no historic influence from the comparatively analytical German.

The survey by Gruzitis et al. (2010) confirmed other important aspects as well that should be addressed, in order to make controlled Latvian more natural and intuitive:

- Due to the rich morphology, there are various alternatives and certain reductions possible in the syntactic realization of a sentence, while preserving both the information structure and the abstract syntax tree (in terms of GF), e.g., making of complex attributes instead of relative clauses may lead to more concise and intelligible sentences[3].
- Explicit determiners ("articles") in certain cases are preferred: an indefinite pronoun ("a") improves the reading of a singular SVO sentence, if the object is not restricted by a relative clause, but a demonstrative pronoun ("the") helps in complex rule statements (in addition to the word order).
- Sentences in the plural are often preferred over their counterparts in the singular.

[1] In this paper we consider only TBox axioms.

[2] Note that any other CNL could be used instead of ACE. We have chosen ACE because of its easily available infrastructure (open source tools and web services) and the active developer community (see `http://attempto.ifi.uzh.ch`).

[3] Such transformations can be applied to a limited extent also in English (e.g., *"animal that eats an animal"* can be expressed as *"animal-eating animal"*).

- Limitations of the OWL expressivity (SVO triples only, no time dimension etc.) to some extent can be lessened on the surface level of the CNL (while preserving the deterministic interpretation), e.g., by using (where appropriate) non-SVO constructions, like adverbial modifiers of place instead of direct objects, and nouns (roles) instead of verbs (actions), and by using the present perfect tense instead of the simple tense (to express a past event that has present consequences).

Therefore, in addition to a grammar that generates the best possible (default) verbalization patterns (taking into account the information structure), we have developed a parallel grammar that allows for completely optional use of determiners and accepts the various syntactic alternatives and extensions[4]. We have also developed a parallel prototype grammar for controlled English that is based on the full ACE[5] with some improvements: we have extended support for the present perfect tense (e.g., by allowing phrases like *"has done something"*), and we have taken a pattern from the Sydney OWL Syntax (Schwitter et al., 2008) to provide an alternative way for expressing inverse nominalized properties (e.g., *"everything has something as a part"* instead of *"everything has-part something"* or *"for everything its part is something"*). It should be mentioned that in the highly inflective controlled Latvian both direct and inverse nominalized properties are verbalized in a more flexible and uniform way.

To achieve a full compliance with the Latvian counterpart, the controlled English grammar has to be further extended with respect to non-SVO sentences (clauses): although adverbial modifiers of place (prepositional constructions) are allowed in the full ACE (e.g., *"someone lives in something"*), there is no support for inverse use of a property in such cases, i.e., it is neither allowed to start a relative clause with the relative pronoun "where", nor to change the fixed word order (like in *"something is a place where someone lives in"*). Again, in controlled Latvian the support for the various relative clauses is ensured in a uniform way.

3 Implementation

The possible steps of our approach that can be performed during the roundtrip from CNL to OWL and vice versa are illustrated in Figure 1. `LavDefSg` is a grammar that defines the default verbalization patterns using Latvian singular sentences, `LavDefPl` is its counterpart for plural sentences, and `LavVar` is an extended combination of both, extensively allowing for free variations (at both the syntactic and lexical level). `LavVar` is used for robust, still predictable parsing (in the ontology authoring direction), while one of the default grammars (depending on the choice of the end-user) — for paraphrasing `LavVar` sentences and for verbalizing existing ontologies. `EngDef` implements the ACE-based English grammar, and `EngVar` provides few lexical and syntactic alternatives. Finally, `AceOwl` implements the chosen interlingua, i.e., accepts/generates sentences that are generated/accepted by the ACE-OWL verbalizer/parser. All these grammars are implemented in GF and are related by a common abstract syntax. Note that translation (reduction) to/from `AceOwl` is an internal step of which the end-user is not aware.

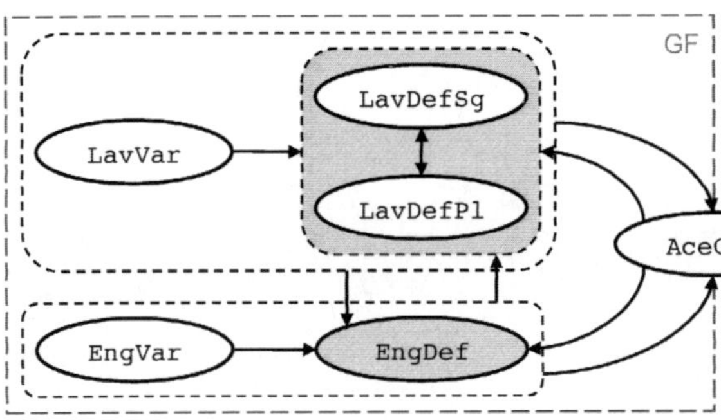

Figure 1: The overall data flow of the automatic translation process among controlled Latvian, English, and OWL. Existing tools are exploited for the transition to/from OWL, using ACE-OWL as an interchange format (covered by the `AceOwl` grammar). Other transitions are ensured by the parallel GF grammars.

[4]An online demo is available at `http://eksperimenti.ailab.lv/cnl/`. Support for plural sentences is being developed.

[5]The full ACE supports prepositional phrases, adjectives and other constructions that are not allowed in ACE-OWL.

Table 1: A sample wildlife ontology, automatically verbalized in controlled English (by `EngDef`) and Latvian (by `LavDefSg`). Underlined are properties that are expressed by nouns (roles) instead of verbs (explicit predicates).

1	Everything that *eats* something is **an** *animal*.	Tas, kas kaut ko *ēd*, ir *dzīvnieks*.
2	Every *carnivore* is **an** *animal* that *eats* **an** *animal*. Every *animal* that *eats* **an** *animal* is **a** *carnivore*.	Ikviens *plēsējs* ir *dzīvnieks*, kas *ēd* **kādu** *dzīvnieku*. Ikviens *dzīvnieks*, kas *ēd* **kādu** *dzīvnieku* ir *plēsējs*.
3	Every *herbivore* is **an** *animal* that *eats* nothing but things that are **a** *plant* or that are **a** *part* of nothing but *plants*.	Ikviens *zālēdājs* ir *dzīvnieks*, kas *ēd* tikai kaut ko, kas ir *augs* vai kas ir tikai *auga daļa*.
4	Every *giraffe* is **a** *herbivore*.	Ikviena *žirafe* ir *zālēdājs*.
5	Everything that is *eaten* by **a** *giraffe* is **a** *leaf*.	Tas, ko *ēd* **kāda** *žirafe*, ir *lapa*.
6	Everything that has **a** *leaf* as **a** *part* is **a** *branch*.	Tas, kura *daļa* ir **kāda** *lapa*, ir *zars*.
7	Every *tasty plant* is **a** *nourishment* of **a** *carnivore*.	Ikviens *garšīgs augs* ir **kāda** *plēsēja barība*.
8	No *animal* is **a** *plant*.	Neviens *dzīvnieks* nav *augs*.
9	If X *eats* Y then Y is **a** *nourishment* of X.	Ja X-s *ēd* Y-u, tad Y-s ir X-a *barība*.

For a demonstration we use a sample African wildlife ontology that is verbalized in Table 1.

During the translation from Table 1 to ACE-OWL (Table 2), all non-SVO statements are reduced to artificial SVO statements (e.g., *"lives in something"* to *"lives-in something"*, *"part of something"* to *"part-of something"*), and all terms are normalized into fixed forms that are conveyed as is to the ontology[6]. The result, in general, is ungrammatical (from the linguistic perspective), but we do not try to make it more grammatical where possible (e.g., the past participle form could be used in the 5th statement) — we use it only as a technical interchange format that normally is not visible to the end-user. However, it is a good illustration that explicitly unveils the nature and limitations of OWL.

Note that certain conversions are done at the end-user level (while paraphrasing from `Var` to `Def`) and are further reflected in OWL. For instance, the present perfect tense can be converted to the simple tense (e.g., *"has done something"* to *"does something"*) or vice versa, if such alternatives are listed in the domain lexicon (individually for each language and property).

Table 2: An automatically generated ACE-OWL text, translated from Table 1 (by the `AceOwl` grammar), or verbalized from the original OWL ontology (by the ACE verbalizer). The prefixes that indicate the POS categories, although accepted by the ACE parser, are used here only for the sake of clarity. The semantic interpretation is acquired by the ACE parser and is given in parallel (in the Manchester notation).

1	Everything that **v:eats** something is an n:animal.	`ObjectProperty: eats Domain: animal`
2	Every n:carnivore is an n:animal that **v:eats** an n:animal. Every n:animal that **v:eats** an n:animal is a n:carnivore.	`Class: carnivore EquivalentTo: animal and (eats some animal)`
3	Every n:herbivore is an n:animal that **v:eats** nothing but things that are a n:plant or that **v:part-of** nothing but n:plant.	`Class: herbivore SubClassOf: animal and (eats only (plant or (part-of only plant)))`
4	Every n:giraffe is a n:herbivore.	`Class: giraffe SubClassOf: herbivore`
5	Everything that is **v:eats** by a n:giraffe is a n:leaf.	`Class: inverse (eats) some giraffe SubClassOf: leaf`
6	Everything that is **v:part-of** by a n:leaf is a n:branch.	`Class: inverse (part-of) some leaf SubClassOf: branch`
7	Every n:tasty-plant **v:nourishment-of** a n:carnivore.	`Class: tasty-plant SubClassOf: nourishment-of some carnivore`
8	No n:animal is a n:plant.	`Class: animal DisjointWith: plant`
9	If X **v:eats** Y then Y **v:nourishment-of** X.	`ObjectProperty: eats InverseOf: nourishment-of`

[6]This is achieved by passing an auto-generated user lexicon to the ACE parser, where all wordforms of each lexical entry are equivalent to that used for the logical symbol.

4 Discussion

The two-level translation approach has allowed us to develop a rather sophisticated multilingual CNL on top of the rather restricted ACE-OWL (in terms of naturalness). Of course, ACE-OWL itself can be developed to be equally natural, but the benefit of our approach is that it allows for more flexible, rapid[7] and independent extensions and adjustments to what users consider the most natural verbalization. The proposed approach enables not only a multilingual, but also a multi-dialect interface to OWL: different CNLs can be mixed together or used in parallel, and the interlingua can be relatively easily changed. It should be reminded that our goal is to ensure a predictable interpretation, therefore we could change the interlingua to CPL-Lite, for instance, but not to CPL, which is non-deterministic (Clark et al., 2010). Also note that GF not only enables the precise cross-grammar translation[8], but also facilitates the application of more flexible and linguistically less restrictive naming conventions at the OWL level.

One might ask why we use an interlingua at all, rather than proceed by translation to and from OWL directly in GF (by providing yet another concrete grammar for the Functional-Style Syntax or some other formal notation of OWL). Indeed, verbalization of existing ontologies could be done in this way, but a problem arises in the reverse direction — form CNL to OWL: the current implementation of GF does not provide support for dealing with anaphors[9]. Thus, by solving the interpretation issues via an interlingua, we get the ontology verbalization functionality for free.

One might also argue that the dependence on a handcrafted domain lexicon is a significant disadvantage. This is the price for flexibility, multilinguality, naturalness and precision. Although it would be possible to generate the English lexicon from a linguistically motivated ontology, the problem is how to acquire the precise translation equivalents. In the case of ontology authoring, common word lexicons could be reused, but, again, the alignment issue arises and specific multi-word units are often used.

In this paper we have considered only terminological (TBox) axioms and rules. It would be interesting to see to what extent the deterministic TFA method can be adjusted for assertional (ABox) statements. However, for populating an ontology with facts (individuals), some other kind of an interface (e.g., GUI forms or tables) could be more appropriate.

References

Angelov, K. and A. Ranta (2010). Implementing controlled languages in GF. In N. E. Fuchs (Ed.), *Controlled Natural Language*, Volume 5972 of *LNAI*, pp. 82–101. Springer.

Barzdins, J., G. Barzdins, K. Cerans, R. Liepins, and A. Sprogis (2010). OWLGrEd: a UML style graphical notation and editor for OWL 2. In *7th International OWLED Workshop*, Volume 614. CEUR.

Clark, P., W. R. Murray, P. Harrison, and J. Thompson (2010). Naturalness vs. predictability: A key debate in controlled languages. In N. E. Fuchs (Ed.), *Controlled Natural Language*, Volume 5972 of *LNAI*, pp. 65–81.

Dimitrova, V., R. Denaux, G. Hart, C. Dolbear, I. Holt, and A. G. Cohn (2008). Involving domain experts in authoring OWL ontologies. In *7th International Conference on the Semantic Web*, Volume 5318 of *LNCS*.

Gruzitis, N. (2010). Word order based analysis of given and new information in controlled synthetic languages. In P. Buitelaar, P. Cimiano, and E. Montiel-Ponsoda (Eds.), *1st International Workshop on the Multilingual Semantic Web*, Volume 571, pp. 29–34. CEUR.

Gruzitis, N., G. Nespore, and B. Saulite (2010). Verbalizing ontologies in controlled Baltic languages. In I. Skadina and A. Vasiljevs (Eds.), *4th International Conference on Human Language Technologies — The Baltic Perspective*, Volume 219 of *Frontiers in Artificial Intelligence and Applications*, pp. 187–194. IOS Press.

Hajicova, E. (2008). What we are talking about and what we are saying about it. In A. Gelbukh (Ed.), *Computational Linguistics and Intelligent Text Processing*, Volume 4919 of *LNCS*, pp. 241–262. Springer.

Horridge, M., N. Drummond, J. Goodwin, A. Rector, R. Stevens, and H. Wang (2006). The Manchester OWL syntax. In *2nd International Workshop on OWL: Experiences and Directions (OWLED)*.

Kaljurand, K. and N. E. Fuchs (2007). Verbalizing OWL in Attempto Controlled English. In *3rd International Workshop on OWL: Experiences and Directions (OWLED)*.

Schwitter, R., K. Kaljurand, A. Cregan, C. Dolbear, and G. Hart (2008). A comparison of three controlled natural languages for OWL 1.1. In *4th International OWLED Workshop*, Volume 496. CEUR.

[7] Especially if the GF resource library is used instead of developing all the concrete grammars from scratch.

[8] In few cases, e.g., in ambiguous coordination of relative clauses, the ACE interpretation rules have to be applied afterwards.

[9] Anaphors (incl. explicit variables) may appear not only in rules, but also in statements that define property axioms.

BALLGAME: A Corpus for Computational Semantics

Ezra Keshet, Terry Szymanski, and Stephen Tyndall

University of Michigan
E-mail: {ekeshet,tdszyman,styndall}@umich.edu

Abstract

In this paper, we describe the Baseball Announcers' Language Linked with General Annotation of Meaningful Events (BALLGAME) project – a text corpus for research in computional semantics. We collected pitch-by-pitch event data for a sample of baseball games and used this data to build an annotated corpus composed of transcripts of radio broadcasts of these games. Our annotation links text from the broadcast to events in a formal representation of the semantics of the baseball game. We describe our corpus model, the annotation tool used to create the corpus, and conclude by discussing applications of this corpus in semantics research and natural language processing.

1 Introduction

The use of large annotated corpora and treebanks has led to many fruitful research programs in computational linguistics. At the time of this writing, Marcus et al. (1993), which introduces the University of Pennsylvania Treebank,[1] has been cited by over 3000 subsequent papers.[2] Such treebanks are invaluable for the training and testing of large-scale syntactic parsers and numerous other applications in the field of Computational Syntax.

Unfortunately for the field of Computational Semantics, there are few corresponding annotated corpora or treebanks representing the formalized meaning of natural language sentences, mainly because there is very little agreement on what such a representation of meaning would look like for arbitrary text. To overcome this obstacle, several recent studies have turned to the arena of sports, pairing natural language with game statistics in several domains, including RoboCup soccer (Liang et al., 2009; Chen et al., 2010), soccer (Theune and Klabbers, 1998; Saggion et al., 2003), American football (Barzilay and Lapata, 2005; Liang et al., 2009), and baseball (Fleischman, 2007).

We have adapted this approach in the creation of a semantics-oriented corpus, using the domain of major-league baseball. The information state of a baseball game can be represented with a small number of variables, such as who is on which base, who is batting, who is playing each position, and the current score and inning. There is even a standard way of representing updates to this information state.[3] This makes baseball a logical stepping stone to a fuller representation of the world. We also chose baseball for this corpus because of the volume of data available, in the form of both natural language descriptions of events and language-independent game statistics. Most of professional baseball's thousands of games per year have at least two television broadcasts (home and away) and at least two radio broadcasts, often in multiple languages. The scorecard statistics for each game are also kept and made available on the internet, along with complete ordered lists of in-game events. These resources, coupled with a high-coverage syntactic parser, allow one to link natural language utterances with representations of their syntax and semantics.

[1] http://www.cis.upenn.edu/~treebank/
[2] http://scholar.google.com/scholar?cites=7124559111460341353
[3] See example scorecards at http://swingleydev.com/baseball/tutorial.php.

2 Corpus Design

The basic design of the BALLGAME corpus is a mapping between *spans* of text and *events* in a baseball game. The raw text comes from the transcribed speech of announcers broadcasting the radio play-by-play of a professional baseball game. This text is chunked into spans, and these spans are then labeled according to the following scheme:

- *Event* is the label given to a span that describes an event in our representation of the game for the first time. (Examples of events are simultaneous descriptions of pitches, plays, and stolen bases.)
- *Recap* is the label given to a span that correlates with prior events in the game. (Examples of recaps are when the announcer states the current score or strike count, or summarizes the current batter's previous at-bats.)
- *Banter* is the label given to a span that does not relate to an event in the game. The majority of spans are labeled as banter. (Examples of banters are "color" commentary, any discussion of the day's news, other baseball games, advertisements, etc.)

The term "span" has no linguistic significance, although spans often turn out to be sentences or clauses. Each span from the text that is labeled as an event is linked to one or more events in the model of the game as shown in Figure 1. Not every event is linked to a span of text, since some events go unmentioned by the announcers.

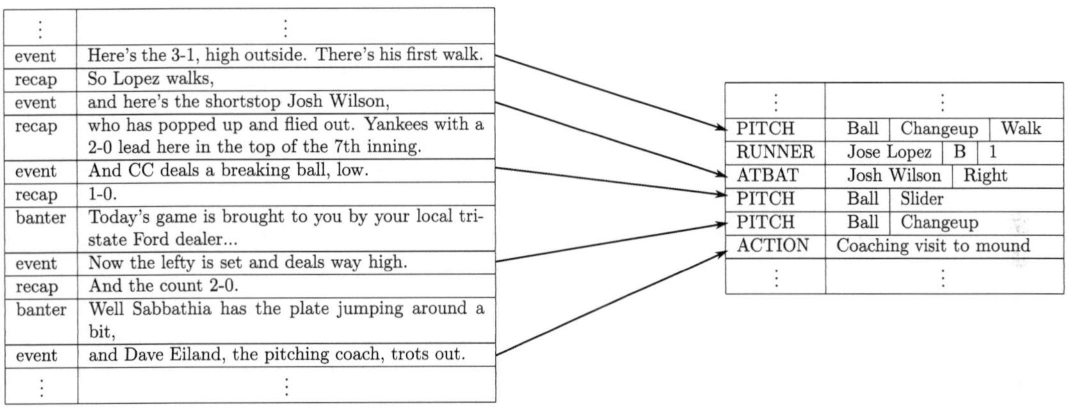

Figure 1: Illustration of a portion of the corpus: event spans of the text (on the left) are associated with events from a standardized description of the ballgame (on the right).

We model each game as a time-ordered sequence of baseball events, designed so that the state of the game at any given point, while not explicitly represented, can be computed given the events from the start of the game up to that point. We use a simple event model inspired by the comprehensive scoring system developed by Retrosheet,[4] but modified to match our needs and data resources. For example, most baseball scoring systems are at-bat-based, but this system is too coarse-grained for our purposes. Therefore, we use a system in which the fundamental event type is the pitch. Every baseball action from the start of the pitcher's motion until the end of the play (a hit or an out) is categorized as a PITCH event. Several other event types exist to accommodate other plays (e.g. balks, pick-offs), non-play actions (e.g. coaching visits to the mound, rain delays), and procedural activities (e.g. ejections, player substitutions).

In addition to a category, each event has multiple attribute values. The possible attributes depend on the category. A PITCH event, for example, has attributes describing the type, speed, and location of the pitch as well as whether it results in a ball, strike, play, etc. If the result is a play, then there are additional

[4] `http://www.retrosheet.org`

attributes describing the fielders involved in the defensive play. On the other hand, a PICKOFF event has different attributes, describing which base the ball was thrown to, whether it resulted in an out, etc.

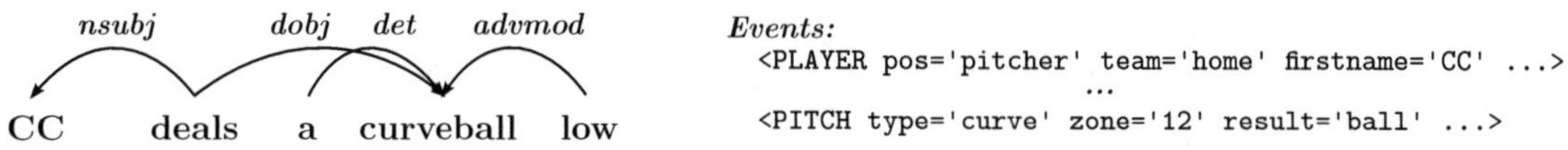

Figure 2: Example of a dependency parsed transcript line and corresponding events.

In the future, we plan to add syntactic parse information for each span such as that generated using the Stanford Parser (De Marneffe et al., 2006). Using an explicit syntactic representation, like the one illustrated in figure 2, it will be possible to label more detailed correlations between the text and the meaning. Even without explicit annotation, statistical learning methods could be used to infer, e.g., that the word "curveball" in the sentence in figure 2 correlates with the semantic attribute `type='curve'`, or that the word "CC" correlates with a specific PLAYER entity. While the annotations in the corpus exist only at the sentence or phrase level, this type of further processing could push the annotation down to the word level, facilitating the study of lexical semantics and semantic transformations of syntactic structures.

3 Corpus Creation

Student transcribers use a custom-created transcription and annotation tool, illustrated in Figure 3, to add data to the corpus. They listen to and transcribe the radio broadcast, while simultaneously chunking the text into spans as described above. Each span is labeled *banter, event*, or *recap*, and, if the span describes an *event*, the student selects the corresponding event(s) from the event column.

Annotators have access to a style guide to encourage consistency. This guide sets out two main principles: first, the transcript of an inning, taken as a whole, should be read like a well-edited, consistently formatted document; and second, all and only the events explicitly mentioned by the radio announcers should be linked to events in the game model.

Although spans are displayed as separate lines in the transcription tool, in order to maintain this first style principle, we ask the students to imagine that all spans of the transcript are pasted together in sequence to form a normal transcript of the game. Thus, they are asked not to put ellipses or dashes at the end of spans nor to capitalize the beginnings of spans that do not begin sentences. Also included in this principle is a standardized formatting style for baseball statistics, such as strike counts, scores, and batting averages, so that, for instance, "the count is two and oh" is transcribed "the count is 2-0".

The second principle set out in the annotation style guide is meant to ensure that the events linked to a particular utterance are as close as possible to the "meaning" of that utterance. Integral to this process is consistently distinguishing the categories of *event, recap* and *banter*. Since recap and banter spans do not relate to events in the model, it is important to keep them separate from the event spans to get the most accurate data. Even given the descriptions of these categories from section 2, ambiguous cases still do arise on occasion. For instance, one common difficulty is distinguishing *event* from *recap* when an announcer discusses a play immediately after it happens. In such cases, in keeping with our annotation principle, we use the rule of thumb that only new information is annotated as *event*; old information is *recap*. We also adopt the rule that only game events that are explicitly stated by the announcer should be linked to spans; for example, if the announcer merely states the name of the batter (e.g. "Cust takes a first-pitch strike") in the process of describing the first pitch of his at-bat, then this should not reference the ATBAT event that indicates the arrival of a new batter at the plate. On the other hand, an explicit mention (e.g. "Here's Cust.") should.

In the final steps of the annotation process, each transcript is reviewed and corrected by a second annotator to reduce errors and further promote consistency across annotators.

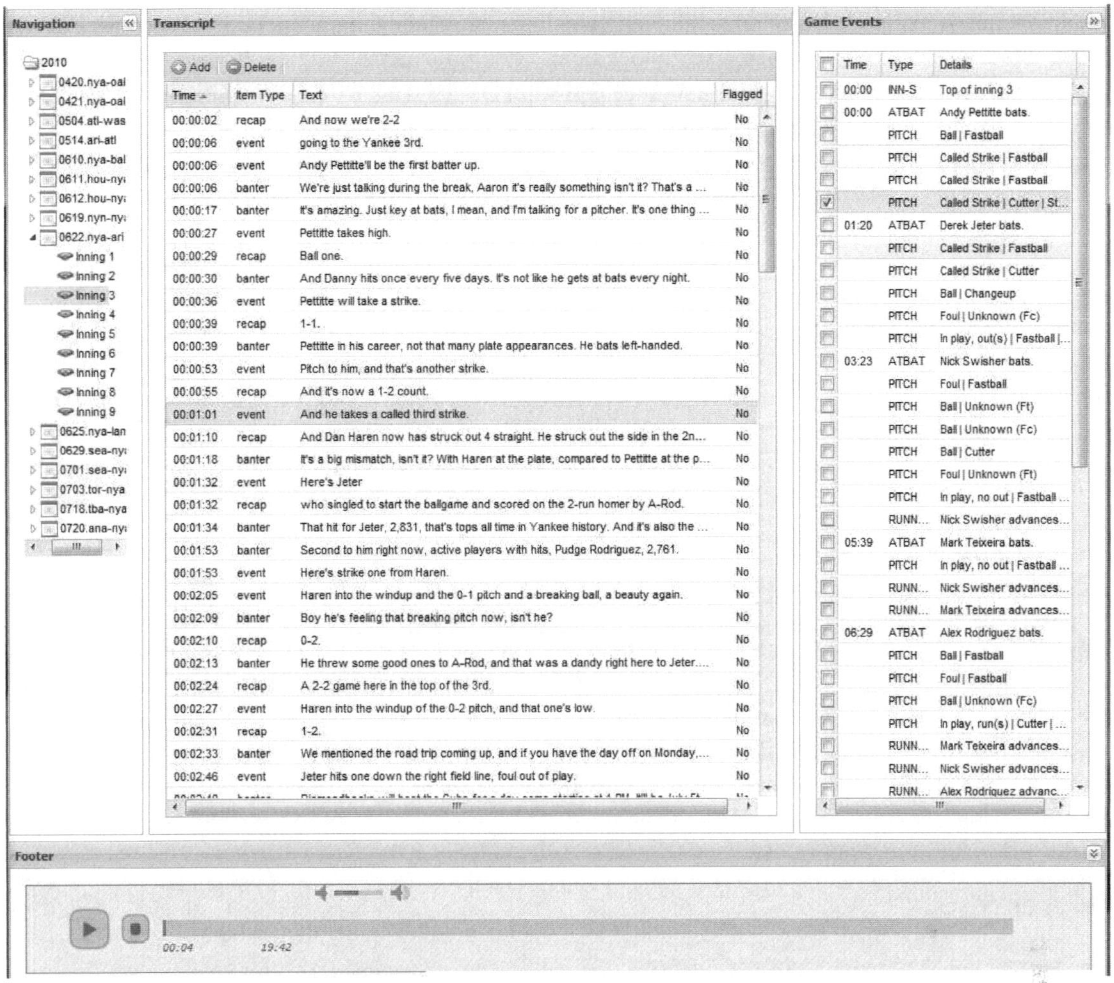

Figure 3: Screen shot of online annotation tool.

4 Potential Applications

Since this corpus links natural language utterances with complete semantic representations which fully describe the state of the baseball game, it has a number of applications for research in computational semantics. While the domain is limited, and the "meaning" of a baseball game does not approach the complexity of the possible "meanings" in the real world, nevertheless this corpus should be a useful resource both for developing NLP tools and for studying theories of language and meaning.

One application domain for this type of data is natural language generation and understanding, and much prior work connecting sports commentaries to statistics or events falls into this domain. One related generation task is to generate textual summaries of complete games: Theune and Klabbers (1998) generated spoken Dutch summaries of soccer matches, and Barzilay and Lapata (2005) investigate the relationship between textual NFL recaps and the box scores of the games. More similar to our project is the RoboCup announcer system of Chen et al. (2010), which produces play-by-play commentary (in English and Korean) of simulated RoboCup soccer matches. Our corpus could certainly be used to train systems that predict the event structure given the text of the commentary, or vice-versa.

In the domain of information extraction, our corpus could be used to train systems to infer representations of meaning from texts. In many domains, the same word or phrase can appear in a variety of different contexts with different ramifications. For example, the phrase "home run" in a baseball commentary may mean that a home run has just occurred, or it may refer to a home run in a previous game, or a player's home-run totals for the season, etc.. Fleischman (2007), using a collection of video broadcasts of baseball games, combines natural language processing with artificial vision technology to resolve when events like home runs actually occur, in order to facilitate retrieval of relevant video clips. Using our corpus, one could design a system to perform the same task based purely on the textual data, perhaps to extend this same task to radio broadcasts as well as television broadcasts. Given the corpus labels of *event*, *recap*, and *banter*, a classifier could be built to identify only the *event* regions, and an extraction system could identify the relevant semantic features (e.g. player names, types of events).

While generation and understanding are tasks most applicable to this corpus, we hope researchers will find additional innovative uses of the corpus. For example, given that we plan to incorporate a number of baseball games with commentary both in English and Spanish, there is a potential connection to machine translation, particularly approaches that utilize comparable (rather than parallel) corpora. In our corpus, the comparable sections (i.e. the *event*-labeled regions) are explicitly aligned with one another, which is not usually the case in comparable corpora. Also, the corpus could prove useful for research on formal semantics, despite the fact the meaning representation is not particularly rich compared to modern semantic theory, and the jargon and speech styles are very specific to the domain of baseball sportscasts.

5 Conclusion

We have presented an overview of the BALLGAME annotated corpus for research in computational semantics, as well as a description of our procedure for annotation and the specialized annotation tool we developed for this purpose. To date, the corpus contains sixteen three- to four-hour-long major league baseball radio broadcasts, transcribed and annotated as described above. This represents 237,100 transcribed words in 13,382 spans (6,511 *banter*; 3,994 *event*; 2,877 *recap*). Work is ongoing, and the goal is to complete fifty games by the end of the year. We believe this corpus, by pairing natural language text with formalized representations of meaning, will prove useful for many types of NLP research.

References

Barzilay, R. and M. Lapata (2005). Collective content selection for concept-to-text generation. In *Proceedings of HLT/EMNLP*, pp. 331–338.

Chen, D., J. Kim, and R. Mooney (2010). Training a multilingual sportscaster: Using perceptual context to learn language. *Journal of Artificial Intelligence Research 37*(1), 397–436.

De Marneffe, M., B. MacCartney, and C. Manning (2006). Generating typed dependency parses from phrase structure parses. In *LREC 2006*.

Fleischman, M. (2007). Situated models of meaning for sports video retrieval. In *NAACL-HLT 2007*, pp. 37–40.

Liang, P., M. Jordan, and D. Klein (2009). Learning semantic correspondences with less supervision. In *Proceedings of the Joint Conference of the 47th Annual Meeting of the ACL and the 4th International Joint Conference on Natural Language Processing of the AFNLP: Volume 1*, pp. 91–99.

Marcus, M., B. Santorini, and M. Marcinkiewicz (1993). Building a large annotated corpus of English: The Penn Treebank. *Computational linguistics 19*(2), 313–330.

Saggion, H., J. Kuper, H. Cunningham, T. Declerck, P. Wittenburg, M. Puts, E. Hoenkamp, F. de Jong, and Y. Wilks (2003). Event-coreference across multiple, multi-lingual sources in the Mumis project. In *Proceedings of the tenth conference on European chapter of the Association for Computational Linguistics: Volume 2*, pp. 239–242.

Theune, M. and E. Klabbers (1998). GoalGetter: Generation of spoken soccer reports. In *Proceedings of the Ninth International Workshop on Natural Language Generation*, pp. 292–295.

An Ontology Based Architecture for Translation

Leonardo Lesmo, Alessandro Mazzei and Daniele P. Radicioni
Dipartimento di Informatica, Università degli Studi di Torino
{lesmo,mazzei,radicion}@di.unito.it

Abstract

In this paper we present some features of an architecture for the translation (Italian – Italian Sign Language) that performs syntactic analysis, semantic interpretation and generation. Such architecture relies on an ontology that has been used to encode the domain of weather forecasts as well as information on language as part of the world knowledge. We present some general issues of the ontological semantic interpretation and discuss the analysis of ordinal numbers.

1 Introduction

In this paper we describe some features of a system designed to translate from Italian into Italian Sign Language (henceforth LIS). The system is being developed within the ATLAS project.[1] This architecture applies a *hard* computational linguistic approach: *knowledge-based restricted interlingua* (Hutchins and Somer, 1992). We perform a deep linguistic processing in each phase of the translation, i.e (1) syntactic analysis of the Italian input sentence, (2) semantic interpretation and (3) LIS generation.[2] The main motivation to adopt this ambitious architecture is that Italian and LIS are very different languages. Moreover, LIS is a poorly studied language, so no large corpus is available and statistical techniques are hardly conceivable. We reduce our ambitions by restricting ourselves to the weather forecasts application domain.

In this paper we describe some major issues of the semantic interpretation and illustrate a case study on ordinal numbers. Our semantic interpretation is based on a syntactic analysis that is a dependency tree (Hudson, 1984; Lesmo, 2007). Each word in the sentence is associated with a node of the syntactic tree. Nodes are linked via labeled arcs that specify the syntactic role of the dependents with respect to their head (the parent node). A key point in semantic interpretation is that the syntax-semantics interface used in the analysis is based on an ontology. The knowledge in the ontology concerns an application domain, i.e. weather forecasts, as well as more general information about the world: the latter information is used to compute the sentence meaning. Indeed, the sentence meaning consists of a complex fragment of the ontology: predicate-argument structures and semantic roles are contained in this fragment and could be extracted by translating this fragment into usual First Order Logic predicates.[3]

The idea to use the ontological paradigm to represent world knowledge as well as sentence meaning is similar to the work by Nirenburg and Raskin (2004) and Buitelaar et al. (2009), but in contrast to these approaches (1) we use a syntactic parser to account for syntactic analysis; and (2) we use a recursive semantic interpretation function similar to Cimiano (2009).

2 The Ontology

The ontological knowledge base is a formal (partial) description of the domain of application. It is formal, since its primitives are formally defined, and it is partial, since it does not include all axioms that provide details about the relationships between the involved concepts. The top level of the domain ontology is illustrated in Fig. 1.[4] The classes most relevant to weather forecasts are *££meteo-status-situation*,

[1] `http://www.atlas.polito.it/`

[2] LIS, as all the signed languages do not have a *natural* writing form. In order to apply linguistic tools designed for written languages, in our project we developed "AEW-LIS", an *artificial* written form for LIS.

[3] However, similar to other approach (among others Bunt et al. (2007); White (2006)), our ontological meaning representation is totally unscoped.

[4] Some conventions have been adopted for ontology names: concepts (classes) have a ££prefix; instances have a £prefix; and relations and relation instances have a & prefix.

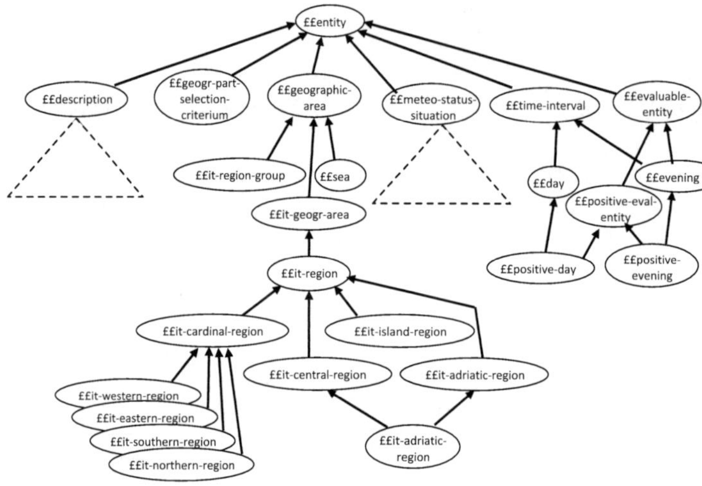

Figure 1: The top ontology used for the weather forecast domain. Dashed triangles represent collapsed regions of the hierarchy.

££geographic-area, *££description*, *££geographic-part-selection-criterium*.
££meteo-status-situation It is the most relevant class in the present setting, since it refers to the possible weather situations, thus providing a starting point –in principle– to every weather forecast. It may concern the sea status, a generic weather status (either stable or not) or possible atmospheric events such as snow, rain or clouds.
££geographic-area* and *££time-interval Any weather situation holds in a specific place; in particular, the relevant places are geographic areas. A *££geographic-area* can be an Italian region, a group of regions, a sea, or may be identified by specifying a cardinal direction (North, South, . . .). Yet, any weather situation holds in a specific temporal interval. Such time interval could last one or more days or a part of a day. Expression as "in the evening" are interpreted anaphorically, i.e. on the basis of current context: if the context is referring to "today", then it is interpreted as "today evening", for "tomorrow" as "tomorrow evening", etc..
££description The actual situation and its description are kept separated. For instance, if *today* is October 28, then "today" is a *££deictic-description* of a particular instance (or *occurrence*) of a *££day*. "April 28, 2010" is another description (absolute) of the same instance. Particular relevance have the deictic descriptions since most temporal descriptions (*today*, *tomorrow*, but also the weekday names, as *Monday*, *Tuesday*, . . .) are deictic in nature.
££geogr-part-selection-criterium In descriptions, a particular instance (or group of instances) can be identified by a general class term (e.g. *area*) and a descriptor (e.g. *northern*). This concept refers to the parts of the reality that can act as descriptors. For instance, the *cardinal direction* can be such a criterium for geographic parts, while a *date* is not.

The last relevant portion of the ontology concerns *relations*. Although the ontology has no axioms, class concepts are connected through relevant relations. In turn, relations constitute the basic steps to form paths (more later on). All relations in the ontology are binary, so that the representation of relations of arity greater than 2 requires that they be reified.

3 Semantic Interpretation

One chief assumption in our work is that words meaning can be expressed in terms of ontology nodes, and the meaning of the sentence is a complex path on the ontology that we call *ontological restriction*. We define the *meaning interpretation function* $\mathcal{M}_{\mathcal{O}}$, that computes the the ontological restriction of a sentence starting from the its dependency analysis and on the basis of an ontology $\mathcal{O}$.

Given a sentence S and the corresponding syntactic analysis expressed as a dependency tree $depTree(S)$, the meaning of S is computed by applying the meaning interpretation function to the root of the tree, that is $\mathcal{M}_{\mathcal{O}}(root(depTree(S)))$. In procedural terms, the meaning for a sentence is computed in two steps: (*i*) we annotate each word of the input sentence with the corresponding lexical meaning; (*ii*) we build the

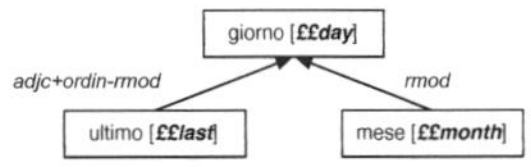

Figure 2: The dependency analysis of *ultimo giorno del mese* (*last day of the month*) enriched with lexical meaning.

actual ontological representation in a quasi-compositional way, by merging paths found in the ontology in a single representation which is a subgraph of the ontology itself. These two steps can be formalized as a meaning interpretation function $\mathcal{M}$ defined as:

$$\mathcal{M}_{\mathcal{O}}(n) := \begin{cases} \mathcal{LM}_{\mathcal{O}}(n) & \text{if } n \text{ is a leaf} \\ \dot{\cup}_{i=1}^{k}(\mathcal{CP}_{\mathcal{O}}(\mathcal{LM}_{\mathcal{O}}(n), \mathcal{M}_{\mathcal{O}}(d_i))) & \text{otherwise} \end{cases}$$

where n is the node of a dependency tree and $d_1, d_2, \ldots, d_k$ are its dependents. $\mathcal{LM}_{\mathcal{O}}(w)$ is a function that extracts the lexical meaning of a word w accessing the dictionary: that is, a class or an individual on the ontology $\mathcal{O}$. $\mathcal{CP}_{\mathcal{O}}(y, z)$ is a function that returns the shortest path on $\mathcal{O}$ that connects y to z. The search for connections relies on the rationale that the shortest path between any two ontology nodes represents the stronger semantic connection between them. In most cases the distance between two concepts is the number of the nodes among them, but in some cases a number of constraints needs to be satisfied too (see the example on ordinal construction). Finally, the operator $\dot{\cup}$ is used to denote a particular merge operator, similar to Cimiano (2009). As a general strategy, shortest paths are composed with the union operation, but each $\mathcal{CP}_{\mathcal{O}}(y, z)$ conveys a peculiar set of ontological constraints: the merge operator takes all such constraints to build the overall complex ontological representation. In particular, a number of semantic clashes can arise from the union operation: we use a number of heuristics to resolve these clashes. For sake of simplicity (and space) in this definition we do not describe the heuristics used in the ambiguity resolution. However, three distinct types of ambiguity exist: (1) lexical ambiguity, i.e. a word can have more than one lexical meaning; (2) shortest path ambiguity, i.e. two nodes can be connected by two equal-length paths; (3) merge ambiguity, i.e. two fragments of ontology can be merged in different manners. Whilst lexical ambiguity has not a great impact due to the limited domain (and could be addressed by standard word sense disambiguation techniques), handling shortest path and merge ambiguities needs heuristics expressed as constraints that rely on general world knowledge.

A particular case of ontological constraints in merge ambiguity is present in the interpretation of ordinal numbers, so further details on the merge operator can be found in Section 4.

4 A case study: the ordinal numbers

In order to translate from Italian into LIS, we need to cope with a number of semantic phenomena appearing in the particular domain chosen as pilot study, i.e. weather forecast. One of the most frequent constructions are ordinal numbers. Consider the simple phrase *l'ultimo giorno del mese* (*the last day of the month*). The (simplified) dependency structure corresponding to this phrase is depicted in Fig. 2: the head word *giorno* (*day*) has two modifying dependents, *ultimo* (*last*) and *mese* (*month*). Since the interpretation relies heavily on the access to the ontology, we first describe the portion of the ontology used for the interpretation and then we illustrate the application of the function $\mathcal{M}$ to the given example.

The relevant fragment of the ontology is organized as shown in Fig. 3, that has been split in two parts. The upper part –labeled *TEMPORAL PARTS*– describes the reified *££part-of* relation and its temporally specialized subclasses. The lower part –labeled *ORDINALS*– is constituted by some classes that account just for ordinal numbers. In the *TEMPORAL PARTS* region of the Fig. we find the *££temporal-part-of* (reified) sub-relation, which, in turn, subsumes *££day-month-part-of*. This specifies that days are parts of months, so that *day of the month* can be interpreted as *the day which is part of the month*. The *££part-of relation* has two roles: we use the term *role* to refer to the binary relation associated with a participant in a reified relation. These roles are "value-restricted" as *&day-in-daymonth* and *&month-in-daymonth* respectively, for what concerns *££day-month-part-of*. The most relevant class in the ORDINALS part of Fig. 3 is the class *££ordinal-description*. It is the *domain* of three roles, *1*) *&ord-described-item*, *2*) *&references-sequence* and *3*) *&ordinal-desc-selector*. The range of the first relation *&ord-described-item* is the item whose position in the sequence is specified by the ordinal, that is a *££sequenceable-entity*. The range of the second relation *&reference-sequence* is the sequence inside which the position makes

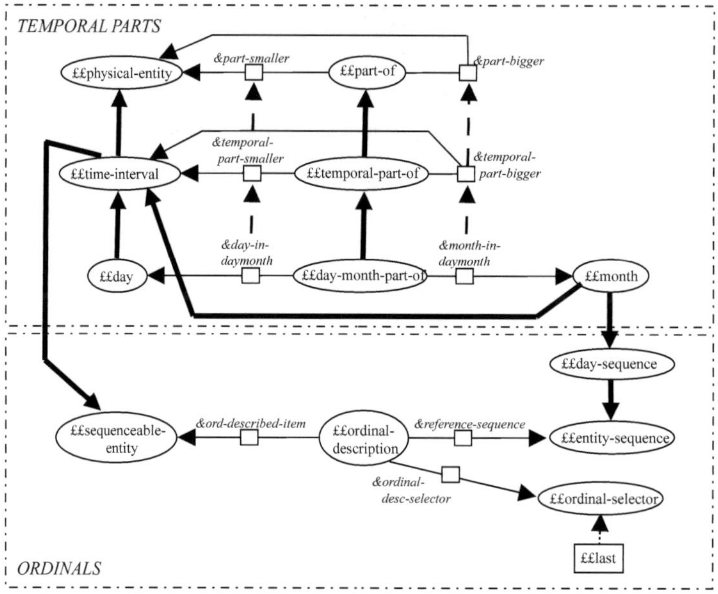

Figure 3: The fragment of the ontology accounting for ordinals.

sense, that is an *££entity-sequence*. The range of the third relation *&ordinal-desc-selector* is item that specifies the position, that is a *££ordinal-selector*. In the example, *£last* is an instance of *££ordinal-selector*. Of course, any (true) ordinal (first, second, thirtythird) can fill that role. The two portions of the ontology are connected by two arcs. The first arc specifies that a *££time-interval* is a subclass of *££sequenceable-entity* (so that one can say *the fourth minute*, *the first year*, and so on). The second arc specifies that *££month* is subclass of *££day-sequence*, which in turn is subclass of *££entity-sequence*. As a consequence it can play the role (can be the range) of the *&reference-sequence*.

We now describe how the meaning interpretation function is applied on the considered example. It consists of three steps: *1.* we compute the connection path between the concepts *££day* and *£last*; *2.* we compute the connection path between *££day* and *££month*; *3.* we merge the connection paths previously computed. In details:

1. By computing $\mathcal{CP}$(*££day*, *£last*) we obtain the connection path in Fig 4-a. Note that this ontological restriction contains the concept *££ordinal-selector*.

2. By computing $\mathcal{CP}$(*££day*, *££month*) we obtain the connection path in Fig 4-b. In this case the shortest path is not actually the "shortest" one, i.e. the presence of the preposition *del* (*of*) constraints the value returned by $\mathcal{CP}$. Moreover, this ontological restriction contains the concept *££day-month-part-of*, which is a sub-concept of *££part-of*.

3. The last step consists of the application of the meaning composition function to $\mathcal{CP}$(*££day*, *£last*) and $\mathcal{CP}$(*££day*, *££month*). The *££ordinal-description* concept is detected in the first ontological restriction; moreover *££day* is recognized as (subclass of) a possible filler for *££ordinal-description*. At this point we need establishing how *££day* fits as the smaller part of a *&part-of* relation. We scan the remaining ontological restriction(s) looking for a bigger part involved in a *&part-of* relation or in any of its sub-relations. The resulting representation (Fig. 4-c) is built by assuming that the larger entity (here *££month*, since *&month-in-daymonth* restricts *&part-bigger*) is the reference sequence for the ordering. So, the direct *££day-month-part-of* of the second ontological restriction is replaced by a path passing through *££ordinal-description*. In such final ontological restriction *££day* is the *&ord-described-item* and *££month* is the *&reference-sequence*.

5 Conclusions and future work

In this paper we illustrated the analysis component of a knowledge-based restricted interlingua architecture for the translation from Italian into LIS. The structure produced by the semantic interpretation of the

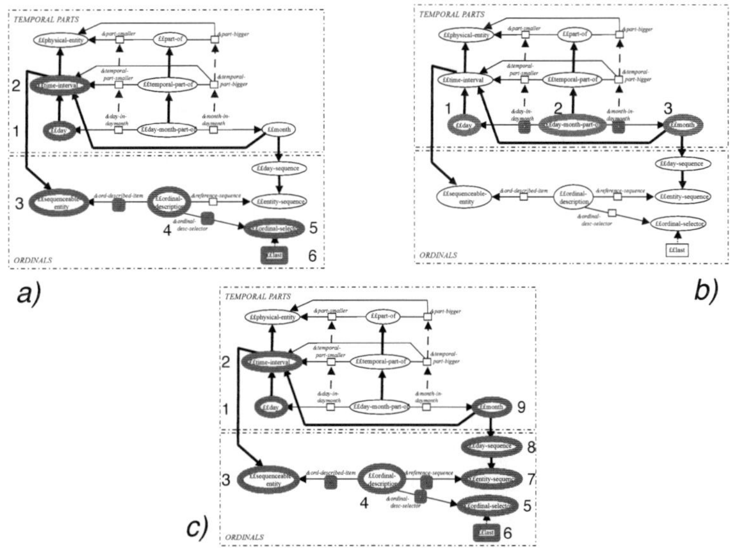

Figure 4: The ontology fragment computed by the semantic interpretation function.

source sentence is a complex ontology fragment obtained by the application of the function $\mathcal{M}_{\mathcal{O}}$. As case study we showed how this function uses the ontology $\mathcal{O}$ to interpret the ordinal numbers. The decision to use an ontology fragment as semantic representation is motivated by theoretical assumptions and has some practical appeals. From a theoretical point of view, we represent language semantics as part of the world knowledge in ontologies (Buitelaar et al., 2009; Galanis and Androutsopoulos, 2007; Nirenburg and Raskin, 2004). From an applicative point of view the ontology restriction produced by the semantic interpretation is used (in logical form) as input of the OpenCCG tool, in the generation component of the translation architecture (White, 2006). As a consequence, similar to Nirenburg and Raskin (2004), we use ontologies in all components of our architecture (cf. Galanis and Androutsopoulos (2007); Sun and Mellish (2007)).

We have currently implemented the main features of the $\mathcal{M}_{\mathcal{O}}$ and the ontology is being developed. Our working hypothesis is that the weather forecast sub-language is characterized by plain and short sentences and this guarantees scalability of our approach. In the next future we plan to broaden the coverage of linguistic phenomena, so to unify ordinals, superlative and comparative adjective analyses.[5]

References

Buitelaar, P., P. Cimiano, P. Haase, and M. Sintek (2009). Towards linguistically grounded ontologies. In *Proceedings of the 6th Annual European Semantic Web Conference (ESWC)*.

Bunt, H., R. M. M. Dzikovska, M. Swift, and J. Allen (2007). *Customizing Meaning: Building Domain-Specific Semantic Representations From A Generic Lexicon*, Volume 83. Springer.

Cimiano, P. (2009). Flexible semantic composition with DUDES. In *Proceedings of the 8th International Conference on Computational Semantics (IWCS'09)*.

Galanis, D. and I. Androutsopoulos (2007). Generating multilingual descriptions from linguistically annotated OWL ontologies: the naturalOWL system. In *In Proceedings of the 11th European Workshop on Natural Language Generation, Schloss Dagstuhl*.

Hudson, R. (1984). *Word Grammar*. Oxford and New York: Basil Blackwell.

Hutchins, W. and H. L. Somer (1992). *An Introduction to Machine Translation*. London: Academic Press.

Lesmo, L. (2007, June). The Rule-Based Parser of the NLP Group of the University of Torino. *Intelligenza Artificiale* 2(4), 46–47.

Nirenburg, S. and V. Raskin (2004). *Ontological Semantics*. The MIT Press.

Sun, X. and C. Mellish (2007). An experiment on "free generation" from single RDF triples. In *Proceedings of ENLG '07*, pp. 105–108. Association for Computational Linguistics.

White, M. (2006). Efficient realization of coordinate structures in combinatory categorial grammar. *Research on Language and Computation 2006*(4(1)), 39—75.

[5]**Acknowledgement:** This work is partly supported from the ATLAS project, that is co-funded by Regione Piemonte within the "Converging Technologies - CIPE 2007" framework (Research Sector: Cognitive Science and ICT).

Corpus-based approaches to processing the scope of negation cues: an evaluation of the state of the art

Roser Morante, Sarah Schrauwen and Walter Daelemans
CLiPS-CL University of Antwerp
{Roser.Morante,Walter.Daelemans}@ua.ac.be
Sarah.Schrauwen@student.ua.ac.be

Abstract

In this paper we summarize existing work on the recently introduced task of processing the scope of negation and modality cues; we analyse the scope model that existing systems can process, which is mainly the model reflected in the annotations of the biomedical corpus on which the systems have been trained; and we point out aspects of the scope finding task that would be different based on observations from a corpus from a different domain and nature.

1 Introduction

Negation and modality are complex aspects of the semantics of language. *Modality* was introduced by Jespersen (1924), who distinguishes between two categories of mood that later have been named as *deontic modality* and *epistemic modality*. Lyons (1996) describes *epistemic modality* as concerned with matters of knowledge and belief, "the speaker's opinion or attitude towards the proposition that the sentence expresses or the situation that the proposition describes". Palmer (1986) defines it as expressing the speaker's degree of commitment to the truth of a proposition. *Polarity* is a discrete category that can take two values: positive and negative. Positive polarity is used by speakers to put information as a fact in the world, whereas negative polarity is used to put information as a counterfact, a fact that does not hold in the world. Negation is a linguistic resource used to express negative polarity.

Although the treatment of these topics in computational linguistics is relatively new compared to other areas like machine translation, parsing or semantic role labeling, incorporating information about modality and polarity has been shown to be useful for a number of applications, such as biomedical text processing (Di Marco and Mercer, 2005; Chapman et al., 2001), opinion mining and sentiment analysis (Wilson et al., 2005), recognizing textual entailment (Snow et al., 2006), and automatic style checking (Ganter and Strube, 2009). In general, the treatment of modality and negation is very relevant for computational applications that process factuality (Saurí, 2008). For example, information extraction systems may be confronted with fragments of texts like the one presented in (1)[1], which contains two negation cues[2] (*not, un-*) and one speculation cue (*likely*) that affect the factuality of the events being expressed:

(1) The atovaquone/proguanil combination has **not** been widely used yet in West Africa so it is **unlikely** that the patient was initially infected with an atovaquone-resistant strain.

So far two main tasks have been addressed within the natural language processing (NLP) community: (i) the detection of various forms of polarity and modality and (ii) the identification of the scope of negation and modality cues. In this paper we reflect on the achievements of the recently introduced scope finding task (Section 2), we analyse the scope model that existing systems can process (Section 3), and we point out aspects of the scope finding task that would be different based on observations from a corpus from a different domain (Section 4).

[1]Example to be found in http://www.biomedcentral.com/content/pdf/1475-2875-1-1.pdf [last consulted 8-10-2010]
[2]A *cue* is the lexical marker that expresses negation or modality.

2 Achievements in scope processing

In the last years, several corpora have been annotated with information related to modality and polarity, which have made it possible to develop machine learning systems. Annotation has been performed at different levels: word (Hassan and Radev, 2010), expression (Baker et al., 2010; Toprak et al., 2010), sentence (Medlock and Briscoe, 2007), event (Saurí and Pustejovsky, 2009), discourse relation (Prasad et al., 2006), text (Amancio et al., 2010), and scope of negation and modality cues (Vincze et al., 2008). Thanks to the existence of the BioScope corpus, the scope processing task was recently introduced. BioScope is a freely available resource, that consists of three parts of medical and biological texts annotated with negation and hedge cues and their scope.

The scope processing task is concerned with determining at a sentence level which tokens are affected by modality and negation cues. It was first modelled as a classification problem by Morante et al. (2008). Later on several systems have been trained on the same corpus (Morante and Daelemans, 2009; Özgür and Radev, 2009; Agarwal and Yu, 2010; Li et al., 2010). Councill et al. (2010) process scopes of negation cues in a different corpus of product reviews, but this corpus is not publicly available.

The CoNLL Shared Task 2010 on *Learning to detect hedges and their scope in natural language text* (Farkas et al., 2010) boosted research on the topic. It consisted of identifying sentences containing uncertainty and recognizing speculative text spans inside sentences. Participating systems would, for example, produce the tagged sentence in (2)[3], in which *propose, suggest* and *possible* are identified as hedge cues and their scope is marked in agreement with the gold standard.

(2) We $[_{propose}$ **propose** that the existence of the alternative alignments, specific to distinct groups of genes, $[_{suggest}$ **suggests** presence of different synchronization modes between the two organisms and $[_{possible}$ **possible** functional decoupling of particular physiological gene networks in the course of evolution $_{possible}]_{suggest}]_{propose}]$.

The best system (Morante et al., 2010) for hedge scope finding in the CoNLL ST 2010 scores 57.32 F-score. Although the results are lower than the scores obtained in other well established tasks (i.e. semantic role labeling, dependency parsing), we can say that setting the first step towards automatic scope processing is an achievement. However, it can be useful to revise the characteristics of the scopes that the systems learn to process, not from a technical machine learning perspective, but from the linguistic annotation perspective, since the annotation model that systems learn determines the quality of the system output and the knowledge that can be inferred from the scopes.

3 Scope model based on the BioScope corpus

Most existing scope labelers have been trained on the BioScope corpus. Thus, the model of scope that these systems learn is determined by the characteristics of scope as they have been annotated in BioScope. Additionally, the systems have been trained for a specific domain, biomedical texts, but it might be the case that negation and speculation cues require different annotation specifications for texts from other domains. In this section we analyze the characteristics of the scope model in the BioScope corpus based on the guidelines (BioScope, 2008) and we propose some changes for further annotation work that we are carrying out. We mark in italics the statements from the BioScope guidelines and we comment on them.

– *The scope is always a continuous sequence of tokens and the cue is included in the scope.* Although most scopes in the corpus are continuous, examples such as (3), in which sentence adverbs do not belong to the scope, suggest that the scopes should be annotated as discontinuous if necessary:

(3) $[_{not}$ The number of glucocorticoid receptors per cell (Ro) and the binding affinity (Kd) for dexamethasone were$_{not}]$, however, $[_{not}$**not** significantly different $_{not}]$

– *Scopes can be determined on the basis of syntax and they extend to the biggest unit possible. If necessary, complements and adjuncts are included in the scope.* It would be useful to furhter specify how different syntactic constructions (coordination, subordination, etc.) should be annotated.

[3]In the examples below, cues will be marked in bold and their scope between brackets.

– *The scope of negative auxiliaries, adjectives and adverbs usually starts with the cue and ends at the end of the phrase, clause or sentence.* In (4) the scope extends to the right of *not*. In our view, the scope should include the subject because the subject contributes to the meaning of the event being negated. If, as Lyons (1996) suggest, we paraphrase the negative connective in (4) with the formula *it is not the case that*, we obtain (5), where the subject is under the scope of the formula.

(4) Once again, the Disorder module does $[_{not}$ **not** contribute positively to the prediction $_{not}]$

(5) Once again, it is not the case that the Disorder module does contribute positively to the prediction

– *Passive voice changes the scope of the cue because the object of the active construction is the subject of the passive construction.* According to the BioScope guidelines, the scope of *not* in 6 and 7 would be annotated differently. As indicated above, we consider that the subject of the active sentence is also under the scope of the negation, so in our view both sentences should be analyzed equally.

(6) $[_{not}$ Levels of RNA coding for the receptor were **not** modulated by exposure to high levels of ligand $_{not}]$

(7) Exposure to high levels of ligand does $[_{not}$ **not** modulate levels of RNA coding for the receptor $_{not}]$

– *Negative conjunctions generally scope over the syntactic unit whose members it coordinates. However, if the complex negative keyword occurs within the subject of the sentence, its scope is extended to the whole sentence.* (8) is the example provided in the guidelines, but paraphrasing the sentence with the *it is not the case* formula as in (9) shows that the subject should also be included in the scope.

(8) In contrast, sodium salicylate (1 mM) inhibited $[_{neither-nor}$**neither** adhesion **nor** expression of these adhesion molecules $_{neither-nor}]$

(9) In contrast, it is not the case that sodium salicylate (1 mM) inhibits either adhesion or expression of these adhesion molecules

– *Prepositions scope over the following (noun) phrase.* (10) is the example provided in the guidelines, where *without* scopes over a noun phrase. Nevertheless, *without* can be followed by a verb phrase, as in (11). In this case, one could argue that the logical subject of the verb should be included in the scope of the preposition, since the negation can be paraphrased as in (12).

(10) $[_{without}$ Mildly hyperinflated lungs **without** focal opacity $_{without}]$

(11) $[_{without}$ CD28 costimulation $_{without}]$ augments IL-2 secretion of activated lamina propria T cells by increasing mRNA stability $[_{without}$ **without** enhancing IL-2 gene transactivation $_{without}]$

(12) It is not the case that CD28 costimulation enhances IL-2 gene transactivation

Possible improvements in the BioScope annotation model are pointed out in Vincze (2010), namely the treatment of elliptic constructions, and discontinuous and intersecting scopes. An additional improvement would be to annotate affixal negation. We consider that (13) is equivalent to (14) and should receive the same analysis, since they can be paraphrased as in (15):

(13) Actually, $[_{un}$ tRNASec and tRNAPyl have **un**usual secondary structures 515 $_{un}]$

(14) Actually, $[_{not}$ tRNASec and tRNAPyl do **not** have usual secondary structures 515 $_{not}]$

(15) Actually, it is not the case that tRNASec and tRNAPyl have usual secondary structures 515

4 Annotating scopes in a different domain

The existing scope labelers have been trained on biomedical texts. However, it is reasonable to expect that texts from other domains contain different phenomena that would affect the systems performance. We are currently analysing negations and their scopes in a complete different corpus, *The Hound of the Baskervilles* (HB) by Conan Doyle. This corpus has been annotated with coreference and semantic roles for the *SemEval Task Linking Events and Their Participants in Discourse* (Ruppenhofer et al., 2010), and will be further annotated with negation and modality cues. Phenomena in this corpus show that whereas the scope of cues can be determined in a similar way as it is determined in biomedical texts, identifying negation cues in certain contexts, which is the first part of the scope finding task, is not only a matter of lexical lookup:

– Not all negative affixes are negation cues. For example the affix *un-* in *unspoken* does not negate its root morpheme. *Unspoken* does not mean 'not spoken', but 'understood without the need for words'. Consequently, in (16) *unspoken* is not a negation cue.

(16) All my unspoken instincts, my vague suspicions, suddenly took shape and centred upon the naturalist

– Fixed expressions like *could not help* in the sentence below do not negate the modified event.

(17) Why about Sir Henry in particular? I could not help asking

– Negation words in tag questions do not have a negation function, but a pragmatic function, since the speaker seeks confirmation from the addressee. A similar case are negation words in dialogue checks like *don't you think* in (19).

(18) You have been inside the house, have you not, Watson?

(19) Don't you think, Watson, that you are away from your charge rather long?

– Negation words in exclamative particles do not have a negation function. In (20), *don't tell me* does not express a negated event. This is a multiword construction used to express surprise.

(20) "Don't tell me that it is our friend Sir Henry!"

– Some modality cues, such as *no doubt*, contain false negation cues. In (21) *no doubt* is a fixed expression that expresses certainty, no event is negated. It is an expression that acts at the discourse level conveying information about the attitude of the speaker towards his statement.

(21) Partly it came no doubt from his own masterful nature, which loved to dominate and surprise those who were around him

– The context influences the effect of the negation cue. The volitive verb *wish* in (22) and the conditional construction in (23) cancel the negative effect of *not*.

(22) Your mission to-day has justified itself, and yet I could almost wish that you had not left his side

(23) In fact, if you had not gone to-day it is exceedingly probable that I should have gone to-morrow

5 Conclusions and future work

In this paper we have briefly presented the achievements in processing the scope of negation and modality cues. There are currently several systems that can process scopes in biomedical texts, however there is a lack of annotated resources, since there is only one publicly available corpus. We have also pointed out that the quality of the systems output depends not only on the technical aspects of the systems, but also on the linguistic model contained in the annotations. Based on annotation work on a literary corpus, we have pointed out some difficulties that existing systems could face in detecting cues.

We are currently annotating texts by Conan Doyle with negation cues and their scopes. For defining the guidelines we take the model of the BioScope corpus as a starting point and we include modifications based on the observations made above. The annotated corpus and the guidelines will be publicly available.

Apart from annotating more data, further work will focus on computing the factuality of statements based on the scopes of negation and modality cues and other contextual features, and studying the interaction between negation and modality.

Acknowledgements

This study was made possible through financial support from the University of Antwerp (GOA project BIOGRAPH). We would like to thank four anonymous reviewers for their suggestions.

References

Agarwal, S. and H. Yu (2010). Detecting hedge cues and their scope in biomedical literature. *Journal of Biomedical Informatics 710.016/j.jbi.2010.08.003*.

Amancio, D. R., R. Fabbri, O. N. Oliveira Jr., M. Nunes, and L. Costa (2010, July). Distinguishing between positive and negative opinions with complex network features. In *Proc. of TextGraphs-5 - 2010 Workshop on Graph-based Methods for Natural Language Processing*, Uppsala, Sweden, pp. 83–87. ACL.

Baker, K., M. Bloodgood, B. Dorr, N. Filardo, L. Levin, and C. Piatko (2010). A modality lexicon and its use in automatic tagging. In *Proceedings of the Seventh conference on International Language Resources and Evaluation (LREC'10)*, Valetta, Malta, pp. 1402–1407. European Language Resources Association (ELRA).

BioScope (2008). Annotation guidelines. http://www.inf.u-szeged.hu/rgai/project/nlp/bioscope/Annotation guidelines2.1.pdf.

Chapman, W., W. Bridewell, P. Hanbury, G. Cooper, and B. Buchanan (2001). A simple algorithm for identifying negated findings and diseases in discharge summaries. *J Biomed Inform 34*, 301–310.

Councill, I., R. McDonald, and L. Velikovich (2010, July). What's great and what's not: learning to classify the scope of negation for improved sentiment analysis. In *Proc. of the Workshop on Negation and Speculation in Natural Language Processing*, Uppsala, Sweden, pp. 51–59. University of Antwerp.

Di Marco, C. and R. Mercer (2005). *Computing attitude and affect in text: Theory and applications*, Chapter Hedging in scientific articles as a means of classifying citations. Dordrecht: Springer-Verlag.

Farkas, R., V. Vincze, G. Szarvas, G. Móra, and J. Csirik (Eds.) (2010, July). *Proc. of the Fourteenth Conference on Computational Natural Language Learning*. Uppsala, Sweden: ACL.

Ganter, V. and M. Strube (2009). Finding hedges by chasing weasels: Hedge detection using wikipedia tags and shallow linguistic features. In *Proc. of the ACL-IJCNLP 2009 Conference Short Papers*, Suntec, Singapore, pp. 173–176.

Hassan, A. and D. Radev (2010, July). Identifying text polarity using random walks. In *Proc. of the 48th Annual Meeting of the ACL*, Uppsala, Sweden, pp. 395–403. ACL.

Jespersen, O. (1924). *The philosophy of grammar*. London: Allen and Unwin.

Li, J., Q. Zhu, and G. Zhou (2010). A unified framework for scope learning via simplified shallow semantic parsing. In *Proc. of EMNLP 2010*.

Lyons, J. (1996). *Semantics*. Cambridge: CUP.

Medlock, B. and T. Briscoe (2007). Weakly supervised learning for hedge classification in scientific literature. In *Proc. of ACL 2007*, pp. 992–999.

Morante, R. and W. Daelemans (2009). Learning the scope of hedge cues in biomedical texts. In *Proc. of BioNLP 2009*, Boulder, Colorado, pp. 28–36.

Morante, R., A. Liekens, and W. Daelemans (2008). Learning the scope of negation in biomedical texts. In *Proc. of the EMNLP 2008*, Honolulu, Hawaii, pp. 715–724.

Morante, R., V. Van Asch, and W. Daelemans (2010, July). Memory-based resolution of in-sentence scopes of hedge cues. In *Proc. of the Fourteenth Conference on Computational Natural Language Learning*, Uppsala, Sweden, pp. 40–47. ACL.

Özgür, A. and D. Radev (2009). Detecting speculations and their scopes in scientific text. In *Proc. of EMNLP 2009*, Singapore, pp. 1398–1407.

Palmer, F. (1986). *Mood and modality*. Cambridge, UK: CUP.

Prasad, R., N. Dinesh, A. Lee, A. Joshi, and B. Webber (2006). Annotating attribution in the penn discourse treebank. In *SST '06: Proc. of the Workshop on Sentiment and Subjectivity in Text*, Morristown, NJ, USA, pp. 31–38. ACL.

Ruppenhofer, J., C. Sporleder, R. Morante, C. Baker, and M. Palmer (2010, July). Semeval-2010 task 10: Linking events and their participants in discourse. In *Proc. of the 5th International Workshop on Semantic Evaluation*, Uppsala, Sweden, pp. 45–50. ACL.

Saurí, R. (2008). *A factuality profiler for eventualities in text*. Ph. D. thesis, Waltham, MA, USA.

Saurí, R. and J. Pustejovsky (2009). FactBank: A corpus annotated with event factuality. *Language Resources and Evaluation 43*(3), 227–268.

Snow, R., L. Vanderwende, and A. Menezes (2006). Effectively using syntax for recognizing false entailment. In *Proc. of HLT NAACL*, Morristown, NJ, USA, pp. 33–40. ACL.

Toprak, C., N. Jakob, and I. Gurevych (2010, July). Sentence and expression level annotation of opinions in user-generated discourse. In *Proc. of the 48th Annual Meeting of the ACL*, Uppsala, Sweden, pp. 575–584. ACL.

Vincze, V. (2010, July). Speculation and negation annotation in natural language texts: what the case of bioscope might (not) reveal. In *Proc. of the Workshop on Negation and Speculation in Natural Language Processing*, Uppsala, Sweden, pp. 28–31. University of Antwerp.

Vincze, V., G. Szarvas, R. Farkas, G. Móra, and J. Csirik (2008). The BioScope corpus: biomedical texts annotated for uncertainty, negation and their scopes. *BMC Bioinformatics 9*((Suppl 11)), S9.

Wilson, T., P. Hoffmann, S. Somasundaran, J. Kessler, J. Wiebe, Y. Choi, C. Cardie, E. Riloff, and S. Patwardhan (2005). Opinionfinder: a system for subjectivity analysis. In *Proc. of HLT/EMNLP on Interactive Demonstrations*, Morristown, NJ, USA, pp. 34–35. ACL.

Classifying Arabic Verbs Using Sibling Classes

Jaouad Mousser
University Of Konstanz
Department of Linguistics
Jaouad.Mousser@uni-konstanz.de

Abstract

In the effort of building a verb lexicon classifying the most used verbs in Arabic and providing information about their syntax and semantics (Mousser, 2010), the problem of classes over-generation arises because of the overt morphology of Arabic, which codes not only agreement and inflection relations but also semantic information related to thematic arity or other semantic information like "intensity", "pretension", etc. The hierarchical structure of verb classes and the inheritance relation between their subparts expels derived verbs from the main class, although they share most of its properties. In this article we present a way to adapt the verb class approach to a language with a productive (verb) morphology by introducing sibling classes.

1 Introduction

Class based approach to lexical semantics such as presented in Levin (1993) provides a straightforward way of describing a large number of verbs in a compact and generalized way. The main assumption is the correlation between the syntactic behaviour of verbs as reflected in diathesis alternations and their semantic properties. Verbs which participate in the same set of diathesis alternations are assumed to share the same meaning facets. Verbs like *abate*, *acidify*, *dry*, *crystallize*, etc. share a meaning component and are grouped into a class (change-of-state), since they participate in the *causative/incoative alternation*, the *middle alternation*, the *instrument subject alternation* and the *resultative alternation* (Levin, 1993). Class based lexica have turned out to be usefull lexical resources such as the English VerbNet (Kipper Schuler, 2005), which provides information about thematic roles, syntactic and semantic structure of 5879 English verbs. Trying to use the same approach to classify verbs of a morphologically rich language like Arabic, the researcher is faced with difficulties because many alternations require morphological operations to express meaning aspects, especially those related to thematic roles.

(1) **Causative/Incoative Alternation in Arabic**

a. *naśśafa* *saliymun* *ālmalābisa.*
dry-*CAUS-PRF* Salim-*SUBJ-NOM* *DEF*-cloth-*PL-OBJ-ACC.*
'Salim dried the clothes.'

b. *naśafati* *ālmalābisu.*
dry-*PRF-PL* *DEF*-cloth-*PL-SUBJ-NOM*
'The colthes dried.'

In example (1) the causative/incoative alternation is realized through an overt morphological change on the head of the sentence (reduplication of the second root consonant in (1a)), in such a way that the verb changes to a new entry, which according to the hierarchical organisation of the class and especially to the inheritance relation between its subparts, cannot longer be kept into the original class. Transporting the new verb entry into a new class risks to loose its connection to the original class, which is an undesired effect, since it does not necessarily reflect the natural organisation of the lexicon of Arabic.

2 Arabic VerbNet and Class Structure

Arabic VerbNet[1] is a large coverage verb lexicon exploiting Levin's classes (Levin, 1993) and the basic development procedure of Kipper Schuler (2005). The current version has 202 classes populating 4707 verbs and 834 frames. Every class is a hierarchical structure providing syntactic and semantic information about verbs and percolating them to subclasses. In the top level of each class there are verb entries represented as tuples. Each tuple contains the verb itself, its root form, the deverbal form and the participle. At the same level thematic roles and their restrictions are encoded. The important information about the class resides in the frames reflecting alternations where the verbs can appear. Every frame is represented as an example sentence, a syntactic structure and a semantic structure containing semantic predicates and their arguments and temporal information in a way similar to Moens and Steedman (1988). Every class can have subclasses for cases where members deviate from the prototypical verb in some non central points. A subclass recursively reflects the same structure as the main class and can (therefore) itself have subclasses. A subclass inherits all properties of the main class and is placed in such a way that the members in the top level are closed for the information it adds. This fact hinders putting derived verbs participating in alternations into the main class or in one of the subclasses.

3 Sibling Classes

Introducing sibling classes is a way to resolve the problem arising from the discrepancy between two derivationally related morphological verb forms which participate in the same set of alternations and therefore share the same semantic meaning. Tables 1 and 2 show two sibling classes and their alternations sets. The incoative alternation introduces a morphological change in the verbs. This fact blocks the derived verbs from entering in any inheritance relation to the base verbs according to the hierarchical structure of the class they belong to. Consequently, a sibling class (Table 2) is created to populate the verbs resulting from alternations requiring morphological changes.

4 Automatic Extension of Arabic VerbNet via Sibling Classes

4.1 Morphological Verb Analyser

In order to generate derived verb forms a Java based morphological analyser was implemented as part of a system in order to generating sibling classes automatically (Sibling class generator SCG). This provides an analyse of the morphological composition of the input verbs. The program is based on regular expressions and identifies the following features:

- *Verb root*: This corresponds to an abstract form of 2–4 consonants carrying a basic semantic meaning of the verb. Thus, *ktb* is the abstract root of the verb *kataba* 'to write' but also of other derivationally related words such as *Iinkataba* 'INC-write', *takaAtaba*, 'RECIP-write' 'to correspond'.
- *Verb pattern*: This corresponds to the verb pattern in the classical Arabic grammar and is represented by a canonical verb form *faEala*[2] where the letters *f*, *E* and *l* correspond respectively to the first, the second and the third root consonant of the input verb. Thus, the pattern of a verb such as *Iinokataba* will be *IinofaEala*, where *f*, *E* and *l* correspond to *k*, *t*, *b* which are the root consonants of the verb.

Table 3 shows the produced morphological analysis of the verbs *kataba* 'to write', *Iinokataba* 'INC-write' and *takaAtaba* 'to correspond'. The extracted features are then used in combination with semantic information of verb classes to generate morpho-semantic derivational forms of verbs and later semantically derived verb classes (sibling classes) as explained in the next sections.

4.2 Identifying Expandable Verb Classes

The input of SCG are the basic verb classes produced in the first stadium of the lexicon building (Mousser, 2010). In order to define which classes are good candidates to be expanded according to

[1] `http://ling.uni-konstanz.de/pages/home/mousser/files/Arabic_VerbNet.php`

[2] Pattern are transliterated using Buckwalter's style. All other Arabic examples are transliterated using Lagally

Table 1: The *change of state* class in Arabic. The causative use.

Class: Change of State			
Members: *ʿaṣrana* 'modernize', *ḫaṣḫaṣa* 'privatize', *ʿawolama* 'globalize', *ʿarraba* 'arabize', etc.			
Roles and Restrictions: Agent [+int_control] Patient Instrument			
Descriptions	**Examples**	**Syntax**	**Semantics**
Basic Intransitive	*naśśafa saliym malābisahu.* (Salim dried his clothes)	V Agent Patient	*cause(Agent, E), state(result(E), Endstate, Patient)*
NP-PP	*naśśafa saliym malaābisahu biālbuḫaā-r.* (Salim dried his clothes with the vapour)	V Agent Patient {bi} Instrument	*cause(Agent, E), state(result(E), Endstate, Patient), use(during(E), Agent, Instrument)*
Instrument Subject	*naśśafa ālbuḫaāru ālmalābisa.* (The vapour dried the clothes.)	V Instrument Patient	*use(during(E), ?Agent, Instrument), state(result(E), Endstate, Patient)*
Subclass			

Table 2: The *change of state* sibling class in Arabic. The incoative use.

Sibling Class: Change of State			
Members: *taʿaṣrana* 'INC-modernize', *taḫaṣḫaṣa* 'INC-privatize', *taʿawolama* 'INC-globalize', *taʿarraba* 'INC-arabize', etc.			
Roles and Restrictions: Agent [+int_control] Patient Instrument			
Descriptions	**Examples**	**Syntax**	**Semantics**
V NP.patient	*naśafati ālmalābisahu.* (The clothes dried)	V Patient	*state(result(E), Endstate, Patient)*
PP	*naśafati ālmalābisahu biālbuḫaār.* (The clothes dried with the vapour.)	V Patient Instrument	*use(during(E), ?Agent, Instrument), state(result(E), Endstate, Patient)*
Subclass			

causativity criteria, thematic role information and semantic predicates of class frames are detected. Classes of verbs with the thematic role *agent* and compositional semantics containing the causative predicate *CAUSE* are selected as in the case of *change-of-state* classes. Additionally, inherently uncausative verb classes involving a change of state are identified according to whether they possess a *patient* theme occupying the subject position and accordingly whether their compositional semantics include the change of state predicate *STATE*.

4.3 Generating Sibling Classes

Generating sibling classes requires generating the appropriate morphological verb forms, new lists of thematic roles and new frames with new syntactic descriptions and new predicate semantics reflecting the derived meaning of the verbs (See Tables 1 and 2).

4.3.1 Generating New Verb Forms

Verbs of the new sibling classes are generated from morphological forms of the base verbs using the following information:

a. The semantic morphological operation required for the input class (causativization, reciprocalization or decausativization).

b. The morphological properties of the input verbs such as root, pattern and segmental material.

c. Rewrite rules defining for each input verb pattern the appropriate derivative form to express the target semantic meaning.

The generation of derived verbs reveals itself to be the reverse of the morphological analysis, as it consists of replacing the consonants *f*, *E* and *l* of the relevant output pattern with the root consonants of the input verb. Thus, the *change-of-state* verb *faḥḥama* 'to carbonize' with the root *fḥm* and the pattern faEāla will produce the derived verb *tafaḥḥama* 'INC-carbonize' according to the decausativization rule 2 in the Table 4 and by replacing the output pattern consonants *f*, *E* and *l* respectively with the root consonants *f*, *ḥ* and *m*.

Table 3: Morphological information

Verb	Root	Pattern	Segments
kataba	ktb	faEala	_a_a_a
Iinokataba	ktb	IinofaEala	Iino_a_a_a
takaAtaba	ktb	taFaAEala	ta_aA_a_a

Table 4: Rewrite rules for decausativization

Input pattern		Output pattern
faEala	⟹	IinofaEala
faEãla	⟹	tafaEãla
faAEala	⟹	tafaAEala
faEolana	⟹	tafaEolana
fawoEala	⟹	tafawoEala

4.3.2 Generating New Lists of Thematic Roles

Building sibling classes is not only a morphological process but also a semantic one with repercussions on the thematic arity of the concerned class. Thus, the simple reciprocal alternation found with social interaction and communication verbs adds a new theme role *actor* which can be used interchangeably with the two symmetrical themes *actor1* and *actor2*. Other operations delete thematic roles in the new class. Thus decausativization deletes the thematic role agent from the list of roles.

4.3.3 Generating New Argument Structures

Adapting thematic structures of the new sibling classes has an influence on their argument structures. Thus, adding a new thematic role while causativizing a verb class is reflected in the syntactic level by adding a new argument with its appropriate restrictions. For instance, the introduction of the theme *actor* in the simple reciprocal alternation of interaction verbs imposes an additional restriction [+*dual*/+plural] on the subject at the syntactic level, whereas the object is omitted from the argument structure of the concerned frame. Additionally, the mapping between thematic roles and grammatical arguments is the subject of change. Thus, change-of-state verbs and other causative verbs are reflexivized by assigning a *agent* role to the *patient* in the causative reading. At the syntactic level this operation is reflected by omitting the subject and promoting the object to the subject position.

4.3.4 Generating New Semantic Descriptions

For sibling classes to reflect the meaning variations introduced by the new morphological material, the semantic description of input classes has to be modified by adding or omitting appropriate semantic predicates. Thus, causativization introduces the predicate *CAUSE* to the semantic description of the class, whereas decausativization is reflected by omitting the same predicate and its argument which corresponds mostly to the *agent* of the concerned frame. In the case of a simple reciprocal alternation the presence of one (plural) *actor* is reflected by introducing two presupposed (implicit) *actor* roles: *actor_i* and *actor_j* in the main semantic description of the verb as shown in (2) in contrast to explicit *actor* roles in (3).

(2) **Implicit symmetrical actor roles**
social_interaction(during(E), $Actor_i$, $Actor_j$*)*

(3) **Explicit symmetrical actor roles**
social_interaction(during(E), Actor1, Actor2)

4.3.5 Generating New Frames

We generate new frames (alternations) on the basis of frames of the base (input) classes. Since operations like decausativization affect only the thematic arity of the class, alternations which are not related to causativity are reproduced in the new classes. For instance, the frame for the instrumental alternation of the causative verb class is reproduced by adapting the thematic structure to the incoative use. Thus, the frame alternation of (4a) will produce the frame alternation (4b), since the instrumental alternation in Arabic can be found with causative verbs as well as with uncausative verbs.

(4)

a. *naśśafa* *saliymun* *ālmalābisa.* *biālbuḫaāri*
dry-*CAUS-PRF* Salim-*SUBJ-NOM* *DEF*-cloth-PL-OBJ-ACC with-*DEF*-vapor.
'Salim dried the clothes with the vapor.'

b. *naśifati* *ālmalābisu.* *biālbuḫaāri*
dry-*PRF* *DEF*-cloth-*PL-SUBJ-NOM* with-*DEF*-vapor.
'The clothes was dried with the vapor.'

5 Results and Discussion

We run SCG on the current version of Arabic VerbNet. The program was able to identify 89 expandable classes with 3005 verbs and 368 frames, 60 of them populate causative and 29 uncausative verbs. For each class one sibling class was generated with a total of 3360 verbs and 368 frames. The high number of generated verbs is due to the fact that some verbs have more than one way to express the causative or the inchoative. After checking the quality of the produced classes, we count 71% accuracy in identifying the patterns of the verbs and 82% in generating their derived forms. After manually adjusting the new sibling classes (deleting unsuitable verb forms and adding the correct ones, adding frame examples, etc.), we noted that Arabic VerbNet counts now 291 classes populating 7937 verbs and 1202 frames, which represents an expansion rate of 44%. Noteworthy, not all verbs formed by the root-pattern system exist synchronically. We observed that inside the same sibling class one verb can be widely found in different Arabic corpora whereas another verb of the same sibling class is not attested in the same corpora. For instance, the verb *nabaḥa* 'to bark' of the class *animal_sounds* has a causative form *anbaḥa* 'cause to bark', but for the most members of the same class the causative form are not attested to be used in the "real world". However, they are potential lexicon entries and native Arabic speakers will most likely recognize their meaning without being exposed to them before. Additionally, given the fact that human lexica are brittle and incomplete, the scope of Levin's class approach (Levin, 1993) can be expanded to explain the derivational behaviour of verbs: Verbs which belong to the same class and share the same syntactic and semantic properties are likely to share the same derivational behaviour, especially when this behaviour is related to the general semantic properties of the class.

6 Conclusion

We presented a way to classify verbs of a language with a productive (verb) morphology like Arabic. Additionally to the traditional classes with a rigid hierarchical structure and a top-down inheritance relation, sibling classes were introduced to classify those verbs which engage in morohological operations during diathesis alternations. Sibling classes are autonomous classes which maintain relations to the class they are issued from consequently reflecting the natural connection between parents element in the lexicon.

References

Kipper Schuler, K. (2005). *VerbNet: A Broad-Coverage, Comprehensive Verb Lexicon.* Ph. D. thesis, University of Pennsylvania.

Korhonen, A. and T. Briscoe (2004). Extended lexical-semantic classification of english verbs. In *The HLT/NACCL wokshop on computational lexical semantics.*

Levin, B. (1993). *English Verb Classes and Alternations. A Preliminary Investigation.* Chicago and London: The University of Chicago Press.

Moens, M. and M. Steedman (1988). Temporal ontology and temporal reference. *Computational Linguistics 14*, 15–28.

Mousser, J. (2010). A large coverage verb taxonomy for arabic. In *Proceedings of the Seventh conference on International Language Resources and Evaluation (LREC'10)*, Valetta, Malta.

Granularity in Natural Language Discourse

Rutu Mulkar-Mehta, Jerry Hobbs and Eduard Hovy
University of Southern California, Information Sciences Institute
me@rutumulkar.com, hobbs@isi.edu, hovy@isi.edu

Abstract

This paper discusses the phenomenon of granularity in natural language[1]. By 'granularity' we mean the level of detail of description of an event or object. Humans can seamlessly shift their granularity perspective while reading or understanding a text. To emulate this mechanism, we describe a set of features that identify the levels of granularity in text, and empirically verify this feature set using a human annotation study for granularity identification. This theory is the foundation for any system that can learn the (global) behavior of event descriptions from (local) behavior descriptions. This is the first research initiative, to our knowledge, for identifying granularity shifts in natural language descriptions.

1 Introduction

Granularity is the concept of breaking down an event into smaller parts or granules such that each individual granule plays a part in the higher level event. For example, the activity of driving to the grocery store involves some fine-grained events like opening the car door, starting the engine, planning the route, and driving to the destination. Each of these may in turn be decomposed further into finer levels of granularity. For instance, planning the route might involve entering an address into GPS and following directions. The phenomenon of granularity is observed in various domains, including scientific literature, game reports, and political descriptions. In scientific literature, the process of photosynthesis on closer examination is made up of smaller individual fine-grained processes such as the light dependent reaction and the light independent reaction.

Granularity is not a new concept. It has been studied actively in various disciplines. In philosophy, Bittner and Smith (2001) have worked on formalizing granularity and part-hood relations. In information retrieval, Lau et al. (2009) have used granularity concepts to extract relevant detail of information resulting from a given search query. In theoretical computer science and ontology development, Keet (2008) has worked on formalizing the concept of entity granularity and hierarchy and applied it biological sciences. In natural language processing, Mani (1998) has worked on applying concepts of granularity to polysemy and Hobbs (1985) has worked on using granularity for decomposing complex theories into simple theories.

Although all of the above work emphasizes the importance of granularity relations for language understanding and formalization, none of it has attempted to observe whether granularity structures exist in natural language texts, explored whether granularity structures can be identified and extracted automatically, or tried to analyze how harvesting granularity relations can possibly help with other NLP problems. This paper focuses on two items: First, we present a model of granularity as it exists in natural language (Section 2); and second, we present an annotation study which we conducted to verify the proposed model of granularity in natural language (Section 3).

[1]This research was supported by the Defense Advanced Research Projects Agency (DARPA) Machine Reading Program under Air Force Research Laboratory (AFRL) prime contract no. FA8750-09-C-0172. Any opinions, findings, and conclusion or recommendations expressed in this material are those of the author(s) and do not necessarily reflect the view of the DARPA, AFRL, ONR, or the US government.

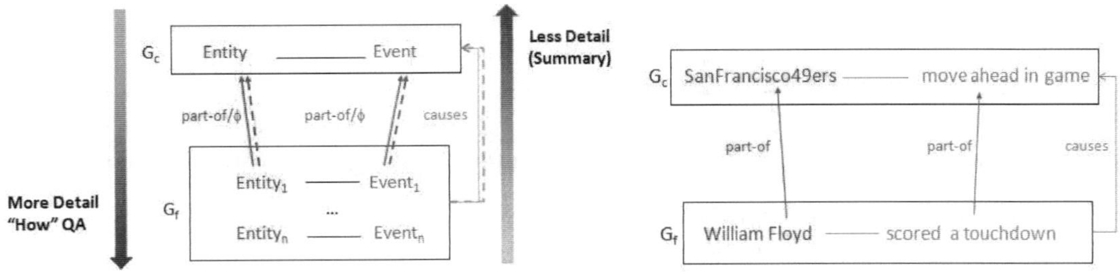

(a) (b)

Figure 1: 1(a): Granularity in Natural Language Descriptions; 1(b): Instantiating Natural Language to the Granularity model

2 Modeling Granularity in Natural Language Texts

Humans can easily shift through various levels of granularity in understanding text. However, for automated granularity identification and extraction, it is necessary to explicitly recognize the identifiers that indicate a shift in granularity. Figure 1(a) illustrates our theory of granularity. A granularity structure exists only if at least two levels of information are present in text, such that the events at the coarse granularity can be decomposed into the events at the fine granularity, and the events at the fine granularity combine together to form at least one segment of the event at the coarse granularity. In Figure 1(a), G_c represents the phrase or sentence with coarse granularity information and G_f represents a phrase or sentence with fine granularity information. Three types of relations can exist between the objects at coarse and fine granularity: *part-whole relationships between entities, part-whole relationships between events*, and *causal relationships between the fine and coarse granularities.* These relations signal a shift in granularity. Instantiating text phrases into this model will expose granularities of text. For example, consider the following sentence:

The San Francisco 49ers moved ahead 7–3 11 minutes into the game when William Floyd scored a two-yard touchdown run.

The event of the player scoring a touchdown (the second clause of the sentence) is a decomposition of the event of the team moving forward in the game (the first clause), and thus a finer granularity representation of the San Francisco 49ers moving ahead in the game. When instantiated in our model of granularity (Figure 1(a)), the graphical representation is shown in Figure 1(b).

Having described the overall model of granularity, we now elaborate on the components of the granularity model, namely *part-whole relations* and *causal relations*.

2.1 Part-Whole Relations

Two types of part-whole relations are present: *meronymic* and *mereologic*. Mereology (for more details read Keet (2008)) is a partial ordering relation that is reflexive, transitive, and antisymmetric. According to the concept of mereology, if *x*, *y* and *z* are three entities, then: *x* is a part of *x*; if *x* is part of *y* and *y* is part of *z* then *x* is part of *z*; and if *x* is part of *y* then *y* cannot be part of *x*. However, various types of part-whole relations that occur in natural language, such as *member of*, do not satisfy the transitivity relation, in which case they will be mereologic but not meronymic: they might be ontologically accurate but not linguistically correct. For instance, *if John's arm is part of John, and John is a member of a football team*, the transitivity relation that *John's arm is part of a football team*, is not a valid meronymic relation. Another instance which is mereologic but not meronymic is the following: *A cup is made of steel, and steel is made of molecules. Therefore a cup is made of molecules.* The concept of mereology does not reflect the way *part of* is used in natural language, and so mereology cannot be used for linguistic based research.

One of the early works on part-whole relations in natural language (meronymy) Winston et al. (1987) was later refined in their empirical experiments Chaffin et al. (1988). Winston et al. discuss meronymic relations and a taxonomy for representing them. They introduce six types of part-whole relationships: (i) Component-Integral (e.g., *pedal* is a component of the integral *bike*), (ii) Member-Collection (e.g., a *ship* is a member of the collection, a *fleet*), (ii) Portion-Mass (e.g., a *slice* is a portion of the mass, a *pie*), (iv) Stuff-Object (e.g., *steel* is one of the ingredients/stuff of the object *car*), (v) Feature-Activity (e.g., *paying* is one of the features of the whole activity of *shopping*), (vi) Place-Area (e.g., *Everglades* is a place within the area of *Florida*). The definition and classification in Winston et al. (1987) for part-whole relations is very relevant for language based analysis of part-whole relations. For granularity identification in our work, the Feature-Activity type relation is used as the part-whole relation for events, and the rest are part-whole relations for entities.

2.2 Causal Relations

Girju and Moldovan (2002) provide a broad compilation of causality research ranging from philosophy, planning in AI, commonsense reasoning, and computational linguistics. Causation in computational linguistics is the only form of causality that is relevant for granularity identification and extraction. The following are the categories of causal constructs relevant for granularity identification and extraction:

- Causal Connectives: These are usually prepositional (such as *because of, thanks to, due to*), adverbial (such as *for this reason, the result that*), or clause links (such as *because, since, for*).
- Causation Verbs: These usually have a causal relation integrated with the verb. For example, *kill, melt* (represent a causal link with the resulting situation), *poison, hang, clean* (represent a causal link with the a part of the causing event)
- Conditionals: Girju and Moldovan (2002) describe conditionals as complex linguistic structures typically of the form *If S1 then S2*. These structures represent causation, temporal relations, among other relations, and are very complex structures in language.

3 Evaluation of the Granularity Model in Natural Language

We conducted an evaluation study to judge the “goodness” of the granularity model proposed. In this study the annotators were asked to annotate granularity relations between two given paragraphs. Paragraph-based analysis was preferred to event-word-based analysis because people reason much more easily with paragraph descriptions than with individual event mentions [2]. The annotation set consisted of paragraph pairs from three domains: travel articles (confluence.org), Timebank annotated data Pan et al. (2006), and Wikipedia articles on games. We selected a total of 37 articles: 10 articles about travel, 10 about games, and 17 from Timebank. Both paragraphs of a given question were selected from the same article and referred to the same overall concept.

3.1 Annotation Task

The articles were uploaded to Mechanical Turk and were annotated by non-expert annotators (regular Turkers). The entire set of 37 articles was annotated by 5 people. The annotators were given a pair of paragraphs and were asked four questions about the relations between them: (i) Is one paragraph a subevent of the other paragraph?, (ii) Did one paragraph cause the other paragraph?, (iii) Is one paragraph less detailed and the other paragraph more detailed?, (iv) Did one paragraph happen after the other paragraph? They were then presented with the comments of other annotators, and asked whether they agreed

[2] This was deduced as a result of an earlier annotation study for granularity identification using individual words as events.

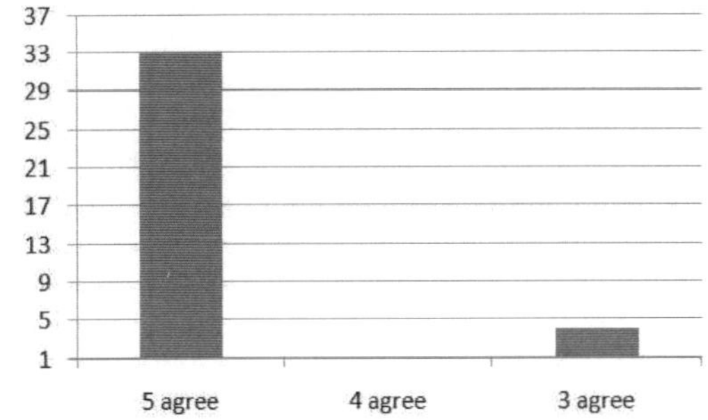

(a)

Annotator ID	A2-K9	A2-CA	A2-GH	A3-CN	A3-FM	Average
A2-K9		0.82	0.76	1	0.76	0.833314
A2-CA	0.82		0.93	0.82	0.93	0.876835
A2-GH	0.76	0.93		0.76	1	0.861683
A3-CN	1	0.82	0.76		0.76	0.833314
A3-FM	0.76	0.93	1	0.76		0.861683

(b)

Figure 2: 2(a) shows the Inter-Annotator agreement for 37 articles and 2(b) shows the Pairwise Kappa Agreement for 37 articles and 5 annotators

with any of the other annotations or explanations. The annotators were asked to provide a justification of their choices.

3.2 Results

The Kappa statistic (Cohen (1960)) is the standard for measuring inter-annotator agreement: $k = \frac{(p(a)-p(e))}{(1-p(e))}$, where *p(a)* is the observed agreement and *p(e)* is the chance agreement between annotators. More refined than simple Percentage Agreement, Kappa corrects for chance agreements.

In our study, two annotators were considered to be in agreement if they agreed with questions (i) Subevents, (iii) More or less detail and (iv) Sequence. Unfortunately question (ii) Causality, as provided to the annotators, could not be taken into account for agreement measurement as individuals had different conceptualizations of causality, and a crisp definition of causality was not provided to them. For instance, consider the following two paragraphs:

1: *I wanted to visit the confluence point located in the extreme southwest of Hunan Province.*
2: *To get to the confluence, I caught the Hong Kong-to-Shanghai intercity train on Friday afternoon.*
Analysis: Some annotators annotated *para2 causes para1*, providing the explanation that the goal para1 could be achieved due to the events of para2. Others annotated *para1 causes para2*, providing the justification that the events of para2 only exist to fulfill the original goal para1. We are interested in the first type of causality, i.e., causality which explains *how* a given event happens. All the annotators agreed that a sub-event explains *how* an event happens, or a sub-event *causes* an event. We counted this in lieu of our causality question (ii).

Figure 2(a) shows the overall agreement of the five annotators on the 37 articles and Figure 2(b) shows the pairwise Kappa agreement for the five annotators. All the annotators agreed in 33/37 cases (23 article pairs were annotated as having a granularity shift, 10 articles were annotated as having no granularity shift). The average pairwise Kappa was 0.85. If the newspaper articles were removed, the overall agreement was 100% for all the annotators. High agreement implied good quality of the annotation guidelines, and provided evidence that people shift through various levels of granularity while reading and understanding text.

3.3 Analysis of the Causes of Disagreement

Where disagreements occurred, different interpretations of the same text were observed to be a major cause. All these disagreements were limited to the newspaper articles. For instance, consider the following:

1: Some 1,500 ethnic Albanians marched Sunday in downtown Istanbul, burning Serbian flags.
2: The police barred the crowd from reaching the Yugoslavian consulate in downtown Istanbul, but allowed them to demonstrate on nearby streets.
Positive Granularity Shift: Some annotators commented that "demonstrations" happen as a part of a "march". So, para2 is a sub-event of para1.
Negative Granularity Shift: Other annotators felt that para2 happened after para1, and so there was no granularity shift.

Overall, we can observe that although disagreement arises due to individual and unique interpretations of text, people agree based on the discriminating features provided to them (part-whole relations and causality) when identifying granularity shifts. This shows that part-whole relations and causality provide a good set of features for identifying granularity shifts.

4 Conclusion and Future Work

In this paper we present the phenomenon of granularity as it occurs in natural language texts. We validate our model of granularity with the help of an annotation study. We are currently developing a system for automatic granularity extraction. We will compare its performance with state of the art techniques for answering causality-style questions to empirically evaluate the significance of granularity structures for automated Question Answering.

References

Bittner, T. and B. Smith (2001). Granular partitions and vagueness. *Proceedings of the international conference on Formal Ontology in Information Systems - FOIS '01*, 309–320.

Chaffin, R., D. J. Herrmann, and M. E. Winston (1988). An empirical taxonomy of part-whole relations: Effects of part-whole relation type on relation identification. *Language and Cognitive Processes 3*(1).

Cohen, J. (1960). A coefficientof agreement for nominal scales. *Educational and Psychological Measurement 20*, 37–46.

Girju, R. and D. Moldovan (2002). Mining Answers for Causation. *Proceedings of American Association of Artificial Intelligence*, 15–25.

Hobbs, J. R. (1985). Granularity. *In Proceedings of the Ninth International Joint Conference on Artificial Intelligence*, 432–435.

Keet, C. M. (2008). *A Formal Theory of Granularity*. Ph. D. thesis, Faculty of Computer Science, Free University of Bozen-Balzano, Italy.

Lau, R. Y. K., C. C. L. Lai, and Y. Li (2009). Mining Fuzzy Ontology for a Web-Based Granular Information Retrieval System. *Lecture Notes in Computer Science*, 239–246.

Mani, I. (1998). A Theory of Granularity and its Application to Problems of Polysemy and Underspecification of Meaning. *In Principles of Knowledge Representation and Reasoning: Proceedings of the Sixth International Conference (KR'98)*, 245–255.

Pan, F., R. Mulkar, and J. R. Hobbs (2006). An Annotated Corpus of Typical Durations of Events. *In Proceedings of the Fifth International Conference on Language Resources and Evaluation (LREC)*, 77–83.

Winston, M. E., R. Chaffin, and D. Herrmann (1987, October). A Taxonomy of Part-Whole Relations. *Cognitive Science 11*(4), 417–444.

Incremental Semantic Construction in a Dialogue System*

Matthew Purver, Arash Eshghi, Julian Hough
Interaction, Media and Communication
School of Electronic Engineering and Computer Science, Queen Mary University of London
{mpurver, arash, jhough}@eecs.qmul.ac.uk

Abstract

This paper describes recent work on the DynDial project* towards incremental semantic interpretation in dialogue. We outline our domain-general grammar-based approach, using a variant of Dynamic Syntax integrated with Type Theory with Records and a Davidsonian event-based semantics. We describe a Java-based implementation of the parser, used within the Jindigo framework to produce an incremental dialogue system capable of handling inherently incremental phenomena such as split utterances, adjuncts, and mid-sentence clarification requests or backchannels.

1 Introduction

Many dialogue phenomena seem to motivate an incremental view of language processing: for example, a participant's ability to change hearer/speaker role mid-sentence to produce or interpret backchannels, or complete or continue an utterance (see e.g. Yngve, 1970; Lerner, 2004, amongst many others). Much recent research in dialogue systems has pursued this line, resulting in frameworks for incremental dialogue processing (Schlangen and Skantze, 2009) and systems capable of mid-utterance backchannels (Skantze and Schlangen, 2009) or utterance completions (DeVault et al., 2009; Buß et al., 2010).

However, to date there has been little focus on semantics, with the systems produced either operating in domains in which semantic representation is not required (Skantze and Schlangen, 2009), or using variants of domain-specific canned lexical or phrasal matching (Buß et al., 2010). Our intention is to extend this work to finer-grained and more domain-general notions of grammar and semantics, by using an incremental grammatical framework, Dynamic Syntax (DS, Kempson et al., 2001) together with the structured semantic representation provided by Type Theory with Records (TTR, see e.g. Cooper, 2005).

	A: I want to go to ...		A: I want to go to Paris ...		A: I want to go to Paris.
(a)	B: Uh-huh	(b)	B: Uh-huh	(c)	B: OK. When do you ...
	A: ... Paris by train.		A: ... by train.		A: By train.

Figure 1: Examples of motivating incremental dialogue phenomena

One aim is to deal with split utterances, both when the antecedent is inherently incomplete (see Figure 1(a)) and potentially complete (even if not intended as such – Figure 1(b)). This involves producing representations which are as complete as possible – i.e contain all structural and semantic information so far conveyed – on a word-by-word basis, so that in the event of an interruption or a hesitation, the system can act accordingly (by producing backchannels or contentful responses as above); but that can be further incremented in the event of a continuation by the user.

Importantly, this ability should be available not only when an initial contribution is intended and/or treated as incomplete (as in Figure 1(b)), but also when it is in fact complete, but is still subsequently extended (Figure 1(c)). Treating A's two utterances as distinct, with separate semantic representations, must require high-level processes of ellipsis reconstruction to interpret the final fragment – for example, treating it as the answer to an implicit question raised by A's initial sentence (Fernández et al., 2004). If,

*The authors were supported by the Dynamics of Conversational Dialogue project (DynDial – ESRC-RES-062-23-0962). We thank Shalom Lappin, Tim Fernando, Yo Sato, our project colleagues and the anonymous reviewers for helpful comments.

instead, we can treat such fragments as continuations which merely add directly to the existing representation, the task is made easier and the relevance of the two utterances to each other becomes explicit.

2 Dynamic Syntax (DS) and Type Theory with Records (TTR)

Our approach is a grammar-based one, as our interest is in using domain-general techniques that are capable of fine-grained semantic representation. Dynamic Syntax (DS) provides an inherently incremental grammatical framework which dispenses with an independent level of syntax, instead expressing grammaticality via constraints on the word-by-word monotonic growth of semantic structures. In DS's original form, these structures are trees with nodes corresponding to terms in the lambda calculus; nodes are decorated with labels expressing their semantic type and formula, and beta-reduction determines the type and formula at a mother node from those at its daughters (Figure 2(a)). Trees can be *partial*, with nodes decorated with requirements for future development; lexical actions (corresponding to words) and computational actions (general capabilities) are defined as operations on trees which satisfy and/or add requirements; and grammaticality of a word sequence is then defined as satisfaction of all requirements (tree *completeness*) via the application of its associated actions – see Kempson et al. (2001) for details.

Previous work in DS has shown how this allows a treatment of split utterances and non-sentential fragments (e.g. clarifications) as extensions of the semantic trees so far constructed, either directly or via the addition of "linked" trees (Purver and Kempson, 2004; Gargett et al., 2009).

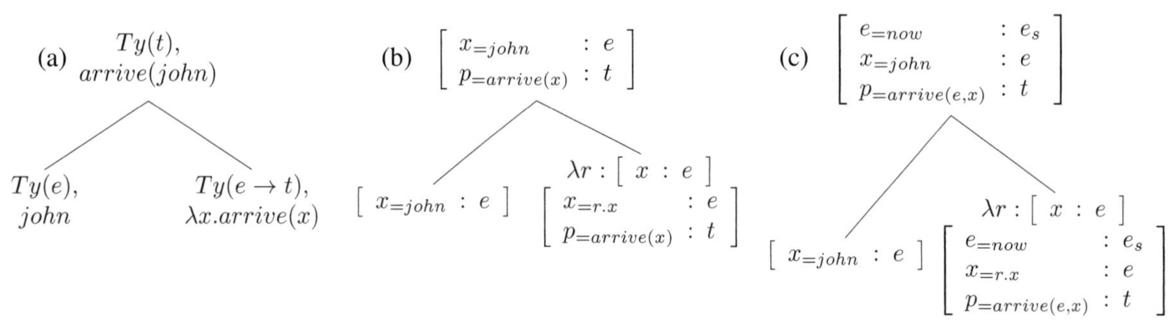

Figure 2: A simple DS tree for *"john arrives"*: (a) original DS, (b) DS+TTR, (c) event-based

2.1 Extensions

More recent work in DS has started to explore the use of TTR to extend the formalism, replacing the atomic semantic type and FOL formula node labels with more complex *record types*, and thus providing a more structured semantic representation. Purver et al. (2010) provide a sketch of one way to achieve this and explain how it can be used to incorporate pragmatic information such as participant reference and illocutionary force. As shown in Figure 2(b) above, we use a slightly different variant here: node record types are sequences of typed labels (e.g. $[x : e]$ for a label x of type e), with semantic content expressed by use of *manifest* types (e.g. $[x_{=john} : e]$ where $john$ is a singleton subtype of e).

We further adopt an event-based semantics along Davidsonian lines (Davidson, 1980). As shown in Figure 2(c), we include an event term (of type e_s) in the representation: this allows tense and aspect to be expressed (although Figure 2(c) shows only a simplified version using the current time now). It also permits a straightforward analysis of optional adjuncts as extensions of an existing semantic representation; extensions which predicate over the event term already in the representation. Adding fields to a record type results in a more fully specified record type which is still a subtype of the original:

$$\begin{bmatrix} e_{=now} & : e_s \\ x_{=john} & : e \\ p_{=arrive(e,x)} & : t \end{bmatrix} \mapsto \begin{bmatrix} e_{=now} & : e_s \\ x_{=john} & : e \\ p_{=arrive(e,x)} & : t \\ p'_{=today(e)} & : t \end{bmatrix}$$

"john arrives" $\mapsto$ *"john arrives today"*

Figure 3: Optional adjuncts as leading to TTR subtypes

3 Implementation

The resulting framework has been implemented in Java, following the formal details of DS as per (Kempson et al., 2001; Cann et al., 2005, *inter alia*). This implementation, DyLan,[1] includes a parser and generator for English, which take as input a set of computational actions, a lexicon and a set of lexical actions (instructions for partial tree update); these are specified separately in text files in the IF-THEN-ELSE procedural (meta-)language of DS, allowing any pre-written grammar to be loaded. Widening or changing its coverage, i.e. extending the system with new analyses of various linguistic phenomena, thus do not involve modification or extension of the Java program, but only the lexicon and action specifications. The current coverage includes a small lexicon, but a broad range of structures: complementation, relative clauses, adjuncts, tense, pronominal and ellipsis construal, all in interaction with quantification.

3.1 The parsing process

Given a sequence of words $(w_1, w_2, ..., w_n)$, the parser starts from the *axiom* tree T_0 (a requirement to construct a complete tree of type t), and applies the corresponding lexical actions $(a_1, a_2, \ldots, a_n)$, optionally interspersing general computational actions (which can apply whenever their preconditions are met). More precisely: we define the parser state at step i as a set of partial trees S_i. Beginning with the singleton axiom state $S_0 = \{T_0\}$, for each word w_i:

1. Apply all lexical actions a_i corresponding to w_i to each partial tree in S_{i-1}. For each application that succeeds (i.e. the tree satisfies the action preconditions), add resulting (partial) tree to S_i.
2. For each tree in S_i, apply all possible sequences of computational actions and add the result to S_i.

If at any stage the state S_i is empty, the parse has failed and the string is deemed ungrammatical. If the final state S_n contains a complete tree (all requirements satisfied), the string is grammatical and its root node will provide the full sentence semantics; partial trees provide only partial semantic specifications.[2]

3.2 Graph representations

Sato (2010) shows how this procedure can be modelled as a *directed acyclic graph*, rooted at T_0, with individual partial trees as nodes, connected by edges representing single actions. While Sato uses this to model the search process, we exploit it (in a slightly modified form) to represent the linguistic *context* available during the parse – important in DS for ellipsis and pronominal construal. Details are given in (Cann et al., 2007; Gargett et al., 2009), but three general mechanisms are available: 1) copying formulae from some *tree* in context (used for e.g. anaphora and strict VP ellipsis); 2) rerunning *actions* in context (for e.g. sloppy VP-ellipsis and fragment corrections); and 3) directly extending/augmenting the current tree (used for most fragment types in (Fernández, 2006)). For any partial tree, then, the context available to the parser must include not only the tree itself, but the sequence of actions and previous partial trees which have gone into its construction. The parse graph (which we call the *tree* graph) provides exactly this information, via the shortest path back to the root from the current node.

However, we can also take a coarser-grained view via a graph which we term the *state* graph; here, nodes are states S_i and edges the sets of action sequences connecting them. This subsumes the tree graph, with state nodes containing possibly many tree-graph nodes; and here, nodes have multiple outgoing edges only when multiple word hypotheses are present. This corresponds directly to the input word graph (often called a word *lattice*) available from a speech recognizer, allowing close integration in a dialogue system – see below. We also see this as a suitable structure with which to begin to model phenomena such as hesitation and self-repair: as edges are linear action sequences, intended to correspond to the time-linear psycholinguistic processing steps involved, such phenomena may be analysed as building further edges from suitable departure points earlier in the graph.[3]

[1] DyLan is short for **Dy**namics of **Lan**guage. Available from `http://dylan.sourceforge.net/`.

[2] Note that only a subset of possible computational actions can apply to any given tree; together with a set of heuristics on possible application order, and the merging of identical trees produced by different sequences, this helps reduce complexity.

[3] There are similarities to chart parsing here: the tree graph edges spanning a state graph edge could be seen as corresponding to chart edges spanning a substring, with the tree nodes in the state S_i as the agenda. However, the lack of a notion of syntactic constituency means no direct equivalent for the active/passive edge distinction; a detailed comparison is still to be carried out.

4 Dialogue System

The DyLan parser has now been integrated into a working dialogue system by implementation as an `Interpreter` module in the Java-based incremental dialogue framework Jindigo (Skantze and Hjalmarsson, 2010). Jindigo follows Schlangen and Skantze (2009)'s abstract architecture specification and is specifically designed to handle units smaller than fully sentential utterances; one of its specific implementations is a travel agent system, and our module integrates semantic interpretation into this.

As set out by Schlangen and Skantze (2009)'s specification, our `Interpreter`'s essential components are a *left buffer* (LB), *processor* and *right buffer* (RB). *Incremental units* (IUs) of various types are posted from the RB of one module to the LB of another; for our module, the LB-IUs are ASR word hypotheses, and after processing, domain-level concept frames are posted as RB-IUs for further processing by a downstream dialogue manager. The input IUs are provided as updates to a word lattice, and new edges are passed to the DyLan parser which produces a state graph as described above in 3.1 and 3.2: new nodes are new possible parse states, with new edges the sets of DS actions which have created them. These state nodes are then used to create Jindigo domain concept frames by matching against the TTR record types available (see below), and these are posted to the RB as updates to the state graph (*lattice updates* in Jindigo's terminology).

Crucial in Schlangen and Skantze (2009)'s model is the notion of *commitment*: IUs are hypotheses which can be revoked at any time until they are *committed* by the module which produces them. Our module hypothesizes both parse states and associated domain concepts (although only the latter are outputs); these are committed when their originating word hypotheses are committed (by ASR) and a type-complete subtree is available; other strategies are possible and are being investigated.

4.1 Mapping TTR record types to domain concepts incrementally

Our `Interpreter` module matches TTR record types to domain concept frames via a simple XML matching specification; TTR fields map to particular concepts in the domain depending on their semantic type (e.g. *go* events map to `Trip` concepts, and the entity of manifest type *paris* maps to the `City[paris]` concept). As the tree and parse state graphs are maintained, incremental sub-sentential extensions can produce TTR subtypes and lead to enrichment of the associated domain concept.

User: I want to go to Paris …

$$\left[\begin{array}{lcl} e_{=\epsilon,e17,PresentState} & : & e_s \\ e1_{=\epsilon,e19,FutureAccomp} & : & e_s \\ x1_{=Paris} & : & e \\ p2_{=to(e1,x1)} & : & t \\ x_{=speaker} & : & e \\ p1_{=go(e1,x)} & : & t \\ p{*}_{=want(e,x,p1)} & : & t \end{array}\right] \quad Trip(to : City[paris])$$

User: … from London

$$\left[\begin{array}{lcl} e_{=\epsilon,e17,PresentState} & : & e_s \\ e1_{=\epsilon,e19,FutureAccomp} & : & e_s \\ x1_{=Paris} & : & e \\ p2_{=to(e1,x1)} & : & t \\ x2_{=London} & : & e \\ p3_{=from(e1,x2)} & : & t \\ x_{=speaker} & : & e \\ p1_{=go(e1,x)} & : & t \\ p{*}_{=want(e,x,p1)} & : & t \end{array}\right] \quad \begin{array}{c} Trip(from : City[london], \\ to : City[paris]) \end{array}$$

Figure 4: Incremental construction of a TTR record type over two turns

Figure 4 illustrates this process for a user continuation; the initial user utterance is parsed to produce a TTR record type, with a corresponding domain concept – a valid incremental unit to post in the RB. The subsequent user continuation *"from London"* extends the parser state graph, producing a new TTR subtype (in this case via the DS apparatus of an adjoining *linked* tree (Cann et al., 2005)), and a more fully specified concept (with a further argument slot filled) as output.

System behaviour between these two user contributions will depend on the committed status of the input, and perhaps some independent prosody-based judgement of whether a turn is finished (Skantze and Schlangen, 2009). An uncommitted input might be responded to with a backchannel (Yngve, 1970); commitment might lead to the system beginning processing and starting to respond more substantively. However, in either case, the maintenance of the parse state graph allows the user continuation to be treated as extending a parse tree, subtyping the TTR record type, and finally mapping to a fully satisfied domain concept frame that can be committed.

5 Conclusions

We have implemented an extension of the Dynamic Syntax framework, integrated with Type Theory with Records, which provides structured semantic representations suitable for use in a dialogue system, and which does so incrementally, producing well-defined partial representations on a word-by-word basis. This has been integrated into a working Jindigo dialogue system, capable of incremental behaviour such as mid-sentence backchannels and utterance continuations, which will be demonstrated at the conference. The coverage of the parser is currently limited, but work is in progress to widen it; the possibility of using grammar induction to learn lexical actions from real corpora is also being considered for future projects. We are also actively pursuing possbilities for tighter integration of TTR and DS, with the aim of unifying syntactic and semantic incremental construction.

References

Buß, O., T. Baumann, and D. Schlangen (2010). Collaborating on utterances with a spoken dialogue system using an ISU-based approach to incremental dialogue management. In *Proceedings of the SIGDIAL 2010 Conference*.

Cann, R., R. Kempson, and L. Marten (2005). *The Dynamics of Language*. Oxford: Elsevier.

Cann, R., R. Kempson, and M. Purver (2007). Context and well-formedness: the dynamics of ellipsis. *Research on Language and Computation 5*(3), 333–358.

Cooper, R. (2005). Records and record types in semantic theory. *Journal of Logic and Computation 15*(2), 99–112.

Davidson, D. (1980). *Essays on Actions and Events*. Oxford, UK: Clarendon Press.

DeVault, D., K. Sagae, and D. Traum (2009). Can I finish? learning when to respond to incremental interpretation results in interactive dialogue. In *Proceedings of the SIGDIAL 2009 Conference*.

Fernández, R. (2006). *Non-Sentential Utterances in Dialogue: Classification, Resolution and Use*. Ph. D. thesis, King's College London, University of London.

Fernández, R., J. Ginzburg, H. Gregory, and S. Lappin (2004). SHARDS: Fragment resolution in dialogue. In H. Bunt and R. Muskens (Eds.), *Computing Meaning*, Volume 3. Kluwer Academic Publishers. To appear.

Gargett, A., E. Gregoromichelaki, R. Kempson, M. Purver, and Y. Sato (2009). Grammar resources for modelling dialogue dynamically. *Cognitive Neurodynamics 3*(4), 347–363.

Kempson, R., W. Meyer-Viol, and D. Gabbay (2001). *Dynamic Syntax: The Flow of Language Understanding*. Blackwell.

Lerner, G. H. (2004). Collaborative turn sequences. In *Conversation analysis: Studies from the first generation*, pp. 225–256. John Benjamins.

Purver, M., E. Gregoromichelaki, W. Meyer-Viol, and R. Cann (2010). Splitting the 'I's and crossing the 'You's: Context, speech acts and grammar. In *Aspects of Semantics and Pragmatics of Dialogue. SemDial 2010, 14th Workshop on the Semantics and Pragmatics of Dialogue*.

Purver, M. and R. Kempson (2004). Incremental context-based generation for dialogue. In *Proceedings of the 3rd International Conference on Natural Language Generation (INLG04)*.

Sato, Y. (2010). Local ambiguity, search strategies and parsing in Dynamic Syntax. In E. Gregoromichelaki, R. Kempson, and C. Howes (Eds.), *The Dynamics of Lexical Interfaces*. CSLI. to appear.

Schlangen, D. and G. Skantze (2009). A general, abstract model of incremental dialogue processing. In *Proceedings of the 12th Conference of the European Chapter of the ACL (EACL 2009)*.

Skantze, G. and A. Hjalmarsson (2010). Towards incremental speech generation in dialogue systems. In *Proceedings of the SIGDIAL 2010 Conference*.

Skantze, G. and D. Schlangen (2009). Incremental dialogue processing in a micro-domain. In *Proceedings of the 12th Conference of the European Chapter of the ACL (EACL 2009)*.

Yngve, V. H. (1970). On getting a word in edgewise. In *Papers from the 6th regional meeting of the Chicago Linguistic Society*.

Extracting Contextual Evaluativity

Kevin Reschke
University of California, Santa Cruz
kreschke@ucsc.edu

Pranav Anand
University of California, Santa Cruz
panand@ucsc.edu

Abstract

Recent work on evaluativity or sentiment in the language sciences has focused on the contributions that lexical items provide. In this paper, we discuss *contextual evaluativity*, stance that is inferred from lexical meaning and pragmatic environments. Focusing on assessor-grounding claims like *We liked him because he so clearly disliked Margaret Thatcher*, we build a corpus and construct a system employing compositional principles of evaluativity calculation to derive that *we* dislikes *Margaret Thatcher*. The resulting system has an F-score of 0.90 on our dataset, outperforming reasonable baselines, and indicating the viability of inferencing in the evaluative domain.

1 Contextual Evaluativity

A central aim of contemporary research on sentiment or evaluative language is the extraction of evaluative triples: ⟨evaluator, target, evaluation⟩. To date, both formal (e.g., Martin and White 2005, Potts 2005) and computational approaches (e.g., Pang and Lee 2008) have focused on how such triples are lexically encoded (e.g., the negative affect of *scoundrel* or *dislike*). While lexical properties are a key source of evaluative information, word-based considerations alone can miss pragmatic inferences resulting from context. (1), for example, communicates that the referent of *we* bears not only positive stance towards the referent of *him*, but also negative stance towards Margaret Thatcher:

(1) We liked him because he so clearly disliked Margaret Thatcher.
LEXICAL EVALUATIVITY: ⟨we, him, +⟩; ⟨he, M.T., -⟩
CONTEXTUAL EVALUATIVITY: ⟨we, M.T., -⟩

This paper argues for a compositional approach to contextual evaluativity similar to the compositional methods adopted for lexical evaluativity in Moilanen and Pulman (2007) and Nasukawa and Yi (2003). At the the heart of the approach is the treatment of verbal predicates (*dislike* in (1)) as evaluativity functors which relate argument/entity-level evaluativity to event-level evaluativity.

As discussed in §2, the utitlity of such a model surfaces in cases where the event-level evaluativity is known from context, and thus new information about the contextual evaluativity of the event participants (e.g. Margaret Thatcher) can be inferred. Consequently, the empirical focus of this paper is on structures like (1), where the second clause provides grounds for the sentiment encoded in the first, and hence has a predictable event-level evaluation from the first clause's evaluator. In §3 we describe the collection and annotation of a corpus of such assessment-grounding configurations from large-scale web data. This annotated corpus serves as a test bed for experimental evaluation of various implementations of the proposed compositional approach. The results of these experiments (§4) strongly support a compositional approach to contextual evaluativity inference. A simple compositional algorithm based on a small, manually created evaluativity functor lexicon demonstrated significantly better precision than non-compositional baselines. Moreover, a method for automatically expanding coverage to novel predicates based on similarity with the manually created lexicon is shown to increase recall dramatically with modest reduction in precision.

2 A Framework For Inferring Contextual Polarity

Evaluativity is concerned with determining private states (e.g., judgment or emotion) that a particular evaluator bears towards a target entity, event, or proposition. This may be represented as a three place

Table 1: Evaluativity functors for verbs of having, withholding, disliking, and liking

x	y	E_{have}	E_{lack}	E_{wthhld}	E_{dprv}	E_{spr}	$E_{dislike}$	E_{like}
+	+	+	-	-	-	#	-	+
+	-	-	+	+	#	+	+	-
-	+	-	+	+	+	#	-	+
-	-	+	-	-	#	-	+	-
x have/lack *y*			*a* withhold/deprive/spare *x* of *y*				*x* dislike/like *y*	

relation, $R \subseteq D_e \times D_\alpha \times D_\mathcal{E}$, where α is of variable type and $\mathcal{E}$ is the type of evaluative stance, assumed here to be binary. Lexical approaches to evaluativity (see Pang and Lee 2008 for a review) have focused on those relations that are determinable from word-internal meaning alone. For example, describing an event e as *coddling* gives rise to two triples: $\langle \text{AGENT}(e), \text{PATIENT}(e), + \rangle$ and $\langle \text{SPEAKER}, e, - \rangle$.[1] These lexical inferences then become part of the feature set for classifying phrasal stance (e.g., the author's overall evaluativity in a sentence). A contrasting line of research (Moilanen and Pulman 2007, Nasukawa and Yi 2003) analyzes phrasal stance as a compositional product of the polarities toward event participants. For example, the evaluative polarity of the speaker toward the event in (2a) is positively correlated with the polarity toward the subject, and negatively so in (2b).

(2) a. My {ally, enemy} was deprived shelter.
 b. My {ally, enemy} was spared a dangerous mission.

Compositional proposals rely on mapping each n-ary predicate P an n-ary evaluativity functor $E_P : D_\mathcal{E}{}^n \rightarrow D_\mathcal{E}$. Anand and Reschke (2011) argue that evaluativity functors largely group into classes, depending on whether the predicates in question entail final states of possession and/or affectedness. For example, the functors for predicates of withholding, including *deprive* and *spare*, are partial cases of the functor for *lack* (partiality reflects lexical idiosyncracies about e.g., deprivation and positive objects), as shown in Table 1.

While compositional systems are designed to compute phrasal stances bottom-up, their calculi straightforwardly allow inference to participant polarities as well, assuming knowledge of the event polarity and all but one participant. Consider the sentence *He disliked Margaret Thatcher*. By the evaluativity conditions in Table 1, $E_{dislike}$ is positive iff the evaluator has negative evaluation of Thatcher. Thus, given knowledge of the event polarity, we can infer the evaluator's stance with respect to Thatcher. In (1), this information is provided by the preceding assessing clause (+, from E_{like}). As the second clause serves as grounds for the assessment in the first clause, the event described in the second clause is predictably also assessed as + by the evaluator *we*. In our experiments we exploited this construction in particular, but the general procedure does not require it (thus, for example, evaluative adverbs such as *fortunately* and *regrettably* could provide an additional construction type). This procedure is sketched for (1) below:

(3) We liked$_{e_{like}}$ him because he so clearly disliked$_{e_{dislike}}$ Margaret Thatcher.
 LEXICAL EVALUATIVITY: ⟨we, him, +⟩; ⟨he, M.T., -⟩
 PRAGMATIC INFERENCE: ⟨we, $e_{dislike}$, +⟩ ($e_{dislike}$ justifies ⟨we, him, +⟩)
 COMPOSITIONAL INFERENCE: $E_{dislike}(+, y) = +$ iff $y = +$
 therefore, y is regarded as $+$, or ⟨we, M.T., -⟩

Note that for this application, we may simplify the compositional picture and treat functors as either preservers or reversers of the polarity of the object of interest, as is done in Moilanen and Pulman (2007) and Nasukawa and Yi (2003): preservers (such as verbs of liking) match the object polarity with the event polarity, and reverses negate it.

When the assessing clause evaluator is not affiliated with the speaker, this procedure can produce markedly different results from lexical markers (which often show speaker evaluativity). Thus, in (4), the speaker's assessment of Obama's cuts (indicated by the lexical *much-needed*) stands in sharp contrast with NASA's (determined by inference):

[1]Here, we simplify regarding potential evaluators outside of the speaker.

(4) NASA got angry at Obama because he imposed some much-needed cuts.
LEXICAL EVALUATIVITY: ⟨NASA, Obama, -⟩; ⟨SPEAKER, some much needed cuts, +⟩
CONTEXTUAL EVALUATIVITY: ⟨NASA, some much needed cuts, -⟩

The assessment-grounding configuration in (1) and (4) is highly productive. Behaviorally, *implicit causality* predicates (including predicates of assessment, as well as praise and scolding) are frequently understood by experimental subjects as describing an event involving the assessment target, especially when followed by *because* (Garvey and Carmazza, 1974; Koornneef and van Berkum, 2006). In addition, Somasundaran and Weibe (2009) exploited a similar construction to gather reasons for people's product assessments from online reviews. These together suggest that such constructions could be simultaneously high-precision sources for evaluativity inference and easily obtainable from large corpora.

3 Data Gathering and Annotation

We developed a corpus of assessment-grounding excerpts from documents across the web to evaluate the potential of the framework in §2. 73 positive and 120 negative assessment predicates (*like*, *adore*, *hate*, *loathe*, etc.) were selected from the MPQA subjectivity lexicon (Wilson et al., 2005). These were expanded accross inflectional variants to produce 826 assessment templates, half with explicit *because*, half without (e.g. *terrified by* X *because he*). These templates were filled with personal pronouns and the names of 26 prominent political figures and issued as websearch queries to the Yahoo! Search API.[2] A total of 440,000 webdocument results were downloaded and processed using an 1152 core Sun Microsystems blade cluster. The relevant sentences from each document were extracted, and those under 80 characters in length were parsed using the Stanford Dependency Parser.[3]

This produced 60,000 parsed assessment-grounding sentences, 6,000 of which (excluding duplicates) passed the additional criterion that the grounding clause should contain a verb with a direct object. This restriction ensured that each item in our corpus had a target for contextual polarity inference. An additional 3,300 cases were excluded because the target in the grounding clause shared possible coreference with the experiencer (subject) of the assessment clause. We avoided these coreferring cases because, from the perspective of a potential application, inferences about an experiencer's stance towards himself are less valuable than inferences about his stance towards others. Finally, the list was manually shortened to include only those sentences marked as assessment-grounding configurations according to two annotators ($\kappa = 0.82$); the classification task of whether this pragmatic connection occurs is beyond the scope of this paper. 57% of the data was removed in this pass, 14% from tokens with *because* and 43% from tokens without. Implicit causality verbs not followed by *because* have been shown experimentally to give rise to a much weaker preference for justification (Au, 1986), and this is confirmed in our corpus search. The result of this procedure was a final corpus size of 1,160.

The corpus was annotated for inferred contextual polarity. One of the authors and another annotator coded sentences for evaluator stance toward the object (+,-, unknown); agreement was high: $\kappa = 0.90$. The 48 unresolved cases were adjudicated by a third annotator. 27 cases were uniformly judged unknown, involving predicates of change, disclosure (*reveal, expose*), and understanding (*know*). These were removed from the corpus, leaving 1,133 sentences for training and testing.

4 System and Experimental Results

Restricting ourselves to the assessment-grounding configuration discussed above, we treat contextual polarity inference as a binary classification problem with two inputs: the INPUT EVENT event-level polarity (derived from the assessment clause) and the main verb of the grounding clause (henceforth FUNCTOR VERB). The goal of the classifier is to correctly predict the polarity of the target NP (direct object to the functor verb) given these inputs.

[2] http://developer.yahoo.com/search/

[3] http://nlp.stanford.edu/software/lex-parser.shtml

Table 2: Examples of verbs marked as preserver/reverser and their sources

EXAMPLE	CLASS	SOURCE
reward	preserver	MPQA subj. lex.
hamper	reverser	MPQA subj. lex.
tutor	preserver (benefit)	FrameNet
batter	reverser (injury)	FrameNet

Table 3: Performance of systems and baselines for contextual evaluativity classification

SYSTEM	PREC.	RECALL	F-SCORE
B-Functor	0.39	0.24	0.30
B-Input	0.69	1.0	0.82
B-MLE	0.75	1.0	0.86
SYS	0.88	0.57	0.69
SYS-MPQA	0.88	0.24	0.38
SYS-Frame	0.89	0.41	0.56
SYS+Maj	0.82	1.0	**0.90**
SYS+Sim	0.84	0.97	**0.90**

As mentioned in §2, we may categorize the functor verbs in our lexicon into preservers and reversers. Two sources populate our lexicon. First, positively subjective verbs from the MPQA subjectivity lexicon were marked as preservers and negatively subjective verbs were marked as reversers (1249 verbs total). For example, $E_{dislike}$ is a reverser. Second, 487 verbs were culled from FrameNet (Ruppenhofer et al., 2005) based on their membership in six entailment classes: verbs of injury, destruction, lacking, benefit, creation, and having. Class membership was determined by identifying 124 FrameNet frames aligning with one or more classes, then manually selecting from these frames verbs whose class membership was unambiguous. Verbs of benefit, creation, and having were marked as preservers. Verbs of injury, destruction, and lacking were marked as reversers (Table 2). Our system (SYS) classifies objects in context as follows: If the functor verb is a preserver, the target NP is assigned the same polarity as the input event polarity. If the functor verb is a reverser, the target NP is assigned the opposite of the input event polarity. This procedure is modulated by the presence of negation, as detected by a *neg* relation in the dependency parse. Under negation, a preserver acts like a reverser, and vice versa.

We tested the performance of this system (SYS) on our annotated corpus against three baselines. The first baseline (B-Functor) attempts to determine the importance of the input event to the calculation. It thus ignores the preceding context, and attempts to classify the target object from the functor verb directly, based on the verb's polarity in the MPQA subjectivity lexicon. It has poor precision and recall,[4] reflecting both the importance of the assessment context for object polarity and the fact that the functor verbs are often not lexically sentiment bearing (e.g., predicates of possession). The second baseline (B-Input), conversely, ignores the functor verb and uses the input event polarity as listed in the MPQA lexicon (modulo negation) for object classification. The purpose of this baseline is to approximate a classifier that predicts target polarity solely from the global/contextual polarity of the preceding clause. This has sharply increased precision, indicating contextual information's importance. The third baseline (B-MLE) picked the majority object class (+), and had the highest precision, indicating the general bias in our corpus for positive objects. Table 3 shows the performance (precision vs. recall) of our system compared to the three baselines. Its precision is significantly higher, but its F-score is limited by the lower coverage of our manually constructed lexicon. SYS-MPQA and SYS-Frame show the performance of the system when the functor lexicon is limited to the MPQA and Framenet predicates, respectively. Both are high precision sources of functor prediction, and pick out somewhat distinct predicates (given the recall gain of combining them). SYS+Maj and SYS+Sim are attempts to handle the low recall of SYS caused by functor verbs in the test data which aren't in the system's lexicon. SYS+Maj simply assigns these out-of-vocabulary verbs to the majority class: preservers. SYS+Sim classifies out-of-vocabulary verbs as preservers or reversers based on their relative similarity to the known preservers and reversers selected from FrameNet – an unknown verb is categorized as a preserver if its average similarity to preservers is greater than its average similarity to reversers. Similarity was determined according to the Jiang-Conrath distance measure (Jiang and Conrath, 1997), which based on links in WordNet (Fellbaum, 1998). (Note: this process cannot occur for words not found in WordNet – e.g. misspellings – hence the

[4]Low recall occurs when items are left unclassified due to out-of-vocabulary functor verbs. Low precision occurs when a + item is classified as – or vice versa.

less than perfect recall). These two systems outperform all baselines, but have indistinguishable F-scores (if misspellings are excluded, SYS+Sim has a Recall of 0.99 and F-score of 0.91).

Most of the precision errors incurred by our systems were syntactic: incorrect parsing, incorrect extraction of the object, or faulty negation handling (e.g., negative quantifiers or verbs). 26% of errors are due to word-sense disambiguation. The verbs *spoil* and *own* each have positive and negative uses (*own* can mean *defeat*), but only one sense was registered in the lexicon, leading to errors. The lion's share of these errors (22%) were due to the use of *hate* and similar expressions to convey jealousy (e.g. *I was mad at him because he had both Boardwalk and Park Place*). In these scenarios, although the assessment is negative, the event-level polarity of the grounding clause event type is positive (because it is desired), a fact which our current system cannot handle. One way forward would be to apply WSD techniques to distinguish jealous from non-jealous uses of predicates of dislike.

5 Conclusion

We have described a system for the extraction of what we termed contextual evaluativity – evaluations of objects that arise from the understanding of pragmatic inferences. This system, once we incorporate procedures to automatically infer evaluativity functor class, significantly outperforms reasonable baselines on a corpus of assessor-grounding extracts from web documents. The system operates by running a compositional approach to phrasal evaluativity in reverse, and is thus an instance of the potential computational value of such treatments of evaluativity.

References

Anand, P. and K. Reschke (2011). Verb classes as evaluativity functor classes. In *Interdisciplinary Workshop on Verbs.* to appear.

Au, T. K. (1986). A verb is worth a thousand words. *Journal of Memory and Language 25*, 104–122.

Fellbaum, C. (1998). *WordNet: An Electronic Lexical Database.* MIT Press.

Garvey, C. and A. Carmazza (1974). Implict causality in verbs. *Linguistic Inquiry 5*, 459–484.

Jiang, J. and C. Conrath (1997). Semantic similarity based on corpus statistics and lexical taxonomy. In *Proceedings of International Conference on Research in Computational Linguistics.*

Koornneef, A. W. and J. J. A. van Berkum (2006). On the use of verb-based implicit causality in sentence comprehension. *Journal of Memory and Language 54*, 445–465.

Martin, J. R. and P. R. R. White (2005). *Language of Evaluation: Appraisal in English.* Palgrave Macmillan.

Moilanen, K. and S. Pulman (2007). Sentiment composition. In *Proceedings of RANLP 2007.*

Nasukawa, T. and J. Yi (2003). Sentiment analysis: Capturing favorability using natural language processing. In *Proceedings of the 2nd international conference on Knowledge capture.*

Pang, B. and L. Lee (2008). Opinion mining and sentiment analysis. *Foundations and Trends in Information Retrieval 2*(1-2), 1–135.

Potts, C. (2005). *The Logic of Conventional Implicature.* Oxford University Press.

Ruppenhofer, J., M. Ellsworth, M. R. L. Petruck, and C. R. Johnson (2005). Framenet ii: Extended theory and practice. Technical report, ICSI Technical Report.

Somasundaran, S. and J. Weibe (2009). Recognizing stances in online debates. In *Proceedings of ACL-47*, pp. 226–234.

Wilson, T., J. Weibe, and P. Hoffman (2005). Recognizing contextual polarity in phrase-level sentiment analysis. In *Proceedings of EMNLP-05.*

Using MMIL for the High Level Semantic Annotation of the French MEDIA Dialogue Corpus.*

Lina Maria Rojas-Barahona
LORIA/INRIA, France
lina.rojas@loria.fr

Thierry Bazillon
Univ. Avignon, France
thierry.bazillon@univ-avignon.fr

Matthieu Quignard
LORIA/INRIA, France
matthieu.quignard@loria.fr

Fabrice Lefevre
Univ. Avignon, France
fabrice.lefevre@univ-avignon.fr

Abstract

The MultiModal Interface Language formalism (MMIL) has been selected as the High Level Semantic (HLS) formalism for annotating the French MEDIA dialogue corpus. This corpus is composed of human-machine dialogues in the domain of hotel reservation and tourist information. Utterances in dialogues have been previously annotated with a concept-value flat semantics for studying and evaluating spoken language understanding modules in dialogue systems. We are now interested in investigating the use of more complex representations to improve the understanding capability. The MMIL intermediate language is a high level semantic formalism that bears relevant linguistic information, from syntax up to discourse. This representation should increase the expressivity of the current annotation though at the expense of the annotation process complexity. In this paper we present our first attempt in defining the annotation guidelines for the HLS annotation of the MEDIA corpus and its effect on the annotation process itself, revealed by annotators' disagreements due to the different levels of hierarchy and the granularity of the features defined in MMIL.

1 Introduction

MMIL is an ontology-oriented representation language that has been used in several natural language processing (NLP) applications, Denis et al. (2010). It permits the integration of divergent resources in distributed systems as well as the representation of various levels of linguistic analysis. In this work we are particularly interested in exploring the representation of these linguistic levels for analyzing utterances in the context of human-machine interactions. To be able to evaluate the representation on a large set of data the French MEDIA dialogue corpus is used, Bonneau-Maynard et al. (2005). The MEDIA corpus collects about 70 hours of spontaneous speech in the task of hotel room reservation and tourist information. It has been created using a Wizard-of-Oz technique, as a consequence, the utterances are made of many disfluencies, hesitations, false starts, truncations or fillers words (e.g., euh or ben). Thus, the syntactic analysis is relevant for keeping valuable information for further processing (e.g., reference resolution). The semantics describe fine grained predicates, arguments and features based on the domain knowledge. Similarly, the possibility of link references for pragmatic analysis and the representation of the illocutionary force of utterances are relevant to improve the understanding in NLP applications. We selected MMIL for the semantic annotation because it supports the representation of all these features.

Although these features enrich the semantic annotation of utterances in the corpus, they also increase the complexity of the annotation and compromise the agreement between annotators. The possibility of representing different instantiations in MMIL has been the main cause of disagreement between annotators. On the one hand, linguists tend to annotate the surface form of the utterance. On the other

*This work is supported by the French *Agence Nationale de la Recherche* (ANR) and is part of the Project PORT-MEDIA (www.port-media.org).

hand, application designers are more biased towards its canonical representation by keeping relevant task oriented actions and features. The trade-off between these two lines of representation is significant for building appropriately the annotation guidelines for the semantic annotation. The annotation would keep the most valuable information in a multilevel representation for enhancing the understanding capability of NLP applications. In this paper we introduce briefly MMIL and we describe the annotation methodology and the inter-annotation agreement.

2 The High Level Representation

MMIL permits the representation of communicative actions that are represented as *components*. A component is a structure that gathers the communicative event and its propositional content. Components are made up of two main types of **entities**: *events*, which are entities anchored in the time dimension, and *participants*, which are entities not bounded by time. Entities are linked together by *relations* and are described by sets of *features* (i.e. pairs of attribute-value), Denis et al. (2010). Every component has a unique communicative event with the illocutionary force represented by means of the *dialogueAct* feature. The propositional content is represented as a *main event* with its arguments, which can be either events or participants, linked to the communicative event by a relation **propContent**. In this representation, predicates are usually represented as events and predicate arguments are usually represented as participants. Relations between participants and events usually describe the thematic roles.

French: "$/_1$euh vous venez de dire que précédemment qu' il n' a y avait plus de chambres disponibles à ces dates et maintenant vous en avez$/_2$ donc je voulais juste m' assurer qu' au Novotel vous avez bien une chambre double euh pour un couple avec un enfant avec une baignoire dans la chambre euh il me il me faut un Parc Ãă proximité et euh cent dix euros maximum la nuit est-ce-que vous pouvez vérifier"
English: "$/_1$um you just said earlier that there are not more rooms available on these dates and now there are$/_2$ so I just wanted to be sure that you have at the Novotel a double room for uh a couple with one child with a bath in the room uh I need a park nearby and uh hundred and ten euros up at night is that you can check"

Figure 1: Example of a complex utterance of the MEDIA Corpus.

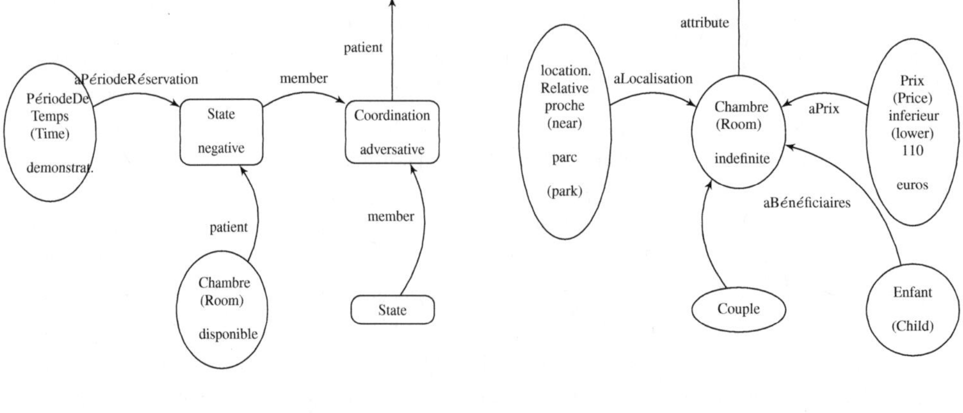

Figure 2: HLS as an abstraction of the meaning of the French utterance shown in Figure 1. Left: this component expresses the inform of a misunderstanding of the first segment ("$/_1$" in Figure 1). Right: this component is a request acknowledgment, representing the second segment("$/_2$" in Figure 1). Note that *events* are exemplify by square boxes while *participants* are exemplify by ellipses.

Let us focus on the MMIL representation for a typical utterance of the MEDIA corpus, given in Figure 1. In this utterance the user first announces an inconsistency, then asks for clarification. Thus, two MMIL components with different communicative actions, *inform* and *request acknowledgment*, have been used, as shown in Figure 2. The component on the left has a main event that describes the misunderstanding expressed in the first segment[1] of the utterance. It is represented by the ontological concept "Understand" and by the syntactic feature *polarity* with the *negative* value. It also contains a coordinated entity mirroring an *adversative* coordination between two events, *state*. The event *state* represents the status of something, therefore the *negated state event* can be understood as "there are not more rooms available on these dates" while the *positive state* represents "now there are". The participants symbolize the arguments "rooms" and "dates" respectively. The component on the right expresses the clarification request of the second segment. It verifies the status of the hotel with the specific constraints.

3 The Annotation Methodology

In the process of defining the annotation guidelines, we elaborated a specification document that describes the representation of dialogue acts, events and exemplifies the high-level semantics. Moreover, it delves into the methodology that might be applied for the automatic and manual annotation. Afterwards, a linguist expert and a project designer were in charge of defining the annotation guidelines. For this purpose, they annotated manually a subset of utterances which were supposed to be representative of the most complex aspects of the HLS annotation, in terms of their semantic constituents. 330 utterances were selected. They are all directly related to the reservation task (first two rows in Figure 4) and mostly occurred in the first 3 turns of the dialogues when the user is describing his goal, defined as an overall objective along with a set of constraints. Hereafter, we present the preliminary evaluation of the experts' agreement on these utterances.

The annotation process has been supported by an annotation tool: `ATool`. It accesses two knowledge-bases, one for the MMIL formalism and the other for the MEDIA domain. The latter is adapted from the MEDIA evaluation campaign, Bonneau-Maynard et al. (2006). ATool permits annotators to navigate through utterances, while displaying the MMIL representation. Annotators can design the MMIL components graphs, define the MMIL entities by associating features, values and segment. ATool will suggest the possible features and values for the MMIL formalism and for the domain according to the knowledge-bases ensuring the integrity of the constructed MMIL components in the annotation.

The MEDIA corpus is rich in expressions that evoke several communicative actions. Figure 4 shows a few examples. For the purpose of the task, we are interested in the underlying meaning of sentences, thus politeness and indirectness are discarded from the HLS representation. For this reason, in *requests* the speaker is the patient, while the hearer is the agent (see Figure 4). Because when translating the utterance into its deep instantiation, the speaker will benefit from the execution of the action, while the hearer has the obligation to perform the action. All the expressions in the corpus that bear the semantics of "command for a reservation" (e.g., *je veux réserver*, *je souhaite réserver*, *je voudrais faire une réservation*, *j'aimerais faire une réservation*, all equivalent to *I would like to reserve*), have been normalized with the deep component shown in Figure 3, exemplifying unequivocally the user's desire to request for a reservation. The possible arguments and roles have been detailed in the domain knowledge-base. As a consequence the knowledge-base defines relations between hotels, rooms, customers, prices, equipments, services, locations and dates. Besides, the grammatical relations and features, such as coordination, have been defined in the MMIL knowledge-base. Coordination is indicated with the "coordtype" feature and it is used in cases of *conjunction* (*je veux une chambre simple et deux chambres double*, *I want a single room and two double bedrooms*), *disjunction* (*Paris ou en proche banlieue*, *in Paris or suburbs*) or *adversation* (*en ville mais pas trop loin de la mer*, *in the city but not too far from the sea*).

For annotating events we can find the main verb in the utterance and represent it as the main event in MMIL by following a domain-specific classification of verbs, from which Figure 4 shows some equivalences among dialogue acts and verbs. For each participant or event, several features can be

[1]Segments are sequence of words that are depicted as "$/_i$", where i is the number of the segment.

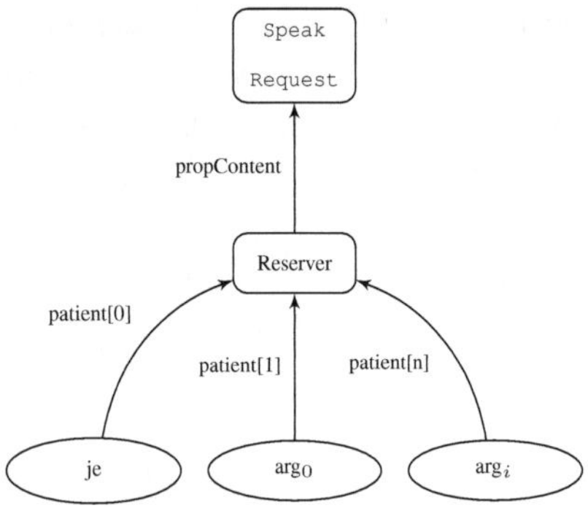

Figure 3: Canonical representation of a booking request in MEDIA.

D. Act	EvType	Examples	Semantic Roles
Request	Reserver	réserver [la chambre]	aObjetRéservé
		réserver [pour le troisième week-end de novembre une nuit] [á Clermont-Ferrand] [pour quatre chambres doubles]	 aPériodeRéservation aLocalisation aObjetRéservé
Inform	Inform	[j'] ai des informations supplémentaires	agent
Request	Inform	[j'] aurais aimÃl' avoir exactement [les dates]	patient[0], patient[1]
Request	State	[Il] est [Ãă combien]	patient, aPrix
Request	Repeter	pouvez-[vous] répéter	agent
Inform	Repeter	[je] vais me répéter	agent
Accept		oui	
Reject		non	

Figure 4: Some of the observed dialogue acts and main events with their arguments in the corpus.

added. The most important of them are "object type" (for participants) or "event type" (for events), which specify their ontological concepts. They may be réserver (reserve), hôtel (hotel), chambre (room), périodedetemps (time), ville (city), person, adulte (adult), enfant (child), localisationnommée (places), among others. There are more specific features, for instance, the journey dates, hotel features (e.g., name, standing, services, etc). Some of these features have predefined values, such as the *gender* of an object (either masculine or feminine). On the other side, features such as *cardinality*, have not predefined values, in that case, the annotator has to manually indicate the correct value.

Obviously, the annotation task difficulty increases with the utterance's complexity. The representation is rather tedious to define in elliptical utterances, such as multiple reservations, in which implicit and explicit information must be taken under consideration. Furthermore, the MMIL formalism does not support the association of discontinuous segments to entities, generating some imprecisions in the HLS annotation. For instance, in *je voudrais une chambre pour deux personnes euh simple* (I would like a room for two people uh simple),"une chambre" (a room) and "simple" should be linked to an unique participant, having as *object type* ("Room") and as *type of room* "simple". However, given that the speaker has not mentioned "simple"right after "chambre", there is a new element imbricated between them: "pour deux personnes". As a result, the annotator must integrate the subsegment 'pour deux personnes" in the "Room" participant. Even though this subsegment is also associated to the "Personne" participant.

4 Results

When analyzing the sample of 330 utterances that were annotated, we found a perfect agreement between annotators in the detection of dialogue-acts, main events, as well as main arguments. In constrast, when measuring fine-grained features inside components we found eight types of disagreement, namely *conjunctions, disjunctions, creation of participant for simple features, groups of features inside entities, features of entities, values of features, relation names* and *relation among entities*. The most frequent cases concern the first two, which refer to coordination: conjunctions (20%) and disjunctions (5%). The inter-annotator agreement for the coordinate entities was computed, obtaining the kappa measure, Carletta (1996), of 0.25 for conjunctions and 0.15 for disjunctions, meaning a fair and slight agreement respectively. Although the other cases were less frequent, the inter-annotator agreement was even lower, indicating no agreement.

In spite of the disagreement, when measuring the global similarity between the MMIL components created by both annotators we found a high score of 98%. This metric measures the graph similarity by computing the similarity between entities and relations, including the fine-grained features inside entities. The speech-act, main-event and main arguments are in compliance with the specifications in both annotations.

Case	Annotator 1	Annotator 2
Conjunctions	68	56
Disjunctions	18	10
Part. for simple feats.	11	0
Grouping feats.	0	2

Case	Discrepancy
Features	4
Features' values	5
Name of relations.	5
Relation among entities.	2

Figure 5: Left: the Table displays the number of utterances by annotator for the listed cases. Annotator 1, is the liguist expert, Annotator 2 is the project designer. Right: fhe Table shows the number of utterances with a completely discrepant annotation: different features for same entities, different values for same features, different relation between same entities and entities related differently in a component.

These issues show that the disagreement cases were less frequent. So far, annotators have not being so rigourous when segmenting the text inside features. Therefore, segmentation needs to be checked in both annotations. After this experiment, we are defining the final certified annotation and deriving the annotation guidelines formally.

5 Discussion

Defining the annotation guidelines for high level semantic representation is controversial. The multiple features that can be represented in the selected MMIL formalism, as well as the multiple instantiations offer different possibilities for representing the same utterance. In general representing spoken utterances is cumbersome, because of the linguist phenomena present in spontaneous speech. As a consequence, annotators have to deal not only with the explicit, but also with the implicit information, and in some cases the representations might be subjective. For these reasons, we defined the standard for the annotation, and based on it, we carried out an annotation experiment on a sample of 330 complex utterances, directly related to the reservation task; involving two annotator profiles i.e., a linguist and a project designer. Afterwards, we measured the similarity between the annotated MMIL components and the inter-annotation agreement obtaining a 98% of similarity and only eight major cases of disagreement, coordination discrepancy being the most frequent. Right now, we are refining the final annotation guidelines based on these results. This first experiment analyzes the most complex and numerous utterances in the corpus covering reservation requests and affirmations. Subsequently, misunderstanding, questions and clarifications will be analyzed following the same methodology. As a result, we will be able to reduce the disagreement between annotators in order to produce the annotation of the whole MEDIA corpus, which will be made freely available to the research community.

References

Bonneau-Maynard, H., C. Ayache, F. Bechet, A. Denis, A. Kuhn, F. Lefèvre, D. Mostefa, M. Quignard, S. Rosset, C. Servan, , and J. Villaneau (2006). Results of the french evalda-media evaluation campaign for literal understanding. In 5th International Conference on Language Resources and Evaluation (LREC2006).

Bonneau-Maynard, H., S. Rosset, C. Ayache, A. Kuhn, and D. Mostefa (2005). Semantic annotation of the french media dialog corpus. In *INTERSPEECH-2005, 3457-3460.*

Carletta, J. (1996). Assessing agreement on classification tasks: the kappa statistic. *Comput. Linguist. 22*(2), 249–254.

Denis, A., L. M. Rojas-Barahona, and M. Quignard. (2010). Extending MMIL semantic representation: Experiments in dialogue systems and semantic annotation of corpora. In *proceedings of the Fifth Joint ISO-ACL/SIGSEM Workshop on Interoperable Semantic Annotation (ISA-5), Hong Kong, January 2010.*

Collecting Semantic Data by Mechanical Turk for the Lexical Knowledge Resource of a Text-to-Picture Generating System

Masoud Rouhizadeh* Margit Bowler* Richard Sproat* Bob Coyne**

*Center for Spoken Language Understanding, Oregon Health and Science University
**Department of Computer Science, Columbia University

Abstract

WordsEye is a system for automatically converting natural language text into 3D scenes representing the meaning of that text. At the core of WordsEye is the Scenario-Based Lexical Knowledge Resource (SBLR), a unified knowledge base and representational system for expressing lexical and real-world knowledge needed to depict scenes from text. To enrich a portion of the SBLR, we need to fill out some contextual information about its objects, including information about their typical parts, typical locations and typical objects located near them. This paper explores our proposed methodology to achieve this goal. First we try to collect some semantic information by using Amazon's Mechanical Turk (AMT). Then, we manually filter and classify the collected data and finally, we compare the manual results with the output of some automatic filtration techniques which use several WordNet similarity and corpus association measures.

1 Introduction

WordsEye (Coyne and Sproat, 2001), (Coyne et al., 2010) is a system for automatically converting natural language text into 3D scenes representing the meaning of that text. A version of WordsEye has been tested online (www.wordseye.com) with several thousand real-world users. The system works by first parsing each input sentence into a dependency structure. These dependency structures are then processed to resolve anaphora and other coreferences. The lexical items and dependency links are then converted to semantic nodes and roles drawing on lexical valence patterns and other information in the Scenario-Based Lexical Knowledge Resource (SBLR) (Coyne et al., 2010). The resulting semantic relations are then converted to a final set of graphical constraints representing the position, orientation, size, color, texture, and poses of objects in the scene. Finally, the scene is composed from these constraints and rendered in OpenGL (http://www.opengl.org).

The SBLR is the core of the text-to-scene conversion mechanism. It is a unified knowledge base and representational system for expressing lexical and real-world knowledge needed to depict scenes from text. The SBLR will ultimately include information on the semantic categories of words; the semantic relations between predicates (verbs, nouns, adjectives, and prepositions) and their arguments; the types of arguments different predicates typically take; additional contextual knowledge about the visual scenes various events and activities occur in; and the relationship between this linguistic information and the 3D objects in our objects library.

To enrich a portion of the SBLR we need to fill out some contextual information about several hundred objects in WordsEye's database, including information about their typical parts, typical location and typical objects nearby them. Such information can in principle be extracted from online corpora (e.g. Sproat (2001)), but such data is invariably noisy and requires hand editing. Furthermore, precisely because much of the information is *common sense* it is rarely explicitly stated in text. Ontologies of common sense information such as Cyc are effectively useless for extracting such information.

This paper explores our proposed methodology to achieve this goal. First we try to collect some semantic information by Amazon's Mechanical Turk (AMT). Then, we manually filter and classify the collected data and finally, we compare the manual results with the output of some automatic filtration techniques which use WN similarity and corpus association measures.

2 Data collection from Amazon's Mechanical Turk

Amazon's Mechanical Turk is an online marketplace that provides a way to pay people small amounts of money to perform tasks that are simple for humans but difficult for computers. Examples of these Human Intelligence Tasks (HITs) range from labeling images to moderating blog comments to providing feedback on the relevance of results for a search query. The highly accurate, cheap and efficient results of several NLP tasks (Callison-Burch and Dredze, 2010) have encouraged us to explore using AMT.

We designed three separate tasks to collect information about typical nearby objects, typical location and typical parts of the objects of our library. For **task 1**, we asked the workers to name 10 common objects that they might typically find around or near a given object. For **task 2**, we asked the workers to name 10 locations in which they might typically find a given object and in **task 3**, we asked the workers to list 10 parts of a given object. Given that some objects might not consist of 10 parts, (i.e, they are very simple objects), we wanted the worker to name as many parts as possible. We collected 17,200 responses from the AMT tasks and paid $106.90 overall for completion of the three tasks. Table 1 shows a summary of the AMT tasks, payments, and completion time.

Task	TW	UI	AA	RPA	EHR	ACT
Objects	342	6850	2′	$0.05	$1.54	5
Locations	342	6850	2′	$0.05	$1.26	5
Parts	245	3500	1′	$0.07	$2.29	5

TW: Number of Target Words; **UI**: Number of User Inputs; **AA**: Average Time Per Assignment; **RPA**: Reward Per Assignment; **EHR**: Effective Hourly Rate; **ACT**: Approximate Completion Days

Table 1: Summary of AMT tasks, payments and the completion time

The data that we collected in this step was in raw format. The next step was filtering out undesirable data entered by the workers and mapping it into entities and relations contained within the SBLR.

3 Manual filtering and classifying the data

Data collected from AMT tasks was manually filtered via removal of undesirable target item-response item pairs and classified via definition of the relations between the remaining target item-response item pairs. Response items given in their plural form were lemmatized to the singular form of the word. A total of 34 relations were defined within the Amazon Mechanical Turk data. Defining relations was completed manually and determined by pragmatic cues about the relationship held between the target item-response item pair. Restricting AMT workers to those within the United States ensured that actions or items which might differ in their typically found location by cultural or geographical context were restricted to the location(s) generally agreed upon by English speakers within the United States.

Generic, widely applicable relations were used in the general case for all sets of Mechanical Turk data (e.g. the containment relation *containing.r* was used for generic instances of containment; the *next-to.r* relation was used for target item-response item pairs for which the orientation of the items with respect to one another was not a defining characteristic of their relationship). Finer distinctions were made within these generic relations, e.g. *habitat.r* and *residence.r* within the overarching containment relation, which specified that the relation held between two items was that of habitat or residence, respectively. More semantically explicit relations were used for target item-response item pairs that tended to occur in more specific relations. Specific relations of this type included those spatial relations from the following target item-response item-relation triples:

javelin - dirt - embedded-in.r
binoculars - case - true-containing.r

Another subsection of relations included functional relations such as those within the following triples:

harmonica - hand - human-grip.r

earmuffs - head - wearing.r

Relation labels for meronymic (part-whole) relations were based off of already defined part-whole classifications (Priss, 1996).

3.1 Data and results for each AMT task

Target item-response item pairs were usually rejected for misinterpretation of the potentially ambiguous target item (e.g. misinterpreting mobile as a cell phone rather than as a decorative hanging structure, prompting *mobile - ear* as an object-nearby object pair). Target item-response item pairs were also discarded if the interpretation of the target item, though viable, was not contained within the SBLR library. This was especially prevalent in instances where the target item was a plant or animal (e.g. *crawfish*) that could be interpreted as either a live plant/animal or as food. With the exception of mushroom, the SBLR does not contain the edible interpretation of these nouns; in the object-nearby object task, target item-response item pairs such as *crawfish - plate* were discarded.

In the object-location task, the most common relation labels were derivatives of the generic spatial containment relation. The *containing.r* relation accounted for 38.01% of all labeled target-response pairs; *habitat.r* accounted for 11.02%, and *on-surface.r* accounted for 10.6%.

In the part-whole task, AMT workers provided responses that were predominantly labeled by part-whole relations. When AMT responses were not relevant for part-whole relations, they tended to fall under the generic containment relation. The *object-part.r* relation accounted for 79.12% of all labeled target-response pairs; *stuff-object.r* accounted for 16.33%, and *containing.r* accounted for 1.48%.

As with the part-whole task, responses in the nearby objects task that were not relevant for the next-to.r relation usually fell under the generic spatial containment relation. In the object-nearby object task, the *next-to.r* relation was the most frequently utilized relation label, accounting for 75.66% of all target-response pairs labeled. The *on-surface.r* relation was the second most common relation, with 5.69%, and *containing.r* accounted for 4.44% of all labeled target-response pairs

4 Automatic filtering undesirable data

Manual processing of the data is a time-consuming and expensive approach. As a result, we are investigating different automatic techniques to filter out the undesirable responses from AMT, using current manually annotated data as a gold standard for evaluation of automatic approaches.

4.1 WordNet Similarity measures

In the first approach, we computed some lexical similarity scores for the target and the response items based on the following WN similarity measures. (It should be noted that not all of the target and responses were present in WN. For such words, we used their nearest hypernyms).

WN Path Distance Similarity between each target word and each received response for that target word. This score denotes how similar two word senses are, based on the shortest path that connects the senses in the is-a (hypernym/hypnoym) taxonomy. We selected the maximum similarity score of different senses of the target and the respond words.

Resnik Similarity between each target word and each of the received responses for that target word. This score denotes how similar the two word senses are, based on the Information Content (IC) of the Least Common Subsumer (most specific ancestor node) (Resnik, 1999).

The Average Pairwise Similarity Score which is computed based on WN path distance similarity score. If we assume $W_1, W_2 ... W_n$ to be n responses for target word T; and S_{ij} to be the WN path distance similarity between W_i and W_j, then the average pairwise similarity score for W_i will be $\frac{S_{i1}+S_{i2}+...+S_{in}}{n}$. This will provide us the average similarity of each response (i.e W_i) with the other responses (i.e. W_j

so that $i \neq j$). In this way we will reward the responses that are more semantically related to each other (regardless of their similarity to the target word).

The WN Matrix Similarity which is a bag of words similarity matrix based on WN path distance similarities. For target word T we have the following similarity matrix:

$$\begin{array}{l} 1 + S_{12} + ... + S_{1n} \\ S_{21} + 1 + ... + S_{2n} \\ \vdots \\ S_{n1} + S_{n2} + ... + S_{nn} \end{array}$$

In this matrix row i is the similarity vector of W_i represented as $\vec{V_i}$ = $[S_{i1} + S_{i2} + ... + S_{in}]$. We use cosine similarity to calculate the similarity measure of two words. So, the similarity measure of W_i and W_j is the cosine of $\vec{V_i}$ and $\vec{V_j}$ and is computed by $CS_{ij} = cos(\theta) = \frac{V_i.V_j}{||V_i||.||V_j||}$. Then the WN matrix similarity score of W_i will be $\frac{CS_{i1}+CS_{i2}+...+CS_{in}}{n}$. The more two words are semantically related to similar set of words, the higher cosine similarity they will have. If a word is related to many different words in the set, it will obtain higher WN matrix similarity score.

4.2 Corpus association measures

The next approach for filtering the raw data was finding association measures of target-response pairs using Google's 1-trillion 5-gram web corpus (LDC2006T13), by counting the frequency of each target and response word in unigram and bigram portions of the corpus and then the number of times the two words co-occur within a +/- 4-word window in the 5-gram portion of the corpus. We also computed the sentential co-occurrences of each target-response pair (i.e. the number of sentences in which the target or the response words appear and the number of sentences in which both words occur together) on the English Gigaword corpus (LDC2007T07) which is a 1 billion word corpus of articles marked up from English press texts (mainly the New York Times). Based on these counts, we used log-likelihood and log-odds ratio (Dunning, 1993) to compute the association between the two words.

4.3 Discussion and evaluation of automatic filtaration techniques

The collected responses of each AMT task were ranked separately by each of the above similarity and association measures. We classify the ranked responses into "keep" (higher-scoring) and "reject" (lower-scoring) classes by defining a specific threshold for each list. Then we evaluated the accuracy of each filtration approach by computing their precision and recall on correct "keep" items (see table 2). In this table the baseline score shows the accuracy of the responses of each AMT task before using automatic filtration techniques. It should be added that collecting data by using AMT is rather cheap and fast, so we are more interested in higher precision (achieving highly accurate data) than higher recall. Lower recall means we lose some data, which is not too expensive to collect.

	Baseline		**Log-likelihood**		**Log-odds**		**WN Path Dist sim**		**Resnik sim**		**WN Pairwise sim**		**WN Matrix sim**	
	Pre	Rec	Pre	Rec	Pre	Rec	Pre	Rec	Pre	Rec	Pre	Rec	Pre	Rec
LOC	0.5527	1.0	0.7832	0.6690	0.7851	0.6684	0.5624	0.9724	0.5674	0.9784	0.6115	0.3657	0.4832	1.0
PAR	0.7887	1.0	0.7921	0.4523	0.8321	0.5022	0.8073	1.0	0.8234	1.0	0.9045	0.2859	0.9010	0.2516
OBJ	0.8934	1.0	0.9015	1.0	0.9286	0.9144	0.9123	1.0	0.9185	1.0	0.9855	0.3215	0.8925	1.0

Table 2: The accuracy of automatic filtering approaches

As can be seen in table 2, within the object-location data set, we gained the best precision (0.7832) by using log-odds with relatively high recall (0.6690). Target-response pairs that were approved or rejected contrary to automatic predictions were due primarily to the specificity of the response location.

In the part-whole task, the best precision (0.9010) was achieved by using WN matrix similarities but again we lost a noticeable portion of data (recall= 0.2516). Rejected target-response pairs from the higher-scoring part-whole set were often due to responses that named attributes, rather than parts, of the target item (e.g. croissant - flaky). Many responses were too general (e.g, gong - material). Many target-response pairs would have fallen under the next-to.r relation rather than any of the meronymic relations. The majority of the approved target-response pairs from the lower-scoring part-whole set were due to obvious, "common sense responses that would usually be inferred rather than explicitly stated, particularly body parts (e.g, bunny - brain).

The baseline accuracy of the nearby objects task is quite high (precision=0.8934, recall=1.0), and we gain the best precision by using WN average pairwise similarity (0.9855) by removing lower-scoring part of AMT responses (recall=0.3215). The high precision in all automatic techniques is due primarily to the fact that the open-ended nature of the task resulted in a large number of target-response pairs that, while not pertinent to the next-to.r relation, could be labeled by other relations. Again, the open-ended nature of the nearby objects task resulted in the lowest percentage of rejected high-scoring pairs.

5 Conclusions

In this paper, we investigated the use Amazon's Mechanical Turk for collecting semantic information for a portion of our lexical knowledge resource. Manual evaluation of the AMT responses (baseline results in table 2) confirms that we can collect highly accurate data in a cheap and efficient way by using AMT. The accuracy of automatic filtration techniques sounds promising as we were able to filter out some undesirable data, most of the time without loosing so much of collected responses.

Overall, we have shown a method which is very good in collecting semantic information and some other methods which are very good at filtering out word pairs that are undesirable in this particular context (i.e locations, nearby object and parts of our object library). This approach seems to have the potential to be extended for more contexts. For the future work, we are planning to apply this methodology to collect semantic information about *action verbs*, such as information about the locations of the action, the participants, their relation to each other, the background objects and so on.

References

Callison-Burch, C. and M. Dredze (2010). Creating speech and language data with amazon's mechanical turk. In *Proceedings of the NAACL HLT 2010 Workshop on Creating Speech and Language Data with Amazon's Mechanical Turk*, Los Angeles, CA, USA, pp. 1–12.

Coyne, B., O. Rambow, J. Hirschberg, and R. Sproat (2010). Frame semantics in text-to-scene generation. In R. Setchi, I. Jordanov, R. Howlett, and L. Jain (Eds.), *Knowledge-Based and Intelligent Information and Engineering Systems*, Volume 6279 of *Lecture Notes in Computer Science*, pp. 375–384. Springer Berlin / Heidelberg.

Coyne, B. and R. Sproat (2001). Wordseye: An automatic text-to-scene conversion system. In *Proceedings of the 28th annual conference on Computer graphics and interactive techniques*, Los Angeles, CA, USA, pp. 487– 496.

Coyne, B., R. Sproat, and J. Hirschberg (2010). Spatial relations in text-to-scene conversion. In *Computational Models of Spatial Language Interpretation, Workshop at Spatial Cognition 2010*, Mt. Hood, OR, USA, pp. 9–16.

Dunning, T. E. (1993). Accurate methods for the statistics of surprise and coincidence. *Computational Linguistics 19*(1), 61–74.

Priss, U. (1996). Classification of meronymy by methods of relational concept analysis. In *Online proceedings of the 1996 Midwest Artificial Intelligence Conference*, Bloomington, IN, USA.

Resnik, P. (1999). Semantic similarity in a taxonomy: An information-based measure and its application to problems of ambiguity in natural language. *Journal of Artificial Intelligence Research*, 95–130.

Sproat, R. (2001). Inferring the environment in a text-to-scene conversion system. In *Proceedings of The First International Conference on Knowledge Capture*, Victoria, BC, Canada, pp. 147–154.

Edge dependent pathway scoring for calculating semantic similarity in ConceptNet

Steve Spagnola
Cornell University
sps34@cs.cornell.edu

Carl Lagoze
Cornell University
lagoze@cs.cornell.edu

Abstract

Most techniques that calculate the relatedness between two concepts use a semantic network, such as Wikipedia, WordNet, or ConceptNet, to find the shortest intermediate pathway between two nodes. These techniques assume that a low number of edges on the shortest pathway indicates conceptual similarity. Although this technique has proven valid in conforming to psychological data, we test the usefulness of additional pathway variables in ConceptNet, such as edge type and user-rated score. Our results show strong evidence for the application of additional pathway variables in calculating semantic similarity.

1 ConceptNet Pathways

ConceptNet 3 is one of the largest commonsense semantic networks in existence, relying on its users to make conceptual assertions and collectively vote on the legitimacy of other users' assertions. ConceptNet is valuable as a semantic resource because it suggests transitive inference between ideas, enabling dissimilar concepts to share a semantic, indirect relationship. Unlike Wikipedia and WordNet, the edges in ConceptNet contain additional semantic information between two concepts. Each edge is assigned a relation type (such as "Is A" or "Located At") and a score that correlates to how well ConceptNet users believe in the validity of the relation [Havasi and Alonso (2007)]. Previous work on calculating semantic relatedness between two concepts ignores these extra edge features, using only the inverse of number of edges on a short path [Rada and Blettner (1989); Wubben and A. (2009)]. Instead of only looking for the shortest pathway from one concept to another we assess all pathways in measuring the semantic similarity of an association. A simple example is shown in Figure 1: two nodes (cat and dog) with two pathways containing varying intermediary nodes and edge types.

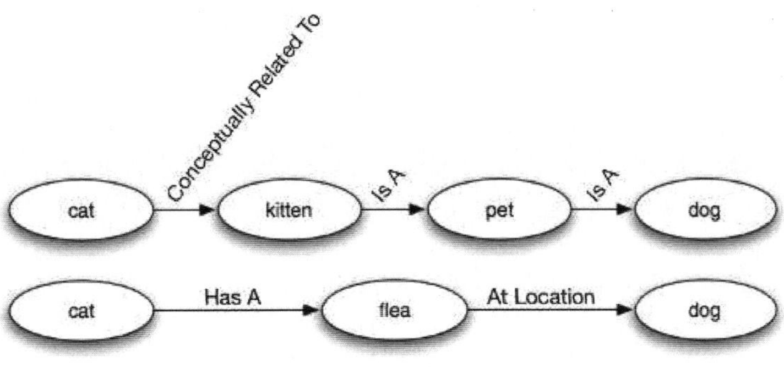

Figure 1: Transitive links between nodes in ConceptNet may occur through a variety of pathways, some being more appropriate than others.

Each possible pathway from one concept to another contains a set of edges, where each edge has a predefined edge type and validity score. Hence, in addition to edge count, we can use the sum of edge scores within a pathway as an additional feature. It may be the case that some pathways have a low number of edges (implying a high relatedness metric by inverse edge count), yet only contain poorly scoring edges that are incorrect or noisy inferences, yielding low aggregate score. In such cases the simple use of edge count may lead to false "low confidence" inferences, which our technique avoids.

In addition to edge score, we also use the 27 predefined edge types in the network to calculate conditional edge type transition probability. We use these edge types to calculate the overall distribution of the 27 edge types as the independent probability of encountering a given edge type on the initial edge traversal within a pathway. Furthermore, we also calculate the conditional probabilities of changing edge types along any given pathway. For example, given that we traverse an "Is A" edge to a concept X, the probability of traversing another "Is A" edge from concept X is .13, whereas the probability of changing to a "Has A" relation is only .05, as shown in Figure 2. These transition probabilities are calculated for all sequential edge pairs within the entire graph, constructing the following Markov Model.

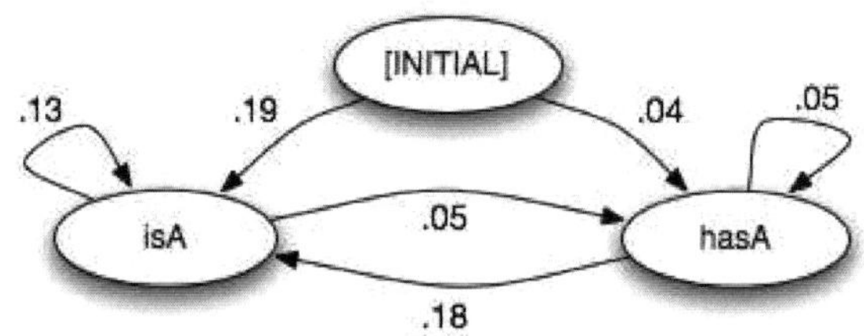

Figure 2: Learned edge transition probabilities (only 2 of 27 edge types shown).

We believe that the inclusion of these two additional variables helps identify edges that not only have a high consensus with respect to the individual triple, but also are contextually appropriate relative to the prior edge traversed. Hence, we are combining the specific attributes of edges with the characteristics of the larger, overall network, edge transition probabilities to assess pathways.

2 Pathway Scoring

We now have two properties for each edge on a given pathway of N nodes: score and transition probability. Using these, we can compose three vectors that can describe any given pathway: SCORES, TRANSITIONS, and EDGES (see equations 1, 2, and 3 respectively).

$$SCORES = [\sqrt[3]{EdgeScore_{1,2}}, \sqrt[3]{EdgeScore_{2,3}}, ..., \sqrt[3]{EdgeScore_{N-1,N}}] \tag{1}$$

SCORES is a vector of size N-1 with the cube root of each edge score in each cell. In initial testing, we found that using the cube root of user ranked scores was necessary to prevent high scoring edges from overshadowing lower scoring edges. We believe that this particular normalization technique is unique to the score distribution of ConceptNet 3, but that the general technique is expandable to other networks based on score distributions.

$$TRANSITIONS = [P(Edge_{1,2}), P(Edge_{2,3}|Edge_{1,2}), ..., P(Edge_{N,N-1}|Edge_{N-1,N-2})] \tag{2}$$

TRANSITIONS is another vector of size N-1 containing the conditional probabilities of observing each edge type within each cell. The first cell in the vector is just the independent probability of encountering the first edge, whereas every cell beyond that calculates the conditional probability of encountering the edge type based on the prior edge type.

$$EDGES = [N - 1] \tag{3}$$

EDGES is a vector of size 1 that simply contains N-1 as its value, or the number of edges in the pathway.

After associating these three vectors with all possible pathways from one concept to another, we now introduce a scoring function for each pathway. The function assigns each possible pathway a score, and the pathway with the highest score is used as the "shortest" semantic pathway from one concept to another. Hence, if a given concept has several pathways to another given concept, we select the pathway with the maximum score and use this score as the similarity metric. We use the maximum score as a metric to follow similar work in the field rather than experimenting with average or minimum pathway strength. Note, that because ConceptNet is directed, the similarity metric between concepts corresponds to a specific direction.

$$PathScore = \frac{< SCORES, TRANSITIONS >}{||EDGES||^2} \tag{4}$$

The scoring function shown in equation 4 is the inner product of SCORES and TRANSITIONS divided by the EDGES, or number of edges, squared. This approach introduces the SCORES and TRANSITIONS values into the traditional inverse edge-count function. We use the inner product to obtain an interaction effect between scores and transitions, where each edge has its score multiplied by its transition probability before being summed. Hence, the inner product will reward edges with both high scores and high transition probabilities as the product grows higher. Our intuition is that this interaction effect will be useful for finding relevant pathways because it ensures that the edges traversed have a high social confidence score, and are ordered in an edge-type sequence that agrees with the overall structure of the network.

We define our function in terms of vectors so we can easily test the effect of ignoring certain features by substituting vectors with all 1s instead of the actual values. For example, to disable the use of the transition probabilities in scoring, we simply set all values in the TRANSITIONS vector to 1. This approach allows us to test all combinations of pathway features to determine which ones are useful, and whether or not an interaction effect exists between scores and transitions.

3 Experiments

We tested all possible combinations of enabling or disabling our three pathway feature vectors in computing pathway scores. To measure how well a scoring function performs, we followed Wubben's approach of comparing ConceptNet shortest path conceptual relatedness to the Finkelstein-353 psychological dataset [Finkelstein and Ruppin (2002)]. This dataset contains 353 word pairs, each with a similarity score from 0 to 10 based on psychological free word association between two words. Because ConceptNet does not contain nodes for all words used in the Finkelstein-353, we ignored word pairs that could not be found in ConceptNet. Wubben calculated the correlation between the word pair rankings in the Finkelstein-353 and ConceptNet similarity (using simple edge count as pathway cost) to obtain a Pearson's correlation of .47 [Wubben and A. (2009)]. Studies using Wikipedia are able to obtain even higher correlations than .47, however we find this work incomparable to our study due to the wider coverage and different structure of Wikipedia [Strube and Ponzetto (2006)].

Our experimental design differs from that of Wubben's on two fronts. Wubben used bidirectional pathways, whereas our work only focuses on directed pathways for each pair in the dataset, ranking the directed pathways from word A to word B in the Finkelstein-353. We chose this approach because psychological subjects were presented with word A first, followed by word B, in which we assume that subjects were more prone to make the directed connections. Furthermore, because we are not using a simple edge-counting algorithm, we were not able to efficiently examine all of ConceptNet due to computational limitations. Instead, we ran several cases in which we examine all pathways between concepts in the Finkelstein set within ConceptNet, subject to a maximum number of pathway nodes. For example, if we only allow a maximum of three pathway nodes, then we only analyze the set of found pathways containing up to three nodes. If a pathway is not found between two concepts within a three node pathway, but we know that the concept exists in ConceptNet, then we set the score equal to 0. We were able to reach a maximum of six pathway nodes before calculations became infeasible.

4 Results

Our experiments were designed to test the usefulness for pathway score and transition probabilities, as well as an interaction effect between the two features, in addition to inverse edge-count. Hence, we aim to prove that using all three vectors in Equation 4 will outperform the traditional approach of only using EDGES. We tested these cases, in addition to all other feature usage combinations, on allowed maximum pathway lengths up to six, hoping to see how allowed pathway length additionally affects our scoring function's usefulness.

Our results from Table 1 show a significant performance gain when using all three vectors in tandem, as opposed to just the number of edges. Furthermore, our results were able to outperform Wubben's results of .47. We also see that the performance gains over the naive edge-only approach increase with the maximum allowed number of nodes in the pathway.

Although we are able to show improvements over edge-only scoring, we replicate previous results that demonstrate that using the inverse of edge length is both necessary and sufficient to obtain acceptable results [Wubben and A. (2009)]. Results become unusable for rows (S), (T), and (ST) beyond a pathway length of 3 when pathway length (E) is not considered. Furthermore, edge only scoring (E) is sufficient by itself to obtain acceptable results, outperforming all other cases aside from (EST).

The most important finding is that if we only add scores or transition probabilities to edge count scoring in cases (ES) and (ET), then performance declines from using only edge counts (E). This suggests that edge scores and transition probabilities are noisy features when considered in isolation. It is only when they are combined, in conjunction with edge count (EST) that we see performance gains, confirming our proposed interaction effect.

5 Discussion

Our results suggest that the interaction effect between edge score and edge type transitioning is useful for improving conceptual similarity calculations in ConceptNet. Our scoring formula provides a strong reward for edges that contain a high user rated score and edge transition probability. We believe that these properties produce stronger results because isolated edge scores are contextualized based on their relative sequence of edge-types within a pathway. For example, a path traversal across an "is A" edge and then to a "has A" edge may not be meaningful if the network as a whole does not contextually support this edge type transition pattern.

For future studies, we would like to extend our experiments beyond pathways of length 6 and see if

Maximum Pathway Length	2	3	4	5	6
Edge (E)	.285	.391	.414	.416	416
Score (S)	.280	.347	.079	-.166	-.120
Transition (T)	.281	.357	.041	-.268	-.097
Edge & Score (ES)	.280	.383	.400	.400	.401
Edge & Transition (ET)	.281	.399	.387	.407	.414
Score & Transition (ST)	.275	.363	.070	-.223	-.093
Edge & Score & Transition (EST)	.275	.416	.473	.496	.507
(EST) Absolute Improvement over (E)	-.010	.025	.059	.080	.091
(EST) Relative Improvement over (E)	-3.51%	6.39%	14.25%	19.23%	21.88%

Table 1: Results: Pearson's correlation for varying formulas and improvement over the traditional edge-only approach. Row labels indicate which feature vectors were activated for the experiment.

performance will begin sinking or will flatten after a given number of allowed nodes. Furthermore, we believe that deeper analysis of ConceptNet is warranted. We noticed that there are many noisy relationships that are illogical at first glance. However, deeper analysis shows that these noisy assertions are often the result of word stemming (such as shortening "building" to "build"), and word sense disambiguation issues. In future work, we would like to revert to the pure lexical assertions within ConceptNet to remove the stemming from the words, preserving the full meaning of the intended relations. We believe that a lexical parser would be able to detect plurals and address stemming issues better than the approach used in ConceptNet. Furthermore, we believe that word sense ambiguity adds noise to the network, and that our results could improve if ambiguous nodes were split into their corresponding senses.

Despite the noise present in ConceptNet, we believe that our approach demonstrates a strong improvement over traditional semantic similarity computations. We hope that future work may resolve the noise and ambiguity issues present in ConceptNet, in which our methodology may provide even stronger results in accurately calculating semantic similarity.

References

Finkelstein, L., G. E. M. Y. R. E. S. Z. W. G. and E. Ruppin (2002). Placing search in context: The concept revisited. In *ACM Transactions on Information Sys- tems.*

Havasi, C. Speer, R. and J. Alonso (2007). Conceptnet 3: a flexi- ble, multilingual semantic network for common sense knowledge. In *Recent Advances in Natural Language Processing.*

Rada, R.; Mili, H. B. E. and M. Blettner (1989). Development and application of a metric to semantic nets. In *IEEE Transactions on Systems, Man and Cybernetics*, Volume 19 of *1*, pp. 17–30.

Strube, M. and S. Ponzetto (2006). Wikirelate! computing semantic relatedness using wikipedia. In *AAAI'06: proceedings of the 21st national conference on Artificial intelligence*, Boston, Massachusetts, pp. 1419–1424. AAAI Press.

Wubben, S. and B. A. (2009). A semantic relatedness metric based on free link structure. In *Proceedings of the 8th International Conference on Computational Semantics*, pp. 355–358. International Conference on Computational Semantics.

Semantic Relatedness from Automatically Generated Semantic Networks

Pia-Ramona Wojtinnek and Stephen Pulman
Oxford University Computing Laboratory
{pia-ramona.wojtinnek, stephen.pulman}@comlab.ox.ac.uk

Abstract

We introduce a novel approach to measuring semantic relatedness of terms based on an automatically generated, large-scale semantic network. We present promising first results that indicate potential competitiveness with approaches based on manually created resources.

1 Introduction

The quantification of semantic similarity and relatedness of terms is an important problem of lexical semantics. Its applications include word sense disambiguation, text summarization and information retrieval (Budanitsky and Hirst, 2006). Most approaches to measuring semantic relatedness fall into one of two categories. They either look at distributional properties based on corpora (Finkelstein et al., 2002; Agirre et al., 2009) or make use of pre-existing knowledge resources such as WordNet or Roget's Thesaurus (Hughes and Ramage, 2007; Jarmasz, 2003). The latter approaches achieve good results, but they are inherently restricted in coverage and domain adaptation due to their reliance on costly manual acquisition of the resource. In addition, those methods that are based on hierarchical, taxonomically structured resources are generally better suited for measuring semantic similarity than relatedness (Budanitsky and Hirst, 2006). In this paper, we introduce a novel technique that measures semantic relatedness based on an automatically generated semantic network. Terms are compared by the similarity of their contexts in the semantic network. We present our promising initial results of this work in progress, which indicate the potential to compete with resource-based approaches while performing well on both, semantic similarity and relatedness.

2 Similarity and Relatedness from semantic networks

In our approach to measuring semantic relatedness, we first automatically build a large semantic network from text and then measure the similarity of two terms by the similarity of the local networks around their corresponding nodes. The semantic network serves as a structured representation of the occurring concepts, relations and attributes in the text. It is built by translating every sentence in the text into a network fragment based on semantic analysis and then merging these networks into a large network by mapping all occurrences of the same term into one node. Figure 1(a) contains a sample text snippet and the network derived from it. In this way, concepts are connected across sentences and documents, resulting in a high-level view of the information contained.

Our underlying assumption for measuring semantic relatedness is that semantically related nodes are connected to a similar set of nodes. In other words, we consider the context of a node in the network as a representation of its meaning. In contrast to standard approaches which look only at a type of context directly found in the text, e.g. words that occur within a certain window from the target word, our network-based context takes into account indirect connections between concepts. For example, in the text underlying the network in Fig. 2, *dissertation* and *module* rarely co-occurred in a sentence, but the network shows a strong connection over *student* as well as over *credit* and *work*.

2.1 The Network Structure

We build the network incrementally by parsing every sentence, translating it into a small network fragment and then mapping that fragment onto the main network generated from all previous sentences. Our translation of sentences from text to network is based on the one used in the ASKNet system (Harrington and Clark, 2007). It makes use of two NLP tools, the Clark and Curran parser (Clark and Curran, 2004) and the semantic analysis tool Boxer (Bos et al., 2004), both of which are part of the C&C Toolkit[1]. The parser is based on Combinatory Categorial Grammar (CCG) and has been trained on 40,000 manually annotated sentences of the WSJ. It is both robust and efficient. Boxer is designed to convert the CCG parsed text into a logical representation based on Discourse Representation Theory (DRT). This intermediate logical form representation presents an abstraction from syntactic details to semantic core information. For example, the syntactical forms *progress of student* and *student's progress* have the same Boxer representation as well as *the student who attends the lecture* and *the student attending the lecture*. In addition, Boxer provides some elementary co-reference resolution.

The translation from the Boxer output into a network is straightforward and an example is given in Figure 1(b). The network structure distinguishes between object nodes (rectangular), relational nodes (diamonds) and attributes (rounded rectangles) and different types of links such as subject or object links.

Students *select* **modules** *from* the published **list** and *write* a **dissertation**. **Modules** usually *provide* 15 **credits** each, but 30 **credits** are *awarded for* the **dissertation**. The **student** must *discuss* the **topic** *of* the final **dissertation** with their appointed **tutor**.

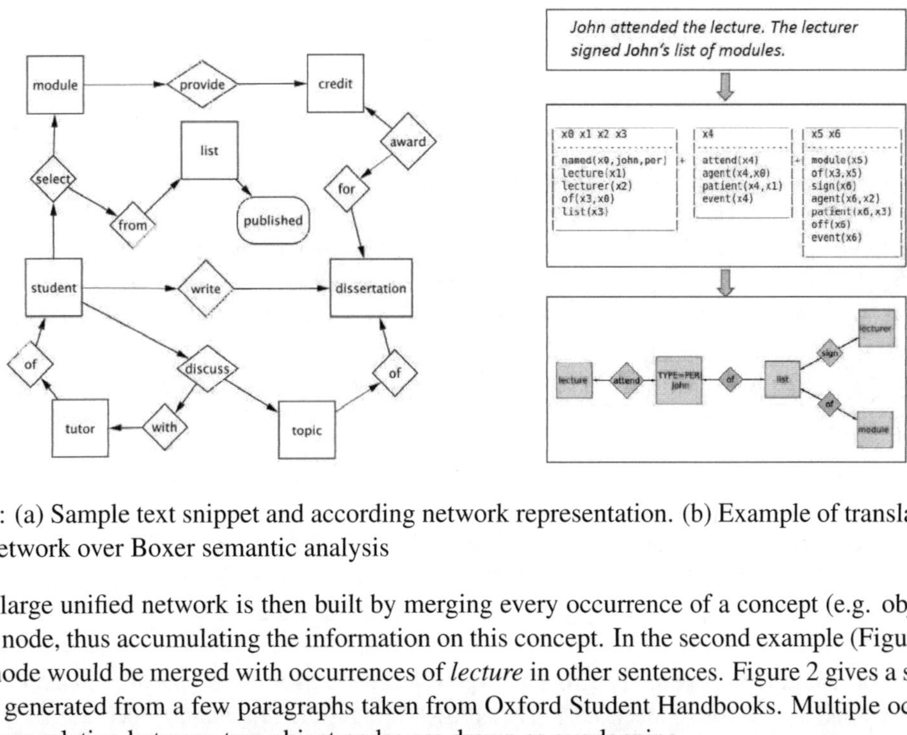

Figure 1: (a) Sample text snippet and according network representation. (b) Example of translation from text to network over Boxer semantic analysis

The large unified network is then built by merging every occurrence of a concept (e.g. object node) into one node, thus accumulating the information on this concept. In the second example (Figure **??**), the *lecture* node would be merged with occurrences of *lecture* in other sentences. Figure 2 gives a subset of a network generated from a few paragraphs taken from Oxford Student Handbooks. Multiple occurrences of the same relation between two object nodes are drawn as overlapping.

2.2 The Vector Space Model

We measure the semantic relatedness of two concepts by measuring the similarity of the surroundings of their corresponding nodes in the network. Semantically related terms are then expected to be connected to a similar set of nodes. We retrieve the network context of a specific node and determine the level

[1] http://svn.ask.it.usyd.edu.au/trac/candc

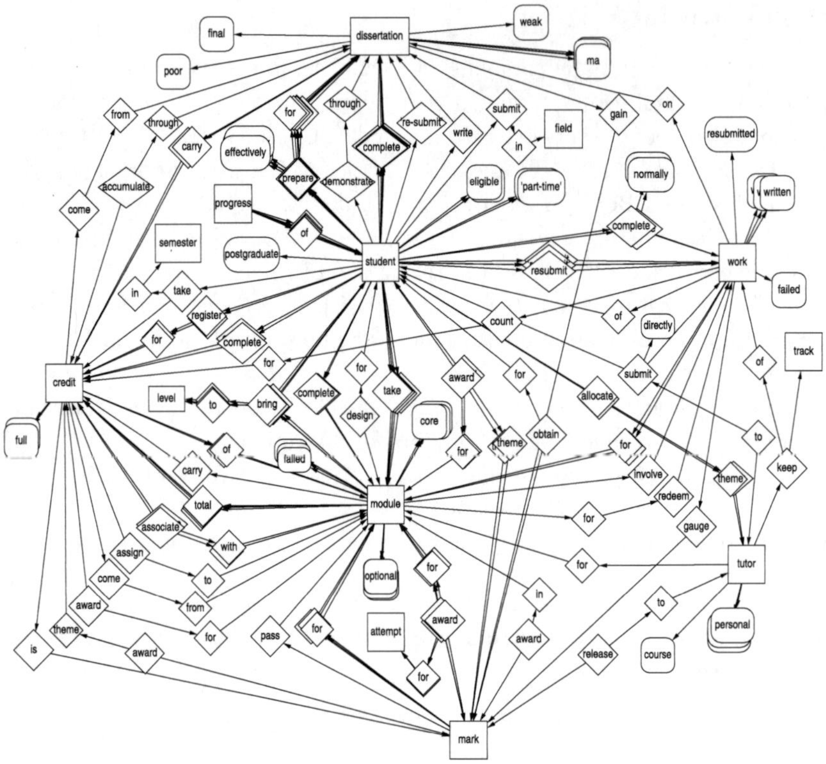

Figure 2: Subgraph displaying selected concepts and relations from sample network.

of significance of each node in the context using spreading activation[2]. The target node is given an initial activation of $a_x = 10{*}\mathit{numberOfLinks}(x)$ and is fired so that the activation spreads over its out- and ingoing links to the surrounding nodes. They in turn fire if their received activation level exceeds a certain threshold. The activation attenuates by a constant factor in every step and a stable state is reached when no node in the network can fire anymore. In this way, the context nodes receive different levels of activation reflecting their significance.

We derive a vector representation $\vec{v}(x)$ of the network context of x including only object nodes and their activation levels. The entries are

$$v_i(x) = act_{x,a_x}(n_i) \qquad\qquad n_i \in \{n \in nodes \mid type(n) = object\_node\}$$

The semantic relatedness of two target words is then measured by the cosine similarity of their context vectors.

$$sim\_rel(x,y) = cos(\vec{v}(x), \vec{v}(y)) = \frac{\vec{v}(x) \cdot \vec{v}(y)}{\|\vec{v}(x)\| \, \|\vec{v}(y)\|}$$

As spreading activation takes several factors into account, such as number of paths, length of paths, level of density and number of connections, this method leverages the full interconnected structure of the network.

3 Evaluation

We evaluate our approach on the WordSimilarity-353 (Finkelstein et al., 2002) test collection, which is a commonly used gold standard for the semantic relatedness task. It provides average human judgments scores of the degree of relatedness for 353 word pairs. The collection contains classically similar word

[2]The spreading activation algorithm is based on Harrington (2010)

Approach		Spearman
(Strube and Ponzetto, 2006)	Wikipedia	0.19-0.48
(Jarmasz, 2003)	Roget's	0.55
(Hughes and Ramage, 2007)	WordNet	0.55
(Agirre et al., 2009)	WordNet	0.56
(Finkelstein et al., 2002)	Web corpus, LSA	0.56
(Harrington, 2010)	Sem. Network	0.62
(Agirre et al., 2009)	WordNet+gloss	0.66
(Agirre et al., 2009)	Web corpus	0.66
(Gabrilovich and Markovitch, 2007)	Wikipedia	0.75
Network (all pairs)		0.38
Network (>100 freq: 293 pairs)		0.46
Network (>300 freq: 227 pairs)		**0.50**

	Similarity	Relatedness
all pairs	0.19 (100 pairs)	0.36 (250 pairs)
>300 freq	**0.50** (60 pairs)	**0.52** (171 pairs)

Table 1: (a) Spearman ranking correlation coefficient results for our approach and comparison with previous approaches. (b) Separate results for similarity and relatedness subset.

pairs such as *street - avenue* and topically related pairs such as *hotel - reservation*. However, no distinction was made while judging and the instruction was to rate the general degree of *semantic relatedness*.

As a corpus we chose the British National Corpus (BNC)[3]. It is one of the largest standardized English corpora and contains approximately 5.9 million sentences. Choosing this text collection enables us to build a general purpose network that is not specifically created for the considered work pairs and ensures a realistic overall connectedness of the network as well as a broad coverage. In this paper we created a network from 2 million sentences of the BNC. It contains 27.5 million nodes out of which 635.000 are object nodes and the rest are relation and attribute nodes. The building time including parsing was approximately 4 days.

Following the common practice in related work, we compared our scores to the human judgements using the Spearman rank-order correlation coefficient. The results can be found in Table 1(a) with a comparison to previous results on the WordSimilarity-353 collection.

Our first result over all word pairs is relatively low compared to the currently best performing systems. However, we noticed that many poorly rated word pairs contained at least one word with low frequency. Excluding these considerably improved the result to 0.50. On this reduced set of word pairs our scores are in the region of approaches which make use of the Wikipedia category network, the WordNet taxonomic relations or Roget's thesaurus. This is a promising result as it indicates that our approach based on automatically generated networks has the potential of competing with those using manually created resources if we increase the corpus size.

While our results are not competitive with the best corpus based methods, we can note that our current corpus is an order of magnitude smaller - 2 million sentences versus 1 million full Wikipedia articles (Gabrilovich and Markovitch, 2007) or 215MB versus 1.6 Terabyte (Agirre et al., 2009). The extent to which corpus size influences our results is subject to further research.

We also evaluated our scores separately on the semantically similar versus the semantically related subsets of WordSim-353 following Agirre et al. (2009) (Table 1(b)). Taking the same low-frequency cut as above, we can see that our approach performs equally well on both sets. This is remarkable as different methods tend to be more appropriate to calculate either one or the other (Agirre et al., 2009). In particular, WordNet based measures are well known to be better suited to measure similarity than relatedness due to its hierarchical, taxonomic structure (Budanitsky and Hirst, 2006). The fact that our system achieves equal results on the subset indicates that it matches human judgement of semantic relatedness beyond specific types of relations. This could be due to the associative structure of the network.

4 Related Work

Our approach is closely related to Harrington (2010) as our networks are built in a similar fashion and we also use spreading activation to measure semantic relatedness. In their approach, semantic relatedness

[3]http://www.natcorp.ox.ac.uk/

of two terms a and b is measured by the activation b receives when a is fired. The core difference of this measurement to ours is that it is path-based while ours is context based. In addition, the corpus used was retrieved specifically for the word pairs in question while ours is a general-purpose corpus.

In addition, our approach is related to work that uses personalized PageRank or Random Walks on WordNet (Agirre et al., 2009; Hughes and Ramage, 2007). Similar the spreading activation method presented here, personalized PageRank and Random Walks are used to provide a relevance distribution of nodes surrounding the target word to its meaning. In contrast to the approaches based on resources, our network is automatically built and therefore does not rely on costly, manual creation. In addition, compared to WordNet based measures, our method is potentially not biased towards relatedness due to similarity.

5 Conclusion and Outlook

We presented a novel approach to measuring semantic relatedness which first builds a large-scale semantic network and then determines the relatedness of nodes by the similarity of their surrounding local network. Our preliminary results of this ongoing work are promising and are in the region of several WordNet and Wikipedia link structure approaches. As future work, there are several ways of improvement we are going to investigate. Firstly, the results in Section 3 show the crucial influence of corpus size and occurrence frequency on the performance of our system. We will be experimenting with larger general networks (e.g. the whole BNC) as well as integration of retrieved documents for the low frequency terms. Secondly, the parameters and specific settings for the spreading activation algorithm need to be tuned. For example, the amount of initial activation of the target node determines the size of the context considered. Thirdly, we will investigate different vector representation variants. In particular, we can achieve a more fine-grained representation by also considering relation nodes in addition to object nodes. We believe that with these improvements our automatic semantic network approach will be able to compete with techniques based on manually created resources.

References

Agirre, E., E. Alfonseca, K. Hall, J. Kravalova, M. Paşca, and A. Soroa (2009). A study on similarity and relatedness using distributional and wordnet-based approaches. In *NAACL '09*.

Bos, J., S. Clark, M. Steedman, J. R. Curran, and J. Hockenmaier (2004). Wide-coverage semantic representations from a ccg parser. In *COLING'04*.

Budanitsky, A. and G. Hirst (2006). Evaluating wordnet-based measures of lexical semantic relatedness. *Computational Linguistics 32*(1), 13–47.

Clark, S. and J. R. Curran (2004). Parsing the wsj using ccg and log-linear models. In *ACL'04*.

Finkelstein, L., E. Gabrilovich, Y. Matias, E. Rivlin, Z. Solan, G. Wolfman, and E. Ruppin (2002). Placing search in context: the concept revisited. *ACM Trans. Inf. Syst. 20*(1), 116–131.

Gabrilovich, E. and S. Markovitch (2007). Computing semantic relatedness using wikipedia-based explicit semantic analysis. In *IJCAI'07*.

Harrington, B. (2010). A semantic network approach to measuring semantic relatedness. In *COLING'10*.

Harrington, B. and S. Clark (2007). Asknet: automated semantic knowledge network. In *AAAI'07*.

Hughes, T. and D. Ramage (2007). Lexical semantic relatedness with random graph walks. In *EMNLP-CoNLL'07*.

Jarmasz, M. (2003). Roget's thesaurus as a lexical resource for natural language processsing. Master's thesis, University of Ottawa.

Strube, M. and S. P. Ponzetto (2006). Wikirelate! computing semantic relatedness using wikipedia. In *AAAI'06*.

Semantic Parsing for Biomedical Event Extraction

Deyu Zhou[1] and Yulan He[2]

[1]School of Computer Science and Engineering, Southeast University,China
[2]Knowledge Media Institute, The Open University, UK

Abstract

We propose a biomedical event extraction system, HVS-BioEvent, which employs the hidden vector state (HVS) model for semantic parsing. Biomedical events extraction needs to deal with complex events consisting of embedded or hierarchical relations among proteins, events, and their textual triggers. In HVS-BioEvent, we further propose novel machine learning approaches for event trigger word identification, and for biomedical events extraction from the HVS parse results. Our proposed system achieves an F-score of 49.57% on the corpus used in the BioNLP'09 shared task, which is only two points lower than the best performing system by UTurku. Nevertheless, HVS-BioEvent outperforms UTurku on the extraction of complex event types. The results suggest that the HVS model with the hierarchical hidden state structure is indeed more suitable for complex event extraction since it can naturally model embedded structural context in sentences.

1 Introduction

In the past few years, there has been a surge of interests in utilizing text mining techniques to provide in-depth bio-related information services. With an increasing number of publications reporting on protein-protein interactions (PPIs), much effort has been made in extracting information from biomedical articles using natural language processing (NLP) techniques. Several shared tasks, such as LLL [7] and BioCreative [4], have been arranged for the BioNLP community to compare different methodologies for biomedical information extraction.

Comparing to LLL and BioCreative which primarily focus on a simple representation of relations of bio-molecules, i.e. protein-protein interaction, the BioNLP'09 Shared Task [5] involves the recognition of bio-molecular events in scientific abstracts, such as gene expression, transcription, protein catabolism, localization and binding, plus (positive or negative) regulation of proteins. The task concerns the detailed behavior of bio-molecules, and can be used to support the development of biomedical-related databases. In the BioNLP'09 shared task evaluation, the system constructed by UTurku [2] achieved an F-score of 51.95% on the core task, the best results among all the participants.

In this paper, we describe a system, called HVS-BioEvent, which employs the hidden vector state model (HVS) to automatically extract biomedical events from biomedical literature. The HVS model has been successfully employed to extract PPIs [9]. However, it is not straightforward to extend the usage of the HVS model for biomedical events extraction. There are two main challenges. First, comparing to the trigger words used for PPIs which are often expressed as single words or at most two words, the trigger words for biomedical event are more complex. For example, controlled at transcriptional and post-transcriptional levels, spanning over 6 words, is considered as the trigger word for the regulation event. In addition, the same word can be the trigger word for different types of biomedical events in different context. Second, biomedical events consist of both simple events and complex events. While simple events are more similar to PPIs which only involve binary or pairwise relations, complex events involve both n-ary ($n > 2$) and nested relations. For example, a regulation event may take another event as its theme or cause which represents a structurally more complex relation. Being able to handle both simple and complex events thus poses a huge challenge to the development of our HVS-BioEvent system.

The rest of the paper is organized as follows. Section 2 presents the overall process of the HVS-BioEvent system, which consists of three steps, trigger words identification, semantic parsing based on the HVS model, and biomedical events extraction from the HVS parse results. Experimental results are discussed in section 3. Finally, section 4 concludes the paper.

2 Biomedical Event Extraction

We perform biomedical event extraction with the following steps. At the beginning, abstracts are retrieved from MEDLINE and split into sentences. Protein names, gene names, trigger words for biomedical events are then identified. After that, each sentence is parsed by the HVS semantic parser. Finally, biomedical events are extracted from the HVS parse results using a hybrid method based on rules and machine learning. All these steps process one sentence at a time. Since 95% of all annotated events are fully annotated within a single sentence, this does not incur a large performance penalty but greatly reduces the size and complexity of the problem. The remainder of the section will discuss each of the steps in details.

2.1 Event Trigger Words Identification

Event trigger words are crucial to biomedical events extraction. In our system, we employ two approaches for event trigger words identification, one is a hybrid approach using both rules and a dictionary, the other treats trigger words identification as a sequence labeling problem and uses a Maximum Entropy Markov Model (MEMM) to detect trigger words.

For the hybrid approach using both rules and a dictionary, firstly, we constructed a trigger dictionary from the original GENIA event corpus [6] by extracting the annotated trigger words. These trigger words were subsequently lemmatized and stemmed. However, the wide variety of potential lexicalized triggers for an event means that lots of triggers lack discriminative power relative to individual event types. For example, in certain context, through is the trigger word for the binding event type and are is the trigger word for localization. Such words are too common and cause potential ambiguities and therefore lead to many false positive events extracted. We could perform disambiguation by counting the co-occurrence of a event trigger and a particular event type from the training data and discard those event triggers whose co-occurrence counts are lower than certain threshold for that event type. After this filtering stage, still, there might be cases where one trigger might representing multiple event types, we thus define a set of rules to further process the trigger words matched from the constructed dictionary.

In the second approach, we treat trigger words identification as a sequence labeling problem and train a first-order MEMM model [8] from the BioNLP'09 shared task training data. As in typical named entity recognition tasks, the training data are converted into BIO format where 'B' refers to the word which is the beginning word of an event trigger, 'I' indicates the rest of the words (if the trigger contains more than one words) and 'O' refers to the other words which are not event triggers. The features used in the MEMM model was extracted from the surface string and the part-of-speech information of the words corresponding to (or adjacent to) the target BIO tags.

2.2 Semantic Parsing using the HVS Model

The Hidden Vector State (HVS) model [3] is a discrete Hidden Markov Model (HMM) in which each HMM state represents the state of a push-down automaton with a finite stack size. State transitions are factored into separate stack pop and push operations constrained to give a tractable search space. The sequence of HVS stack states corresponding to the given parse tree is illustrated in Figure 1. The result is a model which is complex enough to capture hierarchical structure but which can be trained automatically from only lightly annotated data.

In the HVS-based semantic parser, conventional grammar rules are replaced by three probability tables. Let each state at time t be denoted by a vector of D_t semantic concept labels (tags) $c_t = [c_t[1], c_t[2], ..c_t[D_t]]$ where $c_t[1]$ is the preterminal concept label and $c_t[D_t]$ is the root concept label (SS in Figure 3). Given a word sequence W, concept vector sequence $\mathbf{C}$ and a sequence of stack pop operations N, the joint probability of $P(W, \mathbf{C}, N)$ can be decomposed as

$$P(W, \mathbf{C}, N) = \prod_{t=1}^{T} P(n_t|c_{t-1}) P(c_t[1]|c_t[2 \cdots D_t]) P(w_t|c_t) \tag{1}$$

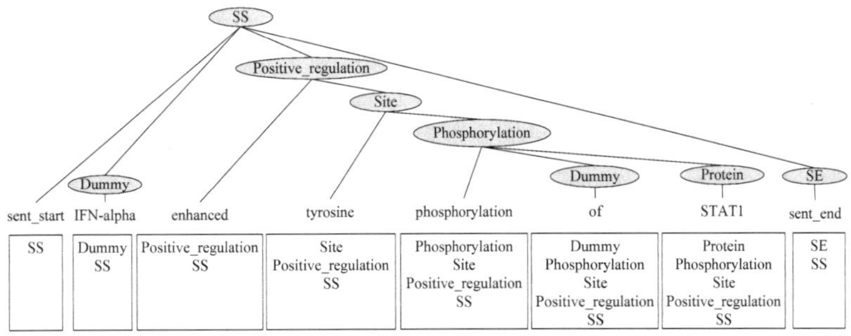

Figure 1: Example of a parse tree and its vector state equivalent.

where n_t is the vector stack shift operation and takes values in the range $0, \cdots, D_{t-1}$, and $c_t[1] = c_{w_t}$ is the new pre-terminal semantic label assigned to word w_t at word position t.

Thus, the HVS model consists of three types of probabilistic move, each move being determined by a discrete probability table: (1) popping semantic labels off the stack - $P(n|c)$; (2) pushing a pre-terminal semantic label onto the stack - $P(c[1]|c[2 \cdots D])$; (3) generating the next word - $P(w|c)$. Each of these tables are estimated in training using an EM algorithm and then used to compute parse trees at run-time using Viterbi decoding. In training, each word string W is marked with the set of semantic concepts C that it contains. For example, the sentence IFN-alpha enhanced tyrosine phosphorylation of STAT1 contains the semantic concept/value pairs as shown in Figure 1. Its corresponding abstract semantic annotation is:

`Positive_regulation(Site(Phosphorylation(protein)))`

where brackets denote the hierarchical relations among semantic concepts[1]. For each word w_k of a training sentence W, EM training uses the forward-backward algorithm to compute the probability of the model being in stack state c when w_k is processed. Without any constraints, the set of possible stack states would be intractably large. However, in the HVS model this problem can be avoided by pruning out all states which are inconsistent with the semantic concepts associated with W. The details of how this is done are given in [3].

For the sentences in the BioNLP'09 shared task, only event information is provided. However, the abstract semantic annotation as shown above is required for training the HVS model. We propose Algorithm 1 to automatically convert the annotated event information into the abstract semantic annotations. An example of how the abstract annotations are generated is given as follows.

Sentence: According to current models the inhibitory capacity of I(kappa)B(alpha) would be mediated through the retention of Rel/NF-kappaB proteins in the cytosol.

Corresponding Events: E1 Negative_regulation: inhibitory_capacity Theme: I(kappa)B(alpha)
E2 Positive_regulation: mediated Theme: E1

Candidate annotation generation (Steps 1-4 of Algorithm 1):
Negative_regulation(Protein) Negative_regulation(Protein(Positive_regulation))

Abstract annotation pruning (Steps 5-14 of Algorithm 1):
Negative_regulation(Protein(Positive_regulation))

2.3 Biomedical Events Extraction From HVS Parse Results

Based on HVS parse results, it seems straightforward to extract the event information. However, after detailed investigation, we found that sentences having the same semantic tags might contain different events information. For example, the two sentences shown in Table 1 have the same semantic parsing results but with different event information.

This problem can be solved by classification. For the semantic tags which can represent multiple event information, we considered each event information as a class and employed hidden Markov support vector machines (HM-SVMs) [1] for disambiguation among possible events. The features used in HM-SVMs are extracted from surface strings and part-of-speech information of the words corresponding to (or adjacent to) trigger words.

[1]We omit SS and SE here which denote sentence start and end.

Algorithm 1 Abstract semantic annotation generation.

Input: A sentence $W =< w_1, w_2, \cdots, w_n >$, and its event information $Ev =< e_1, e_2, \cdots, e_m >$
Output: Abstract semantic annotation A

for each event e_i =<Event_type:Trigger_words Theme:Protein_name ...> **do**
  Sort the Trigger_words, Protein_name, and other arguments based on their positions in W and get a sorted list $t_1, t_2, ..., t_k$
  Generate an annotation as $t_1(t_2(..t_k))$, add it into the annotation list A
end for
for each annotation $a_i \in A$ **do**
  if a_i contains another event **then**
    Replace the event with its corresponding annotation a_m
  end if
end for
for each annotation $a_i \in A$ **do**
  if a_i is a subset of another annotation in A **then**
    Remove a_i from the annotation list A
  end if
end for
Reorder annotations in A based on their positions in W

Sentence	We concluded that CTCF expression and activity is controlled at transcriptional and post-transcriptional levels	CONCLUSION: IL-5 synthesis by human helper T cells is regulated at the transcriptional level
Parse results	SS+Protein(CTCF) SS+Protein+Gene_Expression(expression) SS+Protein+Gene_Expression+Regulation(controlled...levels)	SS+Protein(IL-5) SS+Protein+Gene_Expression(synthesis) SS+Protein+Gene_Expression+Regulation(regulated)
Events	E1 Gene_expression:expression Theme: CTCF E2 Regulation: controlled...levels Theme: E1 E3 Regulation: controlled...levels Theme: CTCF	E1 Gene_expression: synthesis Theme: IL-5 E2 Regulation: regulated Theme: E1

Table 1: An example of the same semantic parse results denoting different event information

3 Results and Discussion

Experiments have been conducted on the training data of the BioNLP'09 shared task which consists of 800 abstracts. After cleaning up the sentences which do not contain biomedical events information, 2893 sentences were kept. We split the 2893 sentences randomly into the training set and the test set at the ratio of 9:1 and conducted the experiments ten times with different training and test data each round.

Method	*Recall (%)*	*Precision (%)*	*F-score (%)*
Trigger Word Identification			
Dictionary+Rules	46.31	53.34	49.57
MEMM	45.43	40.91	42.99
Event Extraction from HVS Parse Results			
No classification	43.57	52.85	47.77
With Classification	46.31	53.34	49.57

Table 2: Experimental results based on 10 fold cross-validation.

Table 2 shows the performance evaluated using the approximate recursive matching method adopted from the BioNLP'09 share task evaluation mode. To evaluate the performance impact of trigger word identification, we also report the overall performance of the system using the two approaches we proposed, dictionary+rules and MEMM. The results show that the hybrid approach combining a trigger dictionary and rules gives better performance than MEMM which only achieved a F-score around 43%. For biomedical event extraction from HVS parse results, employing the classification method presented in Section 2.3 improves the overall performance from 47.77% to 49.57%.

The best performance that HVS-BioEvent achieved is an F-score of 49.57%, which is only two points lower than UTurku, the best performing system in the BioNLP'09 share task. It should be noted that our results are based on 10-fold cross validation on the BioNLP'09 shared task training data only since we don't have the access to the BioNLP'09 test set while the results generated by UTurku were evaluated on the BioNLP'09 test set. Although a direct comparison is not possible, we could still speculate that

Simple Events			*Complex Events*		
Event Class	*HVS-BioEvent*	*UTurku*	*Event Class*	*HVS-BioEvent*	*UTurku*
localization	61.40	**61.65**	binding	**49.90**	44.41
gene expression	72.44	**73.90**	regulation	**36.57**	30.52
transcription	**68.30**	50.23	negative regulation	**40.61**	38.99
protein catabolism	**70.27**	52.17			
phosphorylation	56.52	**77.58**			

Table 3: Per-class performance comparison in F-score (%) between HVS-BioEvent and UTurku.

HVS-BioEvent is comparable to the best performing system in the BioNLP'09 shared task.

The results on the five event types involving only a single theme argument are shown in Table 3 as *Simple Events*. For the complex events such as "binding", "regulation" and "negative regulation" events, the results are shown in Table 3 as *Complex Events*. We notice that HVS-BioEvent outperforms UTurku on the extraction of the complex event types, with the performance gain ranging between 2% and 7%. The results suggest that the HVS model with the hierarchical hidden state structure is indeed more suitable for complex event extraction since it could naturally model embedded structural context in sentences.

4 Conclusions

In this paper, we have presented HVS-BioEvent which uses the HVS model to automatically extract biomedical events from text. The system is able to offer comparable performance compared with the best performing system in the BioNLP'09 shared task. Moreover, it outperforms the existing systems on complex events extraction which shows the ability of the HVS model in capturing embedded and hierarchical relations among named entities. In future work we will explore incorporating arbitrary lexical features into the HVS model training in order to further improve the extraction accuracy.

References

[1] Y. Altun, I. Tsochantaridis, and T. Hofmann. Hidden markov support vector machines. In *International Conference in Machine Learning*, pages 3–10, 2003.

[2] Jari Bjorne, Juho Heimonen, Filip Ginter, Antti Airola, Tapio Pahikkla, and Tapio Salakoski. Extracting complex biological events with rich graph-based feature sets. In *Proceedings of the Workshop on BioNLP*, pages 10–18, 2009.

[3] Yulan He and Steve Young. Semantic processing using the hidden vector state model. *Computer Speech and Language*, 19(1):85–106, 2005.

[4] Lynette Hirschman, Alexander Yeh, Christian Blaschke, and Alfonso Valencia. Overview of biocreative: critical assessment of information extraction for biology. *BMC Bioinformatics*, 2005.

[5] Jin-Dong Kim, Tomoko Ohta, Sampo Pyysalo, Yoshinobu Kano, and Jun'ichi Tsujii. Overview of bionlp'09 shared task on event extraction. In *Proceedings of the Workshop on BioNLP*, pages 1–9, 2009.

[6] Jin-Dong Kim, Tomoko Ohta, and Jun'ichi Tsujii. Corpus annotation for mining biomedical events from literature. *BMC Bioinformatics*, 9(10), 2008.

[7] Claire Nédellec. Learning Language in Logic - Genic Interaction Extraction Challenge. In *Learning Language in Logic workshop (LLL05)*, pages 31–37, 2005.

[8] Nam Nguyen and Yunsong Guo. Comparisons of sequence labeling algorithms and extensions. In *Proceedings of the ICML*, pages 681–688, 2007.

[9] Deyu Zhou, Yulan He, and Chee Keong Kwoh. Extracting protein-protein interactions from medline using the hidden vector state model. *International Journal of Bioinformatics Research and Applications*, 4(1):64–80, 2008.

AUTHOR INDEX

AUTHOR INDEX